VBA FOR MODELERS

DEVELOPING DECISION SUPPORT SYSTEMS WITH MICROSOFT® OFFICE EXCEL®

VBA FOR MODELERS

DEVELOPING DECISION SUPPORT SYSTEMS WITH MICROSOFT® OFFICE EXCEL®

FIFTH EDITION

S. Christian Albright

Kelley School of Business, Indiana University

CENGAGE
Learning·

Australia • Brazil • Mexico • Singapore • United Kingdom • United States

CENGAGE
Learning·

VBA for Modelers: Developing Decision Support Systems with Microsoft® Office Excel®, Fifth Edition
S. Christian Albright

Vice President, General Manager Science, Math, and Quantitative Business: Balraj Kalsi

Product Director: Joe Sabatino

Product Manager: Aaron Arnsparger

Associate Content Developer: Brad Sullender

Manufacturing Planner: Ron Montgomery

Marketing Manager: Heather Mooney

Art and Cover Direction, Production Management, and Composition: Lumina Datamatics, Inc.

Cover Image: © Awstok/Shutterstock

Intellectual Property

   Analyst: Christina Ciaramella

   Project Manager: Betsy Hathaway

Unless otherwise noted, all items © Cengage Learning

For product information and technology assistance, contact us at
Cengage Learning Customer & Sales Support, 1-800-354-9706

For permission to use material from this text or product, submit all requests online at **www.cengage.com/permissions**
Further permissions questions can be emailed to
permissionrequest@cengage.com

Library of Congress Control Number: 2014958175

ISBN: 978-1-285-86961-2

Cengage Learning
20 Channel Center Street
Boston, MA 02210
USA

Cengage Learning is a leading provider of customized learning solutions with employees residing in nearly 40 different countries and sales in more than 125 countries around the world. Find your local representative at **www.cengage.com**.

Cengage Learning products are represented in Canada by Nelson Education, Ltd.

To learn more about Cengage Learning Solutions, visit **www.cengage.com**

Purchase any of our products at your local college store or at our preferred online store **www.cengagebrain.com**

Printed in the United States of America
Print Number: 01   Print Year: 2015

To my wonderful wife, Mary—she is my best friend and constant companion. To our talented son, Sam, his equally talented wife, Lindsay, and our two amazing grandsons, Teddy and Archer. And to Bryn, our dear Welsh corgi who still just loves to play ball.

About the Author

S. Christian Albright

Chris Albright got his B.S. degree in Mathematics from Stanford in 1968 and his Ph.D. degree in Operations Research from Stanford in 1972. Until his retirement in 2011, he taught in the Operations & Decision Technologies Department in the Kelley School of Business at Indiana University. His teaching included courses in management science, computer simulation, and statistics to all levels of business students: undergraduates, MBAs, and doctoral students. He has published over 20 articles in leading operations research journals in the area of applied probability and he has authored several books, including *Practical Management Science, Data Analysis and Decision Making, Data Analysis for Managers, Spreadsheet Modeling and Applications*, and *VBA for Modelers*. He jointly developed *StatTools*, a statistical add-in for Excel, with the Palisade Corporation. In "retirement," he continues to revise his books, he works as a consultant for Palisade, and he has developed a commercial product, Excel Now!, an Excel tutorial.

On the personal side, Chris has been married to his wonderful wife Mary for 43 years. They have a special family in Philadelphia: their son Sam, his wife Lindsay, and their two sons, Teddy and Archer. Chris has many interests outside the academic area. They include activities with his family (especially traveling with Mary), going to cultural events at Indiana University, power walking, and reading. And although he earns his livelihood from statistics and management science, his *real* passion is for playing classical music on the piano.

Contents

8 Working with Other Excel Objects 149

9 Arrays 177

10 More on Variables and Subroutines 204

11 User Forms 231

12 Error Handling

13 Working with Files and Folders

14 Importing Data into Excel from a Database

15 Working with Pivot Tables and Tables

16 Working with Ribbons, Toolbars, and Menus

21 A Product Mix Application   454

22 A Worker Scheduling Application   475

23 A Production-Planning Application   488

24 A Transportation Application   513

33 A Data Envelopment Analysis Application 680

34 An AHP Application for Choosing a Job

You can access chapter 34 at our website, www.CengageBrain.com

35 A Poker Simulation Application

You can access chapter 35 at our website, www.CengageBrain.com

Preface

I wrote *VBA for Modelers* for students and professionals who want to create decision support systems (DSSs) using Microsoft Excel–based spreadsheet models. The book does *not* assume any prior programming experience. It contains two parts. Part I covers the essentials of VBA (Visual Basic for Applications) programming, and Part II provides many applications with their associated programming code. This part assumes that readers are either familiar with spreadsheet modeling or are taking a concurrent course in management science or operations research. There are many excellent books available for VBA programming, many others covering decision support systems, and still others for spreadsheet modeling. However, I have not found a book that attempts to unify these subjects in a practical way. *VBA for Modelers* is designed for this purpose, and I hope you will find it to be an important resource and reference in your own work.

Why This Book?

The original impetus for this book began about 20 years ago. Wayne Winston and I were experimenting with the spreadsheet approach to teaching management as we were writing the first edition of our *Practical Management Science (PMS)* book. Because I have always had an interest in computer programming, I decided to learn VBA, the relatively new macro language for Excel, and use it to a limited extent in my undergraduate management science modeling course. My intent was to teach the students how to wrap a given spreadsheet model, such as a product mix model, into an *application* with a "front end" and a "back end" by using VBA. The front end would enable a user to provide inputs to the model, usually through one or more dialog boxes, and the back end would present the user with a nontechnical report of the results. I found it to be an exciting addition to the usual modeling course, and my students overwhelmingly agreed.

The primary problem with teaching this type of course was the lack of an appropriate VBA textbook. Although there are many good VBA trade books available, they usually go into much more technical VBA details than I have time to cover, and their objective is usually to teach VBA programming as an end in itself. I expect that many adopters of our *Practical Management Science* book will decide to use parts of *VBA for Modelers* to supplement their management science courses, just as I have been doing. For readers who have already taken a management science course, there is more than enough material in this book to fill an entire elective course or to be used for self-study.

However, even for readers with no background or interest in management science, the first part of this book has plenty of value. We are seeing an increasing number of our business students and graduates express interest in automating Excel with macros. In short, they want to become Excel "power users." After the first edition of this book appeared, I taught a purely elective MBA course covering the first part of the book. To my surprise and delight, it regularly attracted about 40 MBA students per year. Yes, it attracted *MBA students*, not computer science majors! (Since I have retired from teaching, the VBA course is still being taught, and it continues to attract these types of audiences.). The students see real value in knowing how to program for Excel. And it is amazing and gratifying to see how far these students can progress in a short 7-week course. Many find programming, especially for Excel, to be as addictive as I find it.

Objectives of the Book

VBA for Modelers shows how the power of spreadsheet modeling can be extended to the masses. Through VBA, complex management science models can be made accessible to nontechnical users by providing them with simplified input screens and output reports. The book illustrates, in complete detail, how such applications can be developed for a wide variety of business problems. In writing the book, I have always concerned myself with the following questions: How much will readers be able to do on their own? Is it enough for readers to see the completed applications, marvel at how powerful they are, and possibly take a look at the code that runs in the background? Or should they be taken to the point where they can develop their *own* applications, code and all? I suspect this depends on the audience, but I know I *can* get students to the point where they can develop modest but useful applications on their own and, importantly, experience the thrill of programming success.

With these thoughts in mind, I have written this book so that it can be used at several levels. For readers who want to learn VBA from scratch and then apply it, I have provided a "VBA primer" in Part I of the book. It is admittedly not as complete as some of the thick Excel VBA books available, but I believe it covers the basics of VBA quite adequately. Importantly, it covers coding methods for working with Excel ranges in Chapter 6 and uses these methods extensively in later chapters, so that readers will not have to use trial and error or wade through online help, as I had to do when I was learning VBA. Readers can then proceed to the applications in Chapters 19 through 35 and apply their skills. In contrast, there are probably many readers who do not have time to learn all of the details, but they can still *use* the applications in Part II of the book for demonstration purposes. Indeed, the applications have been developed for generality. For example, the transportation model in Chapter 24 is perfectly general and can be used to solve *any* transportation model by supplying the appropriate input data.

Approach

I like to teach (and learn) through examples. I have found that I can learn a programming language only if I have a strong motivation to learn it. I suspect that most of you are the same. The applications in the latter chapters are based on many interesting management science models. They provide the motivation for you to learn the material. The examples illustrate that this book is not about programming for the sake of programming. Instead, it is about developing useful applications for business. You probably already realize that Excel modeling skills make you more valuable in the workplace. This book will help you develop VBA skills that make you much *more* valuable.

Contents of the Book

The book is written in two parts. Part I, Chapters 1–18, is a VBA primer for readers with little or no programming experience in VBA (or any other language). Although all of these chapters are geared to VBA, some are more about general programming concepts, whereas others deal with the unique aspects of programming for Excel. Specifically, Chapters 7, 9, and 10 discuss control logic (If-Then-Else constructions), loops, arrays, and subroutines, topics that are common to all programming languages. In contrast, Chapters 6 and 8 explain how to work with some of the most common Excel objects (ranges, workbooks, worksheets, and charts) in VBA. In addition, several chapters discuss aspects of VBA that can be used with Excel and any other applications (Access, Word, PowerPoint, and so on) that use VBA as their programming language. Specifically, Chapter 3 explains the Visual Basic Editor (VBE), Chapter 4 illustrates how to record macros, Chapter 11 explains how to build user forms (dialog boxes), and Chapter 12 discusses the important topic of error handling.

The material in Part I is reasonably complete, but it is available, in greater detail and with a somewhat different emphasis, in several other books. The unique aspect of *this* book is Part II, Chapters 19–35. (Due to length, the last two chapters, Chapter 34, An AHP Application for Choosing a Job, and Chapter 35, A Poker Simulation Application, are available online only. You can find them at www.CengageBrain.com.) Each chapter in this part discusses a specific application. Most of these are optimization and simulation applications, and many are quite general. For example, Chapter 21 discusses a general product mix application, Chapter 23 discusses a general production scheduling application, Chapter 24 discusses a general transportation application, Chapter 25 discusses a stock-trading simulation, Chapter 29 discusses a multiple-server queue simulation, Chapter 30 discusses a general application for pricing European and American options, and Chapter 32 discusses a general portfolio optimization application. (Many of the underlying models for these applications are discussed in *Practical Management Science*, but I have attempted to make these applications stand-alone here.)

The applications can be used as they stand to solve real problems, or they can be used as examples of VBA application development. All of the steps in the development of these applications are explained, and all of the VBA source code is included. Using an analogy to a car, you can simply get in and drive, or you can open the hood and see how everything works.

Chapter 19 gets the process started in a "gentle" way. It provides a general introduction to application development, with an important list of guidelines. It then illustrates these guidelines in a car loan application. This application should be within the grasp of most readers, even if they are not yet great programmers. By tackling this application first, readers get to develop a simple model, with dialog boxes, reports, and charts, and then tie everything together. This car loan application illustrates an important concept that I stress throughout the book. Specifically, applications that really *do* something are often long and have a lot of details. But this does not mean that they are *difficult*. With perseverance—a word I use frequently—readers can fill in the details one step at a time and ultimately experience the thrill of getting a program to work correctly.

Virtually all management science applications require input data. A very important issue for VBA application development is how to get the required input data into the spreadsheet model. I illustrate a number of possibilities in Part II. If only a small amount of data is required, dialog boxes work well. These are used for data input in many of the applications. However, there are many times when the data requirements are much too large for dialog boxes. In these cases, the data are usually stored in some type of database. I illustrate some common possibilities. In Chapter 21, the input data for a product mix model are stored in a separate worksheet. In Chapter 31, the stock price data for finding the betas of stocks are stored in a separate Excel workbook. In Chapter 33, the data for a DEA model are stored in a text (.txt) file. In Chapter 24, the data for a transportation model are stored in an Access database (.mdb) file. Finally, in Chapter 32, the stock price data required for a portfolio optimization model are located on a Web site and are imported into Excel, *at runtime*. In each case, I explain the VBA code that is necessary to import the data into the Excel application.

New to the Fifth Edition

The impetus for writing the fifth edition was the release of Excel 2013. In terms of VBA, there aren't many changes from Excel 2010 to Excel 2013 (or even from Excel 2007 to Excel 2013), but I used the opportunity to incorporate changes that were made in Excel 2013, as well as to modify a lot of the material throughout the book.

- Programmers can never let well enough alone. We are forever tinkering with our code, not just to make it work better, but often to make it more elegant and easier to understand. So users of previous editions will see minor changes to much of the code throughout the book.
- The biggest change, which has nothing to do with the version of Excel, is the way information is passed between modules and user forms. In previous editions, I did this with global variables, a practice frowned upon by many professional programmers. In this edition, I pass the required information through arguments to "ShowDialog" functions in the user forms. This new method is explained in detail in Chapter 11 and is then used in later chapters where user forms appear.

- Chapter 15 contains a brief discussion of the new PowerPivot tool introduced in Excel 2013. This tool can actually be automated with VBA, but because of its advanced nature, I don't discuss the details. Maybe this will appear in the *next* edition of the book, by which time Excel's online help will hopefully be improved.

How to Use the Book

I have already discussed several approaches to using this book, depending on how much you want to learn and how much time you have. For readers with very little or no computer programming background who want to learn the fundamentals of VBA, Chapters 1–12 should be covered first, in approximately that order. (I should point out that it is practically impossible to avoid "later" programming concepts while covering "early" ones. For example, I admit to using a few If statements and loops in early chapters, *before* discussing them formally in Chapter 7. I don't believe this should cause problems. I use plenty of comments, and you can always look ahead if you need to.) After covering VBA fundamentals in the first 12 chapters, the next six optional chapters can be covered in practically any order.

Chapter 19 should be covered next. Beyond that, the applications in the remaining chapters can be covered in practically any order, depending on your interests. However, some of the details in certain applications will not make much sense without the appropriate training in the management science models. For example, Chapter 34 discusses an AHP (Analytical Hierarchy Process) application for choosing a job. The VBA code is fairly straightforward, but it will not make much sense unless you have some knowledge of AHP. I assume that the knowledge of the models comes from a separate source, such as *Practical Management Science*; I cover it only briefly here.

Finally, readers can simply use the Excel application files to solve problems. Indeed, the applications have been written specifically for nontechnical end users, so that readers at all levels should have no difficulty opening the application files in Part II of the book and using them appropriately. In short, readers can decide how much of the material "under the hood" is worth their time.

Premium Web Site Content

The companion Web site for this book can be accessed at www.cengagebrain .com. There you will have access to all of the Excel (.xlsx and .xlsm) and other files mentioned in the chapters, including those in the exercises. The Excel files require Excel 97 or a more recent version, but they are realistically geared to Excel 2007 and later versions. Many of the files from Chapter 17 and later chapters "reference" Excel's Solver. They will not work unless the Solver add-in is installed and loaded. Chapters 14 and 24 uses Microsoft's ActiveX Data Object (ADO) model to import the data from an Access database into Excel. This will work only in Excel 2000 or a more recent version. Finally, Chapter 13 uses the Office File-Dialog object. This works only in Excel XP (2002) or a more recent version.

The book is also supported by a Web site at www.kelley.iu.edu/albrightbooks. The Web site contains errata and other useful information, including information about my other books.

Acknowledgments

I would like to thank all of my colleagues at Cengage Learning. Foremost among them are my current editor, Aaron Arnsbarger, and my former editors, Curt Hinrichs and Charles McCormick. The original idea was to develop a short VBA manual to accompany our *Practical Management Science* book, but Curt persuaded me to write an entire book. Given the success of the first four editions, I appreciate Curt's insistence. I am also grateful to many of the professionals who worked behind the scenes to make this book a success:

- Brad Sullender, Content Developer; Heather Mooney, Marketing Manager; Kristina Mose-Libon, Art Director; and Sharib Asrar as the Project Manager at Lumina Datamatics.

Next, I would like to thank the reviewers of past editions of the book. Thanks go to

- Gerald Aase, Northern Illinois University; Ravi Ahuja, University of Florida; Grant Costner, University of Oregon; R. Kim Craft, Rollins College; Lynette Molstad Gorder, Dakota State University; and Jim Hightower, California State University-Fullerton; Don Byrkett, Miami University; Kostis Christodoulou, London School of Economics; Charles Franz, University of Missouri; Larry LeBlanc, Vanderbilt University; Jerry May, University of Pittsburgh; Jim Morris, University of Wisconsin; and Tom Schriber, University of Michigan.

Finally, I want to thank my wife, Mary. She continues to support my book-writing activities, even when it requires me to work evenings and weekends in front of a computer. I also want to thank our Welsh corgi Bryn, who faithfully accompanies her daddy when he goes upstairs to do his work. She doesn't add much technical assistance, but she definitely adds a lot of motivational assistance.

S. Christian Albright
(e-mail at albright@indiana.edu,
Web site at www.kelley.iu.edu/albrightbooks)
Bloomington, Indiana
January 2015

Part I

VBA Fundamentals

This part of the book is for readers who need an introduction to programming in general and Visual Basic for Applications (VBA) for Excel in particular. It discusses programming topics that are common to practically all programming languages, including variable types and declarations, control logic, looping, arrays, subroutines, and error handling. It also discusses many topics that are specific to VBA and its use with Excel, including the Excel object model; recording macros; working with ranges, workbooks, worksheets, charts, and other Excel objects; developing user forms (dialog boxes); and automating other applications, including Word, Outlook, Excel's Solver add-in, and Palisade's @RISK add-in, with VBA code.

Many of the chapters in Part I present a business-related exercise immediately after the introductory section. The objective of each such exercise is to motivate you to work through the details of the chapter, knowing that many of these details will be required to solve the exercise. The finished files are included in the online materials, but I urge you to try the exercises on your own, before looking at the solutions.

The chapters in this part should be read in approximately the order they are presented, at least up through Chapter 12. Programming is a skill that builds upon itself. Although it is not always possible to avoid referring to a concept from a later chapter in an earlier chapter, I have attempted to refrain from doing this as much as possible. The one small exception is in Chapters 6 (on ranges) and 7 (on control logic and loops). It is almost impossible to do any interesting programming in Excel without knowing about ranges, and it is almost impossible to do any interesting programming in general without knowing about control logic and loops. I compromised by putting the chapter on ranges first and using some simple control logic and loops in it. I don't believe this should cause any problems.

Introduction to VBA Development in Excel

1.1 Introduction

My books *Practical Management Science* (PMS) and *Business Analytics: Data Analysis and Decision Making* (DADM), both co-authored with Wayne Winston, illustrate how to solve a wide variety of business problems by developing appropriate Excel models. If you are familiar with this modeling process, you probably do not need to be convinced of the power and applicability of Excel. You realize that Excel modeling skills will make you a valuable employee in the workplace. This book takes the process one giant step farther. It teaches you how to develop applications in Excel by using Excel's programming language, Visual Basic for Applications (VBA).

In many Excel-modeling books, you learn how to model a particular business problem. You enter given inputs in a worksheet, you relate them with appropriate formulas, and you eventually calculate required outputs. You might also optimize a particular output with Solver, and you might create one or more charts to show outputs graphically. You do all of this through the Excel interface, using its ribbons (as of Excel 2007), menus, and toolbars, entering formulas into its cells, using the chart tools, using the Solver dialog box, and so on. If you are conscientious, you document your work so that other people in your company can understand your completed model. For example, you clearly indicate the input cells so that other users will know which cells they should use for their own inputs and which cells they should leave alone.

Now suppose that your position in a company is to *develop* applications for other less-technical people in the organization to use. Part of your job is still to develop spreadsheet models, but the details of these models might be incomprehensible to many users. These users might realize that they have, say, a product mix problem, where they will have to supply certain inputs, and then some computer magic will eventually determine a mix of products that optimizes company profit. However, the part in between is beyond their capabilities. Your job, therefore, is to develop a user-friendly application with a model (possibly hidden from the user) surrounded by a "front end" and a "back end." The front end will present the user with dialog boxes or some other means for enabling them to define their problem. Here they will be asked to specify input values and possibly other information. Your application will take this information, build the appropriate model, optimize it if necessary, and eventually present the back end to the user—a nontechnical report of the results, possibly with accompanying charts.

This application development is possible with VBA, as I will demonstrate in this book. I make no claim that it is easy or that it can be done quickly, but I do claim that it is within the realm of possibility for people like yourself, not just for professional programmers. It requires a logical mind, a willingness to experiment and take full advantage of online help, plenty of practice, and, above all, perseverance. Even professional programmers seldom accomplish their tasks without difficulty and plenty of errors; this is the nature of programming. However, they learn from their errors (and their colleagues), and they refuse to quit until they get their programs to work properly. Computer programming is essentially a process of overcoming one small hurdle after another. This is where perseverance is so important. But if you are not easily discouraged, and if you love the feeling of accomplishment that comes from getting something to work, you will love the challenge of application development described in the book.

1.2 VBA in Excel 2007 and Later Versions

As you are probably aware, Excel went through a major face lift in 2007. The look of Excel, especially its menus and toolbars, is now much different than in Excel 2003 and earlier. Unfortunately, some users have not converted to Excel 2007 or a later version, so book authors, including myself, are in the uncomfortable position of having to write simultaneously for several audiences. Fortunately, not much about VBA changed in the transition from 2003 to 2007 or from 2007 to 2010 or from 2010 to 2013. I will try to point out the differences as necessary throughout the book, hopefully without interrupting the flow too much.

Perhaps the main difference is in the file extensions you will see. In Excel 2003 and earlier, all Excel files (except for add-ins, not covered here) ended in .xls. It didn't matter whether they contained VBA code or not; they were still .xls files. In Excel 2007 and later versions, there are two new extensions. Files without VBA code now have .xlsx extensions, whereas files with VBA code *must* use .xlsm extensions. If you try to save a file with VBA code as an .xlsx file, you won't be allowed to do so. There is one exception: you can save your new files in the old Excel 2003 format, which is still an option (with Save As), in which case they will have .xls extensions. Why would you do this? The probable reason is that you want to share a file you created in Excel 2007 or a later version with a friend who still uses Excel 2003. Of course, if your file includes features new to Excel 2007 or a later version, your friend won't be able to see them.

I have been using Excel 2007, 2010, and now 2013 since their original releases, and I personally think they are great improvements over earlier versions, at least in most respects. So I will provide my example files in .xlsx and .xlsm formats. If you are using Excel 2003, you will be able to open these if you first install a free Office Compatibility Pack from Microsoft (just search the Web for it). Without this compatibility pack, Excel 2003 users cannot read files in the new .xlsx or .xlsm formats (although users of Excel 2007 and later versions can always read files in the old .xls format).

The fortunate part is that VBA has changed very little. I will usually *not* include new features of Excel 2007 or later versions in my example files that Excel 2003 users (even those with the compatibility pack) could not see. And in the few cases where I need to do so, I will make it clear that these examples are for users of Excel 2007 or later versions only.

1.3 Example Applications

If you have used my PMS or DADM books, you probably understand what a spreadsheet model is. However, you might not understand what I mean by spreadsheet *applications* with front ends and back ends. In other words, you might not understand what this book intends to teach you. The best way to find out is to run some of the applications that will be explained in Part II of the book. At this point, *you* can become the nontechnical user by opening any of the following files that accompany this book: **Product Mix.xlsm, Scheduling.xlsm, Stock Options.xlsm,** and **Transportation.xlsm**. Simply open any of these files and follow instructions. It should be easy. After all, the purpose of writing these applications is to make it easy for a nontechnical user to run them and get results they can understand. Now step back and imagine what must be happening in the background to enable these applications to do what they do. This is what you will be learning in the book. By running a few applications, you will become anxious to learn how to do it yourself. These sample applications illustrate just how powerful a tool VBA for Excel can be.

Security Settings and Trusted Locations

You might encounter annoying messages when you try to open these applications. Microsoft realizes that viruses can be carried in VBA code, so it tries to protect users. First, it sets a macro security level to High by default. This level disallows *any* VBA macros to run. Obviously, this is not good when you are trying to learn VBA programming. The fix is easy.

- For users of Excel 2010 and 2013, open Excel, click the File button, then Options, then the Trust Center tab, then Trust Center Settings, then the Macro Settings tab, and check the "Disable all macros with notification" option.
- For users of Excel 2007, it is the same as for Excel 2010 and 2013 except that you click the Office button, not the File button. (The Office button was replaced by the File button in 2010.)
- For users of Excel 2003 or earlier, open Excel, select the **Tools → Macro → Security** menu item, and select Medium.
- You should need to do this only once. However, even with this macro security setting, you are always asked whether you want to enable macros when you open a file that contains VBA code. Of course, you should typically enable macros. Otherwise, you will be safe from viruses, but none of the VBA code will run!

There is another option, at least in Excel 2007 and later versions, which avoids the security settings altogether. If you find that most of the Excel files with VBA code are in a particular folder on your hard drive, you can add this folder to the list of *trusted locations* on your computer. To do this, a one-time task on a given computer, go to the Trust Center Settings, as explained in the first bullet above, then Trusted Locations, then "Add new location," and browse for the folder you want to add. (In the resulting dialog box, you will probably want to check the "Subfolders of this location are also trusted" option.) From then on, any .xlsm files in this folder (or its subfolders) will open without any warning about enabling macros.

I will make one final comment about enabling macros that pertains to Excel 2007 or later versions only. If you open a file that contains macros, that is, an .xlsm file, and it isn't in a trusted location, you sometimes see the message in Figure 1.1 and you sometimes instead see the button in Figure 1.2 (right above the formula bar). Thanks to John Walkenbach, a fellow VBA author, I finally learned the pattern. If the VB editor (discussed in Chapter 3) is already open when you open the file, you will see the message in Figure 1.1. If it isn't open, you will see the button in Figure 1.2. Why did Microsoft do it this way? I have no idea.

Figure 1.1 Enable Macro Message with VB Editor Open

Figure 1.2 Enable Macro Button with VB Editor Not Open

1.4 Decision Support Systems

In many companies, programmers provide applications called **decision support systems (DSSs).** These are applications, based on Excel or some other package, that help managers make better decisions. They can vary from very simple to very complex, but they usually provide some type of user-friendly interface so that a manager can experiment with various inputs or decision variables to see their effect on important output variables such as profit or cost. Much of what you will be learning, especially in Part II of the book, is how to create Excel-based DSSs. In fact, if you ran the applications in the previous section, you should already understand what decision support means. For example, the Transportation application helps a manager plan the optimal shipping of a product in a logistics network, and the Stock Options application helps a financial analyst price various types of financial options. The value that you, the programmer, provide by developing these applications is that other people in your company can then run them—easily—to make better decisions.

1.5 Required Background

Readers of this book probably vary widely in their programming experience. At one extreme, many of you have probably never programmed in VBA or any other language. At the other extreme, a few of you have probably programmed in Visual Basic but have never used it to automate Excel and build Excel applications. In the middle, some of you have probably had some programming experience in another language such as C or Java but have never learned VBA. This book is intended to appeal to all such audiences. Therefore, a simplified answer to the question, "What programming background do I need?" is "None." You need only a willingness to learn and experiment.

If you ran the applications discussed in Section 1.2, you are probably anxious to get started developing similar applications. If you already know the fundamentals of VBA for Excel, you can jump ahead to Part II of the book. But most of you will have to learn how to walk before you can run. Therefore, the chapters in Part I go through the basics of the VBA language, especially as it applies to Excel. The coverage of this basic material will provide you with enough explanations and examples of VBA's important features to enable you to understand the applications in Part II—and to do some Excel development on your own.

If you want more detailed guidance in VBA for Excel, you can learn from Microsoft's online help or the many user groups on the Web. Indeed, this is perhaps the best way to learn, especially in the middle of a development project. If you need to know one specific detail to overcome a hurdle in the program you are writing, you can look it up quickly in online help or do an online search for it. A good way to do this will be demonstrated shortly.

Part II of the book does presume some modeling ability and general business background. For example, if you ran the Product Mix application, you probably realize that it develops and optimizes a product mix model, a classic linear programming model. One (but not the only) step in developing this application is to develop a product mix model exactly as in Chapter 3 of PMS. As another example, if you ran the Stock Options application, you realize the need to understand option pricing, explained briefly in the second simulation chapter of PMS. Many of the applications in this book are based on examples (product mix, scheduling, transportation, and so on) from PMS or DADM. You can refer to these books as necessary.

1.6 Visual Basic Versus VBA

Before going any further, I want to clarify one common misconception. Visual Basic (VB) is *not* the same as VBA. VB is a software development language that you can buy and run separately, without the need for Excel or Office. Actually, there are several versions of VB available. The most recent is called VB.NET, which comes with Microsoft's Visual Studio software development suite. (The .NET version of VB has many enhancements to the VB language.) Before VB.NET, there was VB6, still in use in thousands of applications. In contrast, VBA comes with Office. If you own Microsoft Office, you own VBA. The VB language is very similar to VBA, but it is not the same. The main difference is that VBA is the language you need to manipulate Excel, as you will do here.

You can think of it as follows. The VBA language consists of a "backbone" programming language with typical programming elements you find in all programming languages: looping, logical If-Then-Else constructions, arrays, subroutines, variable types, and others. In this respect, VBA and VB are essentially identical. However, the "A" in VBA means that any application software package, such as Excel, Access, Word, or even a non-Microsoft software package, can "expose" its *object model* to VBA, so that VBA can manipulate it programmatically. In short, VBA can be used to develop applications for any of these software packages. This book teaches you how to do so for Excel.

Excel's objects are discussed in depth in later chapters, but a few typical Excel objects you will recognize immediately are ranges, worksheets, workbooks, and charts. VBA for Excel knows about these Excel objects, and it enables you to manipulate them with code. For example, you can change the font of a cell, name a range, add or delete a worksheet, open a workbook, and change the title of a chart. Part of learning VBA for Excel is learning the VB backbone language, the elements that have nothing to do with Excel specifically. But another part, the more challenging part, involves learning how to manipulate Excel's objects in code. That is, it involves learning how to write computer programs to do what you do every day through the familiar Excel interface. If you ever take a course in VB, you will learn the backbone elements of VBA, but you will not learn how to manipulate objects in Excel. This requires VBA, and you *will* learn it here.

By the way, there are also VBA for Access, VBA for Word, VBA for PowerPoint, VBA for Outlook, and others. The difference between them is that each has its own specific objects. To list just a few, Access has tables, queries, and forms; Word has paragraphs and footnotes; PowerPoint has slides; and Outlook has mail. Each version of VBA shares the same VB backbone language, but each requires you to learn how to manipulate the objects in the specific application. There is certainly a learning curve in moving, say, from VBA for Excel to VBA for Word, but it is not nearly as difficult as if they were totally separate languages. In fact, the power of VBA, as well as the relative ease of programming in it, has prompted many third-party software developers to license VBA from Microsoft so that they can use VBA as the programming language for their applications. One example is Palisade, the developer of the @RISK and PrecisionTree add-ins for Excel, as will be discussed briefly in Chapter 17. In short, once you know VBA, you know a lot about what is happening in the programming world—and you can very possibly use this knowledge to obtain a valuable job in business.

1.7   Some Basic Terminology

Before proceeding, it is useful to clarify some very basic and important terminology that will be used throughout the book. First, whenever you program in any language, your basic building blocks are lines of **code**, short for **programming code**. Any line of code is intended to accomplish something, and it must obey the rules of syntax for the programming language being used. This book is all about coding in VBA.

Typically, a set of logically related lines of code that accomplishes a specific task is called a **subroutine**, a **procedure**, or a **macro**. In fact, one of the first keywords you will learn in VBA is Sub. This keyword begins all subroutines. The terms *subroutine*, *procedure*, and *macro* are essentially equivalent, although programmers tend to use the terms *subroutine* and *procedure*, whereas spreadsheet users tend to use the term *macro*. I tend to refer to any of these as a sub.

Finally, the term **program** is typically used to refer to all of the subs in an application. When you explore the more complex applications in Part II of the book, you will see that they often include many subs, where each sub is intended to perform one specific task in the overall program. (Chapter 10 discusses why this division of a program into multiple subs makes a lot of sense.)

1.8   Summary

VBA is the programming language of choice for an increasingly wide range of application developers. The main reason for this is that VBA uses the familiar Visual Basic programming language and then adapts it to many Microsoft and even non-Microsoft application software packages, including Excel. In addition, VBA is a relatively easy programming language to master. This makes it accessible to a large number of nonprofessional programmers in the business world—including you. By learning how to program in VBA, you will definitely enhance your value in the workplace.

2

The Excel Object Model

2.1 Introduction

This chapter introduces the Excel object model—the concept behind it and how it is implemented. Even if you have programmed in another language, this will probably be new material, even a new way of thinking, for you. However, without understanding Excel objects, you will not be able to proceed very far with VBA for Excel. This chapter provides just enough information to get you started. Later chapters focus on many of the most important Excel objects and how they can be manipulated with VBA code.

2.2 Objects, Properties, Methods, and Events

Consider the many things you see in the everyday world. To name a few, there are cars, houses, computers, people, and so on. These are all examples of **objects.** For example, let's focus on a car. A car has attributes, and there are things you can do to (or with) a car. Some of its attributes are its weight, its horsepower, its color, and its number of doors. Some of the things you can do to (or with) a car are drive it, park it, accelerate it, crash it, and sell it. In VBA, the attributes of an object are called **properties:** the size property, the horsepower property, the color property, the number of doors property, and so on. In addition, each property has a **value** for any *particular* car. For example, a particular car might be white and it might have four doors. In contrast, the things you can do to (or with) an object are called **methods:** the drive method, the park method, the accelerate method, the crash method, the sell method, and so on. Methods can also have qualifiers, called **arguments,** that indicate *how* a method is performed. For example, an argument of the crash method might be speed—how fast the car was going when it crashed.

The following analogy to parts of speech is useful. Objects correspond to *nouns,* properties correspond to *adjectives,* methods correspond to *verbs,* and arguments of methods correspond to *adverbs.* You might want to keep this analogy in mind as the discussion proceeds.

Now let's move from cars to Excel. Imagine all of the things—objects—you work with in Excel. Some of the most common are ranges, worksheets, charts, and workbooks. (A workbook is really just an Excel file.) Each of these is an object in the Excel object model. For example, consider the single-cell range B5.

This cell is a Range object.[1] Like a car, it has properties. It has a Value property: the value (either text or number) displayed in the cell. It has a HorizontalAlignment property: left-, center-, or right-aligned. It has a Formula property: the formula (if any) in the cell. These are just a few of the many properties of a range.

A Range object also has methods. For example, you can copy a range, so Copy is a method of a Range object. You can probably guess the argument of the Copy method: the Destination argument (the paste range). Another range method is the ClearContents method, which is equivalent to selecting the range and pressing the Delete key. It deletes the contents of the range, but it does not change the formatting. If you want to clear the formatting as well, there is also a Clear method. Neither the ClearContents method nor the Clear method has any arguments.

Learning the various objects in Excel, along with their properties and methods, is a lot like learning vocabulary in English—especially if English is not your native language. You learn a little at a time and generally broaden your vocabulary through practice and experience. Some objects, properties, and methods are naturally used most often, and you will learn quickly. Others you will never need, and you will probably remain unaware that they even exist. However, there are many times when you *will* need to use a particular object or one of its properties or methods that you have not yet learned. Fortunately, there is excellent online help available—a type of dictionary—for learning about objects, properties, and methods. It is called the **Object Browser** and is discussed in the next chapter.

There is one other important feature of objects: **events.** Some Excel objects have events that they can respond to. A good example is the Workbook object and its Open event. This event happens—we say it **fires**—when the workbook is opened in Excel. In fact, you might not realize it, but the Windows world is full of events that fire constantly. Every time you click or double-click a button, press a key, move your mouse over some region, or perform a number of other actions, various events fire. Programmers have the option of responding to events by writing **event handlers.** An event handler is a section of code that runs whenever the associated event fires. In later chapters, particularly Chapter 11, you will learn how to write your own event handlers. For example, it is often useful to write an event handler for the Open event of a Workbook object. Whenever the workbook is opened in Excel, the event handler then runs automatically. It could be used, for example, to ensure that the user sees a certain worksheet when the workbook opens.

2.3 Collections as Objects

Continuing the car analogy, imagine that you enter a used car lot. Each car in the lot is a particular car object, but it also makes sense to consider the *collection* of all

---

[1] From here on, "proper" case, such as Range or HorizontalAlignment, will be used for objects, properties, and methods. This is the convention used in VBA. Also, they appear in this book in a different font.

cars in the lot as an object. This is called a Collection object. Clearly, the collection of cars is not conceptually the same as an individual car. Rather, it is an object that includes all of the individual car objects.

Collection objects also have properties and methods, but they are not the same as the properties and methods of the objects they contain. Generally, there are many *fewer* properties and methods for collections. The two most common are the Count property and the Add method. The Count property indicates the number of objects in the collection (the number of cars in the lot). The Add method adds a new object to a collection (a new car joins the lot).

It is easy to spot collections and the objects they contain in the Excel object model. Collection objects are plural, whereas a typical object contained in a collection is singular. A good example involves worksheets in a given workbook. The Worksheets collection (note the plural) is the collection of all worksheets in the workbook. Any one of these worksheets is a Worksheet object (note the singular). Again, these must be treated differently. You can count worksheets in the Worksheets collection, or you can add another worksheet to the collection. In contrast, typical properties of a Worksheet object are its Name (the name on the sheet tab) and Visible (True or False) properties, and a typical method of a Worksheet object is the Delete method. (Note that this Delete method reduces the Count of the Worksheets collection by one.)

The main exception to this plural/singular characterization is the Range object. There is no "Ranges" collection object. A Range object cannot really be considered singular *or* plural; it is essentially some of each. A Range object can be a single cell, a rectangular range, a union of several rectangular ranges, an entire column, or an entire row. Range objects are probably the most difficult to master in all of their varied forms. This is unfortunate because they are the most frequently used objects in Excel. Think of your own experience in Excel, and you will realize that you are almost always doing something with ranges. An entire chapter, Chapter 6, is devoted to Range objects so that you can master some of the techniques for manipulating these important objects.

2.4 The Hierarchy of Objects

Returning one last time to cars, what is the status of a car's hood, a car's trunk, or a car's set of wheels? These are also objects, with their own properties and methods. In fact, the set of wheels is a collection object that contains individual wheel objects. The point, however, is that there is a natural hierarchy, as illustrated in Figure 2.1. The Cars collection is at the top of the hierarchy. It contains a set of individual cars. The notation Cars (Car) indicates that the collection object is called Cars and that each member of this collection is a Car object. Each car "contains" a number of objects: a Wheels collection of individual Wheel objects, a Trunk object, a Hood object, and others not shown. Each of these can have its own properties and methods. Also, some can contain objects farther down the hierarchy. For example, the figure indicates that an object down the hierarchy from Hood is the HoodOrnament object. Note that each of the rectangles in this

Figure 2.1 Object Model for Cars

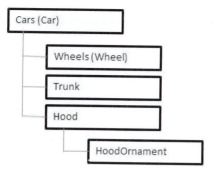

figure represents an *object*. Each object has properties and methods that could be shown emanating from its rectangle, but this would greatly complicate the figure.

The same situation occurs in Excel. The full diagram of the Excel object model appears in Figure 2.2. (This is the Excel 2003 version; versions for Excel 2007 or later are only slightly different.[2]) This figure shows how all objects, including collection objects, are arranged in a hierarchy. At the top of the hierarchy is the Application object. This refers to Excel itself. One object (of several) one step down from Application is the Workbooks collection, the collection of all open Workbook objects. This diagram is admittedly quite complex. All you need to realize at this point is that Excel has a very rich object model—a lot of objects; fortunately, you will need only a relatively small subset of this object model for most of your applications. This relatively small subset is the topic of later chapters.

2.5 Object Models in General

Although the Excel object model is used in this book, you should now have some understanding of what it would take to use VBA for other applications such as Word, Access, or even non-Microsoft products. In short, you would need to learn *its* object model. You can think of each application "plugging in" its object model to the underlying VB language. Indeed, third-party software developers who want to license VBA from Microsoft need to *create* an object model appropriate for their application. Programmers can then use VBA to manipulate the objects in this model. This is a powerful idea, and it is the reason why VBA is the programming language of choice for so many developers—regardless of whether they are working in Excel or any other application.

Figures 2.3 and 2.4 illustrate two other object models. (Again, these are the Office 2003 versions.) The object model in Figure 2.3 is for Word. A few of these objects are probably familiar, such as Sentence, Paragraph, and Footnote. If you

---

[2] For example, if you perform a Web search for "Excel 2013 object model diagram," you will see a number of such diagrams.

Figure 2.2 Excel Object Model

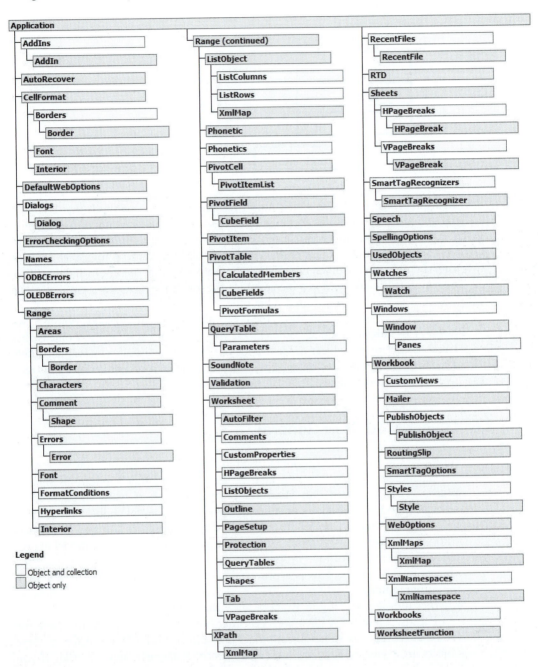

Legend

Object and collection

Object only

Figure 2.3 Word Object Model

were learning VBA for Word, you would need to learn the most common elements of this object model. Figure 2.4 shows part (about 40%) of the object model for Microsoft Office as a whole. You might wonder why Office has a separate object model from Excel or Word. The reason is that Office is an integrated suite, where all of its programs—Excel, Word, PowerPoint, Outlook, and the rest—share a number of features. For example, they all have menus and toolbars, referred to collectively as the CommandBars collection in the object model. Therefore, if you

Figure 2.4 Part of Office Object Model

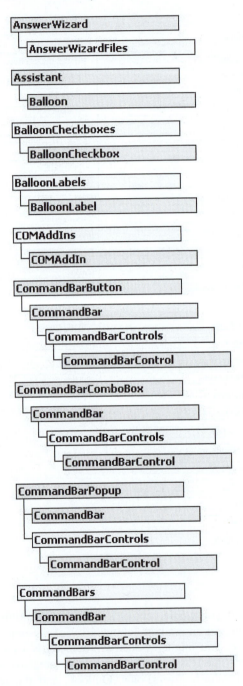

want to use VBA to manipulate toolbars or menus in Excel, as many programmers do, you have to learn part of the Office object model. But then this same knowledge would enable you to manipulate menus and toolbars in Word, PowerPoint, and the others. (Actually, menus and toolbars were replaced for the most part by ribbons in Excel 2007 and later versions, but the CommandBar object is still present. This topic is discussed in Chapter 16.)

The Excel object model continues to evolve as new versions of Excel are released. Sometimes new objects, properties, or methods are added. Other times, some are dropped from the official object model but still continue to work, for backward compatibility. Occasionally, some are dropped completely, so that programs written in an earlier version no longer work. Fortunately, these are the rare exceptions. If you are working in Excel 2007 or later versions and are interested in seeing the types of changes that have been made, open the Visual Basic Editor (Alt+F11 from Excel), press the F1 key for help, and search for "object model changes." Although the list is fairly long, not much in terms of VBA code has changed since this book was originally written for Excel 2003.

2.6 Summary

This chapter has introduced the concept of an object model, and it has briefly introduced the Excel object model that is the focus of the rest of the book. If you have never programmed in an object-oriented environment, you can look forward to a whole new experience. However, the more you do it, the more natural it becomes. It is certainly the dominant theme in today's programming world, so if you want to be part of this world, you have to start thinking in terms of objects. You will get plenty of chances to do so throughout the book.

3

The Visual Basic Editor

3.1 Introduction

At this point, you might be asking where VBA lives. I claimed in Chapter 1 that if you own Excel, you also own VBA, but many of you have probably never seen it. You do your VBA work in the **Visual Basic Editor** (**VBE**), which you can access easily from Excel by pressing the **Alt+F11** key combination. The VBE provides a very user-friendly environment for writing your VBA programs. This chapter walks you through the VBE and shows you its most important features. It also helps you write your first VBA program. By the way, you might also hear the term **Integrated Development Environment** (**IDE**). This is a general term for an environment where you do your programming, regardless of the programming language. The VBE is the IDE for programming with VBA in Excel.

3.2 Important Features of the VBE

To understand this section most easily, you should follow along at your computer. Open Excel and press **Alt+F11** to get into the VBE.[1] It should look something like Figure 3.1, although the configuration you see might be somewhat different. By the time this discussion is completed, you will be able to make your screen look like that in Figure 3.1 or change it according to your own preferences. This is your programming workspace, and you have a lot of control over how it appears. This chapter provides some guidance, but the best way to learn is by experimenting.

The large blank pane on the right is the **Code** window. This is where you write your code. (If any of the windows discussed here are *not* visible on your screen, you can select the View menu from the VBE and then select the window you want to make visible.) The rest of the VBE consists of the top menu, one or more toolbars, and one or more optional windows. Let's start with the windows.

---

[1] In Excel 2003 and earlier, the **Tools → Macro → Visual Basic Editor** menu item also gets you into the VBE, but Alt+F11 is quicker. In Excel 2007 and later versions, you should first make the **Developer** ribbon visible. To do this in Excel 2007, click the Office button and then Excel Options. Under the Popular tab, select the third option at the top: Show Developer tab in the Ribbon. In Excel 2010 and later versions, right-click any ribbon and select Customize the Ribbon. Then check the Developer item in the right pane. You need to do this only once. The Developer tab is a must for programmers. Among other things, you can get to the VBE by clicking on its Visual Basic button, but again, Alt+F11 is quicker.

Figure 3.1 Visual Basic Editor (VBE)

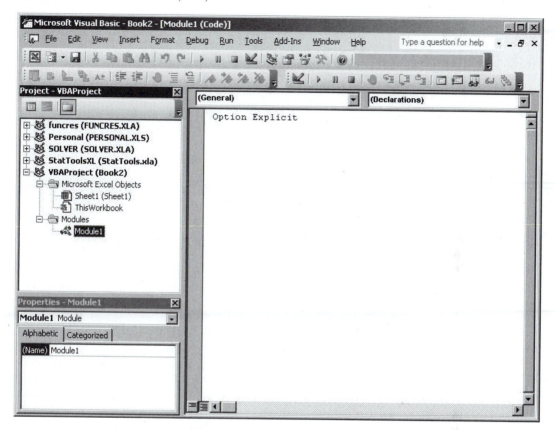

The **Project Explorer** window, repeated in Figure 3.2, shows an Explorer-type list of all open projects. (Your list will probably be different from the one shown here. It depends on the files you have open and the add-ins that are loaded.) For example, the active project shown here has the generic name **VBA-Project** and corresponds to the workbook Book2—that is, the file **Book2.xlsx**.[2] Below a given project, the Project Explorer window shows its "elements." In the Microsoft Excel Objects folder, these elements include any worksheets or chart sheets in the Excel file and an element called ThisWorkbook, which refers to the workbook itself. There can also be folders for modules (for VBA code), user forms (for dialog boxes), and references (for links to other libraries of code you need), depending on whether you have any of these in your project. Modules, user forms, and references are discussed in detail in later chapters.

---

[2] For our purposes, there is no difference between a project and a workbook. However, VBA allows them to have separate names: VBAProject and Book2, for example. If you save Book2 as **Practice.xlsm**, say, the project name will still be VBAProject. Admittedly, it is somewhat confusing, but just think of projects as Excel files.

Figure 3.2 Project Explorer Window

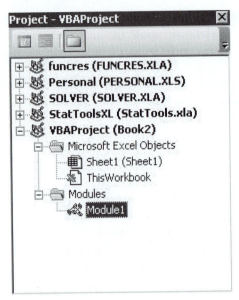

The **Properties** window, shown in Figure 3.3, lists a set of properties. This list depends on what is currently selected. For example, the property list in Figure 3.3 is relevant for the project itself. It indicates a single property only—the project's name. Therefore, if you want to change the name of the project from the generic VBAProject to something more meaningful, such as MyFirstProgram, this is the place to do it. Chapter 11 discusses the use of the Properties window in much more detail. At this point, you don't really need the Properties window, so you can close it by clicking on its close button (the upper right X).

The VBE also has at least three toolbars that are very useful: **Standard, Edit,** and **Debug.** They appear in Figures 3.4, 3.5, and 3.6, where some of the most useful buttons are indicated. (If any of these toolbars are not visible on your

Figure 3.3 Properties Window

Figure 3.4 Standard Toolbar

Figure 3.5 Edit Toolbar

Figure 3.6 Debug Toolbar

computer, you can make them visible through the View menu.) From the Standard toolbar, you can run, pause, or stop a program you have written. You can also display the Project or Properties window (if it is hidden), and you can display the Object Browser or the Control Toolbox (more about these later). From the Edit toolbar, you can perform useful editing tasks, such as indenting or outdenting (the opposite of indenting), and you can comment or uncomment blocks of code, as is discussed later. Finally, although the Debug toolbar will probably not mean much at this point, it is invaluable when you need to debug your programs—as you will undoubtedly need to do. It is discussed in more detail in Chapter 5. For future reference, here are a few menu items of particular importance.

- You usually need at least one module in a project. This is where you will typically store your code. To insert a module, use the **Insert** → **Module** menu item. If you ever have a module you do not need, highlight the module in the Project Explorer window and use the **File** → **Remove Module** menu item. (Answer No to whether you want to export the module.)

- Chapter 11 explains how to build your own dialog boxes. VBA calls these **user forms.** To insert a new user form into a project, use the **Insert → User Form** menu item. You can delete an unwanted user form in the same way you delete a module.
- Under the Insert menu, there is also a **Class Module** item. You can usually ignore this. It is more advanced, but it is discussed briefly in Chapter 18.
- The **Tools → Options** menu item allows you to change the look and feel of the VBE in a variety of ways. You should probably leave the default settings alone—with one important exception. Try it now. Select **Tools → Options,** and make sure the **Require Variable Declarations** box under the Editor tab *is* checked. The effect of this is explained in Chapter 5. You might also want to uncheck the **Auto Syntax Check** box, as I always do. If it is checked, the editor beeps at you each time you make a syntax error in a line of code and then press Enter. This can be annoying. Even if this box is unchecked, the editor will still warn you about a syntax error by coloring the offending line red.
- If you ever want to password-protect your project so that other people cannot see your code, use the **Tools → VBA Properties** menu item and click the **Protection** tab. This gives you a chance to enter a password. (Just don't forget it, or you will not be able to see your *own* code.)
- If you click the familiar **Save** button (or use the **File → Save** menu item), this saves the project currently highlighted in the Project Explorer window. It saves your code *and* anything in the underlying Excel workbook. (It is all saved in the .xlsm file.) You can achieve the same objective by switching back to Excel and saving in the usual way from there. (Note, however, that in Excel 2007 and later versions, if your file started as an .xlsx file without any VBA code, you will have to save it as an .xlsm file once it contains code.)

3.3 The Object Browser

VBA's **Object Browser** is a wonderful online help tool. To get to it, open the VBE and click the Object Browser button on the Standard toolbar (see Figure 3.4). If you prefer keyboard shortcuts, you can press the F2 key. Either way, this opens the window shown in Figure 3.7. At the top left, there is a dropdown list of *libraries* that you can get help on. Our main interest is in the Excel library, the VBA library, and, to a lesser extent, the Office library. The **Excel** library provides help on all of the objects and their properties and methods in the Excel object model. The **VBA** library provides help on the VBA elements that are common to *all* applications that can use VBA: Excel, Access, Word, and others. The **Office** library provides help on objects common to all Office programs, such as CommandBars objects (menus and toolbars).

For now, select the Excel library. In the bottom left pane, you see a list of all objects in the Excel object model, and in the right pane, you see a list of all properties and methods for any object selected in the left pane. A property is designated by a hand icon, and a method is designated by a green rectangular icon. A few objects, such as the Workbook object, also have events they can respond to. An event is designated by a lightning icon.

Figure 3.7 Object Browser

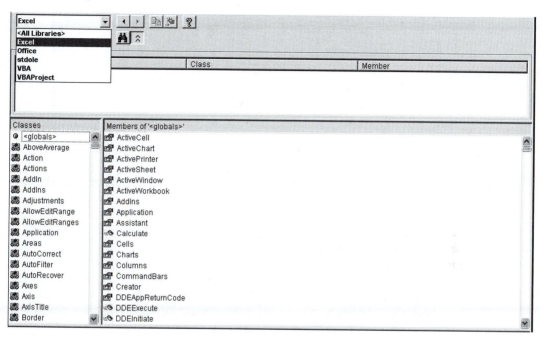

To get help on any of these items, select it and then click the question mark button at the top. It is too early in our VBA discussion to be asking for online help, but you should not forget about the Object Browser. It can be invaluable as you develop your projects. I use it constantly, and you should too. Of course, you can get similar help by performing online searches for specific items, but the Object Browser stores everything in one place.

3.4 The Immediate and Watch Windows

There are two other windows in the VBE that you should be aware of: the **Immediate** and **Watch** windows. Each can be opened through the View menu or the Debug toolbar. (The Immediate window can also be opened quickly with the **Ctrl+g** key combination.) The Immediate window, shown in Figure 3.8, is useful for issuing one-line VBA commands. If you type a command and press Enter, the command takes effect immediately. For example, the first line in Figure 3.8 selects the range A1:B10 of the Data worksheet (assuming there is a Data worksheet in the active workbook). If you type this, press Enter, and switch back to Excel, you will see that the range A1:B10 has been selected. If you precede the command by a question mark, you can get an immediate answer to a question. For example, if you type the second line in the figure, which asks for the address of the range named MyData, and then press Enter, you immediately get the answer on the third line.

Figure 3.8 Immediate Window

```
Immediate                                                    ✕
Worksheets("Data").Range("A1:B10").Select
?Worksheets("Data").Range("MyData").Address
$B$5:$C$20
|
```

Many programmers send information to the Immediate window through their code. If you see the command Debug.Print, followed by something to be printed, the programmer is asking for this to be printed to the Immediate window. This is not a permanent copy of the printed information. It is usually a quick check to see whether a program is working properly.

The Watch window is used for debugging. Programs typically include several variables that change value as the program runs. If the program does not appear to be working as it should, you can put a watch on one or more key variables to see how they change as the program progresses. Debugging in this way is discussed in some detail in Chapter 5.

3.5 A First Program

Although you do not yet know much about VBA programming, you know enough to write a simple program and run it. Besides, sooner or later you will have to stop reading and do some programming on your own. Now is a good time to get started. Although the example in this section is very simple, there are a few details you probably won't understand completely, at least not yet. Don't worry. Later chapters will clarify the details. For now, just follow the directions and realize the thrill of getting a program to work.

This example is based on a simple data set in the file **First Program.xlsx.** It shows sales of a company by region and by month for a 3-year period. (See Figure 3.9, where some rows have been hidden. The range B2:G37 has the range name SalesRange.) Your boss wants you to write a program that scans the sales of each region and, for each, displays a message that indicates the number of months that sales in that region are above a user-selected value such as $150,000. To do this, go through the following steps. (In case you get stuck, the finished version is stored in the file **First Program Finished.xlsm.)**

1. **Open the file.** Get into Excel and open the **First Program.xlsx** file. Because it is going to contain VBA code, save it as **First Program.xlsm.**
2. **Get into the VBE.** Press Alt+F11 to open the VBE. Make sure the Project Explorer Window is visible. If it isn't, open it with the **View → Project Explorer** menu item.

Figure 3.9 Sales by Region and Month

	A	B	C	D	E	F	G
1	**Month**	**Region 1**	**Region 2**	**Region 3**	**Region 4**	**Region 5**	**Region 6**
2	Jan-08	144770	111200	163140	118110	105010	167350
3	Feb-08	155180	155100	129850	133940	140880	104110
4	Mar-08	86230	162310	142950	131490	150160	158720
5	Apr-08	148800	165160	123840	141050	175870	108100
6	May-08	157140	130300	114990	128220	147790	167470
7	Jun-08	126150	163240	149360	152240	167320	181070
31	Jun-10	124320	148410	162310	186440	147200	146200
32	Jul-10	135100	131520	151780	153920	121200	141430
33	Aug-10	150790	151970	168800	144170	140360	139990
34	Sep-10	93740	168100	142040	126440	113500	130500
35	Oct-10	124160	148560	120190	155600	132590	155510
36	Nov-10	109840	189790	127460	135160	149470	163330
37	Dec-10	127100	108640	145300	127920	151130	122900

3. **Add a module.** In the Project Explorer window, make sure the **First Program.xlsm** project is highlighted (select it if necessary), and use the **Insert → Module** menu item to add a module to this project. This module is automatically named Module1, and it will hold your VBA code.

4. **Start a sub.** Click anywhere in the Code window, type Sub CountHighSales, and press Enter. You should immediately see the following code. You have started a program called CountHighSales. (Any other descriptive name could be used instead of CountHighSales, but it shouldn't contain any spaces.) The keyword Sub informs VBA that you want to write a **subroutine** (also called a **procedure** or a **macro),** so it adds empty parentheses next to the name CountHighSales and adds the keywords End Sub at the bottom—two necessary elements of any subroutine. The rest of your code will be placed between the Sub and End Sub lines. Chapters 5 and 10 discuss subroutines in more detail, but for now, just think of a subroutine as a section of code that performs a particular task. For this simple example, there is only one subroutine.

```
Sub CountHighSales( )
End Sub
```

5. **Type the code.** Type the code exactly as shown below between the Sub and End Sub lines. It is important to indent properly for readability. To indent as shown, press the Tab key. Also, note that there is no word wrap in the VBE. To finish a line and go to the next line, you need to press the Enter key. Other than this, the Code window is much like a word processor. You will note that keywords such as Sub and End Sub are automatically colored blue by the VBE. This is a great feature for helping you program. Also, spaces are often inserted for you to make your code more readable. For example, if you

type nHigh=nHigh+1, the editor will automatically insert spaces on either side of the equals and plus signs.

```
Sub CountHighSales( )
    Dim i As Integer
    Dim j As Integer
    Dim nHigh As Integer
    Dim cutoff As Currency

    cutoff = InputBox("What sales value do you want to check for?")
    For j = 1 To 6
        nHigh = 0
        For i = 1 To 36
            If wsData.Range("Sales").Cells(i, j) >= cutoff Then _
                nHigh = nHigh + 1
        Next i
        MsgBox "For region " & j & ", sales were above " & Format(cutoff, "$0,000") _
            & " on " & nHigh & " of the 36 months."
    Next j
End Sub
```

6. **Avoid syntax errors.** Two special characters in this code are the ampersand, &, and the underscore, _. Make sure each ampersand has a space on either side of it, and make sure each line-ending underscore has a space before it. (These spaces are *not* added automatically for you.) There are other syntax errors you could make, but these are the most likely in this short subroutine. Be sure to check your spelling carefully and fix any errors before proceeding.

7. **Run the program from the VBE.** Your program is now finished. The next step is to run it. There are several ways to do so, two of which are demonstrated here. For the first method, make sure the cursor is anywhere within your subroutine and select the **Run → Run Sub/UserForm** menu item. (Alternatively, click the "green triangle" button on the Standard toolbar, or press the F5 key.) If all goes well, you should see the input box in Figure 3.10, where you can enter a value such as 150000. The program will then search for all values greater than or equal to $150,000 in the data set. Next, you will see a series of message boxes such as the one in Figure 3.11. Each message box tells you how many months the sales in some region are above the sales cutoff value you entered. This is exactly what you wanted the program to do.

8. **Run the program with a button.** The run method in the previous step is fine for you, the programmer, but your users won't want to get into the VBE to run the program. They probably don't even want to *see* the VBE. They will instead want to run the program directly from the Excel worksheet that contains the data. You can make this easy for them. First, switch back to Excel (click the Excel button on the taskbar of your screen). Then click the Insert dropdown list on the Developer ribbon (see footnote 1 of this chapter for how to make the Developer tab visible), click the upper left "button" control, and drag a rectangular button somewhere on your worksheet, as

Figure 3.10 InputBox for Sales Cutoff Value

Figure 3.11 MessageBox for Region 2

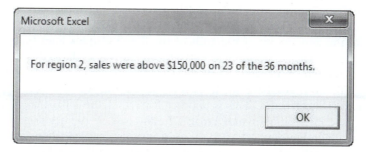

shown in Figure 3.12.[3] You will immediately be asked to assign a macro to this button. This is because the only purpose of a button is to run a macro. You should assign the CountHighSales macro you just wrote. Then you can type a more meaningful caption on the button itself. (Again, see Figure 3.12 for a possible caption.) At this point, the button is "selected"—there is a dotted border around it. To deselect it, just click anywhere else on the worksheet. Now your button is ready to go. To run your program, just click the button.

9. **Save the file.** In case you haven't done so already, save the file under the original (or a new) name. This will save your code and the button you created. Again, make sure you save it with the .xlsm extension.

A note on saving. You have undoubtedly been told to save frequently in all of your computer-related courses. Frequent saving is at least as important in a programming environment. After all the effort you expend to get a program working correctly, you don't want that sinking feeling when your unsaved work is wiped out by a sudden power outage or some other problem. So I will say it, too—save, save, save!

---

[3] In Excel 2003 and earlier, the button control is on the Forms toolbar, which you can make visible by right-clicking any toolbar and checking the Forms option. Although buttons are ready-made for running macros, Excel shapes can also be used. Give it a try. From the Insert menu, select and then drag a shape such as a rectangle. Then right-click, and you will see an Assign Macro menu item.

Figure 3.12 Button on the Worksheet

	A	B	C	D	E	F	G	H	I	J	K	L
1	**Month**	**Region 1**	**Region 2**	**Region 3**	**Region 4**	**Region 5**	**Region 6**					
2	Jan-08	144770	111200	163140	118110	105010	167350					
3	Feb-08	155180	155100	129850	133940	140880	104110					
4	Mar-08	86230	162310	142950	131490	150160	158720					
5	Apr-08	148800	165160	123840	141050	175870	108100					
6	May-08	157140	130300	114990	128220	147790	167470					
7	Jun-08	126150	163360	149360	152240	167320	181070			Count High Sales Values		
8	Jul-08	174010	183360	122120	149730	134220	135530					
9	Aug-08	171780	130050	124130	134510	175590	122230					
35	Oct-10	124160	148560	120190	155600	132590	155510					
36	Nov-10	109840	189790	127460	135160	149470	163330					
37	Dec-10	127100	108640	145300	127920	151130	122900					

Troubleshooting

What if you get an error message when you run your program? First, read your program carefully and make sure the code is exactly like the code shown here. Again, the underscores at the ends of the If and MsgBox lines must be preceded by a space. (Their purpose is to extend long lines of code to the next line.) Also, the ampersand (&) characters in the MsgBox line should have a space on either side of them. If you have any lines colored red, this is a sure sign you have typed something incorrectly. (This is another feature of the VBE that helps programmers. Red lines signify syntax errors.) In any case, if you get some version of the dialog box in Figure 3.13, click the End button. This stops a program with bugs and lets you fix any errors. Alternatively, click the Debug button, and you will see a line of code in yellow. This line is typically the offending line, or close to it. (Again, debugging is discussed in some detail in Chapter 5.)

If your typing is correct and you still get an error, check steps 7 and 8. If you are using step 7 to run the program, make sure your cursor is somewhere *inside* the subroutine. If you are using the button method in step 8, make sure you have assigned the CountHighSales macro to the button. (Right-click the button

Figure 3.13 A Typical Error Dialog Box

and select the Assign Macro menu item.) There are not too many things that can go wrong with this small program, so you should eventually get it to work. Remember, perseverance is the key.

Brief Analysis of the Program

I could not expect you to write this program without my help at this point. But you can probably understand the gist of it. The four lines after the Sub line declare variables that are used later on. The next line displays an InputBox (see Figure 3.12) that asks for a user's input. The section starting with For j = 1 To 6 and ending with Next j is a loop that performs a similar task for each sales region. As you will learn in Chapter 7, loops are among the most powerful tools in a programmer's arsenal. For example, if there were 600 regions rather than 6, the only required change would be to change 6 to 600 in the For j = 1 To 6 line. Computers are excellent at performing repetitive tasks.

Within the loop on regions, there is another loop on months, starting with For i = 1 To 36 and ending with Next i. Within this loop there is an If statement that checks whether the sales value for the region in that month is at least as large as the cutoff value. If it is, the variable nHigh is increased by 1. Once this inner loop has been completed, the results for the region are reported in a MessageBox.

Again, the details might be unclear at this point, but you can probably understand the overall logic of the program. And if you typed everything correctly and ran the program as instructed, you now know the thrill of getting a program to work as planned. I hope you experience this feeling frequently as you work through this book.

3.6 Intellisense

A lot of things are advertised to be the best thing since sliced bread. Well, one of the features of the VBE really is. It is called **Intellisense**. As you were writing the program in the previous section, you undoubtedly noticed how the editor gave you hints and tried to complete certain words for you. You see Intellisense in the following situations:

- Every time you type the first line of a sub and then press Enter, Intellisense adds the End Sub line automatically for you.[4]
- Whenever you start declaring a variable in a Dim statement, Intellisense helps you with the variable type. For example, if you type Dim nHigh As In, it will

[4]There are many other VBA constructs that are bracketed with a beginning line and an ending line: If and End If, For and Next, Do and Loop, and others. You might imagine that if VBA is smart enough to add End Sub for you after you type the Sub line, it is smart enough to add an End If line after an If line, a Next line after a For line, and so on. However, it isn't that smart, at least not yet. My guess is that Microsoft simply hasn't gotten around to it yet. Interestingly, the Visual Studio editor for .NET *is* that smart. It even indents automatically for you.

guess that you want In to be Integer. All you have to do at this point is press the Tab key, and Integer will appear.

- Intellisense helps you with properties and methods of objects. For example, if you type Range("A1:C10"). (including the period), you will see all of the properties and methods of a Range object. At this point you can scroll through the list and choose the one you want.

- Intellisense helps you with arguments of methods. For example, if you type Range("A1:C10").Copy and then a space, you will see all of the arguments (actually, only one) of the Copy method. (Any arguments shown in square brackets in this list are optional. All others are required.)

- Intellisense helps you with hard-to-remember constants. For example, if you type Range("A1").End(, you will see that there are four constants to choose from: xlDown, xlUp, xlToRight, and xlToLeft. (This corresponds to pressing the End key and then one of the arrow keys in Excel. You will learn more about it in Chapter 6.)

- Sometimes you create fairly long variable names like productCost or firstCustomer. Then you need to use them repeatedly in your code. If you start typing one of them, like firs, and then press **Ctrl+Space**, you will get a list of all variables that start with these letters, and you can choose the one you want. In fact, if there is only one variable that starts with these letters, it will be inserted automatically. This can save a lot of typing—and typing errors.

In short, Intellisense is instant online help. It doesn't necessarily help you with the *logic* of your program, but it speeds up your typing, and it helps ensure that you get the syntax and spelling correct. After you get used to Intellisense, you will find that it is absolutely indispensable.

3.7 Color Coding and Case

Another feature of the VBE that enhances readability and helps you get your code correct is color coding.

- All keywords, such as Sub, End, For, and many others, are automatically colored blue.
- All comments (discussed in Chapter 5) are colored green.
- All of the rest of your code is colored black.
- If you make a syntax error in a line of code and then press Enter, the offending line is colored red. This is a warning that you should fix the line before proceeding.

Besides coloring, the editor corrects case for you.

- All keywords start with a capital letter. Therefore, if you type sub and press Enter, the editor changes it to Sub.
- If you declare a variable with the spelling unitCost and then type it as UNIT-Cost later on in the program, the editor automatically changes it to unitCost.

(Whatever spelling you use in the Dim statement is the one used subsequently, even if it is something weird like uNitCost.) Actually, case doesn't matter at all to VBA—it treats unitCost the same as uNitCost or any other variation, but the editor at least promotes consistency.

3.8 Finding Subs in the VBE

For the next few chapters, each of your programs will consist of a single sub, so when you select the file's module in the VBE's Project Explorer, your sub will appear in the Code window. However, in the programs in Part II of the book, there are multiple subs, and not all of them are in modules. In this case, it can be tedious to locate them in the Code window. Fortunately, the VBE provides tools to make this easy.

To follow along, open the **Car Loan.xlsm** file from Chapter 19. It not only has multiple subs in its module, but it has code in other locations, including code behind user forms (discussed in Chapter 11). The point is that it has multiple subs in various places. For now, double-click Module1 in the Project Explorer. You will see the MainProgram sub in the Code window. Now click the right drop-down arrow above the Code window. (See Figure 3.14.) You will see a list of all subs in Module1. To go quickly to any of them, just select the one you want.

Next, right-click the first form, frmInputs, in the Project Explorer and select View Code. This shows the code behind this form. (Again, all of this is explained in Chapter 11.) Now click the left dropdown arrow above the Code window. (See Figure 3.15.) You will see a list of all the controls on the form. Any of these can have associated code that responds to its events. For example, select

Figure 3.14 List of Subs in a Module

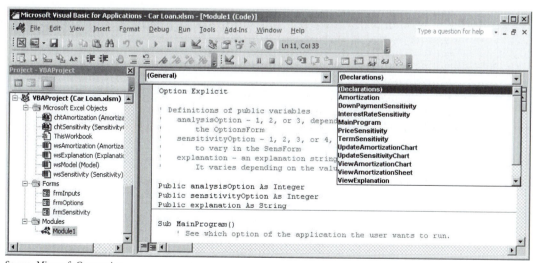

Source: Microsoft Corporation

Figure 3.15 List of Controls on a User Form

the button control cmdOK, and then click the right dropdown list above the Code window. (See Figure 3.16.) You will see a list of all events that the cmdOK control can respond to, and any that have associated code (event handlers) are boldfaced. In this case, the Click event is the only one boldfaced, and if you select it, you will see the corresponding code.

All you need to remember at this point is that these dropdown lists are always available, and they make it easy to navigate around a large program.

Figure 3.16 List of Events That a Control Can Respond To

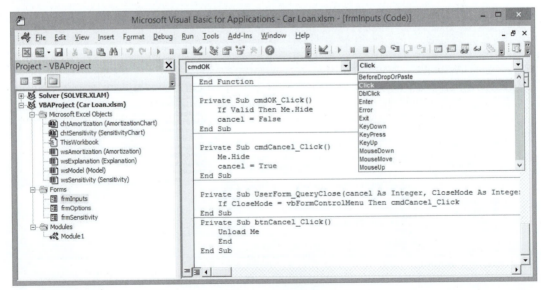

3.9 Summary

This chapter has introduced the Visual Basic Editor (VBE)—its toolbars, some of its menu items, and its windows. It has also briefly discussed online VBA help and the Object Browser. You will be doing most of your development work in the VBE, so you should become familiar with it right away. You will come to appreciate what a friendly and helpful programming environment it provides.

EXERCISES

1. Open Excel and open two new workbooks, which will probably be called Book1 and Book2 (or some such generic names). Get into the VBE and make sure the Project Explorer window is visible. Insert a module into Book1 and click the plus sign next to Modules (for Book1) to see the module you just inserted. Now type the following sub in the Code window for this module and then run it. It should display the name of the workbook.

```
Sub ShowNameO
  MsgBox "The name of this workbook is " & ThisWorkbook.Name
End Sub
```

Finally, go to the Project Explorer window and drag the module you inserted down to Book2. This should create a copy of the module in Book2. Run the sub in the copied module. It should display the name of the second workbook. The point of this exercise is that you can copy code from one workbook to another by copying the module containing the code. Fortunately, copying a module is as simple as dragging in the Project Explorer window.

2. Open the **First Program.xlsm** file you created in Section 3.5, and get into the VBE so that you can look at the code. Select the **Debug → Add Watch** menu item, and type nHigh in the text box. You are adding a watch for the variable nHigh, so that you can see how it changes as the program runs. Next, place the cursor anywhere inside the code, and press the **F8 key** repeatedly. This steps through the program one line at a time. Every time the program sees a sales figure greater than the cutoff value you specify, nHigh will increase by 1, which you should see in the Watch window. (You will probably get tired of pressing F8. You can stop the program prematurely at any time by clicking the blue square **Reset** button on the Standard toolbar. Alternatively, you can click the green triangle **Run** button to run the rest of the program all at once.)

3. Get into the VBE and open the **Immediate** window. (Again, the shortcut for doing so is **Ctrl+g**.) Then type the following lines, pressing the Enter key after each line. You should now understand why it is called the Immediate window.

```
?Application.Name
?Application.DefaultFilePath
?Application.Path
?Application.Version
```

```
?Application.UserName
?IsDate("February 29, 2009")
?IsDate("February 29, 2008")
?Workbooks.Count
?ActiveWorkbook.Name
```

4. Open a new workbook in Excel, get into the VBE, and insert a module into this new workbook. Type the following code in the Code window. Make sure there is no Option Explicit line at the top of the code window. (If there is one, delete it.)

```
Sub EnterUserNameSlowly( )
  Range("A1").Value = "The user of this copy is Excel is listed below."
  yourName = Application.UserName
  nChars = Len(yourName)
  For i = 1 To nChars
    Range("A3").Value = Left(yourName, i)
    newHour = Hour(Now( ))
    newMinute = Minute(Now( ))
    newSecond = Second(Now( )) + 1
    waitTime = TimeSerial(newHour, newMinute, newSecond)
    Application.Wait waitTime
  Next
End Sub
```

Next, return to Sheet1 of this workbook, add a button and assign the EnterUser-NameSlowly sub to it, and then run the program by clicking the button. Can you now explain what the code is doing? (If you like, look up the Wait method of the Application object in the Object Browser for online help.)

5. Open the **First Programs.xlsm** file you created in Section 3.5, and get into the VBE. Use the **Tools → VBAProject Properties** menu item, and click the Protection tab. Check the "Lock project for viewing" option, enter a password in the other two boxes—don't forget it—and click OK. Go back to Excel, save the file, and close it. Now reopen the file and try to look at the code. You have just learned how to password-protect your code. Of course, you have to remember the password. Otherwise, not even you, the author, can look at the code. (If you ever want to remove the protection, just uncheck the "Lock project for viewing" option and delete the passwords from the boxes.)

4

Recording Macros

4.1 Introduction

This chapter illustrates a very quick way to start programming—by *recording* while you perform a task in Excel. Just as you can record yourself singing or playing the piano, you can record your actions as you work in Excel. As the recorder records what you are doing, it generates VBA code in a module. If this sounds too good to be true, it is—at least to an extent. There are certain things you cannot record—loops and control logic, for example—and the recorded code, even though correct, is usually not very "stylish." Still, there are two reasons why recording can be useful. First, it is helpful for beginners. A beginning programmer can immediately generate code and then look at it and probably learn a few things. Second, it is useful even for experienced programmers who need to learn one particular detail of VBA code. For example, what is the VBA code for entering a comment in a cell? You could look it up in online help, but you could also record the process of entering a comment in a cell and then examine the resulting code. Recording often provides the clue you need to overcome a particular coding hurdle.

4.2 How to Record a Macro

Recording is easy. In Excel 2007 and later versions, select **Record Macro** from the Developer ribbon (see Figure 4.1) to display the dialog box in Figure 4.2. (In Excel 2003 and earlier, select the **Tools → Macro → Record New Macro** menu item.) Alternatively, you can click the small button to the right of READY on the status bar at the bottom left of the Excel screen to bring up the same Record Macro dialog box (see Figure 4.3). Then you can give the macro a descriptive name, provide an optional description of the macro, give it an optional shortcut key, and tell Excel where to store the recorded code.[1]

---

[1]A shortcut key is useful if you want to be able to run the macro with a Ctrl+key combination. For example, if you enter the letter k in the box, the macro will run when you press the Ctrl+k key combination. Just be aware that if there is already a Ctrl+key combination, especially one that you use frequently, your new one will override it. For example, many people like to use Ctrl+s to save a file, so it is not wise to override this with your own use of Ctrl+s.

Figure 4.1 Record Macro Button on Developer Ribbon

Figure 4.2 Record Macro Dialog Box

Figure 4.3 Record Macro Button on Status Bar

The storage location for the macro is particularly important. As Figure 4.2 indicates, you can store the macro in the current workbook, in a new workbook, or in a special workbook called your **Personal Macro Workbook**. If you store the macro in the current workbook, you can use it in that workbook but not in others, at least not without some extra work. This is sometimes acceptable, but suppose you want to record macros for tasks you do repeatedly. In fact, suppose your whole purpose in recording these macros is to have them available *at all times* when you are working in Excel. Then the Personal Macro Workbook should be your choice. It is a special file that Excel stores in its **XLStart** folder so that it is opened every time Excel is opened.[2] It is actually opened as a hidden file so that you are not even aware of its presence—but its macros are always available.

Take a look at your Project Explorer window in the VBE to see if you have a **Personal.xlsb** (or **Personal.xls**) item. If you do not, record a macro and select the Personal Macro Workbook option in Figure 4.2 This will create a **Personal.xlsb** (or **Personal.xls**) file on your hard drive, which you can then add to as often as you like. By the way, you can either *record* macros to your Personal Macro Workbook, or you can type code directly into it in the VBE. That is, once you learn to program and not just record, you can add to your Personal Macro Workbook anytime you like. Just select one of its modules in the VBE and start typing your code—and save when you are finished.

After you complete the dialog box in Figure 4.2 and click OK, you should see a **Stop Recording** button on the Developer ribbon. (In Excel 2003 and earlier, this button is in its own toolbar.) Alternatively, you can click the Status Bar button. (Once you start recording, this button becomes a Stop Recording button.) Just remember that the recorder will record virtually *everything* you do until you click a Stop Recording button, so be careful—and don't forget to stop recording when you are finished.

Suppose you already have a module in your current workbook (or your Personal Macro Workbook, if that is where you are storing the recorded macro). Then the chances are that Excel will create a *new* module and place the recorded macro in it. Actually, the rules for whether it opens a new module or uses an existing module are somewhat obscure, but the point is that you might have to search through your modules to find the newly recorded code.

4.3 Changes from Excel 2007 to Later Versions

Some people, especially VBA programmers, have said that Excel 2007 was really just the "beta" for Excel 2010. One reason for this claim is that recording simply doesn't work for certain actions in Excel 2007—Microsoft released the product before it was completely finished. For example, if you record certain actions on charts in Excel 2007, you get no recorded code whatsoever. This is especially frustrating if your whole purpose in recording is to see what the resulting code will look like, as I often do. This seems to be fixed in later versions of Excel, but I haven't tested it completely. There still might be certain actions that produce no recorded code. In such cases, you have to do some detective work, using online help or Web searches, to find the VBA code corresponding to these actions.

4.4 Recorded Macro Examples

This chapter includes two files, **Recording Macros.xlsm** and **Recording Macros Finished.xlsm**, to give you some practice in recording macros. The first file

---

[2] The XLStart folder is way down the directory structure on your hard drive. To see where it is in Excel 2007 or later versions, go to Excel Options, choose the Advanced group, and scroll down to the General options. You will see an "At startup, open all files in:" item, where you can see or change the startup folder location. Actually, if this box is blank, the XLStart folder is in its default location.

includes six worksheets, each with a simple task to perform with the recorder on. The tasks selected are those that most spreadsheet users perform frequently. This section goes through these tasks and presents the recorded code. Although this recorded code gets the job done, it is not very elegant code. Therefore, the finished version of the file contains the recorded code and modifications of it. This is a common practice when using the recorder. You often record a macro to get one key detail. You then modify the recorded code to fit your specific purposes and discard any excess code you do not need. In short, you clean it up.

For the rest of this section, it is best to open the **Recording Macros.xlsm** file and work through each example with the recorder on. Your recorded code might be slightly different from the code in the finished version of the file because you might do the exercises slightly differently. Don't worry about the details of the recorded code or the modified code at this point. Just recognize that recorded code often benefits from some modification, either to make it more general, improve its readability, or delete unnecessary lines.

Exercise 4.1   Entering a Formula

This exercise, shown in Figure 4.4, asks you to name a range and enter a formula to sum the values in this range.

The recorded code and modifications of it appear below in the SumFormula and SumFormula1 subs. If you think about range operations in Excel, you will realize that you usually *select* a range—that is, highlight it—and then do something to it. Therefore, when you record a macro involving a range, you typically see the Select method in the recorded code. This is actually not necessary. When you want to do something to a range with VBA, you do *not* need to select it first. As you can see in the modified version, the Select method is never used. However, there is a reference to the Exercise1 worksheet, just to clarify that the ranges referred to are in *this* worksheet and not one of the others.

Note how the recorded macro names a range. It uses the Add method of the Names collection of the ActiveWorkbook. This Add method requires two arguments: the name to be given and the range being named. The latter is done in

Figure 4.4   Exercise 1 Worksheet

	A	B	C	D	E	F	G	H
1	Naming a range and entering a formula							
2								
3	Month	Cost						
4	Jan-00	$10,897						
5	Feb-00	$11,164		Turn the recorder on, name the range with				
6	Mar-00	$10,062		the numbers MonthlyCosts, then enter the				
7	Apr-00	$12,039		formula =SUM(MonthlyCosts) at the				
8	May-00	$11,111		bottom of the column, then turn the				
9	Jun-00	$10,223		recorder off.				
10	Jul-00	$11,558						
11	Aug-00	$12,553						
12	Total cost							

R1C1 notation. For example, R7C2 refers to row 7, column 2—that is, cell B7. This is a typical example of recorded code being difficult to read. The modified code shown below uses a much easier way of naming a range (by setting the Name property of the Range object). It also uses the code name I gave to the worksheet, wsExercise1. Code names are explained in the next chapter.

Recorded Code

```vba
Sub SumFormula()

' SumFormula Macro
'
    Range("B4:B11").Select
    ActiveWorkbook.Names.Add Name:="MonthlyCosts", RefersToR1C1:= _
        "=Exercise1!R4C2:R11C2"
    Range("B12").Select
    ActiveCell.FormulaR1C1 = "=SUM(MonthlyCosts)"
    Range("B13").Select
End Sub
```

Modified Code

```vba
Sub SumFormula1()
    With wsExercise1
        .Range("B4:B11").Name = "MonthlyCosts"
        .Range("B12").Formula = "=SUM(MonthlyCosts)"
    End With
End Sub
```

Exercise 4.2   Copying and Pasting

This exercise, shown in Figure 4.5, asks you to copy a formula down a column.
The recorded code and modifications of it are shown below in the CopyPaste and CopyPaste1 subs. Here again, you see Select and Selection several times in the

Figure 4.5 Exercise 2 Worksheet

	A	B	C	D	E	F	G	H	I	J
1	Copying and pasting a formula									
2										
3	Month	Region 1 sales	Region 2 sales	Total sales						
4	Jan-00	$14,583	$10,531	$25,114						
5	Feb-00	$10,030	$12,861			Column D is the sum of columns B and C. The				
6	Mar-00	$14,369	$11,172			typical formula is shown in cell D7. Turn on				
7	Apr-00	$13,108	$14,957			the recorder, copy this formula down column				
8	May-00	$14,410	$13,395			D, and turn the recorder off.				
9	Jun-00	$11,439	$12,306							
10	Jul-00	$12,753	$12,593							
11	Aug-00	$13,074	$11,631							
12	Sep-00	$10,957	$11,651							

Source: Microsoft Corporation

recorded code. The recorded code also contains the strange line ActiveSheet.Paste. Why does it paste to the active sheet and not to a particular range? I still find this hard to understand. The modified version is much simpler and easier to read.

Recorded Code

```
Sub CopyPaste()
'
' CopyPaste Macro
'
    Range("D4").Select
    Selection.Copy
    Range("D5:D12").Select
    ActiveSheet.Paste
    Application.CutCopyMode = False
End Sub
```

Modified Code

```
Sub CopyPaste1()
    With wsExercise2
        .Range("D4").Copy Destination:=.Range("D4:D12")
    End With
    ' The next line is equivalent to pressing the Esc key to get
    ' rid of the dotted line around the copy range.
    Application.CutCopyMode = False
End Sub
```

This exercise indicates how you can learn something fairly obscure by recording. Remember that when you copy and then paste in Excel, the copy range retains a dotted border around it? You can get rid of this dotted border in Excel by pressing the **Esc** key. How do you get rid of it in VBA? The answer appears in the recorded code—you finish with the line

```
Application.CutCopyMode = False
```

Exercise 4.3   Copying and Pasting Special as Values

This exercise, shown in Figure 4.6, asks you to copy a range of formulas and then use the Paste Values option to paste it onto itself.

The recorded code and its modifications are listed below in the PasteValues and PasteValues1 subs. This time the recorded code is used as a guide to make a slightly more general version of the macro. Instead of copying a *specific* range (D4:D12), the modification copies the current *selection*, whatever it might be. Also, note that when recorded code contains a method, such as the PasteSpecial method of a Range object, it includes *all* of the arguments of that method. Typically, many of these use the default values of the arguments, so they do not really

Figure 4.6 Exercise 3 Worksheet

	A	B	C	D	E	F	G	H	I	J
1	Copying a range of formulas and pasting onto itself with the PasteSpecial Values option									
2										
3	Month	Region 1 sales	Region 2 sales	Total sales						
4	Jan-00	$14,583	$10,531	$25,114						
5	Feb-00	$10,030	$12,861	$22,891		Column D is the sum of columns B and C.				
6	Mar-00	$14,369	$11,172	$25,541		Replace the formulas in column D with				
7	Apr-00	$13,108	$14,957	$28,065		values. Specifically, turn on the recorder,				
8	May-00	$14,410	$13,395	$27,805		Copy column D, Paste Special (with the				
9	Jun-00	$11,439	$12,306	$23,745		Values option), then turn off the recorder.				
10	Jul-00	$12,753	$12,593	$25,346						
11	Aug-00	$13,074	$11,631	$24,705						
12	Sep-00	$10,957	$11,651	$22,608						

need to be included in the code. The modified code has dropped the Operation, Skip-Blanks, and Transpose arguments because the actions performed in Excel did not change any of these. My point here is that recorded code is often *bloated* code.

Recorded Code

```
Sub PasteValues()
'
' PasteValues Macro
'
    Range("D4:D12").Select
    Selection.Copy
    Selection.PasteSpecial Paste:=xlPasteValues, Operation:=xlNone, SkipBlanks:=False, Transpose:=False
    Application.CutCopyMode = False
End Sub
```

Modified Code

```
Sub PasteValues1()

    ' Note: This macro is somewhat more general. It copies and pastes to the current selection, whatever
    ' range it happens to be.

    With Selection
        .Copy
        .PasteSpecial Paste:=xlPasteValues
    End With
    Application.CutCopyMode = False
End Sub
```

Exercise 4.4   Formatting Cells

This exercise, shown in Figure 4.7, asks you to format a range of labels in several ways. The recorded code and its modifications appear below in the Formatting and

Figure 4.7 Exercise 4 Worksheet

	A	B	C	D	E	F	G	H	I	J	K	L
1	Formatting the cells in a range											
2												
3		Jan	Feb	Mar	Apr	May	Jun					
4								Format the cells to the left so that the font				
5								is Times New Roman, size 12, bold, and red.				
6								Select the range before turning on the				
7								recorder.				
8												

Formatting1 subs. This is a typical example of bloated code generated by the recorder. The exercise changes a few properties of the Font object, but the recorded code shows *all* of the Font properties, whether changed or not. The modified code lists only the properties that are changed.

Recorded Code

```
Sub Formatting()
'
' Formatting Macro
'
    With Selection.Font
        .Name = "Times New Roman"
        .Size = 11
        .Strikethrough = False
        .Superscript = False
        .Subscript = False
        .OutlineFont = False
        .Shadow = False
        .Underline = xlUnderlineStyleNone
        .ColorIndex = 3
        .TintAndShade = 0
        .ThemeFont = xlThemeFontNone
    End With
    With Selection.Font
        .Name = "Times New Roman"
        .Size = 12
        .Strikethrough = False
        .Superscript = False
        .Subscript = False
        .OutlineFont = False
        .Shadow = False
        .Underline = xlUnderlineStyleNone
        .ColorIndex = 3
        .TintAndShade = 0
        .ThemeFont = xlThemeFontNone
    End With
    Selection.Font.Bold = True
    With Selection.Font
        .Color = -16776961
        .TintAndShade = 0
    End With
End Sub
```

Modified Code

```
Sub Formatting1()
    With Selection.Font
        .Name = "Times New Roman"
        .Size = 12
        .Bold = True
        .ColorIndex = 3
    End With
End Sub
```

Exercise 4.5   Creating a Chart

This exercise, shown in Figure 4.8, asks you to create a chart (as shown in Figure 4.9) on the same sheet as the data for the chart.

The recorded code and its modifications are listed in the CreateChart and CreatChart1 subs. It is helpful to use the recorder when you want to use VBA to create or modify a chart. There are too many objects, properties, and methods

Figure 4.8 Exercise 5 Worksheet

	A	B	C	D	E	F	G
1	Creating a chart						
2							
3	Grade	Number					
4	A	25					
5	B	57					
6	C	43					
7	D	10					
8	F	4					

Create a bar chart on this sheet for the grade distribution to the left.

Figure 4.9 Chart on Exercise 5 Worksheet

associated with charts to remember, so you can let the recorder help you. Note that the modified version leaves most of the recorded code alone. It simply inserts some With constructions to avoid repetitive references to the same object. (The With construction is explained in the next chapter.)

If you are using Excel 2007 or 2010, your recorded code will differ from what is shown here, which was recorded in Excel 2013. This is an example of the problem mentioned earlier, where the Excel 2007 recorder does not supply recorded code for all of your actions. Thankfully, this was fixed in Excel 2010, but even so the recorded code is slightly different in Excel 2013 than in Excel 2010.

Recorded Code

```
Sub CreateChart()
'
' CreateChart Macro
'
    Range("A3:B8").Select
    ActiveSheet.Shapes.AddChart2(201, xlColumnClustered).Select
    ActiveChart.SetSourceData Source:=Range("Exercise5!$A$3:$B$8")
    ActiveChart.ChartTitle.Select
    Selection.Caption = "Grade Distribution"
    Range("A1").Select
End Sub
```

Modified Code

```
Sub CreateChart1()
    With wsExercise5
        .Range("A3:B8").Select
        .Shapes.AddChart2(201, xlColumnClustered).Select
        With ActiveChart
            .SetSourceData Source:=Range("Exercise5!$A$3:$B$8")
            .ChartTitle.Caption = "Grade Distribution"
        End With
        .Range("A1").Select
    End With
End Sub
```

Exercise 4.6   Sorting

This final exercise, in Figure 4.10, asks you to sort a range in descending order based on the Total column.

The recorded code and its modifications are listed in the Sorting and Sorting1 subs. This again illustrates how you do not need to select a range before doing something to it. It also shows how the recorded code lists *all* arguments of the Sort method. The ones that have not been changed from their default values are omitted in the modified code.

Figure 4.10 Exercise 6 Worksheet

	A	B	C	D	E	F	G	H
1	Sorting a range							
2								
3	Sales rep	January sales	February sales	Total				
4	Adams	$3,843	$3,848	$7,691				
5	Jones	$2,895	$3,223	$6,118				
6	Miller	$3,707	$2,788	$6,495		Sort on the Total column,		
7	Nixon	$3,544	$2,745	$6,289		from highest to lowest.		
8	Roberts	$3,672	$2,360	$6,032				
9	Smith	$2,825	$2,369	$5,194				
10	Thomas	$2,270	$2,035	$4,305				
11	Wilson	$2,740	$2,625	$5,365				

Recorded Code

```
Sub Sorting()
'
' Sorting Macro
'
    Range("D3").Select
    ActiveWorkbook.Worksheets("Exercise6").Sort.SortFields.Clear
    ActiveWorkbook.Worksheets("Exercise6").Sort.SortFields.Add  Key:=Range("D3"), _
        SortOn:=xlSortOnValues, Order:=xlDescending, DataOption:=xlSortNormal
    With  ActiveWorkbook.Worksheets("Exercise6").Sort
        .SetRange Range("A4:D11")
        .Header = xlNo
        .MatchCase = False
        .Orientation = xlTopToBottom
        .SortMethod = xlPinYin
        .Apply
    End With
End Sub
```

Modified Code

```
Sub Sorting1()
    With  wsExercise6
        .Range("D3").Sort Key1:=.Range("D3"), Order1:=xlDescending, Header:=xlYes
    End With
End Sub
```

As these exercises illustrate, you can learn a lot by recording Excel tasks and then examining the recorded code. However, you often need to modify the code to make it more readable and fit your specific needs. Also, be aware that there are many things you cannot record. Specifically, there is no way to record control logic and loops, two of the most important programming constructs available to a programmer. You have to program these manually—the recorder cannot do it for you. Finally, I repeat my frustration that recording doesn't always work as expected. For example, recording chart manipulations in Excel 2007 often yields no code at al. So don't be surprised if you experience similar recording "errors" from time to time.

The following exercise allows you to try some recording on your own and then create a handy button on your **Quick Access Toolbar** (**QAT**) for the recorded macro.

Exercise 4.7   Recording Print Settings and Modifying Your QAT

We all have our favorite print settings, and I can't count the number of times I have gone through the print settings dialog box to change the settings. This process always includes exactly the same steps, and it takes a number of mouse clicks. In short, it is a bother. This is a perfect situation for a recorded macro that does it once and saves it in the Personal Macro Workbook for easy future use. Here are the steps.

1. Turn the recorder on, give the macro a name such as PrintSettings, and indicate that you want to store it in the Personal Macro Workbook.
2. Open the print settings dialog box, change the settings to the way you want them, and turn the recorder off.
3. Check the code. You will see that every possible print setting has been recorded, not just those you changed. You can leave this as is, or you can streamline the code to change only settings of interest.
4. In Excel 2003 and earlier, you could now create a new toolbar with a new toolbar button to run your PrintSettings macro. (This process was explained in the second edition of the book.) This is no longer possible in Excel 2007 or later versions,[3] but there is an alternative. At the top of the Excel screen, you see the Quick Access Toolbar (QAT). This is where you can create a button to run your favorite macros. The following steps explain the process.
5. Click the dropdown next to the QAT and select **More Commands**.
6. In the top left dropdown, select **Macros**. You should see your PrintSettings macro in the list. Select it, and click the **Add>>** button to add it to your QAT. By default, it will have a generic button icon. To change the icon, click the **Modify** button and choose from the available icons. Then back your way out. (By the way, it would be nice to change the available icons or add to them. This isn't necessarily easy, but it can be done. See Section 16.4 for details.)

This process of recording a macro, saving it to your Personal Macro Workbook, and creating a button on the QAT to run the macro makes you an instant programmer. You will be amazed at how useful simple little macros can be if you design them to automate tasks you perform frequently.

---

[3]Well, this isn't really true in Excel 2010 and later versions, which allow you to create your own customized ribbon with buttons that run your macros. Still, for quick tasks like print settings, the QAT is arguably the preferable way to go.

4.5 Summary

The macro recorder serves two basic purposes: (1) It allows beginning programmers to learn how common Excel operations translate into VBA code; and (2) it allows more advanced programmers to discover the one detail they need to get a program working. However, there are also two drawbacks to the recorder: (1) The recorded code is often far from elegant and is often bloated with unnecessary lines; and (2) it is incapable of capturing logic or loops, two of the most powerful aspects of VBA. In short, the recorder can be very useful, but it has its limits.

EXERCISES

1. VBA can be used to format worksheet ranges in a variety of ways—the font, the interior (background of the cells), the alignment, and others. The recorder can be useful for learning the appropriate properties and syntax. Try the following. Open a new workbook and type some labels or numbers into various cells. Then turn on the recorder and format the cells in any of your favorite ways. Examine the recorded code. You will probably find that it sets many properties that you never intended to set. Delete the code that appears to be unnecessary and run your modified macro.

2. The ThemeColor and TintAndShade properties of the Font object (or the Interior object) determine the color of the font (or the background of a cell). Unfortunately, it is virtually impossible to remember which property values go with which color. Try the following. Open a new workbook and type a label in some cell. Select this cell, turn the recorder on, and change the color of the font (or the cell's background) repeatedly, choosing any colors you like from the color palettes. As you do so, keep track of the colors you have selected and then examine the recorded code. You should be able to match colors with property values. (Actually, this changed in Excel 2007, where "themes" were introduced. When you record these types of actions in Excel 2003 or earlier, you get values of the ColorIndex property. Still, recording is helpful in either case.)

3. Using the recorder can be particularly useful for learning how to use VBA to modify charts. The file **Chart Practice.xlsx** contains a small data set and a chart that is based on it. Open this file, turn the recorder on, and change any of the elements of the chart—the type of chart, the chart title, the axis labels, and so on. (You might be surprised at how many things you can change in a chart.) As you do this, write down the list of changes you make. Then examine the recorded code and try to match the sections of code with the changes you made. (If you want more information on any particular chart property you see in the code, select it and press the F1 key. This provides immediate online help for the element you selected. Alternatively, look it up in the Object Browser.)

4. The previous exercise shows how to use the recorder to learn about properties of an *existing* chart. You can also use the recorder to learn how VBA can create a chart from scratch. Try the following. Open the **Chart Practice.xlsx** file, delete the chart, and then recreate it with the recorder on. Examine the recorded code

to learn even more about how VBA deals with charts. (As with many recording sessions, you might want to practice building a chart *before* turning the recorder on. You don't want the recorder to record your mistakes.)

5. An operation I often perform is to select a range of cells that contain numbers and format them as integers, that is, as numbers with no decimals. This is easy to do with Excel's **Format Cells** menu item, but it takes a few steps. Record a general macro for performing this operation, store it in your Personal Macro Workbook, and create a button on the QAT to run this macro (if you are running Excel 2007 or a later version). Once you are finished, you will always be a click away from formatting a range as integer. *(Hint:* Select a range of numbers *before* turning the recorder on. Your macro will then always work on the currently selected range, whatever it happens to be.)

6. (*Note:* This exercise and the next one are adapted from those in the second edition, which asked you to autoformat a range. Starting with 2007, Excel no longer supports autoformats, at least not officially, but similar functionality is still possible, as indicated here.) Many spreadsheets in the business world contain tables of various types. To dress them up, people often format them in various ways. To do this, select a table of data, including headers, and select an option of your choice from the **Format as Table** dropdown on the Home ribbon. Try it now with the recorder on, using the table in the **Table Data.xlsx** file. Then examine the code. You will see that it first creates a new ListObject object—that is, a table, as discussed in Chapter 15—and it then sets the TableStyle property of the table to one of several built-in Excel styles, such as "TableStyleMedium2". (If you ever need to learn the name of one of these style names, just repeat this exercise. It is a perfect example of how the recorder can be used to learn one critical detail of a program.)

7. Continuing the previous exercise, record a macro that formats a table with your favorite table style option, and store the macro in your Personal Macro Workbook. Then create a button on your QAT that runs this macro. When you are finished, you will be a click away from formatting any table with your favorite style.

8. I like to color-code certain cells in my spreadsheets. For example, I like to make the background of input cells blue, and I like to color cells with decision variables red. This is easy enough with the Fill Color (paint can) dropdown list on the Home ribbon, but it is even easier if I create "color" buttons on my QAT. Try doing this with the recorder. Open a blank file, select any range, turn on the recorder, and color the background a color of your choice. Make sure you store the macro in your Personal Macro Workbook. Then create a button with an appropriate icon on your QAT to run this macro. (*Note:* By selecting the range before you turn the recorder on, your macro will be more general. It will color whatever range happens to be selected when you run it.)

Getting Started with VBA

5

5.1 Introduction

Now it is time to start doing some *real* programming in VBA—not just copying code in the book or recording, but writing your own code. This chapter gets you started with the most basic elements—how to create a sub, how to declare variables with a Dim statement, how to get information from a user with an InputBox, how to display information in a MsgBox, and how to document your work with comments. It also briefly discusses strings, it explains how to specify objects, properties, and methods in VBA code, and it discusses VBA's extremely useful With construction and several other VBA tips. Finally, it discusses techniques for debugging, because programmers virtually never get their programs to work the first time through.

5.2 Subroutines

The logical section of code that performs a particular task is called a **subroutine,** or simply a **sub**. Subroutines are also called **macros,** and they are also called **procedures**. There is also a particular type of subroutine called a **function subroutine** that is discussed in Chapter 10. Subroutines, macros, and procedures are all essentially the same thing. I will call them all **subs.** A sub is any set of code that performs a particular task. It can contain one line of code or it can contain hundreds of lines. However, it is not good programming practice to let subs get too long. If the purpose of your application is to perform several related tasks, it is a good idea to break it up into several relatively short subs, each of which performs a specific task. In this case there is often a "main" sub that acts as the control center—it "calls" the other subs one at a time. The collection of subs that fit together is called a **program.** In other words, a program is a collection of subs that achieves an overall objective.

There are several places you can store your subs, but for now, you should store all of your subs in a **module**. When you look at a new project in the VBE, it will have no modules by default. However, you can add a module through the **Insert** menu, and then you can start adding subs to it. It is also possible to double-click a sheet or ThisWorkbook in the VBE Project Explorer to bring up a code window, but you should *not* enter your subs there, at least not yet. They are reserved for event handlers, which are discussed in Chapter 11. So again, for now, you should place all of your subs in modules.

Each sub has a name, which must be a single word. This word, which can be a concatenation of several words such as GetUserInputs, should indicate the purpose of the sub. You can use generic names such as Sub1 or MySub, but this is a bad practice. You will have no idea in a week what Sub1 or MySub is intended to do, whereas GetUserInputs clearly indicates the sub's purpose.

All subs must begin with the keyword Sub and then the name of the sub followed by parentheses, as in:

```
Sub GetUserInputs()
```

You can type this line directly into a module in the VBE, or you can use the **Insert** → **Procedure** menu item, which will prompt you for a name. (Again, if there is no module for the current project, you must insert one.) The editor will immediately insert the following line for you:

```
End Sub
```

Every sub must start with the Sub line, and it must end with the End Sub line. You will notice that the editor also colors the reserved words Sub and End Sub blue. In fact, it colors all reserved words blue as an aid to the programmer. Now that your sub is bracketed by the Sub and End Sub statements, you can start typing code in between.

Why are there parentheses next to the sub's name? As you will see in Chapter 10, a sub can take **arguments**, and these arguments must be placed inside the parentheses. If there are no arguments, which is often the case, then there is nothing inside the parentheses; but the parentheses still must be included. (This is similar to a few Excel worksheet functions that take no arguments, such as =**RAND()**, where the parentheses are also required.)

If a program contains several logically related subs, it is common to place all of them in a single module, although some programmers put some subs in one module and some in another, primarily for organizational purposes. The subs in a particular module can be arranged in any order. If there is a "main" sub that calls other subs to perform certain tasks, it is customary to place the main sub at the top of the module and then place the other subs below it, in the order they are called. But even this is not necessary; any order is accepted by VBA.

Later sections ask you to run a sub. There are several ways to do this, as explained in Chapter 3. For now, the easiest way is to place the cursor *anywhere* within the sub and click the **Run** button (the green triangle) on the VBE Standard toolbar. Alternatively, you can press the **F5** key, or you can use the **Run** → **Run Sub/UserForm** menu item.

5.3 Declaring Variables and Constants

Virtually all programs use variables. Variables contain values, much like the variables *x* and *y* you use in algebra. For example, the next three lines illustrate a simple use of variables. The first line sets the unitCost variable equal to 1.20, the second line sets the unitsSold variable to 20, and the third line calculates the variable totalCost as the product of unitCost and unitsSold. Of course, the value of totalCost here will be 24.0.

```
unitCost = 1.20
unitsSold = 20
totalCost = unitCost * unitsSold
```

Unlike algebra, you can also have a line such as the following:

```
totalCost = totalCost + 20
```

To understand this, you must understand that each variable has a location in memory, where its value is stored. If a variable appears to the left of an equals sign, then its new value in memory becomes whatever is on the right side of the equals sign. For example, if the previous value of totalCost was 260, the new value will be 280, and it will replace the old value in memory.

Although it is not absolutely required (unless the line Option Explicit is at the top of the module), you should *always* declare all of your variables at the beginning of each sub with the keyword Dim.[1] (Dim is an abbreviation of dimension, a holdover from the old BASIC language. It would make more sense to use the word Declare, but we are stuck with Dim.) Declaring variables has two advantages. First, it helps catch spelling mistakes. Suppose you use the variable unitCost several times in a sub, but in one case you misspell it as unitsCost. If you have already declared unitCost in a Dim statement, VBA will catch your spelling error, reasoning that unitsCost is not on the list of declared variables.

The second reason for declaring variables is that you can then specify the *types* of variables you have. Each type requires a certain amount of computer memory, and each is handled in a certain way by VBA. It is much better for you, the programmer, to tell VBA what types of variables you have than to let it try to determine them from context. The variable types used most often are the following.

- String (for text like "Bob" or "The program ran without errors.")
- Integer (for integer values in the range –32,768 to 32,767)
- Long (for really large integers beyond the Integer range)
- Boolean (for variables that can be True or False)
- Single (for numbers with decimals)
- Double (for numbers with decimals where you require more accuracy than with Single)
- Currency (for monetary values)
- Variant (a catch-all, where you let VBA decide how to deal with the variable)

---

[1] If you declare a variable inside a sub, it is called a **local** variable. It is also possible to declare a variable outside of subs, in which case it is a **module-level** variable. This issue is discussed in Chapter 10.

Variable declarations can be placed anywhere within a sub, but it is customary to include them right after the Sub line, as in the following:

```
Sub Test()
    Dim i As Integer, unitCost As Currency, isFound As Boolean
    Other statements
End Sub
```

Some programmers prefer a separate Dim line for each variable. (I tend to favor this, but I'm not always consistent.) This can lead to a long list of Dim statements if there are a lot of variables. Others tend to prefer a single Dim, followed by a list of declarations separated by commas. You can use either convention or even mix them. However, you *must* follow each variable with the keyword As and then the variable type. Otherwise, the variable is declared as the default Variant type, which is considered poor programming practice. For example, variables i and j in the following line are (implicitly) declared as Variant, not as Integer. Only k is declared as Integer.

```
Dim i, j, k As Integer
```

If you want all of them to be Integer, the following declaration is necessary:

```
Dim i As Integer, j As Integer, k As Integer
```

Symbols for Data Types

It is also possible to declare (some) data types by the symbols in Table 5.1. For example, you could use Dim unitCost@ or Dim nUnits%, where the symbol follows the variable name. This practice is essentially a holdover from older versions of the BASIC language, and you might see it in legacy code (as I recently did). However, I don't recommend using this rather obscure shorthand way of declaring variables. After all, would *you* remember them?

Table 5.1 Symbols for Data Types

Integer	%
Long	&
Single	!
Double	#
Currency	@
String	$

Figure 5.1 Error Message for Undeclared Variable

Using Option Explicit

You should *force* yourself to adopt the good habit of declaring all variables. You can do this by using the tip mentioned in Chapter 3. Specifically, you should select the **Tools** → **Options** menu item in the VBE and check the **Require Variable Declarations** box under the Editor tab. (By default, it is *not* checked. I still have no idea why Microsoft makes this the default setting.) From that point on, every time you open a new module, the line Option Explicit will be at the top. This simply means that VBA will force you to declare your variables. If you forget to declare a variable, it will remind you with an error message when you run the program and it sees an undeclared variable. If you ever see the message in Figure 5.1—and you almost certainly will—you will know that you forgot to declare a variable (or misspelled one).

Object Variables

There is one other type of variable. This is an Object variable, which "points" to an object. For example, suppose you have a Range object, specified by the range name Scores on a worksheet named Data, that you intend to reference several times in your program. To save yourself a lot of typing, you can Set a range object variable named scoreRange to this range with the lines

```
Dim scoreRange As Range
Set scoreRange = ActiveWorkbook.Worksheets("Data").Range("Scores")
```

From then on, you can simply refer to scoreRange. For example, you could change its font size with the line

```
scoreRange.Font.Size = 12
```

This is a lot easier than typing

```
ActiveWorkbook.Worksheets("Data").Range("Scores").Font.Size = 12
```

There are two fundamental things to remember about Object variables.

- They must be declared just like any other variables in a Dim statement. The type can be the generic Object type, as in

```
Dim scoreRange as Object
```

or it can be more specific, as in

```
Dim scoreRange as Range
```

The latter is *much* preferred because VBA does not then have to figure out what *type* of object you want scoreRange to be. (It is *not* enough to include Range in the name of the variable.)

- When you define an Object variable—that is, put it on the left of an equals sign—you must use the keyword Set. In fact, this is the only time you use the keyword Set. The following line will produce an error message because the keyword Set is missing:

```
scoreRange = ActiveWorkbook.Worksheets("Data").Range("Scores")
```

In contrast, assuming that totalCost is a variable of type Currency (or any non-object variable type), the following line will produce an error message because the keyword Set should *not* be included:

```
Set totalCost = 24.0
```

The moral is that you should always use the keyword Set when defining object variables, but you should never use it when defining other variables (numbers, dates, and strings).

Built-In Objects and Code Names

In previous editions of the book, I often referred to a particular worksheet in code with lines like the following:

```
Dim wsData as Worksheet
Set wsData = Worksheets("Data")
```

That is, I declared a Worksheet variable wsData and then Set it to refer to the worksheet named Data. (I use prefix ws to remind me that this is a Worksheet variable.) This practice is fine, but I now believe there is a better way, and I have used it in virtually all of the examples in the rest of the book. This method relies on the **code names** of built-in worksheet (and chart sheet) objects in any Excel file.

Every worksheet in an Excel file is a Worksheet object with two properties (among others): Name and CodeName. The Name property is the name you see on the worksheet's tab. If you manually change the name of the tab, the Name property changes automatically. Alternatively, if you wanted to change the name with VBA from Sheet1 to Data, say, you could use a line like the following:

```
Worksheets("Sheet1").Name = "Data"
```

Now, imagine that you write code that includes the following reference: Worksheets("Data"). This is fine, but what happens if the user manually changes the name on the worksheet's tab to something else, like Data1? This will create an error in your code, because the Data reference no longer works.

Fortunately, the CodeName property provides a safer method. If you look at the Project Explorer in the VBE (see Figure 5.2), you will see the built-in

Figure 5.2 Names and Code Names

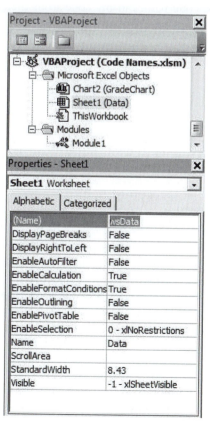

worksheet, chart sheet, and workbook objects. In the figure, for example, there is one worksheet listed as Sheet1 (Data). This indicates that the worksheet's name (the one that appears on its tab) is Data, but that its code name is currently Sheet1. Below, in the Properties window, you see two properties on the left: (Name) and Name. The (Name) property is really the CodeName property, and it can be changed as indicated. In this case, it is being changed to wsData. So why would you bother to do this? There are two very good reasons.

First, you can refer to the code name directly in code. For example, you can refer to its cell A1 as wsData.Range("A1"). There is no need to declare a Worksheet variable and then use a Set statement, so this saves two lines of code. In fact, as soon as you type a worksheet's code name and then a period, you immediately get Intellisense. The second reason is that if a user changes the worksheet's tab name, your code will still work. You might argue that they could break the code by changing the worksheet's code name, and this is true, but they would have to visit the VBE to do so, and this is much less likely to happen.

Therefore, the practice you will see in almost all examples from here on is to change the default code names from their default generic names like Sheet1 to more meaningful names like wsData. (Again, I always use the ws prefix to remind me that this is a worksheet.) When I created the examples, I had to make the changes as shown in Figure 5.2, which required a little extra work up front, but then I was able to refer to the code names in my code from then on—without worrying that a user might change the worksheet tab names.

Interestingly, the CodeName property is a *read* but not a *write* property. This means that you can find the code name of a worksheet with a line like

```
If ActiveSheet.CodeName = "wsData" Then
```

However, the following line produces an error. If you want to change a worksheet's code name, you have to do so through the Properties window, as in Figure 5.2.

```
ActiveSheet.CodeName = "wsData"  ' Produces an error
```

The same comments apply to chart sheets. As you can see in Figure 5.2, there is a chart sheet with the generic code name Chart2 but with tab name GradeChart. If I wanted to refer to this chart in code, I would probably change its code name to something like chtGrades, using the prefix cht to remind me of the sheet's type.

Finally, you see one other built-in object in Figure 5.2, ThisWorkbook. This is the code name for the file itself. You could again change it in the Properties window, but there is no good reason to do so. In later examples where an application involves several Excel files (for example, files with data that you want your application to import), you always know that ThisWorkbook refers to the workbook that contains your code. As an example, ThisWorkbook.Path returns the path to the folder containing the file with your code.

Intellisense with Variable Names: Ctrl+Space

I discussed this in Chapter 3, but it is so handy that I will briefly mention it again. After you have declared your variables in Dim statements, you will then refer to them in lines of code. To save yourself typing and avoid spelling mistakes, start typing your variable name and then press **Ctrl+Space**. If there is only one variable that starts with the letters you typed, it will be inserted automatically. If there are several candidates, you can choose the one you want. If you tend to use long variable names, you will love this feature.

Variable Naming Conventions

Programmers have surprisingly strong feelings about variable naming conventions. The one thing they all agree on is that variable names should indicate what the variables represent. So it is much better to use a name such as taxRate than to use a generic name like x. Your code becomes much easier to read, both for others and for yourself, if you use descriptive names.

Beyond this basic suggestion, however, there are at least three naming conventions used in the programming world, and each has its proponents. The **Pascal** convention uses names like TaxRate, where the first letter in each "word" in the name is upper case. The **camel** convention is similar, but it does not capitalize the *first* word. Therefore, it would use the name taxRate. (The term *camel* indicates that the hump is in the middle, just like a camel.) Finally, the **Hungarian** convention, named after a Hungarian programmer, prefixes variables with up to three characters to indicate their variables types. For example, it might use the name sngTaxRate to indicate that this variable is of type Single. Other commonly used prefixes are int (for Integer), bln (for Boolean), str (for String), and so on. The proponents of the Hungarian convention like it because it is self-documenting. If you see the variable sngTaxRate in the middle of a program, you immediately know that it is of type Single, without having to go back to the Dim statement that declares the variable.

Which convention should you use? This seems to depend on which convention is currently in style, and this changes over time. For a while, it seemed that the Hungarian convention was the "in thing," but it results in some rather long and ugly variable names. At present, the camel convention appears to be the most popular, so I have adopted it throughout this book. But if you end up programming for your company, there will probably be a corporate style that you will be required to follow.

Constants

The term *variable* means that it can change. Specifically, the variables discussed earlier can change values as a program runs—and they often do. There are times, however, when you want to define a *constant* that never changes during the program. The reason is usually the following. Suppose you have a parameter such as a tax rate that plays a role in your program. You know that its value is 28% and that it will never change (at least, not within your program). You could type the value 0.28 every place in your program where you need to use the tax rate. However, suppose the tax rate changes to 29% next year. To use your old program, you would need to search through all of the lines of code and change 0.28 to 0.29 whenever it appears. This is not only time-consuming, but it is prone to errors. (Maybe one of the 0.28 values you find is not a tax rate but is something else. You don't want to change it!)

A better approach is to define a constant with a line such as the following.

```
Const taxRate = 0.28
```

This line is typically placed toward the beginning of your sub, right below the variable declarations (the Dim statements). Then every place in your sub where you need a tax rate, you type taxRate rather than 0.28. If the tax rate does happen to change to 29% next year, all you have to change is the value in the Const line.[2]

Another advantage to using constants is that your programs don't have "magic numbers." A magic number is a number found in the body of a program that seems to appear out of nowhere. A person reading your program probably has no idea what a number such as 0.28 represents (unless you explain it with a comment or two). In contrast, if the person sees taxRate, there is no question what it means. So try your best to use constants and avoid magic numbers.[3]

5.4 Built-in Constants

There are many built-in constants that you will see in VBA. They are either built into the VBA language, in which case they have the prefix vb, they are built into the Excel library, in which case they have the prefix xl, or they are built into the Microsoft Office library, in which case they have the prefix mso. Actually, these constants all have integer values, and they are all members of **enumerations**. A simple example illustrates the concept of an enumeration. Consider the Color property of a Font object. It can be one of eight possible integer values, and no one on earth would possibly memorize these eight values. (They are *not* 1 through 8.) Instead, you remember them by their constant names: vbBlack, vbBlue, vbCyan, vbGreen, vbMagenta, vbRed, vbWhite, and vbYellow. Using these constants, you can change the color of a font in a line such as

```
Range("A1").Font.Color = vbBlue
```

---

[2] Some programmers like to spell their constants with all uppercase letters, such as TAXRATE, to emphasize that they are constants. However, I have not adopted this convention.
[3] The same idea applies to formulas in Excel. You should avoid embedding numbers in formulas. Instead, you should list these numbers in input cells and cell reference the input cells in your formulas.

Similarly, Excel has a number of enumerations. One that is useful when dealing with ranges is the set of possible directions, corresponding to the four arrow keys: xlDown, xlUp, xlToRight, and xlToLeft. Again, these constants are really integer values that no one in the world remembers. You remember them instead by their more suggestive names.

To view the many enumerations for VBA, Excel, and Office, open the Object Browser, select the VBA, Excel, or Office library, and search the class list for items starting with Vb, Xl, or Mso. Each of them is an enumeration that holds a number of built-in constants. For example, the XlDirection enumeration holds the constants xlDown, xlUp, xlToRight, and xlToLeft, and the VbMsgBoxStyle enumeration holds all the constants that correspond to message box icons and buttons. You will see a few of these in the next section.

5.5 Input Boxes and Message Boxes

Two of the most common tasks in VBA programs are to get inputs from users and to display messages or results in some way. There are many ways to perform both tasks, and many of them are illustrated in later chapters. This section illustrates a very simple way to perform these tasks. It takes advantage of two built-in VBA functions: the InputBox and MsgBox functions. They are not complex or fancy, but they are very useful.

The InputBox function takes at least one argument: a prompt to the user.[4] A second argument that is often used is the title that appears at the top of the dialog box. An example is the following:

```
price = InputBox("Enter the product's unit price.", "Selling price")
```

If you type this line in a sub and run the sub, the dialog box in Figure 5.3 will appear.

Figure 5.3 Typical InputBox

---

[4] If you look up InputBox in the VBA online help, you will see two items: the InputBox *method* and the InputBox *function*. The discussion here is really about the *function*, the one most commonly used. The InputBox method differs from the InputBox function in that it allows selective validation of the user's input, and it can be used with Microsoft Excel objects, error values, and formulas. Notice that Application.InputBox calls the InputBox method; InputBox with no object qualifier calls the InputBox function.

This generic dialog box has OK and Cancel buttons, a title (which would be Microsoft Excel if you didn't supply one), a prompt, and a textbox for the user's input. When the user enters a value and clicks the OK button, the user's input is assigned to the variable price.

The MsgBox function takes at least one argument: a message that you want to display. Two other optional arguments often used are a button indication and a title. A typical example is the following:

```
MsgBox "The product's unit price is $2.40.", vbInformation, "Selling price"
```

The first argument is the text "The product's unit price is $2.40." The second argument is vbInformation, a built-in VBA constant that inserts an "i" icon in the message box. The third argument is the title, "Selling price". If you type this line in a sub and run the sub, the message box in Figure 5.4 will appear.

I will finish this section with some rather advanced code involving InputBox. You can ignore it at this point if you like, but my own students always ask about it. Suppose you prompt a user for a value with an InputBox, and the user either clicks the OK button without entering anything in the text box or clicks the Cancel button (or the upper right X). Try it out, and you will find that Excel produces an obscure error message. As a good programmer, you should anticipate this and handle it nicely.

It turns out that InputBox returns an empty string, "" , if the user does any of the preceding actions. So you can check (by using an If construction) whether the response is an empty string. Furthermore, by using an undocumented VBA function, StrPtr, it is possible to check whether the user clicked the OK button or the Cancel (or the X) button. Finally (and this is optional), you can embed the check in a loop so that you allow the user to "quit the game" by clicking the Cancel (or the X) button, but you keep asking for an input if the user clicks the OK button with no input in the text box. The code in the file **OK vs Cancel in InputBox.xlsm** contains the required code. Open it, and try all the possibilities you can think of. I call this *bulletproof* code. It forces the user to do something correctly—and there are no obscure error messages. I will return to bulletproofing in Chapter 11.

Figure 5.4 Typical Message Box

5.6 Message Boxes with Yes and No Buttons

The previous section illustrates the most common use of MsgBox: to display a message. However, MsgBox can be used for simple logic by including the appropriate buttons. For example, the following line not only displays the message with Yes and No buttons (see Figure 5.5), but it also captures the button pressed in the result variable. In this case, the second argument, vbYesNo, indicates that Yes and No buttons will be included. The value of result will be vbYes or vbNo, two built-in VBA constants. You could then use a logical If statement to proceed appropriately, depending on whether the result is vbYes or vbNo.

```
result = MsgBox("Do you want to continue?", vbYesNo, "Chance to quit")
```

You can even use the InputBox and MsgBox functions in the same line, as in

```
MsgBox InputBox("Type your name.", "User's name"), vbInformation, "User's Name"
```

The first argument of the MsgBox function is now the *result* of the InputBox function. When I ran this, I first saw the input box and typed my name, as in Figure 5.6. I then saw the message box in Figure 5.7, the message being my name.

Here are a couple of other points that apply to InputBox and MsgBox, as well as to other VBA statements.

Figure 5.5 Message Box with Yes and No Buttons

Figure 5.6 InputBox

Figure 5.7 Message Box

- **Continuing statements on more than one line.** Lines of code can often get long and run past the right side of the screen, particularly with messages. You can continue them on another line by using the **underscore** character, _, preceded by a space. (Don't forget the space.) For example, you can write

```
MsgBox InputBox("Type your full address: city, state, zip code.", "User's address"), _
    vbInformation, "User's Address"
```

This is treated as a *single* line of code. Actually, a line can be broken as many times as you like with the underscore character. When I do this, I typically indent the continuation lines for readability.

- **Whether to use parentheses.** If you have been paying close attention, you have noticed that the arguments of InputBox and MsgBox are sometimes included in parentheses, but sometimes they are not. For example, compare the line

```
MsgBox "Thank you for supplying your name.", vbExclamation, "Name accepted"
```

to the line

```
result = MsgBox("Do you want to continue?", vbYesNo, "Chance to quit")
```

The first simply displays a message. The second captures the result of MsgBox (vbYes or vbNo) in the result variable. The rule for parentheses, for the Input-Box function, the MsgBox function, and other VBA functions, is that parentheses are *required* when the result is captured in a variable or used in some way. In contrast, parentheses are *optional* (and are usually omitted) when no result is being captured or used in some way. This parentheses rule is rather difficult to understand until you become more proficient in VBA. However, if your program fails to work and you cannot find anything else wrong, check whether you have violated this rule. Then remove the parentheses or add them, and hopefully the bug will disappear.

Exercise 5.1 Displaying a Message

Before proceeding, try the following exercise. Open a new workbook and save it as **Input Output 1.xlsm**. Then create a sub called RevenueCalc that does the following: (1) It asks the user for the unit price of some product and stores it in the variable unitPrice, defined as Currency type; (2) it asks the user for the number of items sold and stores it in the variable quantitySold, defined as Integer type; (3) it calculates the revenue from this product and stores it in the variable revenue, defined as Currency type; and (4) it displays a message such as "The revenue from this product was $380."

Try to do as much of this as you can without help. Then consult the file **Input Output 1.xlsm** for a solution. You will probably have trouble with the MsgBox line. The message consists of two parts: a literal part ("The revenue from this product was ") and a variable part (the calculated revenue).[5] These two parts need to be concatenated with the ampersand symbol, &, a *very* common operation that is explained later in the chapter. The solution also contains a Format function to display the revenue as, say, $380 rather than 380. This is also explained in a later section.

5.7 Using Excel Functions in VBA

Excel has hundreds of functions you commonly use in Excel formulas: SUM, MIN, MAX, SQRT, VLOOKUP, SUMIF, and so on.[6] It would be a shame if programmers had to reinvent this rich set of functions with their own VBA code. Fortunately, you do not have to. You can "borrow" Excel functions with a line such as

```
WorksheetFunction.SUM(Range("A1:A10"))
```

When you type WorksheetFunction and then a period, a list of most Excel functions appears. For example, if you choose SUM, as above, you have to supply the same type of argument (a range or ranges) that you would in an Excel formula. (*Note*: In early editions, I said to use Application.WorksheetFunction instead of simply WorksheetFunction, where Application refers to Excel itself. Either version works fine, but Application is not necessary.)

There is one peculiar "gotcha" with borrowing Excel functions.[7] It turns out that the VBA language has a few functions of its own. For example, open the Object Browser, choose the VBA library, and look at the **Math** class. Three

---

[5] It also has a third part if you want to end the sentence with a period.
[6] When I refer to Excel functions in this book, I capitalize them, as in SUM. This is primarily to distinguish them from VBA functions. Of course, you don't need to capitalize them when you enter them into Excel formulas.
[7] I almost deleted this part. I tried the line ?WorksheetFunction.Ln(1) in the Immediate Window, and it worked fine, returning the correct value 0. Therefore, I guessed that the problem discussed here had been fixed. However, I then realized that WorksheetFunction.Ln(1) in a sub still *does* produce an error. Very strange!

notable VBA math functions you will see are log (natural logarithm), sqr (square root), and rnd (random number). You probably know that Excel also has these functions, except that they are spelled LN, SQRT, and RAND. The "gotcha" is that if VBA has a function, you are *not* allowed to borrow Excel's version of that function. Therefore, the statement WorksheetFunction.SQRT(4) produces an error. If you want the square root of 4 in VBA, you must get it with sqr(4).

Fortunately, there are not many of these duplicated functions. You just have to be aware that a few, such as LN, SQRT, and RAND, will not work in VBA.

5.8 Comments

You might think that once you get your program to run correctly, your job is finished. This is not the case. Sometime in the future, you or someone else might have to modify your program as new situations arise. Therefore, it is extremely important that you *document* your work. There are several ways to document a program, including the use of meaningful names for subs and variables. However, the best means of documentation is the liberal use of comments. A comment is text that you type anywhere in your program to indicate to yourself or someone else what your code means or how it works. It is very easy to insert a comment anywhere in the program, inside a sub or outside a sub. You start the line with a single quote. That line is then colored green and is ignored by VBA. However, comments are *not* ignored by those who read your program. For them, the comments are often the most interesting part.

The following line is a typical comment:

```
' The purpose of the following section is to calculate revenue.
```

It is also possible to include a comment in the same line as a line of code. To do so, type the code, follow it with one or more spaces, then a single quote, and then the comment, as in

```
Range("A1").Value = "March Sales" ' This is the title cell for the worksheet.
```

There is a tendency on the part of programmers (myself included) to wait until the last minute, after the code has been written, to insert comments—if they insert them at all. Try instead to get into the good habit of inserting comments as you write your code. Admittedly, it takes time, but it also aids your logical thought process if you force yourself to explain what you are doing as you are doing it. Of course, comments can also be overdone. There is usually no point in documenting every single line of code. Use your discretion on what *really* needs to be documented. My best advice is that if you believe you or someone else might have trouble understanding what a block of code is supposed to do or how it works, add a comment. When you revisit your code in a few weeks or a few years, you will *really* appreciate the comments.

5.9 Indenting

Besides comments, the best thing you can do to make your programs more readable is to indent religiously. You will see numerous examples to emulate in the rest of the book, but for now, take a look at the two following subs. They are completely equivalent, and VBA treats each of them in an identical way. But which of the two would you rather read?

This version indents properly:

```vba
Sub CountHighSales()
    Dim i As Integer
    Dim j As Integer
    Dim nHigh As Integer
    Dim cutoff As Currency
    cutoff = InputBox("What sales value do you want to check for?")
    For j = 1 To 6
        nHigh = 0
        For i = 1 To 36
            If wsData.Range("Sales").Cells(i, j) >= cutoff Then _
                nHigh = nHigh + 1
        Next i
        MsgBox "For region " & j & ", sales were above " & Format(cutoff, "$0,000") _
            & " on " & nHigh & " of the 36 months."
    Next j
End Sub
```

This version doesn't indent at all.

```vba
Sub CountHighSales()
Dim i As Integer
Dim j As Integer
Dim nHigh As Integer
Dim cutoff As Currency
cutoff = InputBox("What sales value do you want to check for?")
For j = 1 To 6
nHigh = 0
For i = 1 To 36
If wsData.Range("Sales").Cells(i, j) > = cutoff Then _
nHigh = nHigh + 1
Next i
MsgBox "For region " & j & ", sales were above " & Format(cutoff, "$0,000") _
& " on " & nHigh & " of the 36 months."
Next j
End Sub
```

It is easy to indent, so you should start doing it right away in *all* of your programs.[8] To indent a single line, use the **Tab** key; *don't* simply insert spaces.

---

[8] Microsoft's Visual Studio .NET, its integrated development environment, automatically indents for you. Unfortunately, the VBE for Excel is not quite up to this level yet, so you have to indent manually.

To outdent (the opposite of indent) a single line, use the **Shift+Tab** key combination. To indent or outdent entire blocks of code, highlight the block and then use the indent and outdent buttons on the VBE's **Edit** toolbar.

5.10 Strings

The InputBox function takes at least one argument, a prompt such as "Enter your name." Similarly, the MsgBox function takes at least one argument, a message such as "Thank you for the name." Technically, each of these is called a **string.** A string is simply text, surrounded by double quotes. Strings are nearly always arguments to InputBox, MsgBox, and other functions, and they are also used in many other ways in VBA. For example, because a string essentially corresponds to a label in Excel, if you want to use VBA to enter a label in a cell, you set the Value property of the Range object representing the cell to a string. You will see many examples of this throughout the book. The point now is that strings are used in practically all VBA programs.

Often a string is a literal piece of text, such as "The user's name is Chris Albright." (Again, remember that the double quotes are part of the string and cannot be omitted.) Many times, however, a string cannot be written literally and must be pieced together in sections. This is called **string concatenation**. As an example, suppose the following InputBox statement is used to get a product name:

```
product = InputBox("Enter the product's name.")
```

The user types the product's name into the text box, and it is stored as a string, "LaserJet 1100" for example, in the product variable. Now suppose you what to display a message in a message box such as "The product's name is LaserJet 1100." What should the first argument of the MsgBox be? It cannot be the literal "The product's name is LaserJet 1100." This is because you, the programmer, do not know what product name will be entered in the InputBox. Therefore, you must "build" the message string by concatenating three strings: the literal "The product's name is ", the *variable* string product, and the literal period ".". To concatenate these, you use the ampersand concatenation character, &, surrounded on either side by a space (and the spaces *are* necessary). The resulting MsgBox statement is

```
MsgBox "The product's name is " & product & "."
```

Note how the ampersand is used twice to separate the *variable* information from the literal parts of the string. String concatenation—the alternation of literal and variable parts of a string—is extremely important and is used in practically all programs.

A completed sub that gets a product's name and then displays it in a message box appears below, along with the results from running it, in Figures 5.8 and 5.9.

Figure 5.8 InputBox

Figure 5.9 MessageBox

```
Sub GetProductName()
    Dim product As String
    product = InputBox("Enter the product's name.")
    MsgBox "The product's name is " & product & ".", vbInformation
End Sub
```

One tricky aspect of string concatenation occurs when you use the underscore character to break a long string, even a totally literal one, into two lines. You might think that the following would work:

```
MsgBox "This is a long string, long enough to extend _
    beyond the screen, so it is broken up into two lines." ' This produces an error.
```

However, this produces an error message. If you break a string across two lines, you *must* concatenate it:

```
MsgBox "This is a long string, long enough to extend " & _
    "beyond the screen, so it is broken up into two lines."
```

(Note that there is a space after the word *extend,* so that *extend* and *beyond* will not run together in the message. There is also a space on each side of the ampersand, as required by VBA.) Alternatively, you could place the ampersand on the second line:

```
MsgBox "This is a long string, long enough to extend " _
    & "beyond the screen, so it is broken up into two lines."
```

Whether you put the ampersand at the end of the first line or the beginning of the second line is a matter of taste.

Exercise 5.2   Displaying a Message

Return to Exercise 5.1 from Section 5.4. There you obtained a unit price and a quantity sold from input boxes, calculated the revenue, and then displayed a message such as "The revenue from this product was $380." You should now understand that the last part of this message, the actual revenue, requires string concatenation. (See my **Input Output 1.xlsm** file.) Now try expanding your program slightly (and save your results in the file **Input Output 2.xlsm).** Start by using an input box to get the product's name. Then use input boxes to get the product's unit price and the quantity sold, and include the product's name in the prompts for these inputs. For example, a prompt might be "Enter the unit price for LaserJet 1100." Next, calculate the revenue. Finally, display a message that contains all of the information, something like "For the LaserJet 1100, the unit price is $500, the quantity sold is 25, and the revenue is $12,500." Do as much as you can on your own. If you need help, look at the file **Input Output 2.xlsm.**

Formatting Strings

If the revenue is 12500, how do you get it to appear as $12,500 in a message? This can be done with VBA's Format function. This function takes two arguments: the number to be formatted and a **format code** string that indicates how to format the number. To format 12500 in the usual currency format (with a dollar sign and comma separators), you can use Format(12500,"$#,##0"). If the variable revenue holds the actual revenue, then you would use Format(revenue,"$#,##0"). Using the Format function is tricky. Rather than memorizing formatting codes, it is best to select the Format option in Excel (right-click any cell and choose Format Cells, or press Ctrl+1) and choose the **Custom** option. It will list a number of formatting codes you can use in VBA.

Useful String Functions

String concatenation is useful when you need to piece together several small strings to create one long string. You might also need to get *part* of a string. There are three useful VBA string functions for doing this: Right, Left, and Mid. They are illustrated in the following lines.

```
shortString1 = Right("S. Christian Albright", 8)
shortString2 = Left("S. Christian Albright", 12)
shortString3 = Mid("S. Christian Albright", 4, 5)
```

The first line returns "Albright". In general, the Right function takes two arguments, a string and an integer *n*, and it returns the rightmost *n* characters of the string. The Left function is similar. It returns the leftmost *n* characters. In the second line, it returns "S. Christian". (The space after "S." is considered a character.) Finally, the Mid function takes a string and two integer arguments. The first integer specifies the starting character and the second specifies the number of characters to return. Therefore, the third line returns "Chris". Starting at the fourth character, "C", it returns the next five characters. Note that the third argument of Mid can be omitted, in which case Mid returns all characters until the end of the string. For example, Mid("Albright",3) returns "bright".

Another useful string function is the Len function. It takes a single argument, a string, and returns the number of characters in the string. For example, the following line

```
nCharacters = Len("S. Christian Albright")
```

returns 21. Again, remember that spaces count.

One other string function that can come in handy is the Instr function. It checks whether a substring is anywhere inside a given string, and if it is, where it begins within the string. For example, the following line returns 9 because the comma is the ninth character. (The first argument indicates where to start the search. It is optional and is assumed to be 1 if omitted.)

```
Instr(1,"Albright, Chris",",")
```

If the substring isn't found, Instr returns 0. For example, this would occur with the line

```
Instr(1,"Albright, Chris",".")
```

These string functions can be used in many combinations. Suppose you want all but the last two characters of some string called thisString, but you don't know the number of characters in thisString. Then the following combination of Len and Left will do the job.

```
allBut2 = Left(thisString, Len(thisString) - 2)
```

For example, if thisString turns out to have 25 characters, allBut2 will contain the leftmost 23 characters.

The VBA string functions discussed here are only several of those available. To see others, open the Object Browser in the VBE, select the VBA library, and click the Strings category on the left. On the right, you can scan for functions, such as Join, Replace, and Trim, that might look useful. By the way, you can ignore those that end with a dollar sign, such as Mid$. They are essentially the same as the corresponding functions without the dollar sign.

5.11 Specifying Objects, Properties, and Methods

Objects, properties, and methods were introduced in Chapter 2. Now it is time to see how they are implemented in VBA code. This is important material. Virtually nothing can be done in VBA for Excel without knowing how to manipulate its objects in code. The basic rules are as follows.

Specifying a Member of a Collection

To specify a particular member of a collection, you use the *plural* name of the collection, with the particular member specified in parentheses and enclosed inside quotes, as in Worksheets("Data"). (Remember from Section 5.3 that you could also refer to a worksheet by its code name.) In the special case of the Range object, where there is no plural, you just write Range, followed by a specification of the range inside parentheses. (The next chapter is devoted entirely to Range objects because they are so important—and tricky.) You can generally specify any particular member of a collection in one of two ways: by index (a number) or by name (a string). For example, you can specify Worksheets(2) or Worksheets("Data").[9] The name method is *much* preferred. After all, if someone inserts a new worksheet or moves an existing worksheet, the worksheet in question might no longer be the *second* one. It is much easier to understand the reference to the worksheet's name. Note that the argument 2 actually refers to the second sheet from the left, not necessarily the second sheet created.

Specifying Objects down a Hierarchy

To specify objects down a hierarchy, you separate them with a period, with objects farther down the hierarchy to the right, as in

```
Workbooks("Sales").Worksheets("March").Range("A1")
```

You essentially read this line backward. It specifies cell A1 from the March worksheet of the Sales workbook. We say that an object is **qualified** by any objects listed to its left. It is possible that you have several worksheets and even workbooks open. The above line specifies the cell you want: cell A1 in the March worksheet of the Sales workbook.

This rule has a number of variations. For example, if you refer simply to Range("A1"), do you need to qualify it with a particular workbook and worksheet? Let's just say that you are safer to specify at least the worksheet. The rule is very simple. If you refer simply to Range("A1"), you are referring to the *active* sheet of the *active* workbook, whatever they happen to be at the time. Actually, there are built-in VBA objects called ActiveWorkbook and ActiveSheet (but no ActiveWorksheet). They refer to the workbook and sheet currently selected. If you refer simply to Range("A1"), this is equivalent to

---

[9] For a worksheet, you can again refer to it by its code name. I usually prefer this to either of the other two methods.

```
ActiveWorkbook.ActiveSheet.Range("A1")
```

If this is what you want, the shorter Range("A1") is perfectly acceptable. However, if you do it this way, make sure that the *active* worksheet of the *active* workbook contains the cell A1 you are interested in. In other words, if you do not qualify Range("A1"), VBA will guess which cell A1 you mean, and it might not guess correctly. It is safer to qualify it, as in Worksheets("Data").Range("A1"), for example. Alternatively, you can qualify it by the worksheet's code name, as in wsData.Range("A1"). This is how I will do it in most examples.

Specifying a Property

To specify a property of an object, you list the property name to the right of the object, separated by a period, as in

```
Range("A1").Value
```

This refers to the Value property of the range A1—that is, the contents of cell A1. A property can be set or returned. For example, the following line enters the string "Sales for March" in cell A1:

```
Range("A1").Value = "Sales for March"
```

In contrast, the following line gets the label in range A1 and stores it as a string in the variable title:

```
title = Range("A1").Value
```

Specifying a Method

To specify a method for an object, you list the method name to the right of the object, separated by a period:

```
Range("A1:D500").ClearContents
```

Specifying Arguments of a Method

If a method has arguments, you list them, separated by commas, next to the method's name. Each argument should have the name of the argument (which can be found from online help), followed by :=, followed by the value of the argument. For example, the following copies the range A1:B10 to the range D1: E10. Here, Destination is the name of the argument of the Copy method.

```
Range("A1:B10").Copy  Destination:=Range("D1:E10")
```

It is possible to omit the argument name and the := and to write

```
Range("A1:B10").Copy  Range("D1:E10")
```

However, this can be dangerous and can lead to errors unless you know the rules well. It is better to supply the argument name and :=. Even if you are an experienced programmer, this practice makes your code more readable for others.[10]

By the way, when methods have arguments, Intellisense helps a great deal. In the above line, as soon as you type .Copy and then a space, Intellisense shows you a list of the arguments, both required and optional, of the Copy method. In this case, there is only one argument, Destination, and Intellisense shows it in square brackets, indicating that is optional.

These are the rules, and you can return to this section as often as you like to refresh your memory. They are reinforced with many examples in later chapters.

Exercise 5.3   Calculating Ordering Costs

The file **Input Output 3_1.xlsx** is a template for calculating the total order cost for ordering a product with quantity discounts. The table, range-named LTable, in the range A4:C8 contains unit costs for various order quantity intervals. The range B11:B13 contains a typical order cost calculation, where the input is the order quantity in cell B11 and the ultimate output is the total cost in cell B13. Take a look at this file to see how a VLOOKUP function is used to calculate the appropriate unit cost in cell B12.

The file **Input Output 3_2.xlsm** indicates what the exercise is supposed to accomplish. Open it now and click the "Create table" button. It asks for three possible order quantities, and then it fills in the table in the range D12:E14 with these order quantities and the corresponding total costs. Basically, it plugs each potential order quantity into cell B11 and transfers the corresponding total cost from cell B13 to column E of the table. If you then click the "Clear table" button, the information in this table is deleted.

---

[10] Methods often have multiple arguments, listed in a certain order. If you omit the argument names, you *must* supply the arguments in that order. However, if you use argument names and :=, you are allowed to list the arguments in any order.

Now that you see what the finished application should do, go back to the **Input Output 3_1.xlsx** file, save it as an .xlsm file, and attempt to write two subs, CreateTable and ClearTable, which will eventually be attached to buttons. Go as far as you can on your own. If you need help, look at the code in my **Input Output 3_2.xlsm** file.

This exercise will undoubtedly leave you wishing for more. First, even with only three order quantities, there is a lot of repetitive code. By copying and pasting your code (and then making suitable modifications), you can minimize the amount of typing required. Second, the program ought to allow *any* number of entries in the table, not just three. To see how these issues can be addressed, open the file **Input Output 3_3.xlsm**, click its buttons, and look at its code. There are probably a few lines you will not understand yet, but at least this gives you something to strive for. You will eventually understand all of the code in this file. In fact, you will eventually appreciate that it is quite straightforward.

5.12 With Construction

There is an extremely useful shortcut you can use when working with objects and their properties and methods. This is the With construction. Unless you have programmed in VBA, you have probably never seen it. The easiest way to explain the With construction is by using an example. Suppose you want to set a number of properties for the range A1 in the March worksheet of the Sales workbook. You could use the following code.

```
Workbooks("Sales").Worksheets("March").Range("A1").Value = "Sales for March"
Workbooks("Sales").Worksheets("March").Range("A1").HorizontalAlignment = xlLeft
Workbooks("Sales").Worksheets("March").Range("A1").Font.Name = "Times New Roman"
Workbooks("Sales").Worksheets("March").Range("A1").Font.Bold = True
Workbooks("Sales").Worksheets("March").Range("A1").Font.Size = 14
```

As you can see, there is a lot of repetition in these five lines, which means a lot of typing (or copying and pasting). The With construction enables you to do it much more easily:

```
With Workbooks("Sales").Worksheets("March").Range("A1")
    .Value = "Sales for March"
    .HorizontalAlignment = xlLeft
    With .Font
        .Name = "Times New Roman"
        .Bold = True
        .Size = 14
    End With
End With
```

The first line has the keyword With, followed by an object reference. The last line brackets it with the keywords End With. In between, any object, property, or method that starts with a period "tacks on" the object following With. For example, .Value in the second line is equivalent to

```
Workbooks("Sales").Worksheets("March").Range("A1").Value
```

This example also illustrates how With constructions can be *nested*. The line With .Font is equivalent to

```
With Workbooks("Sales").Worksheets("March").Range("A1").Font
```

Then, for example, the .Name reference inside this second With is equivalent to

```
Workbooks("Sales").Worksheets("March").Range("A1").Font.Name
```

With (and nested With) constructions can save a lot of typing, and they improve readability. They also speed up the execution of your programs slightly. However, there are two things to remember. First, remember that the End With line must accompany each With line. A good habit is to type the End With line immediately after typing the With line. That way, you don't forget. Second, you should indent appropriately. As mentioned earlier, indenting is not required—your programs will run perfectly well without it—but errors are much easier to catch (and avoid) if you indent, and your programs are *much* easier to read. Compare the above code to the following version:

```
With Workbooks("Sales").Worksheets("March").Range("A1")
.Value = "Sales for March"
.HorizontalAlignment = xlLeft
With .Font
.Name = "Times New Roman"
.Bold = True
.Size = 14
End With
End With
```

Although it is correct, this version without indenting is certainly harder to read, and if you forgot the next-to-last line, it could be difficult to find the error.

Exercise 5.4   Using With Constructions

Open the file **Input Output 3_2.xlsm** (or your own finished version in **Input Output 3_1.xlsm**) from the previous exercise and save it as **Input Output 3_4.xlsm**. Then use the With construction wherever possible. For one possible solution, see the file **Input Output 3_4.xlsm**.

5.13 Other Useful VBA Tips

This section illustrates a few miscellaneous features of VBA that are frequently useful.

Screen Updating

A VBA program for Excel sometimes makes many changes in one or more worksheets before eventually showing results. During this time the screen can flicker, which wastes time and is certainly annoying. The following line turns off screen updating. It essentially says, "Do the work and just show me the results at the end."

```
Application.ScreenUpdating = False
```

To appreciate how this works, open the file **Screen Updating.xlsm**. It has two buttons, each attached to a sub. Each sub performs the same operations, but one turns off screen updating and the other leaves it on. Unless you have a really fast machine, you will notice the difference.

If you do decide to turn off screen updating (typically at the beginning of a sub), it is good programming practice to turn it back on just before the end of the sub. You do this with the line

```
Application.ScreenUpdating = True
```

Display Alerts

If you use the Excel interface to delete a worksheet, you get a warning, as shown in Figure 5.10. In some applications you don't want this warning; you just want the worksheet to be deleted. In this case (and other cases where you don't want an Excel warning), you can use the following line:

```
Application.DisplayAlerts = False
```

This can actually be a bit dangerous—you might *want* a warning later on—so it is a good idea to turn display alerts back on immediately, as in the following lines:

```
Application.DisplayAlerts = False
wsReport.Delete
Application.DisplayAlerts = True
```

Figure 5.10 Excel Warning Message

Timer Function

Programmers often like to see how long their programs (or parts of their programs) take to run. This is easy to do with VBA's Timer function. It returns the current clock time. If it is used twice, once at the beginning of some code and once later on, then the difference in the two times is the elapsed run time. The following lines illustrate how it can be used. The start time is captured in the variable startTime. This is followed by any number of programming lines. Finally, the variable elapsedTime captures the current time (from Timer) minus the start time. Note that these times are measured in *seconds*.

```
startTime = Timer
' Enter any code in here.
elapsedTime = Timer - startTime
MsgBox "This section took " & elapsedTime & " seconds to run."
```

5.14 Good Programming Practices

As a programmer, your primary goal is to write code that works correctly to accomplish a specified task. However, good programmers are not satisfied with accuracy. They want their programs to be readable and easy to maintain, so that if changes are necessary sometime in the future, they won't be too difficult to make. (Keep in mind that the person responsible for making these changes is often *not* the original programmer.) Therefore, good programmers consistently follow a set of good habits. Even if you are a beginning programmer, you should follow these good habits right from the start. Admittedly, you can practice poor habits and still write programs that work, but your programs will probably not be very readable or easy to maintain. Besides, poor habits typically lead to more programming errors.

Not all programmers agree completely on a programming style that should be followed, but they would almost certainly agree on the following list.

- **Provide sufficient comments.** As discussed earlier in this chapter, providing a liberal number of comments is the best way to make your programs understandable, both to others and to yourself (at a later date). It is always better to include too many comments than too few.
- **Indent consistently.** This was also mentioned earlier, but it bears repeating. Some programmers write code with no indenting—all lines are left-aligned on the page. Unless the program is short and simple, this type of code is practically impossible to read, and the potential for errors increases dramatically. Indenting provides a logical structure to your program, and it indicates that you are *aware* of this logical structure. You will have plenty of

chances to see the proper use of indenting as you read through the examples in the book.

- **Use white space liberally.** Don't be afraid to insert blank lines in your subs, which are ignored by VBA. Like indenting, this tends to provide a more logical structure to your code, and it is greatly appreciated by those who try to read your code. Generally, lines of code fall into logical blocks. Therefore, it is a good idea to separate these blocks by white space.

- **Break long lines into multiple lines.** It is no fun to read a line of code that scrolls off to the right of the screen. Therefore, keep your lines short enough that they fit inside the Code window. When necessary, use the underscore character, _, to break long lines.

- **Name your variables appropriately.** I already discussed this earlier in the chapter, but it also bears repeating. Thankfully, the days when programmers could get away with meaningless variable names like KK, X, and PR, are gone. (Don't laugh. Programs in the old days were filled with variables like this.) Variable names like fixedCost and lastName produce much more readable code.

- **Declare all of your variables, usually at the beginnings of subs.** I already stated that Option Explicit should be at the top of each of your modules. This *forces* you to declare your variables with Dim statements. Actually, these Dim statements can be placed just about anywhere within a sub (before the variable is used), but it is a good programming practice to place them right after the Sub line. This makes it easy to find a list of all your variables. (This doesn't count **module-level** variables, which must be declared *before* any subs. They are discussed in Chapter 10.)

- **Use the Variant type as little as possible.** Remember that a Variant type is a catch-all; it can hold any type of variable. The way a Variant variable is stored and manipulated depends on the context of the program. Essentially, you are making the computer determine the type of variable you have, and this is not efficient. If you know that your variable is really an integer, for example, then declare it as Integer, not as Variant. The use of Variant types is usually a sign of sloppy programming. And remember that not specifying a type at all is the same as specifying a Variant type.

- **Break a complex program into small subs.** This is the topic of Chapter 10, but even at this point it should make sense. It is much more difficult to read and debug a long complex sub than to work with a series of shorter subs, each devoted to performing a single task. Think of this as the "divide and conquer" rule.

As you start writing your own programs, refer back to this list from time to time. If you find that you are consistently violating one or more of these rules, you know that you have room to improve—and you should strive to do so.

5.15 Debugging

Some programmers are more skillful and careful than others, but the sad fact is that we *all* make errors, known in the programming world as **bugs**. The art of finding and getting rid of bugs, **debugging**, is almost as important as programming itself. Debugging is basically detective work, and, like programming, it takes practice. This section gets you started.

There are really three types of errors: **syntax** errors, **runtime** errors, and **logic** errors.

Syntax Errors

Syntax errors are usually the easiest to spot and fix. They occur when you spell something wrong, omit a keyword, or commit various other "grammatical" errors. They are easy to spot because the VBE typically detects them immediately, colors the offending line red, and displays a warning in a message box.[11] You have probably experienced this behavior several times already, but in case you haven't, type the following line of code and press the Enter key:

```
If FirstNumber > SecondNumber
```

You will be reminded immediately that this line contains a syntax error—the keyword Then is missing. Sometimes the resulting error message tells you in clear terms what the error is, and other times it is misleading. But at least you know that there is something wrong with your syntax, you know approximately where the error is, and you have a chance to fix it right away. There is no excuse for not doing so. If you are not sure of the correct syntax, you can search online help.

Runtime Errors

Runtime errors are more difficult to spot and fix. They occur when there is something wrong with your code, but the error is not discovered until you *run* your program. The following is a typical example.

```
Option Explicit
Option Base 1

Sub Test()
    Dim myArray(10) As Integer, i As Integer, nReps As Integer
    nReps = InputBox("Enter the number of replications.")
    For i = 1 To nReps
        myArray(i) = 20 * i
    Next
End Sub
```

---

[11] This is the default behavior of the VBE, and you can leave it as is. However, if you get tired of the warnings, you can select VBE's **Tools**→**Options** menu item and uncheck Auto Syntax Check under the Editor tab.

Figure 5.11 Error Dialog Box

This code has no syntax errors, but it is likely to produce a runtime error. The user is asked to enter a number of replications, which is stored in the variable nReps. If the user enters a value less than or equal to 10, the program will run fine. However, if the user enters a number greater than 10, the program will try to fill an array with more values than it is dimensioned for. (Arrays are covered in Chapter 9.) If you run this program and enter 15 in the input box, you will get the error message shown in Figure 5.11. It is one of Microsoft's cryptic error messages that you will come to despise, both because it means that *you* made an error and because you can't understand the message.

At this point, you have the three options indicated by the enabled buttons: (1) You can ask for help, which is almost never helpful; (2) you can end the program, which doesn't do anything to help you locate the bug; or (3) you can click the Debug button. This latter option displays the offending line of code and colors it yellow. If you then move the cursor over variables, you can see their current values, which often provides the clue you need. Figure 5.12 shows what happens if you click the Debug button and then place the cursor over the

Figure 5.12 Code After Clicking Debug

```
(General)                                      Test

    Option Explicit
    Option Base 1
    Sub Test()
        Dim myArray(10) As Integer, i As Integer, nReps As Integer
        nReps = InputBox("Enter the number of replications.")
        For i = 1 To nReps
            myArray(i) = 20 * i
        Next            i = 11
    End Sub
```

variable i in the offending line. Its current value is 11, and the array is dimensioned for only 10 elements.

This is the clue you need to fix the program, as shown below. The trick is to redimension the array *after* discovering the value of nReps. The details of the fix are not important at this point. The important thing is that you found the location of the bug, and that is often all you need to fix the problem.

```
Option Explicit
Option Base 1

Sub Test()
    Dim myArray() As Integer, i As Integer, nReps As Integer
    nReps = InputBox("Enter the number of replications.")
    ReDim myArray(nReps)
    For i = 1 To nReps
        myArray(i) = 20 * i
    Next
End Sub
```

The problem with runtime errors is that there is an infinite variety of them, and the error messages provided by Microsoft can sometimes be misleading. Consider the following sub, which purposely violates the cardinal rule of indenting to mask the bug in the program. Can you spot it?

```
Sub Test()
Dim cell As Range
For Each cell In Range("A1:D10")
If cell.Value > 10 Then
With cell.Font
.Bold = True
.Italic = True
End If
Next
End Sub
```

The properly indented version listed below clearly indicates the problem—the With construction is missing an End With line.

```
Sub Test()
    Dim cell As Range
    For Each cell In Range("A1:D10")
        If cell.Value > 10 Then
            With cell.Font
                .Bold = True
                .Italic = True
        End If
    Next
End Sub
```

However, if you run this program (either version), you will get the error message in Figure 5.13, and the End If line of the sub will be highlighted in yellow. As you can imagine, this type of misleading information can drive a programmer

Figure 5.13 Misleading Error Message

crazy. Of course, some snooping around indicates that the problem is *not* with End If but is instead with End With. However, an unsuspecting programmer could be led down a time-consuming blind alley searching for the bug. Therefore, it is best to interpret runtime error messages with caution. They typically point you in the general *neighborhood* of the offending code, but they do not always pinpoint the problem. And, as you can probably guess, the Help button in this case is not of any help at all.

When you get any of these runtime error messages, your program goes into **break mode,** which essentially means that it is on hold. You always know a program is in break mode when a line of code is highlighted in yellow. Sometimes you can fix a line of code while in break mode and then click the **Run Sub/UserForm** button on the VBE Standard toolbar to let the program finish. (See Figure 5.14.) Other times, it is impossible to continue. You need to click the **Reset** button, fix the bug, and then rerun the program. It is usually best to do the latter. If you ever get a message to the effect that something can't be done because the program is in break mode, get back into the VBE and click the Reset button. In this case, the reason you can't run your program is that it is already running.

Logic Errors

The third general type of error, a logic error, is the most insidious of the three because you frequently don't even know that you *made* an error. You run the program, it produces some results, and you congratulate yourself on work well done. However, if your program contains any logic errors, even a single tiny error, the results can be totally wrong. You might or might not get an error message to alert you to the problem.

Here is a typical example. (This file is not included with the book, but you might want to create it for practice.) You want to average the numbers in column

Figure 5.14 VBE Standard Toolbar

Figure 5.15 Scores to Average

	A	B
1	Scores	
2	87	
3	78	
4	98	
5	82	
6	77	
7	99	
8	80	
9	85	
10	76	
11		
12	84.67	

Figure 5.16 Display of Incorrect Average

A (through row 10) in Figure 5.15 and display the average in a message box. The correct average, calculated with Excel's AVERAGE function, appears in cell A12.

The AverageScores sub listed below contains no syntax errors and no runtime errors.[12] If you run it, it will display the message in Figure 5.16—with the *wrong* average! Unless you have read ahead to the next chapter, you probably don't know enough about **Range** objects to spot the problem, but there is a bug, and it is quite subtle.

```
Sub AverageScores()
    Dim scoreRange As Range, cell As Range, sum As Single

    With Range("A1")
        Set scoreRange = Range(.Offset(0, 0), .End(xlDown))
    End With

    For Each cell In scoreRange
        If IsNumeric(cell.Value) Then sum = sum + cell.Value
    Next

    MsgBox "The average of the scores is " & sum / scoreRange.Cells.Count
End Sub
```

[12] Of course, you would never write such complex code to perform such a simple task. It is done here only to illustrate a point.

Figure 5.17 VBE Debug Toolbar

Toggle breakpoint Step into Step over Step out Quick watch

There are actually two problems. The first problem, and probably the more important one, is that if the correct average had not been calculated separately in cell A12, you would probably have accepted the answer in the message as being correct. (How many programs in the real world contain errors that no one is even aware of? I suspect the number is huge. Is it possible, for example, that there are errors in the gigantic programs used by the IRS to check your tax returns? It's a scary thought!)

However, assuming that you are suspicious of the answer in the message box, the second problem is that you have to find the error and fix it. Fortunately, the VBE has some powerful tools for debugging your programs. One of the most useful methods is to **step through** a program one line at a time, possibly keeping a **watch** on one or more key variables. VBE's **Debug** toolbar is very handy for doing this. (See Figure 5.17.) Equivalently, you can use menu items and shortcut keys to perform the same tasks.

Let's use this method to find the faulty logic in the average example. To do this—and you should follow along at your own computer—get into the VBE and put a watch on the key variable sum. The easiest way to do this is to put the cursor anywhere on the sum variable (anywhere it appears in the code) and click the **Quick watch** button. The **Watch window** then opens, as shown in Figure 5.18. It allows you to watch the contents of sum as the program executes. In general, you can put watches on as many variables as you like.

At this point, sum has not yet been defined, so its value is listed as "out of context." But it changes as you step through the program. To do this, put the cursor anywhere inside the sub and repeatedly click the **Step into** button. (Alternatively, press the **F8** key repeatedly.) This executes a line of code at a time. If the line changes the value of **sum,** the updated value will appear in the Watch window. By the time the For Each loop is finished, the Watch window appears as in Figure 5.19.

If you sum the numbers in the range A2:A10 of Figure 5.15, you will find that the sum is indeed 762. This means that the problem is *not* with the logic for calculating sum. The only other possible problem is with the number that sum is divided by to obtain the average. (Now do you see the error?) A careful

Figure 5.18 Watch Window

Watches				
Expression	Value	Type	Context	
δδ Sum	<Out of context>	Empty	Module1.AverageScores	

Figure 5.19 Watch Window After For Each Loop

look at the code shows that scoreRange includes the label in cell A1. Therefore, scoreRange.Cells.Count returns 10, not 9. The correct average is 762/9, not 762/10. (You might recall that Excel's COUNT worksheet function counts only cells with numbers. In contrast, VBA's Count property, as used here, counts all cells, even empty cells or cells with labels.)

The general point made by this example is that stepping through a program, together with a careful use of the Watch window, can localize a problem and enable you to fix it. You can also employ some other debugging tools to fine-tune your search for bugs. This is particularly important if you have a large program with several subs and you are confident that most of them are bug-free. You then can use the following tools.

- **Set breakpoints.** Place the cursor on any line of code and click the **Toggle breakpoint** button. This puts a red dot in the left-hand margin of the Code window (or it removes the red dot if one was already there). If you now run the program, it will execute until it encounters this line of code, at which time it goes into break mode. Then you can examine values of variables or step through the program from this point on. In general, whenever you click the **Run Sub/Userform** button, the program advances to the *next* breakpoint. (If there isn't another breakpoint, the program runs to completion.)
- **Step over subs.** As you are stepping through a program, you might get to a line that **calls** another sub. (Calling other subs is discussed in Chapter 10.) If you do not want to step through that sub line by line (because you are confident it is bug-free), click the **Step over** button. This executes the sub all at once, without stepping through it line by line.
- **Step out of subs.** Similarly, if you are stepping through a sub and decide there is no point in stepping through the rest of it, click the **Step out** button. The rest of the sub is executed all at once and control passes back to the calling sub, which you can then continue to step through.

These tools are great for debugging, but they are not magic bullets. Incorrect logic creeps into almost all programs of any reasonable size, and it is the programmer's task to find them. This requires a thorough knowledge of the program, a lot of detective work, and perseverance. The easy way out is to seek immediate help from someone else (your instructor?) as soon as something goes wrong. However, you should try to find the bugs yourself, using the tools described here. It is probably the most effective way to become a good programmer. You will learn at least as much from your errors as from any programming manuals.

5.16   Summary

This chapter has covered a lot of VBA programming fundamentals, including subroutines (subs); variables; the InputBox and MsgBox functions; comments; strings and string operations; specification of objects, properties, and methods; With constructions; a few other VBA elements; and debugging. All of these fundamentals are used repeatedly in later chapters. Don't worry if they are not yet completely clear. It takes plenty of practice to master these VBA fundamentals.

EXERCISES

1. Open a new workbook, get into the VBE, insert a module, and enter the following code:

```
Sub Variables()
    Dim nPounds As Integer, dayOfWeek As Integer
    nPounds = 17.5
    dayOfWeek = "Monday"
    MsgBox nPounds & " pounds were ordered on " & dayOfWeek
End Sub
```

There are two problems here. One causes the program to fail, and the other causes an incorrect result. Explain what they are and then fix them.

2. Open a new workbook, get into the VBE, insert a module, and enter the following code:

```
Sub CalculateExpenses()
    customerName = InputBox("Enter the name of a customer.")
    nPurchases = InputBox("Enter the number of purchases made by " _
        & customerName & " during the month.")
    totalSpent = 0
    For counter = 1 To nPurchases
        amountSpent = InputBox("Enter the amount spent by " & customerName _
            & " on purchase " & counter)
        totalSpent = totalSpent + amountSpent
    Next
    MsgBox customerName & " spent a total of " & Format(totalSpent, _
        "$#,##0.00") & " during the month.", vbInformation
End Sub
```

a. Make sure there is no Option Explicit line at the top of the module. (If there is, delete it.) Then run the program. It should work fine. (If it doesn't, check your spelling.)

b. Enter an Option Explicit line at the top of the module. Now run the program. It should produce an error message. The problem is that the Option Explicit statement forces you to declare variables, and none of the variables in this sub have been declared. Declare them appropriately with a Dim statement (or several Dim statements) and rerun the program. Now it should work.

3. Write a program, and store it in a file called **Travel Expenses.xlsm**, that does the following: (a) It asks for a person's first name and stores it in firstName; (b) it asks for a person's last name and stores it in lastName; (c) it asks for the number of miles the person traveled on a recent trip and stores it in nMiles; (d) it asks for the average miles per gallon the person got on the trip and stores it in milesPerGallon; (e) it asks for the average price per gallon paid for gas on the trip and stores it in avgPrice; (f) it calculates the cost of the trip and stores it in tripCost; and (g) it displays a message such as "Bob Jones traveled 800 miles, got 31.3 miles per gallon on average, paid $3.49 per gallon on average, and paid a total of $89.20 for gas." Make sure there is an Option Explicit line at the top of the module and that you declare all of your variables appropriately.

4. Write a program, and store it in a file called **String Funtions.xlsm**, that does the following: (a) It asks the user for a word with at least 10 characters and stores it in myWord; (b) it displays a message indicating the number of characters in the word; (c) it displays a message showing the first four characters of the word; (d) it displays a message showing the last six characters of the word; (e) it displays a message showing the fifth character in the word; (f) it displays a message showing all but the first two and last two characters in the word; and (g) it displays the word in reversed order. (*Hint:* For the last part, look up Strings in the VBA library of the Object Browser.)

5. The file **Formatting 1.xlsm** contains the following code for formatting some data. It is all correct. Rewrite the code so that there are no With constructions, and then run the modified program to make sure it still works. Can you see how With constructions reduce repetitive code?

```
Sub Formatting()
    With ActiveWorkbook.Worksheets("Sheet1")
        With .Range("A1")
            .Value = "Expenses for March"
            With .Font
                .Name = "Arial"
                .Bold = True
                .ColorIndex = 5
                .Size = 14
            End With
            .HorizontalAlignment = xlLeft
        End With
        With Range("A3:A6")
            .InsertIndent 1
            With .Font
                .Italic = True
                .Bold = True
            End With
        End With
        With .Range("B3:B6")
            .Interior.Color = vbBlue
            .NumberFormat = "$#,##0"
        End With
    End With
End Sub
```

6. The file **Formatting 2.xlsm** contains the following code for formatting some data. This code works perfectly well, but it is quite repetitive. Rewrite it by using as many With constructions as make sense, using appropriate indentation, and then run your modified code to make sure it still works.

```
Sub Formatting()
    ActiveWorkbook.Worksheets("Sheet1").Range("A1").Font.Bold = True
    ActiveWorkbook.Worksheets("Sheet1").Range("A1").Font.Size = 14
    ActiveWorkbook.Worksheets("Sheet1").Range("A1").HorizontalAlignment = xlLeft
    ActiveWorkbook.Worksheets("Sheet1").Range("A3:A6").Font.Bold = True
    ActiveWorkbook.Worksheets("Sheet1").Range("A3:A6").Font.Italic = True
    ActiveWorkbook.Worksheets("Sheet1").Range("A3:A6").Font.Color = vbGreen
    ActiveWorkbook.Worksheets("Sheet1").Range("A3:A6").InsertIndent 1
    ActiveWorkbook.Worksheets("Sheet1").Range("B2:D2").Font.Bold = True
    ActiveWorkbook.Worksheets("Sheet1").Range("B2:D2").Font.Italic = True
    ActiveWorkbook.Worksheets("Sheet1").Range("B2:D2").Font.Color = vbBlue
    ActiveWorkbook.Worksheets("Sheet1").Range("B2:D2").HorizontalAlignment = xlRight
    ActiveWorkbook.Worksheets("Sheet1").Range("B3:D6").Font.Color = vbRed
    ActiveWorkbook.Worksheets("Sheet1").Range("B3:D6").NumberFormat = "$#,##0"
End Sub
```

7. The file **Formatting 3.xlsm** contains code that is very difficult to read. Besides that, it contains an error. Reformat it with indenting, white space, and comments, and fix the error so that it runs correctly.

8. The file **Count Large.xlsm** has quantities sold for 1000 products for each of 60 months, for a total of 60,000 values. The following code counts the number of these that are greater than 100. Check how long it takes to do this by inserting Timer functions appropriately in the code and displaying the elapsed time in a message box.

```
Sub CountLarge()
    Dim cell As Range, nLarge As Long
    For Each cell In Range("Sales")
        If cell.Value > 100 Then nLarge = nLarge + 1
    Next
    MsgBox nLarge & " cells in the Sales range have a quantity larger than 100.", _
        vbInformation
End Sub
```

9. Write single lines of code for each of the following.
   a. Set the value of cell A17 in the Sales sheet of the active workbook to 1325.
   b. Capture the value of cell B25 in the Quantities sheet of the workbook **Sales.xlsx** in the variable marchSales.
   c. Clear the contents of the range named Sales.
   d. Copy the range A1:A10 on the Sheet1 worksheet of the active workbook to the range A1:A10 of the MarchSales sheet in the **Sales.xlsx** workbook. Assume that **Sales.xlsx** is *not* the active workbook.

10. The file **Exam Scores.xlsx** has scores for an exam in the range A1:A100. Write a sub that reports the average, standard deviation, minimum, and maximum of the scores in a message box. Use Excel's functions (with WorksheetFunction) to do the arithmetic.

11. Open a new workbook, name it **Random Number.xlsm**, and delete all but the first sheet if necessary. Write a sub that enters a random number in cell A1. Try this two ways. First, use Excel's RAND function (with WorksheetFunction) to set the Value property of this cell. Does this work? It shouldn't. Second, set the Value property of the cell to VBA's rnd function. Does this work? It should. The moral is that if VBA has a function that does something, you have to use it; you can't borrow Excel's function that does the same thing.

6

Working with Ranges

6.1 Introduction

This chapter focuses on ways to work with ranges in VBA. This is a particularly important topic because the majority of operations in Excel are *range* operations. You select ranges, you enter values and formulas in ranges, you format ranges in various ways, you copy ranges, and so on. Therefore, it is important to be able to automate these common tasks with VBA. Unfortunately, it can be difficult to do even the simplest tasks unless you know the correct techniques, and online help is sometimes more confusing than helpful. This chapter presents sample VBA code that accomplishes many common tasks. You can then adapt this code to your own programs.

6.2 Exercise

The following exercise illustrates the type of problem you will be able to solve once you master the techniques in this chapter. You should probably not try this exercise yet, but you should keep it in mind as you read through the rest of the chapter. By the end, you should have more than enough tools to solve it—one way or another.

Exercise 6.1

The file **Calculate NPV.xlsx** contains a model for calculating the net present value (NPV) from an investment. (See Figure 6.1.) Five inputs are listed in the range B4:B8. These are used to implement the calculations for cash inflows in row 12, and the NPV is then calculated with the formula **=NPV(B8,B12:K12)-B4** in cell B14. All of the logic to this point is incorporated in the worksheet and does not need to be changed at all. When you enter different inputs in the B4:B8 range, the NPV in cell B14 automatically recalculates.

Rows 18–22 contain possible values of the inputs, where each row is sorted in increasing order. The values shown are for illustration only—you can change them if you like. The goal of the exercise is to ask the user for any *two* of the five inputs. Then the application should find the minimum and maximum values for these two inputs from the corresponding 18–22 rows, substitute each combination (minimum of first and minimum of second, minimum of first and maximum of second, maximum of first and minimum of second, and

Figure 6.1 Setup for Exercise

	A	B	C	D	E	F	G	H	I	J	K	L
1	Calculating the net present value of a stream of cash flows											
2												
3	Inputs											
4	1. Cash outflow, beginning of year 1	$40,000										
5	2. Cash inflow, end of year 1	$12,000										
6	3. Pct increase in cash inflow per year	12%										
7	4. Number of years of cash inflows	10										
8	5. Discount rate	16%										
9												
10	Model of cash inflows (all occur at the ends of years)											
11	Year	1	2	3	4	5	6	7	8	9	10	
12	Cash inflow	$12,000	$13,440	$15,053	$16,859	$18,882	$21,148	$23,686	$26,528	$29,712	$33,277	
13												
14	Net present value (NPV)	$48,787		Note that the values in each of rows 18-22 are in increasing order, so that the								
15				minimum value is at the left and the maximum value is at the right. Even if more								
16	Possible values of the inputs to test			values are added, you can assume that they will always be placed in increasing order.								
17												
18	1. Cash outflow, beginning of year 1	$10,000	$15,000	$20,000	$25,000	$30,000	$35,000	$40,000				
19	2. Cash inflow, end of year 1	$4,000	$5,000	$6,000	$7,000	$8,000	$9,000	$10,000	$11,000	$12,000		
20	3. Pct increase in cash inflow per year	2%	3%	4%	5%	6%	7%	8%	9%	10%	11%	12%
21	4. Number of years of cash inflows	5	6	7	8	9	10					
22	5. Discount rate	8%	9%	10%	11%	12%	13%	14%	15%	16%		
23												
24	Sensitivity table (NPV for combinations of min and max of two selected inputs)											
25			NPV									

Figure 6.2 Completed Solution

	A	B	C	D	E	F	G	H	I	J	K	L
1	Calculating the net present value of a stream of cash flows											
2												
3	Inputs											
4	1. Cash outflow, beginning of year 1	$40,000										
5	2. Cash inflow, end of year 1	$12,000										
6	3. Pct increase in cash inflow per year	12%										
7	4. Number of years of cash inflows	10										
8	5. Discount rate	16%										
9												
10	Model of cash inflows (all occur at the ends of years)											
11	Year	1	2	3	4	5	6	7	8	9	10	
12	Cash inflow	$12,000	$13,440	$15,053	$16,859	$18,882	$21,148	$23,686	$26,528	$29,712	$33,277	
13												
14	Net present value (NPV)	$48,787		Note that the values in each of rows 18-22 are in increasing order, so that the minimum								
15				value is at the left and the maximum value is at the right. Even if more values are added,								
16	Possible values of the inputs to test			you can assume that they will always be placed in increasing order.								
17												
18	1. Cash outflow, beginning of year 1	$10,000	$15,000	$20,000	$25,000	$30,000	$35,000	$40,000				
19	2. Cash inflow, end of year 1	$4,000	$5,000	$6,000	$7,000	$8,000	$9,000	$10,000	$11,000	$12,000		
20	3. Pct increase in cash inflow per year	2%	3%	4%	5%	6%	7%	8%	9%	10%	11%	12%
21	4. Number of years of cash inflows	5	6	7	8	9	10					
22	5. Discount rate	8%	9%	10%	11%	12%	13%	14%	15%	16%		
23												
24	Sensitivity table (NPV for combinations of min and max of two selected inputs)											
25		Input 3	Input 5	NPV								
26		0.02	0.08	$47,074								
27		0.02	0.16	$22,029								
28		0.12	0.08	$91,583								
29		0.12	0.16	$48,787								

maximum of first and maximum of second) in the appropriate cells in the B4:B8 range, and finally report the input values and corresponding NPVs in a table, starting in row 25. As an example, if the user selects inputs 3 and 5, the final result should appear as in Figure 6.2. Note that the values for the third input go from 2% to 12%, whereas the values for the fifth input go from 8% to 16%. Of course, these limits could change if the values in rows 18–22 are changed. The VBA should be written to respond correctly, regardless of the values in rows 18–22, assuming they are always listed in increasing order from left to right.

Figure 6.2 is taken from the file **Calculate NPV Finished.xlsm**. You can open this file and click the Run Sensitivity Analysis button to see in more detail how the application should work. (Don't forget to *enable* the macros when you open the file.) However, try not to look at the code in this file until you have tried to develop the application on your own, starting with the file **Calculate NPV.xlsx**. (This example is obviously limited. Why only *two* of the five inputs? Why not three or more? For a more ambitious version, take a look at the file **Calculate NPV Finished with Loops.xlsm**.)

6.3 Important Properties and Methods of Ranges

This section lists several of the more important and frequently used properties and methods of Range objects. You can skim over it on a first reading, because it is primarily for reference. However, you should find this section useful as you work through the exercises and examples in this chapter and later chapters. Of course, you can find all of this information (and much more) online or in the Object Browser.

Properties

The following properties of a Range object are listed alphabetically, not necessarily in order of their importance or usefulness (and there are many other properties not listed here).

- Address. This returns the address of a range as a string, such as "B2:C6".
- Cells. This returns a reference to a Range object and is often used to refer to a particular cell. For example, Range("D1:D10").Cells(3) refers to the third cell in the range, D3, whereas Range("E10:G15").Cells(3,2) refers to the cell in the third row and second column of the range, cell F12. If the range has multiple rows and columns, then it is customary to use two arguments in Cells, where the first is the row and the second is the column. However, if the range is only part of a single column or a single row, a single argument of Cells suffices.

Before proceeding, you might have noticed a subtle point in the definition of the Cells property. Many objects, including the Range object, have *properties* that are in fact references to *objects* down the hierarchy. The Cells property is an example. If you look up the Range object in the Object Browser, you will see that Cells is classified as a *property*. However, the purpose of this property is to return an *object*. For example, consider the code Range("A1:G10").Cells(3,5).Value. Here, Cells(3,5) is a property of the Range("A1:G10") object, but it returns an *object*, Range("E3"), a reference to cell E3. The Value property then returns the contents of cell E3. Another example is the Font property of a Range object. The code Range("A1").Font.Bold = True uses the Font property to reference a Font object, and then its Bold property is set to True. Again, this distinction between objects and properties is subtle, especially for beginners. Fortunately, it has little impact on you as you do your actual programming.

- Column. This returns the index of the first column in the range, where column A has index 1, column B has index 2, and so on.
- CurrentRegion. This returns a reference to a range bounded by any combination of blank rows and blank columns. For example, the current region of cell A3 in Figure 6.2 is the range A3:B8. As another example, if the range consists of A1:B10 and C5:D8, the current region is the smallest rectangular region enclosing all of this, A1:D10.[1]
- EntireColumn. This returns a reference to the range consisting of the entire column(s) in the range. For example, Range("A1").EntireColumn returns the entire column A.
- Font. This returns a reference to the font of the range, and then the properties (such as Size, Name, Bold, Italic, and so on) of this font can be changed, as in Range("A1:D1").Font.Bold = True.
- Formula. This returns or sets the formula in the range as a string, such as "=SUM(A1:A10)". Note that this string includes the equals sign. Surprisingly, the Formula property can be used even if a cell doesn't contain a formula. For example, if cell A1 contains the value 10, Range("A1").Formula returns 10. However, you are most likely to use the Formula property for ranges that do indeed contain formulas.
- FormulaR1C1. This returns the formula in a range as a string in R1C1 (row-column) notation. This is particularly useful for formulas that are copied down or across. As an example, suppose each cell in the range C3:C10 is the sum of the corresponding cells in columns A and B. For example, cell C3 is the sum of cells A3 and B3. Then the FormulaR1C1 property of the range C3:C10 is "=RC[–2]+RC[–1]". The R by itself means to stay in the *same* row. The [–2] and [–1] next to C reference two cells to the left and one cell to the left, respectively. To gain some experience with R1C1 notation, try the following. Enter some numbers in the range A1:D10 and calculate row sums and column sums with the SUM function in column E and row 11, respectively. Now go to Excel Options, and under the Formulas group, check the R1C1 reference style option. (To get there in Excel 2003, use the **Tools** → **Options** menu item, and click the General tab.) You might be surprised at how your formulas now appear. (You can then uncheck the R1C1 reference style option to get back to the usual "A1" notation.)
- HorizontalAlignment. This returns the horizontal alignment of the cells in the range. The three possible values are xlRight, xlLeft, and xlCenter.
- Interior. This returns a reference to the interior of the cells in a range. It is often used to color the background of the cells, as in Range("A1").Interior. Color = vbRed. (This colors cell A1 red, because vbRed is a built-in constant that corresponds to red.)

---

[1] If you have ever used Excel's pivot tables, the current region is how Excel guesses where your data set lives, assuming the cursor is somewhere within the data set. It returns the current region of the cursor location. The same goes for Excel tables in Excel 2007 and later versions.

- Name. This returns the name of the range (if any has been specified). If it is used in a line such as Range("B3:E20").Name = "Sales", it creates a range name for the specified range.
- NumberFormat. This returns the format code (as a string) for the range. This is usually used to specify the number format for a range, as in Range ("C3:C10").NumberFormat = "#,##0.00". However, it is difficult to remember these format codes, so you might try the following. Format a cell such as A1 manually in some way and then use the line Debug.Print Range("A1").NumberFormat. (Alternatively, type the line ?Range("A1").NumberFormat in the Immediate Window of the VBE.) This will print the number format of cell A1 to the Immediate Window. You can then see the appropriate format code.
- Offset. This returns a reference relative to a range, where the range is usually a single cell. This property is *very* useful and is used constantly in the applications in later chapters. It is explained in more detail in the next section.
- Row, EntireRow. These are similar to the Column and EntireColumn properties.
- Value. This is usually used for a single-cell range, in which case it returns the value in the cell, which could be a label, a number, or the result of a formula. Note that the syntax Range("A1").Value can be shortened to Range("A1"). That is, if .Value is omitted, it is taken for granted. This is because the Value property is the *default* property of a Range object. When I was first learning VBA programming, I used this shortcut a lot. Now I try to remember to include .Value, even though it isn't necessary, because it makes my code more readable.

Methods

The following list, again shown in alphabetical order, indicates some of the more useful methods of a Range object.

- Clear. This deletes everything from the range—the values *and* the formatting.
- ClearContents. This can be used instead of Clear to delete only the values (and formulas) and leave the formatting in place.
- Copy. This copies a range. It has a single (optional) argument called Destination, which is the paste range. For example, the line Range("A1:B10").Copy Destination:=Range("E1:F10") copies the range A1:B10 to the range E1:F10. Note that if the Destination argument is omitted, the range is copied to the clipboard.
- PasteSpecial. This pastes the contents of the clipboard to the range according to various specifications spelled out by its arguments. A frequently used option is the following. Suppose you want to copy the range C3:D10, which contains formulas, to the range F3:G10 as *values*. The required code is as follows.

```
Range("C3:D10").Copy
Range("F3:G10").PasteSpecial Paste:=xlPasteValues
```

The Paste argument, which can be one of several built-in Excel constants, indicates *how* you want to paste the copy. (To appreciate how many ways you can "paste special," copy a range in Excel and then click the Paste drop-down on the Home ribbon. You will see quite a few possibilities.)

- Resize. This takes two integer arguments, RowSize and ColumnSize. Start from the upper left cell in the range; this returns a range with RowSize rows and ColumnSize columns.
- Select. This selects the range, which is equivalent to highlighting the range in Excel.
- Sort. This sorts the range. The specific way it sorts depends on the arguments used. For a typical example, suppose you want to sort the data set in Figure 6.3 (see section 6.5) in ascending order on Score 2 (column C). The following line does the job. The Key1 argument specifies which column to sort on, the Order1 argument indicates whether to sort in ascending or descending order (with the built-in constants xlAscending and xlDescending), and the Header argument specifies that there are column headings at the top of the range that should *not* be part of the sort.

```
Range("A1:F19").Sort Key1:=Range("C2"), Order1:=xlAscending, Header:=xlYes
```

The lists shown here indicate only a fraction of the properties and methods of the Range object, but they should suffice for many of your programming needs. If you want to learn more, or if you want to look up any specific property or method, the best way is to open the Object Browser in the VBE, select the Excel library, select the Range object in the left pane, select any property or method in the right pane, and click the question mark button for help.

6.4 Referencing Ranges with VBA

Once a range is referenced properly in VBA code, it is relatively easy to set (or return) properties of the range or use methods of the range. In my experience, the hard part is usually referencing the range in the first place. Part of the reason is that there are so many ways to do it. This section describes the basic syntax for several of these methods, and the next section presents a number of small subs that implement the methods. Like the previous section, the material here is mostly for reference. However, keep the exercise in section 6.2 in mind as you read this section and the next. You will need to implement some of these ideas to do the exercise.

The most common ways to reference a range are as follows:

- **Use an address.** Follow Range with an address in double quotes, such as Range("A1") or Range("A1:B10").
- **Use a range name.** Follow Range with the name of a range in double quotes, such as Range("Sales"). This assumes there *is* a range with the name Sales in the active workbook.
- **Use a variable for a range name.** Declare a string variable, such as salesName, and set it equal to the name of the range. This would be done with a line such as

```
salesName = Range("Sales").Name
```

Then follow **Range** with this variable, as in **Range(salesName)**. Note that there are now no double quotes. They are already included in the variable **salesName** (because it is a **String** variable).

- **Use a Range object variable.** Declare a variable, such as **rngSales**, as a **Range** object and define it with the keyword **Set**. This can be done with the following two lines:

```
Dim rngSales as Range
Set rngSales = Range("Sales")
```

Then simply refer to **rngSales** from then on. For example, to change the font size of the range, you could write **rngSales.Font = 12**. The advantage of doing it this way is that as soon as you type **rngSales** and then a period, you get Intellisense. Once you get used to Intellisense, you will really miss it when it doesn't appear—which *does* happen in some cases.

- **Use the Cells property.** Follow **Range** with the **Cells** property, which takes one or two arguments. For example,

```
Range("B5:B14").Cells(3)
```

refers to the third cell in the range B5:B14—that is, cell B7. In contrast,

```
Range("C5:E15").Cells(4,2)
```

refers to the cell in the fourth row and second column of the range C5:E15—that is, cell D8. In the first case, B5:B14 is a single-column range, so it suffices to use a single argument for the **Cells** property. (The same is true for a single-row range.) However, in the second case, where C5:E15 spans multiple rows and columns, it is more natural to use two arguments for the **Cells** property. The first argument refers to the row, the second to the column. Actually, the **Cells** property (a property of the **Application** object) can be used all by itself, as in **Cells(3,2)**. This refers to cell B3.

- **Use the Offset property.** Follow **Range** with the **Offset** property, which takes two arguments. For example, the reference

```
Range("A5").Offset(2,3)
```

says to start in cell A5, then go 2 rows down and 3 columns to the right. This takes you to cell D7. The first argument of **Offset** indicates the *row* offset. Use a positive offset to go down and a negative offset to go up. The second argument indicates the *column* offset. Use a positive offset to go to the right and a negative offset to go to the left. Either argument can be 0, as in

```
Range("A5").Offset(0,3)
```

This refers to cell D5. As you will see in later chapters, the Offset property is one of my favorites. I use it all the time.

- **Use top left and bottom right arguments.** Follow Range with two arguments, a top left cell and a bottom right cell, separated by commas. This corresponds to the way you often select a range in Excel. You select the top left cell, hold down the Shift key, and select the bottom right cell. For example,

```
Range(Range("C1"),Range("D10"))
```

returns the range C1:D10. Another example, which uses a With construction to save typing, is as follows:

```
With Range("A1")
    Range(.Offset(1, 1), .Offset(3, 3)).Select
End With
```

This code selects the range B2:D4. The top left cell is the cell offset by 1 row and 1 column from A1, namely, B2. Similarly, the bottom right cell is the cell offset by 3 rows and 3 columns from A1, namely, D4. Note, for example, that .Offset(1,1) is equivalent to Range("A1").Offset(1,1) because it is inside the With construction.

- **Use the End property.** You have probably used the End-Arrow key combinations to select ranges in Excel, particularly if they are large ranges. For example, if the range A1:M100 is filled with values and you want to select it, you can select cell A1, hold down the Shift key, then press the End and down arrow keys in succession (not at the same time), and finally press the End and right arrow keys in succession. (You might prefer the **Ctrl+Arrow** or **Shift+Ctrl+Arrow** key combinations to do the same thing. But in either case, this is *much* better than scrolling, especially with large data ranges.) The question is how to do this in VBA. It is easy once you know the End property. This takes one argument to determine the direction. It can be any of the built-in constants xlDown, xlUp, xlToRight, or xlToLeft. The following example is typical, where the goal is to select a data set that starts in cell A1.

```
With Range("A1")
    Range(.Offset(0,0), .End(xlDown).End(xlToRight)).Select
End With
```

The middle line selects a range that is specified by a top left cell and a bottom right cell. The first argument, .Offset(0,0), which is equivalent to Range("A1").Offset(0,0) because it is inside a With, is simply cell A1. The second argument, .End(xlDown).End(xlToRight), which is equivalent to Range ("A1").End(xlDown).End(xlToRight) again because it is inside a With, is at the bottom right of the rectangular range that begins in cell A1. The advantage of using the End property is that you do not need to know the *size* of the range. The above code specifies the correct range regardless of whether the data set range is A1:B10 or A1:M500.

To use the End property correctly in VBA, you have to understand exactly how the End-Arrow key combinations work in Excel. Depending on the position of blank cells in your worksheet, it is easy to make mistakes. See the file **Using End-Down Correctly.xlsm** for an illustration of the pitfalls you might experience. They are fairly easy to avoid if you know how to recognize them.

- **Use the Resize property.** Starting with a given range and RowSize and ColumnSize arguments for Resize, this returns the range with the upper left cell of the given range, but with RowSize rows and ColumnSize columns. For example, the following line refers to the range C1:D10.

```
Range("A1").Offset(0,2).Resize(10,2)
```

- **Use square brackets**. Surprisingly, the code ["A1:B10"].Select has the same effect as Range("A1:B10").Select. (Actually, the square bracket code is equivalent to Application.Evaluate("A1:B10").Select.) I mention this option only because you might see it in someone else's code. I don't recommend it because it's less efficient in terms of computing time, and it's not recognized by most users.

6.5 Examples of Ranges with VBA

It is one thing to know the information in the previous two sections in an abstract sense. It is another to use this information correctly to perform useful tasks. This section presents a number of small subs for illustration. (All of these subs are listed in Module1 of the file **Ranges.xlsm**.) When presenting example subs that actually *do* something, it is difficult to avoid aspects of VBA that have not yet been covered. Whenever this occurs, I include a brief explanation of anything new.

Watching Your Subs Run

It is very informative to run these subs and watch what they do. Here is a useful strategy. First, make sure that only Excel and the VBE are open. (You might want to close any programs other than Excel.) Then position the Excel and VBE windows so that they are side by side. (It helps if you have a large monitor or two

Figure 6.3 Employee Data

	A	B	C	D	E	F	G	H
1	Employee	Score1	Score2	Score3	Score4	Score5		Extra junk
2	1	90	87	76	95	86		
3	2	78	90	99	84	84		
4	3	72	60	84	58	69		
5	4	82	66	81	69	72		
6	5	95	85	82	77	93		
7	6	90	93	66	88	93		
8	7	90	100	57	70	89		
9	8	90	98	61	56	83		
10								
11	Employee	SSN						
12	1	677-56-3523						
13	2	368-18-8238						
14	3	767-97-6963						
15	4	597-60-9462						
16	5	469-96-1823						
17	6	577-68-8445						
18	7	755-43-1476						
19	8	161-82-2041						

monitors.) Next, place the cursor anywhere within a sub you want to run, and press the **F8** key repeatedly. This steps through your sub one line at a time. By having the Excel window visible, you can immediately see the effect of each line of code.

The Data Set

Most of the examples in this section are based on a small database of performance scores on various activities and Social Security Numbers for a company's employees. These data are in the **Ranges.xlsm** file and are listed in Figure 6.3. The subs in this section all do something with this data—perhaps nothing earthshaking, but illustrative of the methods you can use to work with ranges. (The label in cell H1 is used to indicate that the performance scores are separated by a blank column from other data that might be on the worksheet.)

Note that there is only one worksheet in this file, the Data sheet. Therefore, there is no real need to qualify ranges such as Range("A1") with a worksheet name; there is only one cell A1 in the file. However, to set the stage for more complex examples, I gave the code name wsData to the Data sheet (remember from the last chapter that you do this in the VBE Properties window), and I qualified all ranges by wsData, as in wsData.Range("A1"). Again, this isn't really necessary, but I think it is a good habit to get into. I could even qualify the ranges by ThisWorkbook, as in ThisWorkbook.wsData.Range("A1"), but I think this is excessive. Remember that qualifying ranges is only *really* necessary when there a chance for ambiguity, where there are multiple A1 cells in open workbooks.

EXAMPLE 6.1 Using Addresses

The Range1 sub refers to ranges by their literal addresses. This is the easiest method if you know that the location and size of a data range are not going to change. For several ranges, this sub displays the address of the range in a message box by using the **Address** property of a **Range** object. For example, the line

```
MsgBox Range("A2:A19").Address
```

displays the address of the range "A2:F19" in a message box.

```
Sub Range1()
    ' This sub refers to ranges literally. It would be used if you
    ' know the size of a data range is not going to change.
    With wsData
        MsgBox .Range("A1").Address
        MsgBox .Range("B1:F1").Address
        MsgBox .Range("A2:A19").Address
        MsgBox .Range("B2:F19").Address

        ' The following two lines are equivalent because the Value
        ' property is the default property of a Range object. Note
        ' how string concatenation is used in the message.
        MsgBox "The first employee's first score is " & .Range("B2").Value
        MsgBox "The first employee's first score is " & .Range("B2")
    End With
End Sub
```

Toward the end of this sub, note how **.Value** can be used but is not necessary. Many programmers tend to take advantage of this shortcut. I try to avoid it for two reasons. First, your code is more straightforward if you include all properties explicitly, including default properties. Second, if you move from VBA to Microsoft's newer programming language, VB.NET, you will find that there are no default properties; you are required to include all properties explicitly.

EXAMPLE 6.2 Creating and Deleting Range Names

The Range2 sub first uses the **Name** property of a **Range** object to create several range names. Then to restore the workbook to its original condition, which is done for illustration purposes only, these range names are deleted. To delete a range name, you first set a reference to a particular name in the **Names** collection of the **ActiveWorkbook**. Then you use the **Delete** method.

```
Sub Range2()
    ' This sub creates range names for various ranges, again
    ' assuming the data range is not going to change.
    With wsData
        .Names.Add Name:="ScoreNames", RefersTo:=.Range("B1:F1")
```

```
        .Names.Add Name:="EmployeeNumbers", RefersTo:=.Range("A2:A19")
        .Names.Add Name:="ScoreData", RefersTo:=.Range("B2:F19")
    End With
    MsgBox "Sheet names have been created.", vbInformation

    ' Delete these range names if you don't really want them.
    With wsData
        .Names("ScoreNames").Delete
        .Names("EmployeeNumbers").Delete
        .Names("ScoreData").Delete
    End With
    MsgBox "Names have been deleted.", vbInformation

    ' Alternatively, delete them all with the following lines.
    Dim nm As Name
    For Each nm In wsData.Names
        nm.Delete
    Next
End Sub
```

If there were, say, 50 names in the Names collection, it would be tedious to write 50 similar lines of code to delete each one. The For Each construction at the bottom of the sub illustrates a much quicker way. For Each loops are not discussed formally until the next chapter, but you can probably see what this one is doing. It goes through each member of the Names collection, using a generic variable name nm for a typical member. Then nm.Delete deletes this range name from the collection.

There is a subtle issue with range names in the Range2 sub. (See Section 6.6 for more details.) The beginning section uses wsData.Names.Add to add three range names. Because this starts with the worksheet reference wsData, these range names have worksheet-level scope. (You can see this in Excel's Name Manager dialog box.) Therefore, these range names can be deleted later on by again referencing the worksheet, as in wsData.Names("ScoreNames").Delete, and the program works correctly.

However, if I used the more common way of adding range names, as in wsData. Range("B1:F1").Name = "ScoreNames", the range names would have workbook-level scope, and lines such as wsData.Names("ScoreNames").Delete would fail, essentially because this range name belongs to the workbook, not to the worksheet. Such lines would need to be replaced by Activeworkbook.Names("ScoreNames").Delete.

Admittedly, this is pretty obscure, but it is exactly the type of thing that can drive you crazy when you keep getting an error message you can't understand. Of course, once you figure it out, you have really learned something and you are unlikely to make the same error again.

EXAMPLE 6.3   Formatting Ranges

The Range3 sub first names a range, then it uses the range name to turn the Bold property of the font of this range to True. For illustration (and to restore the sheet to its original condition), it then sets the Bold property to False. Note that the Bold property of a Font object is one of many Boolean properties in Excel. A Boolean property has only two possible values, True and False.

```
Sub Range3()
    ' If a range has a range name, you can refer to it by its name.
    With wsData
        .Names.Add Name:="ScoreData", RefersTo:=.Range("B2:F19")
        .Range("ScoreData").Font.Bold = True
    End With
    MsgBox "The ScoreData range has been boldfaced."

    ' Now turn bold off, and delete the range name.
    With wsData
        .Range("ScoreData").Font.Bold = False
        .Names("ScoreData").Delete
    End With
    MsgBox "The ScoreData range is no longer boldfaced."
End Sub
```

Note the object hierarchy in the line

```
Range("ScoreData").Font.Bold = True
```

Each Range object has a Font object down the hierarchy from it, and the Font object then has a Bold property. This line shows the proper syntax for referring to this property.

EXAMPLE 6.4   Using a String Variable for a Range Name

The Range4 sub is almost identical to the Range3 sub, except that it uses the string variable rngName to capture and then use the name of a range.

```
Sub Range4()
    ' This is the same as the previous sub except that the range name
    ' has been stored in the string variable rngName. Note the lack of
    ' double quotes except in the line defining rngName. Being a string
    ' variable, rngName already includes the double quotes, so they
    ' aren't needed later on.
    Dim rngName As String
    rngName = "ScoreData"
    With wsData
        .Names.Add Name:=rngName, RefersTo:=.Range("B2:F19")
        .Range(rngName).Font.Bold = True
    End With
    MsgBox "The ScoreData range has been boldfaced."

    ' Now turn bold off, and delete the range name.
    With wsData
        .Range(rngName).Font.Bold = False
        .Names(rngName).Delete
    End With
    MsgBox "The ScoreData range is no longer boldfaced."
End Sub
```

Note the lack of double quotes around rngName in the line

```
Range(rngName).Font.Bold = True
```

Because rngName is a string variable, it already includes the double quotes, so they shouldn't be entered in the code.

EXAMPLE 6.5   Using the Cells Property and the Top Left, Bottom Right Combination

The Range5 sub refers to ranges with the Cells property. Remember that if the Cells property uses two arguments, the first refers to the row and the second to the column. This sub also shows how to refer to a range by its top left and bottom right cells. As explained in the comments, it is a good idea to use a With construction to save typing.

```
Sub Range5()
    ' This sub illustrates how to refer to a range with the Cells property.
    With wsData
        .Names.Add Name:="ScoreData", RefersTo:=Range("B2:F19")

        ' The following displays the address of the 2nd row,
        ' 3rd column cell of the ScoreData range. (This is cell D3.)
        With .Range("ScoreData").Cells(2, 3)
            .Select
            MsgBox "The address of the selected cell is " & .Address
        End With

        ' The following shows how to specify a range in the format
        '       Range(TopLeft,BottomRight)
        ' where TopLeft refers to the top left cell in the range,
        ' BottomRight refers to the bottom right cell in the range. The top
        ' left in the following is cell C3, the bottom right is cell E4.
        With Range(.Range("ScoreData").Cells(2, 2), _
                .Range("ScoreData").Cells(3, 4))
            .Select
            MsgBox "The address of the selected range is " & .Address
        End With

        ' A better method is to Set a range object variable first
        ' and then refer to it as follows.
        Dim scoreRange As Range
        Set scoreRange = .Range("ScoreData")
        With Range(scoreRange.Cells(2, 2), scoreRange.Cells(3, 4))
            .Select
            MsgBox "The address of the selected range is " & .Address
        End With

        .Names("ScoreData").Delete
        .Range("A1").Select
    End With
End Sub
```

EXAMPLE 6.6   Using the End Property and the Offset Property

The Range6 sub uses the End property to specify the bottom right cell of a range that might expand or contract as data are added to, or deleted from, a worksheet. It also uses the Offset property as a convenient way to specify other ranges relative to some "anchor" cell. In the middle of the sub, the Count property of the Columns collection is used to count the columns in a range. Similarly, .Rows.Count counts the rows. Finally, note how string concatenation is used in the MsgBox statements.

```
Sub Range6()
    ' Up to now, there has been an implicit assumption that the range
    ' of the data will not change, so that it can be referred to literally
    ' (e.g., B2:F19). But a more general approach is to assume the number
    ' of rows and/or columns could change. This sub shows how to find the range.
    ' Think of cell A1 as an anchor that everything else is offset relative to.
    Dim a1 As Range

    Set a1 = wsData.Range("A1")
    With wsData
        .Names.Add Name:="ScoreNames", RefersTo:=Range(a1.Offset(0, 1), _
            a1.End(xlToRight))
        .Names.Add Name:="EmployeeNumbers", RefersTo:=Range(a1.Offset(1, 0), _
            a1.End(xlDown))
        .Names.Add Name:="ScoreData", RefersTo:=Range(a1.Offset(1, 1), _
            a1.End(xlDown).End(xlToRight))
    End With

    ' Alternatively, we could first find the number of columns and the number
    ' of rows in the data set, and then use these.
    Dim nScores As Integer, nEmployees As Integer
    With a1
        nScores = Range(.Offset(0, 1), .End(xlToRight)).Columns.Count
        MsgBox "There are " & nScores & " scores for each employee.", _
            vbInformation, "Number of scores"
        nEmployees = Range(.Offset(1, 0), .End(xlDown)).Rows.Count
        MsgBox "There are " & nEmployees & " employees in the data set.", _
            vbInformation, "Number of employees"

        ' Now (just for variety) include row 1, column A in the range.
        wsData.Names.Add Name:="EntireDataSet", _
            RefersTo:=Range(.Offset(0, 0), .Offset(nEmployees, nScores))
        MsgBox "The entire data set is in the range " & _
            Range("EntireDataSet").Address, vbInformation, "Address"
    End With

    ' Delete all range names.
    Dim nm As Name
    For Each nm In wsData.Names
        nm.Delete
    Next
End Sub
```

EXAMPLE 6.7   Other Ways to Refer to Ranges

The Range7 sub illustrates some other methods to refer to ranges. Note that the range of SSNs in Figure 6.3 is separated by a blank row from the range of performance scores. Therefore, the easiest way to refer to the SSN range is to start at the *bottom* of the worksheet, not the top. Here, Cells(Rows.Count, 1) refers to the last cell in column A (cell A1048576 in Excel 2013), .End(xlUp) zooms up to the last SSN row, and the Row property returns the row number, 19. Next, .End(xlUp) is used again to find the row number of the first SSN, 12. After nEmployees is found by simple arithmetic, the Resize property is used to find the address, B12:B19, of the range containing the SSNs. Keep in mind that the variables in this sub could be found in many different ways, but the method used here results in very compact code.

```
Sub Range7()
    ' This sub shows an easy way to find the range that holds the
    ' SSNs. Because it is separated from the top score data set by
    ' a blank row, End(xlDown), starting at cell A1, would have to
    ' be used multiple times to get to the SSN data set. It is easier
    ' to use End(xlUp), starting at the bottom of the worksheet.
    Dim firstRow As Integer, lastRow As Integer
    Dim nEmployees As Integer
    Dim SSNAddress As String

    lastRow = Cells(Rows.Count, 1).End(xlUp).Row
    firstRow = Cells(lastRow, 1).End(xlUp).Row + 1
    nEmployees = lastRow - firstRow + 1

    ' For variety, use the Resize property.
    SSNAddress = Cells(firstRow, 2).Resize(nEmployees, 1).Address

    MsgBox "There are " & nEmployees & " with SSNs, and the range " _
        & "that contains these SSNs is " & SSNAddress & ".", vbInformation
End Sub
```

EXAMPLE 6.8 Referring to Rows and Columns

It is often necessary to refer to a row or column of a range. It might also be necessary to refer to an *entire* row or column, as you do when you select a row number of a column label in the margin of a worksheet. The Range8 sub shows how to do either. For example, .Rows(12) refers to the 12th row of a range, whereas .Columns(4).EntireColumn refers to the entire column corresponding to the 4th column in the range (in this case, column D). The end of this sub indicates that you cannot refer to multiple columns with numbers, such as .Columns("4:5"). However, it is possible to refer to a *single* column with a number, such as .Columns(4).

```
Sub Range8()
    ' This sub shows how to select rows or columns.
    With wsData
        With .Range("A1:F19")
            .Rows(12).Select
            MsgBox "12th row of data range has been selected."
            .Rows(12).EntireRow.Select
            MsgBox "Entire 12th row has been selected."
            .Columns(4).Select
            MsgBox "4th column of data range has been selected."
            .Columns(4).EntireColumn.Select
```

```
            MsgBox "Entire 4th column has been selected."
        End With
        .Rows("4:5").Select
        MsgBox "Another way to select rows."
        .Columns("D:E").Select
        MsgBox "Another way to select columns."

        ' The following line does NOT work; it produces an error.
        '    .Columns("4:5").Select
        .Range("A1").Select
    End With
End Sub
```

EXAMPLE 6.9   Formatting Cells in a Range

One of the most useful things you can do with VBA is format cells in a range. The Range9 sub illustrates how to apply various formats to a range. Note in particular the Color property of the Font or Interior of a range. This property can be specified as one of the eight VBA constants (vbBlack, vbBlue, vbCyan, vbGreen, vbMagenta, vbRed, vbWhite, and vbYellow), or as any of more than 16 million combinations of red-green-blue (RGB) values. For example, red is equivalent to RGB(255,0,0), so instead of the line .Color = vbRed, you could use the line .Color = RGB(255,0,0). Each RGB argument is an integer from 0 to 255 and indicates the amount of red, blue, and green in the color.

You can also specify "theme" colors by their ThemeColor and TintAndShade properties, as has been done toward the bottom of the sub. In fact, these two properties are set if you color a font or interior with the recorder on. (Themes were introduced in Excel 2007.) To understand these better, look at a color palette in Excel 2007 or a later version. In the Theme Colors section, each column corresponds to a ThemeColor value, such as xlThemeColorAccent2, and each TintAndShade value is a percentage for the lightness or darkness of this color. If you specify theme colors and then change the theme (from Excel's Page Layout ribbon), the colors in the worksheet will change automatically to those in the new theme. I found the ThemeColor and TintAndShade values from recording. This is the best way to find them.

This whole topic of colors in Excel and VBA is rather complex, so I created the file **Colors in Excel.xlsm** to help you out. Note that Microsoft changed the theme colors in Excel 2013 for reasons we can only surmise. If you prefer those in Excel 2007 and 2010, you can specify the "Excel 2007–2010" theme in the Colors dropdown of the Page Layout ribbon.

```
Sub Range9()
    ' Here are some common ways to format data in ranges.
    Dim a1 As Range

    Set a1 = wsData.Range("A1")
    With wsData
        .Names.Add Name:="ScoreNames", RefersTo:=Range(a1.Offset(0, 1), _
            a1.End(xlToRight))
        .Names.Add Name:="EmployeeNumbers", RefersTo:=Range(a1.Offset(1, 0), _
            a1.End(xlDown))
```

```
        .Names.Add Name:="ScoreData", RefersTo:=Range(a1.Offset(1, 1), _
            a1.End(xlDown).End(xlToRight))
    ' Do some formatting.
    With .Range("ScoreNames")
        .HorizontalAlignment = xlRight
        With .Font
            .Bold = True
            .Color = vbRed
            .Size = 16
        End With
        .EntireColumn.AutoFit
    End With
    With .Range("EmployeeNumbers").Font
        .Italic = True
        .Color = vbBlue
        .Size = 12
    End With
    With .Range("ScoreData")
        .Interior.Color = vbYellow
        .Font.Name = "Times Roman"
        .NumberFormat = "0.0"
    End With
    MsgBox "Formatting has been applied"

    ' Restore the original style (called "Normal"
    .Range("ScoreNames").Style = "Normal"
    .Range("EmployeeNumbers").Style = "Normal"
    .Range("ScoreData").Style = "Normal"
    MsgBox "Original formatting restored"

    ' Apply theme colors (there are many to choose from).
    With .Range("B2")
        With Range(.Offset(0, 0), .End(xlDown).End(xlToRight)).Interior
            .ThemeColor = xlThemeColorDark1
            .TintAndShade = -0.149998474074526
        End With
        With Range(.Offset(0, 0), .End(xlDown).End(xlToRight)).Font
            .ThemeColor = xlThemeColorAccent2
            .TintAndShade = -0.249977111117893
        End With
    End With
    MsgBox "Theme colors have been applied."

    ' Restore the original style.
    .Range("A1").Style = "Normal"
    .Range("ScoreNames").Style = "Normal"
    .Range("EmployeeNumbers").Style = "Normal"
    .Range("ScoreData").Style = "Normal"
    MsgBox "Original formatting restored"
End With

' Delete all range names.
Dim nm As Name
For Each nm In wsData.Names
    nm.Delete
Next
End Sub
```

This is a particularly good example for tiling the Excel and VBE windows vertically and then stepping through the code one line at a time with the F8 key. You can then see the code in one window and the effect of the formatting in the other window.

EXAMPLE 6.10 Entering Formulas

The Range10 sub illustrates how to enter formulas in cells with VBA. There are two properties you can use, the Formula property and the FormulaR1C1 property. The Formula property requires a string that matches what you would type if you were entering the formula directly into Excel. For example, to enter the formula =**AVERAGE(Score1)**, you set the Formula property equal to the string "=Average(Score1)".

The FormulaR1C1 property is less obvious, but it is sometimes more natural because of the way relative addresses work in Excel. For example, suppose you have two columns of numbers and you want to form a third column to their right where each cell in this third column is the sum of the two numbers to its left. You would then set the FormulaR1C1 property of this range equal to "=Sum(RC[–2]:RC[–1])". The R with no brackets next to it means to stay in the *same* row. The C with brackets next to it means, in this case, to go from 2 columns to the left to 1 column to the left. That is, using square brackets is equivalent to relative addressing in Excel. Remember that for rows, plus means down, minus means up. For columns, plus means to the right, minus means to the left. If you want an *absolute* address in R1C1 notation, you omit the square brackets and use numbers to refer to rows and columns. For example, R2C4 is equivalent to $D$2.

Note that this sub uses a couple of For loops in the middle. For loops are discussed in detail in the next chapter. All you need to know here is that the variable i goes from 1 to the number of scores. First it is 1, then 2, then 3, and so on. You should study this sub carefully. It is probably the most difficult example so far. Also, it is another excellent candidate for placing the Excel and VBE windows next to one another and then using the F8 key to step through the code one line at a time.

```
Sub Range10()
    ' This sub shows how to enter formulas in cells. You do this with
    ' the Formula property or the FormulaR1C1 property of a range.
    ' Either property takes a string value that must start with an equals
    ' sign, just as you enter a formula in Excel. First, I name a range
    ' for each column of scores, and then I use the Formula property to
    ' get the average of each column below the scores in that column.
    Dim nScores As Integer, nEmployees As Integer, i As Integer
    Dim a1 As Range

    Set a1 = wsData.Range("A1")
    ' Determine the number of score columns and the number of employees.
    ' Then name the score ranges Score1, Score2, and so on.
    With a1
        nScores = Range(.Offset(0, 1), .End(xlToRight)).Columns.Count
        nEmployees = Range(.Offset(1, 0), .End(xlDown)).Rows.Count
        For i = 1 To nScores
            wsData.Names.Add Name:="Score" & i, _
                RefersTo:=Range(.Offset(1, i), .Offset(1, i).End(xlDown))
        Next
    End With

    ' For each score column, enter the average formula below the last score.
    ' Note how string concatenation is used. For i = 1, for example, the
```

```
' string on the right will be "=Average(Score1)".
For i = 1 To nScores
    a1.Offset(nEmployees + 1, i).Formula = "=Average(Score" & i & ")"
Next

' Now use the FormulaR1C1 property to find the average score for each
' employee. Note how each cell in the column of averages has the SAME
' formula in R1C1 notation. It is the average of the range from nScores
' cells to the left to 1 cell to the left. For example, if nScores is 4,
' this is RC[-4]:RC[-1]. The lack of brackets next to R mean that these
' scores all come from the same row as the cell where the formula is
' being placed.
With a1.Offset(0, nScores + 1)
    Range(.Offset(1, 0), .Offset(nEmployees, 0)).FormulaR1C1 = _
        "=Average(RC[-" & nScores & "]:RC[-1])"
End With

MsgBox "All row and column averages have been entered as formulas."

' Delete averages.
With a1
    For i = 1 To nScores
        .Offset(nEmployees + 1, i).Clear
    Next
    For i = 1 To nEmployees
        .Offset(i, nScores + 1).Clear
    Next
End With

MsgBox "All row and column averages have been deleted."

' Delete all range names.
Dim nm As Name
For Each nm In wsData.Names
    nm.Delete
Next
End Sub
```

If you want to enter a formula in a cell through VBA, it seems natural to use the Formula (or FormulaR1C1) property. However, the following two lines have exactly the same effect—they both enter a formula into a cell:

```
Range("C1").Formula = "=SUM(A1:B1)"
Range("C2").Value = "=SUM(A1:B1)"
```

Given that this is true—and you can check it yourself—why should you bother with the Formula property at all? The only time it makes a difference is if you *read* the property in VBA. In the above lines, I have *written* the Formula and Value properties, that is, I have specified the values for these properties. But suppose I enter the following two lines after the above two lines:

```
MsgBox Range("C1").Formula
MsgBox Range("C2").Value
```

The first will return "=SUM(A1:B1)", and the second will return 10 (assuming that cells A1 and B1 each contain 5). Here, I am *reading the* properties, and here it makes a difference.

Another related property of a range is the Text property. It is very similar to the Value property. Let's say that cell Dl is the average of several values, and this average turns out to be 38.33333... However, you format cell Dl to have only two decimals. Then the following two lines will return 38.33333... and 38.33, respectively. In words, the Text property returns what you see in the cell after formatting.

```
MsgBox Range("D1").Value
MsgBox Range("D2").Text
```

The Text property is a *read only* property. If you try to use it to *write* a value to a range, you will get an error. For example, the following line will *not* work. You would have to use the Value property instead.

```
Range("A1").Text = "Sales"
```

EXAMPLE 6.11   Referring to Other Range Objects

The Range11 sub introduces the CurrentRegion and UsedRange properties, as explained in the comments. It also demonstrates the Union property for referring to possibly noncontiguous ranges. Finally, it illustrates the Areas property of a range. Of all these properties, CurrentRegion is probably the one you will use most frequently in your own programs.

```
Sub Range11()
    ' Here are some other useful range properties. The CurrentRegion
    ' and UsedRange properties are rectangular ranges. The former is
    ' the range "surrounding" a given range. The latter is a property
    ' of a worksheet. It indicates the smallest rectangular range
    ' containing all nonempty cells.
    Dim a1 As Range, a21 As Range, h1 As Range

    Set a1  = wsData.Range("A1")
    Set a21 = wsData.Range("A21")
    Set h1  = wsData.Range("H1")

    MsgBox "The range holding the dataset is " & a1.CurrentRegion.Address, _
        vbInformation, "Current region"
    MsgBox "The range holding everything is " & wsData.UsedRange.Address, _
        vbInformation, "Used range"

    ' It is sometimes useful to take the union of ranges that are not
    ' necessarily contiguous.
    Dim unionRange As Range
    Set unionRange = Union(a1.CurrentRegion, a21, h1)
    With unionRange
```

```
        MsgBox "The address of the union is " & .Address, vbInformation, _
            "Address of union"

        ' The Areas property returns the "pieces" in the union.
        MsgBox "The union is composed of " & .Areas.Count & " distinct areas.", _
            vbInformation, "Number of areas"
    End With
End Sub
```

EXAMPLE 6.12   Adding or Deleting Comments

The Range12 sub shows how to add a comment to a cell or delete a comment from
a cell. You do this with the AddComment method of a range and the Delete method
of a Comment object. A Comment object, like all other objects, has a rather bewildering number of properties and values, and I have illustrated some of them. As usual,
you can learn more about comments from the Object Browser or by recording.

I have introduced error checking in this example, which is discussed in more
detail in Chapter 12. Specifically, the line On Error Resume Next can be used to
anticipate errors. Without it, the line b1.Comment.Delete would produce an error
(assuming that cell B1 has no comment). However, On Error Resume Next says to
turn on error checking and ignore any errors that might be encountered. Once
you are past the code where you anticipate errors, you can turn off error checking
with the really strange line On Error GoTo 0.

```
Sub Range12()
    ' This sub shows how you can enter a comment in a cell or delete
    ' a comment in a cell. Inserting is easy, but deleting is trickier.
    ' Before you delete a comment, you should handle the situation where
    ' there is no comment to delete. If you try to delete a cell comment
    ' that doesn't exist, you will get an error (unless you perform the
    ' appropriate error checking).
    Dim a1 As Range, b1 As Range
    Dim cmt As Comment

    Set a1 = wsData.Range("A1")
    Set b1 = wsData.Range("B1")

    ' Insert a comment.
    a1.AddComment "This is a data set of employee scores on 5 aptitude tests."
    Set cmt = a1.Comment
    With cmt.Shape
        .Left = wsData.Range("B1").Left
        .Top = wsData.Range("B2").Top
    End With
    MsgBox "A comment has been added to cell A1."

    ' Delete a comment, but error check in case there is none to delete.
    On Error Resume Next
    a1.Comment.Delete
    b1.Comment.Delete
    On Error GoTo 0
    MsgBox "The comments in cells A1 and B1, if any, have been deleted."
End Sub
```

6.6 Range Names and Their Scope

The easiest way to name a range through the Excel interface is to select a range, type a name in the Name box (to the left of the formula bar), and press Enter. However, the topic of range names is considerably more complex than this, especially in VBA. The range names you create by typing a name in the Name box are called **workbook-level** range names. There are also **worksheet-level** range names. To create one of these in the Name box, you type the name of the worksheet, then an exclamation point, and then the name, as in **Sheet2!UnitCost**. You can also create range names in Excel's Name Manager, available from the Defined Names dropdown arrow on the Formulas ribbon. After clicking the New button in the Name Manager, you get the dialog box in Figure 6.4. You type a name, select the scope to be the workbook or any of the worksheets, and point to a range. The scope determines whether the name is workbook-level or worksheet-level.

Why does Microsoft allow this level of complexity? The main reason is that it allows you to use the *same* name in multiple worksheets. For example, suppose you have multiple worksheets set up approximately the same way, with a unit cost cell in each. You would like each of these cells to be range-named UnitCost. Worksheet-level names allow you to do this by setting the scope of each to the corresponding worksheet. Then your Name Manager might look something like Figure 6.5.[2] If you want a formula in Sheet1 to refer to *its* UnitCost cell, you can write =**UnitCost**. But if you want the formula on Sheet1 to refer to the Unit-Cost on Sheet2, you must write =**Sheet2!UnitCost**.

Figure 6.4 Adding a Range Name in the Name Manager

---

[2] You *could* have a Sheet2-level range name that refers to a range in Sheet1, but you would be going out of your way to confuse yourself and your users!

Figure 6.5 Multiple Worksheet-Level Range Names Using the Same Name

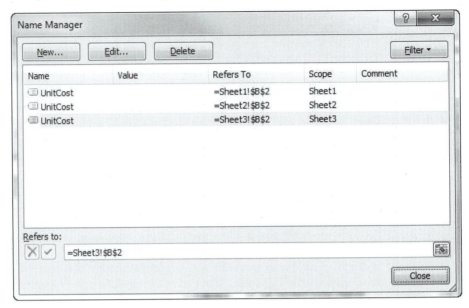

If you don't need multiple versions of the same name, you can use all workbook-level range names, as most of us do. If TotalRevenue is a workbook-level range name, the formula =**TotalRevenue** can be used unambiguously in *any* of the worksheets, even though TotalRevenue refers to a range in a particular worksheet.

In terms of Excel's object model, each workbook-level range name is a member of the **Names** collection of the **Workbook** object, and each worksheet-level range name is a member of the **Names** collection of the corresponding **Worksheet** object. In other words, there are separate **Names** collections for the workbook and for each worksheet in the workbook. This has a big impact on how you refer to, add, or delete to range names in VBA code.

To provide a prototype of what you can and can't do, I developed the file **Range Names.xlsm**. There are three worksheets named Sheet1, Sheet2, and Sheet3. Sheet1 and Sheet2 have exactly the same data (see Figure 6.6), and Sheet3 is blank. Cell E1 of Sheet1 has the workbook-level name Total_spent, and Sheet2 has Sheet2-level name Total_spent.

The following RangeName1 sub indicates how you can refer to existing range names of either scope. You might be surprised (like I was) that some of these lines work the way they do.

Figure 6.6 Data in Sheet1 and Sheet2

	A	B	C	D	E
1	Person	Spent		Total spent	6827
2	1	402			
3	2	751			
4	3	541			
5	4	941			
6	5	783			
7	6	857			
8	7	897			
9	8	707			
10	9	948			

```
Sub RangeName1( )
    ' This sub shows how to reference named ranges. These range
    ' names were created through the Excel interface. One is a
    ' workbook-level name for a cell in Sheet1, and the other is
    ' a Sheet2-level name for a cell in Sheet2. Both names are Total_spent.
    ' No ranges in Sheet3 are named.

    ' Note that ws1 and ws2 are the code names for Sheet1 and Sheet2.
    ' The following gives the total in the active sheet unless the
    ' active sheet is Sheet3. Then it gives the total in Sheet1, which
    ' has the workbook-level name.
    MsgBox "Total spent: " & Range("Total_spent").Value

    ' The following both give the total in Sheet1, regardless
    ' of which sheet is active. Surprisingly, the second works even
    ' though there is no Sheet1-level name Total_spent.
    MsgBox "Total spent: " & ws1.Range("Total_spent").Value
    MsgBox "Total spent: " & Range("Sheet1!Total_spent").Value

    ' The following both give the total in Sheet2, regardless
    ' of which sheet is active.
    MsgBox "Total spent: " & ws2.Range("Total_spent").Value
    MsgBox "Total spent: " & Range("Sheet2!Total_spent").Value
End Sub
```

The RangeName2 sub indicates how you can add and then delete new range names of either scope. It indicates one thing that will not work and will produce an error—namely, if you try to delete something from the Names collection of a worksheet when that collection is empty.

```
Sub RangeName2( )
    ' This sub shows how to create and then delete workbook-level
    ' and worksheet-level range names.

    ' Note that ws1 and ws2 are the code names for Sheet1 and Sheet2.
```

```
Const name1 = "Indexes"
Const name2 = "Expenses"
Const addr1 = "A2:A10"
Const addr2 = "B2:B10"

' Here are two ways to add workbook-level names.
ws1.Range(addr1).Name = name1
ActiveWorkbook.Names.Add Name:=name2, RefersTo:="Sheet1!" & addr2
' Here are two ways to add worksheet-level names.
ws2.Range(addr1).Name = "Sheet2!" & name1
ws2.Names.Add Name:=name2, RefersTo:="Sheet2!" & addr2

MsgBox "Range names have been added."

' The following two lines delete the two workbook-level names.
' However, they can't be replaced by the two commented-out
' lines because there are no Sheet1-level names, i.e.,
' the Names collection belonging to Sheet1 is empty.
ActiveWorkbook.Names(name1).Delete
ActiveWorkbook.Names(name2).Delete
'    ws1.Names(name1).Delete ' produces an error
'    ws1.Names(name2).Delete ' produces an error

' The following two lines delete the two worksheet-level names.
' They could be replaced by the two commented-out lines.
ws2.Names(name1).Delete
ws2.Names(name2).Delete
'    ActiveWorkbook.Names("Sheet2!" & name1).Delete
'    ActiveWorkbook.Names("Sheet2!" & name2).Delete
End Sub
```

If you plan to use range names extensively in multiple-worksheet applications, you should keep these subs handy for reference. Or you can do what I did—experiment with trial and error.

6.7 Summary

The examples in this chapter present a lot of material, more than you can probably digest on first reading. However, they give you the clues you need to complete Exercise 6.1 and to understand the applications in later chapters. Indeed, you can borrow any parts of these examples for your own work, either for exercises or for later development projects. As stated in the introduction, most of the operations you perform in Excel are done with ranges, and one of my primary objectives in the book is to show you how to perform these operations with VBA. Therefore, I expect that you will frequently revisit the examples in this chapter as you attempt to manipulate ranges in your own VBA programs.

EXERCISES

1. The file **Employee Scores.xlsx** contains the same data set as in the **Ranges.xlsm** file (the file that was used for the examples in Section 6.5). However, the VBA code has been deleted. Also, there is now a heading in cell A1, and the data set

begins in row 3. Save a copy of this file as **Employee Scores 1.xlsx** and work with the copy to do the following with VBA. (Place the code for all of the parts in a single sub.)

   a. Boldface the font of the label in cell A1, and change its font size to 14.

   b. Boldface and italicize the headings in row 3, and change their horizontal alignment to the right.

   c. Change the color of the font for the employee numbers in column A to blue (any shade you like).

   d. Change the background (the Interior property) of the range with scores to gray (any shade you like).

   e. Enter the label Averages in cell A22 and boldface it.

   f. Enter a formula in cell B22 that averages the scores above it. Copy this formula to the range C22:F22.

2. Repeat the previous exercise, starting with a fresh copy, **Employee Scores 2.xlsx**, of the original **Employee Scores.xlsx** file. Now, however, begin by using VBA to name the following ranges with the range names specified: cell A1 as Title, the headings in row 3 as Headings, the employee numbers in column A as EmpNumbers, and the range of scores as Scores. Refer to these range names as you do parts a-f of the previous exercise.

3. Repeat Exercise 1 once more, starting with a fresh copy, **Employee Scores 3.xlsx**, of the original **Employee Scores.xlsx** file. Instead of naming ranges as in Exercise 2, declare Range object variables called titleCell, headingRange, empNumbersRange, and scoresRange, and Set them to the ranges described in Exercise 2. Refer to these object variables as you do parts a–f.

4. Repeat the previous three exercises. However, write your code so that it will work even if more data are added to the data set—new scores, new employees, or both. Try your programs on the original data. Add an extra column of scores and some extra employees, and see if it still works properly.

5. Write a reference (in VBA code) to each of the following ranges. You can assume that each of these ranges is in the active worksheet of the active workbook, so that you don't have to qualify the references by worksheet or workbook.

   a. The third cell of the range A1:A10.

   b. The cell at the intersection of the 24th row and 10th column of the range A1:Z500.

   c. The cell at the intersection of the 24th row and 10th column of a range that has the range name Sales.

   d. The cell at the intersection of the 24th row and 10th column of a range that has been Set to the Range object variable salesRange.

   e. The entire column corresponding to cell D7.

   f. The set of entire columns from column D through column K.

   g. A range of employee names, assuming the first is in cell A3 and they extend down column A (although you don't know how many there are).

   h. A range of sales figures in a rectangular block, assuming that region labels are to their left in column A (starting in cell A4) and month labels are above them in row 3 (starting in cell B3). You don't know how many regions or months there are, and you want the range to include only the sales figures, not the labels.

    i.   The cell that is 2 rows down from and 5 columns to the right of the active cell. (The active cell is the cell currently selected. If a rectangular range is selected, the active cell is the *first* cell that was selected when the range was selected. It can always be referred to in VBA as ActiveCell.)

  6.   The file **Product Sales.xlsx** has sales totals for 12 months and 10 different products in the range B4:M13. Write a VBA sub to enter formulas for the totals in column N and row 14. Use the FormulaR1C1 property to do so. (You should set this property for two ranges: the one in column N and the one in row 14.)

  7.   Repeat the previous exercise, but now assume the data set could change, either by adding more months, more products, or both. Using the FormulaR1C1 property, fill the row below the data and the column to the right of the data with formulas for totals. (*Hint:* First find the number of months and the number of products, and store these numbers in variables. Then use string concatenation to build a string for each FormulaR1C1 property. Refer to the Range10 sub in the **Ranges.xlsm** file for a similar formula.)

  8.   Do the previous two exercises by using the Formula property rather than the FormulaR1C1 property. *(Hint:* Enter a formula in cell N4 and then use the Copy method to copy down. Proceed similarly in row 14. Do *not* use any loops.)

  9.   The file **Exam Scores.xlsx** has four exam scores, in columns B through E, for each of the students listed in column A.

    a.   Write a VBA sub that sorts the scores in increasing order on exam 3.

    b.   (More difficult, requires an If statement and can be postponed until after reading Chapter 7.) Repeat part **a**, but now give the user some choices. Specifically, write a VBA sub that (1) uses an InputBox to ask for an exam from 1 to 4, (2) uses an InputBox to ask whether the user wants to sort scores in ascending or descending order (you can ask the user to enter A or D), and (3) sorts the data on the exam requested and the order requested. Make sure the headings in row 3 are *not* part of the sort.

7

Control Logic and Loops

7.1 Introduction

All programming languages contain logical constructions for controlling the sequence of statements through a program, and VBA is no exception. This chapter describes the two constructions used most often: the If and Case constructions. The If construction has already been used informally in previous chapters—it is practically impossible to avoid in any but the most trivial programs—but this chapter discusses it in more detail. The Case construction is an attractive alternative to a complex If construction when each of several cases requires its own code.

This chapter also discusses the extremely important concept of loops. Have you ever had to stuff hundreds of envelopes? If you have ever had to perform this or any similar mind-numbing task over and over, you will appreciate loops. Perhaps the single most useful feature of computer programs is their ability to loop, that is, to repeat the same type of task any number of times—10 times, 100 times, even 10,000 or more times. All programming languages have this looping ability, the only difference being their syntax. VBA does it with For loops, For Each loops, and Do loops, as this chapter illustrates. Fortunately, it is quite easy. It is amazing how much work you can make the computer perform by writing just a few lines of code.

The material in this chapter represents essential elements of almost all programming languages, including VBA. Without control logic and loops, computer programs would lose much of their power. Therefore, it is extremely important that you master the material in this chapter. You will get a chance to do this with the exercise in the next section and the exercises at the end of the chapter. Beyond this, you will continue to see control logic and loops throughout the rest of the book.

7.2 Exercise

The following exercise is typical in its need for control logic and loops. You can keep it in mind as you read through this chapter. It is not too difficult, but it will keep you busy for a while. Even more important, it will give you that wonderful feeling of accomplishment once you solve it. It is a great example of the power of the tools in this chapter.

Exercise 7.1   Finding Record Highs and Lows for Stock Prices

The file **Records.xlsx** contains two worksheets. The Prices worksheet contains monthly closing prices (adjusted for dividends and stock splits) for several large companies from January 2002 to August 2014. The Records worksheet is a template for calculating the record highs and lows for any one of these companies. It is shown in Figure 7.1 (with a number of hidden rows). The Walmart prices in column B have been copied from the WMT column of the Prices worksheet.

You can first choose a month in cell F1 from a dropdown list. Then the purpose of the exercise is to scan column B from top to bottom. If you see a price that is higher than any price so far, it is called a "record high." Similarly, if a price is lower than any price so far, it is called a "record low." The objective is to find each record high and record low that occurs from the selected month on and record these record highs and lows in columns D, E, and F. Column D records the date, column E records the price, and column F records whether it is a record high or a record low. Note that the records are based on *all* of the data, but records are listed only from the selected date on.

The file **Records Finished 1.xlsm** contains the finished application. You can open it, copy (manually) any stock's price data from the Prices worksheet to the Records worksheet, and then click the button. Figures 7.2 and 7.3 indicate the results you should obtain for Walmart. The message box in Figure 7.2 summarizes the results, whereas columns D, E, and F show the details of the record prices. Feel free to run the program on other stocks' prices, but do *not* look at the VBA code in the file until you have given it your best effort.

If you like, you can extend this exercise in a natural direction. Modify your code so that there is now a loop over all stocks in the Prices worksheet. For each stock, your modified program should copy the prices from the Prices worksheet to the Records worksheet and *then* continue as in the first part of the exercise. Essentially,

Figure 7.1   Template for Record Highs and Lows for Walmart

	A	B	C	D	E	F
1	**Adjusted closing prices**			**Record values from**		**Jan-04**
2	Date	WMT		Date	Price	High or Low
3	Jan-02	48.27				
4	Feb-02	49.91				
5	Mar-02	49.39				
6	Apr-02	45.01				
7	May-02	43.59				
151	May-14	76.77				
152	Jun-14	75.07				
153	Jul-14	73.58				
154	Aug-14	73.54				

Figure 7.2   Summary of Record Results

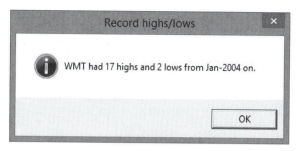

Figure 7.3   Detailed Record Results

	D	E	F
1	**Record values from**		**Jan-04**
2	Date	Price	High or Low
3	Aug-05	37.310	Low
4	Sep-05	36.370	Low
5	Apr-08	50.150	High
6	Jul-08	50.920	High
7	Aug-08	51.520	High
8	Sep-08	52.230	High
9	Oct-11	53.020	High
10	Nov-11	55.060	High
11	Dec-11	56.210	High
12	Jan-12	57.720	High
13	Mar-12	57.950	High
14	May-12	62.750	High
15	Jun-12	66.470	High
16	Jul-12	70.960	High
17	Oct-12	71.910	High
18	Mar-13	72.590	High
19	Apr-13	75.390	High
20	Jul-13	76.060	High
21	Nov-13	79.530	High

the code from the first part of the exercise should be placed inside a loop on the stocks. The finished version of this part of the exercise is in the file **Records Finished 2.xlsm**. Again, feel free to open the file and click the button to see the results you should obtain, but do not look at the code until you have attempted it yourself.

7.3 If Constructions

An If construction is useful when there are one or more possible conditions, each of which requires its own code. Here, a **condition** is any expression that evaluates to either True or False. Typical conditions are Total <= 200, SheetName = "Data", and isFound (where isFound is a Boolean variable that evaluates to True or False). You often need to check whether a condition is true or false and then proceed accordingly. This is the typical situation where an If construction is useful.

There are several versions of the If construction, in increasing order of complexity.

- **Single-line If.** The simplest version can be written on a single line. It has the form

```
If condition Then statement1 [Else statement2]
```

Here, *condition* is any condition and *statement1* and *statement2* are any statements. (The convention in writing generic code like this is that any parts in square brackets are *optional*. In other words, the Else part of this statement is optional. Note that you do *not* actually type the square brackets.) This simple form requires only a single line of code (and there is no End If). An example is

```
If numberOrdered <= 200 Then unitCost = 1.30
```

Another example is

```
If numberOrdered <= 200 Then unitCost = 1.30 Else unitCost = 1.20
```

- **If-Then-Else-End If**. A more common version of the If construction requires several lines and has the form:

```
If condition Then
    statements1
[Else
    statements2]
End If
```

(Again, the square brackets denote that the lines within them are optional.) In this form, *condition* is first tested. If it is true, the statements denoted by *statements1* are executed. You might also want to execute another set of statements, denoted by *statements2*, in case the condition does not hold. If so, you must insert these after the keyword Else. In fact, there are four keywords in this form: If, Then, Else, and End If. (Note the required space between End and If. However, the editor will enter the space for you if you omit it.) An example of this construction is the following:

```
If numberOrdered <= 200 Then
    unitCost = 1.3
    MsgBox "The unit cost is " & unitCost
Else
    unitCost = 1.25
    MsgBox "The unit cost is " & unitCost
End If
```

- **If-Then-ElseIf-Else-End If.** The most general version of the If construction allows more than a single condition to be tested by using one or more ElseIf keywords. (Note that there is *no* space between Else and If. It is all one word.) The general form is

```
If condition1 Then
    statements1
[ElseIf condition2 Then
    statements2
ElseIf condition3 Then
    statements3
...
Else
    other statements]
End If
```

This construction performs exactly as it reads. There can be as many ElseIf lines as needed (denoted by the...), and the Else part is not required. It is used only if you want to execute some statements in case all of the above conditions are false. An example of this version is the following:

```
If numberOrdered <= 200 Then
    unitCost = 1.3
ElseIf numberOrdered <= 300 Then
    unitCost = 1.25
ElseIf numberOrdered <= 400 Then
    unitCost = 1.2
Else
    unitCost = 1.15
End If
```

In this version, the program goes through the conditions until it finds one that is true. Then it executes the corresponding statement(s) and jumps down to the End If line. If none of the conditions hold and there is an Else line, the statement(s) following it are executed.

- **Nested If statements.** It is also possible to *nest* If constructions, in which case proper indentation is *crucial* for readability. Here is an example:

```
If Product = "Widgets" Then
    If numberOrdered <= 200 Then
        unitCost = 1.3
    Else
        unitCost = 1.2
    End If
ElseIf product = "Gadgets" Then
    If numberOrdered <= 500 Then
        unitCost = 2.7
    ElseIf numberOrdered <= 600 Then
        unitCost = 2.6
    Else
        unitCost = 2.5
    End If
Else
    unitCost = 2
End If
```

The meaning of this code should be self-evident, but only because the lines are indented properly. Try to imagine these lines without any indentation, and you will understand why the indentation is crucial. Besides indentation, make sure you follow every If with an eventual End If (unless the If construction is of the simple one-line version). In fact, it is a good practice to type the End If line right after you type the If line, just so you don't forget. Also, every condition must be followed by the keyword Then. If you mistakenly type something like If numberOrdered <= 200 and press Enter, you will immediately see your mistake—the offending line will be colored red. You can fix it by adding Then.

- **Immediate If function.** There is one other function you might occasionally find useful: the "immediate" If function. It has the syntax IIf(*condition,statement1,statement2*), where the arguments are the same as in Excel's IF function. Its advantage is that it can be used to evaluate an expression in the midst of any line of code, such as the following:

```
MsgBox "The unit price is " & IIf(unitsSold > 100, 20, 25) & " dollars."
```

The file **If Examples.xlsm** contains several examples to illustrate If constructions. They are all based on the small data set shown in Figure 7.4. Each example changes the formatting of the data in some way. The Restore button is attached to a sub that restores the data to its original plain vanilla formatting. In each example there is a For Each loop that goes through all of the cells in some range. (For Each loops are discussed in detail in Section 7.6.) There is then at least one If construction that decides how to format cells in the range. (*Note:* In all of these If subs, I use the variable cell. This is *not* a keyword in VBA. I could just as well have used cel or cl or cll, or any other spelling.)

Figure 7.4   Data Set for If Examples

	A	B	C	D
3	Employee	Score1	Score2	Score3
4	1	90	87	76
5	2	78	90	99
6	3	72	60	84
7	4	82	66	81
8	5	95	85	82
9	6	90	93	66
10	7	90	100	57
11	8	90	98	61
12	9	96	67	85
13	10	87	69	77
14	11	81	68	61
15	12	58	57	72
16	13	70	92	59
17	14	69	71	89
18	15	85	94	66
19	16	55	79	99
20	17	60	75	63
21	18	83	93	88

EXAMPLE 7.1   Single-Line If Construction

The If1 sub illustrates a one-line If construction. If an employee's first score (in column B) is greater than 80, the corresponding employee number is bold-faced. Note that the range A4:A21 has been range-named Employee.

```
Sub IfStatement1()
    ' Example of a one-line If (note there is no End If).
    Dim cell As Range
    Const cutoff = 80

    ' Go down the Employee column. If the Employee's first score is
    ' greater than the cutoff, boldface the font of the Employee number.
    For Each cell In wsData.Range("Employee")
        If cell.Offset(0, 1).Value > cutoff Then cell.Font.Bold = True
    Next
End Sub
```

EXAMPLE 7.2   If-ElseIf-End If Construction

The If2 sub illustrates an If with a single ElseIf (and no Else). If an employee's first score is less than 70, the sub colors the corresponding employee number red. Otherwise, if it is greater than 85, the sub colors the employee number blue. If the score is from 70 to 85, no action is taken. Hence there is no need for an Else.

```
Sub IfStatement2()
    ' Example of a typical If-ElseIf-End If construction. Note that
    ' ElseIf is one word, but End If is two words.
    Dim cell As Range
    Const cutoff1 = 70, cutoff2 = 85

    ' Go down the Employee column. If the Employee's first score is
    ' less than cutoff1, color the Employee number red; if greater
    ' than cutoff2, color it blue. Because there is no Else condition,
    ' nothing happens for scores between cutoff1 and cutoff2.
    For Each cell In wsData.Range("Employee")
        If cell.Offset(0, 1).Value < cutoff1 Then
            cell.Font.Color = vbRed
        ElseIf cell.Offset(0, 1).Value > cutoff2 Then
            cell.Font.Color = vbBlue
        End If
    Next
End Sub
```

EXAMPLE 7.3   If-ElseIf-Else-End If Construction

The If3 sub extends the If2 sub. Now there is an Else part to handle scores from 70 to 85. All such scores are colored green.

```
Sub IfStatement3()
    ' Example of a typical If-ElseIf-Else-End If construction.
    Dim cell As Range
    Const cutoff1 = 70, cutoff2 = 85

    ' Go down the Employee column. If the Employee's first score is
    ' less than cutoff1, color the Employee number red; if greater than
    ' cutoff2, color it blue. Otherwise, color it green.
    For Each cell In wsData.Range("Employee")
        If cell.Offset(0, 1).Value < cutoff1 Then
            cell.Font.Color = vbRed
        ElseIf cell.Offset(0, 1).Value > cutoff2 Then
            cell.Font.Color = vbBlue
        Else
            cell.Font.Color = vbGreen
        End If
    Next
End Sub
```

EXAMPLE 7.4   Nested If Constructions

The If4 sub illustrates how a nested If construction allows you to test whether all three of an employee's scores are greater than 80 (in which case the employee's number is boldfaced). Note that the statement setting Bold to True is executed only if *each* of the three conditions is true.

```
Sub IfStatement4()
    ' Example of nested If's.
    Dim cell As Range
    Const cutoff = 80

    ' Go down Employee column. If all scores for a Employee are greater
    ' than cutoff, boldface the Employee number. Note the indenting.
    ' It is crucial for readability!
    For Each cell In wsData.Range("Employee")
        If cell.Offset(0, 1).Value > cutoff Then
            If cell.Offset(0, 2).Value > cutoff Then
                If cell.Offset(0, 3).Value > cutoff Then
                    cell.Font.Bold = True
                End If
            End If
        End If
    Next
End Sub
```

EXAMPLE 7.5   Compound (And, Or) Conditions

Conditions can be of the *compound* variety, using the keywords And and Or. It is often useful to group the conditions in parentheses to eliminate any ambiguity. For example, the compound condition in the line

```
If condition1 And (condition2 Or condition3) Then
```

is true if *condition1* is true and at least one of *condition2* and *condition3* is true. Note that the individual conditions must be spelled out completely. For example, it is tempting to write

```
If Range("A1").Font.Color = vbRed Or vbBlue Then
```

However, this will generate an error message. The corrected line is

```
If Range("A1").Font.Color = vbRed Or Range("A1").Font.Color = vbBlue Then
```

The If5 sub illustrates a typical compound condition. It first checks whether an employee's first score is greater than 80 *and* at least one of the employee's last two scores is greater than 85. If this compound condition is true, it boldfaces the employee's number, it colors the first score red, and it colors blue any second or third score that is greater than 85.

```
Sub IfStatement5()
    ' Example of compound conditions (with And/Or).
```

```
    Dim cell As Range
    Const cutoff1 = 80, cutoff2 = 85

    ' Boldface Employee numbers who did well on the first score and even
    ' better on at least one of the last two scores. Note the indenting
    ' for clear readability.
    For Each cell In wsData.Range("Employee")
        If cell.Offset(0, 1).Value > cutoff1 And _
            (cell.Offset(0, 2).Value > cutoff2 _
            Or cell.Offset(0, 3).Value > cutoff2) Then
            cell.Font.Bold = True
            cell.Offset(0, 1).Font.Color = vbRed
            If cell.Offset(0, 2).Value > cutoff2 Then _
                cell.Offset(0, 2).Font.Color = vbBlue
            If cell.Offset(0, 3).Value > cutoff2 Then _
                cell.Offset(0, 3).Font.Color = vbBlue
        End If
    Next
End Sub
```

7.4 Case Constructions

If constructions can become fairly complex, especially when there are multiple Elself parts. The Case construction discussed here is often used as a less complex alternative. Suppose the action you take depends on the value of some variable. For example, you might have a product index that can have values from 1 to 10, and for each product index you need to take a different action. This could be accomplished with an If construction with multiple Elself lines. However, the Case construction provides an alternative. The general form of this construction is

```
Select Case variable
    Case value1
        statements1
    Case value2
        statements2
    ...
    [Case Else
        statementsElse]
End Select
```

(As usual, the square brackets are not typed. They indicate only that the Else part is optional.) Here, the keywords are Select Case, Case, and End Select, and *variable* is any variable on which the various cases are based. Then *value1, value2*, etc., are mutually exclusive values of *variable* that require different actions, as specified by *statements1, statements2*, and so on. Actually, these values can be single values or ranges of values. For example, if *variable* is named productIndex, you might need to do one thing if productIndex is from 1 to 5, another thing if productIndex is 6, and still another if productIndex is from 7 to 10. You can also include a Case Else, although it is not required. It specifies the action(s) to take if none of the other cases hold.

The following is a typical example of how the cases can be specified.

```
Select Case productIndex
    Case Is <= 3
        unitPrice = 1.2 * unitCost
    Case 4 To 6
        unitPrice = 1.3 * unitCost
    Case 7
        unitPrice = 1.4 * unitCost
    Case Else
        unitPrice = 1.1 * unitCost
End Select
```

Note the three ways the values are specified after the keyword Case: Is <= 3, 4 To 6, and 7 (where Is and To are keywords). You can find the precise rules in VBA help, or you can mimic the examples shown here. Alternatively, there is nothing you can accomplish with Case constructions that you cannot also accomplish with (somewhat complex) If constructions. The construction chosen is often a matter of programming taste.

The file **Case Examples.xlsm** illustrates Case constructions. It is based on the small data set in Figure 7.5. As with the If examples, the examples here change the formatting of the data, so the Restore button is attached to a macro that restores the formatting to its original form. Note that the range A4:A21 has been named Family.

Figure 7.5   Data Set for Case examples

	A	B
3	Family	Income
4	1	$43,800
5	2	$40,200
6	3	$23,100
7	4	$47,400
8	5	$39,700
9	6	$27,700
10	7	$43,600
11	8	$51,300
12	9	$37,600
13	10	$37,200
14	11	$74,800
15	12	$57,400
16	13	$38,000
17	14	$55,400
18	15	$44,800
19	16	$55,400
20	17	$41,400
21	18	$54,500

EXAMPLE 7.6   Single Statement After Each Case

The Case1 sub uses a For Each loop to go through each cell in the Family range. The Case construction is then based on the family's income, that is, the value in cell.Offset(0,1). Depending on which of four income ranges the family's income is in, the income is colored red, green, blue, or magenta. (I assume that all values are listed to the nearest dollar; there are no values such as $50,000.50.) The data are then sorted according to Income, so that all of the incomes of a particular color are adjacent to one another.

```
Sub Case1( )
    Dim cell As Range
    Const cutoff1 = 35000, cutoff2 = 50000, cutoff3 = 65000

    ' Go through families, color the income a different color
    ' for different income ranges, then sort on income.
    For Each cell In wsData.Range("Family")
        With cell
            Select Case .Offset(0, 1).Value
                Case Is <= cutoff1
                    .Offset(0, 1).Font.Color = vbRed
                Case cutoff1+1 To cutoff2
                    .Offset(0, 1).Font.Color = vbGreen
                Case cutoff2+1 To cutoff3
                    .Offset(0, 1).Font.Color = vbRed
                Case Else ' above cutoff3
                    .Offset(0, 1).Font.Color = vbMagenta
            End Select
        End With
    Next

    With wsData
        .Range("B3").Sort Key1:=.Range("B4"), Order1:=xlAscending, _
            Header:=xlYes
    End With
End Sub
```

EXAMPLE 7.7   Multiple Statements After Cases

The Case2 sub is very similar to the Case1 sub. The main difference is that it shows that multiple statements can follow any particular case. Here, the incomes less than or equal to 35,000 are colored red. In addition, if they are less than 30,000, they are also italicized. Similarly, incomes greater than 65,000 are colored magenta, and if they are greater than 70,000, they are boldfaced.

```
Sub Case2()
    ' This is the same as Case1, but if shows how multiple statements
    ' can be used in any particular case.
    Dim cell As Range
    Const cutoff1 = 35000, cutoff2 = 50000, cutoff3 = 65000
```

```
Const cutoff0 = 30000, cutoff4 = 70000

For Each cell In wsData.Range("Family")
    With cell
        Select Case .Offset(0, 1).Value
            Case Is <= cutoff1
                .Offset(0, 1).Font.Color = vbRed
                If .Offset(0, 1) < cutoff0 Then _
                    .Offset(0, 1).Font.Italic = True
            Case cutoff1+1 To cutoff2
                .Offset(0, 1).Font.Color = vbGreen
            Case cutoff2+1 To cutoff3
                .Offset(0, 1).Font.Color = vbBlue
            Case Else ' above cutoff3
                .Offset(0, 1).Font.Color = vbMagenta
                If .Offset(0, 1) > cutoff4 Then _
                    .Offset(0, 1).Font.Bold = True
        End Select
    End With
Next
With wsData
    .Range("B3").Sort Key1:=.Range("B4"), Order1:=xlAscending, _
        Header:=xlYes
End With
End Sub
```

If you find that you favor **Case** constructions to **If** constructions in situations like these, just remember the following: The construction must begin with **Select Case**, it must end with **End Select**, and every case line in between must start with **Case**.

Using a Colon to Separate Two VBA Lines

When you see **Case** constructions, they often include two lines of VBA code on a single physical line. This is allowable if you separate the two lines with a **colon**. This is usually done when the lines are very short. The following is a typical example.

```
With Range("A1")
    Select Case .Value
        Case 1: .Font.Color = vbRed
        Case 2: .Font.Color = vbBlue
        Case 3: .Font.Color = vbGreen
    End Select
End With
```

Actually, a colon can be used to separate *any* two short VBA lines on a single physical line. However, I have seen it most often in **Case** constructions.

7.5 For Loops

Loops allow computers to do what they do best—repetitive tasks. There are actually two basic types of loops in VBA: **For** loops and **Do** loops. Of these two types, **For** loops are usually the easier to write, so I will discuss them first.

For loops take the following general form, where the keywords are For, To, Step, and Next.

```
For counter = first To last [Step increment]
    statements
Next [counter]
```

(As usual, square brackets indicate optional elements. You should not type the brackets.) There is always a *counter* variable. Many programmers, including myself, name their counters i, j, k, m, or n, although any variable names can be used. The first line states that the counter goes from *first* to *last* in steps of *increment*. For each of these values, the *statements* in the body of the loop are executed. The default value of the Step parameter is 1, in which case the Step part can be omitted (as it usually is). The loop always ends with Next. It is possible, but not required, to write the counter variable at the end of the Next line. This is sometimes useful when there are multiple For loops and there could be some ambiguity about which Next goes with which For.

The following is a simple example of a For loop that sums the first 1000 positive integers and reports their sum. This is actually a very common operation, where you accumulate a total within a loop. It is always a good idea to *initialize* the total to 0 just before starting the loop, as is done here.

```
sum = 0
For i = 1 To 1000
    sum = sum + i
Next
MsgBox "The sum of the first 1000 positive integers is " & sum
```

Virtually any types of statements can be used in the body of the loop. The following example illustrates how If logic can be used inside a loop. Here, you can assume that the worksheet with code name wsSalaries has 500 employee names in column A (starting in row 2) and that their corresponding salaries are in column B. This code counts the number of employees with salaries greater than $50,000. The loop finds this number, nHigh, by adding 1 to the current value of nHigh each time it finds a salary greater than $50,000. Note how the counter variable i is used in .Offset(i, 1) to find the salary for employee i.

```
nHigh = 0
With wsSalaries.Range("A1")
    For i = 1 To 500
        If .Offset(i, 1) > 50000 Then nHigh = nHigh + 1
    Next
End With
MsgBox "The number of employees with salaries greater than $50,000 is " & nHigh
```

Exiting a For Loop Prematurely

Sometimes you need to exit a For loop prematurely. This is possible with the Exit For statement. It immediately takes you out of the loop. For example, suppose again that 500 employee names are in column A, starting in row 2, and you want to know whether there is an employee named James Snyder. The following code illustrates one way to do this. It uses a Boolean variable isFound that is initially set to False. The program then loops through all employees. If it finds James Snyder, it sets isFound to True, exits the loop, and reports that James Snyder has been found. However, if it gets through the loop *without* finding Snyder, then isFound is still False, and it displays a message to this effect.

```
Dim isFound As Boolean
isFound = False
With wsSalaries.Range("A1")
    For i = 1 To 500
        If .Offset(i, 0).Value = "James Snyder" Then
            isFound = True
            Exit For
        End If
    Next
End With
If isFound Then
    MsgBox "James Snyder is in the employee list."
Else
    MsgBox "James Snyder is not in the employee list."
End If
```

By the way, most beginning programmers (and even some experienced programmers) would write the fifth from last line as

```
If isFound = True Then
```

This is technically correct, but the = True part is not necessary. Remember that a condition in an If statement is any expression that evaluates to True or False. Therefore, the condition isFound, all by itself, works just fine. It is Boolean, so its value is True or False. Similarly, the line

```
If Not isFound Then
```

could be used for the opposite condition. The keyword Not in front of a condition switches True to False and vice versa. Therefore, an equivalent way to end this example is as follows:

```
If Not isFound Then
    MsgBox "James Snyder is not in the employee list."
Else
    MsgBox "James Snyder is in the employee list."
End If
```

Again, the point of this discussion is that if you use a Boolean variable as the condition in an If statement, you do *not* have to include = True or = False in the condition.

Nested For Loops

It is also common to *nest* For loops. This is particularly useful if you want to loop through all of the cells in a rectangular range. Then there is one counter such as i for the rows and another counter such as j for the columns.[1] The following example illustrates nested loops.

EXAMPLE 7.8   Nested For Loops

Consider the worksheet code-named wsSales with the data in Figure 7.6. (This data set and accompanying code are in the file **For Loop Examples.xlsm**.) Each row corresponds to a sales region, and each column corresponds to a month. The numbers in the body of the table are sales figures for various regions and months, and the goal is to find the total sales over all regions and months. Then the nested For loops in the following GetGrandTotal sub do the job. Note how the sales figure for region i and month j is captured by the offset relative to cell A3. Note also how the counter variables are included in the Next lines (Next i and Next j) for clarity. Actually, the indentation achieves the same effect—easy readability.

```
Sub GetGrandTotal()
    ' Calculate and display the total of all sales.
    Dim total As Single
    Dim iRow As Integer
    Dim iCol As Integer

    ' The following line is not absolutely necessary because numeric
    ' variables are initialized to 0. But it never hurts to play it safe.
    total = 0

    ' Loop through all rows and all columns within each row.
    With wsSales.Range("A3")
        For iRow = 1 To 13
            For iCol = 1 To 9
                total = total + .Offset(iRow, iCol)
            Next iCol
        Next iRow
    End With

    MsgBox "Total sales for the 13 regions during this 9-month period is " _
        & total
End Sub
```

---

[1] I sometimes use more meaningful counter names, such as iRow and iCol. However, the generic names i and j are most often used by programmers, including myself, in such situations.

Figure 7.6   Monthly Sales by Region

	A	B	C	D	E	F	G	H	I	J
1	Sales by region and month									
2										
3		Jan-08	Feb-08	Mar-08	Apr-08	May-08	Jun-08	Jul-08	Aug-08	Sep-08
4	Region 1	2270	1290	1600	2100	1170	1920	1110	2060	3130
5	Region 2	1730	3150	1180	740	1650	900	1830	1220	1620
6	Region 3	1840	1700	2170	3300	1390	1660	1720	2090	880
7	Region 4	3280	1920	2000	1270	1510	2280	2730	2160	1380
8	Region 5	2090	2110	2040	2270	1650	1910	2220	3380	1850
9	Region 6	1820	2570	2060	2190	1840	3310	1920	1080	940
10	Region 7	2400	1880	2980	2370	1910	2580	3470	2220	2200
11	Region 8	1680	1680	3120	1010	1550	2880	1410	2800	1520
12	Region 9	2230	2960	2240	2120	1870	2790	1390	2290	1620
13	Region 10	2040	2310	2120	2750	1220	1270	2080	2150	2650
14	Region 11	1430	2970	1800	2510	1660	1900	2910	770	2740
15	Region 12	1760	1590	1610	1550	1730	1150	3660	1670	3440
16	Region 13	1870	1330	1930	2080	2210	1850	3360	1930	1100

Continuing this example, suppose you want to append a Totals row to the bottom, where you sum sales across regions for each month, and a Totals column to the right, where you sum sales across months for each region. The following GetTotals sub accomplishes this. It is actually quite general. It first finds the number of months and number of regions in the data set so that it will work for any numbers of months and regions, not just those in Figure 7.6. For example, the following line, inside With wsSales.Range("A3"), shows how to count the number of month labels to the right of cell A3.

```
nMonths = Range(.Offset(0, 1), .Offset(0, 1).End(xlToRight)).Columns.Count
```

This is a very common operation for counting columns (or rows), so you should examine it carefully.

```
Sub GetTotals()
    Dim nMonths As Integer, nRegions As Integer
    Dim iRow As Integer, iCol As Integer
    Dim regionTotal As Single, monthTotal As Single

    With wsSales.Range("A3")
        ' Capture the number of months and number of regions.
        nMonths = Range(.Offset(0, 1), .Offset(0, 1).End(xlToRight)) _
            .Columns.Count
        nRegions = Range(.Offset(1, 0), .Offset(1, 0).End(xlDown)) _
            .Rows.Count

        ' Insert labels.
        .Offset(0, nMonths + 1) = "Totals"
```

```
            .Offset(nRegions + 1, 0) = "Totals"

        ' Get totals in right column.
        For iRow = 1 To nRegions
            regionTotal = 0  ' This is absolutely necessary!
            For iCol = 1 To nMonths
                regionTotal = regionTotal + .Offset(iRow, iCol)
            Next iCol
            ' Display total.
            .Offset(iRow, nMonths + 1) = regionTotal
        Next iRow
        ' Get totals in bottom row.
        For iCol = 1 To nMonths
            monthTotal = 0  ' This is also absolutely necessary.
            For iRow = 1 To nRegions
                monthTotal = monthTotal + .Offset(iRow, iCol)
            Next iRow
            ' Display total.
            .Offset(nRegions + 1, iCol) = monthTotal
        Next iCol
    End With
End Sub
```

Pay particular attention in this sub to the initialization statements for region-Total and monthTotal. For example, in the first pair of loops, where the totals in the right column are calculated, the outer loop goes through all of the rows for the regions. For a particular region, you *must* first reinitialize regionTotal to 0, and *then* loop through all of the months, adding each month's sales value to the current regionTotal value. Make sure you understand why the regionTotal = 0 and monthTotal = 0 statements are not only necessary, but why they must be placed exactly where they have been placed for the program to work properly.

In fact, a good way to learn how this works is to purposely do it wrong and see what happens. For example, delete (or comment out) the regionTotal = 0 and monthTotal = 0 lines in the **For Examples.xlsm** file, run the program, and step through the code, periodically checking the value of regionTotal. You really *can* learn from your mistakes. (I have been programming for years, but I still have to think through this type of initialization logic each time I do it. It is *very* easy to do it wrong.)

In all of the For loop examples to this point, the counter has gone from 1 to some fixed number in steps of 1. Other variations are possible, including the following:

- **Variable upper limit**. It is possible for the upper limit to be a *variable* that has been defined earlier. In the following lines, the number of customers is first captured in the variable nCustomers (as the number of rows in the Data range). Then nCustomers is used as the upper limit of the loop.

```
Dim nCustomers As Integer
nCustomers = Range("Data").Rows.Count
For i = 1 To nCustomers
    statements
Next
```

- **Lower limit other than 1**. It is possible for the lower limit to be an integer other than 1, or even a variable that has been defined earlier, as in the following lines. Here, the minimum and maximum scores in the Scores range are first captured in the minScore and maxScore variables. Then a loop uses these as the lower and upper limits for its counter.

```
Dim minScore As Integer, maxScore As Integer
minScore = WorksheetFunction.Min(Range("Scores"))
maxScore = WorksheetFunction.Max(Range("Scores"))
For i = minScore To maxScore
    statements
Next
```

- **Counting backward**. It is possible to let the counter go backward by using a negative value for the Step parameter, as in the following lines. Admittedly, this is not common, but there are times when it is very useful. Here is a typical example. Suppose you have numbers in the range A2:A21. You want to delete all rows where the number is greater than 100. The following code will do this correctly.

```
Sub DeleteRowsCorrectly()
    Dim i As Integer
    With Range("A1")
        For i = 20 To 1 Step -1
            If .Offset(i, 0).Value > 100 Then
                .Offset(i, 0).EntireRow.Delete
            End If
        Next
    End With
End Sub
```

However, the following code will do it incorrectly. Can you see why? It is far from obvious. If you are curious, open the file **Deleting Rows.xlsm** and step through each of the subs. You will learn a lot!

```
Sub DeleteRowsIncorrectly()
    Dim i As Integer
    With Range("A1")
        For i = 1 To 20
            If .Offset(i, 0).Value > 100 Then
                .Offset(i, 0).EntireRow.Delete
            End If
        Next
    End With
End Sub
```

- **Lower limit greater than upper limit**. Another relatively uncommon situation, but one that *can* occur, is when the lower limit of the counter is greater than the upper limit (and the Step parameter is positive). This occurs in the following lines. What does the program do? It never enters the body of the loop at all; it just skips over the loop entirely. And, unlike what you might expect, there is no error message. It is instructive to understand why this is the case. When VBA encounters a For loop, it sets the counter equal to the lower limit. Then it checks whether the counter is less than or equal to the upper limit. If it is, the body of the loop is executed, the counter is incremented by the step size, and the same check is made again. As soon as this check is *not* satisfied, execution passes to the line right after the loop.

```
lowLimit = 10
highLimit = 5
For i = lowLimit To highLimit
    statements
Next
```

7.6 For Each Loops

There is another type of For loop in VBA that is not present in all other programming languages: the For Each loop. Actually, this type of loop has been used a few times in this and previous chapters, so you are probably somewhat familiar with it by now. It is used whenever you want to loop through all *objects* in a *collection*, such as all cells in a Range object or all worksheets in a workbook's Worksheets collection. Unlike the For loops in the previous section, you (the programmer) might have no idea how many objects are in the collection, so you don't know how many times to go through the loop. Fortunately, you don't need to know. The For Each loop figures it out for you. For example, if there are three worksheets, it goes through the loop three times. If there are 15 worksheets, it goes through the loop 15 times. The burden is not on you, the programmer, to figure out the number of objects in the collection.

The typical form of a For Each loop is the following.

```
Dim item As object
For Each item In collection
    statements
Next
```

Here, the declaration of the object variable *item* is shown explicitly. Also, *item*, *object*, and *collection* have been italicized to indicate that they will vary depending on the type of collection. In any case, *item* is a generic name for a particular item in the collection. Programmers generally use a short variable name, depending on the type of item. For example, if you are looping through all worksheets, you might use the variable name ws. Actually, any name will do. In this case, *object* should be replaced by Worksheet, and *collection* should be replaced by Worksheets (or ActiveWorkbook.Worksheets). The following code illustrates how you could search through all worksheets of the active workbook for a sheet code-named wsData. If you find one, you can exit the loop immediately. Note that you must declare the generic ws variable as an object—specifically, a Worksheet object.

```
Dim ws As Worksheet
Dim isFound As Boolean

isFound = False
For Each ws In ActiveWorkbook.Worksheets
    If ws.CodeName = "wsData" Then
        isFound = True
        Exit For
    End If
Next

If isFound Then
    MsgBox "There is a worksheet named Data."
Else
    MsgBox "There is no worksheet named Data."
End If
```

The important thing to remember about For Each loops is that the generic item, such as ws in the above code, is an *object* in a collection. Therefore, it has the same properties and methods as any object in that collection, and they can be referred to in the usual way, such as ws.CodeName. Also, there is no built-in loop counter unless you want to create one—and there *are* situations where you will want to do so. As an example, the code below generalizes the previous code slightly. It counts the number of worksheets with a name that starts with "Sheet". (To do this, it uses the string function Left. For example, Left("Sheet17",5) returns the leftmost 5 characters in "Sheet17", namely, "Sheet".)

```
Dim ws As Worksheet
Dim counter As Integer

counter = 0
For Each ws In ActiveWorkbook.Worksheets
    If Left(ws.Name, 5) = "Sheet" Then
        counter = counter + 1
    End If
Next
MsgBox "There are " & counter & " sheets with a name starting with Sheet."
```

For Each with Ranges

One special type of collection is a Range object. Remember that there is no Ranges collection, but the singular Range acts like a collection, and you can use it in a For Each loop. Then the individual items in the collection are the cells in the range. The following is a typical example. It counts the number of cells in a range that contain formulas. To do so, it uses the built-in HasFormula property, which returns True or False. Note again that cell is *not* a keyword in VBA. It is used here to denote a typical member of the Range collection—that is, a typical cell. Instead of cell, any other name (such as cl) could have been used for this generic object. In any case, this generic member must first be declared as a Range object.

```
Dim cell As Range
Dim counter As Integer

counter = 0
For Each cell In Range("Data")
    If cell.HasFormula Then counter = counter + 1
Next
MsgBox "There are " & counter & " cells in the Data range that contain formulas."
```

If you have programmed in another language, but not in VBA, it might take you a while to get comfortable with For Each loops. They simply do not exist in programming languages that do not have objects and collections. However, they can be extremely useful. For examples, refer back to any of Examples 7.4–7.7 in this chapter. They all use a For Each loop to loop through all cells in a range.

To see a few more For Each examples, examine the code in the file **For Each Examples.xlsm**. This code illustrates how you can loop through the Worksheets collection, the Charts collection (that includes chart sheets), the Sheets collection (that includes worksheets and chart sheets), and the Names collection (that includes range names). Actually, there are many more collections in Excel that you can loop through with For Each loops.

7.7   Do Loops

For loops (not For each loops) are perfect for looping a fixed number of times. However, there are many times when you need to loop *while* some condition holds or *until* some condition holds. You can then use a Do loop. Do loops are somewhat more difficult to master than For loops, partly because you have to think through the logic more carefully, and partly because there are four possible variations of Do loops. Usually, *any* of these variations can be used, but you have to decide which one is most natural and easiest to read.

The four variations are as follows. In each variation, the keyword Do appears in the first line of the loop, and the keyword Loop begins the last line of the loop. The first two variations check a condition at the top of the loop, whereas the last two variations check a condition at the bottom of the loop.

Variation 1: Do Until … Loop

```
Do Until condition
    statements
Loop
```

Variation 2: Do While … Loop

```
Do While condition
    statements
Loop
```

Variation 3: Do … Loop Until

```
Do
    statements
Loop Until condition
```

Variation 4: Do … Loop While

```
Do
    statements
Loop While condition
```

Here are some general comments that should help you understand Do loops.

- **Conditions at the top**. In the first two variations, the program checks the condition just before going through the body of the loop. In an Until loop, the statements in the body of the loop are executed only if the condition is *false;* in a While loop, the statements are executed only if the condition is *true.* If you stop and think about it, this is not something you need to memorize; it makes sense, given the meaning of the words "until" and "while."
- **Conditions at the bottom**. The same holds in variations 3 and 4. The difference here is that the program decides whether to go through the loop *again.* The effect is that the statements in the loop will certainly be executed *at least once* in the last two variations, whereas they might *never* be executed in the first two variations.
- **Exit Do statement**. As with a For loop, you can exit a Do loop prematurely. To do so, you use an Exit Do statement inside the loop.
- **Possibility of infinite loops**. A Do loop has no built-in counter as in a For loop. Therefore, you as a programmer *must* change something within the loop to give it a chance of eventually exiting. Otherwise, it is easy to be caught in an **infinite loop** from which the program can never exit. The following is a simple example. It shows that it is easy to get into an infinite loop. It happens to all of us. You can assume that isValid has been declared as a Boolean variable—it is either True or False.

```
Sub Test()
    Dim isvalid As Boolean, password As String
    isvalid = False
    Do Until isvalid
        password = InputBox("Enter a valid password.")
    Loop
End Sub
```

Go through the logic in these statements to see if you can locate the problem. Here it is. The Boolean variable isValid is never changed inside the loop. It is initialized to False, and it never changes. But the loop continues until isValid is True, which will never occur. If you type this code into a sub and then run it, the sub will never stop.

Breaking Out of an Infinite Loop: A Lifesaver

This might not sound too bad, but suppose you have spent the last hour writing a program, you have not saved your work (shame on you!), and you decide to test your program by running it. All of a sudden, you realize that you are in an infinite loop that you cannot get out of, and panic sets in. How can you save your work? Fortunately, there is a way to break out of an infinite loop (or terminate a program that has been running too long)—you can use the **Ctrl+Break** key combination. (The Break key is at the top right of most keyboards. However, some keyboards, including those on Macs, don't have a Break key. In this case, you can press the **Esc** key, which appears to do the same thing.[2]) This allows you to exit the program and save your work. This brush with disaster also reminds you to save more often. Try it now. Run the above password program and see whether you can break out of the loop.

How do you avoid the infinite loop in this example? Let's suppose that any password of the form "VBAPass" followed by an integer from 1 to 9 will be accepted. In this case, the following code will do the job. It checks whether the user enters one of the valid passwords, and if so, it sets isValid to True, allowing an exit from the loop. But there is still a problem. What if the poor user just doesn't know the password? She might try several invalid passwords and eventually give up, either by entering nothing in the input box or by clicking on the Cancel button (or the X button). The program checks for this by seeing whether password, the string returned from the InputBox statement, is an empty string, "". (Clicking the Cancel button or the X button of an input box returns an empty string.) In this case, the program not only exits the loop, but it ends abruptly because of the keyword Exit Sub. After all, you don't want the user to be able to continue if she doesn't know the password.

```
Sub Test()
    Dim isvalid As Boolean, password As String
    isvalid = False
    Do Until isvalid
        password = InputBox("Enter a valid password.")
        If password = "" Then
            MsgBox "Sorry, but you cannot continue."
            Exit Sub
        Else
            For i = 1 To 9
                If password = "VBAPass" & i Then
```

---

[2] Unfortunately, as I just discovered when I lost some of my own unsaved code, this doesn't necessarily work. First, my keyboard on a Windows 8 machine doesn't have a Break key. Second, pressing the Esc key has no effect at all. If you search the Web for "VBA infinite loops," you will see that other programmers have discovered the same problem, along with some possible remedies.

```
                        isvalid = True
                        Exit For
                    End If
                Next
            End If
        Loop
End Sub
```

Study this code carefully. Note that the Exit For statement provides an exit from the For loop, because the program has found that the user entered a valid password such as VBAPass3. In this case there is no need to check whether she entered VBAPass4, VBAPass5, and so on. In addition, by this time, isValid has just been set to True. Therefore, when control passes back to the top of the Do loop, the condition will be true, and the Do loop will be exited.

There is an important lesson in this example. It is easy to get into an infinite loop—we all do it from time to time. If you run your program and it just seems to hang, the chances are good that you are in an infinite loop. In that case, press Ctrl +Break (or Esc) to stop the program, save your file, and check your loops carefully.

EXAMPLE 7.9   Locating a Name in a List

The file **Do Loop Examples.xlsm** illustrates a typical use of Do loops. It starts with a database of customers in a Data worksheet, as shown in Figure 7.7 (with several hidden rows). Column A contains a company's customers last year, and column B contains the customers this year. Next year has not yet occurred, so the company doesn't know its customers for next year—hence the empty list in column C. The user first selects a

Figure 7.7   Customer Lists

	A	B	C
1	**Customer last year**	**Customer this year**	**Customer next year**
2	Barlog	Aghimien	
3	Barnett	Bang	
4	Bedrick	Barnett	
5	Brulez	Bedrick	
6	Cadigan	Brulez	
7	Castleman	Cadigan	
8	Chandler	Castleman	
92	Yablonka	Tracy	
93	Zick	Ubelhor	
94	Ziegler	Usman	
95		Vicars	
96		Villard	
97		Wendel	
98		Wier	
99		Wise	
100		Yablonka	
101		Yeiter	
102		Zakrzacki	
103		Zhou	

column from 1 to the number of columns (here 3, but the program is written more generally for any number of columns). The goal of the program is to check whether a customer with a user-selected name is in the selected column. (The blank "Customer next year" column is included here for illustration. It shows what happens if you try to locate a particular name in a *blank* list.)

The DoLoop1 sub shows how to perform the search with a Do Until loop. It searches down the selected column for a user-supplied name until it finds the name or it runs into a blank cell, the latter signifying that it has checked the entire customer list for that column. If it finds the name along the way, it exits the loop prematurely with an Exit Do statement. Note that the program works even if column C is chosen. You should reason for yourself exactly what the program does in this case—and why it works properly.

```
Sub DoLoop1()
    Dim selectedColumn As Integer
    Dim nColumns As Integer
    Dim rowCount As Integer
    Dim foundName As Boolean
    Dim requestedName As String

    ' Count the columns.
    With wsData.Range("A1")
        nColumns = Range(.Offset(0, 0), .End(xlToRight)).Columns.Count
    End With

    ' Ask for a name to be searched for.
    requestedName = InputBox("What last name do you want to search for?")

    ' No error checking -- assumes user will enter an appropriate value!
    selectedColumn = InputBox("Enter a column number from 1 to " & nColumns)

    ' Go to the top of the selected column.
    With wsData.Range("A1").Offset(0, selectedColumn - 1)
        rowCount = 1
        foundName = False

        ' Keep going until a blank cell is encountered. Note that if there
        ' are no names at all in the selected column, the body of this loop
        ' will never be executed.
        Do Until .Offset(rowCount, 0).Value = " "
            If UCase(.Offset(rowCount, 0).Value) = UCase(requestedName) Then
                foundName = True
                MsgBox requestedName & " was found as name " & rowCount _
                    & " in column " & selectedColumn & ".", vbInformation
                ' Exit the loop prematurely as soon as a match is found.
                Exit Do
            Else
                ' Unlike a For loop, any counter must be updated manually
                ' in a Do loop.
                rowCount = rowCount + 1
            End If
        Loop
    End With

    ' Display appropriate message if no match is found.
    If Not foundName Then
```

```
            MsgBox "No match for " & requestedName & " was found.", vbInformation
        End If
End Sub
```

Probably the most important parts of this loop are the row counter variable, rowCount, and the updating statement, rowCount = rowCount + 1. Without these, there would be an infinite loop. But because rowCount increases by 1 every time through the loop, the condition following Do Until is always based on a *new* cell. Eventually, the program will find the requested name or it will run out of customers in the selected column. In either way, it will eventually end.

VBA's UCase and LCase Functions

The condition that checks for the requested name uses VBA's built-in UCase (uppercase) function. This function transforms any string into one with all uppercase characters. This is often useful when you are not sure whether names are capitalized fully, partially, or not at all. By checking for uppercase only, you take all guesswork out of the search. Similarly, VBA has an LCase (lowercase) function that transforms all characters to lowercase.

Changing Do Until to Do While

It is easy to change a Do Until loop to a Do While loop or vice versa. You just change the condition to its opposite. The **Do Loop Examples.xlsm** file contains a DoLoop2 sub that uses Do While instead of Do Until. The only change is that the Do Until line becomes the following. (Note that <> means "not equal to.")

```
Do While .Offset(rowCount, 0).Value <> ""
```

Putting Conditions at the Bottom of the Loop

It is also possible to perform the search for the requested name using variation 3 or 4 of a Do loop—that is, to put the conditions at the *bottom* of the loop. The DoLoop3 and DoLoop4 subs of the **Do Loop Examples.xlsm** file illustrate these possibilities. However, for this particular task (of finding a particular name), it is probably more natural to place the condition at the top of the loop. This way, if the first element of the selected column's list is blank, as for the next year column, the body of the loop is never executed at all.

7.8 Summary

The programming tools discussed in this chapter are arguably the most important tools in VBA or any other programming language. It is hard to imagine many interesting, large-scale applications that do not require some control logic and loops. They appear everywhere. Fortunately, they are not difficult to master, and you will see them in numerous examples in later chapters.

EXERCISES

1. Write a sub that requests a positive integer with an InputBox. Then it uses a For loop to sum all of the odd integers up to the input number, and it displays the result in a MsgBox.
2. Change your sub from the previous exercise so that it enters all of the odd integers in consecutive cells in column A, starting with cell A1, and it shows the sum in the cell just below the last odd integer.
3. The file **Sales Data.xlsx** contains monthly sales amounts for 40 sales regions. Write a sub that uses a For loop to color the interior of every other row (rows 3, 5, etc.) gray. Color only the data area, columns A to M. (Check the file **Colors in Excel.xlsm** to find a nice color of gray.)
4. Starting with the original **Sales Data.xlsx** file from the previous exercise, write a sub that italicizes each monthly sales amount that is greater than $12,000 and changes the font color to red for each label in column A where the yearly sales total for the region is greater than $130,000.
5. Starting with the original **Sales Data.xlsx** file from the previous exercise, write a sub that examines each row for upward or downward movements in quarterly totals. Specifically, for each row, check whether the quarterly totals increase each quarter and whether they decrease each quarter. If the former, color the region's label in column A red; if the latter, color it blue.
6. An InputBox statement returns a string—whatever the user enters in the box. However, it returns a blank string if the user enters nothing and clicks the OK or Cancel button (or the X button). Write a sub that uses an InputBox to ask the user for a product code. Embed this in a Do loop so that the user has to keep trying until the result is *not* a blank string.
7. Continuing the previous exercise, suppose all valid product codes start with the letter P and are followed by four digits. Expand the sub from the previous exercise so that the user has to keep trying until a *valid* code has been entered.
8. In Exercise 6, you chose one of the four possible versions of Do loops in your code: using a While or Until condition, and placing the condition at the top of the loop or the bottom of the loop. Regardless of how you did it, rewrite your sub in each of the three other possible ways.
9. Write a sub that displays a MsgBox. The message should ask whether the total receipt for a sale is greater than $100, and it should display Yes and No buttons. If the result of the MsgBox is vbYes (the built-in VBA constant that results from clicking the Yes button), a second message box should inform the user that she gets a 10% discount.
10. Write a sub that asks for the unit cost of a product with an InputBox. Embed this within a Do loop so that the user keeps being asked until she enters a positive numeric value. (*Hint:* Use VBA's IsNumeric function. Also, remember that if the user clicks the Cancel button or the X button, an empty string is returned.)

11. Write a sub that asks for a product index from 1 to 100. Embed this within a Do loop so that the user keeps being asked until he enters an integer from 1 to 100. (*Hint:* Use a For loop for checking.)

12. All passwords in your company's system must be eight characters long, start with an uppercase letter, and consist of uppercase letters and digits—no spaces. Employees are issued a password, but then they are allowed to change it to one of their own choice.
    a. Write a sub to get a user's new password. It should use an InputBox, embedded within a Do loop, to get the password. The purpose of the loop is to check that they indeed enter a *valid* password.
    b. Expand your sub in part **a** to include a second InputBox that asks the user to verify the password in the first input box (which by then is known to be valid). Embed the whole procedure within an outer Do loop. This outer loop keeps repeating until the user provides a valid password in the first InputBox and enters the *same* password in the second InputBox.

13. Repeat the previous exercise, but now assume that, in addition to the other restrictions on valid passwords, passwords can have at most two digits—the rest must be uppercase letters.

14. Repeat Exercise 12, but now perform a second check. Use the file **Passwords.xlsx**, which has a single worksheet called Passwords. This sheet has a list of all passwords currently being used by employees in column A, starting in cell A1. If the new employee selects one of these passwords, an appropriate warning message is displayed, and the user has to choose another password. When the user finally chooses a valid password that is not being used, a "Congratulations" message should be displayed, and the new password should be added to the list at the bottom of column A.

15. Write a sub that asks the user for three things in three InputBox lines: (1) a last name, (2) a "first" name (which can actually be their middle name if they go by their middle name), and (3) an initial. Use Do loops to ensure that the first name and last name are all letters—no digits, spaces, or other characters. Also, check that the initial is a single letter or is blank (because some people don't like to use an initial). If an initial is given, ask the user in a MsgBox with Yes and No buttons whether the initial is a *middle* initial. (The alternative is that it is a *first* initial.) Then display a MsgBox listing the user's full name, such as "Your full name is F. Robert Jacobs", "Your name is Wayne L. Winston", or "Your name is Seb Heese".

16. Assume you have a mailing list file. This file is currently the active workbook, and the active sheet of this workbook has full names in column A, starting in cell A1, with last name last and everything in uppercase letters (such as STEPHEN E. LEE). Write a sub that counts the number of names in the list with last name LEE and then displays this count in a MsgBox. Note that there might be last names such as KLEE, which should not be counted.

17. The file **Price Data.xlsx** has a single sheet that lists your products by product code. For each product, it lists the unit price and a discount percentage that customers get if they purchase at least a minimum quantity of the product. For example, the discount for the first product is 7%, and it is obtained if the customer

purchases at least 20 units of the product. Write a sub that asks for a product code with an input box. This should be placed inside a Do loop that checks whether the code is one in the list. It should then ask for the number of units purchased, which must be a positive number. (You don't have to check that the input is an *integer*. You can assume that the user doesn't enter something like 2.73.) Finally, it should display a message something like the following: "You purchased _ units of product _. The total cost is _. Because you purchased at least _ units, you got a discount of _ on each unit." Of course, your code will fill in the underscores in this message. Also, the last sentence should not be displayed if the user didn't purchase enough units to get a discount. (*Note:* You should write this sub, and the subs in the next two exercises, so that they are valid even if the list of products expands in the future.)

18. Continuing the previous exercise, write a sub that first asks the user for the number of different products purchased. Then use a For loop that goes from 1 to this number, and place the code from the previous exercise, modified if necessary, inside this loop. That is, each time through the loop you should get and display information about a particular product purchased. At the end of the sub, a message should be displayed that shows the total amount spent on all purchases.

19. Again, use the **Price Data.xlsx** file described in Exercise 17. Write a sub that asks the user for a purchase quantity that can be any multiple of 5 units, up to 50 units. Then enter a label in cell E3 something like "Cost of _ units", where the underscore in the message is filled in by the user's input. Below this, enter the total cost of this many units for each product. For example, cell E4 will contain the purchase cost of this many units of the first product in the list. Enter these as values, not formulas.

20. The file **Customer Accounts.xlsx** contains account information on a company's customers. For each customer listed by customer ID, the Data worksheet has the amount the customer has purchased during the current year and the amount the customer has paid on these purchases so far. For example, the first customer purchased an amount worth $2466 and has paid up in full. In contrast, the second customer purchased an amount worth $1494 and has paid only $598 of this. Write a sub to create a list on the Results worksheet of all customers who still owe more than $1000. (It should first clear the contents of any previous list on this worksheet.) The list should show customer IDs and the amounts owed. This sub should work even if the data change, including the possibility of more or fewer customer accounts.

21. (More difficult) The file **Customer Orders.xlsx** shows orders by date for a company's customers on the Data worksheet. Many customers have ordered more than once, so they have multiple entries in the list. Write a sub that finds the total amount spent by each customer on the list and reports those whose total is more than $2000 on the Report worksheet. As part of your sub, sort the list on the Report worksheet in descending order by total amount spent. (*Hint:* The orders in the Data worksheet are currently sorted by date. It might be helpful to use VBA to sort them by Customer ID. Then at the end of the sub, restore the list to its original condition by sorting on date.)

22. You are a rather paranoid business executive, always afraid that a competitor might be snooping on your sensitive e-mail messages. Therefore, you decide to use a very simple form of encryption. The table in the file **Scramble.xlsx** shows your scheme. For example, all instances of the letter "a" are changed to the letter "e", all instances of "b" are changed to "v", and so on. Note at the bottom of the table that uppercase letters are scrambled differently than lowercase letters. For example, all instances of "A" are changed to "D". (Spaces, periods, and other nonalphabetic characters are not changed.) Write two subs, Scramble and Unscramble. In each, ask the user for a message in an InputBox. In the Scramble sub, this will be an original message; in the Unscramble sub, it will be a scrambled message. Then in the Scramble sub, scramble the message and display it. Similarly, in the Unscramble sub, unscramble the message and display it. (Of course, in a real situation, you and the person you are e-mailing would each have the **Scramble.xlsm** file. You would use the Scramble sub, and the person you are e-mailing would use the Unscramble sub.)

23. (More difficult) A prime number is one that is divisible only by itself and 1. The first few prime numbers are 2, 3, 5, 7, 11, and 13. Note that 2 is the only *even* prime number.

    a. Write a sub that finds the first *n* prime numbers, where you can choose *n*, and lists them in column B of the First_n worksheet of the **Primes.xlsx** file. The first few are already listed for illustration. (*Hint:* You should use VBA's Mod function. It returns the remainder when one number is divided by another. For example, 45 Mod 7 returns 3. A number *n* is *not* prime if n Mod $k = 0$ for some integer *k* between 1 and *n*. For example, 39 is not prime because 39 Mod 3 = 0.)

    b. Change the sub in part **a** slightly so that it now finds all prime numbers less than or equal to some number *m*, where you can choose *m*, and lists them in the UpTo_m worksheet of the **Primes.xlsx** file.

24. (More difficult) The cipher in Exercise 22 is a really simple one that hackers would break in no time. The file **Cipher.xlsx** explains a much more sophisticated cipher. (It has been around for centuries, and it too can be broken fairly easily by experts, but it is safe from most onlookers.) Write a sub that first asks the user for a *key*, a word with all uppercase letters. Then it asks the user for a message that contains only lowercase words and spaces. The sub should delete all of the spaces from this message and then encode what remains, using the explanation in the file and the given key. It should report the encoded message, without any spaces, in a MsgBox. (You can test it on the following. If the key is VBAMODELERS and the message is "the treasure is buried in the garden", the encoded message, with spaces reinserted, is "OIE FFHEDYTW DT BGFLIO ME LCF GMFGIY". In the same sub, and using the same encoded message and key, decode the message and report it in a message box. Of course, it should be the same as the original message.

25. (More difficult) Consider the following model of product preferences. Assume that a retailer can stock any of products 1 through *n*. Each customer is one of several customer segments. The customers in a given segment all rank the products in the same way. For example, if $n = 5$ and a segment has ranked preferences

{2, 1, 4}, any customer in this segment would purchase any of products 1, 2, and 4, but not products 3 or 5. Furthermore, any such customer prefers product 2 to product 1 and product 1 to product 4. So if the retailer stocks products 1, 3, 4, and 5, this customer will purchase her highest ranked stocked product, product 1. (She would prefer product 2, but it isn't stocked.) But if the retailer stocks only products 3 and 5, this customer won't purchase anything. The file **Preferences.xlsx** has instructions, where your task is to write a sub that takes (1) a customer population size, (2) any given set of customer segments, (3) the proportions of all customers in the customer segments, (4) the profit margin for each product, and (5) the products offered by the retailer. It should then find (1) which product each customer segment purchases, if any; (2) the number of customers who purchase each offered product; and (3) the retailer's total profit. (*Note*: You might think that with all profit margins being positive, it would certainly make sense for the retailer to offer all *n* products. However, this is not necessarily true. For example, imagine that product 1 has a relatively small profit margin, product 2 has a relatively large profit margin, and a lot of the customers' first and second preferences, in that order, are products 1 and 2. Then by *not* offering product 1, a lot of customers would go to their second preference, product 2, and the retailer would probably earn a larger profit.)

Working with Other Excel Objects

8.1 Introduction

This chapter extends the information given in Chapters 6 and 7. Chapter 6 focused on ranges. This chapter illustrates how to work with three other common objects in Excel: workbooks, worksheets, and charts. In doing so, it naturally illustrates further uses of control logic and loops, which were discussed in Chapter 7. Workbooks, worksheets, and charts are certainly not the only objects you will encounter in Excel, but if you know how to work with these objects, along with ranges, you will be well along the way. (Although they aren't discussed here, the files Comments.xlsm, Hyperlinks.xlsm, and Web Queries.xlsm illustrate how VBA can be used to manipulate other fairly common Excel objects.) All of the objects in this chapter have many properties and methods, and only a small fraction of them are illustrated. As usual, you can learn much more from online help, particularly the Object Browser.

8.2 Exercise

The exercise in this section illustrates the manipulation of multiple workbooks, worksheets, and ranges. It is fairly straightforward, although you have to be careful to keep your bearings as you move from one workbook or worksheet to another. You should work on this exercise, or at least keep it in mind, as you read through the rest of this chapter. All of the tools required to solve it are explained in this chapter or were already explained in a previous chapter. When you finally get it working, you can consider yourself a legitimate Excel programmer.

Exercise 8.1   Consolidating Data from Multiple Sheets

Consider a company that sells several of its products to five large customers. The company currently has a file with two worksheets, Revenues and Costs, for each customer. These files are named **Customer1.xlsx** through **Customer5.xlsx**. Each worksheet shows the revenues or costs by day for all products sold to that customer. For example, a sample of the revenue data for customer 1 appears in Figure 8.1. Each of the customer files has data for the *same* dates (currently, from January 2015 through June 2015, although new data could be added in the future). In contrast, different customers have data for *different* numbers of products. For example, customer 1 purchases products 1 to 4, customer 2 purchases products 1 to 6, and so on.

Figure 8.1 Sample Revenue Data for Customer 1

	A	B	C	D	E
1	Date	Product 1	Product 2	Product 3	Product 4
2	25-Jan-15	1890	2010	1150	2480
3	26-Jan-15	2880	2670	2280	3520
4	27-Jan-15	1520	2400	3430	1710
5	28-Jan-15	2270	2530	3220	2050
6	31-Jan-15	3280	2730	2080	2670
7	01-Feb-15	2630	1970	2900	1930
8	02-Feb-15	3030	3250	2410	3260
9	03-Feb-15	1990	1600	2360	2220
10	04-Feb-15	2800	1970	2650	2450

Figure 8.2 Template for Consolidated File

	A	B	C	D	E	F	G	H	I	J	K	L	M
1		Customer 1		Customer 2		Customer 3		Customer 4		Customer 5		Total all customers	
2	Date	Revenues	Costs	Revenues	Costs	Revenues	Costs	Revenues	Costs	Revenues	Costs	Revenues	Costs
3													

The purpose of the exercise is to consolidate the data from these five workbooks into a single Summary worksheet in a workbook named **Consolidating.xlsm**. This file already exists, but it includes only headings, as shown in Figure 8.2. When finished, the dates will go down column A, the revenues and costs for customer 1 will go down columns B and C, those for customer 2 will go down columns D and E, and so on. The revenues and costs for all customers combined will go down columns L and M. Note that the revenues and costs in columns B and C, for example, are totals over all products purchased by customer 1.

Figure 8.3 shows part of the results for the finished application. There is a button to the right that runs the program. The program should have a loop over the customers that successively opens each customer's file, sums the revenues and costs for that customer, places the totals in the consolidated file, and then closes that customer's file. Finally, after entering all of the information in Figure 8.3 through column K, the program should enter *formulas* in columns L and M to obtain the totals.

Figure 8.3 Results from Finished Application

	A	B	C	D	E	F	G	H	I	J	K	L	M
1		Customer 1		Customer 2		Customer 3		Customer 4		Customer 5		Total all customers	
2	Date	Revenues	Costs	Revenues	Costs	Revenues	Costs	Revenues	Costs	Revenues	Costs	Revenues	Costs
3	25-Jan-15	7530	5730	13810	8740	5290	2960	6520	5400	13310	7470	46460	30300
4	26-Jan-15	11350	5500	15860	9080	5510	3100	7100	4290	12610	7380	52430	29350
5	27-Jan-15	9060	5770	14840	9190	5000	3410	7250	4990	12570	7570	48720	30930
6	28-Jan-15	10070	5750	14910	9270	4800	2770	8500	4650	12900	7900	51180	30340
7	31-Jan-15	10760	6180	13540	9180	4050	2700	7650	3550	12880	7050	48880	28660
8	1-Feb-15	9430	5750	18810	9410	4770	2510	8830	3960	12000	7890	53840	29520
9	2-Feb-15	11950	6010	16550	9760	4150	2690	8540	4720	11390	7010	52580	30190
10	3-Feb-15	8170	5830	15040	8960	4300	2830	7610	5180	11900	8490	47020	31290
11	4-Feb-15	9870	6240	17660	9120	5750	2720	7220	4070	12460	6800	52960	28950

To see how this application works, make sure none of the individual customer's files is open, open the **Consolidating Finished.xlsm** file, and click the button. Although you will have to watch closely to notice that anything is happening, each of the customer's files will be opened for a fraction of a second before being closed, and the results in Figure 8.3 will appear. As usual, you can look at the VBA code in the finished file, but you should resist doing so until you have given it your best effort.

8.3 Collections and Members of Collections

Collections and members of collections (remember, plural and singular?) were already discussed in Chapter 5, but these ideas bear repeating here as I discuss workbooks, worksheets, and charts. There are actually two ideas you need to master: (1) specifying a member of a collection, and (2) specifying a hierarchy in the object model.

The three collections required for this chapter are the Workbooks, Worksheets, and Charts collections.[1] The Workbooks collection is the collection of all open workbooks. (It does *not* include Excel files on your hard drive that are not currently open.) Any member of this collection—a particular workbook—can be specified with its name, such as Workbooks("Customers.xlsx"). This refers to the **Customers.xlsx** file (assumed to be open in Excel). Similarly, a particular worksheet such as the Data worksheet can be referenced as Worksheets("Data"), and a particular chart sheet such as the Sales chart sheet can be referenced as Charts("Sales"). The point is that if you want to reference any particular member of a collection, you must spell out the plural collection name and then follow it in parentheses with the name of the member in double quotes.

It is possible to refer to a member with a numeric index, such as Worksheets(3), but this method is typically not used. It is difficult to remember what the *third* worksheet is, for example. By the way, *third* refers to the third sheet from the left.

As discussed in Chapter 5, you can also refer to worksheets and chart sheets by their code names, and I will do this frequently in this chapter. Remember that there are two primary advantages of doing it this way. First, if a user changes the tab name of a worksheet from Data to Data1, the code name stays fixed, so programs are less likely to be broken by such changes. Second, you can refer directly to a code name such as wsData, with a line like wsData.Range("A1"). You don't need to declare a Worksheet object and then Set it, as in the following two lines:

```
Dim ws as Worksheet
Set ws = Worksheets("Data")
```

As for hierarchy, it works as follows. The Workbooks collection consists of individual Workbook objects. Any particular Workbook object *contains* a Worksheets

---

[1] The **ChartObjects** collection is also mentioned in Section 8.6.

collection and a Charts collection. If a particular worksheet, such as the Data worksheet, belongs to the *active* workbook, you can refer to it simply as Worksheets("Data"). You can also refer to it as ActiveWorkbook.Worksheets("Data"). However, there are times when you need to spell out the workbook, as in Workbooks("Customers.xlsx").Worksheets("Data"). This indicates explicitly that you want the Data worksheet from the Customers workbook.

In a similar way, you can specify the Sales chart sheet as Charts("Sales") or, if the Sales sheet is in the active workbook, as ActiveWorkbook.Charts("Sales"). Alternatively, to designate the Sales chart sheet in the Customers workbook, you can write Workbooks("Customers.xlsx").Charts("Sales"). Finally, you can refer to the code names of chart sheets exactly like you do with worksheets. I like to prefix these code names with cht, as in chtSales.

The Worksheets collection is one step down the hierarchy from the Workbooks collection. Range objects are one step farther down the hierarchy. Suppose you want to refer to the range A3:C10. If this is in the active worksheet, you can refer to it as Range("A3:C10") or as ActiveSheet.Range("A3:C10"). If you want to indicate explicitly that this range is in the Data sheet, you should write Worksheets("Data").Range("A3:C10") or wsData.Range("A3:C10") if wsData is the code name of the worksheet. But even this assumes that the Data sheet is in the active workbook. If you want to indicate explicitly that this sheet is in the Customers file, then you should write Workbooks("Customers.xlsx").Worksheets("Data"). Range("A3:C10"). You always read this type of reference from right to left—the range A3:C10 of the Data sheet in the Customers file.

Once you know how to refer to these objects, you can easily refer to their properties by adding a dot and then a property or method after the reference. Some examples are:

```
ActiveWorkbook.Worksheets("Data").Range("C4").Value = "Sales for 2009"
```

and

```
Charts("Sales").Delete
```

Many other examples appear throughout this chapter.

One final concept mentioned briefly in Chapter 2 is that the Workbooks, Worksheets, and Charts *collections* are also objects and therefore have properties and methods. Probably the most commonly used *property* of each of these collections is the Count property. For example, ActiveWorkbook.Worksheets.Count returns the number of worksheets in the active workbook. Probably the most commonly used *method* of each of these collections is the Add method. This adds a new member to the collection, which then becomes the *active* member. For example, consider the following lines:

```
ActiveWorkbook.Worksheets.Add
ActiveSheet.Name = "NewData"
```

The first line adds a new worksheet to the active workbook, and the second line names this new sheet NewData. (This new worksheet also has a generic code name such as Sheet2, but you cannot change it with VBA code because it is a *read only* property; you can change it only in the Properties window of the VBE.)

Before proceeding to examples, I want to make some comments about reference to objects and Intellisense. Once you type an object and then a period, if VBA recognizes the *type* of object (range, worksheet, or whatever), Intellisense *should* provide a list of its properties and methods. It is very disconcerting when this list doesn't appear. In fact, I usually assume I have made an error when Intellisense doesn't appear. But VBA doesn't seem to be totally consistent about providing Intellisense for objects. For example, I opened a new workbook and entered the code Worksheets ("Sheet1"). (including the period), but no Intellisense appeared. Why not? I have no idea. There shouldn't be any doubt that this refers to a Worksheet object, but Intellisense acts as if it isn't sure.

There are two remedies for this. The first is to Set object variables and then refer to them. If you declare ws as a Worksheet object, then type the line Set ws = Worksheets("Sheet1"), and finally type ws. (including the period), you will get Intellisense. Maybe this is why experienced programmers declare and use so many object variables. The second remedy is to use code names for worksheets and chart sheets. (Other objects don't have code names.) In fact, this has led me to use code names much more than in earlier editions.

8.4 Examples of Workbooks in VBA

The file **Workbooks.xlsm** illustrates how to open and close workbooks, how to save them, how to specify the paths where they are stored, and how to display several of their properties, all with VBA. It is the basis for the following examples.

EXAMPLE 8.1   Working with Workbooks

The Workbooks1 sub shows how to open and close a workbook. It also uses the Count property of the Worksheets collection to return the number of worksheets in a workbook, and it uses the Name property of a Workbook to return the name of the workbook. As illustrated in the sub, the opening and closing operations are done slightly differently. To open a workbook, you use the Open method of the Workbooks collection, followed by the Filename argument. This argument specifies the name (including the path) of the workbook file. To close a workbook, you use the Close method of that Workbook object without any arguments.[2]

---

[2] This is not precisely true. The Open and Close methods both have optional arguments I have not mentioned here. You can find details in online help.

Note that the file you are trying to open must exist in the location you specify. Otherwise, you will obtain an error message. Similarly, the file you are trying to close must currently be open.

```
Sub Workbooks1()
    ' This sub shows how to open or close a workbook. They are done
    ' differently. To open a workbook, use the Open method of the
    ' Workbooks collection, followed by the name of the workbook file.
    ' To close a workbook, use the Close method of that workbook.

    ' The following line assumes there is a file called Text.xlsx in the
    ' C:\Temp folder. If you want to run this (without an error message),
    ' make sure there is such a file.
    Workbooks.Open Filename:="C:\Temp\Test.xlsx"

    ' Count the worksheets in this file and display this in a message box.
    MsgBox "There are " & ActiveWorkbook.Worksheets.Count _
        & " worksheets in the " & ActiveWorkbook.Name & " file."

    ' Close the workbook.
    Workbooks("Test.xlsx").Close
End Sub
```

If you run this sub, then assuming the **Test.xlsx** file exists in the C:\Temp folder and has three worksheets, the message in Figure 8.4 will be displayed.

As I mentioned earlier, you will get an error if you try to open a workbook that doesn't exist (at least not in the path specified), and you will also get an error if you try to close a workbook that isn't currently open. The following sub shows how to avoid the latter error. It uses the On Error Resume Next statement to turn on error checking but to ignore any errors encountered. (This statement is covered in more detail in Chapter 12.) However, if an error is encountered, the built-in Err object captures details about the error, including the Number property. This property is nonzero if there is an error, and it is zero if there is no error. So if the workbook to be closed isn't open, this code provides a nice message to this effect—not a nasty error message.

Figure 8.4 Information About Opened File

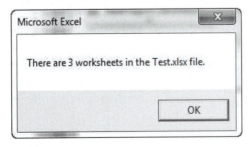

```
Sub Workbooks1a()
    ' This sub illustrates a way you can avoid an error when you
    ' try to close a workbook that might not be open.

    On Error Resume Next
    Workbooks("Test.xlsx").Close
    If Err.Number <> 0 Then _
        MsgBox "The Test.xlsx workbook can't be closed. It isn't open."
End Sub
```

It is slightly more difficult to provide an error check for opening a workbook that might not exist. A method for doing this is presented in Chapter 13.

EXAMPLE 8.2   Saving a Workbook

The Workbooks2 sub illustrates how to save an open workbook. This requires either the Save method or the SaveAs method, both of which mimic the similar operations in Excel. The Save method requires no arguments—it simply saves the file under its current name—whereas the SaveAs method typically has arguments that specify how to perform the save. There are quite a few optional arguments for the SaveAs method. The code below illustrates two of the more common arguments: Filename (the name and path of the file) and FileFormat (the type of format, such as the .xls or .xlsx format, to save the file as). The type for .xls format is xlWorkbookNormal; for .xlsx format, it is xlOpenXMLWorkbook; and for .xlsm, it is xlOpenXMLWorkbookMacroEnabled. You can look up other arguments in online help.

```
Sub Workbooks2()
    ' This sub shows how to save an open workbook. It mimics the familiar
    ' Save and SaveAs menu items.
    With ActiveWorkbook
        ' This saves the active workbook under the same name, no questions asked.
        .Save

        ' The SaveAs method requires as arguments information you would
        ' normally fill out in the SaveAs dialog box.
        .SaveAs Filename:="C:\Temp\Test", _
            FileFormat:=xlOpenXMLWorkbookMacroEnabled

        ' Check the name of the active workbook now.
        MsgBox "The name of the active workbook is " & .Name
    End With
End Sub
```

If you run this sub from the **Workbooks.xlsm** file, the SaveAs method will save a copy of this file in the C:\Temp folder as **Test.xlsm** and the message in Figure 8.5 will be displayed.

Figure 8.5 Confirmation of Saved Name

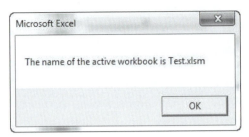

EXAMPLE 8.3   Locating the Path of a Workbook

When you open a workbook in Excel through the usual interface, you often need to search through folders to find the file you want to open. This example illustrates how the path to a file can be specified in VBA. Suppose, as in Exercise 8.1, that you are writing a sub in one workbook that opens another workbook. Also, suppose that both of these workbooks are in the *same* folder on your hard drive. Then you can use ThisWorkbook.Path to specify the path of the workbook to be opened. Remember that ThisWorkbook always refers to the workbook containing the VBA code. It then uses the Path property to specify the path to this workbook. For example, if the workbook containing the code is in the folder C:\VBA Examples\Chapter 8, then ThisWorkbook.Path returns the string "C:\VBA Examples\Chapter 8". If another file in this same folder has file name **Test.xlsx**, then you can refer to it with the concatenated string

```
ThisWorkbook.Path  &  "\Test.xlsx"
```

Note that the second part of this string starts with a backslash. The Path property does *not* end with a backslash, so the backslash required for separating the folder from the filename must begin the literal part of the string.

The Workbooks3 sub illustrates the entire procedure. It assumes that another file named **Customer1.xlsx** exists in the same folder as the one in which the workbook containing the VBA resides.

```
Sub Workbooks3()
    ' This sub assumes a file named Customer1.xlsx exists in the
    ' same folder as the file containing this code. Otherwise,
    ' an error message will be displayed.
    Workbooks.Open ThisWorkbook.Path & "\Customer1.xlsx"
    MsgBox "The Customer1.xlsx file is now open.", vbInformation

    Workbooks("Customer1.xlsx").Close
    MsgBox "The Customer1.xlsx file is now closed.", vbInformation
End Sub
```

EXAMPLE 8.4   Checking Properties of a Workbook

The Workbooks4 sub illustrates a few properties you can check for an open workbook. These include its name, its file format, whether it is password-protected, whether it is an add-in, its path, whether it is read only, and whether it has been changed since the last time it was saved. Most of these properties will find limited use, but it nice to know that they are available.

```
Sub Workbooks4()
    ' This sub shows some properties you can obtain from an open workbook.
    With ActiveWorkbook
        ' Display the file's name.
        MsgBox "The active workbook is named " & .Name

        ' Check the file format (.xlsx, .xlsm, .csv, .xla, and many others).
        ' Actually, this will display an obscure number, such as 52 for .xlsm.
        ' You have to search online help to decipher the number.
        MsgBox "The file format is " & .FileFormat

        ' Check whether the file is password protected.
        MsgBox "Is the file password protected? " & .HasPassword

        ' Check whether the file is an add-in, with an .xla extension.
        MsgBox "Is the file an add-in? " & .IsAddin

        ' Check the file's path.
        MsgBox "The path to the file is " & .Path

        ' Check whether the file is ReadOnly.
        MsgBox "Is the file read only? " & .ReadOnly

        ' Check whether the file has been saved since the last change.
        MsgBox "Has the file been changed since the last save? " & .Saved
    End With
End Sub
```

8.5 Examples of Worksheets in VBA

This section presents several examples to illustrate typical operations with worksheets. Each example is included in the file **Worksheets.xlsm**. It contains an AllStates worksheet (with code name wsAllStates) that lists states in column A where a company has offices, as shown in Figure 8.6. Then for each state in the list, there is a sheet for that state that shows where the company's headquarters are located, how many branch offices it has, and what its sales in the current year were. For example, there is a sheet named Texas, and it contains the information in Figure 8.7. (Actually, the year listed in Figure 8.7 is dynamic; it is the year when you open the file. See the formula in cell A3.)

Figure 8.6 State List

	A	B	C
1	States where the company has offices		
2	Michigan		
3	Illinois		
4	Ohio		
5	Massachusetts		
6	California		
7	Minnesota		
8	New York		
9	Indiana		
10	Pennsylvania		
11	Texas		

Figure 8.7 Information for a Typical State

	A	B
1	Headquarters	Dallas
2	Branch offices	4
3	Sales in 2014	$17,500

EXAMPLE 8.5   Displaying Information on All States

The Worksheets1 sub loops through all sheets other than the AllStates sheet and displays information about each state in a separate message box. A typical state's worksheet is referred to as ws, although any other generic variable name could be used. The loop excludes the AllStates worksheet by using an If statement to check whether the worksheet's code name is not wsAllStates. If this condition is true—the worksheet's code name is not wsAllStates—the message is displayed. (Again, remember that <> means "not equal to.")

```
Sub Worksheets1()
    Dim ws As Worksheet

    ' Go through each state and display info for that state.
    For Each ws In ActiveWorkbook.Worksheets
        With ws
            If .CodeName <> "wsAllStates" Then
                MsgBox "The headquarters of " & .Name & " is " _
                    & .Range("B1").Value & ", there are " _
                    & .Range("B2").Value & " branch " _
                    & "offices, and sales in " & Year(Date) & " were " _
                    & Format(.Range("B3").Value, "$#,##0") & ".", _
                    vbInformation, .Name & " info"
            End If
        End With
    Next
End Sub
```

Figure 8.8 Information About a Typical State

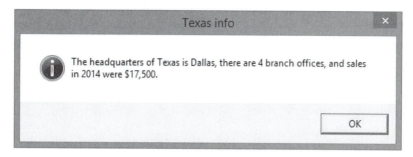

If you run this sub, you will see a message such as the one in Figure 8.8 for each state.

EXAMPLE 8.6   Displaying States and Headquarters

The Worksheets2 sub is similar to the Worksheets1 sub. It lists all states in the workbook and their headquarters in a *single* message box, with each state on a different line. The new line is accomplished with the built-in constant vbCrLf (short for carriage return and line feed, from ancient typewriters). Another built-in constant vbTab is used to indent. Note how string concatenation is used to build the long message variable.

```
Sub Worksheets2()
    ' This sub just lists all of the states and their headquarters.

    Dim ws As Worksheet
    Dim message As String

    message = "The states and their headquarters in this workbook are:"

    ' Note the built-in vbCrLf constant. It codes in a line break.
    For Each ws In ActiveWorkbook.Worksheets
        With ws
            If .CodeName <> "wsAllStates" Then _
                message = message & vbCrLf & .Name & ": " & .Range("B1")
        End With
    Next

    MsgBox message, vbInformation, "State info"
End Sub
```

When you run this sub, the message in Figure 8.9 is displayed.

Figure 8.9 State and Headquarters Information

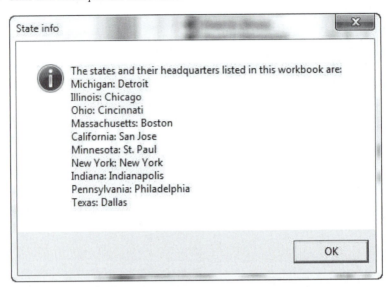

─────────

EXAMPLE 8.7   Adding a New State

The Worksheets3 sub allows a new state to be added. It first asks the user to specify a new state not already in the list and then asks the user for information about this new state. The sub then copies an existing state's sheet to create a new sheet (essentially a template), it names the new sheet appropriately, and puts its information in cells B2, B3, and B4. Note how the Do loop is used to keep asking the user for a new state until one not already on the current list is provided.

```
Sub Worksheets3()
    ' This sub asks the user for a new state and its information,
    ' then creates a new sheet for the new state.

    Dim isNew As Boolean
    Dim newState As String
    Dim headquarters As String
    Dim nBranches As Integer
    Dim sales As Currency
    Dim ws As Worksheet
    Dim wsNew As Worksheet

    ' Keep asking for a new state until the user provides one that is new.
    Do
        newState = InputBox("Enter a new state.", "New state")
        isNew = True
        For Each ws In ActiveWorkbook.Worksheets
            If newState = ws.Name Then
                MsgBox "This state already has a worksheet. " _
                    & "Enter another state.", vbExclamation
                isNew = False
                Exit For
```

```
            End If
        Next
    Loop Until isNew

    ' Get the required information for the new state. There is
    ' no error checking here. It probably should be added to
    ' check for improper inputs.
    headquarters = InputBox("Enter the headquarters of " & newState)
    nBranches = InputBox("Enter the number branch offices in " & newState, _
        "Branch offices")
    sales = InputBox("Enter sales in " & Year(Date) & " in " & newState)

    ' Add the name of the new state to the list in the AllStates sheet.
    wsAllStates.Range("A1").End(xlDown).Offset(1, 0).Value = newState

    ' Copy the second sheet (or any other state's sheet) to obtain a new
    ' sheet, which becomes the active sheet. Then change its name and info.
    Worksheets(2).Copy after:=Worksheets(Worksheets.Count)
    With ActiveSheet
        .Name = newState
        .Range("B1").Value = headquarters
        .Range("B2").Value = nBranches
        .Range("B3").Value = sales
    End With
End Sub
```

Examine the line

```
wsAllStates.Range("A1").End(xlDown).Offset(1, 0).Value = newState
```

Starting in cell A1, this line uses .End(xlDown) to go to the bottom of the current list. Then it uses .Offset(1,0) to go one more row down. This is the first blank cell, where the name of the new state is placed.

Note also the line

```
Worksheets(2).Copy after:=Worksheets(Worksheets.Count)
```

This line makes a copy of the second sheet, the one used as a template, and it places the copy after the worksheet referred to as Worksheets(Worksheets.Count). To see the effect of this, assume there are currently eight worksheets. Then Worksheets.Count is 8, so the copy is placed after Worksheets(8). This means it is placed just after (to right of) all existing worksheets. This provides the rare example where it *is* useful to refer to a worksheet by number rather than by name.

EXAMPLE 8.8   Sorting Worksheets

The Worksheets4 sub illustrates how to sort the worksheets for the individual states in alphabetical order. The trick is to use VBA's Sort method to sort the states in column A of the AllStates sheet. It then uses the Move method of a worksheet, with the After argument, to move the sheets around according to the sorted list in the AllStates sheet.

```vba
Sub Worksheets4()
    ' This sub puts the state sheets (not including the AllStates sheet)
    ' in alphabetical order. It first sorts the states in the AllStates
    ' sheet, then uses this order.

    Dim shtName1 As String
    Dim shtName2 As String
    Dim cell As Range

    ' Sort the states in the AllStates sheet.
    With wsAllStates
        .Range("A1").Sort Key1:=.Range("A1"), Order1:=xlAscending, _
            Header:=xlYes
        With .Range("A1")
            Range(.Offset(1, 0), .End(xlDown)).Name = "States"
        End With
    End With

    ' Rearrange the order of the other sheets according to the sorted
    ' list in the AllStates sheet. shtName1 is always the name of the
    ' "current" sheet, whereas shtName2 is always the name of the next
    ' sheet in alphabetical order.
    shtName1 = "AllStates"
    For Each cell In Range("States")
        shtName2 = cell.Value
        Worksheets(shtName2).Move after:=Worksheets(shtName1)
        shtName1 = shtName2
    Next

    With wsAllStates
        .Activate
        .Range("A1").Select
    End With
    MsgBox "State sheets are now in alphabetical order."
End Sub
```

Pay very close attention to how the For Each loop works because it is typical of the way programmers learn to think. The worksheet that shtName1 refers to is initially the AllStates worksheet. After that, shtName1 always refers to the current worksheet in alphabetical order, and shtName2 refers to the *next* worksheet in alphabetical order, which is moved to the right of shtName1. After the move, the value of the variable shtName1 is replaced by the value of shtName2 to get ready for the *next* move. This logic is a bit tricky, especially if you are new to programming. To understand it better, try the following. Open the **Worksheets.xlsm** file, get into the VBE, and create watches for the shtName1 and shtName2 variables. (You do this with the **Debug → Add Watch** menu item.) Then put your cursor anywhere inside the Worksheets4 sub and step through the program one line at a time by repeatedly pressing the F8 key. Once you get toward the bottom of the sub, you can see in the Watch window how the values of shtName1 and shtName2 keep changing.

8.6 Examples of Charts in VBA

The Chart object is one of the trickiest Excel objects to manipulate with VBA. The reason is that a chart has so many objects associated with it, and each has a large number of properties and methods. If you need to create charts in VBA, it is probably best to record most of the code and then modify the recorded code as necessary, making frequent visits to online help. Alternatively, you can use the Excel's chart tools to create the chart, and then use VBA only to modify the existing chart in some way.

Another reason for the difficulty is that Microsoft keeps changing the rules. As you are almost certainly aware, both the Excel tools for manipulating charts and the look of the charts themselves have changed in each new version of Excel: from 2003 to 2007, from 2007 to 2010, and from 2010 to 2013. The VBA code, including recorded code, hasn't changed as much, but it has changed. Specifically, if you are using the recorder to learn VBA code for creating or manipulating charts in one version of Excel, you might generate some code that will *not* work in previous versions.[3] For example, if you insert a line chart with the recorder on in Excel 2013, you will generate a line something like the following:

```
ActiveSheet.Shapes.AddChart2(332, xlLineMarkers).Select
```

When I did this, I was surprised at the AddChart2 method, which I'd never seen before. I looked it up in online help, and I learned that it was added to the object model in Excel 2013. So not only do you need to learn something new, but if you use this method to create a chart, your code won't work in previous versions of Excel!

This state of affairs presents obvious difficulties for programmers, but there is no option except to learn as much as possible through recording and online help, and to be careful that you program for your intended users. For example, if your intended users are still using Excel 2007 or 2010, you should avoid using code, like the AddChart2 method, that won't work in those versions.

The following four examples indicate some of the possibilities. They are based on the file **Modifying Charts.xlsm**. This file has monthly sales for several products; a portion is shown in Figure 8.10. I first used Excel 2013's chart tools manually (no VBA) to create a line chart on the same sheet as the data. This chart shows the monthly time series movement of two of the products, as illustrated in Figure 8.11. VBA could be used to create this chart from scratch, as I will illustrate shortly, but it is easier to use VBA to modify an existing chart.

Location of a Chart

The first issue is the location of the chart. As you probably know, a chart can be placed on a separate **chart sheet** (a special type of sheet reserved only for charts, with no rows and columns), or it can be embedded in a worksheet. The choice is

---

[3] Actually, as mentioned in Chapter 4, if you are recording in Excel 2007, you might not get any recorded code at all.

Figure 8.10 Monthly Product Sales Data

	A	B	C	D	E	F	G	H
1	Month	Product1	Product2	Product3	Product4	Product5	Product6	Product7
2	Jan-13	791	613	450	434	488	400	559
3	Feb-13	781	649	646	548	442	652	423
4	Mar-13	520	631	488	622	513	545	726
5	Apr-13	635	615	568	709	686	461	629
6	May-13	418	463	433	523	548	655	420
7	Jun-13	431	504	580	540	767	487	631
8	Jul-13	786	534	490	408	653	704	708
9	Aug-13	695	734	618	564	620	453	553
10	Sep-13	547	671	699	721	657	448	760

Figure 8.11 Sales Chart of Two Selected Products

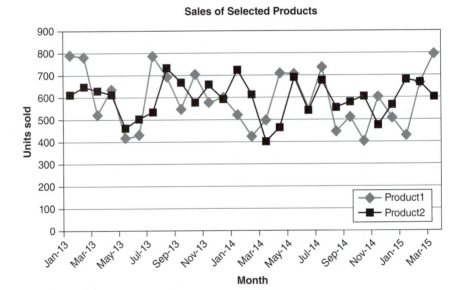

usually a matter of taste. (If you are using Excel's tools, you make this choice in the Design ribbon under the Chart Tools group.) In the first case, assuming the name of the chart sheet is SalesChart, you would refer to it in VBA as Charts ("SalesChart"). Here, Charts is the collection of all chart sheets, and it is followed by the name of the particular chart sheet. Alternatively, if you give it a code name such as chtSales, you can refer directly to the code name.

In the second case, assuming this chart has been named Sales and the code name of the worksheet is wsSales, you must first refer to the object "containing" the chart.[4] This container is called a ChartObject object. The Chart object itself is

---

[4]You can change the name of the chart by selecting the chart and entering a name in the Name box to the left of the Formula bar.

then one step down the hierarchy from the ChartObject object, and you can refer to it in code as wsSales.ChartObjects("Sales").Chart. Admittedly, it is confusing and probably sounds like double-talk, but just think of a ChartObject object as floating above a worksheet's cells. This object's only purpose is to hold a Chart object. You can resize and move the ChartObject containers, and then you can manipulate the properties of the underlying chart, such as its axes and its legend. Finally, just to make sure the point is clear, remember that the ChartObject object is relevant only for charts placed on a worksheet. It is not relevant for chart sheets.

EXAMPLE 8.9   Displaying Properties of a Chart

The Charts1 sub works with the Sales chart in the Sales worksheet of the **Modifying Charts.xlsm** file. Remember that the chart itself was *not* created with VBA. The VBA below simply displays properties of the chart that already exists. It first refers to the ChartObject container and displays its Left, Top, Height, and Width properties. These are properties of many objects in Excel that can be moved and resized, and they are always measured in points, where a **point** is 1/72 of an inch. Top is the distance from the top of the container to the top of row 1, Left is the distance from the left of the container to the left of column A, and Height and Width are the height and width of the container.

The Charts1 code indicates the hierarchy in charts. At the top is the ChartObject object. Below it is the Chart object. Below it are a number of objects: the two Axis objects (xlCategory for the horizontal axis, xlValue for the vertical axis), a Series object for each series plotted, a SeriesCollection object for the collection of all series plotted, a Legend object, and others. Of course, all of these have plenty of properties and a few methods. The Charts1 sub indicates only a few of them.

When working with charts in VBA, I find it very useful to Set object variables for the various objects down the hierarchy, in this case chtObj, cht, ser, axH and axV. As I have learned from many frustrating sessions, this has two benefits. First, it makes the code more readable. Second and perhaps more important, it guarantees Intellisense. In this example, if you type cht.Axes(xlValue) and then a period, you won't get any Intellisense to help with Axis objects. However, if you Set an Axis object, such as axH, you *will* get Intellisense when you type axH followed by a period. With so many confusing properties for objects in charts, this Intellisense help is invaluable.

When you run this sub, you will get some strange results, due to built-in Excel constants. For example, the ChartType property in this example returns 65, the index for a line chart of the type shown. Fortunately, you never have to learn these numbers. When you want to set the chart type, you can type cht.ChartType and then a period, and Intellisense will give you a list of all the built-in constant names. In this case, 65 is equivalent to xlLineMarkers. (In more technical terms, when you *read* a property, as has been done here, you will see a number that makes no sense. But when you *write* a property, you can refer to it by its meaningful name.)

```
Sub Charts1()
    ' This sub illustrates some of the properties of a chart. The chart already
    ' exists (was built with Excel's chart tools) on the Sales sheet.
    Dim message As String
    Dim chtObj As ChartObject
    Dim cht As Chart
    Dim ser As Series, serCount As Integer
    Dim axH As Axis, axV As Axis

    Set chtObj = wsSales.ChartObjects("Sales")
    Set cht = chtObj.Chart
    Set axH = cht.Axes(xlCategory)
    Set axV = cht.Axes(xlValue)

    message = "Here are some properties of the chartobject." & vbCrLf
    With chtObj
        message = message & vbCrLf & "Left: " & .Left
        message = message & vbCrLf & "Top: " & .Top
        message = message & vbCrLf & "Height: " & .Height
        message = message & vbCrLf & "Width property: " & .Width
        message = message & vbCrLf & "Name: " & .Name
    End With
    MsgBox message, vbInformation

    message = "Here are some properties of the chart." & vbCrLf
    With cht
        message = message & vbCrLf & "ChartType: " & .ChartType
        message = message & vbCrLf & "HasLegend: " & .HasLegend
        message = message & vbCrLf & "HasTitle: " & .HasTitle
        If .HasTitle Then _
            message = message & vbCrLf & "Title: " & .ChartTitle.Text
        message = message & vbCrLf & "Number of series plotted: " _
            & .SeriesCollection.Count
    End With
    MsgBox message, vbInformation

    message = "Here are some properties of the series in the chart." & vbCrLf
    For Each ser In cht.SeriesCollection
        serCount = serCount + 1
        With ser
            message = message & vbCrLf & "Name of series " _
                & serCount & ": " & .Name
            message = message & vbCrLf & "MarkerSize for series " _
                & serCount & ": " & .MarkerSize
            message = message & vbCrLf & "MarkerBackgroundColor for series " _
                & serCount & ": " & .MarkerBackgroundColor
            message = message & vbCrLf & "MarkerForegroundColor for series " _
                & serCount & ": " & .MarkerForegroundColor
            message = message & vbCrLf & "MarkerStyle for series " _
                & serCount & ": " & .MarkerStyle
            message = message & vbCrLf
        End With
    Next
    MsgBox message

    message = "Some properties of the horizontal axis:" & vbCrLf
    With axH
        message = message & vbCrLf & "Format of tick labels: " _
```

```
                  & .TickLabels.NumberFormat
        If .HasTitle Then
            message = message & vbCrLf & "Title: " & .AxisTitle.Text
            message = message & vbCrLf & "Font size of title: " _
                  & .AxisTitle.Font.Size
        Else
            message = message & vbCrLf & "Horizontal axis has no title."
        End If
    End With
    MsgBox message

    message = "Some properties of the vertical axis:" & vbCrLf
    With axV
        If .HasTitle Then
            message = message & vbCrLf & "Title: " & .AxisTitle.Text
            message = message & vbCrLf & "Font size of title: " _
                  & .AxisTitle.Font.Size
        Else
            message = message & vbCrLf & "Vertical axis has no title."
        End If
        message = message & vbCrLf & "Minimum scale: " & .MinimumScale
        message = message & vbCrLf & "Maximum scale: " & .MaximumScale
    End With
    MsgBox message
End Sub
```

EXAMPLE 8.10   Changing Properties of a Chart

The previous sub simply *displays* the current values of various chart properties. The Charts2 sub *modifies* the chart. Specifically, it allows the user to choose which two products (out of the seven available) to plot. It uses the SeriesCollection object, which is one step down the hierarchy from the Chart object. In general, a chart plots a number of Series objects, labeled SeriesCollection(1), SeriesCollection(2), and so on. The properties of each series can be changed, as described in the comments in the sub, to plot different data. Specifically, the Values property designates the data range for the series (a Range object), the XValues property designates the range for the values on the horizontal axis (another Range object), and the Name property is a descriptive name for the series that is used in the legend. Note that the data ranges in the Sales sheet have already been range-named Product1 through Product7. These range names are used in the sub. Also, note how the line

```
.Name = Range("Product" & productIndex1).Cells(1).Offset(-1, 0).Value
```

uses .Cells(1) to go to the first sales figure in a product range and then uses .Offset (−1,0) to go one row above to find the product's name, such as Product1.

```
Sub Charts2()
    ' This sub allows you to change the product columns (two of them)
    ' charted. It assumes the chart currently has two series plotted.
```

```
    Dim productIndex1 As Integer
    Dim productIndex2 As Integer
    Dim chtObj As ChartObject
    Dim cht As Chart
    Dim ser As Series

    MsgBox "You can choose any two of the products to plot versus time."
    productIndex1 = InputBox("Enter the index of the first " _
        & "product to plot (1 to 7)")
    productIndex2 = InputBox("Enter the index of the second product " _
        & "to plot (1 to 7, not " & productIndex1 & ")")

    ' Note that the columns of data already have range names
    ' Product1, Product2, etc.
    Set chtObj = wsSales.ChartObjects("Sales")
    Set cht = chtObj.Chart

With cht
    Set ser = .SeriesCollection(1)
    With ser
        ' The Values property indicates the range of the data
        ' being plotted. The XValues property indicates the values
        ' on the X-axis (in this case, the months). The Name property
        ' is the name of the series (which is shown in the legend).
        ' This name is found in row 1, right above the first cell in
        ' the corresponding Product range.
        .Values = Range("Product" & productIndex1)
        .XValues = Range("Month")
        .Name = Range("Product" & productIndex1) _
            .Cells(1).Offset(-1, 0).Value
    End With

    ' The XValues property doesn't have to be set again, since
    ' both series use the same values on the horizontal axis.
    Set ser = .SeriesCollection(2)
    With .SeriesCollection(2)
        .Values = Range("Product" & productIndex2)
        .Name = Range("Product" & productIndex2) _
            .Cells(1).Offset(-1, 0).Value
    End With
    End With
    End With
End Sub
```

EXAMPLE 8.11   More Properties and Methods of Charts

The Charts3 sub indicates some further possibilities when working with charts. Try running it to see the effects on the chart. I got the part about the plot area and grid lines from recording. However, something strange occurs. If you run this sub by clicking the Run Charts3 button on the worksheet, the plot area and grid lines do *not* change as they should. However, if you step through the code in the VBE, they *do* change. This same behavior occurred in Excel 2010 (as mentioned in the previous edition of the book), and it still occurs in Excel 2013. I still don't know why, or how to fix it.

```
Sub Charts3()
    ' This sub shows some other things you can do to
    ' fine tune charts. In general, you learn some of the
    ' coding from recording, some from the Object Browser.

    Dim red1 As Integer, green1 As Integer, blue1 As Integer
    Dim red2 As Integer, green2 As Integer, blue2 As Integer
    Dim chtObj As ChartObject
    Dim cht As Chart
    Dim ser As Series
    Dim ax As Axis

    ' Use this next statement so that the random colors chosen
    ' later on will be different from run to run.
    Randomize

    Set chtObj = wsSales.ChartObjects("Sales")
    Set cht = chtObj.Chart

    With cht
        ' Change properties of plot area.
        With .PlotArea.Format.Fill
            MsgBox "The plot area will be changed from blank to gray."
            .ForeColor.ObjectThemeColor = msoThemeColorBackground1
            .ForeColor.Brightness = -0.150000006
            .Visible = msoTrue
        End With

        MsgBox "It will now be restored to blank."
        .PlotArea.Format.Fill.Visible = msoFalse

        ' Remove and restore grid lines.
        Set ax = .Axes(xlValue)
        With ax.MajorGridlines.Format.Line
            MsgBox "The horizontal grid lines will be deleted."
            .Visible = msoFalse

            MsgBox "They will now be restored."
            .Visible = msoTrue
        End With

        ' Generate two random colors (with no green in the first,
        ' no red in the second).
        MsgBox "The two series will now change to some random colors."
        red1 = Int(Rnd * 255)
        green1 = 0
        blue1 = Int(Rnd * 255)
        red2 = 0
        green2 = Int(Rnd * 255)
        blue2 = Int(Rnd * 255)

        ' Change some colors in the chart.
        Set ser = .SeriesCollection(1)
        With ser
            .Border.Color = RGB(red1, green1, blue1)
            .MarkerBackgroundColor = RGB(red1, green1, blue1)
            .MarkerForegroundColor = RGB(red1, green1, blue1)
        End With
        Set ser = .SeriesCollection(2)
```

```
        With ser
            .Border.Color = RGB(red2, green2, blue2)
            .MarkerBackgroundColor = RGB(red2, green2, blue2)
            .MarkerForegroundColor = RGB(red2, green2, blue2)
        End With
    End With
End Sub
```

EXAMPLE 8.12   Adding Multiple Series to the Chart

The Charts4 sub generalizes the Charts2 sub. It allows the user to choose which of the seven products to chart. It begins by clearing all series from the chart. Then for the first series chosen, it inserts the horizontal axis month labels. (This needs to be done only for the first series; the other series share the same months.) Then the user gets to choose which series to chart. Note that the Do loop forces the user to select at least one series to chart.

```
Sub Charts4()
    ' This sub generalizes Charts2 to allow any number of
    ' products to be charted.
    Dim i As Integer, nChosen As Integer
    Dim nProducts As Integer
    Dim chtObj As ChartObject
    Dim cht As Chart
    Dim ser As Series
    Dim serColl As SeriesCollection
    Dim isFirst As Boolean
    Dim dataRange As Range
    Dim monthRange As Range

    Set chtObj = wsSales.ChartObjects("Sales")
    Set cht = chtObj.Chart

    ' Count number of products.
    With wsSales.Range("A1")
        nProducts = Range(.Offset(0, 1), .End(xlToRight)).Columns.Count
    End With

    ' Clear all series from chart.
    For Each ser In cht.SeriesCollection
        ser.Delete
    Next

    ' Only need to set the date range for X axis for the first series.
    isFirst = True
    With wsSales.Range("A1")
        Set monthRange = Range(.Offset(1, 0), .End(xlDown))
    End With

    Do
        nChosen = 0
        For i = 1 To nProducts
            If MsgBox("Do you want to plot product " & i & "?", vbYesNo) = vbYes Then
                nChosen = nChosen + 1
                With wsSales.Range("A1")
```

```
                Set dataRange = Range(.Offset(1, i), .Offset(1, i).End(xlDown))
            End With
            Set serColl = cht.SeriesCollection
            Set ser = serColl.NewSeries
            With ser
                .Name = "Product" & i
                .Values = dataRange
                If isFirst Then
                    .XValues = monthRange
                    isFirst = False
                End If
            End With
        End If
    Next
    If nChosen = 0 Then _
        MsgBox "Try again. You must choose at least one product.", vbExclamation
    Loop Until nChosen >= 1
End Sub
```

EXAMPLE 8.13   Creating a Chart

This example is based on the file **Creating Charts.xlsm**. It starts with the data in
Figure 8.12 and nothing else—no existing charts. It illustrates how you can create
a chart from scratch with VBA, and it illustrates two other useful features of charts.
First, different series can have different chart types. Second, if two series of very different magnitudes are charted, they can have different vertical axes, one on the left
and one on the right. The axis on the right is then called a secondary axis. After
running the code in this file, the chart in Figure 8.13 is created.

There are two keys to the code for this example. The first is the line

```
Set chtObj = wsSales.ChartObjects.Add(l, t, w, h)
```

Figure 8.12 Data for Chart

	A	B	C
1	Month	Product1	Product2
2	Jan-13	791	613000
3	Feb-13	781	649000
4	Mar-13	520	631000
5	Apr-13	635	615000
6	May-13	418	463000
7	Jun-13	431	504000
8	Jul-13	786	534000
9	Aug-13	695	734000
10	Sep-13	547	671000
11	Oct-13	703	580000
12	Nov-13	579	658000
13	Dec-13	601	592000

Figure 8.13　Chart Created with VBA

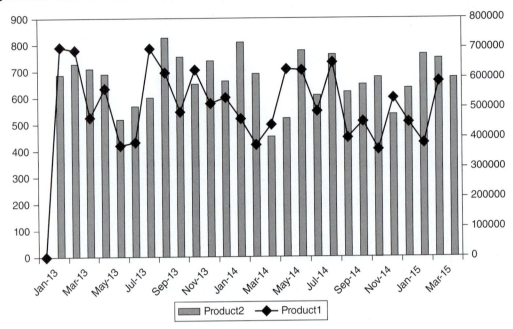

This line creates a new **ChartObject** object and stores it in the object variable chtObj.[5] This requires the left, top, width, and height arguments for positioning and sizing the chart. After this line executes, you will see an empty rectangle on the worksheet, but no chart. The rest of the code fills in the chart.

The second key is the following code:

```
Set serColl = .SeriesCollection
Set ser = serColl.NewSeries
```

The first line defines the object variable **serColl**, which ensures that you get Intellisense in the second line. The second line creates a new series and stores it in the object variable **ser**. From then on, when you type ser followed by a period, you get Intellisense on **Series** objects.

Here is the entire **CreateChart** sub:

```
Sub CreateChart()
    ' This sub creates a chart from scratch.
    Dim topCell As Range
    Dim chtObj As ChartObject
    Dim cht As Chart
```

---

[5] Remember from earlier in this section that you can use the **AddChart2** method in Excel 2013, but then your code wouldn't work in previous versions of Excel.

```
Dim serColl As SeriesCollection
Dim ser As Series

' Delete the old chart (if there is one).
On Error Resume Next
wsSales.ChartObjects("Sales").Delete

' The following (left, top, width, height) are for positioning and
' sizing a chart. They are used (always in this order) for positioning
' and sizing a lot of objects that "float above" the worksheet.
Dim l As Single, t As Single, w As Single, h As Single

Set topCell = wsSales.Range("A1")

' Start one column to the right of the data and in row 3.
l = topCell.End(xlToRight).Offset(0, 2).Left
t = Rows(3).Top
w = 500
h = 250

Set chtObj = wsSales.ChartObjects.Add(l, t, w, h)
With chtObj
    .Name = "Sales"
    Set cht = .Chart
End With

With cht
    .HasLegend = True
    Set serColl = .SeriesCollection
    Set ser = serColl.NewSeries
    With ser
        .Name = topCell.Offset(0, 1).Value
        .XValues = Range(topCell.Offset(1, 0), topCell.End(xlDown))
        .Values = Range(topCell.Offset(0, 1), topCell.Offset(0, 1).End(xlDown))
        ' Each series can have its own chart type.
        .ChartType = xlLineMarkers
    End With
    Set ser = serColl.NewSeries
    With ser
        .Name = topCell.Offset(0, 2).Value
        .Values = Range(topCell.Offset(0, 2), topCell.Offset(0, 2).End(xlDown))
        .ChartType = xlColumnClustered
        ' Use a secondary axis on the right for this series.
        .AxisGroup = xlSecondary
    End With
End With
End Sub
```

Speaking from extensive experience in getting chart code wrong in every conceivable way, I urge you to mimic the code in the above examples. By using object variables for chartobjects, charts, series, and so on, you avoid the frustration of typing a perfectly good reference, like cht.SeriesCollection(1) and then a period, and *not* getting Intellisense. I hope this will improve in future versions of Excel, but for now, object variables are definitely the way to go.

8.7   Summary

This chapter has built upon your knowledge of Range objects from Chapter 6. It is necessary to be able to manipulate workbooks, worksheets, and charts with VBA code in many applications, and this chapter has illustrated some of the most useful techniques for doing so. At this point, it is not important that you memorize all the properties and methods of these objects. It is more important that you have some feeling for what is *possible* and that you know how to find help when you need it. You can always revisit the examples in this chapter to search for key details, and you can always try the recorder or visit the Object Browser for online help.

EXERCISES

1. Suppose you have a lot of Excel files currently open. You would like to count the number of these files that contain a worksheet with the name Revenues. Write a sub that reports the result in a MsgBox.

2. Repeat the previous exercise, but now count the number of files that contain a worksheet with Revenue somewhere in the name. For example, this would include sheets with names "2005 Revenues" and "Revenues for Quarter 1".

3. Write a general purpose sub that opens a particular workbook, such as **C:\MyFiles\Company Data.xlsx**, adds a new worksheet named **Formula List** after the original worksheets, and then goes through all of the original worksheets hunting for cells with formulas. Each time it finds a formula, it enters information about it in a new row of the Formula List worksheet. Specifically, it records the worksheet's name in column A, it enters the formula as a string in column B, and it enters the formula's value in column C. (*Hint:* To check whether a cell contains a formula, use VBA's HasFormula property of a range.)

4. Write a sub that counts the number of worksheets in a particular (open) workbook and also counts the number of sheets. Note that the Worksheets collection includes only worksheets (those with rows and columns), whereas the Sheets collection contains worksheets *and* chart sheets. Then test your sub by creating a workbook with some worksheets and at least one chart sheet and running your sub on it.

5. The file **Chart Example.xlsx** contains two sheets. The first sheet is a worksheet that contains some data and four column charts based on the data. The second sheet is a chart sheet that is also based on the data. Write a sub that counts the number of ChartObject objects in the workbook and also counts the number of Chart objects in the workbook. The counts should be 4 and 5, respectively.

6. Open a new workbook and insert a module in this workbook. Then write a sub that does the following: (1) It opens some workbook that you know exists on your hard drive—you can choose which one; (2) it displays a message indicating the number of worksheets in this workbook; (3) it closes the workbook; and (4) it tries to open a workbook that you know does not exist on your hard drive. What happens when it tries to open this latter workbook?

7. Open a new workbook and save it under any name you like. Then write a sub that displays a message like: "The name of this workbook is _, and it was created by _." The underscores in this message should be filled in by appropriate properties of the ActiveWorkbook (or the Application) object. (*Hint*: Look up the BuiltinDocumentProperties property of a workbook. This provides one way to get the author's name, but this isn't the only way.)

8. Suppose you have a folder on your hard drive that contains a number of Excel files with the names **Customer1.xlsx**, **Customer2.xlsx**, and so on. You are not sure how many such files there are, but you know they are named this way, with consecutive integers. Write a sub to open each file, one at a time, save it under a new name, and then close it. The new names should be **CustomerOrders1.xlsx**, **CustomerOrders2.xlsx**, and so on.

9. Continuing the previous exercise, suppose you want to check whether the Customer files are "read only." Write a sub that counts the number of Customer files in the folder and the number of them that are read only and then displays this information in a message.

10. The file **Cities.xlsx** contains an AllCities sheet that lists all cities where a company has offices. Write a sub that does the following: (1) For each city in the list, it checks whether there is a worksheet with the name of that city in the workbook, and if there isn't one, it adds one; and (2) it deletes any city worksheet if the worksheet's name is not in the current AllCities list. The sub should be written so that it can be run at any time and will always respond with the current list of cities in the AllCities sheet. (*Note*: Your sub should also work if the AllCities list contains exactly one city or no cities.)

11. The Data worksheet in the file **Product Info.xlsx** lists information on various software packages a company sells. Each product has an associated category listed in column B. Write a sub that creates a worksheet for each category represented in the list, with the name of the worksheet being the category, such as Business. For each category worksheet, it should enter the product names and their prices in columns A and B, starting in row 4. Each category worksheet should have an appropriate label, such as "Products in the Business category", in cell A1; it should have labels "Product" and "Price" in cells A3 and B3; and the column width for its column A should be the same as the column width of column A in the Data worksheet. (Note that there are only three categories represented in the current data. However, the program should be written so that it works for any number of categories—and any number of products—that might be present.)

12. The Data worksheet in the file **Product Purchases.xlsx** has unit prices for all software packages a mail-order company sells. It also has an Invoice worksheet. Whenever the company takes an order from a customer, the order taker gets the customer's name, the date, and the quantity of each product the customer wants to purchase. These quantities are written in column C of the Data worksheet. The information in this worksheet is then used to create an invoice for the customer in the Invoice worksheet. The current Invoice worksheet is a "template" for a general invoice. You should write two subs, ClearOld and CreateInvoice, and attach them to the buttons at the top of the Data worksheet. They should do the following.

a.   The ClearOld sub should clear any quantities from a previous order from column C of the Data worksheet. It should also clear any old data from the Invoice worksheet from row 5 down.

b.   The CreateInvoice sub should be run right after the order taker has gotten the information from the customer and has entered quantities in column C of the Data worksheet. (When you test your macro, you should first enter some quantities in column C.) The sub should use input boxes to ask for the customer's name and the date, and it should use these to complete the labels in cells A1 and A2 of the Invoice worksheet. It should then transfer the relevant data about products (only those ordered) to the Invoice worksheet, it should calculate the prices for each product ordered (unit price times quantity ordered), and it should calculate the tax on the order (5% sales tax) and the total cost of the order, including tax, in column D, right below the prices of individual products, with appropriate labels in column C (such as "5% sales tax" and "Total Cost").

c.   As a finishing touch, add some code to the CreateInvoice sub to *print* the finished invoice. (Although the chapter didn't discuss printing, you should be able to discover how to do it, either by using the recorder or by looking it up in online help.)

13. The file **Sales Chart Finished.xlsm** has monthly data on two products, a corresponding chart and four buttons. The ranges of the product data in columns B and C are range-named Product1 and Product2. To understand what you are supposed to do, open this file and click the buttons. It should be clear what's going on. However, the code behind the buttons is password-protected. Your job is to create similar code yourself in the file **Sales Chart.xlsx**. This file has the same chart and same buttons, but there is no code yet (which means that the buttons aren't attached to any macros). This code is tricky, and you will probably have to look through the code in the examples a few times, as well as online help, to get everything working correctly. (I did!)

9 Arrays

9.1 Introduction

Chapter 7 emphasized the benefits of loops for performing repeated tasks. Loops are often accompanied by the topic of this chapter, arrays. Arrays are lists, where each element in the list is an indexed element of the array. For example, suppose you need to capture the names and salaries of your employees, which are currently listed in columns A and B of a worksheet. Later on in the program, you plan to analyze them in some way. You might use a loop to go through each employee in the worksheet, but how do you can store the employee information in memory for later processing? The answer is that you can store it in employee and salary arrays. The name and salary of employee 1 are stored in employee(1) and salary(1), those for employee 2 are stored in employee(2) and salary(2), and so on.

A useful analogy is to the small mailboxes you see at a post office. An array is analogous to a group of mailboxes, numbered 1, 2, and so on. You can put something into a particular mailbox—that is, into an array element—in a statement such as

```
employee(5) = "Bob Jones"
```

Similarly, you can read the contents of a particular mailbox with a statement such as

```
MsgBox "The fifth employee is " & employee(5)
```

In other words, array elements work just like normal variables, except that they are indexed. This indexing makes them particularly suitable for looping, as this chapter illustrates.

9.2 Exercise

The following exercise is typical in its use of arrays. Although there are certainly ways to do the exercise *without* arrays, they make the job much easier. Actually, this exercise is simpler than the examples discussed later in this chapter, but you should still study the examples before attempting it.

Exercise 9.1   Aggregating Sales Data

Consider a large appliance/electronics store with a number of salespeople. The company keeps a spreadsheet listing the names of the salespeople and the dollar amounts of individual sales transactions. This information is in the file **Transactions.xlsx**, as illustrated in Figure 9.1 (with many hidden rows). Periodically, salespeople are hired and fired. The list in column A is always the most current list, and it is always shown in alphabetical order. Column B lists the corresponding Social Security numbers. The sales data in columns D to F are sorted by date. Also, some of these sales are for salespeople who are no longer with the company. That is, some of the Social Security numbers in column D have no corresponding values in column B.

The purpose of the exercise is to write a program to fill columns H and I with aggregate dollar amounts for each salesperson currently employed. You can open the file **Transactions Finished.xlsm** and click its button to see the results, which should appear as in Figure 9.2. However, do not look at the VBA code until you have tried writing the program yourself. Make sure you think through a solution method before you begin programming. Most important, think about what arrays you will need and how they will be used.

Figure 9.1 Salespeople and Transaction Data

	A	B	C	D	E	F	G	H	I
1	Data on sales people			Individual sales				Aggregated sales	
2	Name	SS#		Salesperson SS#	Date	Dollar amount		Salesperson	Dollar amount
3	Adams	776-61-4492		640-34-5749	1-Mar-15	$323			
4	Barnes	640-34-5749		365-99-1247	1-Mar-15	$260			
5	Cummings	115-12-5882		365-99-1247	1-Mar-15	$305			
6	Davis	736-95-5401		932-62-4204	1-Mar-15	$366			
7	Edwards	880-52-9379		986-38-6372	1-Mar-15	$217			
8	Falks	348-79-3515		449-44-7141	1-Mar-15	$294			
9	Gregory	546-44-7576		640-34-5749	1-Mar-15	$289			
10	Highsmith	467-86-5786		769-79-9580	1-Mar-15	$460			
11	Invery	765-85-7850		932-62-4204	1-Mar-15	$567			
12	Jacobs	986-38-6372		449-44-7141	1-Mar-15	$970			
13	Ketchings	769-79-9580		919-58-6925	1-Mar-15	$426			
14	Leonard	468-38-8871		115-12-5882	1-Mar-15	$214			
15	Moore	919-58-6925		546-44-7576	1-Mar-15	$306			
16	Nixon	126-27-9832		467-86-5786	1-Mar-15	$258			
17	Price	631-55-5579		546-44-7576	1-Mar-15	$287			
18	Reynolds	529-61-3561		765-85-7850	2-Mar-15	$183			
19	Stimson	474-60-8847		640-34-5749	2-Mar-15	$196			
20	Travis	449-44-7141		365-99-1247	2-Mar-15	$322			
21	Vexley	539-55-4012		640-34-5749	3-Mar-15	$180			
22	Wheaton	833-44-9683		474-60-8847	3-Mar-15	$205			
23	Zimmerman	932-62-4204		126-96-8510	3-Mar-15	$286			
24				126-96-8510	3-Mar-15	$264			
781				348-79-3515	23-Jul-15	$333			
782				932-62-4204	23-Jul-15	$167			
783				952-12-3694	24-Jul-15	$253			
784				776-61-4492	24-Jul-15	$211			
785				952-12-3694	24-Jul-15	$56			

Figure 9.2 Results

	H	I	J	K
1	**Aggregated sales**			
2	Salesperson	Dollar amount	First sale	Last sale
3	Adams	$12,429	3/4/2015	7/24/2015
4	Barnes	$11,308	3/1/2015	7/1/2015
5	Cummings	$8,117	3/1/2015	7/20/2015
6	Davis	$9,831	3/7/2015	7/22/2015
7	Edwards	$7,602	3/6/2015	7/16/2015
8	Falks	$9,223	3/4/2015	7/23/2015
9	Gregory	$7,112	3/1/2015	7/18/2015
10	Highsmith	$7,234	3/1/2015	7/14/2015
11	Invery	$9,436	3/2/2015	7/17/2015
12	Jacobs	$12,012	3/1/2015	7/21/2015
13	Ketchings	$10,935	3/1/2015	7/23/2015
14	Leonard	$8,765	3/7/2015	7/17/2015
15	Moore	$8,551	3/1/2015	7/22/2015
16	Nixon	$11,374	3/4/2015	7/20/2015
17	Price	$8,055	3/5/2015	7/6/2015
18	Reynolds	$9,246	3/10/2015	7/19/2015
19	Stimson	$10,161	3/3/2015	7/15/2015
20	Travis	$8,202	3/1/2015	7/6/2015
21	Vexley	$8,594	3/7/2015	7/22/2015
22	Wheaton	$9,030	3/14/2015	7/17/2015
23	Zimmerman	$10,224	3/1/2015	7/23/2015

9.3 The Need for Arrays

Many beginning programmers think that arrays are difficult to master, and they react by arguing that arrays are not worth the trouble. They are wrong on both counts. First, arrays are not that difficult. If you keep the mailbox analogy in mind, you should catch on to arrays quite easily. Second, arrays are definitely not just a luxury for computer programmers; they are absolutely necessary for dealing with lists. Consider a slightly different version of the employee salary example from the introduction. Now suppose you would like to go through the list of employees in columns A and B (again inside a loop) and keep track of the names and salaries of all employees who make a salary greater than $50,000. Later on, you might want to analyze these employees in some way, such as finding their average salary.

The easiest way to proceed is to go through the employee list with a counter initially equal to 0. Each time you encounter a salary greater than $50,000, you add 1 to the counter and store the employee's name and salary in hiPaidEmp and hiSalary arrays. Here is how the code might look (assuming the employees start in row 2 and the number of employees in the data set is known to be nEmployees).

```
counter = 0
With Range("A1")
    For i = 1 To nEmployees
        If .Offset(i, 1).Value > 50000 Then
            counter = counter + 1
            hiPaidEmp(counter) = .Offset(i, 0).Value
            hiSalary(counter) = .Offset(i, 1).Value
        End If
    Next
End With
```

After this loop is completed, you will know the number of highly paid employees—it is the final value of counter. More important, you will know the identities and salaries of these employees. The information for the first highly paid employee is stored in hiPaidEmp(1) and hiSalary(1), the information for the second is stored in hiPaidEmp(2) and hiSalary(2), and so on. You are now free to analyze the data in these newly created lists in any way you like.

Admittedly, there is a nonarray solution to this example. Each time you find a highly paid employee, you could immediately transfer the information on this employee to another section of the worksheet (columns D and E, say) rather than storing it in arrays.[1] Then you could analyze the data in columns D and E later. In other words, there is usually a way around using arrays—especially if you are working in Excel, where you can store information in cells of a worksheet. However, most programmers agree that arrays represent the best method for working with lists, not only in VBA but in all other programming languages. They offer power and flexibility that simply cannot be achieved without them.

9.4 Rules for Working with Arrays

When you declare a variable with a Dim statement, VBA knows from the variable's type how much memory to set aside for it. The situation is slightly different for arrays. Now, VBA must know how *many* elements are in the array, as well as their variable type, so that it can set aside the right amount of memory for the entire array. Therefore, when you declare an array, you must indicate to VBA that you are declaring an *array* of a certain type, not just a single variable. You must also tell VBA how many elements are in the array. You can do this in the declaration line or later in the program. Finally, you must indicate what index you want the array to begin with. Unlike what you might expect, the default first index is *not* 1; it is 0. However, you can override this if you like.

Here is a typical declaration of two arrays named employee and salary:

```
Dim employee(100) As String, salary(100) As Currency
```

---

[1] This same type of comment is true for the other examples in this chapter. However, if the lists are really long, the array solutions will be considerably faster. Besides, in situations where the lists are *extremely* long, the contents might not even fit in a worksheet.

This line indicates that (1) each element of the employee array is a string variable, (2) each element of the salary array is a currency variable, and (3) each array has 100 elements. (This assumes an Option Base of 1. See below.)

The Option Base Statement

Surprisingly, unless you add a certain line to your code, the first employee will *not* be employee(1) and the last employee will not be employee(100); they will be employee(0) and employee(99). This is because the default in VBA is called **0-based indexing**.

This means that the indexes of an array are 0, 1, 2, and so on. There is a technical reason for having 0-based indexing as the default; however, most of us do not think this way. Most of us prefer 1-based indexing, where the indexes are 1, 2, 3, and so on. The simple reason is that when we count, we typically begin with 1. If you want your arrays to be 1-based, you can use the following Option Base line:

```
Option Base 1
```

This line should be placed at the top of each of your modules, right below the Option Explicit line (which, if you remember, forces you to declare your variables).

Alternatively, if 0-based indexing is in effect, you can override it by indicating explicitly how you want a particular array to be indexed. The following line shows how you can do this for the employee and salary arrays.

```
Dim employee(1 To 100) As String, salary(1 To 100) As Currency
```

Now the first employee will be employee(1) and the last will be employee(100), regardless of any Option Base line at the top of the module.[2] By the way, if you do *not use* an Option Base 1 line and declare an array, say, as salary(100), the array will have 101 elements, indexed 0 to 100. In other words, if you include only one number inside parentheses, it specifies the largest index, not necessarily the number of elements in the array.

Dynamic Indexing and Redim

There are many times where you know you need an array, but when you are writing the code, you have no way of knowing how many elements it will contain. For example, you might have an InputBox statement near the top of your sub asking the user for the number of employees at her company. Once she tells you that there are

---

[2] Interestingly, Microsoft's .NET technology *requires* programmers to use 0-based indexing—it cannot be overridden. I doubt that this will happen to VBA in the future because it would break too many existing VBA programs.

150 employees, then, but not until then, you will know you need an array of size 150. So how should you declare the array in this case? You can do it in two steps. First, you declare that you need an *array,* as opposed to a single variable, in the Dim statement by putting empty parentheses next to the variable name, as in

```
Dim employee() as String
```

Then in the body of the sub, once you learn how many elements the array should have, you use the Redim statement to set aside the appropriate amount of memory for the array. The following two lines illustrate a typical example.

```
nEmployees = InputBox("How many employees are in your company?")
Redim employee(1 to nEmployees)
```

If the user enters 10, the employee array will be of size 10. If she enters 1000, it will be of size 1000. The Redim statement enables the array to adjust to the precise size required.

You can actually use the Redim statement as many times as you like in a sub to readjust the size of the array. (The examples later in the chapter illustrate why you might want to do this. It is actually quite common.) The only problem is that when you use the Redim statement to change the size of an array, all of the previous *contents* of the array are deleted. This is usually not what you want. Fortunately, you can override this default behavior with the keyword Preserve, as in the following lines.

```
nEmployees = nEmployees + 1
Redim Preserve employee(1 to nEmployees)
```

These lines would be appropriate if you just discovered that you have one extra employee, so that you need one extra element in the employee array. To keep from deleting the names of the previous employees when you redimension the array, you insert the keyword Preserve in the Redim line. This gives you an extra array element, but the previous elements retain their current values. If you ever use Redim somewhere in your program and nothing seems to work properly, the chances are that you forgot a Preserve and your data were deleted. (It has happened to me often.)

Multiple Dimensions

Arrays can have more than one dimension. (The arrays so far have been one-dimensional.) For example, a two-dimensional array has two indexes, as in employee(2,18). This might be appropriate if you want to index your employees by location and by number, so that this refers to the 18th employee at location 2. The main difference in working with multidimensional arrays is that you must indicate the number of elements for *each* dimension. As an example, the following line indicates that the employee array requires 10 elements for the first dimension and 100 for the second dimension:

```
Dim employee(1 to 10, 1 to 100) As String
```

Therefore, VBA will set aside 10*100 = 1000 locations in memory for this array.

Note that this *could* be quite wasteful. If the first dimension is the employee location and the second is the employee number at a location, suppose there are 100 employees at location 1 but only 5 at location 2. Then the array elements employee(2,6) through employee(2,100) are essentially wasted. Even though today's computer memory is cheap and abundant, computer programmers worry about this sort of thing. Therefore, they warn against using multidimensional arrays unless it is really necessary. You will sometimes see code with two-dimensional arrays, but you will rarely see arrays with three or more dimensions.

9.5 Examples of Arrays in VBA

The best way to understand arrays—and to appreciate the need for them—is to look at some examples. The first example is a fairly simple one. The next three are more challenging and interesting. They are typical of the examples that *really* benefit from arrays.

EXAMPLE 9.1   Looking Up a Price

The VLOOKUP and HLOOKUP functions in Excel are very useful for looking up information in a table. This example illustrates how you can accomplish the same thing with VBA and arrays. The file **Unit Prices.xlsm** contains a table of product codes and unit prices, as shown in Figure 9.3 (with many hidden rows). We want to write a program that asks the user for a product code. It then searches the list of product codes for a matching product code. If it finds one, it displays an appropriate message, such as in Figure 9.4. If it does not find a match, it displays a message to this effect.

Although there are many ways to write the required program, the LookupPrice sub listed below illustrates how it can be done with arrays. The number of products is found first, then the productCode and unitPrice arrays are redimensioned appropriately and a For loop is used to populate these arrays with the data in columns A and B of the worksheet. Next, after a user specifies a product code, another For loop searches the productCode array for a match to the requested code. If one is found, the corresponding element of the unitPrice array is stored in the requestedPrice variable. In either case an appropriate message is displayed at the end. Note that the line Option Base 1 is *not* used at the top of the module, although it could be. Instead, the two ReDim statements specify the indexing explicitly.

Figure 9.3 Table of Product Information

	A	B	C
1	Table of unit prices for products		
2			
3	Product code	Unit price	
4	L2201	50.99	
5	N1351	34.99	
6	N7622	10.95	
7	B7118	99.95	
8	R1314	105.99	
1212	D8665	51.95	
1213	R7932	93.95	
1214	R8509	14.95	
1215	L4701	3.95	

Figure 9.4 Unit Price of Requested Product

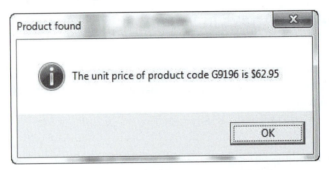

Product found

The unit price of product code G9196 is $62.95

OK

```
Option Explicit

Sub LookupPrice()
    Dim productCode() As String
    Dim unitPrice() As Currency
    Dim i As Integer
    Dim found As Boolean
    Dim requestedCode As String
    Dim requestedPrice As Currency
    Dim nProducts As Integer

    ' Find the number of products, redimension the arrays, and fill them
    ' with the data in the lists.
    With wsData.Range("A3")
        nProducts = Range(.Offset(1, 0), .End(xlDown)).Rows.Count
        ReDim productCode(1 To nProducts)
        ReDim unitPrice(1 To nProducts)
        For i = 1 To nProducts
            productCode(i) = .Offset(i, 0).Value
            unitPrice(i) = .Offset(i, 1).Value
        Next
    End With
```

```
' Get a product code from the user (no error checking).
requestedCode = InputBox("Enter a product code (an uppercase letter " _
    & "followed by four digits).")

' Look for the code in the list. Record its unit price if it is found.
found = False
For i = 1 To nProducts
    If productCode(i) = requestedCode Then
        found = True
        requestedPrice = unitPrice(i)
        Exit For
    End If
Next

' Display an appropriate message.
If found Then
    MsgBox "The unit price of product code " & requestedCode & " is " & _
        Format(requestedPrice, "$0.00"), vbInformation, "Product found"
Else
    MsgBox "The product code " & requestedCode & " is not on the list.", _
        vbInformation, "Product not found"
End If
End Sub
```

EXAMPLE 9.2   Keeping Track of Products Sold

A company keeps a spreadsheet of each sales transaction it makes. These transaction data, sorted by date, are listed in columns A to C of the **Product Sales.xlsm** file. (See Figure 9.5, which has many hidden rows.) Each row shows the four-digit code of the product sold, plus the date and dollar amount of the transaction. Periodically, the company wants to know how many separate products have been sold, and it wants a list of all products sold, the number of transactions for each product sold, and the total dollar amount for each product sold. It wants this list to be placed in columns E, F, and G, and it wants the list to be sorted in descending order by dollar amount.

Figure 9.5 Transaction Data

	A	B	C
1	Individual sales data		
2	Product Code	Date	Amount ($)
3	2508	1/2/2015	469
4	1111	1/5/2015	481
5	1107	1/6/2015	434
6	1119	1/6/2015	596
190	2515	12/23/2015	532
191	1104	12/25/2015	524
192	1111	12/26/2015	535
193	2510	12/30/2015	512

Figure 9.6 Number of Products Sold

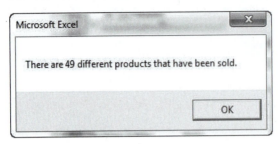

The ProductSales sub listed below does the job. When a button is clicked to run this sub, the message in Figure 9.6 appears, and the list in Figure 9.7 is created. (This figure does not show all 49 products sold. Some rows have been hidden.)

The idea behind the program is to loop through the product codes in column A, which are stored in an array called productCodesData, one at a time. These are used to build an array called productCodesFound. It eventually contains the *distinct* product codes in column A. At each step of the loop, a product code in column A is compared with all product codes already found. If this product code has already been found, 1 is added to its number of transactions, and the dollar amount of the current transaction is added to the total dollar amount for this product. Otherwise, if the product code has not already been found, an item is added to the productCodesFound array, the number of transactions for this new product is set to 1, and its total dollar amount is set to the dollar amount of the current transaction. Three other arrays facilitate the bookkeeping. The dollarsData array stores the data in column C, and the transactionsCount and dollarsTotal arrays store the numbers of transactions and total dollar amounts for all product codes found.

Figure 9.7 Results

	E	F	G
1	Summary data		
2	Product Code	Quantity	Amount ($)
3	1118	7	3818
4	1106	8	3764
5	2520	7	3696
6	1120	6	3415
7	2505	6	3306
45	2517	2	861
46	1113	1	735
47	2518	1	637
48	1102	1	581
49	2510	1	512
50	1109	1	451
51	2514	1	342

Once all product codes in column A have been examined, the data from the productCodesFound, transactionsCount, and dollarsTotal arrays are stored in columns E, F, and G, and they are sorted on column G in descending order.

Again, no **Option Base 1** statement is used. Instead, the arrays are dimensioned explicitly (as **1 to nSales**, for example).

```
Option Explicit

Sub ProductSales()
    ' These are inputs: the number of transactions, the product code for each
    ' sale, and the dollar amount of each sale.
    Dim nSales As Integer
    Dim productCodesData() As Integer
    Dim dollarsData() As Single

    ' The following are outputs: the product codes found, the number of transactions
    ' for each product code found, and total dollar amount for each of them.
    Dim productCodesFound() As Integer
    Dim transactionsCount() As Integer
    Dim dollarsTotal() As Single
    ' Variables used in finding unique product codes.
    Dim isNewProduct As Boolean
    Dim nFound As Integer

    ' Counters.
    Dim i As Integer
    Dim j As Integer

    ' Clear any old results in columns E to G.
    With wsData.Range("E2")
        Range(.Offset(1, 0), .Offset(0, 2).End(xlDown)).ClearContents
    End With

    ' Find number of sales in the data set, redimension the productCodesData and
    ' dollarsData arrays, and fill them with the data in columns A and C.
    With wsData.Range("A2")
        nSales = Range(.Offset(1, 0), .End(xlDown)).Rows.Count
        ReDim productCodesData(1 To nSales)
        ReDim dollarsData(1 To nSales)
        For i = 1 To nSales
            productCodesData(i) = .Offset(i, 0).Value
            dollarsData(i) = .Offset(i, 2).Value
        Next
    End With

    ' Initialize the number of product codes found to 0.
    nFound = 0

    ' Loop through all transactions.
    For i = 1 To nSales

        ' Set the Boolean isNewProduct to True, and change it to False only
        ' if the current product code is one already found.
        isNewProduct = True
        If nFound > 0 Then
            ' Loop through all product codes already found and compare them
            ' to the current product code.
```

```
            For j = 1 To nFound
                If productCodesData(i) = productCodesFound(j) Then
                    ' The current product code is not a new one, so update
                    ' its transactionsCount and dollarsTotal values appropriately,
                    ' and exit this inner loop.
                    isNewProduct = False
                    transactionsCount(j) = transactionsCount(j) + 1
                    dollarsTotal(j) = dollarsTotal(j) + dollarsData(i)
                    Exit For
                End If
            Next
        End If

        If isNewProduct Then
            ' The current product code is a new one, so update the list of
            ' codes found so far, and initialize the transactionsCount and
            ' dollarsTotal values for this new product.
            nFound = nFound + 1
            ReDim Preserve productCodesFound(1 To nFound)
            ReDim Preserve transactionsCount(1 To nFound)
            ReDim Preserve dollarsTotal(1 To nFound)
            productCodesFound(nFound) = productCodesData(i)
            transactionsCount(nFound) = 1
            dollarsTotal(nFound) = dollarsData(i)
        End If
    Next

    ' Place the results in columns E to G.
    For j = 1 To nFound
        With wsData.Range("E2")
            .Offset(j, 0).Value = productCodesFound(j)
            .Offset(j, 1).Value = transactionsCount(j)
            .Offset(j, 2).Value = dollarsTotal(j)
        End With
    Next

    ' Sort on column G in descending order, and display an appropriate message.
    wsData.Range("E3").Sort Key1:=wsData.Range("G3"), _
        Order1:=xlDescending, Header:=xlYes
    MsgBox "There are " & nFound & " different products that have been sold."
End Sub
```

Although there are numerous comments in the code, some further explanation might be useful.

- The productCodesData and dollarsData arrays are redimensioned *without* the keyword Preserve, whereas the CodesFound, transactionsCount, and dollarsTotal arrays are redimensioned with it. The reason is that the former two arrays are redimensioned only once, so there is no need to worry about deleting previous contents—there aren't any. However, the latter three arrays are redimensioned every time a new product code is found, and when this happens, the previous contents should *not* be deleted.

- When a new product code is found, nFound is increased by 1, and the productCodesFound, transactionsCount, and dollarsTotal arrays are redimensioned by adding an extra element to each. After doing this, the appropriate values are placed in the newly created elements of these arrays. For example, if nFound increases from 34 to 35, element number 35 of each array is specified.

- To specify a range to be sorted, it suffices to specify any cell within this range. Similarly, to specify the column to sort on (in the Key1 argument), it suffices to specify any cell within this column.

EXAMPLE 9.3 Traveling Salesperson Heuristic

This example deals with a famous problem in management science, the traveling salesperson problem. A salesperson starts in a certain city, visits a number of other cities exactly once, and returns to the original city. The problem is to find the route with the minimum total distance. Although this problem is easy to state, it is extremely difficult to solve optimally, even for a moderately small number of cities such as 50. Therefore, management scientists have developed heuristics that usually give good, but not necessarily optimal, solutions. The advantage of heuristics is that they are quick and easy to implement. This example illustrates the "nearest-neighbor" heuristic. It is very easy to state: The salesperson always goes next to the closest city not yet visited. Finally, he must return to the original city (labeled here as city 1) at the end.

The **Traveling Salesperson.xlsm** file implements this heuristic for any number of cities. There are actually two subs in this file. The first, GenerateDistances, generates random distances between the cities. It doesn't use any arrays, but it provides a good illustration of For loops. By running this sub repeatedly, you can generate many problems, each with a *different* set of distances. Figure 9.8 shows a matrix of distances generated by the GenerateDistances sub. Note that the distances are symmetric. For example, the distance from city 5 to city 10 is the same as the distance from city 10 to city 5. This is guaranteed by the way the GenerateDistances sub is written.

Figure 9.8 Distances for Traveling Salesperson Problem

	A	B	C	D	E	F	G	H	I	J	K	L	M	N	O	P
11	Distance matrix (symmetric, so values above the diagonal are the same as values below)															
12		City 1	City 2	City 3	City 4	City 5	City 6	City 7	City 8	City 9	City 10	City 11	City 12	City 13	City 14	City 15
13	City 1		66	3	48	35	29	73	55	47	59	45	95	41	13	8
14	City 2	66		29	42	19	26	50	25	76	1	40	33	97	56	95
15	City 3	3	29		31	4	10	7	80	24	44	61	66	60	89	73
16	City 4	48	42	31		68	49	25	43	1	68	96	96	58	26	80
17	City 5	35	19	4	68		32	82	32	77	1	50	81	57	63	95
18	City 6	29	26	10	49	32		62	1	75	71	41	99	8	6	74
19	City 7	73	50	7	25	82	62		14	21	45	12	87	76	91	92
20	City 8	55	25	80	43	32	1	14		7	68	64	59	76	85	94
21	City 9	47	76	24	1	77	75	21	7		25	29	43	60	30	23
22	City 10	59	1	44	68	1	71	45	68	25		39	35	34	25	96
23	City 11	45	40	61	96	50	41	12	64	29	39		99	37	32	66
24	City 12	95	33	66	96	81	99	87	59	43	35	99		62	53	99
25	City 13	41	97	60	58	57	8	76	76	60	34	37	62		54	64
26	City 14	13	56	89	26	63	6	91	85	30	25	32	53	54		66
27	City 15	8	95	73	80	95	74	92	94	23	96	66	99	64	66	

```
Sub GenerateDistances()
    ' This sub enters random integers from 1 to 100 above the diagonal and
    ' then enters values below the diagonal to make the matrix symmetric.

    Dim i As Integer ' row counter
    Dim j As Integer ' column counter
    Dim nCities As Integer
    Dim response As String
    Dim isValid As Boolean

    ' Clear everything from previous run (if any).
    ActiveSheet.UsedRange.ClearContents

    ' Turn off screen updating.
    Application.ScreenUpdating = False

    ' Restore labels.
    wsModel.Range("A1").Value = "Traveling salesperson model"
    wsModel.Range("A11").Value = "Distance matrix (symmetric, so values above " _
        & "the diagonal are the same as values below)"

    ' Find size of problem. Keep asking until an integer >= 2 is entered.

    Do
        isValid = True
        response = InputBox("Enter the number of cities, an integer >= 2.")
        If Not IsNumeric(response) Then
            isValid = False
        Else
            If Int(response) <> response Or response < 2 Then
                isValid = False
            End If
        End If
    Loop Until isValid
    nCities = response

    ' Fill up the distance matrix with random numbers.
    With wsModel.Range("A12")
        ' Enter labels.
        For i = 1 To nCities
            .Offset(i, 0).Value = "City " & i
            .Offset(i, 0).HorizontalAlignment = xlLeft
            .Offset(0, i).Value = "City " & i
        Next

        ' First fill up above the diagonal.
        For i = 1 To nCities - 1

            ' Generate random distances from 1 to 100. (Note: This uses Excel's
            ' RandBetween function, which is new to Excel 2007.)
            For j = i + 1 To nCities
                .Offset(i, j).Value = WorksheetFunction.RandBetween(1, 100)
            Next
        Next

        ' Now fill up below the diagonal to make the matrix symmetric.
        For i = 2 To nCities
            For j = 1 To i - 1
                .Offset(i, j).Value = .Offset(j, i).Value
            Next
        Next
    End With

    Application.ScreenUpdating = True
End Sub
```

Here are a couple of notes about the GenerateDistances sub.

- In early editions of the book, I used the VBA function Rnd to generate random distances. Now I have used Excel's RANDBETWEEN function, introduced in Excel 2007. Either works fine.
- The first set of nested For loops fills up the matrix *above* the diagonal, and the second set creates a mirror image *below* the diagonal.

The second sub, NearestNeighbor, uses arrays to implement the nearest-neighbor heuristic. Once the distances are known, the NearestNeighbor sub can be run (by clicking the second button in the file) to generate the nearest-neighbor route. When it is run (for the distances in Figure 9.8), the route and total distance are specified in the worksheet, as shown in Figure 9.9. For this solution, the traveler first goes from city 1 to city 3, then to city 5, and so on, until he eventually returns to city 1. The total distance of this route is 307. (For this rather small problem, you can check manually, using Figure 9.8 as a guide, that this is indeed the solution to the nearest-neighbor heuristic.)

The NearestNeighbor code is listed below. Although there are numerous comments, a few explanations should be helpful.

- This is the probably the most complex program so far, so I have added comments at the top of the sub to explain the variables. This is always a good idea, especially when the variable names might not be totally self-explanatory.
- The Option Base 1 statement is not used, but 1-based indexing is used by specifying the dimensions explicitly.

Figure 9.9 Route from Nearest-Neighbor Algorithm

	A	B	C
29	Nearest neighbor route		
30		Stop #	City
31		1	1
32		2	3
33		3	5
34		4	10
35		5	2
36		6	8
37		7	6
38		8	14
39		9	4
40		10	9
41		11	7
42		12	11
43		13	13
44		14	12
45		15	15
46		16	1
47			
48	Total distance is 307		

- There are two arrays, the Boolean array wasVisited and the integer array route. If wasVisited(6) is True, for example, this means that city 6 has been visited, so it cannot be visited again. Otherwise, if wasVisited(6) is False, then city 6 is a candidate for the next visit. The route array identifies the cities on the different stops of the route. For example, if route(8) equals 3, this means that city 3 is the 8th city to be visited.

- The arrays wasVisited and route are dimensioned initially with empty parentheses, just to make the sub more general. Once the number of cities is known, these arrays are redimensioned appropriately. The Preserve keyword is not necessary because the arrays are empty at the time they are redimensioned.

- Several variables need to be initialized appropriately before the real work can be done. They include route(1), route(nCities+1), nowAt, totalDistance, and the wasVisited array.

- The heuristic is performed with two nested For loops. The outer loop goes over the "steps" of the route. Its purpose is to discover which city will be the second visited, which will be third, and so on. The inner loop finds the nearest neighbor city for that step. It does this with a "running minimum," where it finds the smallest distance to all cities from the current city (nowAt) among all those not yet visited. The best of these is stored in the variable nextAt. After this inner loop is completed, nowAt becomes nextAt in preparation for the *next* pass through the outer loop.

- After the loops are completed, the distance back to city 1 is added to the totalDistance variable, and the contents of the route array and the total distance are entered in the worksheet.

```
Sub NearestNeighbor()
  ' This sub runs the nearest neighbor heuristic.

  ' Definition of variables:
  '  nCities - number of cities in the problem
  '  distance - array of distances between pairs of cities
  '  wasVisited - a Boolean array: True only if a city has been visited so far
  '  step - a counter for the number of cities visited so far
  '  route - an array where element i is the i-th city visited
  '      Note that Route(1) and Route(NCities+1) must both be 1.
  '  nowAt - city currently at
  '  nextAt - city to visit next
  '  totalDistance - total distance traveled
  '  minDistanceance - the minimum distance to the nearest (yet unvisited) neighbor
  '  i, j - counters

  Dim nCities As Integer
  Dim distance() As Integer
  Dim wasVisited() As Boolean
  Dim step As Integer
  Dim route() As Integer
  Dim nowAt As Integer
  Dim nextAt As Integer
  Dim totalDistance As Integer
  Dim minDistance As Integer
  Dim i As Integer
  Dim j As Integer
```

```
' Get the size of the problem (number of nodes) and redimension the various
' arrays appropriately.
With wsModel.Range("A12")
    nCities = Range(.Offset(1, 0), .Offset(1, 0).End(xlDown)).Rows.Count
End With

ReDim distance(1 To nCities, 1 To nCities)
ReDim wasVisited(1 To nCities)
ReDim route(1 To nCities + 1)

' Enter the distances into the Distance matrix.
With wsModel.Range("A12")
    For i = 1 To nCities
        For j = 1 To nCities
            If i <> j Then distance(i, j) = .Offset(i, j).Value
        Next
    Next
End With

' Start and end at city 1.
route(1) = 1
route(nCities + 1) = 1

' Only city 1 has been visited so far.
wasVisited(1) = True
For i = 2 To nCities
    wasVisited(i) = False
Next

' Initialize other variables.
nowAt = 1
totalDistance = 0

' Go through the steps on the route, one at a time, to see which cities
' should be visited in which order.
For step = 2 To nCities

    ' Find which city should be visited next by finding a 'running minimum'
    ' of distances from the current city to all other cities. The next
    ' city is a candidate only if it is not the current city and it has
    ' not yet been visited. Start the running minimum (minDistance) at a
    ' LARGE value, so that anything will beat its initial value.
    minDistance = 10000
    For j = 2 To nCities
        If j <> nowAt And Not wasVisited(j) Then
            If distance(nowAt, j) < minDistance Then
                ' Capture the best candidate so far and its associated
                ' distance from the current city.
                nextAt = j
                minDistance = distance(nowAt, nextAt)
            End If
        End If
    Next

    ' Store the city to go to next in Route, record that this city has
    ' been visited, and update the total distance.
    route(step) = nextAt
    wasVisited(nextAt) = True
    totalDistance = totalDistance + minDistance
```

```
          ' Get ready for the next time through the loop.
            nowAt = nextAt
      Next step

      ' Update the total distance to include the return to city 1
      totalDistance = totalDistance + distance(nowAt, 1)

      ' Start entering output two rows down from distance matrix.
      With wsModel.Range("B12").Offset(nCities + 2, 0)

          ' Enter labels.
          .Offset(0, -1).Value = "Nearest neighbor route"
          .Offset(1, 0).Value = "Stop #"
          .Offset(1, 1).Value = "City"

          ' Record the route from city 1 back to city 1 in the spreadsheet.
          For step = 1 To nCities + 1
              .Offset(step + 1, 0).Value = step
              .Offset(step + 1, 1).Value = route(step)
          Next step

          ' Record the total distance.
          .Offset(nCities + 4, -1).Value = "Total distance is " & totalDistance
      End With
End Sub
```

You should go through this code line by line until you understand how it works. It is structured to do exactly what you would do if you had to perform the nearest-neighbor heuristic manually. Of course, its advantage is that it is extremely fast—and it doesn't make mistakes.

EXAMPLE 9.4   Merging Lists

Like the previous example, this example is easy to describe but no less challenging to develop. It is an example of merging two lists and is contained in the file **Merging Lists.xlsm**. As in all applications in Part II of the book, there is an Explanation sheet (see Figure 9.10) that users see when they open the file. It explains the purpose of the application, and it has a button that runs a macro to take them to the Data worksheet. The code attached to this button is very simple:

```
Sub ViewData()
    With wsData
        .Activate
        .Range("A2").Select
    End With
End Sub
```

The lists (with some hidden rows) in the Data worksheet are already sorted in alphabetical order and appear in Figure 9.11. Note that some customers are in

Figure 9.10 Explanation of Merging Example

Merging Customer Lists

You have two lists of customers: those who bought last year and those who bought this year. Each of these lists is in alphabetical order (by last name of customer). To simplify the application, we'll assume that no two last names in the database are identical. For example, if you see Smith on last year's list and this year's list, you can assume that it is the same Smith in both cases. You want to create a new list that merges the names from these two lists into a common customer list.

Go to Data Sheet

Figure 9.11 Lists To Be Merged

	A	B	C	D
1	**Existing lists**	Merge Lists		**Merged list**
2				
3	Customers last year	Customers this year		Customers
4	Barlog	Aghimien		
5	Barnett	Bang		
6	Bedrick	Barnett		
7	Brulez	Bedrick		
8	Cadigan	Brulez		
9	Castleman	Cadigan		
93	Wyatt	Theodas		
94	Yablonka	Tracy		
95	Zick	Ubelhor		
96	Ziegler	Usman		
97		Vicars		
98		Villard		
99		Wendel		
100		Wier		
101		Wise		
102		Yablonka		
103		Yeiter		
104		Zakrzacki		
105		Zhou		

last year's list only, some are in this year's list only, and some are in both. The merged list in column D should include each customer in either list exactly once.

A Conceptual Method

Before discussing any VBA code, you need to have a mental picture of how you would do the merging manually. It is pointless to try to write code for a procedure unless you thoroughly understand the steps you would take to perform it manually. Here is one reasonable approach.

1. Start at the top of each of the existing lists and compare the names.
   - If they are the same, transfer this common name to column D and move down one row in both column A and column B for the next comparison.
   - If the name in column A comes before the name in column B in alphabetical order, transfer the name in column A to column D and move down one row in column A (but *not* in column B) for the next comparison. Proceed similarly if the name in column B comes before the name in column A in alphabetical order. For example, the second comparison in the given lists will be between Barlog and Bang.
2. Continue as in step 1, always making a comparison between a name in column A and a name in column B, until you have transferred all of the names from at least one of the column A and column B lists. Then if there are names left in one of the lists, transfer all of them to column D.

Try this procedure on the lists in Figure 9.11, and you will see that it works perfectly. Even though the list in column B is longer, you will finish transferring the names from column B first, with Zick and Ziegler left in the column A list. The last step of the procedure is to move these two names to the bottom of the merged list in column D.

Coding the Method

Now it is time to code this procedure. The MergeLists sub listed below contains the relevant code. It is written to work for *any* two lists in columns A and B, not just the ones shown in Figure 9.11. (The only assumptions are that the names are unique, in the sense that there is only one Smith, say, in either list, and if Smith appears in both lists, it is the same Smith. Duplicated names raise other issues that are not addressed here.) Again, there are plenty of comments, but a few explanations should help.

- There are three arrays, list1, list2, and list3, with sizes listSize1, listSize2, and listSize3. The first two are filled with the two known customer lists. The third is filled by the merging procedure.
- The array sizes listSize1 and listSize2 can be obtained immediately by looking at the existing customer lists. The array size listSize3 will be known only at the end of the procedure. We could redimension list3 right away with size listSize1+listSize2 (this will certainly be large enough—do you see why?), but instead we redimension list3 with one extra element every time a new customer is added to the merged list. This means that the final list3 will be dimensioned exactly as large as it needs to be. To keep from deleting previous customers from the merged list, the Preserve keyword is necessary.
- The sub first deletes any previous merged list from column D with the ClearContents method. Next, the list sizes of the existing lists are found, and the list1 and list2 arrays are filled with existing customer names. Finally, the merging procedure is used to fill the list3 array, which is eventually written to column D.

- Note how the conceptual method described earlier is implemented in VBA. The sub uses the index1 and index2 integer variables to indicate how far down the existing customer lists the procedure is. The corresponding customer names are name1 and name2. A comparison between them indicates which to add to the merged list, as well as which of index1 and index2 to increment by 1. A Do While loop is arguably the most natural approach here. It says to keep going through the lists while there is at least one name remaining in each list.

- After the Do loop is completed, the contents of the list not yet completed (if either) are transferred to the merged list. Then the contents of list3 are written to column D of the worksheet.

```
Sub MergeLists()
    ' The listSizex variables are list sizes for the various lists (x from 1 to 3).
    ' The listx arrays contains the members of the lists (again, x from 1 to 3).
    ' The lists are indexed from 1 to 3 as follows:
    '   list1 - customers from last year (given data)
    '   list2 - customers from this year (given data)
    '   list3 - customers who bought in either or both years (to be found)

    Dim i1 As Integer, i2 As Integer, i3 As Integer ' counters
    Dim listSize1 As Integer, listSize2 As Integer, listSize3 As Integer
    Dim list1() As String, list2() As String, list3() As String
    Dim index1 As Integer, index2 As Integer
    Dim name1 As String, name2 As String

    ' Delete the old merged list (if any) in column D.
    With wsData.Range("D3")
        Range(.Offset(1, 0), .Offset(1, 0).End(xlDown)).ClearContents
    End With

    ' Get the list sizes and the names for the given data in columns A, B.
    With wsData.Range("A3")
        listSize1 = Range(.Offset(1, 0), .End(xlDown)).Rows.Count
        ReDim list1(1 To listSize1)
        For i1 = 1 To listSize1
            list1(i1) = .Offset(i1, 0).Value
        Next
        listSize2 = Range(.Offset(1, 1), .Offset(0, 1).End(xlDown)).Rows.Count
        ReDim list2(1 To listSize2)
        For i2 = 1 To listSize2
            list2(i2) = .Offset(i2, 1).Value
        Next
    End With

    ' Create the merged list. First, initialize new list size to be 0.
    listSize3 = 0

    ' Go through list1 and list2 simultaneously. The counters index1 and index2
    ' indicate how far down each list we currently are, and name1 and name2 are
    ' the corresponding customer names. First, initialize index1 and index2.
    index1 = 1
    index2 = 1

    ' Keep going until we get past at least one of the lists.
    Do While index1 <= listSize1 And index2 <= listSize2
```

```
            name1 = list1(index1)
            name2 = list2(index2)

            ' Each step through the loop, add one customer name to the merged list, so
            ' update the list size and redim list3 right now.
            listSize3 = listSize3 + 1
            ReDim Preserve list3(1 To listSize3)

            ' See which of the two names being compared is first in alphabetical order.
            ' It becomes the new member of the merged list. Once it's added, go to the
            ' next name (by updating the index) in the appropriate list. In case of a tie,
            ' update both indexes.
            If name1 < name2 Then
                list3(listSize3) = name1
                index1 = index1 + 1
            ElseIf name1 > name2 Then
                list3(listSize3) = name2
                index2 = index2 + 1
            ElseIf name1 = name2 Then
                list3(listSize3) = name2
                index1 = index1 + 1
                index2 = index2 + 1
            End If
    Loop

    ' By this time, we're through at least one of the lists (list1 or list2).
    ' Therefore, add all leftover names from the OTHER list to the merged list.
    If index1 > listSize1 And index2 <= listSize2 Then
            ' Some names remain in list2.
        For i2 = index2 To listSize2
            listSize3 = listSize3 + 1
            ReDim Preserve list3(1 To listSize3)
            list3(listSize3) = list2(i2)
        Next
    ElseIf index1 <= listSize1 And index2 > listSize2 Then
            ' Some names remain in list1.
        For i1 = index1 To listSize1
            listSize3 = listSize3 + 1
            ReDim Preserve list3(1 To listSize3)
            list3(listSize3) = list1(i1)
        Next
    End If

    ' Record the merged list in column D of the worksheet.
    With wsData.Range("D3")
        For i3 = 1 To listSize3
            .Offset(i3, 0).Value = list3(i3)
        Next
    End With

    ' End with the cursor in cell A2.
    wsData.Range("A2").Select
End Sub
```

The introduction to this chapter claimed that arrays are useful for working with lists. This merging example is a perfect example of this claim. The merging could certainly be done without arrays, but arrays provide the perfect means for accomplishing the job.

9.6 Array Functions

This chapter concludes with a brief description of a rather curious construct in VBA: the Array function. The following code illustrates how the Array function works.

```
Option Base 1

Sub ArrayFunctionExample()
    Dim days As Variant
    days = Array("Mon", "Tues", "Wed", "Thurs", "Fri", "Sat", "Sun")
    MsgBox "The first day in the array is " & days(1)
End Sub
```

The keyword Array, followed by a list inside parentheses, is used to populate the variable days. Then days acts like a typical array. For example, days(1) in the message box statement will be "Mon". (It would be "Tues" if the Option Base 1 statement were not included. Remember, the default is 0-based indexing.) However, days is not *declared* like a typical array. It must be declared as Variant, with no empty parentheses in the Dim statement. VBA figures out that you want days to be an array only after you set days equal to the Array function in the third line of the sub.

You might not use the Array function very often, but as this example code shows, it provides a quick and convenient way to populate an array.

9.7 Summary

You already know from previous chapters how powerful looping can be in computer programs. Arrays increase this power tremendously, especially when processing lists in some way. This power has been illustrated by a variety of examples, and I will continue to illustrate the power of arrays in later chapters. Arrays are well worth the effort required to master them.

EXERCISES

1. Write a sub that creates an array day of size 7 and then populates it with the days of the week: Monday, Tuesday, and so on. It should then loop through this array and write its elements to the range A1:G1 of the first worksheet.
2. Write a sub that creates two arrays month and daysInMonth, each of size 12. It should then populate the first array with the months January, February, and so on, and it should populate the second with the number of days in these months: 31, 28 (assume it is not a leap year), and so on. Then it should loop through these arrays and write their elements to the range A1:L2. For example, cells A1 and A2 will have January and 31.
3. Do the previous exercise in a slightly different way. Instead of two one-dimensional arrays, create one two-dimensional array monthInfo of size 12 by 2.

The first dimension should contain the month and the second should contain the number of days in the month. For example, monthInfo(6,1) should be June and monthInfo(6,2) should be 30. Use nested loops to fill the range A1:L2 as in the previous exercise. (*Note:* You will need to declare this array as Variant because it contains two different types of data, strings and integers.)

4. Write a sub that asks the user for an integer such as 100 and stores it in the variable upperLimit. It then asks the user for another integer such as 3 and stores it in the variable factor. It then creates an array called multiple, of the appropriate size, that contains all the multiples of factor no greater than upperLimit. Finally, it uses a loop to sum all of the elements in the array and reports this sum with an appropriate message in a MsgBox. For example, if the two inputs are 100 and 3, it should report "The sum of all multiples of 3 no greater than 100 is 1683."

5. Write a sub that creates an array card of size 52. Its first 4 elements should be 1, its next 4 elements should be 2, its next 4 elements should be 3, and so on. You should be able to do this with a pair of nested For loops. You should *not* do it by brute force with 52 statements or 13 For loops. (This type of array is used in a later online chapter to simulate poker hands. You are essentially setting up the deck here.)

6. The file **Random Numbers.xlsx** contains 50,000 random numbers in column A. (To generate these, I used Excel's RAND function and then froze them by copying values over the formulas.) Write a sub that creates an array called frequency of size 10. It should then populate the array by looping over the random numbers and putting them into "bins." Specifically, frequency(1) should contain the count of all random numbers from 0 to 0.1, frequency(2) should contain the count of all random numbers from 0.1 to 0.2, and so on. Because every random number has to be in one of these bins, the counts should sum to 50,000, which you should check. Report the final contents of the array in a MsgBox. (How should you deal with the breakpoints such as 0.1? It doesn't really matter because there is virtually no chance that a random number will fall *exactly* on one of the breakpoints.)

7. Write a sub that does the following: (1) It declares an array called practiceArray of size 100; (2) it stores the value i in element i (for i from 1 to 100); and (3) it uses a For loop to switch the contents of the elements i and i+1 for each i from 1 to 99. At the end, transfer the contents of practiceArray to column A of a worksheet. The effect of all the switching should be to push the 1 down to the bottom of the list. Is that what you got? (*Hint:* When you switch two array elements, you need a third "temporary" variable. I usually call it temp.)

8. The file **High Spenders.xlsx** contains a list of customers and the amounts they spent during the past month. Write a sub that captures the existing lists in two arrays and then creates two new arrays of customer names and amounts spent for customers who spent at least $500. After these new arrays have been filled, write their contents to columns D and E of the worksheet.

9. The file **Customer Lists.xlsx** contains two lists of customers: those who purchased from our company last year and those who purchased this year. Write a sub that captures: the existing lists in two arrays and then creates three new arrays of customers those who purchased only last year; those who purchased only this year; and those who purchased in both years. After these new arrays have been filled, the sub should write their contents to columns D, E, and F of the worksheet.

10. The file **Flights.xlsx** contains a list of flights in columns A, B, and C flown by EastWest Airlines. The list includes the flight number, the origin, and the destination of each flight. You are interested in flights that leave from any city in column E and end up at any city in column F. You need to list such flights in columns H, I, and J. Write a VBA program to do so, using arrays. Your program should work even if the lists in columns A to C and in E to F change. To see how it should work, look at the **Flights Finished.xlsm** file. Its code is password-protected.

11. Suppose you have a list of customers, labeled from 1 to *n*, and you want to choose a random subset of them of size *m* (where *m* < *n*). Write a sub to do this. It should first ask the user for *n* and *m*, using two input boxes. It should then fill an array of size *m* called chosen, where chosen(1) is the index of the first person chosen, chosen(2) is the index of the second person chosen, and so on. No person can be chosen more than once, so no two elements of the chosen array should have the same value. Finally, the sub should list the values of the chosen array in column A of a worksheet. Note that you can borrow Excel's RANDBETWEEN function to generate a random integer from 1 to *n*.

12. The file **Incomes.xlsx** contains annual incomes for many households in a particular town. As in the previous exercise, choose a random subset of *m* households. Then report the average of *all* incomes in the file and the average of the incomes in the subset in a message box. Unlike the previous exercise, the user cannot select *n*; it is the number of households listed in the file. However, the user should be allowed to choose the sample size *m*.

13. Consider the following state lottery. Five random digits are selected. This is the winning number. You can buy as many lottery cards as you like at $1 per card. Each card contains five random digits. If you get a card that matches the winning number, you win $100,000. (Assume that order matters. For example, if the winning number is 21345, then 12345 doesn't win.) Write a sub that does the following. It first generates a random winning number and stores it in a string variable (so that you can use string concatenation), and it asks the user how many cards he wants to buy. It then uses a For loop to generate this many cards and store their numbers in a card array (which should be a string array). Next, it uses a Do loop to keep checking cards until a winner has been found or no more cards remain. Finally, it displays a message stating whether you are a winner and your net gain or loss. Note that you can generate a single random digit from 0 to 9 with Excel's RANDBETWEEN function.

14. The previous exercise is realistic because a lottery player must commit to the number of cards purchased *before* learning the winning number. However, suppose you want to see how many cards you would have to buy, on average, before getting a card with the winning number. Write a sub that does the following. It has an outer For loop that goes from 1 to 100, so that you can repeat the whole process 100 times, each with a different winning number. Each time you go through this loop, you generate a winning card, you use a Do loop to keep generating cards until you get a winner, and you keep track of the number of cards required in an element of the requiredCards array (of size 100). At the end of the program, you should display summary measures of requiredCards in a message box: the average of its elements, the smallest of its elements, and the largest of

its elements. For example, the latter is the most cards you ever had to buy in any of the 100 lotteries. (*Note:* Although you will be working with integers, they will likely be very *large* integers. Therefore, declare them as Long, not Integer, types. Also, don't be surprised if this program takes a while to run. It took mine about a minute.)

15. If you have ever studied relational databases, you have heard of joins. This exercise illustrates what a join is. The file **Music CDs 1.xlsx** contains data on a person's classical music CD collection. There are three worksheets. The Labels worksheet lists all music labels (such as Philips), where they are indexed with consecutive integers. The CDs worksheet lists the person's CDs. Specifically, it shows for each CD the index of the music label, the composer, and the piece(s) on the CD. We say that the tables on these two worksheets are related through the label indexes. Write a sub, using arrays, to join the information on these two worksheets. The joined information should be placed on the Join worksheet. As the headings indicate, for each CD, it should show the music label (its name, not its index), the composer, and the piece(s).

16. The previous exercise demonstrated a one-to-many relationship. This means that each CD has only one music label, but many CDs can have the same label. Relationships can also be many-to-many, as this exercise illustrates. The file **Music CDs 2.xlsx** contains four worksheets. The Works worksheet lists works of music, along with the composers, and they are indexed by consecutive integers. The Conductors worksheet lists conductors, which are also indexed by consecutive integers. The CDs worksheet has an entry for each CD owned. For each entry, it shows the index of the work and the index of the conductor. The relationship is now many-to-many because it is possible to have more than one CD of a given work, each conducted by a different conductor, and it is possible to have more than one CD with a given conductor, each conducting a different work. Write a sub, using arrays, to fill the Join worksheet, which currently has only headings. As these headings indicate, each row should list the composer, the work, and the conductor for a particular CD. (This worksheet should end up with as many rows as the CDs worksheet.) Finally, the sub should keep track of any works on the Works worksheet that you do not own, and it should display these in some way—you can decide how.

17. (More difficult) Your company makes steel rods of a fixed diameter and length 50 inches. Your customers request rods of the following lengths (all in inches): 5, 8, 12, 15, 20, and 25. Write a sub to find all ways to cut the rods so that any leftovers are unusable. For example, one way to do it is with one 5-inch rod, one 8-inch rod, and three 12-inch rods. This uses 49 inches of the rod, and the other inch is unusable. As you find usable patterns, list them in the **Patterns.xlsx** file. (One possible pattern is already shown in row 5 for illustration.)

18. Practically all computer science majors are required at some time in their college careers to write a sort routine. You start with an array of numbers (or even strings), and you need to write a sub that ends with this same array but in increasing order. For example, if the array elements are A(1)=17, A(2)=12, A(3)=19, and A(4)=7, the end result will have A(1)=7, A(2)=12, A(3)=17, and A(4)=19.

   a. Given access to Excel, there is a very easy way to do this. Write a sub that does the following. It first populates an array of any size with any set of numbers. (You can choose these.) It then stores the first number in cell A1 of a worksheet, the second in cell A2, and so on. Next, it uses the Sort method of a Range object to sort this range. Finally, it uses a loop to store the contents of the range into the array, overwriting the previous contents. In essence, you get Excel to do the hard part of sorting.

b. (More difficult) Repeat part **a**, but do it without the help of Excel's Sort method. To do this, you need a strategy. Here is a fairly simple one, although it is quite inefficient for large arrays. Loop through the array to find the smallest number. Let's say A(15) is the smallest. Then exchange the contents of A(1) and A(15). This exchange requires a variable I will call temp. Put A(15) into temp, put A(1) into A(15), and put temp into A(1). Next, find the smallest of the elements from A(2) on. Let's say this is A(7). Then exchange elements A(2) and A(7). Do you see the pattern? It is called a **bubble sort** because the small numbers bubble up to the top of the array. You should code this algorithm, using a set of nested loops.

19. (More difficult) The Data worksheet in the **Variable Number of Lists.xlsx** file contains three lists of varying lengths. The Combinations worksheet shows all combinations of these lists. Write a sub, using arrays, to generate the data on the Combinations worksheet. It should work for *any* number of lists of any lengths.

20. (*Very* useful for dumping data to a worksheet). Suppose your program fills a large two-dimensional array called results with values, and you would like it to dump these values into an Excel range. For example, if results is *m* by *n*, you would like the program to dump the values into a range with *m* rows and *n* columns. One way is to use two nested loops to dump the data one element at a time into the appropriate cell. This approach turns out to be *extremely* slow. A much better approach is to set the Value property of an *m*-row, *n*-column range to results, that is, one statement with no loops. To compare these two methods, initialize the *i, j* element of an *m* by *n* array to $i+j$. (Any values would do.) Now use both methods just described to dump the results to an *m*-row, *n*-column Excel range. You should find a *huge* difference. (On my computer, with $m=2500$, $n=500$, the looping method took several *minutes*, whereas the single-statement method took less than a *second*. Note that the "trick" illustrated in this problem works only for two-dimensional arrays. However, if you want to dump a one-dimensional array into a column, you can first store it in a two-dimensional array with constant second dimension equal to 1 and then use the trick.)

10

More on Variables and Subroutines

10.1 Introduction

To this point, all programs have been single, self-contained subs. This chapter illustrates how individual subs can be part of an overall program, which is very important for the applications discussed in Part II of the book. A typical program can have many subs in one or more modules, and they can be related. First, they can share the same variables. For example, one sub might use an input box to capture an employee's salary in the variable salary. Then another sub might use this same variable in some way. Both subs need to know the value of this salary variable. In technical terms, the salary variable must have the appropriate *scope*.

Subs can also call one another, and they can pass arguments (share information) when they make the call. As programs become longer and more complex, it is common to break them down into smaller subs, where each sub performs a specific task. There is often a "main" sub that calls the other subs. In effect, the main sub acts as a control center. Making programs modular in this way makes them easier to read. Perhaps even more important, it makes them easier to debug. In addition, there is a better chance that the smaller subs can be reusable in other programs. In fact, one of the most important ideas in computer programming is the idea of reusable code. Professional programmers attempt to make their subs as general and self-contained as possible so that they or other programmers can use existing code rather than having to reinvent the wheel every time they write a program.

Finally, this chapter introduces a particular type of subroutine called a function subroutine. Unlike the subroutines discussed so far, the purpose of a function subroutine is to return a value. Actually, all of the Excel functions you use in formulas, such as SUM and MAX, are really function subroutines. This chapter illustrates how you can develop your *own* custom functions and then use them in VBA programs or even in Excel worksheets.

10.2 Exercise

The emphasis in this chapter is on dividing an overall program into several subroutines, each of which performs a particular task. The following exercise is typical. It could be written in one fairly long sub, but a much better way is to modularize it. By the time you have finished reading this chapter, you should be able to solve this exercise according to the specific instructions without much difficulty.

Exercise 10.1   Updating Customer Accounts

Consider a company that services air conditioners and heaters. It currently has 30 residential customers in a certain region, and it keeps track of service charges for these customers in the file **Customer Accounts.xlsx**. This file contains a worksheet called New Charges. Each month the company deletes the charges from the previous month and adds charges for the current month to this worksheet. Figure 10.1 shows the charges for the most recent month.

The file also contains a separate worksheet for each customer, where the worksheet name is the customer's account number. For example, the worksheet for customer Stevens (account number S3211) appears in Figure 10.2 (with

Figure 10.1   New Charges

	A	B	C	D
1	Information on new charges			
2				
3	Date	Customer	Account #	Charge
4	2-Jul-15	Astrid	A1865	$89.42
5	6-Jul-15	Bricker	B1808	$70.94
6	10-Jul-15	Allenby	A1151	$87.11
7	13-Jul-15	Argos	A1225	$71.15
8	14-Jul-15	Exley	E3597	$96.15
9	18-Jul-15	Owens	O2752	$77.94
10	19-Jul-15	Stevens	S3211	$133.12
11	20-Jul-15	Spinaker	S2378	$81.17
12	22-Jul-15	West	W3697	$152.77

Figure 10.2   Typical Customer Account Sheet

	A	B	C	D	E	F	G
1	Stevens account						
2							
3	All charges			Summary by year			
4	Date	Charge		Year	Total	Discount	Net
5	28-Apr-07	$140.20		2007	$296.41	$12.23	$284.18
6	24-Aug-07	$156.21		2008	$523.50	$29.26	$494.24
7	9-Jan-08	$130.51		2009	$459.42	$24.46	$434.97
8	2-May-08	$160.87		2010	$519.48	$28.96	$490.52
9	8-Sep-08	$109.23		2011	$531.14	$29.84	$501.31
10	25-Dec-08	$122.88		2012	$528.74	$29.66	$499.09
11	19-May-09	$112.77		2013	$652.02	$38.90	$613.11
12	8-Sep-09	$126.00		2014	$450.48	$23.79	$426.70
13	21-Oct-09	$110.60		2015	$143.19	$2.16	$141.03
14	23-Nov-09	$110.05					
15	23-Jan-10	$93.75					
35	31-May-14	$161.20					
36	28-Sep-14	$121.42					
37	25-Feb-15	$143.19					

several rows hidden). Columns A and B list all of Stevens's charges since the account was opened, and columns D to G summarize the yearly totals. The totals in column E are sums of charges for the various years. The discounts in column F are based on the company's discount policy: no discount on the first $100 (for any year), 5% discount on the next $100, and 7.5% discount on all charges over $200. The net in column G is the total minus the discount.

The purpose of the exercise is to update the customer account worksheets with the charges on the New Charges worksheet. This includes new entries in columns A and B, plus updates of the total and discount for the current year (2015) in columns E and F. As an example, after running the program, the Stevens account worksheet should appear as in Figure 10.3. Of course, if a customer has no charge in the New Charges worksheet, this customer's account worksheet does not need to be updated.

This exercise can be done in many ways, but to get the most benefit from it, it should be done as follows. There should be a Main sub that loops through all of the charges in the New Charges worksheet. For each charge, an Update sub should be called that takes three arguments: the customer's account number, the date of the charge, and the amount of the charge. This Update sub should add the new charge to the end of the customer's charges (as in cells A38 and B38 in Figure 10.3 for Stevens), and it should update the Total and Discount cells for the current year. To find the discount, it should call a function subroutine called Discount that calculates the discount for any yearly total passed to it. (When writing this program, you can assume that all new charges are indeed for the year 2015.)

Figure 10.3 Updated Account Sheet

	A	B	C	D	E	F	G
1	Stevens account						
2							
3	All charges			Summary by year			
4	Date	Charge		Year	Total	Discount	Net
5	28-Apr-07	$140.20		2007	$296.41	$12.23	$284.18
6	24-Aug-07	$156.21		2008	$523.50	$29.26	$494.24
7	9-Jan-08	$130.51		2009	$459.42	$24.46	$434.97
8	2-May-08	$160.87		2010	$519.48	$28.96	$490.52
9	8-Sep-08	$109.23		2011	$531.14	$29.84	$501.31
10	25-Dec-08	$122.88		2012	$528.74	$29.66	$499.09
11	19-May-09	$112.77		2013	$652.02	$38.90	$613.11
12	8-Sep-09	$126.00		2014	$450.48	$23.79	$426.70
13	21-Oct-09	$110.60		2015	$276.31	$10.72	$265.59
14	23-Nov-09	$110.05					
15	23-Jan-10	$93.75					
36	28-Sep-14	$121.42					
37	25-Feb-15	$143.19					
38	19-Jul-15	$133.12					

As usual, you can try running the program in the completed file **Customer Accounts Finished.xlsm**, but you should not look at the code until you have tried writing the VBA code yourself. Also, if you are interested in a more challenging version of this problem, see the code in the file **Customer Accounts Extra.xlsm**, which allows the new charges to go into the next year.

10.3 Scope of Variables and Subroutines

This section discusses the important concept of **scope**, or "Which parts of a program have access to which other parts?" Variables and subroutines both have scope. I will discuss each.

Scope of Variables

You already know how to declare a variable with a Dim statement. Here is a typical example:

```
Sub Test1()
    Dim salary As Currency
    salary = 50000
    ' Other lines of code would go here.
End Sub
```

When a variable such as salary is declared *inside* a sub in this way, it is called a **procedure-level variable**, or a **local variable**. The only sub that recognizes this variable is the sub that contains it. Suppose there is another sub with the following lines:

```
Sub Test2()
    MsgBox "The value of salary is " & salary
    ' Other lines of code would go here.
End Sub
```

If you run Test1 and then Test2, the message box in Test2 will *not* display "The value of salary is 50000". This is because Test2 does not know the value of the salary variable; only Test1 knows it. In fact, Test2 can have its own salary variable, as in

```
Sub Test2()
    Dim salary As Currency
    salary = 40000
    MsgBox "The value of salary is " & salary
    ' Other lines of code would go here.
End Sub
```

If you run Test1 and then Test2, Test2 will have no memory that salary was 50000 in Test1. It knows only about *its* version of salary, defined as 40000. In other words, local variables in different subs can have the same names, but they lead independent existences. Technically, they have different memory locations.

What if you want different subs to have access to common variables? Then you can declare these variables at the *top* of a module, before any subs. Actually, you have two options. First, you can declare a variable at the top of a module with the usual Dim keyword, as in

```
Dim salary As Currency
```

This variable is then a **module-level variable**, which means that every sub in the module has access to it. (An alternative to the keyword Dim is the keyword Private. A **private variable** also has module-level scope.) The second possibility is to declare a variable at the top of a module with the keyword Public, as in

```
Public salary As Currency
```

Then salary is a **public variable** with **project-level scope**, which means that *all* modules in the entire project have access to it.[1] This is often useful when you have two or more modules in your project. (It is also useful when you have *event handlers* for user forms, as explained in Chapter 11. Then public variables are also recognized by the event handlers. However, as you will read in Chapter 11, I try to avoid the use of such public variables.)

If you declare a variable to have module-level or project-level scope, you almost surely do *not* want to declare the same variable inside a sub with a Dim statement. For example, consider the following code:

```
Public salary As Currency

Sub Test1()
    salary = 50000
End Sub

Sub Test2()
    Dim salary As Currency
    MsgBox "Salary is " & salary
End Sub
```

If you run Test1 and then Test2, the message box in Test2 will *not* display "Salary is 50000" as you might expect—it will display "salary is 0". The reason is that the Dim statement in Test2 creates a local version of salary that *overrides* the public version. This local version is initialized to 0 by default. Hence the message

---

[1] Some programmers use the term **global variable** rather than public (or project-level) variable. This is the term used in some other programming languages.

says that salary is 0, which is probably not what you want. Actually, if you know what you're doing, you can have public and local variables with the same name, but it is still likely to cause confusion.

Scope of Subroutines

Subroutines also have scope. As discussed in the next section, one sub can call another inside a program. Scope then determines which subs can call which others. The default is that all subs have *public* scope unless specified otherwise. This means that when you define a sub as in

```
Sub Test()
```

any other sub in the entire project can call this Test sub. To make this more explicit, you can precede Sub with the keyword Public, as in

```
Public Sub Test()
```

However, this is not really necessary because a sub's scope is public by default.
    Now suppose that you want Test to be callable only by subs within its module. Then you *must* precede Sub with the keyword Private, as in

```
Private Sub Test()
```

Then any sub in the same module as Test can call Test, but subs outside of the module containing Test have no access to Test. By the way, the scoping rules for subs are exactly the same for function subroutines, the topic of section 10.6.

10.4 Modularizing Programs

There is a tendency for beginning programmers to write one long sub in a program—a sub that does it all. This is a bad habit for at least three reasons:

- Long subs are hard to read. Would you like to read a book with a single long chapter or a chapter with a single long paragraph?
- Long subs are hard to debug. There are too many lines with possible bugs.
- It is difficult to reuse the code from long subs in other programs.

A preferred approach is to modularize programs so that they become a sequence of relatively short subs, each with a specific task to perform. These short subs then overcome the three criticisms above: (1) Their brevity and focus make them easier to read; (2) they can be tested independently, or at least in sequence, so that bugs are easier to detect and fix; and (3) there is a much greater chance that they can be reused in other programs.

The question, then, is how to tie the subs together into an overall program. Fortunately, this is quite easy. You have one sub *call* another sub. Here is a typical setup:

```
Sub Main()
    Call Task1
    Call Task2
End Sub

Sub Task1()
    Call Task3
    ' Other lines of code would go here.
End Sub

Sub Task2()
    ' Lines of code would go here.
End Sub

Sub Task3()
    ' Lines of code would go here.
End Sub
```

The Main sub does nothing but call the Task1 sub and then the Task2 sub. The Task1 sub in turn calls the Task3 sub, and it then executes some other statements. We say that Main passes control to Task1, which then passes control to Task3. When Task3 is completed, it passes control back to Task1. When Task1 is completed, it passes control back to Main, which immediately passes control to Task2. Finally, when Task2 is completed, it passes control back to Main. At this point, the program ends. This code also indicates how easy it is to call another sub. You simply type the keyword Call, followed by the name of the sub being called.

It is also possible to omit the keyword Call, and many programmers do so. Instead of writing, say, Call Test1, they simply write Test1. I realize that I might be in the minority, but I prefer to use the keyword Call, mostly to remind myself that a sub is being called. Here is my reasoning. Suppose you see the following line in the middle of a sub:

```
TaxCalc
```

You might think that this is some variable name you had forgotten about, rather than a call to a sub called TaxCalc. But if the line includes Call, as in

```
Call TaxCalc
```

there is no doubt that a subroutine named TaxCalc is being called. Still, you can choose: include Call or omit it.

There is a trade-off when modularizing a program. At one extreme, you can have a single long sub. At the other extreme, you can create a separate sub for every small task your program performs. You typically need to find a middle ground that breaks an overall program into reasonable chunks. Different programmers argue about the term "reasonable." For example, I have heard one programmer say he doesn't like subs with more than 10 lines, which I believe is overly restrictive. However, all programmers agree that some modularizing is appropriate in long programs.

EXAMPLE 10.1   Traveling Salesperson Model Revisited

To see how modularizing works, I rewrote the code for the traveling salesperson nearest-neighbor heuristic from the previous chapter. The modified code is the file **Traveling Salesperson Modified.xlsm**. Now instead of one long Nearest-Neighbor sub, there is a short NearestNeighbor "main" sub that calls four other subs, GetProblemData, Initialize, PerformHeuristic, and DisplayResults, to do the work. The code appears below. (The comments have been omitted to emphasize the overall structure.) Note how the names of the subs indicate the basic tasks to be performed. This is always good programming practice.

Compare the code below with the one-sub code in the original **Traveling Salesperson.xlsm** file. You will probably agree that the divide-and-conquer strategy used here makes the program easier to understand. It not only helps you see the big picture, but it also helps you to understand the details by presenting them in bite-sized chunks.

```vba
Option Explicit

Dim nCities As Integer
Dim distance() As Integer
Dim wasVisited() As Boolean
Dim route() As Integer
Dim totalDistance As Integer

Sub NearestNeighbor()
    Call GetProblemData
    Call Initialize
    Call PerformHeuristic
    Call DisplayResults
End Sub

Sub GetProblemData()
    Dim i As Integer, j As Integer
    With wsModel.Range("A12")
        nCities = Range(.Offset(1, 0), .Offset(1, 0).End(xlDown)).Rows.Count
        ReDim distance(1 To nCities, 1 To nCities)
        For i = 1 To nCities
            For j = 1 To nCities
                If i <> j Then distance(i, j) = .Offset(i, j).Value
            Next
        Next
    End With

    ReDim wasVisited(1 To nCities)
    ReDim route(1 To nCities + 1)
End Sub
```

```
Sub Initialize()
    Dim i As Integer
    route(1) = 1
    route(nCities + 1) = 1
    wasVisited(1) = True
    For i = 2 To nCities
        wasVisited(i) = False
    Next
    totalDistance = 0
End Sub

Sub PerformHeuristic()
    Dim step As Integer
    Dim i As Integer
    Dim nowAt As Integer
    Dim nextAt As Integer
    Dim minDistance As Integer

    nowAt = 1
    For step = 2 To nCities
        minDistance = 10000
        For i = 2 To nCities
            If i <> nowAt And Not wasVisited(i) Then
                If distance(nowAt, i) < minDistance Then
                    nextAt = i
                    minDistance = distance(nowAt, nextAt)
                End If
            End If
        Next i
        route(step) = nextAt
        wasVisited(nextAt) = True
        totalDistance = totalDistance + minDistance
        nowAt = nextAt
    Next step

    totalDistance = totalDistance + distance(nowAt, 1)
End Sub

Sub DisplayResults()
    Dim step As Integer
    With wsModel.Range("B12").Offset(nCities + 2, 0)
        .Offset(0, -1).Value = "Nearest neighbor route"
        .Offset(1, 0).Value = "Stop #"
        .Offset(1, 1).Value = "City"

        For step = 1 To nCities + 1
            .Offset(step + 1, 0).Value = step
            .Offset(step + 1, 1).Value = route(step)
        Next step

        .Offset(nCities + 4, -1).Value = "Total distance is " & totalDistance
    End With
End Sub
```

When you divide a program into multiple subs, you have to be careful with variable declarations. If a particular variable is required by more than one of the subs, it should be declared at the top of the module. The module-level variables above are nCities, totalDistance, and the distance, wasVisited, and route arrays.

Other variables that are needed only in a specific sub, such as the step variable in the DisplayResults sub, should be declared locally. In general, this forces you to examine your variables (and the logical structure of your program) carefully to see what belongs where. You *could* take the easy way out by declaring *all* variables at the top as module-level variables, but this is considered very poor programming practice. It signals that you haven't thought very carefully about the overall structure of your program.

10.5 Passing Arguments

In a typical modular program, a particular sub can be called several times. Each time it is called, the sub performs the same basic task, but possibly with different inputs (and different outputs). As a very simple example, suppose a main sub calls a display sub to display a customer's name in a message box. You want the display sub to be very general so that it will display any name given to it. The question is how you get the customer's name from the main sub to the display sub. There are two ways: (1) by using module-level variables and (2) by **passing arguments**. These two methods are compared next.

Module-Level Variables Method

The following program illustrates the use of module-level variables. It assumes there is a range called Names that contains the last names and first names of 10 customers. I want to display each customer's full name in a message box. To do so, I declare module-level variables lastName and firstName in the first line. Then the Main sub loops through the rows of the Names range, stores the last and first names of the current customer in the lastName and firstName variables, and calls the DisplayName sub to display the customer's full name. The Display-Name sub knows the current values of lastName and firstName because they are module-level variables.

```
Dim lastName As String, firstName As String

Sub Main()
    Dim i As Integer
    For i = 1 To 10
        lastName = Range("Names").Cells(i, 1)
        firstName = Range("Names").Cells(i, 2)
        Call DisplayName
    Next
End Sub

Sub DisplayName()
    Dim customerName As String
    customerName = firstName & " " & lastName
    MsgBox "The customer's full name is " & customerName
End Sub
```

Passing Arguments Method

Alternatively, you can pass arguments (in this case, names) from the Main sub to the DisplayNames sub. In this context, you refer to the Main sub as the *calling* sub and the DisplayNames sub as the *called* sub. To implement this method, the variables lastName and firstName are no longer declared as module-level variables. They are now declared locally in the Main sub, and they are passed to the Display-Name sub as arguments in the second-to-last line of Main. Specifically, to pass arguments, you type the name of the called sub (DisplayName) and then list the variables being passed, separated by commas and included within parentheses. The first line of the called sub then indicates the arguments it expects to receive.

```
Sub Main()
    Dim i As Integer, firstName As String, lastName As String
    For i = 1 To 10
        lastName = Range("Names").Cells(i, 1)
        firstName = Range("Names").Cells(i, 2)
        Call DisplayName(lastName, firstName)
    Next
End Sub

Sub DisplayName(lName As String, fName As String)
    Dim customerName As String
    customerName = fName & " " & lName
    MsgBox "The customer's full name is " & customerName
End Sub
```

Note that the arguments in the first line of the DisplayName sub are lName and fName. They are *not* the same as the names passed to it, lastName and firstName. This is perfectly legal. The variables being passed from the calling sub and the arguments in the called sub do not need to have the same names, although they often do. The only requirements are that *they must match in number, type, and order*. If Main passes two string variables to DisplayName, then DisplayName must have two arguments declared as string type. Otherwise, VBA will display an error message. Also, if the last name is the first variable in the passing statement, it must be the first argument in the argument list of the called sub.[2]

Summarizing, here are the rules for passing arguments:

- To call a sub with arguments, type its name and follow it with arguments separated by commas and included within parentheses. The arguments should be declared locally within the calling sub, as in:

```
Dim lastName as String, firstName as String
Call DisplayName(lastName, firstName)
```

---

[2] Actually, this is not quite true. It is possible to include the *names* of the arguments when calling the sub, in which case the arguments can come in a different order, but I will not use this variation here.

- The called sub should declare its arguments inside parentheses next to the name of the sub, as in:

```
Sub DisplayName(lName As String, fName As String)
```

- The names of the variables in the calling sub do not need to be the same as the names of the arguments in the called sub, but they must match in number, type, and order.

Now you have two ways to deal with shared variables. You can declare them as module-level (or project-level with the keyword Public) variables at the top of a module, or you can pass them as arguments from one sub to another. Which method is better? Most professional programmers favor passing arguments whenever possible. The reason is that this makes a sub such as DisplayName totally self-contained. It can be reused exactly as it stands in a different program, because it is not dependent on a list of module-level variables that might or might not exist. However, passing variables is a somewhat more difficult concept, and it is sometimes more awkward to implement than the "global variable" approach. Therefore, both methods can be used, and you will see both in the applications in Part II of the book.

EXAMPLE 10.2   Formatting Extremes

The file **Format Extremes.xlsm** contains monthly sales values for a company's sales regions. (See Figure 10.4.) The company wants to highlight the extreme sales in each month. Specifically, it wants to color the minimum sale in each month red and italicize it, and it wants to color the maximum sale in each month blue and boldface it.

Figure 10.4 Sales Data

	A	B	C	D	E	F	G	H	I	J	K	L	M
1	Sales by region and month												
2													
3		Jan	Feb	Mar	Apr	May	Jun	Jul	Aug	Sep	Oct	Nov	Dec
4	Region 1	25630	19660	15270	33810	19360	15770	22490	8350	18310	18160	14040	10680
5	Region 2	18490	10060	13150	17350	12120	16940	24120	4550	13920	11020	10370	8590
6	Region 3	13360	12630	20350	10850	17650	20570	18500	36460	7530	11880	18110	18760
7	Region 4	17280	22930	19310	12230	16490	6760	12850	18930	16640	13590	8180	10830
8	Region 5	10970	10550	11780	7210	23280	7320	15840	19690	19280	8690	9810	10540
9	Region 6	7990	14690	20680	17130	12620	7400	8420	13810	7090	8990	12570	15260
10	Region 7	40310	10820	18310	13900	6390	13290	12980	28440	15530	25940	16600	18160
11	Region 8	10770	18250	29580	21020	10200	9380	15210	5750	13710	11770	10820	23160
12	Region 9	10530	14170	24630	16910	21670	11750	10470	19150	20170	20600	26180
13	Region 10	8600	22950	14080	16760	17270	16670	18650	10370	12040	13810	8000	11690
14	Region 11	11510	15660	16870	17930	15110	7760	12090	10260	23240	14760	15430	16540
15	Region 12	10360	11490	15000	14060	9770	13110	24320	24500	13300	15610	21040	12620
16	Region 13	18670	12350	20450	9860	16730	10100	12870	11390	16220	11760	18480	13330
17	Region 14	16360	18640	17050	25080	10760	14420	16730	17260	22470	11980	10710	19640
18	Region 15	20760	13610	6340	12510	14570	11930	26490	21130	21530	20390	24960	16100
19	Region 16	18690	23710	10530	18050	17730	7230	20750	23370	18070	10490	18980	12390

This task is accomplished with the Main and ChangeFont subs listed below. The Main sub is attached to the button on the worksheet. It loops through all of the cells in the sales range with a pair of nested For loops. For each cell, it calls the ChangeFont sub to change the font of the cell appropriately if the sales value in this cell is an extreme for the month. Four arguments are passed to ChangeFont sub: the cell (a range object), the sales value in the cell, the minimum sales value for the month, and the maximum sales value for the month. All of these arguments have the same names in the called sub as in the calling sub, but they could have different names and the program would still work correctly.

```vba
Sub Main()
    Dim nMonths As Integer, nRegions As Integer
    Dim i As Integer, j As Integer
    Dim minVal As Single, maxVal As Single, salesVal As Single
    Dim cell As Range

    With wsData.Range("A3")
        nMonths = Range(.Offset(0, 1), .Offset(0, 1).End(xlToRight)).Columns.Count
        nRegions = Range(.Offset(1, 0), .Offset(1, 0).End(xlDown)).Rows.Count
        ' Restore to normal.
        With Range(.Offset(1, 1), .Offset(nRegions, nMonths)).Font
            .Color = vbBlack
            .Bold = False
            .Italic = False
        End With
        ' Look for extremes (those that match the min or max in any column).
        For j = 1 To nMonths
            minVal = WorksheetFunction.Min(Range(.Offset(1, j), .Offset(nRegions, j)))
            maxVal = WorksheetFunction.Max(Range(.Offset(1, j), .Offset(nRegions, j)))
            For i = 1 To nRegions
                Set cell = .Offset(i, j)
                salesVal = cell.Value
                Call ChangeFont(cell, salesVal, minVal, maxVal)
            Next
        Next
    End With
End Sub

Sub ChangeFont(cell As Range, salesVal As Single, minVal As Single, maxVal As Single)
    With cell
        If salesVal = minVal Then
            .Font.Color = vbRed
            .Font.Italic = True
        ElseIf salesVal = maxVal Then
            .Font.Color = vbBlue
            .Font.Bold = True
        End If
    End With
End Sub
```

Note how general the ChangeFont sub is. You could easily use it in any other program that needs to change the font of particular cells. All you need to pass to it are the cell (again, as a Range object), a sales value, and minimum and maximum sales values to compare to.

Passing by Reference and by Value

When you pass a variable such as lastName from one sub to another, the default method is **by reference**. This means that the variables in the calling and the called subs share the same memory location so that any changes to lastName in the called sub will be reflected in the calling sub. For example, suppose lastName has value "Jones" when it is passed, and then the called sub changes it in a line such as

```
lastName = "Smith"
```

Then the value of lastName will be "Smith" when control passes back to the calling sub.

If this is *not* the behavior you want, you can pass the variable **by value**. This sends a *copy* of lastName to the called sub, so that any changes made there to last-Name are *not* reflected in the calling sub. In the above example, lastName would remain "Jones" in the calling sub. If you want to pass by value, the called sub must have the keyword ByVal (all one word) next to the argument, as in

```
Sub DisplayName(ByVal lastName As String, ByVal firstName As String)
```

On the other hand, if you want to emphasize that you are passing by reference, you can write

```
Sub DisplayName(ByRef lastName As String, ByRef firstName As String)
```

However, the keyword ByRef is never really necessary because passing by reference is the default method. It is the method I use in all later examples, so you will never see either keyword, ByRef or ByVal.[3]

Passing Arrays

Consider the following scenario. You have written a general-purpose sub called SortNames that takes any array of last names and sorts them in alphabetical order. (The details of how it does this are irrelevant for now.) You would like to be able to call SortNames from any sub by passing any array of last names to it. In particular, you want this to work regardless of the *size* of the array being passed. That is, it should work for a 10-element array, a

---

[3] Interestingly, in its .NET technology, Microsoft passes *by value* by default. This means you have to specify ByRef explicitly if you want to pass by reference.

1000-element array, or an array of any other size. What is the appropriate way to proceed?[4]

The following code does the job. (The next-to-last line indicates the detailed code for sorting. It is irrelevant for this discussion.)

```
Sub CallingSub()
    Dim names(100) As String
    For i = 1 To 100
        names(i) = Range("Names").Cells(i).Value
    Next
    Call SortNames(names)
End Sub

Sub SortNames(names() As String)
    Dim nNames As Integer
    nNames = UBound(names)
    ' Other lines of code would go here.
End Sub
```

The calling sub stores 100 names in an array of size 100. (It populates this array by pulling the names from a worksheet range, which is assumed to be filled with 100 last names.) It then passes the names array to the SortNames sub with the line

```
Call SortNames(names)
```

Note that there are no parentheses next to the names argument in this line. VBA knows that names is an array because it was declared earlier to be an array. On the other end, the first line of the SortNames sub uses empty parentheses next to the names argument to indicate that it is expecting an array. It will know how large an array to work with only when an array of a specific size is passed to it.

Note that you can determine the size of the array that has been passed to SortNames with the line

```
nNames = UBound(names)
```

somewhere inside the SortNames sub, as was done here. The VBA UBound function returns the largest index in the array. Therefore, when an array of size 100 is passed to SortNames, nNames becomes 100. If an array of size 1000 were passed instead, nNames would be 1000. The point is that this procedure works regardless of the size of the array that is passed.[5]

---

[4] I have included this section because passing arrays is a common operation and not all VBA books tell you how to do it.

[5] If the default 0-based indexing is in effect, UBound returns 1 less than the number of array elements. That is, UBound returns the largest *index* of the array.

10.6 Function Subroutines

The subroutines to this point—the subs—can perform virtually any task. They can sort numbers in a worksheet, they can create and manipulate charts, they can add or delete worksheets, and so on. This section discusses a special type of subroutine called a **function subroutine** that has a more specific objective: It returns a value.[6] The following simple example illustrates one possibility. It returns the larger of two numbers passed to it (number1 and number2) in the variable Larger.

```
Function Larger(number1 As Single, number2 As Single) As Single
    If number1 >= number2 Then
        Larger = number1
    Else
        Larger = number2
    End If
End Function
```

This function subroutine looks a lot like a typical sub. For example, it can take arguments, in this case number1 and number2, both of Single type. However, it has some important differences:

- Instead of beginning with Sub and ending with End Sub, it begins with Function and ends with End Function.
- It returns a certain *type* of variable, in this case Single. This type is specified in the first line, after the argument list.
- It returns the value assigned to its name. In the example, the return value will come from one of the two lines that begin Larger =. For example, if the numbers 3 and 5 are passed to this function, it will return 5. (The common practice is to capitalize the first letter of a function name, such as Larger.)

A function subroutine can be used in one of two ways. It can be called by another sub (or even another function subroutine), or it can be used as a new function in an Excel formula. Here is an example of the first method, where the calling sub calls Larger in the next-to-last line.

```
Sub CallingSub()
    Dim firstNumber As Single, secondNumber As Single
    firstNumber = 3
    secondNumber = 5
    MsgBox "The larger of the two numbers is " & _
        Larger(firstNumber, secondNumber)
End Sub
```

The message box will report that the larger number is 5. Note once again that the variables being passed can have different names from the arguments of

---

[6]Actually, a function subroutine can return a "value" of any type: Integer, Single, String, Boolean, and so on. It can even return an object, such as a Range object.

the function, but they should agree in number, type, and order. In this case, Larger is expecting two arguments of type Single.

To illustrate the second method, open a new workbook in Excel, get into the VBE, insert a new module, and type the code for the Larger function exactly as above. Now enter the formula =**Larger(5,3)** in any cell. It will recognize your new function, and it will correctly enter 5 in the cell. In fact, as you start typing the formula in Excel, you will even get some help from Intellisense. However, it doesn't list the arguments it expects, as it does with built-in Excel functions.

This creates a whole new realm of possibilities for you as a programmer. You can define your own functions and then use them in Excel formulas. You might not need to do this very often because Excel already includes a rich list of its own functions. However, there might be a *few* times when you want to create your own functions. Here are some things you should know.

- If you write the code for a function in workbook1 and then try to use this function in a formula in workbook2, it won't be recognized. The problem is that workbook2 recognizes only the functions written in *its* modules. There are at least two solutions to this problem. First, you can set a reference to workbook1 in workbook2. To do so, make sure workbook1 is open. Then activate workbook2, get into the VBE, select the **Tools → References** menu item, and check the workbook1 box.[7] The problem with this method is that workbook1 must be open. A better method is to put all of your favorite functions in your Personal Macro Workbook (recall Chapter 4), and then set a reference to it, again through **Tools → References**, in any workbook where you want to use these functions. The advantage of this method is that your Personal Macro Workbook is always open (unless you deliberately close it).
- Suppose you want to write a function that accepts one or more *lists* as arguments. In particular, these lists might come from worksheet ranges. For example, suppose you want to emulate Excel's SUM function. Then the following code will work. (You can find it in the **Functions.xlsm** file.)

```
Public Function MySum(values As Variant) As Single
    Dim v As Variant, total As Single
    For Each v In values
        total = total + v
    Next
    MySum = total
End Function
```

The point here is that the values argument, which contains the list of values to be summed, must be declared as Variant, even though it acts like a collection. This enables you to use the For Each loop inside the function. Importantly, this list could come from a worksheet range, as illustrated in Figure 10.5. The gray cells contain

---

[7] Actually, you will see the Project Name of workbook1 in the list, which still might be the generic name VBAProject. This provides a good reason to change this generic name, which you can do through the Properties Window.

Figure 10.5 Using the MySum Function in a Worksheet

	A	B	C	D
1	Illustration of MySum function			
2				
3	98	35	68	201
4	12	87	77	176
5	59	23	39	121
6	40	37	46	123
7	19	98	20	137
8	73	95	94	262
9	31	38	43	112
10	332	413	387	
11				
12				
13				
14				
15				

Formula in cell B10 is:
=MySum(B3:B9)

row and column sums, indicated by the typical formula in the text box. It is even possible to copy this formula across and down, just like any other Excel formula.

EXAMPLE 10.3   Concatenating Names

This example illustrates a useful string function I developed called FullName. It is *not* a built-in Excel function. It is defined by the code listed below. (You can find this code in the **Functions.xlsm** file.) The function takes four arguments: a person's first name, last name, initial (if any), and a Boolean variable. The Boolean variable is True if the initial is the person's *middle* initial, and it is False if the initial is the initial of the person's first name (in which case, the "first name" argument is really the person's middle name). The initial argument can have a period after it, or it can have no period. (The code uses VBA's Left function, with last argument 1, to delete the period in case there is one. Then it adds a period, just to ensure that there is one after the initial.) Also, the initial argument can be an empty string (no initial in the name), in which case the Boolean value is irrelevant. (Those of us who go by our middle names wish everyone would use this type of function to ensure that they get our names correct.)

```
Public Function FullName(firstName As String, lastName As String, _
      initial As String, Optional isMiddleInitial As Boolean = True) As String
   If initial = "" Then
      FullName = firstName & " " & lastName
   ElseIf isMiddleInitial Then
      FullName = firstName & " " & Left(initial, 1) & ". " & lastName
   Else ' must be first initial
      FullName = Left(initial, 1) & ". " & firstName & " " & lastName
   End If
End Function
```

Figure 10.6 FullName Examples

	A	B	C
1	**Concatenating names**		
2			
3	S.	Wayne	Abraham
4	Christian	L	
5	Albright	Winston	Lincoln
6			
7	S. Christian Albright	Wayne L. Winston	Abraham Lincoln

Figure 10.6 illustrates the use of this function. The inputs to the function are in rows 3-5. The formulas in cells A7 to C7 are

= FullName(A4,A5,A3,FALSE)

= FullName(B3,B5,B4,TRUE)

and

= FullName(C3,C5,C4,TRUE)

Note that the arguments after FullName must be in the correct order: first name, last name, initial, and Boolean; however, they could come from any cells in the spreadsheet. Also, note that Abraham Lincoln has no middle initial. Therefore, the Boolean value in the cell C7 formula is irrelevant—it could be TRUE or FALSE.

The Boolean argument could even be omitted because it is declared as optional. When you see an argument such as

Optional isMiddleInitial As Boolean = True

this indicates that argument does not need to be included, in which case its default value is the value provided, in this case, True. You can have number of optional arguments. The only restriction is that all optional arguments have to come after required arguments, that is, they must be at the end of the argument list.

EXAMPLE 10.4   Generating Random Numbers

If you have done any spreadsheet simulation, you know the need for random numbers from various probability distributions. Some simulation add-ins such as @RISK have their own collections of random number functions. This example illustrates a simple function you can use in your own simulations, *without* the need for an add-in such as @RISK. It generates random values from *any* discrete distribution, where you supply the possible values and their corresponding probabilities. Its code is listed below. (It is stored in the file **Functions.xlsm**.)

```
Public Function Discrete(value As Variant, prob As Variant)
   ' We assume that the value array contains integers in ascending order.
   Dim i As Integer
   Dim cumProb As Single
   Dim uniform As Single

   ' The following line ensures that we'll get different random numbers
   ' each time we run this procedure.
   Randomize

   ' The following line ensures that the function recalcs (with new random
   ' numbers) if it's entered as a formula in a worksheet.
   Application.Volatile

   ' Generate a uniform random number.
   uniform = Rnd

   ' Find the first cumulative probability that's greater than uniform,
   ' and return the corresponding value.
   cumProb = prob(1)
   i = 1
   Do Until cumProb > uniform
      i = i + 1
      cumProb = cumProb + prob(i)
   Loop
   Discrete = value(i)
End Function
```

Several points might require some explanation.

- The Application.Volatile line ensures that if this function is entered in a worksheet, it will recalculate (and thereby generate a *different* random number) each time the worksheet recalculates.
- The Randomize line ensures that you won't get the *same* random number each time this function is called. (This would certainly destroy the function's usefulness in simulation.)
- The Rnd function is a built-in VBA function similar to Excel's RAND function. It generates random numbers uniformly distributed between 0 and 1.
- The loop finds the place where the uniform random number "fits" in the probability distribution. For example, with the probabilities given in Figure 10.7, the cumulative probabilities are 0.1, 0.4, 0.9, and 1.0, so if the uniform random number is 0.532, then the function returns the third value (3) because 0.532 is between 0.4 and 0.9.
- The value and prob arrays must be declared as Variant types with no parentheses. This is a rather obscure rule, but it is the only way that allows you to use such a function in an Excel formula.

Figure 10.7 Random Numbers from a Discrete Distribution

	A	B	C	D	E	F
1	Generating random numbers from a discrete distribution					
2						
3	Value	Probability				
4	1	0.1				
5	2	0.3				
6	3	0.5				
7	4	0.1				
8						
9	Random numbers					
10		2				
11		3				
12		3				
13		2				
14		1				
15		3				
16		3				
17		3				
18		1				
19		3				

The following code indicates how you could call such a function in a VBA module (as opposed to using it in an Excel formula):

```
Sub TestDiscrete()
    ' This sub tests the Discrete random number generator above.
    Dim value As Variant, prob As Variant, i As Integer
    value = Array(1, 2, 3, 4)
    prob = Array(0.1, 0.3, 0.5, 0.1)
    For i = 1 To 30
        MsgBox Discrete(value, prob)
    Next
End Sub
```

This function is illustrated in Figure 10.7, where several random numbers are generated. (See the Discrete worksheet in the **Functions.xlsm** file.) The formula in cell B10, which is then copied down, is

```
=Discrete($A$4:$A$7,$B$4:$B$7)
```

If you open this file and recalculate (by pressing the F9 key, for example), you will see that all of the random numbers change.

If you want to use this function or develop your own random number functions, you will probably want it to be available regardless of which files are open. As discussed earlier, a good option is to place the code in your Personal Macro Workbook, and then set a reference to this workbook in any file where you want to use the function. (Remember, you set a reference in the VBE from the **Tools** → **References** menu item.)

The file **Functions.xlsm** contains the function subroutines discussed above, plus others. It also asks you to develop a couple of your own.

10.7 The Workbook_Open Event Handler

In Chapter 2, I briefly discussed events and event handlers. An event handler is a sub that runs whenever a certain event occurs, that is, when it *fires*. Event handlers are discussed in much more detail in the next chapter when you learn about user forms. However, there is one simple event handler that you can use right away. It responds to the event where a workbook is opened. In short, if you want anything to occur when you open an Excel workbook, you can write the appropriate code in this event handler.

Event handlers have built-in names—you have no control over the names given to these subroutines. The particular event handler discussed here has the name Workbook_Open. Also, it is a Private sub by default. Therefore, its first line is always the following:

```
Private Sub Workbook_Open()
```

Another distinguishing feature of this subroutine is that you do *not* place it in a module. Instead, you store it in the ThisWorkbook code window. To get to this window, double-click the ThisWorkbook item in the VBE Project Explorer (see Figure 10.8). This opens a code window that looks just like a module code window, except that it is reserved for event handlers having to do with workbook events.

The code in a Workbook_Open sub is usually not very elaborate. A typical use of this sub is to ensure that a worksheet code-named wsExplanation is activated when a user opens the workbook. (I use it for this purpose in all of the applications in Part II of the book.) The following sub is all that is required:

```
Private Sub Workbook_Open()
    wsExplanation.Activate
End Sub
```

Figure 10.8 ThisWorkbook Item in Project Explorer

Of course, you could place other statements in this sub—to hide certain worksheets, for example. Again, if there are any actions you want to occur when a workbook opens, the Workbook_Open sub is the place to put them.

As you might guess, there is also an event handler for the event where a workbook is *closed*. It is named Workbook_BeforeClose. Because this subroutine is somewhat more complex—it takes a rather obscure argument, for example—and is not used in later applications, I will not discuss it here. However, if you are interested, you can find online help for it in the Object Browser.

10.8 Summary

Long programs should not be written in a single long sub; this is considered poor style. In this chapter I illustrated how to organize long programs into a sequence of shorter subs, each of which performs a specific task. The resulting code is easier to read and debug, and pieces of it are more likely to be reusable in other programs. I discussed how it is a good programming practice to pass arguments from one sub to another whenever possible. When this is done, the called subs can often be written in a totally self-contained manner, which allows them to be reused in other programs. I also introduced function subroutines. Their purpose is to return a value, and they can be called by other subs (even other function subroutines), or they can be used as new spreadsheet functions. Finally, I briefly discussed event handlers. Specifically, I illustrated how the Workbook_Open sub can be used to perform any desired actions when a workbook is opened.

EXERCISES

1. Write a sub called GetName that asks the user to type a first name and last name in an input box, which is captured in a string variable fullName. It should then call a sub called ProperCase that takes a single argument, a string, and converts this argument to proper case. For example, if the user enters the name gEORge buSH, the sub should return George Bush. The GetName sub should then display the result, such as George Bush, in a message box.
2. Repeat the previous exercise, but now ask for two separate names, firstName and lastName, in two separate input boxes, and pass these *two* arguments to the ProperCase sub (which will need to be modified).
3. Write a Function subroutine called Tax that takes a single argument grossIncome of type Currency. It should calculate the tax on any income using the following tax schedule: (1) if income is less than or equal to $15,000, there is no tax; (2) if income is greater than $15,000 and less than or equal to $75,000, the tax is 15% of all income greater than $15,000; and (3) if income is greater than $75,000, the tax is 15% of all income between $15,000 and $75,000 plus 20% of all income greater than $75,000. Then write a CalcTax sub that asks a user for his income, gets the function subroutine to calculate the tax on this income, and reports the tax in a message box.

4. Expanding on the previous exercise, the file **Tax Schedule.xlsx** has a tax schedule. Write a CalcTax sub, just as in the previous exercise, that asks for an income and passes it to a Tax function. However, the Tax function now finds the tax by using the tax schedule in the worksheet. (This tax schedule is similar to the one in the previous exercise and is illustrated with the sample tax calculation on the worksheet.) The Tax function should be flexible enough to work even if more rows (breakpoints) or different breakpoints or percentages are added to the tax schedule.

5. Write a function subroutine called Add that mimics Excel's SUM function. It should accept an array of type Single, and it should return the sum of the elements of the array. Then write a short Test sub that sets up an array, passes it to the function, and reports the result.

6. Write a function subroutine called AddProduct that mimics Excel's SUMPRODUCT function. It should accept two arrays of type Single, both of the same size, and it should return the sum of the products of the two arrays. For example, if you pass it the arrays (3,5,1) and (4,3,6), it should return 3*4 + 5*3 + 1*6 = 33.

7. Write a function subroutine called NextCell that takes a string argument Address, which should look like the address of a cell, such as C43. The function should return True or False depending on whether the cell to the right of this one contains a formula. For example, if you pass it C43, it checks whether cell D43 contains a formula.

8. Write a function subroutine called NameExists of type Boolean that takes two arguments of type Range and String, respectively. It should search all of the cells in the given range and check whether any of them have their Value property equal to the given string. For example, if the string is "Davis", it should check whether "Davis" is in any of the cells. (A cell containing "Sam Davis" wouldn't count. The contents have to be "Davis" exactly, including case.) If so, it should return True. Otherwise, it should return False.

9. Open a new workbook and add several worksheets. Each worksheet should be named as some state, such as Pennsylvania. Write a States sub that creates an array called capital. It should have as many elements as the number of worksheets, and it should be populated with the capitals of the states. For example, if Pennsylvania is the third worksheet, you should set capital(3) equal to Harrisburg. Now write a sub called EnterLabel that takes two string arguments, a state and a capital, and enters a label, such as "The capital of Pennsylvania is Harrisburg", in that state's cell A1. Finally, use a loop in the States sub to go through the worksheets and send the worksheet name and the appropriate element of the array to the EnterLabel sub. After the States sub runs, there should be an appropriate label in cell A1 of each worksheet.

10. Open a new workbook with a single worksheet, and enter some integers in the range A1:B10. (Any integers will do.) Write a ColorMax sub that has a For loop from i=1 to i=10. Each time through this loop, a sub Process should be called with three arguments: i and the two numbers in columns A and B of row i. The Process sub should enter the larger of the two numbers in column C of row i, and it should color its font red if the number in row A is the larger. Otherwise, it should color the font blue.

11. The file **Customer Lists.xlsx** contains lists of customers from last year and this year in columns A and B. Write a sub called FindMatch that takes a single argument customerName (a string variable). It should check whether this

customer is in both lists. If so, it should display a message to this effect, and it should boldface both instances of the customer's name. Otherwise, it should display a message that the customer's name is *not* on both lists. Next, write a Test sub that uses an input box to ask for a customer name and then calls FindMatch with this customer's name as the argument.

12. The file **Stock Prices.xlsx** contains monthly adjusted closing prices, adjusted for dividends and stock splits, for WalTech's stock from 2007 to early 2015. (WalTech is a fictitious company.)

   a. Write a sub called RecordHigh1 that takes a single argument called searchPrice. This sub searches down the list of prices for the first price that exceeds the search-Price argument. If it finds one, it displays the corresponding date in a message, something similar to, "The first date WalTech stock price exceeded _ was _." If the price never exceeded the argument searchPrice, it displays a message to this effect. Next, write a Records sub that uses an input box to ask the user for a price and then calls RecordHigh1 with this price as the argument.

   b. Write another sub called RecordHigh2 that takes a single argument called specifiedMonth. This sub searches down the list of prices for the last time up until (and including) the specified month where the stock reached a record high (that is, it was larger than all prices before it, going back to the beginning of 2007). It then displays a message such as, "The most recent record, up until _, was in _, when the price reached _." (Note that Jan-2007 is a record high by default, so at least one record high will always be found.) Change the Records sub from part **a** so that the input box now asks for a month and then calls RecordHigh2 with this month as an argument.

13. The file **Boy Girl Finished.xlsm** contains a worksheet with scores for boys and girls. Open the file and click the button. You will see that it asks the user for 1 (boys) or 2 (girls). It then names the range of the scores for the chosen gender as DataRange, it enters a label and the average score for the chosen gender (as a *formula*) in cells D9 and E9, and it formats the D9:E9 range appropriately (blue font for boys, red font for girls). The code in this file is password-protected. Now open the **Boy Girl.xlsx** file, which contains only the data, and write your own code to perform the same tasks. It should contain a Main sub that calls the following subs: (1) GetResponse (to show the input box and get the user's response), (2) NameGenderRange (to name the appropriate range as DataRange), (3) FormatOutputRange (to format the output range D9:E9 appropriately), and (4) EnterOutput (to enter a label in D9 and a formula in E9). Write your subs so that there are no module-level variables. Instead, a string variable gender should be an argument of each called sub, where gender can be "boys" or "girls". Also, write the program so that it will work even if more data are added to the data set.

14. Open a new workbook and write a sub called GetWorkbookInfo that takes an argument called fileName (a string). This sub should attempt to open the file called fileName. Assuming that it is successful (the file exists), a message box should display the creator of the file and the number of worksheets in the file. It should then close the file. Next, write an OpenFile sub that uses an input box to ask for the name of a file, including its path, and then calls GetWorkbookInfo with this file name as the argument. (Your GetWorkbookInfo will have one serious deficiency—it

will bomb if the requested file doesn't exist, at least not in the specified path. Don't worry about this for now. You will see how to check for it in Chapter 12.)

15. The program in the **Merging Lists.xlsm** file from the previous chapter (see Example 9.4) is written as a single sub.
    a. Break it into several shorter subs, all called from a Main sub. The called subs should be (1) ClearOld (to clear the old merged list in column D, if any), (2) GetData (to put the data in the current lists in arrays), and (3) CreateMergedList (to create the merged list in column D). Don't pass any variables; use all module-level variables for any shared variables.
    b. Repeat part **a**, but pass variables. In particular, the listSize1 and listSize2 variables and the list1 and list2 arrays should be arguments of both GetData and CreateMergedList. (*Hint:* Refer to the section in this chapter dealing with passing arrays as arguments.)

16. The program in the **Product Sales.xlsm** file from the previous chapter (see Example 9.2) is written as a single sub. Break it into at least three shorter subs, all called from a Main sub. You can decide how to break it up and whether you want to use module-level variables or pass arguments.

17. The file **Recent Sales Finished.xlsm** contains a list of a company's sales reps in the Sales Reps worksheet. For each of several Midwest states, there is a worksheet showing recent sales by the sales reps in that state. Open this file and click the button on the Sales Reps worksheet. You will see that it asks for a sales rep and then a state, and it summarizes sales by that rep in that state in a message box. Run this several times (including queries for reps and states not in the company's list) to see all the functionality built into it. The code in this file is password-protected. Now open the file **Recent Sales.xlsm**, which contains only the data and a Main sub that calls some yet-to-be-written subs. Your job is to write the subs, using the arguments indicated in the Main sub, to achieve the same functionality. (*Note:* Make sure that when you do a search for, say, Arnett, you don't also find information for Barnett. Check out the various arguments for the Find function in VBA.)

18. The file **Transactions Finished.xlsm** contains two worksheets. The Customers_Products worksheet lists a company's customers and its products. The Transactions worksheet lists information about recent transactions involving these customers and products. Open this file and click the button on the Customers_Products worksheet. You will be asked for a last name and a first name of a customer. If this customer is found on the list, you will be asked for the name of a product. If this product is found in the list, a message will be displayed summarizing the sales of this product to this customer. Try it a few times (including queries for customers or products not in the lists) to see how it works. The code in this file is password-protected. Now open the file **Transactions.xlsm**, which contains only the data and a Main sub that calls some yet-to-be-written subs. Your job is to write the subs, using the arguments indicated in the Main sub, to achieve the same functionality.

19. The file **Errors 1.xlsx** contains a list of forecasting errors in column A made by some forecasting method. Write a function subroutine called MAE that finds the mean absolute error, that is, the average of the absolute values of the errors. It should be written to work on *any* range of errors such as the one in column A. Then try it out by entering the appropriate formula in cell E1.

20. The file **Errors 2.xlsx** contains a time series of monthly sales in column A and a series of forecasts of these sales in column B. Write a function subroutine called MAPE that finds the mean absolute percentage error of the forecasts, that is, the average of the absolute percentage errors. For example, the absolute percentage error in row 2 is $|713 - 738|/713 = 0.035$, or 3.5%. Write this function so that it will work with *any* two ranges of observations and corresponding forecasts. Then try it out by entering the appropriate formula in cell E1.

21. The triangular distribution is a probability distribution commonly used in business spreadsheet simulations. It is literally triangularly shaped. There are three parameters of this distribution, labeled *a*, *b*, and *c*. The parameters *a* and *c* are the minimum and maximum possible values, and the parameter *b* is the most likely value (where you see the high point of the triangle). This is a simple distribution for people to understand, but it is not straightforward to generate random numbers from this distribution. The method is as follows:

- Calculate $d = (b - d)/(c - a)$
- Generate a uniformly distributed random number U between 0 and 1 (with VBA's Rnd function).
- If $U < d$, return $a + (c - a)\sqrt{dU}$ as the random number.
- If $U > d$, return $a + (c - a)[1 - \sqrt{(1 - d)(1 - U)}]$ as the random number.

(Note that VBA has a built-in sqr function for calculating square roots.) Write a function subroutine called Triangular that takes three arguments corresponding to *a*, *b*, and *c* and returns a triangularly distributed random number. (Use the Application.Volatile and Randomize statements that were used in Example 10.4.) Then try out your random number generator in a worksheet by entering the formula and copying it down to generate a large number of these random numbers. You might also want to create a histogram of these random numbers, just to verify that it has an approximate triangular shape.

User Forms

11.1 Introduction

This chapter introduces user forms, or what you know as dialog boxes. Everyone who has ever used a Windows program is familiar with dialog boxes. They are the primary means for getting users' inputs. In fact, they are so familiar that you probably take them for granted, never stopping to think how they actually work. This chapter explains how to create user forms for your own applications.[1] This entails two distinct operations. First, you have to *design* the user form to have the required functionality and look attractive. Second, you have to write **event handlers** that sit behind the user form waiting to respond appropriately to whatever the user does. For example, many user forms have OK and Cancel buttons. During the design stage, you have to place and resize these buttons on the form. You then have to write VBA code to respond appropriately when a user clicks one of these buttons. Specifically, when the user clicks the Cancel button, you typically want the dialog box to disappear. When the user clicks the OK button, you typically want to capture the user's inputs and then have the dialog box disappear.

Working with user forms is arguably the most fun part of VBA application development. You can use your creative and artistic talents to design the dialog boxes that users will interact with. You can then use your logical skills to ensure that everything works properly when users click buttons, select items from a list box, check "radio" buttons, fill in text boxes, and so on. In short, you get to *create* what you have been using for years—dialog boxes—and you start to see why there is a "V" in VBA.

11.2 Exercise

Working with user forms is not difficult, but there are many small steps to master, and practice is the key to mastering these. The following exercise is typical. It requires very little in the way of calculation, but you must put all of the pieces of

---

[1] Throughout this chapter, I use the terms "dialog box" and "user form" interchangeably. The former term is used by most users, whereas the latter term is used by programmers. In fact, some programmers spell "user form" as UserForm, all one word with two capital letters. I will use the less formal spelling here. Finally, I will usually simply reference a "form." This reference is equivalent to "user form."

the application together in just the right way. By the time you have read through the rest of this chapter and have studied its examples, this exercise will be fairly straightforward—but it is exactly the type your boss will appreciate.

Exercise 11.1 Summarizing Monthly Sales

Consider a company that has regional stores in Atlanta, Charlotte, and Memphis. Each region sells a variety of products, although the products vary from region to region. The file **Sales Summary.xlsm** contains a separate worksheet for each region that shows monthly sales for a three-year period for each product the region sells. Part of the Atlanta worksheet appears in Figure 11.1. Note that the product codes sold in any region always appear in row 4.

The file also contains an Explanation worksheet, as shown in Figure 11.2. This summarizes what the exercise is supposed to accomplish. (Similar Explanation

Figure 11.1 Sample Data for Atlanta

	A	B	C	D	E	F	G	H
1	Sales for Atlanta							
2								
3		Product code						
4	Month	U394K71	B350B99	Y342H72	Q253I61	W311E65	F822G38	M228M28
5	Jan-13	105	477	492	873	424	97	582
6	Feb-13	102	433	528	904	445	111	1149
7	Mar-13	99	591	612	835	553	87	917
8	Apr-13	116	538	546	1143	571	84	898
9	May-13	52	670	573	987	536	97	994
10	Jun-13	97	671	520	720	507	82	1069
11	Jul-13	82	398	501	701	402	95	1170
12	Aug-13	92	559	523	966	388	142	396
13	Sep-13	107	402	432	1161	506	116	881
14	Oct-13	98	419	448	1232	454	116	1138

Figure 11.2 Explanation Sheet

Monthly Sales

The next three sheets show monthly sales of various products for a company's three sales regions. The purpose of this application is to summarize the sales for a particular region and a particular product. The scores can be summarized by any of the following: count, average, median, standard deviation, minimum, and maximum. The user first chooses a region and a set of summary measures. Then the user chooses a product from a list of products for that region. The results should be shown in a message box.

Find summary measures

worksheets appear in all of the applications in Part II of the book. It is always good to tell users right away what an application is all about.) The button on this worksheet should eventually be attached to a macro that runs the application.

It is easier to show what this application is supposed to do than to explain it in detail. In fact, you can try it out yourself by opening the **Sales Summary Finished.xlsm** file and clicking the button. The form in Figure 11.3 is first displayed, where the user must select a region and a set of summary measures. By default, the Atlanta button and the Median and Average boxes are selected when the user sees this form. The user can then make any desired selections.

Next, the user sees the form in Figure 11.4. It contains a message specific to the region chosen and a list of all products sold in that region. (When you write the program, you find this list of product codes by scanning across row 4 of the region's sales worksheet.) By default, the first product code is selected. The user can then select any product code by scrolling through the list.

When the user clicks the OK button, the application summarizes the sales of the product and region chosen and displays the results in a message box. For example, if the user chooses Atlanta, product W620X96, and the average and median summary measures, the message in Figure 11.5 appears.

To develop this application, you need to create the forms in Figures 11.3 and 11.4, place the appropriate controls on them, give these controls appropriate properties, and write appropriate event handlers. You also have to insert a module that contains the non-event code. Specifically, this code must "show" the forms, perform any necessary calculations, and display the final message. One hint that will come in handy is the following. To calculate the required summary measures, you can borrow any of Excel's worksheet functions: COUNT, AVERAGE, MEDIAN, STDEV, MIN, or MAX. For example,

Figure 11.3 First User Form

Figure 11.4 Second User Form

Figure 11.5 Results

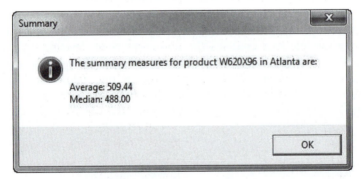

to calculate the average for some range, you can use WorksheetFunction.Average (*range*), where *range* is a reference to the range you want to average. (WorksheetFunction was explained in Chapter 5.)

11.3 Designing User Forms

The first step in developing applications with user forms is designing the forms. This section explains how to do it, but the explanations are purposely kept fairly brief. The more you read about designing forms, the harder you will think it is. It is actually very easy. With a half hour of practice, you can learn how to design user forms. (It will take longer to make them look really professional, but that too is mostly a matter of practice.) So let's get started. As you read this section, you should follow along on your own computer.

Figure 11.6 New User Form

First, open a new workbook in Excel, get into the VBE, and make sure the Project Explorer and Properties windows are visible. (If they aren't visible, click the appropriate buttons on the Standard toolbar or use the appropriate menu items from the View menu.) To add a user form, use the **Insert → UserForm** menu item. A blank form will appear, and your screen will appear as in Figure 11.6. If it doesn't look exactly like this, you can resize windows and dock the Project Explorer and Properties windows at the left side of the screen. In fact, you can move and resize windows any way you like. Also, when you insert the form, the **Toolbox** at the bottom right should appear. If it ever disappears, you can always redisplay it by selecting the **View → Toolbox** menu item or clicking the "hammer and wrench" button on the Standard toolbar.

To design user forms, you need to know three things:

- Which controls are available
- How to place, resize, and line up controls on a form
- How to changes properties of controls in the Properties window

Available Controls

The available controls are those in the Toolbox in Figure 11.7. The arrow at the top left is used only for pointing. The rest, starting with the A and going from left to right, have the following generic names:[2]

- First row—Label, TextBox, ComboBox, ListBox
- Second row—CheckBox, OptionButton, ToggleButton, Frame, CommandButton

---

[2] This list uses the technical single-word names for the controls, such as TextBox (all one word). Throughout the discussions, I usually revert to less formal names, such as text box.

Figure 11.7 Toolbox

- Third row—TabStrip, MultiPage, ScrollBar, SpinButton, Image
- Fourth row—RefEdit

Each of these controls has a certain behavior built into it. Without going into details, I will simply state that this standard behavior is the behavior you are familiar with from working with dialog boxes in Windows applications. For example, if there are several option (radio) buttons on a form and you select one of them, the others are automatically unselected. The following list describes the functionality of the most frequently used controls.

- CommandButton—used to run subs (the user clicks a button and a sub runs)
- Label—used mainly for explanations and prompts
- TextBox—used to obtain any type of user input (the user types something in the text box)
- ListBox—lets the user choose one or more items from a list
- ComboBox—similar to a list box, except that the user can type an item that isn't on the list in a box
- CheckBox—lets the user check whether an option is desired or not (any or all of a set of check boxes can be checked)
- OptionButton—often called a radio button, lets the user check which of several options is desired (only one of a set of option buttons can be checked)
- Frame—usually used to group a related set of options buttons, but can be used to organize any set of controls into logical groups
- RefEdit—similar to a TextBox control, but used specifically to let the user select a worksheet cell or range

The controls in Figure 11.7 are the "standard" controls that are available to everyone who uses Excel. However, there are actually many more controls you might want to experiment with. To do so, right-click anywhere in the middle of the Toolbox in Figure 11.7 and select **Additional Controls**. You will see a fairly long list. Just check any that look interesting, and they will be added to your Toolbox. However, don't expect much help on what these additional controls do or how they work. You are essentially on your own.

A particularly useful control is the Calendar control. It not only allows you to put a calendar on a form, but this calendar is *smart*, so it needs virtually no programming on your part. If you add a calendar control to a form, you can find information about its properties and methods by going to the Object Browser and viewing the MSACAL library. Check it out. Students love it.

Note about the Calendar control in Excel 2010 and later versions. I was quite upset to learn, upon trying some of my Excel 2007 applications in Excel 2010, that the Calendar control was no longer there. In fact, applications I developed in Excel 2007 that contained Calendar controls no longer worked! Fortunately, as I discovered from Web searches (and from similar unhappy programmers), the Calendar control is still available; it is just not available by default in Excel 2010 and later versions. You need to install and register it on your computer. Then you can use it, and any of my applications that contain this control will work in Excel 2010 and later versions. You can find the necessary files, along with installation instructions, in the Calendar Control folder of the book files.

However, there is still another "gotcha" with this Calendar control (MSCAL), at least as of the time of this writing: It doesn't work with 64-bit versions of Office. This is stated clearly in a number of Web sites. If you have a 64-bit version of Office 2010 or later, you might try exploring the Web for a 64-bit compatible Calendar control. The only possibility I found was at http://www.x64bitdownload.com /downloads/t-64-bit-calendar-activex-control-download-gteojqqn.html, but even it didn't show up in the additional controls list in my 64-bit version of Excel 2013. Maybe we should all follow the advice of a number of Web bloggers: Don't install 64-bit Office yet, even if you are running 64-bit Windows, because too many things are still incompatible with it.

Adding Controls to a User Form

To add any control to a form, click the control in the Toolbox and then drag a shape on the form. That's all there is to it. Try the following step-by-step exercise, and don't be afraid to experiment. When you are finished, your form should appear approximately like the one in Figure 11.8.

Figure 11.8 Controls on Practice User Form

1. Resize the user form (make it wider and taller).
2. Add a command button at the top right. While it is still selected, press the Ctrl key and drag the button down to make a copy. You will know you are copying, not moving, when you see a plus sign as you drag. This is the general way to copy controls—select them and then drag them with your finger on the Ctrl key. (If you take your finger off the Ctrl key too early, you will move, not copy. I make this mistake all the time.)
3. Add a wide label to the left of the command buttons. This is a good place for explaining what your dialog box does.
4. Add a label (shown as Label2) and a corresponding text box to its right. A text box typically has a corresponding label that serves as a prompt for what the user is supposed to enter in the text box.
5. Add a fairly large frame below the text box. Next, add an option button inside the frame, and make a copy of this option button. Make sure that both option buttons fit entirely within the frame boundary. You want both of them to *belong* to the frame.
6. Drag over the frame to select it, put your finger on the Ctrl key, and drag the whole thing to the right to make a copy. Note that you get not only a new frame, but also a new set of option buttons. The option buttons in a frame are essentially part of the frame, so when you copy the frame, you also copy the option buttons. In addition, the option buttons in any frame are a logical set in the sense that only one button *in each frame* can be checked. For example, the top button in the left frame could be checked, *and* the bottom button in the right frame could be checked. If option buttons are not inside frames, then only one option button on the whole form can be checked.
7. Add a check box at the lower left and make a copy of it to its right. Any number of these can be checked, including none of them.
8. Add a list box at the bottom right. No list appears yet; you will add one later.
9. Resize and align the controls to make the form visually appealing. This is quite easy, if a bit tedious. Just experiment with the menu items under the Format menu, such as **Format → Align** and **Format → Make Same Size**. The key is that you can drag over several controls to select them. The selected controls are then treated as a group for the purpose of aligning and resizing. The *first* one selected is the one that the others are aligned or resized to. (It is the one with the white handles; the others have black handles.)

When you design a form in an application that others will use, keep in mind that users tend to be very critical of design flaws. If your application is complex and does a lot great things, users still might complain that a set of radio buttons aren't quite aligned with one another. In fact, they might not trust your entire application if they aren't impressed with the design. So spend some time making your forms look professional. Probably the best advice is to mimic dialog boxes you see in various Microsoft applications.

11.4 Setting Properties of Controls

The user form in Figure 11.8 doesn't do anything yet. In fact, it isn't even clear what it is supposed to do. You can fix the latter problem by setting some properties

Figure 11.9 Properties Window for User Form

of the controls. You do this in the **Properties** window. (If the Property window isn't visible, usually right below the Project Explorer window, you can make it visible from the View menu in the VBE or by clicking on the "hand" button on the Standard toolbar.) Like Excel ranges, worksheets, and workbooks, controls are objects with properties, and these are listed in the Properties window. The items in the Properties window change depending on which control is selected, because different types of controls have different sets of properties. Figure 11.9 shows the Properties window for the user form itself. (To select the user form, click anywhere on its gray area where there are no controls.) The names of the properties are listed on the left, and their values are listed on the right.

Microsoft provides a bewildering number of properties for user forms and controls. Fortunately, you can ignore most properties and concentrate on the few you need to change. For example, you will typically want to change the Name and Caption properties of a user form. The Name property is used in general for referring to the user form (or any control) in VBA code. The default names are generic, such as UserForm1, CommandButton1, and so on. It is typically a good idea to change the Name property only if you plan to refer to the object in VBA code; otherwise, you can keep the default name. The Caption property is what you see on the screen. The caption of the form itself appears in the title bar. For now, go through the following steps to change certain properties. (See Figure 11.10 for the finished user form.) For each step, select the control first (click it), so that the Properties window shows the properties for *that* control.

Before going through these steps, I want to make a point about naming user forms and controls. In Chapter 5, I mentioned several conventions for naming variables, and I said I favored the camel convention, with names like unitCost. I have been using this convention consistently ever since, and I use it in the rest of the book. However, for user forms and controls, I favor the Hungarian convention, which uses short prefixes in the name to indicate what type of control it is. I adopt this convention because it is used by most programmers. Here are some common prefixes: frm for user form, lbl for label, cmd for command button (some people prefer btn), txt for text box, lb for list box, cbo for combo box, opt for option button, chk for check box, and rfe for ref edit. These prefixes make

Figure 11.10 User Form with Changed Properties

your code much more readable. They not only distinguish one type of control from another, but perhaps more important, they distinguish controls from variables like unitCost.

1. **User form.** Change its Name property to frmInputs and its Caption property to Product Inputs.
2. **Top command button.** Change its Name property to cmdOK, change its Caption property to OK, and change its Default property (yes, it is listed as Default in the left pane of the Properties window) to True. This Default setting gives the OK button the functionality you expect once the form is operational—you can click it *or* press the Enter key to accomplish the same thing.
3. **Bottom command button.** Change its Name property to cmdCancel, change its Caption property to Cancel, and change its Cancel property to True. The effect of this latter property is to allow the user to press the Esc key instead of clicking on the Cancel button. Again, this is standard behavior in Windows dialog boxes.
4. **Top label.** Usually, the only property you will change for a label is its Caption property—the text that appears in the label. You can do this through the Properties window, or you can click the label once to select it and then again to put a dark border around it.[3] This allows you to type the label directly on the form. For this label, enter the caption This is for practice only, to see how controls on user forms work.
5. **Label to the left of the text box.** Change its Caption property to Product.

---

[3] If you accidentally double-click the label or any other controls during the design stage, you will open the event code window, which is discussed later in the chapter. To get back to the user form design, select the **View → Object** menu item.

Figure 11.11   MultiSelect Property for List Boxes

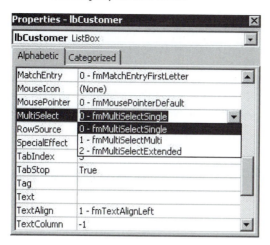

6. **Text box.** Change the Name property to txtProduct.
7. **Frames.** Change their Caption properties to Region of Origin and Shipping Method, respectively. These captions appear at the top borders of the frames.
8. **Option buttons.** Change the Name properties of the option buttons in the left frame to optEast and optWest, and change their Caption properties to East and West. These captions are the text you see next to the buttons. Similarly, change the Name properties of the other two option buttons to optTrain and optTruck, and change their Caption properties to Train and Truck.
9. **Check boxes.** These are similar to option buttons. Change their Name properties to chkPerish and chkFragile, and change their Caption properties to Perishable and Fragile.
10. **List box.** Change its Name property to lbCustomer. A list box does not have a Caption property, so add a label control above it with the caption Customers. Otherwise, the user will not know what the list is for. There is another property you should be aware of for list boxes: the MultiSelect property. Its default value is 0-fmMultiSelectSingle. This indicates that the user is allowed to select only one item from the list. Sometimes you will want the user to be able to select *more* than one item from a list. If so, you should select option 2-fmMultiSelectExtended. (See Figure 11.11.) For now, accept the first (default) option. (The middle option is virtually never used. I have no idea why they even include it.)

Tab Order

There is one final touch you can add to make your user form more professional—the tab order. You are probably aware that most dialog boxes allow you to move from one control to another by pressing the Tab key. To give your form this functionality, all you need to do is change the Tab Index property of each control, using any ordering you like and starting with index 0. There are two things you should know about tabbing.

- Any control with the TabStop property set to False cannot be tabbed to. This is typically the case for labels.
- When there is a frame with embedded controls such as option buttons, you set the TabIndex for the *frame* relative to the order of the other controls on the form, but the tab order for the controls within the frame is set separately. For example, a frame might have index 6 in the tab order of *all* controls, but its two option buttons would have indexes 0 and 1. Essentially, the user first tabs to the frame and then tabs through the controls inside the frame.

The easiest way to set the tab order is to select the **View → Tab Order** menu item. This allows you to move any of the controls up or down in the tab order. Just remember that if you select **View → Tab Order** when a frame is selected, you will see the tab order only for the controls inside that frame.

Testing the Form

Now that you have designed the form, you can see how it will look to the user. To do this, make sure the user form, not some control on the form, is selected, and click the **Run Sub/UserForm** button (the blue triangle button) or press the F5 key. This displays the user form. It doesn't *do* anything yet, but it should at least look nice. Note that the *focus* (the cursor location) is set to the control at the top of the tab order (tab index 0). For example, if you set the tab index of the text box to 0, the cursor will be in the text box, waiting for the user to type something. You can see how the tab order works by pressing the Tab key repeatedly. To get back to design view, click the Close button of the form (the X button at the top right). Note that you cannot yet close the form by clicking the Cancel button, because the Cancel button is not yet "wired." You will remedy this shortly.

11.5 Creating a User Form Template

If you design a lot of forms, you will quickly get tired of always having to design the same OK and Cancel buttons that appear on most forms. This section illustrates a handy shortcut. Open a new workbook and go through the procedure in the previous two sections to design a user form with an OK and a Cancel button and having the properties listed earlier in steps 2 and 3. It should look something like Figure 11.12. Now select the **File → Export File** menu item, and save the form under a name such as **OK_Cancel.frm** in some convenient folder.[4] Later on, whenever you want a user form with ready-made OK and Cancel buttons, select the **File → Import File** menu item and open the **OK_Cancel.frm** file. This can save you about a minute each time you design a form.

---

[4]You will note that this also saves a file called **OK_Cancel.frx** in your folder. You don't need to be concerned about this file, except that if you ever move the .frm file to a different folder, you should also move the .frx file to the same folder.

Figure 11.12 User Form Template

11.6 Writing Event Handlers

Much of Windows programming is built around events, where an event occurs whenever the user does something. This could mean clicking a button, entering text in a text box, checking an option button, selecting a worksheet, right-clicking a cell, mousing over a cell—in short, doing just about anything. Each of these events has a built-in **event handler**. This is a sub where you can add code so that appropriate actions are taken when the event occurs. These subs are always available—*if* you want the program to respond to certain events. Of course, there are many events that you don't want to bother responding to. For example, you *could* respond to the event where the mouse is dragged over a command button, but you probably have no reason to do so. In this case, you simply ignore the event. On the other hand, there are certain events you *do* want to respond to. For these, you have to write the appropriate event handler. This section illustrates how to do this in the context of user forms.

First, you have to understand where the event handler is placed. Also, you have to understand naming conventions. All of the VBA code to this point has been placed in modules, which are inserted into a project with the **Insert →
Module** menu item.[5] Event handlers are *not* placed in these modules. Instead, they are placed in a user form's code window. To get to a user form's code window, make sure you are viewing the form's design window, and select the **View → Code** menu item. In general, the **View → Code** and **View → Object** menu items toggle between the form's design and its code window. There are also two handy buttons at the top left of the Project Explorer for toggling between code and design (see Figure 11.13), and if you prefer keystrokes, the F7 and Shift-F7 keys do the same thing.

Another way to get from the design window to the code window is to double-click a control. (You might already have experienced this by accident.) This not only opens the code window, but it inserts a "stub" for the event handler. For example, by double-clicking the OK button in design view, the code window opens and the following stub is inserted:

---

[5] There was one exception, where you learned to create an event handler, the Workbook_Open sub, behind the ThisWorkbook object.

Figure 11.13 Buttons for Toggling Between Code and Design

```
Private Sub cmdOK_Click()
End Sub
```

Each control has many such subs available. The sub names all start with the name of the control, followed by an underscore and an event type. The one you get by double-clicking the control depends on which event is the *default* event for that control. To understand this better, get into the code window for the form you created in Section 11.3. You will see two dropdown lists at the top of the window. The one on the left lists all controls on the form, including the form itself, as shown in Figure 11.14. Select any of these and then look at the dropdown list on the right. It lists all events the selected control can respond to. Figure 11.15 illustrates this list for a command button.

If you double-click any of the items in the list in Figure 11.15, you get a sub into which you can write code. For example, if you double-click the MouseUp item, you get the following sub:

```
Private Sub cmdOK_MouseUp(ByVal Button As Integer, ByVal Shift As Integer, _
    ByVal X As Single, ByVal Y As Single)
End Sub
```

Figure 11.14 List of Controls

Figure 11.15 List of Events for a Command Button

You have no choice over the format of the Sub line. The sub must be named as shown (control name, underscore, event type), and it must contain any arguments that are given. But how would you ever know what this sub responds to (what is a MouseUp event, anyway?), and how would you know what the arguments are all about? The best way is to consult the Object Browser. Try it out. Open the Object Browser and select the **MSForms** library. This library provides help for all objects in user forms. (It appears in the list of libraries only if you have inserted a user form.) Specifically, it provides a list of controls on the left and their properties, methods, and events on the right, as shown in Figure 11.16. The events are designated by **lightning** icons. By selecting any of these and clicking the question mark button, you can get plenty of help.

This information about getting help works for most controls, but not for the RefEdit control, the one that allows a user to select a cell or a range. For some reason, there is no information about the RefEdit control in the MSForms library, evidently because it is not part of that library. Instead, it is in its own **RefEdit** library, with itself as the only member and with virtually no online help. If you want to use RefEdit controls, your best bet is to perform a Web search for information about them—or experiment with them.[6]

In general, you need to decide which events you want to respond to with code. This chapter illustrates the ones that are used most often for the applications in later chapters, but you should realize that the floodgates are wide open—you can respond to just about any action the user takes. This can be bewildering at first, but it is the reason Windows programming is so powerful. The following example illustrates some possibilities.

---

[6]The RefEdit control is indeed strange—and not totally trustworthy—although I still use it a lot. To see its library, you need to check **Ref Edit Control** under **Tools → References**. Then you can see a list of its properties and methods in the Object Browser, but without any online help. Strangely, you do *not* need to set this reference to actually use a RefEdit control on your form. It suffices to have the default reference to the **MSForms** library, even though the RefEdit control doesn't show up in its list. A programming colleague at Palisade told me that they distrust the RefEdit control so much that they discontinued using it and developed their own version instead.

Figure 11.16 Object Browser

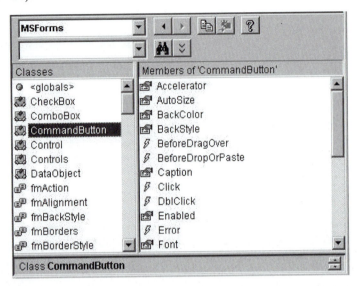

EXAMPLE 11.1

Consider the dialog box in Figure 11.17. (See the file **StatPro Location Form.xlsm**.) It gives the user three choices of where to place results from some analysis—to the right of a data set, on a new worksheet, or in a selected cell.[7] The three option buttons are named optToRight, optNewSheet, and optCell. If the user chooses the second option, the text box txtNewSheet next to this option is enabled so that the user can enter the name of the new worksheet. Otherwise, this text box is disabled. Similarly, if the user chooses the third option, the refedit control rfeCell next to this option is enabled so that the user can select the desired cell. Otherwise, this control is disabled.

Figure 11.17 Location Dialog Box

---

[7] It is taken from my old StatPro add-in, available free from http://www.kelley.iu.edu/albrightbooks. However, I no longer support this add-in.

The following three event handlers implement the desired logic. Each responds to the Click event of an option button. They set the Enabled property of the txtNewSheet and rfeCell controls to True or False, and they use the SetFocus method to select the appropriate control. For example, if the user clicks the optNewSheet button, the txtNewSheet text box is enabled and selected, and the rfeCell box is disabled. These subs should give you a taste of the power you have over your applications.

```vba
Private Sub optToRight_Click()
    ' Explain this option, and disable the newsheet and cell boxes.
    lblExplain.Caption = "The results will " _
        & "be placed in newly inserted columns just to the right of " _
        & "the data range. Any data already to the right of the " _
        & "data range will be moved over."
    txtNewSheet.Enabled = False
    refCell.Enabled = False
End Sub

Private Sub optNewSheet_Click()
    ' Explain this option, enable the newsheet option, set
    ' the focus to it, and disable the cell box.
    lblExplain.Caption = "BE CAREFUL!!! The output will " _
        & "be placed on a new sheet with the name you enter. " _
        & "If a sheet with this name exists, " _
        & "it will be replaced (and any charts based on it will " _
        & "be lost)."
    With txtNewSheet
        .Enabled = True
        .SetFocus
    End With
    refCell.Enabled = False
End Sub

Private Sub optCell_Click()
    ' Explain this option, enable the cell option, set
    ' the focus to it, and disable the newsheet box.
    lblExplain.Caption = "BE CAREFUL!!! The output will be placed " _
        & "in a range starting in the cell you specify. " _
        & "The output will overwrite anything already in this range."
    txtNewSheet.Enabled = False
    With refCell
        .Enabled = True
        .SetFocus
    End With
End Sub
```

EXAMPLE 11.2

This example illustrates event handlers for the user form you created in sections 11.3 and 11.4. (The completed version is in the file **Practice Form.xlsm**.) It is typical of the forms you will see in later chapters. There are two event handlers: cmdOK_Click and cmdCancel_Click. These two determine what occurs when the user clicks the OK and Cancel buttons.

Overview of the Procedure

If you are used to the event handlers in previous editions of the book, you will see significant changes in this edition. The changes were made to avoid the global variables that were used to share information between the main sub and the event handlers. The code in previous editions still works fine, but the code used in this edition is more professional. It passes variables as arguments rather than using global variables. This new procedure is briefly explained here.[8] (The previous files are still available. Their file names all end with "_old".)

The typical code behind a form begins with a Public function with a name such as ShowInputsDialog (or any name you prefer). This function takes arguments that need to be shared by the main sub and the form's code, usually the user's choices from the form, and it returns a Boolean value: False if the user clicks the Cancel button (or the upper right X button) and True otherwise. A module-level Boolean variable named cancel keeps track of whether the user cancels or not, and the ShowInputsDialog function gets its value from this cancel variable.

Besides the usual cmdOK_Click and cmdCancel_Click event handlers, plus any other event handlers such as you saw in the StatPro Location code, there are typically three other subs in the form's code:

- The UserForm_QueryClose event handler, which is used to capture the event where the user cancels by clicking the upper right X button
- An Initialize sub, which is used to initialize the form for when the user first sees it
- Optionally, a Boolean Valid function, which checks whether the user's inputs are valid and makes the user try again if they aren't

Finally, everything is started in motion from the main sub with a line such as

```
If frmInputs.ShowInputsDialog(arguments) Then
```

This line transfers control to the form's code, passing the necessary arguments to the form and showing the form to the user. Then if the user *doesn't* cancel, ShowInputsDialog returns True, and lines after the above If statement process the user's inputs in some way. However, if the user *does* cancel, ShowInputsDialog returns False, and the program typically ends quietly.

Now this procedure will be illustrated for the Practice Form example.

Main Sub Code

The sub in the module declares the variables that will capture the user's inputs as procedure-level variables, *not* as global variables. Then with the If line, it passes these to the form's code. Finally, assuming the user doesn't cancel, it displays the user's choices.

---

[8] I thank my colleague Erik Westwig at Palisade Corp for showing me this better way of passing variables. As always, the best way to learn programming is from other programmers!

```
Sub Main()
    Dim productIndex As Integer, region As String, shipping As String, _
        isPerishable As Boolean, isFragile As Boolean, customer As String
    ' Display the inputs form to get the user's inputs,
    ' but quit if the user clicks the Cancel (or X) button.
    If frmInputs.ShowInputsDialog(productIndex, region, _
            shipping, isPerishable, isFragile, customer) Then
        MsgBox "The user chose the following:" &vbCrLf _
            & "Product index: "&productIndex&vbCrLf _
            & "Region of origin: "& region &vbCrLf _
            & "Shipping method: "& shipping &vbCrLf _
            & "Perishable? "&isPerishable&vbCrLf _
            & "Fragile? "&isFragile&vbCrLf _
            & "Customer: "& customer, vbInformation, "User inputs"
    ' The rest of the program would then act on the user's inputs.
    End If
End Sub
```

ShowInputsDialog Function Code

First, note that this function is declared as Public. This is necessary so that it can be called from the main sub in the module. However, everything else in the form code, including the module-level cancel variable, is declared as Private. The function's arguments match those passed from the main sub. The Initialize sub is called to fill the form with initial values, and the form is then made visible to the user with the Me.Show line. (The keyword Me anywhere inside the form code refers to the form itself.) If the user doesn't cancel, the user's inputs are captured from the values of the form's controls. Finally, the value of the function is the opposite of cancel, and the form is unloaded from memory with the line Unload Me.

```
Private cancel As Boolean

Public Function ShowInputsDialog(productIndex As Integer, region As String, _
        shipping As String, isPerishable As Boolean, _
        isFragile As Boolean, customer As String) As Boolean
    Call Initialize
    Me.Show
    If Not cancel Then
        ' Capture the user's inputs.
        productIndex = txtProduct.Text
        If optEast.Value Then region="East" Else region="West"
        If optTruck.Value Then shipping="Truck" Else shipping="Train"
        isPerishable = chkPerish.Value
        isFragile = chkFragile
        customer = lbCustomer.Value
    End If
    ShowInputsDialog = Not cancel
    Unload Me
End Function
```

Although more will be said about list boxes later in the chapter, note for now that the Value property of a list box indicates the item selected—in this case, the name of the customer. In contrast, the ListIndex property indicates the position in the list of the selected item, starting with 0. For example, it returns 3 if the fourth item is chosen. If no item is selected, ListIndex is 1.

Hide Versus Unload. There is a subtle difference between hiding and unloading a form. When you hide a form, using the line Me.Hide, the form disappears from the screen, but it is still in memory. In contrast, when you unload a form, using the line Unload Me, the form disappears from the screen *and* it is deleted from memory. It is a common practice among programmers to hide a form and then unload it, as I will do from now on.

Initialize Code

For this application, I want the following behavior when the form initially appears: the East and Truck buttons should be checked, the Perishable box should be unchecked, the Fragile box should be checked, and the customer list box should be filled with a list of customers, with the first customer selected. (Of course, the programmer gets to make these decisions, which the user can then override when the form appears.) Except for the last requirement, this is easy. Each control has properties that can be set with VBA code. Also, each type of control has a default property.[9] If you want to set the default property, you don't even have to list the property's name. For example, the Value property is the default property of an option button and a check box. It is True or False, depending on whether the control is checked or not. To set this property, you can write

```
optEast.Value = True
```

or you can use the shortened version

```
optEast = True
```

Similarly, the Value property is the default property of a text box control. It indicates the value, treated as a string, in the box.[10] For example, to make a text box blank, you can write

```
txtProduct.Value = ""
```

or

```
txtProduct = ""
```

---

[9] The default property for a control has a small blue dot above it in the Object Browser. For example, if you select OptionButton in the Object Browser and scan its list of properties, you will see a blue dot above the Value property.

[10] A text box also has a Text property. From what I can uncover in online help, the Text and Value properties are virtually identical for a text box. You can use either.

Figure 11.18 Customer List on a Worksheet

	A
1	Customer list
2	Adobe
3	Altaire
4	Canon
5	Compaq
6	Diamond
7	Epson
25	Symantec
26	Toshiba
27	Visioneer
28	Xerox

I strongly prefer the first version in each case. Even though the default property can be omitted, I believe the code is much more readable if the default property is shown explicitly.

List boxes are trickier. You can populate them in several ways. Two methods are illustrated here. For both, I assume that there is a worksheet with a list of customers in a range named Customers. This list might appear as in Figure 11.18, where the Customers range is A2:A28.

Then the AddItem method of the list box can be used inside a For loop to add the customers to the list box, one at a time. The only required argument of the AddItem method is the name of the item to be added.

The completed Initialize code appears below.

```
Private Sub Initialize()
    Dim cell As Range

    txtProduct.Text = ""
    optEast.Value = True
    optTruck.Value = True
    chkPerish.Value = False
    chkFragile.Value = True

    With lbCustomer
        For Each cell In Range("Customers")
            .AddItem cell.Value
        Next
        ' Select first customer (0-based indexing).
        .ListIndex = 0
    End With
End Sub
```

Alternatively, the RowSource property of the list box can be set to Customers at design time (in the Properties window). This tells VBA to populate the list box

Figure 11.19 Initialized User Form

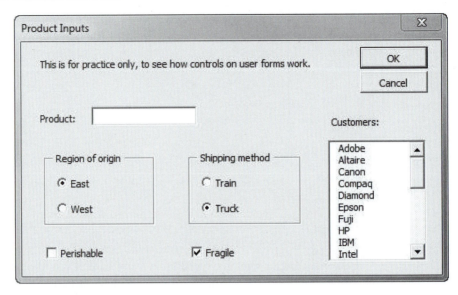

with the list in the named Customers range. As a result, the For Each loop in the above code would not be necessary.

When the form is shown initially, it will appear as in Figure 11.19. Of course, the user is then free to make any desired selections.

Valid Function Code

The Valid function checks whether the user's inputs are valid. In this case, it checks whether the product index in the text box is a number from 1 to 1000. Note that by selecting the first customer in the Initialize sub, there is no way for the user to *not* select a customer in the list box, so there is no need to include a check for this in the Valid code.

cmdOK_Click Code

Because the user's choices are captured in the ShowInputsDialog function, the only purpose of this event handler is to hide the form and set cancel to False. However, the Valid function is called first. If it is False, so that the user's inputs aren't valid, the form is *not* hidden, and the user has to try again.

```
Private Sub cmdOK_Click()
    If Valid Then Me.Hide
    cancel = False
End Sub
```

cmdCancel_Click Code

There is usually not much you want to happen when the user clicks the Cancel button. This is the user's way of saying she doesn't want to continue, so the typical cmdCancel_Click code is the following.

```
Private Sub cmdCancel_Click()
    Me.Hide
    cancel = True
End Sub
```

UserForm_QueryClose Code

This code handles the situation where the user cancels by clicking the upper right X button on the form. (The condition CloseMode = vbFormControlMenu means that the X is clicked.) It can be used, as is, for virtually all of your forms. It assumes that there is a Cancel button on your form and that you want the same behavior for clicking the X as for clicking Cancel.

```
Private Sub UserForm_QueryClose(cancel As Integer, CloseMode As Integer)
    If CloseMode = vbFormControlMenu Then cmdCancel_Click
End Sub
```

When you run this program and don't cancel, the result should be a message something like the one in Figure 11.20.

Figure 11.20 Display of User's Inputs

User inputs

The user chose the following:
Product index: 235
Region of origin: East
Shipping method: Train
Perishable? True
Fragile? False
Customer: Epson

OK

A Note on Extraneous Event Handler Stubs

Don't be surprised if you find a couple of lines like the following in your event code:

```
Private Sub txtProduct_Change()
End Sub
```

I got these by inadvertently double-clicking on the txtProduct text box while in design mode. This happens frequently. Whenever you do it, you get the beginnings of an event handler for the control's default event, in this case the Change event. This "stub" causes no harm if you leave it in your program, but if you don't really need it, you should get rid of it. I wouldn't be surprised if I have one or two of these stubs in the files included in this book. If so, I simply forgot to delete them.

11.7 Looping Through the Controls on a User Form

There are many times when you would like to loop through controls of a certain type to perform some action. For example, you might want to loop through a group of check boxes, one for each region of the country, to see which of them are checked. The easiest way to do this would be to form an *array* of controls and then go through the array elements with a For loop. Unfortunately, however, VBA does not allow you to form arrays of controls. An alternative method that *is* possible is to use a For Each loop to loop through the Controls collection on the user form. This loops through *all* controls—text boxes, labels, command buttons, and so on. If you want to perform some action on only a particular type of control, such as the text boxes, you can use the TypeName function, as illustrated in the following code.

```
Dim ctl As Control
Valid = True
For Each ctl In Me.Controls
    If TypeName(ctl) = "TextBox" Then
        If ctl.Value = "" Or Not IsDate(ctl) Then
            Valid = False
            MsgBox "Enter valid dates in the text boxes.", _
                vbInformation, "Invalid entry"
            ctl.SetFocus
            Exit For
        End If
    End If
Next
```

Note that ctl is declared as a generic control. The For Each loop goes through all controls in the collection Me.Controls (where Me is again a reference to the form itself). The If TypeName(ctl) = "TextBox" statement then checks whether the control is a text box. (Note that it requires the formal name, TextBox, spelled exactly as shown.) If it is, certain actions are taken. If it is not, no actions are taken. This looping method is not as convenient as being able to loop through an array of controls, but it is the best method available. (By the way, you will *not* get Intellisense when you type ctl and then a period. This is because the different types of controls have different properties and methods, and with ctl being a *generic* control, VBA doesn't know which list of properties and methods to list.)

11.8 Working with List Boxes

List boxes are among the most useful controls for forms, but they are also tricky to work with. This section explains methods for populating list boxes and capturing users' choices.

First, list boxes come in two basic types: **single** and **multi**. The type is determined by the MultiSelect property. A single-type list box allows the user to select only one item from the list, whereas a multi-type list box allows the user to select *any* number of items (including no items) from the list. Of course, the context of the application determines which type to use, but you should know how to work with both.

Single List Boxes

If you want a list box to be of the single type, you do *not* have to change its MultiSelect property. By default, a list box is of the single type—the MultiSelect setting is 0-fmMultiSelectSingle in the Properties window. For this single type, there are two properties you are likely to use: the Value property and the ListIndex property. These properties were illustrated in Example 11.2. For example, if the user selects Compaq from the list in Figure 11.19, which is the fourth customer in the list, the Value property is the string "Compaq" and the ListIndex property is 3. (It is 3, not 4, because indexing always starts with 0.) If no item is selected, then ListIndex is –1, which can be used for error checking. (You typically want the user to select *some* item.)

Multi List Boxes

Multi-type list boxes are slightly more complex. First, you have to set the MultiSelect property appropriately (the correct setting is 2-fmMultiSelectExtended in the Properties window) at design time. Second, it no longer makes much sense to use Value and ListIndex properties. Instead, you need to know *which* items the user has selected. You do this with the Selected property of the list box, which acts as a 0-based Boolean array, as illustrated below. You can also take advantage of the ListCount property, which returns the number of items in the list. The following sample code is typical. It uses a public Boolean array variable isChosen (passed from a module) to capture the user's choices for later use. Because I prefer 1-based arrays, isChosen starts with index 1. Unfortunately, it is not possible to make the built-in Selected array 1-based; it is *always* 0-based. This accounts for the difference between the indexes of Selected and isChosen in the code.

```
For i = 1 To lbProducts.ListCount
    isChosen(i) = lbProducts.Selected(i - 1)
Next
```

For example, if there are five items in the list and the user selects the first, second, and fifth, then isChosen(1), isChosen(2), and isChosen(5) will be True, and isChosen(3) and isChosen(4) will be False. This information can then be used in the rest of the program.

There is more to say about list boxes. For example, they can have multi-column lists. However, this is enough information for now. Other list box features will be explained as needed in later chapters.

11.9 Modal and Modeless Forms

All of the forms (dialog boxes) you have seen so far, including InputBox and MsgBox, have been **modal**. This means that you have to dismiss them (make them disappear) before you can do any other work in Excel. For example, if a MsgBox is visible, you can't select a cell or a chart on a worksheet. Starting with Excel 2000, it is also possible to create **modeless** forms, at least for the ones *you* create (as opposed to ones built-in like MsgBox and InputBox). You can do this with the Show method, as in

```
frmTest.Show vbModeless
```

Because the built-in constant **vbModeless** equals 0, the following line also works:

```
frmTest.Show 0
```

Although it is possible to show a form as modeless, I can't think of many reasons why you would want to do so. I certainly don't see any reason to do so for the applications in Part II of the book or any of the smaller applications in this chapter. However, one possible situation where a modeless form makes sense is when you want to show a "progress indicator" form. This can be done with the following steps. (See the file **Modeless Form.xlsm**.)

1. Create a form called frmProgress, and change its Caption property to Progress Indicator. (See Figure 11.21.)
2. Create a label control called lblFixedLength. Change its Caption property to a blank string—no caption—and change its BackColor property to white.
3. Create a second label control called lblVariableLength. Change its Caption property to a blank string and change its BackColor property to blue. Make sure that the two labels lie on top of one another. You can force this by making their Top, Left, Height, and Width properties the same.
4. Type the following code behind the form. This isn't an event handler, but it should be placed in the same code window where you would put an event handler for the form. Essentially, this sub becomes a *method* of the form, so

Figure 11.21 Modeless Form with Two Labels

that the line Call frmProgress.ChangeWidth(i / 1000000) in the module is possible.

```
Public Sub ChangeWidth(pct As Single)
    ' Change the width to be a percentage of the fixed width.
    lblVariableWidth.Width = pct * lblFixedWidth.Width

    ' The following is necessary to allow the operating
    ' system to refresh the screen.
    DoEvents
End Sub
```

5. In a module, enter the following code (or something similar depending on your application):

```
Sub TestWithProgress()
    Dim i As Long, val As Single

    frmProgress.Show vbModeless

    ' Perform some task that takes awhile.
    For i = 1 To 1000000

        ' Every so often, change the width of the variable
        ' width bar to show the progress
        If i Mod 100 = 0 Then
            Call frmProgress.ChangeWidth(i / 1000000)
        End If

        ' Do something that takes at least a little time.
        val = Application.NormInv(Rnd, 1000, 100)
    Next

    ' Now that the task is complete, unload the form.
    Unload frmProgress
End Sub
```

When you run the TestWithProgress sub, the progress indicator will go from all white to all blue, and then the form will disappear. The DoEvents line in the ChangeWidth sub is technical, but it is necessary. If you omit it, the dialog box will appear, but nothing inside it will be visible. The DoEvents line allows Windows to refresh the screen.

11.10 Working with Excel Controls

By now, you are probably used to placing buttons on your worksheets. As described in Chapter 3, you typically click the upper-left button icon in Figure 11.22, drag a button on your worksheet, and then assign a macro to the button. The controls shown in Figure 11.22 are accessed from the Insert dropdown list on the Developer ribbon in Excel 2007 and later versions. (They were in two separate toolbars in Excel 2003 and earlier.) These controls have the same purposes and functionality as those in the VBE, but they are placed directly in Excel worksheets.

The **Forms** controls at the top of Figure 11.22 are a leftover from older versions of Excel (version 95 and before). These controls, often referred to as *lightweight* controls, are simple and easy to use. Microsoft changed its Excel programming environment rather dramatically in version 97, but it decided to keep the Forms controls for backward compatibility—and because users like them. Fortunately (in my opinion), these Forms controls are still available.

You don't need to know any VBA programming to use the Forms controls. All you need to do is click one of them, drag it on a worksheet, and then right-click it to change a few properties. The following example is typical of the useful applications you can create with Forms controls.

EXAMPLE 11.3

The file **Home Loan.xlsx** is a template for the monthly mortgage payment for a home loan. (Note that it is an .xlsx file, not an .xlsm file. It contains *no* VBA code.) As shown in Figure 11.23, the user enters inputs in cells B3, B4, and B5, and the monthly payment is calculated in cell B7 with the PMT function. With the Forms controls in Figure 11.22 visible, drag a spinner control (fourth from the left in the top row) approximately as in the figure. Then right-click it, select **Format Control**, select the **Control** tab, and set its properties as shown in Figure 11.24. This says that the spinner's possible values are integers from 5 to 30, in increments of 1, and that the spinner's value is stored in cell B5,

Figure 11.22 Excel Controls

Figure 11.23 Home Loan Calculation

	A	B	C	D	E
1	**Home loan application**				
2					
3	Amount financed	$125,000		Spinner for term	
4	Annual interest rate	6.25%		▲	
5	Term (years)	15		▼	
6					
7	Monthly payment	$1,071.78			

the term of the loan. Now click anywhere else on the worksheet to deselect the spinner. Finally, click the up or down arrows of the spinner and watch what happens. The term increases or decreases, and the monthly payment changes accordingly—all with no programming.

Now you should appreciate why Microsoft kept the Forms controls. They are extremely easy to use, and users like to employ them to automate their work-sheets, as in this home loan example. However, these controls are not "modern" controls because they do not respond to events as discussed earlier in this chapter. Therefore, beginning in version 97 of Excel, Microsoft introduced the **ActiveX** controls listed at the bottom of Figure 11.22. They have the same basic function-ality as the Forms controls, but you implement them differently.

Figure 11.24 Spinner Properties

Format Object					? ✕

Size	Protection	Properties	Alt Text	**Control**

Current value: 14

Minimum value: 5

Maximum value: 30

Incremental change: 1

Page change:

Cell link: $B$5

☑ 3-D shading

OK   Cancel

To see how the ActiveX controls work, click the ActiveX spinner control and drag it to a worksheet. You will get a spinner in design mode. There will be "handles" around the spinner, and the Design Mode button on the Developer ribbon will be highlighted, as shown in Figure 11.25 This button toggles a given control, such as the spinner, in or out of design mode. You need to be in design mode to "wire up" the control. You need to be out of design mode to make it work—to make it spin, for example.

In design mode, right-click the control and select **Properties** from the resulting menu to see the Properties window in the VBE, as in Figure 11.26. This is exactly like the Properties window discussed earlier in this chapter. It is available for ActiveX controls, but not for Forms controls. You can experiment with the various properties. For example, you can change the Orientation property to make the spinner point north-south versus east-west (change it to 0-frmOrientationVertical), or you can change the Min, Max, SmallChange, and Value properties to mimic the behavior of the spinner used in the home loan example.

Figure 11.25 Design Mode Button Highlighted

Figure 11.26 Spinner Control and Associated Properties Window

Spinner for term		

Properties	
SpinButton1 SpinButton	
Alphabetic	Categorized

Property	Value
(Name)	SpinButton1
AutoLoad	False
BackColor	&H8000000F8
Delay	50
Enabled	True
ForeColor	&H800000128
Height	21
Left	536.25
LinkedCell	
Locked	True
Max	100
Min	0
MouseIcon	(None)
MousePointer	0 - fmMousePoint
Orientation	-1 - fmOrientatio
Placement	2
PrintObject	True
Shadow	False
SmallChange	1
Top	158.25
Value	0
Visible	True
Width	60.75

Figure 11.27 Event Handler for Change Event

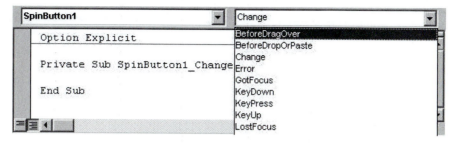

Next, close the Properties window and double-click the spinner. You get an event handler for the Change event of the spinner. (See Figure 11.27.) In general, you get the event handler for the default event of the control you double-click. The Change event is the natural default event for a spinner, because you want to react in some way when the user clicks the up or down arrow of the spinner. You can also write event handlers for other events associated with the spinner. Just select any of the other events from the list in Figure 11.27. The chances are that you won't have any reason to do so, but you can if you like. The point is that you have as much control over these ActiveX controls as you have in the controls you place in user forms in the VBE. The difference is that the controls discussed earlier in this chapter are placed on a user form. The ones from the Developer ribbon (Figure 11.22) are placed directly on a worksheet.

To use an ActiveX spinner in the home loan example, proceed as follows.

1. Drag a spinner to the worksheet, exactly as in Figure 11.23.
2. Right-click the spinner, choose Properties from the resulting menu, and change the Min, Max, SmallChange, and Value properties to 5, 30, 1, and 15, respectively. If you like, change the Orientation property to 0-frmOrientationVertical. Close the Properties window.
3. Double-click the spinner to get into the code window. Add the following line to the sub in Figure 11.27. As before, this links the value in cell B5 to the spinner value.

```
Range("B5").Value = SpinButton1.Value
```

4. Get back into Excel, and click the Design Mode button on the controls toolbar to get out of design mode.
5. Click the spinner to make the term, and hence the monthly payment, change.
6. The spinner is now fully operational. If you want to make any further changes, click the Design Mode button to get back into design mode.

You might ask where the event handler lives. Go into the VBE and double-click the worksheet name in Project Explorer where the spinner resides, for example, Sheet1. You will see your event handler. In general, the event handlers for ActiveX controls reside "behind" the sheets they are on—not in modules.

You can decide whether you want to use Forms controls or ActiveX controls—or both. Forms controls are definitely easier to work with, but ActiveX controls give you a much greater degree of control over their look and behavior. Besides, once you get used to working with controls in user forms, you should have no problems with ActiveX controls.[11]

11.11 Summary

With the material in this chapter, you have taken the first steps to becoming a real *Windows* programmer. I have discussed how to design user forms by placing various types of controls on them, and I have illustrated how to write event handlers that respond to events triggered by a user's actions. Once you have designed a user form and have made any necessary changes in the Properties window, you need to write the appropriate event handlers in the form's code window. Typically, this means capturing user selections that can be analyzed later with the code in a module. You will see many examples of how this is done in Part II of the book, most of which employ forms. Finally, I compared the Forms and ActiveX controls you can place directly on your worksheets.

EXERCISES

1. Suppose you have a form with quite a few text boxes and possibly some other controls. Write an Initialize sub that loops through all controls and, if they are text boxes, sets their Value property to a blank string.
2. Create a form that contains the usual OK and Cancel buttons. It also should contain two sets of option buttons, each set placed inside a frame. The captions on the first set should be Baseball, Basketball, and Football. The captions on the second set should be Watch on TV and Go to games. Then write appropriate code so that when the program runs, the user sees the form. If the user makes a couple of choices and clicks OK, he should see a message like, "Your favorite sport is basketball, and you usually watch on TV." If the user clicks Cancel or the X button, the message "Sorry you don't want to play." should appear.
3. Repeat the previous exercise, but now make the controls checkboxes, not option buttons. Change the message in case the user clicks OK to something appropriate, such as, "You like baseball and basketball, and you like to watch on TV and go to games." The message should be appropriate, regardless of which checkboxes are checked (including none being checked).
4. Create a form that contains the usual OK and Cancel buttons. It should also contain a list box of the type where the user is allowed to select only one item from the list. Write an Initialize sub that populates the list with the states Illinois, Indiana, Iowa, Maryland, Michigan, Minnesota, Nebraska, New Jersey, Ohio,

---

[11] With that said, I must admit that I rarely use ActiveX controls on worksheets. Forms controls are much easier and usually get the job done.

Pennsylvania, and Wisconsin (in this order), and selects Indiana by default. Then write appropriate code so that when the program runs, the user sees the form. If she chooses an item from the list and then clicks OK, she should see a message such as, "You live in Ohio." If she clicks Cancel or the X button, she should see the message, "You must not live in a Big Ten state."

5. Repeat the previous exercise, but now start with the file **Big Ten States.xlsx**, which contains a list of the states in a range named States. When you create the list box, set its RowSource property to States. This will populate the list box automatically, so that you don't need to do it in an Initialize sub.

6. Repeat Exercise 4, but now change the listbox to the type where the user can select multiple items from the list. The resulting message for OK should now be something like, "You have lived in Indiana, Illinois, and Ohio." For Cancel, it should be "You have never lived in a Big Ten state."

7. The file **Big Ten Teams.xlsx** contains the school and mascot names for the Big Ten teams in a range named Teams. Create a form that contains the usual OK and Cancel buttons. It should also contain a list box of the type where the user is allowed to select only one item from the list. Set its RowSource property to Teams, so that the list box is automatically populated from the list in the Teams range. Also, set its ColumnCount property to 2, so that schools and mascots both appear in the list box, and set its ColumnHeads property to True, so that each column has an appropriate heading. Write an Initialize sub that selects Indiana by default. Then write the appropriate code so that when the program runs, the user sees the form. If he chooses an item from the list and then clicks OK, he should see a message such as, "You must root for the Indiana Hoosiers." If he clicks Cancel or the X button, he should see the message, "You must not be a Big Ten fan." (*Hint:* In online help, look up the BoundColumn property of a list box and how it controls the Value property.)

8. The file **Receivables.xlsx** contains data on a company's receivables from its customers. Each row corresponds to a particular customer. It indicates the size of the customer (1 for small, 2 for medium, 3 for large), the number of days the payment has been outstanding, and the amount of the payment due. Develop a form that has the usual OK and Cancel buttons, plus two sets of option buttons. The first set allows the user to choose the size of the customer (using captions Small, Medium, and Large), and the second set allows the user to choose the Days or the Amount column to summarize. Then write appropriate code that captures these choices and displays a message listing the appropriate average. For example, if the user chooses Small and Amount, the message box should display the average amount owed by all small customers.

9. Repeat the preceding exercise, but now use check boxes instead of option buttons. Now a separate message should be displayed for each combination the user checks. For example, if the user checks the Small check box and the Days and Amount check boxes, one message should display the average of Days for the small customers and another should display the average of Amount for the small customers.

10. The file **Stock Returns.xlsx** contains stock returns for many large companies. Each worksheet contains the returns over a five-year period for a certain stock, with the ticker symbol of the stock used as the worksheet name. Write a sub that

presents the user with a form. This form should have the usual OK and Cancel buttons, and it should have a list box with a list of all the stock ticker symbols. The user should be allowed to choose only one stock in the list. The sub should then display a message box that reports the average monthly return for the selected stock.

11. Repeat the previous exercise, but now allow the user to select multiple stocks from the list. Use a For loop to display a separate message box for each selected stock.

12. The file **Exceptions Finished.xlsm** contains monthly sales totals for a number of sales regions. Open the file and click the button. It allows you to choose two colors and two cutoff values. When you click OK, all sales totals below the minimum cutoff are colored the first color, and all totals above the maximum cutoff are colored the other color. The VBA in this file has been password-protected. Your job is to create this same application, starting with the file **Exceptions.xlsx**. This file contains only the data. Make sure you do some error checking on the inputs in the form. Specifically, the text boxes must have numeric values, the minimum cutoff should not exceed the maximum cutoff, and the two chosen colors should not be the same. (*Note*: If you assign a built-in constant like vbGreen to an Integer variable, you will get an error because the integer value of vbGreen is outside the Integer range. Assign it instead to a Long variable.)

13. The file **Scores Finished.xlsm** contains scores for various assignments in three courses taught by an instructor. Open the file. You will see an Explanation worksheet and a button. Click the button to run the program. It shows one form where you can choose a course and any of six summary measures. When you click OK, you see a second form where you can choose an assignment for that course. (Note the list of assignments varies from course to course. Also, the label at the top includes the course number chosen in the first form.) When you click OK, a message box is displayed summarizing the scores on that assignment. The VBA in this file has been password-protected. Your job is to create this same application, starting with the file **Scores.xlsx**. This file contains only the data.

14. The file **Book Reps Finished.xlsm** contains data on a number of sales representatives for a publishing company. The data on each rep include last name, first name, gender, region of country, age, years of experience, and performance rating. Open the file and click the button. It presents two forms. The first asks for the last name and first name of a rep. After the user enters these, the program searches for a rep with this name. If none is found, a message to this effect is displayed and the program ends. If the rep is found, a second form is displayed with the rep's current characteristics. The user can then change *any* of these and click OK. The changes are then reflected in the data range. The VBA in this file has been password-protected. Your job is to create this same application, starting with the file **Book Reps.xlsx**. This file contains only the data.

15. The file **Country Form Finished.xlsm** contains a form. The user can select any of three option buttons, named optUSA, optCanada, and optEurope. When any of these is selected, the labels and text boxes should change appropriately. Specifically, if the USA button is clicked, the caption of the top label, named lblLocation, should change to State, and the bottom text box, named txtLanguage, should be disabled, with English entered in the text box. (Presumably, English

is the common language in the USA.) If the user chooses the Canada option, txtLanguage should be enabled, with the text box cleared, and the caption of lblLocation should change to Province. Similarly, if the user chooses the Europe option, txtLanguage should be enabled, with the text box cleared, and the caption of lblLocation should change to Country. The code in this file has been password-protected. Starting with the codeless form in the file **Country Form.xlsm**, write event handlers for the Click event of the option buttons to guarantee this behavior.

16. Open a new workbook and develop a form that asks for a beginning date and an ending date in text boxes. It should instruct the user (with an appropriate label) to enter dates from January 1, 1990, to the current date. Create a Valid function to perform the following error checks: (1) the date boxes should not be blank; (2) they should contain valid dates (use the IsDate function for this); (3) the first date shouldn't be before January 1, 1990; (4) the last date shouldn't be after the current date (use the Date function for this—it returns the current date); and (5) the first date should be before the last date. If any one of these error checks is not passed, the form should not be hidden, and the focus should be set to the offending text box so that the user can try again. If all error checks are passed, the dates should be displayed in an appropriate message box, such as "You chose the dates 1/1/2000 and 2/2/2002."

17. Continuing the previous exercise, it might take you several tries to get everything, especially the error checking, working properly. Dates are tricky! Once you go to all of this work, you shouldn't have to do it again. The purpose of this exercise, therefore, is to write a Public Boolean function called ValidDate that does the error checking for this type of situation automatically. You could then use this general sub any time you need it in the future. Structure it as follows. It should take four arguments: txtDate1 (a text box for the first date), txtDate2 (a text box for the second date), earliestDate (a Date variable, corresponding to the January 1, 1990 date in the previous exercise), latestDate (a Date variable corresponding to the current date in the previous exercise). This sub should check for all errors. If it finds any, it should set the focus to the offending text box and set ValidDate to False. Otherwise, it should set ValidDate to True. Write this ValidDate function, which should be placed in a *module,* and then use it to solve the previous exercise. (*Hint:* The code in this exercise will be very similar to the code in the previous exercise. However, the ValidDate function is now in a module, and there is no Valid function in the form code. This presents some interesting problems on how to pass variables, and you can decide the best way to do it—preferably without global variables. Also, if you try to make a TextBox control the argument of a function in a module, you can't just type something like txtDate1 As TextBox. You must also include a reference to the library that has information about text boxes. Therefore you must type txtDate1 As MSForms.TextBox. You learn such details through extensive trial and error.)

18. This chapter has explained only the most frequently used controls: command buttons, labels, text boxes, option buttons, check boxes, and so on. However, there are a few others you might want to use. This exercise and the next one let you explore two of these controls. In this exercise, you can explore the SpinButton control. Open a new

workbook, get into the VBE, add a user form, and place a spin button on the form. You can probably guess the functionality this button should have. If the user clicks the up arrow, a counter should increase. If the user clicks the down arrow, the counter should decrease. To operationalize the button, set its Min, Max, SmallChange, and Value properties to 1, 10, 1, and 5 in the Properties window. This will allow the user to change the counter from 1 to 10 in increments of 1, with an initial value of 5. But how would a user know the value of the counter? The trick is to put a text box right below the spin button and make the text box's Value property equal to the spin button's Value property (which is the counter). To keep them in sync, write a line of code in the spin button's Change event handler that sets the text box's value equal to the spin button's value. Similarly, write an event handler for the text box's Change event, so that if the user changes the value in the text box, the spinner's counter stays in sync with it. Try it out by running the form (by clicking the blue triangle run button in the VBE). How can you make sure that the two controls *start* in sync when the form is first displayed?

19. Continuing the previous exercise, put a spin button to work on the **Car Loan.xlsx** file. This file contains a template for calculating the monthly payment on a car loan, given the amount financed, the annual interest rate, and the term of the loan (the number of months to pay). Develop an application around this template that does the following: (1) It has a button on the worksheet to run a VaryTerm sub in a module; (2) the VaryTerm sub "shows" a form with the usual OK and Cancel buttons, a spin button and corresponding text box, and appropriate label(s) that allow(s) the user to choose a term for the loan (allow only multiples of 12, up to 60); and (3) the VaryTerm sub then places the user's choice of term in cell B5, which automatically updates the monthly payment.

20. This exercise continues the previous two exercises, but it now asks you to explore the ScrollBar control. Open a new workbook, get into the VBE, add a user form, and place a scrollbar on the form. (You can make it vertical or horizontal. Take your pick.) As you can probably guess, the scrollbar's Value property indicates the position of the slider. It can go from the Min value to the Max value. The SmallChange property indicates the change in the slider when the user clicks one of the arrows. The LargeChange property indicates the change when the user clicks somewhere inside the scrollbar. You could proceed as with spin buttons to place a text box next to the scrollbar that shows the current value of the scrollbar. However, try another possibility this time. Place *labels* at the ends of the scrollbar and around the middle, as illustrated in Figure 11.28. These labels provide guidance for the user and will never change. Now try all of this out on a variation of the previous exercise, using the same **Car Loan.xlsx** file. Write a VaryAmount sub that shows a user form with a scrollbar. The Min, Max, SmallChange, LargeChange, and Value properties of the scrollbar should be 10000, 50000, 500, 2000, and 30000 (set in the Properties window at design time). The goal is the same as in the previous exercise, except that now the sensitivity analysis is on the amount financed. When the form first shows, make the value of the scrollbar whatever value is in cell B3 of the spreadsheet.

21. The previous two exercises employed a user form with either a spinner or a scrollbar. In this exercise, don't use a user form. Instead, obtain the same

Figure 11.28 Scrollbar with Informational Labels

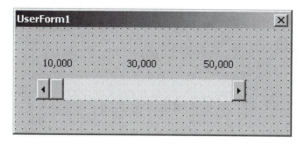

functionality with controls from the Forms controls on the Developer ribbon. Then repeat, using ActiveX controls.

22. When you use text boxes, you often do some error checking in the Valid function to ensure that the user enters valid values. For example, if you ask for a date, then 12/46/1996 is clearly not appropriate. In this case, you typically have code something like the following:

```
Valid = False
MsgBox "Please enter a valid date.",vbExclamation
txtDate.SetFocus
```

This indicates what was wrong, sets the focus back in the date box, and makes the user try again. For example, if the user enters 12/46/1996, the cursor will be right after 1996. You can add an even more professional touch by having your code highlight the whole 12/46/1996. Then the user can simply start typing to enter a new date. Create a small application that does this. (*Hint:* Get into the Object Browser and check the properties of a TextBox object that start with Sel. Note that online help in Object Browser is available for controls from the **MSForms** library, and this library is in the list only when your project contains a user form.)

23. Open the file **Baseball Favorites Finished.xlsm** and click the button. The form should be self-explanatory, but notice what is enabled and what is disabled, and how this changes as you make selections. For example, you can't type in the "Other" text boxes until you choose an "Other below" option. Eventually, make a choice and click OK to see a resulting message. The code in this finished version is password-protected. Now open the file **Baseball Favorites.xlsm**. The form has already been designed. Your job is to write the code, including the event handlers for the form—and quite a few are necessary to make sure everything is enabled or disabled at the appropriate times.

24. You see many Windows and Web applications where a combo box is used with a prompt. Open the file **Combo Box with Prompt Finished.xlsm** to see how this should work. Note that you *can* highlight the prompt and type over it. However, this user behavior is unlikely, so the code doesn't check for it (although you can if you like). The code in this finished version is password-protected. Try creating it yourself.

12

Error Handling

12.1 Introduction

The important topic of debugging was discussed in Chapter 5. You debug to find and fix the errors in your code. Unfortunately, you have to be concerned about more than your *own* errors. The applications you will be developing are typically interactive. An application displays one or more dialog boxes for the user to fill in, and it then responds to the user's inputs with appropriate actions. But what if the user is asked to enter a percentage as a decimal between 0 and 1, and he enters 25? Or what if a user is asked for a date and she enters 13/35/2011? Your code should check for these types of errors that a *user* might make. VBA will not do it automatically for you. It is up to you to include the appropriate error-trapping logic.

In addition to watching for inappropriate user inputs, you must be on the watch for situations where your code performs an action that cannot be performed in the current context. For example, you might have a line that deletes a worksheet named Results. But suppose that when this line executes, there is no worksheet named Results. If you, the programmer, do not include error-trapping logic, this line will cause your program to crash.

12.2 Error Handling with On Error Statement

This section discusses methods for trapping the types of errors discussed in the previous paragraph. The most common way to do this is with the On Error statement. There are several forms of this statement. They all essentially watch for errors and then respond in some way. The following code is typical.

```
On Error Resume Next
Application.DisplayAlerts = False
Worksheets("Results").Delete
MsgBox "Now the program can continue."
```

The objective here is to delete the Results sheet. However, there might not *be* a Results sheet, in which case the Delete line will cause a run-time error. The On Error Resume Next statement says, "If an error is encountered, ignore it and go on to the next statement." In this case, if there is no Results sheet, no error message is displayed, and the MsgBox statement is executed. More specifically, when you include an On Error Resume Next statement, the program goes into

Figure 12.1 Error Code Message

error-checking mode from that point on. If it comes to a statement that would lead to an error, it ignores that statement—it doesn't try to execute it—and goes on to the next statement.

A variation of this is listed below. If an error is encountered, control still passes to the next statement, but the default Number property of the built-in Err object has a *nonzero* value that an If statement can check for. Actually, each specific type of error has a particular error code that is stored in the Err object. For example, this particular error (trying to delete a worksheet that doesn't exist) returns error code 9. You can discover this by running the following code to obtain the message in Figure 12.1. However, unless you plan to do *a lot* of programming, you don't need to learn these error codes. Just remember that Err.Number is nonzero if an error occurs, and it is 0 if there is no error. (Because Number is the default property of the Err object, you could write If Err <> 0 rather than If Err.Number <> 0. The shortened version is often used.)

```
On Error Resume Next
Application.DisplayAlerts = False
Worksheets("Results").Delete
If Err.Number <> 0 Then MsgBox "The Results worksheet couldn't be deleted " _
    & "because it doesn't exist. This is error code " & Err.Number
```

The On Error Resume Next statement is useful when you want to ignore an "unimportant" error. However, there are some errors that you definitely do *not* want to ignore. The following code illustrates a typical method that programmers use to handle errors.

```
Sub TryToOpen()
    On Error GoTo ErrorHandling
    Workbooks.Open "C:\VBABook\Ranges.xlsm"
    On Error GoTo 0

    ' Other statements would go here.
    Exit Sub

ErrorHandling:
    MsgBox "The Ranges.xlsm file could not be found."
End Sub
```

The purpose of this sub is to open the **Ranges.xlsm** file, located in the VBABook folder on the C drive, and then perform some actions on this file (designated by the commented line). However, there is always the possibility that this file does not exist, at least not in the specified location. The On Error GoTo ErrorHandling line handles this possibility. It says, "Watch for an error. If an error is encountered, go to the ErrorHandling label farther down in the sub. Otherwise, continue with the normal sequence of statements." You can have any number of labels in a sub, each followed by a colon, and you can give them any names you like. Each label acts like a bookmark that you can "GoTo."[1]

The Exit Sub statement is necessary in case there is no error. Without it, the **Ranges.xlsm** file would be opened and the statements indicated by the commented line would be executed—so far, so good. But then the MsgBox statement would be executed, saying that the file couldn't be found—not exactly what the programmer has in mind.

If you have an On Error GoTo statement somewhere in a sub, it is active throughout the entire sub, always monitoring for errors. If you want to turn off this monitoring, you can use the On Error GoTo 0 statement, as shown in the above code. This disables any error checking. Admittedly, this line doesn't make much sense, and it is undoubtedly left over from the "bad old days" of programming, but it hasn't been changed yet.

12.3 Handling Inappropriate User Inputs

In addition to On Error statements, you should check explicitly for invalid user inputs. This is done in most of the cmdOK_Click event handlers in later chapters to check that the user has entered appropriate values in a user form. A typical example of this is the following. The dialog box in Figure 12.2 contains two text boxes that the user must fill in. They are named txtDate1 and txtDate2. There are several inappropriate inputs that could be given: the boxes could be left blank, the entries could be invalid dates such as 6/31/2010 (or not dates at all), or the beginning date could be *after* the ending date. You hope the user will not provide any such invalid inputs, but you as a programmer should not leave it to chance.

The following code uses no error checking. It simply captures the user's inputs in the variables begDate and endDate and hopes for the best. If invalid dates are supplied, there is no telling what might go wrong in the rest of the program.

---

[1] Many programs from a few decades ago contained multiple GoTo statements, resulting in code that was practically impossible to decipher. GoTo statements are now frowned upon, except in these special error handling situations. Even here, many programmers try to avoid GoTo statements. For example, in Microsoft .NET, there is a better error handling structure called **Try/Catch** that avoids GoTo statements altogether.

Figure 12.2 Dialog Box for Dates

```
Private Sub cmdOK_Click()
    begDate = txtDate1.Value
    endDate = txtDate2.Value
    Unload Me
End Sub
```

A much better way is to check for possible invalid dates, as illustrated in the code below. It goes through all of the controls on the user form and checks whether they are text boxes. For the text boxes, it checks whether they are blank or contain invalid dates (with VBA's *very* handy IsDate function). In either case, an error message is displayed, the focus is set to the offending text box, and Valid is set to False. If these error checks are passed, a later error check is performed to see if the beginning date is after the ending date. If it is, another error message is displayed, the focus is set to the first date box, and Valid is again set to False. As usual in form code, when Valid is False, the form is *not* unloaded and the user has to try again. By the time this form is eventually unloaded, the programmer can be sure that begDate and endDate contain valid dates.

```
Private Function Valid() As Boolean
    Dim ctl As Control
    Dim begDate As Date, endDate As Date

    Valid = True
    For Each ctl In Me.Controls
        If TypeName(ctl) = "TextBox" Then
            If ctl.Value = "" Or Not IsDate(ctl.Value) Then
                MsgBox "Enter a valid date.", vbInformation, "Invalid entry"
                ctl.SetFocus
                Valid = False
                Exit Function
            End If
        End If
    Next
```

```
        begDate = txtDate1.Value
        endDate = txtDate2.Value
        If begDate >= endDate Then
            MsgBox "The beginning date should be before the ending date.", _
                vblnformation, " Invalid dates"
            txtDate1 .SetFocus
            Valid = False
        End If
End Function
```

Writing this error-checking code is not a lot of fun, but it is necessary for any professional program. It not only prevents the program from accepting invalid inputs and then proceeding blindly, but it also provides users with helpful error messages so that they can change their responses appropriately. You might not be able to check for all conceivable errors, but you should attempt to anticipate the most likely ones.

Actually, if you want a user to specify dates, there is a simpler and more foolproof approach. Rather than having the user type dates in a text box, you can use controls where the user can't do it wrong. The Calendar control used in some later chapters is a perfect example. The user sees a calendar and simply selects a date, so that no error checking is necessary. (Well, you still might need to check that a "beginning" date is before an "ending" date.) You also see a lot of applications, especially on the Web, where you choose a month, day, and year from spinners or lists. Any of these approaches is much better than having a user type a date in a text box—and very possibly having them type it wrong.

This idea can be generalized. When you are developing a form to get user inputs, you should always try to choose the controls that give the user the smallest chance of making a mistake. This certainly applies to dates, but it applies in other situations as well. For example, if you want the user to input the term of a loan, you could use a text box for the term. But a better approach is to use option (radio) buttons for the distinct possibilities, such as 12, 24, 36, 48, and 60, and select one of these by default (in the Initialize code). Then there is no possibility that the user can choose an invalid term (or none at all).

12.4   Summary

Error handling is probably no one's favorite programming topic, but it is necessary if you want to consider yourself a professional programmer. You need to include code that anticipates things that could go wrong, anything from an attempt to open a file that doesn't exist to a user providing an input of "abc" when asked for a birth date. To write bulletproof code—code that (almost) never crashes—you have to take an active role in defeating Murphy's law: If it *can* go wrong, it *will* go wrong. Otherwise, Murphy's law will bite you!

EXERCISES

1. Open a new workbook and make sure it has two worksheets in it named Sheet1 and Sheet2. Write a sub that has three lines. The first should be Application.DisplayAlerts = False. (See section 5.13 to recall what this does.) The second line should delete Sheet2, and the third should delete Sheet3. What happens when you run the program? Change your code so that if it tries to delete a worksheet that doesn't exist, nothing happens—and no error message appears.

2. Open a new workbook and make sure it has two worksheets named Sheet1 and Sheet2. Write a sub that has three lines. The first should be Application.DisplayAlerts = False. (See section 5.13 to recall what this does.) The second line should delete Sheet2, and the third should delete Sheet1. What happens? The problem is that Excel won't allow you to delete a worksheet if it is the only worksheet left. Restore Sheet2. Then add an appropriate On Error GoTo line and an associated label in your sub to trap for the error. Take an appropriate action when it occurs. Use a message box to learn the code for this error (from the Number property of the built-in Err object).

3. Open a new workbook, insert a module, and write a sub that does the following: (1) it uses an input box to ask the user for the path and name of an Excel file to open, and (2) it then tries to open the file. Run this sub and enter the name of a file that you know exists. It should open the file with no problem. Then run it again and enter a file that you know does not exist. What happens? Rewrite the sub with the appropriate error-handling capability to take care of this possibility— and present a "nice" message to the user in either case.

4. The file **Shaq.xlsm** contains hypothetical data on Shaquille O'Neal's success from the free throw line. (In case you are not a basketball fan, Shaq was a notoriously poor free throw shooter.) For each of several games, it lists the number of free throws attempted and the number made. It then divides the number made by the number attempted to calculate his free throw percentage for that game. Unfortunately, this results in a **#DIV/0!** error in games where he didn't take any free throws. The question explored here is how you can recognize and react to this cell error in VBA code. There is already a DisplayPcts sub in this file that goes through each cell in the "Pct made" column and displays the cell's value in a message box. Run the sub and watch how it bombs. Now rewrite the code so that if this error ever occurs, a message is displayed to the effect that no percentage can be reported because no free throws were attempted—and no nasty error messages are displayed. Do this by checking only the cells in column D; don't check the cells in column B. (*Hint:* Use VBA's IsError function. You can learn how it works in the Object Browser.)

5. Open a new workbook, get into the VBE, insert a user form, add a text box named txtLastName, and add a Last Name label to its left. This text box is supposed to capture a person's last name. Therefore, it should contain alphabetical characters only. You could perform an error check in a Valid function subroutine, but you might want to check for nonalphabetical characters at the same time the user is typing the name. You can do this with the Change event for a text box. In this case, the event handler's name is txtLastName_Change. This event fires

each time any change occurs to the contents of the text box, including the insertion of a new character. Write the appropriate code for this event handler. It should check whether the *last* character (the one most recently typed) is alphabetical. If not, it should display an appropriate message box telling the user to type alphabetical characters only, set the focus to the text box, and exit the sub. For example, if the user types Smi7, it should recognize that the fourth character is nonalphabetical and respond accordingly.

The following five exercises deal with debugging. Although this is not exactly the topic of the current chapter, it is still in the spirit of error checking.

6. The file **State Sales.xlsm** lists sales by some company in a number of states. Each state has its own worksheet, with the name of the state used as the worksheet name. There is a module that contains the sub ListStates. The purpose of this sub is to display a message that lists all of the states. Unfortunately, it has a few bugs. Find them and correct them.

7. Continuing the previous exercise, the module in **State Sales.xlsm** contains the subs StateSearch and FindState. The StateSearch sub should get the name of a state from the user, call the FindState sub, and then display a message saying whether that state is one of the worksheets in the workbook. The FindState sub searches for the state passed to it and returns the Boolean variable isFound, which should be True if the state is found and False otherwise. Again, these subs have bugs. Find them and correct them.

8. Continuing Exercise 6 once more, the module in **State Sales.xlsm** contains the sub CountSales. The purpose of this sub is to ask the user for a state and a sales rep. It should then count the number of sales by this sales rep in this state and report the result in a message box. An On Error statement is supposed to trap for the error that the given state is not one of the states in the workbook. As you can see, this sub is in bad shape. The red lines indicate syntax errors. Find and fix all of the errors, syntax and otherwise.

9. Continuing Exercise 6 again, the module in **State Sales.xlsm** contains the sub TotalSales1. The purpose of the sub is to ask the user for a date. Then the total of all sales in all states up to (and including) this date should be found and displayed in a message box, with the date and the total suitably formatted. Again, this sub is full of bugs, including syntax errors. Find and fix all of the errors, syntax and otherwise.

10. Continuing Exercise 6 one last time, the module in **State Sales.xlsm** contains a sub TotalSales2. There is also a user form called frmInputs. The purpose of these is to let the user choose a state and a sales rep from list boxes on the user form. The TotalSales2 sub should then calculate the total of all sales made by this sales rep in the selected state and display it in a message box. Before showing the user form, the TotalSales2 sub creates an array of all states and an array of all sales reps (in all worksheets). It uses these to populate the list boxes. The logic in the TotalSales2 sub and the event handlers for the user form is basically correct, but there are numerous small errors that keep the program from running correctly. Find all of them and fix them. When you think you have everything fixed and running correctly, check your total sales (for some state and some rep) manually, just to make sure you have it correct.

Working with Files and Folders

13.1 Introduction

The focus of this chapter is on working with files and folders, not on manipulating Excel objects. There are many times when you need to find a file or folder and, perhaps, manipulate it. For example, you might want to check whether a particular file exists, or you might want to rename a file in a particular folder. Of course, you can open Windows Explorer and perform the required file or folder operations there. However, you can also perform these operations with VBA, as discussed in this chapter. You might also want to work with text files. For example, you might want to import the contents of a text file into Excel, or you might want to write the contents of an Excel worksheet into a text file for use by some other program. These text file operations can also be performed with VBA and are discussed here.

13.2 Exercise

The following exercise requires the types of file operations that you will learn in this chapter.

Exercise 13.1 Retrieving SoftBed Sales Data

The SoftBed Company has historical sales data for several of its customers for the years 2014 and 2015. They are stored in tab-delimited text files in various folders. Each file has a name such as **Clark Sales Q1 2014.txt**, which identifies the customer name, the quarter, and the year. Each file is structured as shown in Figure 13.1. The first row identifies product numbers, such as P3254, and the other rows list the date and sales figures. Your boss would like you to write a program that asks for a customer name, a product code, a quarter, and a year; imports the appropriate data from the text file into an Excel workbook; and saves it under a name such as **Clark Sales P3254 Q3 2014.xlsx**. The resulting file should be structured as shown in Figure 13.2. You can assume that all text files for a given customer are in the same folder, but you don't know which folders contain which files. Therefore, you should present your boss with a dialog box for finding the appropriate folder for any selected customer.

This exercise illustrates the type of operations discussed in this chapter. First, it requires you to obtain a dialog box for finding the appropriate folder. Next, it requires you to find the appropriate files in the selected folder. Finally, it requires you to import the appropriate data into Excel format. By the time you have read

Figure 13.1 Text File Data

```
Date    P3254   P7417   P3416
25-Jan-14    1960    2710    1850
26-Jan-14    2290    2640    2170
27-Jan-14    2610    2270    2370
28-Jan-14    3130    2720    2650
31-Jan-14    2500    2610    2540
01-Feb-14    3430    2360    3040
02-Feb-14    3480    3140    1920
03-Feb-14    2050    2460    3100
04-Feb-14    3170    1840    2210
07-Feb-14    2050    2830    1680
08-Feb-14    2390    2920    2020
09-Feb-14    1320    2930    2390
10-Feb-14    2060    2360    1700
11-Feb-14    1670    2930    2550
14-Feb-14    1740    2490    2810
15-Feb-14    1330    2700    3640
```

Figure 13.2 Imported Data in Excel File

	A	B	C
1	Clark sales of P3254 for Q3 2014		
2			
3	Date	Sales	
4	7/18/2014	$2,530	
5	7/19/2014	$2,780	
6	7/20/2014	$2,880	
7	7/21/2014	$2,310	
8	7/24/2014	$1,780	
9	7/25/2014	$2,910	
10	7/26/2014	$2,030	
11	7/27/2014	$1,740	
12	7/28/2014	$2,990	
13	7/31/2014	$2,360	
14	8/1/2014	$1,820	
15	8/2/2014	$1,560	

this chapter, you will be able to perform all of these operations in VBA. Eventually, you should try doing this application on your own, but if you want to see the finished application, it is in the file **Sales Import Finished.xlsm**.[1]

---

[1] If you used the second edition of this book, you will see significant differences in the code for this example. In the second edition, I used the very handy **FileSearch** object to find a file with a given name and given content. For reasons that are not clear, Microsoft not only discontinued FileSearch in Office 2007, but it broke all existing applications like mine that used FileSearch. The current application is forced to use a workaround: the VB Script **FileSystemObject** object. I will explain it in Section 13.4.

13.3 Dialog Boxes for File Operations

Creating dialog boxes can be fun and rewarding, but it definitely takes time. Fortunately, VBA includes a few built-in dialog boxes that you can use directly. You are already well aware of two of these: InputBox and MsgBox. Neither is a very fancy way of getting a user input or displaying output, but they are certainly easy to use. This section briefly describes several additional built-in dialog boxes you can use for performing common file or folder operations. The first of these, FileDialog, is the most powerful. It is actually part of the Office object model, so that it can be used in any Office VBA application. However, it was introduced only in Excel XP (version 2002). Therefore, for backward compatibility, I also discuss two methods of the Application object that were available before Excel XP and are still available: GetOpenFileName and GetSaveAsFileName. (You can find help for them in the Object Browser by going to the Excel library and searching for methods of the Application object.)

FileDialog

The FileDialog object provides file functionality similar to that of the standard Open and Save As dialog boxes in all Microsoft Office applications. With these dialog boxes, users can easily specify the files and folders they wish to use. There are actually four versions of FileDialog specified by the following constants (where mso stands for Microsoft Office):

- msoFileDialogOpen—lets the user select one or more files that can then be opened in Excel with the Execute method
- msoFileDialogSaveAs—lets the user select a pathname that the current file can be saved as using the Execute method
- msoFileDialogFilePicker—lets the user select one or more files that are stored in the SelectedItems collection
- msoFileDialogFolderPicker—lets the user select a folder that is stored in the SelectedItems collection (as item 1)

The following OpenFiles sub is typical. (This sub and the others in this section are in the **FileDialog Examples.xlsm** file.) It allows a user to select one or more files and then open each file selected. Note that fd is first declared as an Office.FileDialog object. It is then Set to an Application.FileDialog of type msoFile-DialogOpen. The Show method opens the familiar File Open dialog box in Figure 13.3, at which time the user can select one or more files in the usual way. The Show method returns True or False depending on whether the user clicks Open or Cancel in the dialog box. If the user clicks Open, the Execute method opens each of the selected files in Excel. (If the user selects a file type such as a .docx file that Excel doesn't recognize, an error occurs.) If the user clicks Cancel, the sub is exited quietly. Note that the files the user selects are in the SelectedItems collection, and a typical file in this collection *must* be declared as Variant, not as String.

```
Sub OpenFiles()
    Dim fd As Office.FileDialog
    Dim file As Variant
    Dim notCancel As Boolean
```

Figure 13.3 File Open Dialog Box

```
    ' This lets you select one or more files, and it
    ' tries to open them in Excel. Strange things can happen
    ' if the selected files aren't files that Excel can read.
    Set fd = Application.FileDialog(msoFileDialogOpen)
    With fd
        notCancel = .Show
        If notCancel Then
            For Each file In .SelectedItems
                .Execute
            Next
        End If
    End With
End Sub
```

The following **SaveFileAs** sub allows the user to save the file that contains the code in a selected folder with a specified name. It opens the usual File Save As dialog box seen in Figure 13.4, and, unless the user clicks Cancel, it saves the file with the **Execute** method.

```
Sub SaveFileAs()
    Dim fd As Office.FileDialog
    Dim notCancel As Boolean

    ' This lets you save the current file under
    ' a different name and/or location.
    Set fd = Application.FileDialog(msoFileDialogSaveAs)
    With fd
        notCancel = .Show
        If notCancel Then
            .Execute
        End If
    End With
End Sub
```

Figure 13.4 File Save Dialog Box

The msoFileDialogFolderPicker version of FileDialog is especially useful. The following FolderPicker sub allows the user to select a folder from the dialog box in Figure 13.5, and, unless the user clicks Cancel, stores it as SelectedItems(1). Based on the folder chosen in the figure, the message in Figure 13.6 is shown.

```
Sub FolderPicker()
    Dim fd As Office.FileDialog
    Dim path As String
    Dim notCancel As Boolean

    ' This lets you select a folder. It gives you access to
    ' the path name of the selected folder.
    Set fd = Application.FileDialog(msoFileDialogFolderPicker)
    With fd
        notCancel = .Show
        If notCancel Then
            path = .SelectedItems(1)
            MsgBox "The selected folder is " & path, vbInformation
        End If
    End With
End Sub
```

The msoFilePicker option is similar to the msoFolderPicker option, except that the user can select multiple files, not just a single folder. All selected files are stored in the SelectedItems collection and can be looped through with a For Each construction, exactly as in the earlier FileOpen sub.

Figure 13.5 Folder Picker Dialog Box

Figure 13.6 Selected Folder

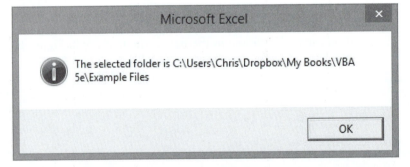

GetOpenFileName Method[2]

The GetOpenFileName method displays the usual Open dialog box you see when you click the Open button in Excel. Although there are a number of optional arguments for this method (see online help), you can call it without any arguments, as in the following line:

---

[2] If you are running Excel XP (version 2002) or a more recent version, you can skip the rest of this section, because FileDialog is superior to the GetOpenFileName and GetSaveAsFileName methods. However, you can still use these "old" methods if you like.

Figure 13.7 Open Dialog Box

Application.GetOpenFileName

The user then sees the typical Open dialog box, such as in Figure 13.7, and he can maneuver around in it in the usual way to find the file he wants to open.

However, the behavior is not quite what you might expect. If the user selects a file and then clicks Open, the selected file is *not* opened. Instead, the GetOpenFileName method returns the file name of the selected file as a string. Therefore, the typical way you would use this method is illustrated in the following code lines.

```
Dim fileToOpen As String
fileToOpen = Application.GetOpenFilename
Workbooks.Open fileToOpen
```

In this case, fileToOpen holds the name of the selected file (actually, the full path name of this file). The last line actually opens this file in Excel.

GetSaveAsFileName

Similarly, the GetSaveAsFileName method mimics Save As in Excel. It opens the usual Save As dialog box, as shown in Figure 13.8. Now the user maneuvers to where she wants to save the file and enters a file name in the File name box. When she clicks Save, the file is not actually saved. Instead, the full path name of

Figure 13.8 Save As Dialog Box

her selection is stored as a string. Then an extra line of code is required to actually save the file. The typical use of this method is illustrated in the following code lines:

```
Dim nameToSaveAs As String
nameToSaveAs = Application.GetSaveAsFilename
ActiveWorkbook.SaveAs Filename:=nameToSaveAs
```

The next-to-last line opens the Save As dialog box and captures the name of the file to be saved. The last line actually saves the file with this name.

Other Built-in Dialog Boxes

There are many dialog boxes you see when you select various Excel menu items. You can get to these dialog boxes in VBA with the Dialogs property of the Application object. The code in Figure 13.9 indicates how to do it. When you type Application.Dialogs followed by a left paren, you see a list of all available dialog boxes from Excel—and there are a lot of them. Once you select an available dialog box, you can then use the Show method to display it. For example, the following line shows the Page Setup dialog box, at which time the user can make the usual choices for printing. Eventually, the user will click OK or Cancel. The variable result will be True (for OK) or False (for Cancel).

Figure 13.9 Dialogs Property

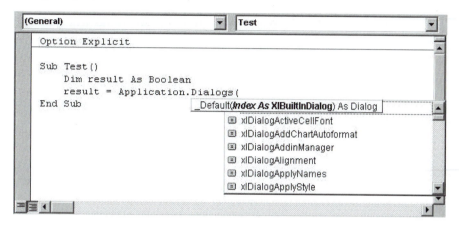

```
result = Application.Dialogs(xlDialogPageSetup).Show
```

You might not use these built-in dialog boxes very often in your VBA code. After all, once the Page Setup (or whatever) dialog box appears, the user is free to make any choices she likes, and you (the programmer) have no control over her choices. Nevertheless, you might want to experiment with these built-in dialog boxes.

13.4 The FileSystemObject Object

There are many times when you might like to write code to check whether a file exists, rename a file, or other common file operations. In Excel 2003, there was a very handy object, FileSearch, part of the Office library, that could be used to perform file operations easily. I discussed the FileSearch capabilities in the second edition of this book. Unfortunately, Microsoft discontinued the FileSearch object in Excel 2007. It is simply *gone*, and any applications that used it, such as a few files in the second edition, are now broken—they give an error message when you try to run them. If you do a Web search for "FileSearch Office 2007," you will see that a number of programmers were not very happy about this unfortunate state of affairs. I have no idea why Microsoft did it, but I will offer an alternative in this section.

This alternative uses a library that has been around for a long time and comes with Windows, so that you already own it. It is called the **Scripting** library. In particular, it contains a FileSystemObject object that has much of the functionality of FileSearch. To use the Scripting library in a VBA project, you must first set a reference to it. To do so, you select the **Tools** → **References** menu item in the VBE, scroll down the list for **Microsoft Scripting Runtime**, and check it (see Figure 13.10). As you can see, its functionality is stored in a file called **scrrun. dll**, located somewhere in your Windows folder. Once you set this reference, you can visit the Object Browser to learn more about the Scripting library. Figure 13.11 shows the objects available, including FileSystemObject, the one used here. As usual, you can select a property or method of this object and then click the question mark to get help. Actually, if you click the question mark, you are taken to a generic help screen, but if you then search for FileSystemObject, you will get real help.

I will not try to explain all of the functionality of the FileSystemObject object, but I will show how I used it in the opening example of this chapter. The relevant part of the code is listed below. (There is other code in the file, but this is the part relevant for the current discussion.) The declarations section illustrates two ways to declare the FileSystemObject (or, to be more precise, as explained in Chapter 17, to create an *instance* of the FileSystemObject class). You can do it all in one line, using the New keyword, or you can do it in two lines, where you first declare the fso variable and then Set it with the CreateObject function. The only use I make of the fso variable is when I use the FileExists method later on to check whether a file of a given name exists in a specified folder. The FileExists method returns True or

Figure 13.10 Setting Reference to Scripting Library

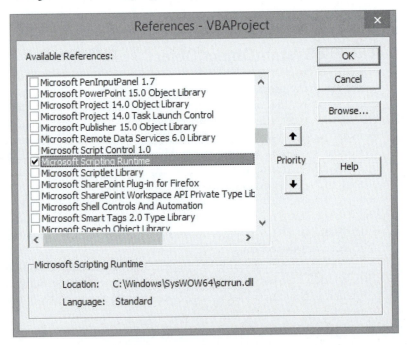

Figure 13.11 Scripting Library Objects

False. If it returns False, I provide a message to this effect and then quit. If it returns True, I then open the text file and search for the given product code. With the (now discontinued) FileSearch object, it was possible to perform this latter search *inside* the file with a line or two of code. However, the FileSystemObject object doesn't have this capability, so the only alternative is to open the text file and parse through it with the last few lines of code. I will discuss parsing in more detail in Section 13.6.

```
Dim fd As Office.FileDialog
Dim fso As New Scripting.FileSystemObject

' The following two lines are an alternative to the
' preceding line for declaring the FileSystemObject.
' You tend to see the following version in online help.
'Dim fso as Scripting.FileSystemObject
'Set fso = CreateObject("Scripting.FileSystemObject")
```

```
' Get the user inputs (customer, product, quarter, year).
If frmInputs.ShowInputsDialog(customer, product, year, quarter) Then

    ' Get the folder where the files are stored.
    MsgBox "In the following dialog box, browse for the " _
        & "folder where the " & customer & " sales files are stored."
    Set fd = Application.FileDialog(msoFileDialogFolderPicker)
    With fd
        If .Show Then
            path = .SelectedItems(1)
        Else
            Exit Sub
        End If
    End With

    Application.ScreenUpdating = False
    With fso
        ' First check whether there is a customer file in the selected location
        ' for this quarter and year.
        textFile = path & "\" & customer & " Sales Q" & quarter & " " & year & ".txt"
        isFound = .FileExists(textFile)
        If Not isFound Then
            MsgBox "There is no sales file for customer " & customer & _
                " in Q" & quarter & " " & year & ".", vbInformation, "No file"
            Exit Sub
        Else
            ' File is found, so now open it and search for selected product code.
            Open textFile For Input As #1
            Line Input #1, dataLine
            Call GetProductIndex(dataLine, index, product)
        End If
    End With
End If
```

We programmers hate to see our applications broken because functionality that used to be there is no longer available, but this is exactly what happened with the FileSearch object. Microsoft must have had a reason for discontinuing it, but that reason is difficult to locate. Fortunately, most of the same functionality is available with the Scripting library's FileSystemObject.

13.5 A File Renaming Example[3]

There are probably times when you have many similarly named files in a particular folder and you would like to rename all of them in some way. For example, if they have underscores in their names, such as **Product_B3211.xlsx**, you might want to replace all underscores by spaces to obtain **Product B3211.xlsx**. The file **Rename Files.xlsm** gives you several options for such renaming. If you want

---

[3] In this section of a previous edition, I discussed a considerably more complex file *renumbering* application. That application is still available in the book files with this edition, but a simpler file *renaming* application is discussed here. Actually, the example files folder includes a simpler renaming application, **Rename Files Simple Version.xlsm**, that you can check out as well.

Figure 13.12 File Renaming Dialog Box

to rename in other ways, it shouldn't be difficult to modify the code in this file to do it the way you want.

When you click the Rename files button in this file, you eventually see the dialog box in Figure 13.12, where you can choose from one of five renaming options. Your choice is stored in a variable renameOption, which has possible values 1 to 5. The RenameFile sub shown below uses this option to rename all files in a specified folder.

```
Sub RenameFiles()
    Dim renameOption As Integer ' 1 to 5
    Dim fd As FileDialog
    Dim searchFolder As String
    Dim oldName As String, newName As String
    Dim nChanges As Integer
    Dim period As Integer, i As Integer
    Dim char As String, newChar As String

    Dim fso As New Scripting.FileSystemObject
    Dim srchFolder As Scripting.folder
    Dim file As Scripting.file

    ' Open a dialog box to let user select a folder,
    MsgBox "In the next dialog box, select the folder where files to be " _
        & "renamed are stored.", vbInformation
    Set fd = Application.FileDialog(msoFileDialogFolderPicker)
    If fd.Show Then
        ' Capture the selected folder (as a string).
        searchFolder = fd.SelectedItems(1)
    Else
```

```
                ' User clicked on Cancel, so end.
            Exit Sub
        End If

        ' Get user option on how to rename.
        If frmOptions.ShowOptionsDialog(renameOption) Then

                ' Search for all files of desired type from selected folder.
                Set srchFolder = fso.GetFolder(searchFolder)
                For Each file In srchFolder.files
                    oldName = file.Name
                    Select Case renameOption
                        Case 1: newName = Replace(oldName, "_", " ")
                        Case 2: newName = Replace(oldName, " ", "_")
                        Case 3
                            newName = Replace(oldName, " ", "")
                            newName = Replace(newName, "_", "")
                        Case 4 To 5
                            If renameOption = 4 Then newChar = " " Else newChar = "_"
                            ' Get position of period before extension.
                            period = Len(oldName) - InStr(1, StrReverse(oldName), ".") + 1
                            For i = period - 1 To 2 Step -1
                                ' Check only uppercase characters that don't already
                                ' have a space or underscore to their left.
                                char = Mid(oldName, i, 1)
                                If char >= "A" And char <= "Z" _
                                        And Mid(oldName, i - 1, 1) <> " " _
                                        And Mid(oldName, i - 1, 1) <> "_" Then
                                    oldName = Left(oldName, i - 1) & newChar _
                                            & Right(oldName, Len(oldName) - i + 1)
                                End If
                            Next
                            newName = oldName
                    End Select
                    If oldName <> newName Then
                        file.Name = newName
                        nChanges = nChanges + 1
                    End If
                Next

                Select Case nChanges
                    Case 0
                        MsgBox "No files were renamed.", vbInformation
                    Case 1
                        MsgBox "one file was renamed successfully.", vbInformation
                    Case Else
                        MsgBox nChanges & " files were renamed successfully.", vbInformation
                End Select
        End If
End Sub
```

Here are some comments about the code.

- The FileDialog variable fd of the type msoFileDialogFolderPicker is used to ask the user for the folder to search in.
- The FileSystemObject variable fso is used to get the folder Object variable. Then a For Each loop goes through each file in this folder. Note how the generic Object variable file is used in this loop.

- The file object has the Name property, which returns the name of the file (but not the path to it).
- The strings oldName and newName are then manipulated depending on the user's option. Then the line before Next sets the file name to newName.

13.6 Working with Text Files

The last type of file operation discussed in this chapter concerns importing text from a text file into Excel or exporting Excel data to a text file. It is not uncommon to find data in a text file because this format represents a lowest common denominator—all you need is NotePad or any other text editor to read a text file. Usually the extension for a text file is .txt, although .csv (comma-delimited), .dat, and .prn are also used. When data are stored in a text file, each line typically includes information about a particular record. This could be information about a particular order, a particular customer, a particular product, and so on. The individual pieces of data in a line, such as first name, last name, address, and so on, are typically separated with a **delimiter** character. The most common delimiters are tabs and commas, although others are sometimes used.

If you look at a line in a tab-delimited text file, it might look like

01-Feb-02   3430   2360   3040

This is a bit misleading. There are four pieces of data in this line, but there is only a *single* character between each piece of data—a tab character, or vbTab in VBA. If you want to import this line into the first four cells of a row in Excel, you must parse the line into its individual pieces of data. Essentially, you must go through the line, character by character, searching for vbTab characters. This parsing operation is at the heart of working with text files. (It is also at the heart of all word processors.)

Importing a Text File into Excel

To import a text file into Excel, perform the following steps.

1. Open the text file for input with the line

```
Open file For Input As #1
```

Here, file is declared as String, which by this time has a value such as "C:\My Files\Sales.txt". You can have several text files open at the same time, in which case you number them consecutively as #1, #2, and so on.

2. Loop over the lines with the statements

```
Do Until EOF(1)
    Line Input #1, dataLine
    ' Code for parsing the line
Loop
```

This loops until it reaches the end of file (EOF) for input file #1. The first line inside the loop reads a new line of data and stores it in the string variable dataLine. Then this line must be parsed appropriately.

3. Close the text file with the line

```
Close #1
```

Parsing the line is where most of the work is involved. The following sub is fairly general.[4] (It is stored in the file **Parse.xlsm**.) It accepts two arguments, a dataLine to be read and a delimiter character, and it returns two results, the number of pieces of data and an array of these pieces of data. The comments spell out the individual steps. Whether you use this sub as is or you write your own parser, the logic is always the same. You have to go through the line character by character, searching for the delimiters and the text between them. (This sub has been written for 1-based indexing.)

```
Option Explicit

' Note that the indexing for the returnArray array is set up
' for 1-based indexing.

Sub ParseLine(dataLine As String, delimiter As String, _
        nValues As Integer, returnArray() As String)
    ' This sub parses a line of data from the text file into individual pieces of data.
    ' It returns an array of the pieces of data and number of pieces (in nValues).

    Dim i As Integer
    Dim char As String
    Dim counter As Integer ' counts the pieces of data in the line
    Dim currentText As String ' text since last comma

    ' Counter counts the number of pieces of data in the line.
    counter = 1
    ReDim returnArray(counter)

    ' currentText is any piece of data in the line, where the pieces
    ' are separated by commas.
    currentText = ""

    ' Go through the string a character at a time.
    For i = 1 To Len(dataLine)

        ' Get the character in position i.
        char = Mid(dataLine, i, 1)

        ' Check if the character is a comma or the last character in the string.
        If char = delimiter Then
            returnArray(counter) = currentText

            ' Get ready for the next piece of data.
            currentText = ""
```

---

[4] See the last exercise in this chapter for a much easier alternative to this parsing sub.

```
            counter = counter + 1
            ReDim Preserve returnArray(counter)

      ElseIf i = Len(dataLine) Then
            ' Capture this last piece of data and return the number of pieces.
            currentText = currentText & Mid(dataLine, i, 1)
            returnArray(counter) = currentText
            nValues = counter

      Else
            ' Add this character to the currentText string.
            currentText = currentText & Mid(dataLine, i, 1)
      End If
   Next i
End Sub
```

Exporting Excel Data to a Text File

Writing Excel data to a text file is not as common as reading from a text tile, but it is sometimes useful. The steps required are as follows.

1. Open the text file for output with the line

```
Open txtFile For Output As #1
```

Here, txtFile is declared as String, which by this time has a value such as "C:\Temp\Sales.txt". As with importing, you can have several text files open at the same time, in which case you number them consecutively as #1, #2, and so on.

2. Loop over the lines you will be storing. Inside the loop create a line (in the dataLine variable), and store it with the code

```
Write #1, dataLine
```

3. Close the text file with the line

```
Close #1
```

In this case there is no parsing. Each dataLine is typically created by reading cells from an Excel worksheet and separating them with a delimiter. For example, suppose the Excel file is structured as in Figure 13.13. Then the

Figure 13.13   Excel Data to be Exported

⊿	A	B	C	D
1	Date	P3254	P7417	P3416
2	25-Jan-15	1960	2710	1850
3	26-Jan-15	2290	2640	2170
4	27-Jan-15	2610	2270	2370
5	28-Jan-15	3130	2720	2650
6	31-Jan-15	2500	2610	2540

following WriteSalesToText sub could be used to store the data in the file C:\Temp\Sales.txt. (This sub is stored in the file **Write Sales.xlsm.**)

```
Sub WriteSalesToText()
    Dim txtFile As String
    Dim row As Integer, column As Integer
    Dim nRows As Integer, nColumns As Integer
    Dim dataLine As String

    ' Substitute the appropriate path and filename in the next line.
    txtFile = "C:\Temp\Sales.txt"
    Open txtFile For Output As #1

    With wsSales.Range("A1")
        nRows = Range(.Offset(0, 0), .End(xlDown)).Rows.Count
        nColumns = Range(.Offset(0, 0), .End(xlToRight)).Columns.Count
        For row = 1 To nRows
            ' Build data line from data in this row, separated by tabs.
            dataLine = ""
            For column = 1 To nColumns
                dataLine = dataLine & .Cells(row, column).Value
                ' Don't add a tab after the last piece of data in the row.
                If column < nColumns Then _
                    dataLine = dataLine & vbTab
            Next
            ' Write this line to the text file.
            Write #1, dataLine
        Next
    End With
    Close #1
End Sub
```

The resulting text file is shown in Figure 13.14. Note that double-quotes are automatically inserted around each line of text (because each line is considered a string by VBA). These double-quotes could be a potential nuisance for a programmer who later intends to *import* this text data into Excel. The moral is that you should always check text files before you try to import the data. Text files are notorious for containing messy data.

Figure 13.14   Resulting Text File

13.7 Summary

Although this chapter is not geared as specifically to Excel operations as the other chapters, it provides a lot of useful information for dealing with files and folders. For example, by using the FileDialog object, you can easily let a user specify a folder. Or by using the FileSystemObject object, you can easily test whether a file exists in a specific folder. In addition to the file/folder operations you typically perform in Windows Explorer, this chapter has briefly illustrated how to work with text files, either for importing or exporting. An example of importing text data for use in an optimization model appears in Chapter 33.

EXERCISES

1. Write an application that uses a FileDialog object of the msoFileDialogFilePicker type. It should allow the user to select one or more files, and then it should list the chosen files in column A of a worksheet. (The worksheet should be in the same workbook as your code. A typical file name will include the path, such as C:\My Files\Sales.xlsx.)

2. Write an application that uses a FileDialog object of the msoFileDialogOpen type. It should allow the user to select a *single* Excel (.xlsx) file, which should then be opened in Excel. (*Hint:* Look up the AllowMultiSelect and Filters properties of the FileDialog object in the Object Browser.)

3. Write an application that uses a FileDialog object of the msoFileDialogSaveAs type. After it saves the file in a name chosen by the user, it should display the new file name in a message box.

4. Write an application that uses a FileDialog object of the msoFileDialogFolderPicker type. After the user selects a folder, the application should then use a FileSystem-Object object to find all of the files in that folder (and its subfolders) with extension .xlsx or .docx, and these files should all be listed in column A of a worksheet. (The worksheet should be in the same workbook as your code. A typical file name will include the path, such as C:\My Files\Sales.xlsx.)

5. (*Note:* I left this exercise from the second edition here to illustrate how much we are missing by not having FileSearch. There is no easy way to do it! My solution uses the AltFileSearch object from Codematics, which you have to purchase. Even with it, there is no easy way to answer the second part of the exercise.) Write an application that asks the user for an extension, such as .xlsx, and then uses a FileSearch object to count the number of files on the C drive with this extension. The count should be displayed in a message box. Try it out on your own computer, say, with the extension .docx. Then modify the application so that only files that have been modified during the current month are listed.

6. Write an application that asks the user to pick a folder. The application should then open all Excel files (.xls or .xlsx) in that folder, if any, with **Forecast** in the file name. For example, these would include **Forecasting the Weather.xls** and **Company Forecasts for March.xlsx**.

7. Suppose a company has a lot of Excel files for its customers. You can assume that all files for a given customer are in the same folder, and all of these customer files begin the customer's name, such as **Davidson_Sales_2010.xlsx**. You don't know the exact naming convention; you only know that the file begins with the customer's name. Write an application that asks for a customer's name and the folder where this customer's files are stored and then lists all of the file names for this customer in column A of a worksheet. (The worksheet should be in the same workbook as your code. A typical file name will include the path, such as **C:\My Files\Davidson_Sales_2010.xlsx**.)

8. Starting with the same setup as in the previous exercise, suppose that a customer's name changes. Create an application that asks for the customer's old name, new name, and the folder where this customer's files are stored, and then renames all of the files appropriately.

9. Sometimes I renumber entire chapters. For example, Chapter 14 might become Chapter 17. Then various files for the chapter need to be renumbered. If there are a lot of files of the form **Figure 14_xx.gif**, say, they would all need to renumbered as **Figure 17_xx.gif**. Write an application to do this.

10. Use NotePad to create a text (.txt) file that contains one long list of words, where the individual words are separated by the space character. (In NotePad, use the Format menu to turn word wrap off, so your text will physically appear in one long line.) Write a sub that opens this text file, parses the single line with the space character as the delimiter, returns the number of words in a message box, returns the number of words with more than five characters in a second message box, and finally closes the file.

11. The file **Revenue Data.xlsx** has a single worksheet. This worksheet has headings in row 1 and revenues for various products on various dates in the remaining rows. Write a sub that exports these data in tab-delimited format to a text file that should be named **Revenue Data.txt** and stored in the same folder as the Excel file. Once you get the data exported, write another sub that imports the tab-delimited data back into an Excel file, just like the original Excel file, but with name **Revenue Data 1.xlsx**. You can create this new file manually, name it, and make sure it contains only a single worksheet named Revenues, but your code should open it before doing the importing.

12. The ParseLine sub in section 13.6 is a great exercise in computing logic (which is why I included it), but it is actually not necessary. The VBA library has a powerful string function called Split that does the parsing logic for you. Look it up in the Object Browser and then use it instead of the GetData sub in the **Sales Import Finished.xlsm** file to parse the data.

Importing Data into Excel from a Database

14

14.1 Introduction

An important theme throughout this book is that Excel applications often need to access data. Sometimes the data are obtained from one or more user forms, and sometimes the data reside in an Excel worksheet, either in the application's workbook or in another Excel file. However, in the corporate world, the chances are that the data are stored in a relational database, possibly on a database server. Therefore, applications typically need to import data into Excel for analysis. This chapter illustrates how to do this with VBA code. Fortunately, because this is such a common need, Microsoft has developed several technologies for importing data from relational databases. In fact, an "alphabet soup" of technologies for importing data has emerged over the past 20 years: ODBC, DAO, RDO, OLE DB, ADO, ADO.NET, and possibly others that are currently emerging. This chapter discusses a fairly recent technology that is available with Excel VBA: ActiveX Data Objects (ADO).[1]

14.2 Exercise

The **Sales Orders.mdb** file is an Access database included in the book files. (Access files created in Access 2007 or later versions have a new .accdb extension. However, I will continue to use files with the old .mdb extensions here.) As discussed in the next section, this database includes a number of related tables that store information about a company's orders for its products. The structure of this database appears in Figure 14.1. Specifically, there is a row in the Orders table for each order taken by the company, there is a row in the Products table for each product the company sells, and there is a row in the LineItems table for each line item in each order. For example, if a customer places an order for three units of product 7 and two units of product 13, there will be a single row in the Orders table for this order, and there will be two rows in the LineItems table, one for each of the two products ordered.

---

[1] A more recent technology is ADO.NET, part of Microsoft's .NET initiative. Although ADO.NET *can* be used to develop VBA applications for Excel, it requires more software than simply Microsoft Office, so it is not covered here. The "old" ADO works just fine.

Figure 14.1   Structure of Sales Orders Database

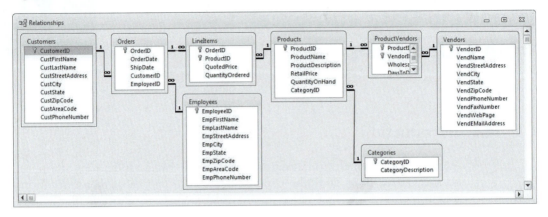

Figure 14.2   Dialog Box with List of Products

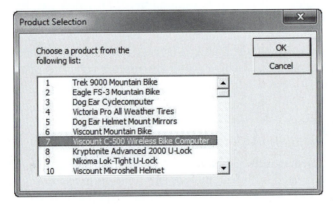

The purpose of this exercise is to develop an application where a user can select a product from a list box in a user form (see Figure 14.2) and then see details about all orders that include this product (see Figure 14.3, which shows the first few rows). This exercise requires two uses of the material in this chapter. It must first query the Products table to populate the list box in Figure 14.2. Then, once the user selects a product from the list, it must query the Orders and LineItems tables to obtain the order information for this product in Figure 14.3.

As you read through this chapter, you can try to develop this application on your own. The details will eventually be discussed in Section 14.5. Once you understand the material in the next two sections—relational databases, Structured Query Language (SQL), and ADO—you will see that applications such as this one are not as difficult to develop as you might expect.

Figure 14.3 Information on Orders for Selected Product

⩗	A	B	C	D	E
1	Orders for product:	Viscount C-500 Wireless Bike Computer			
2					
3	Order ID	Order Date	Unit Price	Quantity	Extended Price
4	6	1-Jul-2015	$49.00	2	$98.00
5	17	2-Jul-2015	$47.53	6	$285.18
6	22	3-Jul-2015	$47.53	6	$285.18
7	26	4-Jul-2015	$47.53	6	$285.18
8	27	4-Jul-2015	$49.00	3	$147.00
9	28	4-Jul-2015	$49.00	4	$196.00
10	32	5-Jul-2015	$49.00	1	$49.00
11	33	5-Jul-2015	$47.53	6	$285.18
12	44	7-Jul-2015	$49.00	1	$49.00
13	58	9-Jul-2015	$49.00	4	$196.00

14.3 A Brief Introduction to Relational Databases

The two main purposes of databases are to (1) store data efficiently, and (2) allow users to request the data they want, in a suitable form. Various forms of databases have existed, including those that predate computers. Several decades ago, researchers formalized the **relational** form of databases that is still the predominant method of storing data electronically. Many packages have been developed by various companies to implement relational databases, and many are in daily use in organizations. Some packages, such as the well-known Microsoft Access package, are **desktop** systems. If you own Microsoft Office (for Windows), then you own Access. It resides on your desktop (or laptop) machine, and you can create databases as files that reside on your hard drive. Other more heavy-duty software packages, referred to as **relational database management systems** (**RDBMS**), are **server-based**. The software and the associated databases are not likely to reside on an individual's computer, except possibly as a scaled-down version for testing purposes. Instead, they reside on a server, where users can access the data through network connections. Three well-known server-based packages are Microsoft's SQL Server, Oracle, and IBM's DB2—and there are others.

The purpose of this section is to describe the essential ideas behind relational databases. These ideas are relevant regardless of the software package that implements them, although I will illustrate the concepts with Microsoft Access so that you can follow along on your computer.

Tables, Fields, and Records

The essential element of any relational database is a **table**. A table stores data in a rectangular array of rows and columns—yes, much like a spreadsheet. In database terminology, however, the rows are usually called **records**, and the columns are

Figure 14.4 Customers Table

usually called **fields**. If you were storing information about customers in a table, each field would include some characteristic of a customer, so you might have fields such as FirstName, LastName, BirthDate, Address, City, State, Phone, EMailAddress, and possibly others. Any row (record) contains all of this information for a particular customer. In other words, each row has to do with a single customer, whereas each field lists a particular characteristic of the customer. Part of the Customers table from the Sales Orders database is shown in Figure 14.4.

Many databases consist of a single table. These types of databases are often called **flat files**. Suppose you want to store information about all of the books you read. You might store the title, the author (or authors, one per field), the year you read it, and whether it is fiction or nonfiction. A single-table database for such a simple collection of data would probably suffice. (For example, I have a flat-file database for all the books I have read.)

However, most real-world databases contain multiple tables, sometimes *many* tables. These tables are typically related in some way, which leads to the concept of *relational* database. In a well-designed relational database, each table should contain information about a particular entity. For example, in the Sales Orders database discussed in the previous section, the data center around a company's orders for its products. Several tables include: (1) the Customers table, with information about the customers who place the orders, (2) the Employees table, with information about the employees who take the orders, (3) the Orders table, with information about the orders taken, (4) the Products table, with information about the products the company sells, and (5) the Vendors table, with information about the company's suppliers.

Why aren't all of these data stored in a *single* table? This is the crucial question. Presumably, if a single table were used, each record would have data about a single order: which customer placed the order, which employee took the order, when the order was placed, and so on. Now imagine that customer Jim Smith has placed 100 orders. If the database includes personal information about the customers, then that information for Jim Smith will be repeated in 100 records of the single table. This introduces an immense amount of redundancy. Not only will the size of the database be much larger than necessary, but there will be many possibilities for errors. First, if you are a data entry person, you will need to enter

Jim Smith's personal data many times, and you are likely to make errors. Second, what if Jim Smith's phone number changes? You will then have to search through all of the records for Jim Smith and change the phone number in each. This means a lot of work and many chances for errors.

You probably do not need to be convinced that this level of redundancy—storing a customer's personal information in multiple places—is a bad idea, but what is the alternative? The answer is to have a Customers table that stores *only* information about customers, with one record per customer. Then if Jim Smith's phone number changes, you need to change it in exactly one place—in the single record for Jim Smith. This sounds like a great idea for avoiding redundancy and errors, and it is, but it introduces a potential problem. In the Orders table, where information about orders is stored, how do you know which customers placed which orders? This question is answered next. It is the key to relational databases.

Many-to-One Relationships, and Primary and Foreign Keys

Consider the Categories and Products tables in the Sales Orders database. The Categories table lists all product categories, and the Products table lists information about each product, including its category. The relationship between these tables is called a **many-to-one** relationship, because each product is in exactly *one* category, but each category can contain *many* products.

The two tables are related by fields called keys. Let's start with the Categories table, the "one" side of the many-to-one relationship. It contains a field called a **primary key**. A primary key is a *unique identifier* of the records in the table. In other words, no two records are allowed to have the same value in the primary key field. For some entities, there are "natural" primary keys. For example, a unique identifier for US citizens is their Social Security Number (SSN). For books, a unique identifier is their ISBN. But even if there is no ready-made unique identifier, it is always possible to generate one as an **autonumber** field. This is a field that numbers the records consecutively—1, 2, 3, and so on—as the data are entered into the table. If the most recently entered record has autonumber 347, the next one will have autonumber 348. This guarantees uniqueness and provides an easy way to create a primary key. The primary key for the Categories table is an example of an autonumber field named CategoryID.

To relate the Categories and Products table, a **foreign key** field, also called CategoryID, is placed in the Products table.[2] For example, it turns out that the category Clothing has CategoryID 3. Therefore, for every product in the Clothing category, the foreign key value is 3. This clearly indicates that foreign key fields are not unique. If there are, say, 250 products in the Clothing category, there will be 250 rows in the Products table with CategoryID equal to 3.

---

[2] The field names of the primary key and associated foreign key are often the same, simply to avoid confusion. However, there is no requirement that they be the same. For example, the primary key could be named CategoryID and the foreign key could be named CatID.

Figure 14.5 Categories Table

Figure 14.6 Products Table

ProductID	ProductName	ProductDescription	RetailPrice	QuantityOnHand	CategoryID
1	Trek 9000 Mountain Bike		$1,200.00	6	2
2	Eagle FS-3 Mountain Bike		$1,800.00	8	2
3	Dog Ear Cyclecomputer		$75.00	20	1
4	Victoria Pro All Weather Tires		$54.95	20	4
5	Dog Ear Helmet Mount Mirrors		$7.45	12	1
6	Viscount Mountain Bike		$635.00	5	2
7	Viscount C-500 Wireless Bike Compute		$49.00	30	1
8	Kryptonite Advanced 2000 U-Lock		$50.00	20	1

Record: 1 of 40   No Filter   Search

The actual data for these two tables appear in Figures 14.5 and 14.6 (with the first few rows showing for the Products table). Note how the CategoryID field in Figure 14.6 allows you to perform a table lookup in Figure 14.5 to find the category for any given product. Alternatively, you could use the primary key values in Figure 14.5 to find all products, say, in the Clothing category.

Referential Integrity

An extremely important idea in relational databases is that of keeping the links between primary and foreign keys valid. The technical term for this is **referential integrity**. Again, consider the Clothing category with primary key 3. Referential integrity could be violated in the following ways:

- The Clothing row in the Categories table could be deleted. Then there would be a lot of "dangling" products, with links to a category that is no longer in the database.
- The primary key value for Clothing in the Categories table could be changed to, say, 9. Then all of the clothing products with foreign keys equal to 3 would be wrong; they should now be 9.

Figure 14.7 Dialog Box with Referential Integrity Option

- Some product's foreign key could be changed from 3 to a new value. This might or might not violate referential integrity. If you realize that this product's category is not Clothing but is instead Accessories, with primary key 1, then you *should* change the foreign key to 1. However, if you change the foreign key to a value such as 15, which is not the primary key for *any* category, you will violate referential integrity.

Fortunately, database packages such as Access allow you to check an option that enforces referential integrity. (See Figure 14.7, the dialog box in Access.) With this option checked, you are not *allowed* to inadvertently make a change that would violate referential integrity. There are usually additional options, such as cascading deletions. With this option checked, if you delete the Clothing record in the Categories table, then all of the associated clothing products in the Products table will also be deleted automatically. For obvious reasons, you want to be sure you know what you are doing before you check this option.

Many-to-Many Relationships

Not all entities are related in a many-to-one manner. There are also **many-to-many** relationships. (In addition, there are **one-to-one** relationships, but they are less common, and I will not discuss them here.) A perfect example of a many-to-many relationship is the relationship between orders and products. Any order can include several products, and any product can be included in multiple orders.

The way to deal with such relationships again uses primary and foreign keys, but now an extra table is required. This table is often called a **linking table**. The Orders table has primary key OrderID, and the Products table has primary key ProductID. Then the linking table, which has been named LineItems, has two foreign keys, OrderID and ProductID. The linking table for this database has a couple of extra fields, QuotedPrice and QuantityOrdered, but it is often just a set of foreign keys. There is a row in this linking table for *each* combination of order and product. So, for example, if an order is for four products, there will be four associated rows in the linking table. Or if a product is a part of 25 orders, there will be 25 associated rows in the linking table. Because of this, linking tables tend to be tall and narrow.

The linking table allows you to look up information on orders or products. For example, if you want to know when the product King Cobra Helmet has been ordered, you look up its ProductID in the Products table, which happens to be 25. Then you search the ProductID column of the LineItems table for values of 25 and keep track of the corresponding OrderID values. Then you look up these latter values in the Orders table to find the order dates.

Many database experts insist that all tables have a primary key. What is the primary key for the LineItems table? It cannot be OrderID because of duplicates in this field. For the same reason, it cannot be ProductID. In this case, a *combination* of fields, OrderID and ProductID, is used as the primary key. This works fine, because no two records in the LineItems table have the same combination of these two fields. The point is that if there is no single field with unique values, it is usually possible to find a combination of fields that can serve as the primary key.

14.4   A Brief Introduction to SQL

As relational databases became the standard several decades ago, a language called **Structured Query Language**, or **SQL**, was developed to retrieve data from relational databases. In database terminology, SQL statements are used to **query** a database. The SQL language, known as "the language of databases," applies in some form to all database systems, whether they be Access, SQL Server, Oracle, or others. If you have worked with Access, you are probably not familiar with SQL because Access provides a user-friendly graphical interface for developing queries. However, when you use this interface, an SQL statement is created in the background, and this SQL statement is used by Access to retrieve the data you want.

Whole books (thick ones at that) have been written on SQL, but you can learn the essentials of SQL fairly quickly. First, there are several types of SQL statements. The most common type is called a **SELECT** query. A SELECT query asks for certain data from the database. For example, a SELECT statement could be used to find information on all orders placed after the year 2013. A SELECT statement allows you to view data; it doesn't *change* the data. Other SQL statements allow you to change the data. These include **INSERT**, **UPDATE**, and **DELETE** queries. However, this section discusses SELECT queries only.

A SELECT query is analogous to a single sentence with several clauses. There are only a few possible types of clauses:

- The SELECT clause lists the fields you want data on.
- The FROM clause specifies the table or tables that hold the data you want.
- The WHERE clause lists criteria that you specify. Only the data that meet these criteria are returned.

Figure 14.8   Relationships Diagram for Sales Orders Database

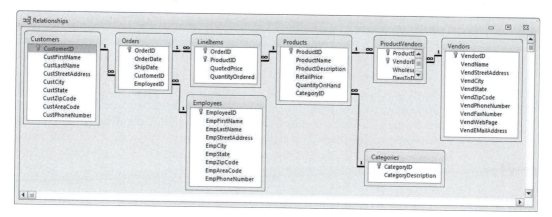

- The GROUP BY clause allows you to get subtotals, such as the total revenue from each order. In this case, you "group by" the orders.[3]
- The ORDER BY clause allows you to specify sort orders for the data returned.

Only the SELECT and FROM clauses are necessary. If any of the others are used, they must be listed in the order just shown.

Single-Table Queries

The simplest SELECT statements are queries from a single table, such as the information on all customers who live in California. Because all of this information resides in the Customers table, the query is called a **single-table query**. (See the relationships diagram in Figure 14.8, a copy of Figure 14.1 repeated here for convenience.) The corresponding SQL statement might look something like the following:[4]

```
SELECT CustFirstName, CustLastName, CustPhoneNumber
FROM Customers
WHERE CustState = 'CA'
ORDER BY CustLastName, CustFirstName
```

Although this is a *single* SELECT statement, it is customary to put each clause on one or more separate lines to improve readability. The SELECT clause lists the fields you are interested in retrieving. The FROM clause lists the single table that contains the customer data. The WHERE clause includes a criterion: the customer's state should be 'CA'. Finally, the ORDER BY clause states that data should

---

[3] There is also a HAVING clause that can follow a GROUP BY clause, but I won't discuss it here.
[4] Case is not important in SQL statements, but it is common, especially when learning the language, to capitalize keywords such as SELECT. I will do so in this section.

be returned alphabetically on last name, and in case of ties, on first name. Note the single quotes around CA in the WHERE clause. The rules in SQL for Access are that: (1) single quotes should be placed around literal text, such as CA; (2) pound signs (#) should be placed around literal dates, such as WHERE OrderDate > #12/31/2013#; and (3) nothing should placed around numbers, as in WHERE QuantityOrdered >= 5.

There are many variations of single-table SQL statements. Rather than present a long list here, I refer you to the file **Sales Order Queries.docx** available with the book. This file presents a number of examples, along with some explanation. I will just mention two variations here. First, you can include calculated fields in the SELECT clause. Here are two examples:

```
SELECT QuotedPrice * QuantityOrdered AS ExtendedPrice
```

and

```
SELECT CustFirstName & ' ' & CustLastName AS CustName
```

The first example calculates the product of QuotedPrice and QuantityOrdered and calls the result ExtendedPrice. Then ExtendedPrice acts just like any other field. The second example concatenates CustFirstName and CustLastName, with a literal space in between, and calls the result CustName.

The second variation is to use aggregate functions in the SELECT clause. The aggregate functions available are COUNT, SUM, AVERAGE, MIN, MAX, and a few others. For example, suppose you want to show the number of line items and the total amount spent in the order corresponding to OrderID 17. Then the following SQL statement does the job:

```
SELECT COUNT(ProductID) AS NumberItems, SUM(QuotedPrice * QuantityOrdered) AS TotalSpent
FROM LineItems
WHERE OrderID = 17
```

The COUNT function counts the rows in the LineItems table where OrderID equals 17, and the SUM function sums the products of QuotedPrice and QuantityOrdered for these line items. For the Sales Orders database, this query returns a single row with two numbers: 6 and 4834.98.

Often a SELECT statement with aggregate functions is accompanied by a GROUP BY clause. For example, suppose you want to know how many of the company's customers are in each state. Then the following SQL statement is appropriate:

```
SELECT CustState, COUNT(CustomerID) AS CustomerCount
FROM Customers
GROUP BY CustState
```

Figure 14.9   Results of GROUP BY Query

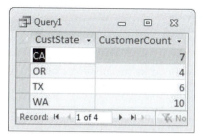

Note that the SELECT clause includes a mix. There is an individual field name (CustState) and an aggregate (the COUNT function). In this case, the rule is that you *must* GROUP BY each *individual* field in the list. The result of this query for the Sales Orders database is shown in Figure 14.9. It shows a count of customers in each of the four states represented in the database.

Multitable Queries and Joins

One principal goal of relational databases is to separate data into individual, but related, tables so that data redundancy can be avoided. However, queries often need to access data from two or more tables. In database terminology, the related tables must be **joined**. For example, if you want information on all orders that include the King Cobra Helmet product, a quick look at the relationships diagram in Figure 14.8 shows that you need data from three tables: Orders, Line-Items, and Products. The resulting SQL statement might look as follows:

```
SELECT Orders.OrderDate, LineItems.QuotedPrice, LineItems.QuantityOrdered
FROM (Orders INNER JOIN LineItems ON Orders.OrderID = LineItems.OrderID)
INNER JOIN Products ON LineItems.ProductID = Products.ProductID
WHERE Products.ProductName = 'King Cobra Helmet'
```

The middle two lines make up the FROM clause. The basic syntax for joining two tables is:

```
Table1 INNER JOIN Table2 ON Table1.KeyField1 = Table2.KeyField2
```

The two key fields are typically the primary key from one table and the corresponding foreign key from the other table. Note that each field in the above SQL statement is preceded by a table name and a period, as in Orders.OrderDate. This avoids ambiguity, in case the same field name is used in more than one table, and it is a good practice in all multitable queries.

Because this SQL requires a lot of typing, it is common to use **aliases** (short nicknames) for tables, as in the following version of the preceding query.

```
SELECT O.OrderDate, L.QuotedPrice, L.QuantityOrdered
FROM (Orders O INNER JOIN LineItems L ON O.OrderID = L.OrderID)
INNER JOIN Products P ON L.ProductID = P.ProductID
WHERE P.ProductName = 'King Cobra Helmet'
```

Here, the aliases O, L, and P are defined in the FROM clause. The rule is that if table aliases are defined in a FROM clause, they *must* be used throughout the entire SQL statement.

One final note about multitable queries is that Access requires parentheses in the FROM clause, as shown in the preceding query, if more than two tables are being joined. Essentially, these parentheses indicate that *two* tables are joined at a time. If you wanted information on customers in addition to information on orders and products, the following FROM clause, including the parentheses, would be relevant.

```
FROM ((Customers C INNER JOIN Orders O ON C.CustomerID = O.CustomerID)
INNER JOIN LineItems L ON O.OrderID = L.OrderID)
INNER JOIN Products P ON L.ProductID = P.ProductID
```

Admittedly, the syntax is tricky at first, but the idea is fairly simple. You check which tables contain the data you need, you consult the relationships diagram, and you follow the links.

It takes some time to master SQL, but it is time well spent. If you study the sample queries in the **Sales Orders Queries.docx** file, you will see that SQL is a relatively simple language, at least for the majority of common queries.

14.5 ActiveX Data Objects (ADO)

To understand the code in this chapter, you must understand relational databases and SQL, but you must also understand the way Microsoft enables VBA programmers to retrieve data from an external database. Its current standard is called **OLE DB**. This is a library of code written in another language (C++) that retrieves data from practically any type of database and transforms the results into a common row-column format. Because OLE DB is too complex for most programmers to work with, several technologies, including **Data Access Objects (DAO)** and **ActiveX Data Objects (ADO)**, have been developed as a go-between. Each of these exposes an object model to VBA programmers. DAO came first, and there are still many corporate applications that use it. Later, Microsoft developed ADO. Its object model is "flatter" than DAO's, meaning that there are fewer objects to learn. Both of these technologies allow a programmer to write relatively simple code in VBA to retrieve data from an external database. Because ADO is both simpler and more "modern," this chapter focuses entirely on it.

It is important to realize that neither DAO nor ADO is part of the Excel (or Office or VBA) object model. Therefore, the first step in using either DAO or ADO in your

Figure 14.10 Setting Reference to ADODB Library

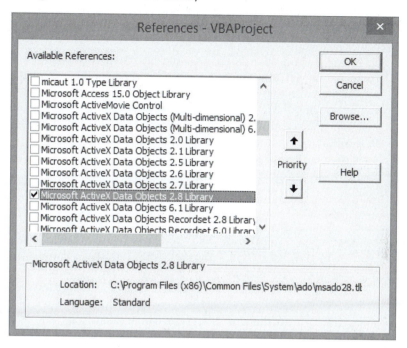

VBA code is to set a reference in the VBE. Try it now. Open a blank workbook, get into the VBE, and select the **Tools** → **References** menu item. You will see a long list of libraries, with a few items at the top checked by default. Now scroll down to the Microsoft ActiveX Data Objects x.x Library items. As the technology evolves, newer versions are added to this list. My computer lists versions 2.0, 2.1, 2.5, 2.6, 2.7, 2.8, and 6.1; yours might list others. (See Figure 14.10.)[5] You can check any of these and click on OK. Now you have access to the ADO object model. However, to avoid confusion with other possible libraries, you should refer to ADO objects with the prefix ADODB, such as ADODB.Connection. (Why ADODB and not simply ADO? I have no idea.) In fact, once you set a reference to the library and then type ADODB and a period in your code, you will get help about this library from Intellisense. (Also, once you set the reference, the Object Browser provides help about the ADODB library.)

Once a reference to ADO is set, you need to create a **connection** to the database. This requires, at the very least, a reference to the name and location of the database file and information above the data provider. Each type of database has a data provider. A **data provider** is code stored somewhere on your computer that knows how to deal with a particular type of database. It is analogous to the drivers that are provided for various types of printers. There is a provider for Access,

---

[5] New versions of ADO appear with new versions of Windows. The latest version in my list, 6.1, came with Windows 8. However, older versions work just fine.

Oracle, SQL Server, and other database systems. An older provider for Access is called **Microsoft Jet 4.0 OLE DB Provider**. A more recent one is **Microsoft. ACE.OLEDB.12.0**, which I will use here. (If this doesn't work for you, try the earlier provider.)

Once a connection is formed, the next step is usually to open a recordset based on an SQL statement. A **recordset** is a temporary database table (temporary in the sense that it resides only in memory, not as a file on a hard drive). It can be an entire table from the database, or it can be the result of a query.

After the recordset is opened, it is easy to go through its records with a Do loop and retrieve information from any of its fields. A common practice is to use code such as the following:

```
With rs
    Do Until .EOF
        statements
        .MoveNext
    Loop
End With
```

Here, rs is a Recordset object variable. One of its properties is EOF (end of file), and one of its methods is MoveNext. Very simply, these lines tell the program to go through the rows of the recordset, one at a time, taking some actions in the part called *statements,* and quitting when the end of the file is reached. The MoveNext method moves to the next row of the table. To capture the data in a field named ProductName, say, a reference to .Fields("ProductName") can be made inside this loop.

If you use a Do loop in this manner, the .MoveNext line is crucial—and easy to forget. If you forget to include it, as I have done many times, the loop will stay forever in the *first* row of the table, and you will be in an infinite loop. Remember to press **Ctrl+Break** or **Esc** to exit the infinite loop if this happens to you.

How to Open a Connection

To open a connection to a database, you first declare a Connection object, as in the following line:

```
Dim cn as ADODB.Connection
```

Here, cn is the name of the Connection object variable—any generic name could be used—and ADODB indicates that this Connection object comes from the ADODB library. Second, the line

```
Set cn = New ADODB.Connection
```

creates a new instance of a Connection object. Alternatively, these two lines can be combined into the single line.

```
Dim cn as New ADODB.Connection
```

This single line performs two actions: (1) it declares cn as an ADODB.Connection object; and (2) it creates a new instance of a Connection object. We say that it **instantiates** a Connection object. Whether you use two separate lines or a single line, the keyword New is required. This is an object-oriented programming concept (discussed in more detail in Chapter 17). Before you can work with an object from the ADODB library, you must first create an instance of one.

Next, the ConnectionString and Provider properties are used to specify information about the connection (what type of database it is and where it lives), and the Open method of the Connection object is used to actually open the connection. The next few lines illustrate how to open the connection to the **Sales Orders.mdb** file. (Note that this code resides in an Excel file, so ThisWorkbook.Path refers to the folder where the Excel file lives. For the connection to succeed, the Access file must be in the *same* folder as the Excel file. Alternatively, you could replace ThisWorkbook.Path with the actual path to the .mdb file, assuming that you know what it is.)

```
With cn
    .ConnectionString = "Data Source=" & ThisWorkbook.Path & "\SalesOrders.mdb"
    .Provider = "Microsoft.ACE.OLEDB.12.0"
    .Open
End With
```

The ConnectionString property in the second line must begin with "Data Source=" and be followed by the path and name of the Access database file. The Provider property is the name of the data provider for Access. The Open method opens the connection. Once the data have been obtained, the following line should eventually be used to close the connection.

```
cn.Close
```

How to Open a Recordset

Similarly, a new Recordset object with a generic name such as rs must be declared and instantiated with the lines

```
Dim rs As ADODB.Recordset
Set rs = New ADODB.Recordset
```

or the single line

```
Dim rs as New ADODB.Recordset
```

It can then be opened with the line

```
rs.Open SQL, cn
```

Here, SQL is a string variable that contains an SQL statement. In general, the first two arguments of a recordset's Open method are an SQL string (or a table name) and the Connection object that has already been opened. (There are other optional arguments, but they are not discussed here.) As with a Connection object, a Recordset object should eventually be closed with the line

```
rs.Close
```

Then the Close method of the Connection object should be called.

Note that Access does not need to be open to do any of this. In fact, Access doesn't even need to be installed on your computer. All you require is the Access database file (the .mdb file) and the knowledge of its location on your hard drive and its structure (table names and field names). Of course, if you want to create your own Access database, you *do* need Access.

On a first reading, this discussion of connections, recordsets, data providers, and so on can be intimidating. However, the code varies very little from one application to the next, so there is not as much to learn as you might expect. Besides, the effort required to learn ADO is well worth it due to the power it provides for retrieving external data for your Excel applications.

Importing from Other Database Packages

The examples in this book retrieve data only from Access databases. However, you should be aware that most corporate databases are not stored in Access files that reside on an employee's computer. They are typically stored on a database server—not on a desktop—using either SQL Server, Oracle, or some other server-based database system.[6] Fortunately, ADO can be used with these server-based database systems as well as with Access. The only differences are in the Connection-String and Provider properties of the Connection object. For the ConnectionString, you must specify the server name, the database name, credentials (username and password), and possibly other information. For the Provider, you must specify the type of database system—SQL Server, Oracle, or whatever. (Actually, the provider information can be included as part of the ConnectionString property, as it often is. Then no Provider property is necessary.)

The credentials in the ConnectionString are particularly important. A company doesn't want unauthorized people accessing its corporate data, so it is the job of

---

[6] SQL Server is Microsoft's server-based database system, whereas Oracle is the flagship product of Oracle Corporation.

the database administrator (DBA) to set up various permissions for company employees. Then, once you enter your username and password in the Connection-String, the settings in the database system check whether you have permission to do what you are trying to do. For example, you might have permission to run SQL queries that *retrieve* data from tables in a database, but not to run queries that *change* data in tables.

The main point, however, is that once you set the ConnectionString and Provider properties for a particular database, whatever type of database it might be, the rest of the ADO code is *exactly the same* as illustrated in this chapter for Access databases.[7] This is why ADO is so powerful—it applies with very few changes to all relational database systems.

14.6 Discussion of the Sales Orders Exercise

Now that you know the steps required to use ADO in an Excel VBA application, this section explains how to create the Sales Orders application described in Section 14.2. If you want to follow along on your computer, open the file **Sales Orders.xlsx**, which contains a template for getting started. Otherwise, you can open the **Sales Orders Finished.xlsm** file, which contains the completed application.

The first step is to design and write event handlers for the user form, called frmProducts, so that it appears as in Figure 14.11 (a copy of Figure 14.2 repeated here for convenience). This form includes the usual OK and Cancel buttons, as well as a list box named lbProducts. You should set the list box's ColumnCount to 2 so that the user sees both the product ID and the product name. This is not just for cosmetic purposes. The rest of the application uses both the ProductID and ProductName fields from the Products table of the database, so they need to be shown in the list box.

Figure 14.11   Product Selection Dialog Box

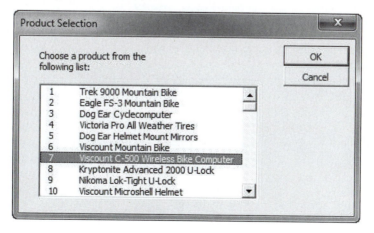

---

[7]This isn't quite true. SQL statement syntax varies slightly from one database system to another. A few of these variations are illustrated in the **Sales Orders Queries.docx** file.

The event handlers for this form are listed below. By the time the dialog box appears, code in the Main and GetOrderInfo subs (shown later) will have filled the recordset object variable rs with product IDs and product names from the Products table. The Initialize sub populates the list box with the contents of rs. This is a bit tricky. According to online help, a multicolumn list box should be populated by setting its List property to a Variant array. Therefore, a 100×2 array, productArray, is first filled by looping through the rows of the recordset. The first column of the array is filled with the ProductID field, and the second column is filled with the ProductName field. (Note that the indexes of rows and columns in a list box necessarily start at 0, not 1.)

The last line of this sub selects the *first* product in the list by default. Then the ShowProductsDialog function stores the contents of the selected row of the list box in the variables productID and productName for use in the Main sub. Recall from Chapter 11 that the selected row of the list box is provided by the ListIndex property.

```
Private cancel As Boolean

Public Function ShowProductsDialog(cn As ADODB.Connection, _
        productID As Integer, productName As String) As Boolean
    Call Initialize(cn)
    Me.Show
    If Not cancel Then
        productID = lbProducts.List(lbProducts.ListIndex, 0)
        productName = lbProducts.List(lbProducts.ListIndex, 1)
    End If
    ShowProductsDialog = Not cancel
    Unload Me
End Function

Private Sub Initialize(cn As ADODB.Connection)
    Dim rs As New ADODB.Recordset
    Dim rowCount As Integer, SQL As String
    Dim productArray(100, 2) As Variant ' Assume no more than 100 products.

    ' Populate the two-column list box with items from the recordset.
    SQL = "SELECT ProductID, ProductName FROM Products"
    rs.Open SQL, cn
    rowCount = 0
    With rs
        Do Until .EOF
            productArray(rowCount, 0) = .Fields("ProductID")
            productArray(rowCount, 1) = .Fields("ProductName")
            rowCount = rowCount + 1
            .MoveNext
        Loop
    End With
    lbProducts.List = productArray
    lbProducts.ListIndex = 0
    rs.Close
    Set rs = Nothing
End Sub

Private Sub cmdOK_Click()
    Me.Hide
    cancel = False
End Sub

Private Sub cmdCancel_Click()
    Me.Hide
```

```
    cancel = True
End Sub

Private Sub UserForm_QueryClose(cancel As Integer, CloseMode As Integer)
    If CloseMode = vbFormControlMenu Then cmdCancel_Click
End Sub
```

The application's single module begins by declaring several public variables, including the Connection object cn and the Recordset object rs. Note that these objects are both declared and instantiated in single lines of code.

```
Public cn As New ADODB.Connection
Public rs As New ADODB.Recordset
Public productID As Integer
Public productName As String
Public topCell As Range
```

The Main sub in the module clears any possible previous results (refer back to Figure 14.3), opens the connection to the database, shows the form, calls the GetOrderInfo sub to do the work, and finally closes the connection.

```
Sub Main()
    Dim cn As New ADODB.Connection
    Dim productID As Integer
    Dim productName As String

    ' Delete any previous results.
    wsOrders.Range("B1") = ""
    With wsOrders.Range("A3")
        Range(.Offset(1, 0), .Offset(1, 4).End(xlDown)).ClearContents
    End With

    ' Open connection to database.
    With cn
        .ConnectionString = "Data Source=" & ThisWorkbook.Path & "\Sales Orders.mdb"
        .Provider = "Microsoft.ACE.OLEDB.12.0"
        .Open
    End With

    ' This is set up so that GetOrderInfo is called only if the user
    ' doesn't cancel from the Products form.
    If frmProducts.ShowProductsDialog(cn, productID, productName) Then
        Call GetOrderInfo(cn, productID, productName)
    End If

    ' Close the connection.
    cn.Close
    Set cn = Nothing

    wsOrders.Range("A2").Select
End Sub
```

Finally, the GetOrderInfo sub queries the database for information on all orders that include the selected product. It then uses this data to fill the Orders worksheet. It begins by putting the selected product's name in cell Bl. Then it defines an SQL statement. Note that the required data are stored in two related tables, Orders and LineItems. (Refer back to Figure 14.8 for table names and field names.) Therefore, an inner join of these tables is required. (Because the product ID is *known*, there is no need to include the Products table in the join.) To save typing, I use the aliases O and L for the two tables. The SELECT clause lists the desired fields, including the calculated ExtendedPrice field (price times quantity). The WHERE clause indicates that results should be returned only for the selected product. Pay particular attention to the WHERE clause condition. The variable **productID** contains the ProductID field's value for the selected product, and this field is a foreign key in the LineItems table. Therefore, the condition is on this foreign key field. Finally, the ORDER BY clause sorts the returned rows by OrderDate and then OrderID.

```
Sub GetOrderInfo(cn As ADODB.Connection, productID As Integer, productName As String)
    Dim rs As New ADODB.Recordset
    Dim SQL As String
    Dim rowCount As Integer
    Dim topCell As Range

    Range("B1").Value = productName
    Set topCell = wsOrders.Range("A3")

    ' Define SQL statement to get order info for selected product.
    SQL = "SELECT O.OrderID, O.OrderDate, L.QuantityOrdered, " _
        & "L.QuotedPrice, L.QuantityOrdered * L.QuotedPrice AS ExtendedPrice " _
        & "FROM Orders O INNER JOIN LineItems L ON O.OrderID = L.OrderID " _
        & "WHERE L.ProductID =" & productID & " " _
        & "ORDER BY O.OrderDate, O.OrderID"

    ' Run the query and use results to fill Orders sheet.
    With rs
        .Open SQL, cn
        rowCount = 0
        Do While Not .EOF
            rowCount = rowCount + 1
            topCell.Offset(rowCount, 0).Value = .Fields("OrderID")
            topCell.Offset(rowCount, 1).Value = .Fields("OrderDate")
            topCell.Offset(rowCount, 2).Value = .Fields("QuotedPrice")
            topCell.Offset(rowCount, 3).Value = .Fields("QuantityOrdered")
            topCell.Offset(rowCount, 4).Value = .Fields("ExtendedPrice")
            .MoveNext
        Loop
        .Close
    End With
    Set rs = Nothing
End Sub
```

The last half of this sub opens the recordset **rs**, based on the SQL statement and the still-open connection, and then loops through its rows to enter the data from the five fields into the Orders worksheet. All cell references are relative to cell A3, indicated by the range variable **topCell**. Once the results have been transferred to the worksheet, the recordset is closed. Then, in the **Main** sub, the connection to the database is closed.

When building a fairly long SQL string by string concatenation across several lines, a common error is to run clauses together. In the above SQL statement, note the empty set of double quotes at the end of the next-to-last line. I initially forgot to include this literal space, so the last part of the SQL statement became something like WHERE L.ProductID=6ORDER BY O.OrderDate, O.OrderID. This created a syntax error—there must be spaces between the clauses—and it caused the program to bomb. Unfortunately, this common error can be hard to locate. The best way is to run the program to this point with a watch on the SQL variable and then look at the syntax of this variable closely.

Although there are a number of details that you have to get just right to make this type of application work properly (such as populating the two-column list box correctly), it is amazing that so much can be accomplished with so little code. As you see, ADO is not only powerful, but it results in very compact VBA code.

14.7 Summary

As demonstrated throughout this book, the ability to automate Excel with VBA programs makes you a very valuable employee. Given the importance of corporate databases in today's business environment, your value elevates to a whole new level when you can write programs to import external data into your Excel applications. Fortunately, a little knowledge of relational databases, SQL, and ADO goes a long way toward getting you to this level.

EXERCISES

1. Based on the Sales Orders database, write SQL statements to implement the following queries. Run them in Access to ensure that they work properly.
   a. Find the OrderDate for all orders placed by the customer with CustomerID 13.
   b. Find the OrderDate for all orders placed by the customer with first name Mark and last name Rosales.
   c. Find the number of orders placed by the customer in part **b**.
   d. Find the ProductName for all products supplied by the vendor with VendorID 3.
   e. Find the ProductName for all products supplied by the vendor Armadillo Brand.
   f. Find the number of products in each product category.
   g. Find the total dollar value of all products in each product category. (Dollar value is RetailPrice times QuantityOnHand.) The results should be grouped by category. That is, there should be a row in the result for each category.
2. The trickiest part of the Sales Orders application (at least for me) was filling the two-column list box correctly in the Initialize sub. Here is an alternative. In the Properties window for the list box, set the RowSource property to ProductList. Then write code in the Initialize sub to fill a range starting in cell AA1 of the Orders sheet with the product numbers (column AA) and product names

(column AB) from the Products table. Then name the resulting two-column range ProductList. Now much of the code in the Initialize sub can be omitted except the last line that sets the ListIndex property to 0.

3. Change the Sales Orders application so that it asks the user for the location and name of the database file. After all, there is no reason to believe that it resides in the same folder as the application itself. You could do this with an input box (and risk having the user spell something wrong), but Excel provides an easier way with the FileDialog object, as illustrated in Chapter 13 (or the GetOpenFilename method of the Application object if you prefer). Use either of these to change the application so that it prompts the user for the name and location of the database file. Actually, you should probably precede the above line with a MsgBox statement so that the user knows she is being asked to select the file with the data. Then try the modified application with a renamed version of the .mbd file, stored in a folder *different* from the folder containing the Excel application.

4. Develop an application similar to the Sales Orders application that again uses data from the Sales Orders database. This application should show a user form that lists the CategoryID and CategoryDescription fields from the Categories table in a two-column list box. Once the user selects a category, the application should display all information about the products (all fields in the Products table) for the selected product category. This information should be placed in a worksheet called Products.

5. Develop an application similar to the Sales Orders application that again uses data from the Sales Orders database. This application should show a user form that lists the CustomerID field and a CustomerName calculated field from the Customers table in a two-column list box. (The calculated field should be a concatenation of the CustFirstName and CustLastName fields. It should be defined in an SQL statement.) Once the user selects a customer, the application should display all information about the orders placed by the selected customer. Specifically, it should show the OrderDate and TotalCost for each order, sorted by OrderDate. TotalCost should be a calculated field, the sum over all items in the LineItems table of QuantityOrdered times QuotedPrice. In other words, for each order, TotalCost is the total amount the customer spent for the order. This information should be placed in a worksheet called CustomerOrders.

6. Develop an application that is a combination of the application in the chapter and the previous problem. Specifically, a userform should show *two* two-column list boxes, one for customers (as in the previous problem) and one for products. When the user selects a customer and a product, the application should display OrderDate, QuotedPrice, QuantityOrdered, and ExtendedPrice for each order for the selected product placed by the selected customer.

Working with Pivot Tables and Tables

15

15.1 Introduction

Excel's pivot tables and associated pivot charts are among its best features. They let you view data sets in all sorts of ways. For example, if a data set shows a daily company's sales in each state where it has stores, you can easily view sales totals by month, by state, or by both. Pivot tables are not only useful, but they are extremely powerful, and they are quite easy to use. All you need to do is drag and drop to obtain summary results in a matter of seconds. With such a simple user interface, it might appear that there is no need to manipulate pivot tables with VBA code, and this is often the case. However, everything you can do manually with pivot tables, you can also do with VBA. This could be particularly useful if your job is to develop an executive information system for your boss, who wants to obtain results quickly and easily with the click of a button or two. In this chapter I briefly discuss the manual way of creating and manipulating pivot tables, just in case you have never been introduced to them, and then I illustrate the pivot table object model that allows you to create and manipulate pivot tables with VBA. I also briefly discuss the extension to pivot tables, PowerPivot, introduced in Excel 2013.

In addition to pivot tables, Microsoft introduced tables in Excel 2007. These are especially useful for sorting and filtering a data set. Much of the functionality of tables has been in Excel for years, but it is now more powerful and easier to use. Interestingly, no new Table object was introduced to the Excel 2007 object model, but there is a ListObject object for working with tables, and this ListObject object is *not* new to Excel 2007. Tables were called *lists* in previous versions of Excel, and it was possible to manipulate them with VBA. Now there are more possibilities, as I discuss briefly in this chapter.

15.2 Working with Pivot Tables Manually

To create a pivot table, you must start with a data set. This data set can reside in an Excel worksheet or in an external database, such as Access, SQL Server, or Oracle. For simplicity, I assume in this chapter that the data set resides in an Excel worksheet. In that case, it should be in the form shown in Figure 15.1 (with many rows hidden). This data set contains sales transactions, one per row, for a direct marketing company over some period of time. (It is in the **Sales Data.xlsx** file.) There is

Figure 15.1 Sales Data Set

	A	B	C	D	E	F	G	H
1	Age	Gender	OwnHome	Married	Salary	Catalogs	NumberOrders	AmountSpent
2	Young	Female	No	No	Low	12	4	$1,508
3	Middle-aged	Female	Yes	Yes	High	18	3	$651
4	Middle-aged	Male	Yes	Yes	High	12	4	$1,045
5	Senior	Male	Yes	Yes	Low	12	1	$175
6	Young	Male	No	No	Low	6	2	$432
7	Middle-aged	Female	No	No	Medium	12	1	$62
8	Middle-aged	Female	No	No	Medium	18	3	$890
999	Middle-aged	Male	Yes	Yes	High	18	5	$1,505
1000	Middle-aged	Female	No	Yes	High	24	6	$824
1001	Middle-aged	Male	Yes	Yes	High	24	1	$258

one row for each transaction, and each column contains some attribute of the transaction. In database terminology, the columns are often called fields.

This is the typical type of data set where pivot tables are useful. There are some numeric fields, such as NumberOrders and AmountSpent, that you would like to summarize, and there are categorical fields, such as Age and Gender, that you would like to break the summary measures down by.

To create a pivot table, select any part of the data range and click the Pivot-Table button on the Insert ribbon.[1] You will see the dialog box in Figure 15.2,

Figure 15.2 Pivot Table Dialog Box

---

[1] The user interface for creating and working with pivot tables changed significantly in Excel 2007 and slightly in later versions. All screen shots and explanations in this chapter are geared to Excel 2013.

Figure 15.3 Blank Pivot Table and PivotTable Fields Pane

and you should fill it out as shown. The data set in this example lives in an Excel worksheet (you can override Excel's guess for the data range, but it is usually correct), and you want the results to be placed on a new worksheet. Note the bottom checkbox for adding to the data model. This is new to Excel 2013.

When you click the OK button, you get a new worksheet with a blank pivot table, shown on the left of Figure 15.3. (This worksheet has a generic sheet name, which you might want to change.) This blank pivot table sheet is accompanied by the PivotTable Fields pane on the right of Figure 15.3 and two Pivot-Table Tools ribbons, Analyze (called Options in previous versions) and Design, in Figures 15.4 and 15.5. (If you ever lose either of these, just select a cell inside the pivot table, and they will reappear.) The pivot table has four "areas": Rows, Columns, Filters, and Values. The first three are typically for categorical fields

Figure 15.4 PivotTable Tools Analyze Ribbon

Figure 15.5 PivotTable Tools Design Ribbon

Figure 15.6 Typical Pivot Table

	A	B	C	D
1	Married	(All)		
2				
3	Sum of AmountSpent	Column Labels		
4	Row Labels	Female	Male	Grand Total
5	Middle-aged	178087	267211	445298
6	Senior	109529	64067	173596
7	Young	156296	102596	258892
8	Grand Total	443912	433874	877786

you want to summarize by. The Values area is typically for numeric fields you want to summarize. You can move any of the fields to any of the areas by dragging from the field list to the appropriate pivot table area.

The pivot table in Figure 15.6 is typical. I dragged Age to the Rows area, Gender to the Columns area, Married to the Filters area, and AmountSpent to the Values area. (See Figure 15.7.) The results show the sum of AmountSpent for each combination of Age and Gender. For example, the total of all orders from middle-aged females is $178,087, whereas the total of all orders from young people of both genders is $258,892.

If you want this breakdown for married people only, click the dropdown arrow in cell B1 and select Yes. The results for this subset of married people appear in Figure 15.8, which illustrates the role of the Filters area. However, the Filters field is optional; you don't have to have a field in this area.

If you don't care about Gender, drag Gender from the pivot table field list to get the results in Figure 15.9. This illustrates that you don't need both a Rows field and a Columns field; you can have only one or the other. Actually, you can have more than one Rows or Columns field, but the pivot table becomes more difficult to read when you have multiple fields in either area.

If you would rather have Gender in the Rows area and Age in the Columns area, this is easy. Just drag Gender to the Rows area and then drag Age to the

Figure 15.7 Corresponding Fields Pane

PivotTable Fields ▼ ✕

Choose fields to add to report: ⚙ ▼

- ☑ **Age**
- ☑ **Gender**
- ☐ OwnHome
- ☑ **Married**
- ☐ Salary
- ☐ Catalogs
- ☐ NumberOrders
- ☑ **AmountSpent**

MORE TABLES...

Drag fields between areas below:

▼ FILTERS	▥ COLUMNS
Married ▼	Gender ▼

≡ ROWS	Σ VALUES
Age ▼	Sum of Amou... ▼

☐ Defer Layout Update   UPDATE

Figure 15.8 Results for Married People Only

	A	B	C	D
1	Married	Yes 🔽		
2				
3	Sum of AmountSpent	Column Labels ▼		
4	Row Labels ▼	Female	Male	Grand Total
5	Middle-aged	102809	156800	259609
6	Senior	64468	48479	112947
7	Young	36709	39193	75902
8	Grand Total	203986	244472	448458

Figure 15.9 Results After Dragging Gender Off Column Area

	A	B
1	Married	Yes
2		
3	Row Labels ▼	Sum of AmountSpent
4	Middle-aged	259609
5	Senior	112947
6	Young	75902
7	**Grand Total**	**448458**

Figure 15.10 Menu for Changing Various PivotTable Items

Columns area. Now you should be starting to see why pivot tables are so powerful and easy to use.

Recall that AmountSpent was dragged to the Values area. When you do this with a numeric variable such as AmountSpent, it is automatically summarized by the Sum operator. There are several other possible summary operators. Right-click on any number in the pivot table to get the menu in Figure 15.10. From the Summarize Values By item, you can choose any of the summary operators, such as Average. Also, if you want to change the number formatting in the pivot table, here is the place to do so. You can select the Number Format item and change the formatting, say, to currency with two decimals. The results appear in Figure 15.11. Now each dollar figure is an average of the corresponding category. For example, the young married people spent an average of $948.78 per

Figure 15.11 Average of AmountSpent Formatted as Currency

	A	B	
1	Married	Yes	🔽
2			
3	Row Labels 🔽	Average of AmountSpent	
4	Middle-aged	$883.02	
5	Senior	$882.40	
6	Young	$948.78	
7	Grand Total	$893.34	

transaction. (The Value Field Settings item in Figure 15.10 opens a dialog box where you can change all of these settings. You might prefer to use it.)

Working with Counts

Note that one of the summary operators is Count. This operator requires some explanation. If you summarize by Count, it doesn't matter at all which variable is in the Values area. For example, Figure 15.12 shows the same pivot table as in Figure 15.6, but summarized by Count, not Sum. Each number in the pivot table is now a count of the transactions for each category combination. For example, 116 of the 1,000 transactions were made by young males, and 205 of the transactions were made by seniors. The variable in the Values area is still AmountSpent, but this is completely irrelevant; any other variable in the Values area would produce exactly the same counts. For this reason, I changed the label in cell A3 from "Count of AmountSpent" to "Count".

Suppose you want to know the percentage of transactions made by females versus males for each age group. Starting from the pivot table in Figure 15.12, right-click any of the counts and select Show Values As. You see the options in Figure 15.13. For now, select the % of Row Total option. (You can experiment with the other options.) This produces the results in Figure 15.14. For example, almost 63% of all transactions made by seniors were made by females.

Figure 15.12 Pivot Table with Counts

	A	B	C	D
1	Married	(All)	🔽	
2				
3	Count	Column Labels 🔽		
4	Row Labels 🔽	Female	Male	Grand Total
5	Middle-aged	206	302	508
6	Senior	129	76	205
7	Young	171	116	287
8	Grand Total	506	494	1,000

Figure 15.13 Show Data As Options

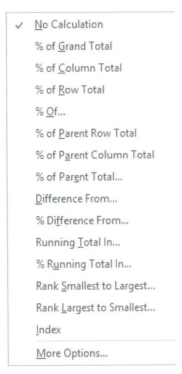

- ✓ No Calculation
- % of Grand Total
- % of Column Total
- % of Row Total
- % Of...
- % of Parent Row Total
- % of Parent Column Total
- % of Parent Total...
- Difference From...
- % Difference From...
- Running Total In...
- % Running Total In...
- Rank Smallest to Largest...
- Rank Largest to Smallest...
- Index
- More Options...

Figure 15.14 Counts Shown as Percentages of Row Total

	A	B	C	D
1	Married	(All) ▾		
2				
3	Count	Column Labels ▾		
4	Row Labels ▾	Female	Male	Grand Total
5	Middle-aged	40.55%	59.45%	100.00%
6	Senior	62.93%	37.07%	100.00%
7	Young	59.58%	40.42%	100.00%
8	Grand Total	50.60%	49.40%	100.00%

As mentioned earlier, it is common to put categorical variables in the Rows and Columns areas and numeric variables in the Values area. But this is not required. Try the following. Drag everything off the current pivot table, and then drag AmountSpent to the Rows area and any categorical variable such as Salary to the Values area. Note that when you drag a categorical (nonnumeric) variable to the Values area, it is automatically summarized by Count, which is what you want here, but the resulting pivot table isn't very informative. Every distinct value of AmountSpent is listed in column A, so you get a very "tall" pivot table. Fortunately, this can be fixed.

Figure 15.15 Group Dialog Box

Right-click any value in column A, and select Group to bring up the dialog box in Figure 15.15. You can change the default settings if you like. For example, I changed the bottom entry to 200 and obtained the pivot table shown in Figure 15.16.

Remember that when the data area is summarized by Count, the variable in the values area is irrelevant. So although the label in cell A3 is "Count of Salary", the numbers in column B are really just counts of the various AmountSpent groupings. For example, 116 of the transactions had an amount spent from $1,024 to $1,223 (inclusive). For this reason, you might want to change the label in cell A3 from "Count of Salary" to "Count", as discussed earlier.

Pivot Charts

Once you have a pivot table, you can easily create a corresponding pivot chart. To do so, select any cell inside the pivot table, and click the PivotChart button on the PivotTable Tools/Analyze ribbon. (See Figure 15.4.) From there, you can choose

Figure 15.16 Pivot Table Grouped by AmountSpent

	A	B
1		
2		
3	Row Labels ▼	Count of Salary
4	24-223	91
5	224-423	142
6	424-623	142
7	624-823	108
8	824-1023	131
9	1024-1223	116
10	1224-1423	104
11	1424-1623	79
12	1624-1823	52
13	1824-2023	24
14	2024-2223	6
15	2224-2423	4
16	2424-2623	1
17	Grand Total	1000

Figure 15.17 Pivot Chart

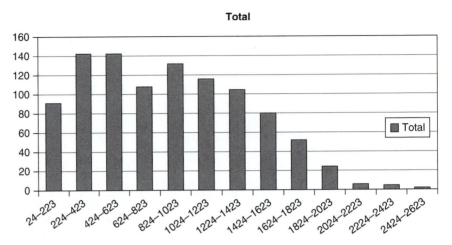

the type of chart you want. When you make changes to the pivot table, the pivot chart updates accordingly—and automatically. For example, the pivot chart corresponding to the pivot table in Figure 15.16 is shown in Figure 15.17. This pivot chart is as "interactive" as the pivot table. You can drag fields to or from its areas, and you can select items from its dropdown lists. Whatever changes you make to the pivot chart are made to the pivot table as well, and vice versa. In addition, the chart is just like any other Excel chart, so, for example, you can change the type of chart from a column chart to a line chart, you can change the chart title, and so on.

Formulas Based on Pivot Table Data

Once you have formed a pivot table, you might want to enter formulas in other cells that refer to the pivot table data. This can lead to some very strange-looking formulas. For example, starting with the pivot table in Figure 15.6, I entered a formula in cell F3 by typing = and then pointing to cell B5. I got the following formula:

```
=GETPIVOTDATA("AmountSpent",$A$3,"Age","Middle-aged","Gender","Female")
```

Excel does this to remind you exactly what information is being referenced. However, if you would prefer the more familiar formula, =**B5**, go to Excel options, select the Formulas group, and uncheck the "Use GetPivotData functions for PivotTable references" option. From then on, you won't see any more ugly GETPIVOTDATA formulas.

This discussion has barely scratched the surface of what you can do with pivot tables. However, it has already given you a glimpse of how powerful they are and how easy they are to manipulate. In the next section, I illustrate how these same operations can be performed with VBA.

15.3 Working with Pivot Tables Using VBA

You might remember the discussion of charts and VBA in Chapter 8. I mention this discussion because you can manipulate so many parts of charts in so many ways. The part of Excel's object model that deals with charts is quite complex. There are numerous objects, they belong to a hierarchy, and each has many properties and methods. The same applies to pivot tables and pivot charts. If you want to learn the part of VBA that deals with pivot tables, you could spend a lot of time exploring the various objects and their properties and methods. I will try to keep it simple here, exploring only the parts you are most likely to use in applications.

First, just as with charts, you can use VBA to build a pivot table from scratch and then manipulate it. Alternatively, and more easily, you can form a blank pivot table (as in Figure 15.3) manually and then use VBA to populate it. I will briefly illustrate pivot table creation with VBA, and then I will discuss pivot table manipulation with VBA in more depth.

Creating a Pivot Table with VBA

When you create a pivot table manually, Excel actually stores the data that the pivot table is based on in a **cache** (short-term memory). The notion of a cache for your pivot table data is important in understanding the VBA required to create a pivot table. There are two key objects: the PivotCache object and the PivotTable object. To create a pivot table in VBA, you first create a PivotCache object, and then you create a PivotTable object based on the PivotCache object. Actually, you can create multiple pivot tables from the *same* cache.

The code below is a slightly modified version I obtained by turning the recorder on and creating a pivot table. This pivot table is based on a data set with range name Data. There were no pivot tables yet in this workbook, so a PivotCache had to be created first. Then the pivot table was created from the cache. Although I named both the new worksheet and the new pivot table as PT1, they could have different names. (Note that version 14 refers to Excel 2010. The Version and DefaultVersion arguments are optional.)

```
Sub CreatePivotTable()
    Sheets.Add
    ActiveSheet.Name = "PT1"
    ActiveWorkbook.PivotCaches.Create(SourceType:=xlDatabase, _
        SourceData:="Data", Version:=xlPivotTableVersion15) _
        .CreatePivotTable TableDestination:=Range("A3"), _
        TableName:="PT1", DefaultVersion:=xlPivotTableVersion15
    Range("A3").Select
End Sub
```

I then wrote the following code to create another pivot table. It uses the pivot cache associated with PivotTable1 to create the second pivot table. I could have based it on a new cache, but this would have been a waste of memory.

```
Sub CreateAnotherPivotTable()
    Sheets.Add
    ActiveSheet.Name = "PT2"
    ActiveWorkbook.Worksheets("PT1").PivotTables("PivotTable1").PivotCache _
        .CreatePivotTable TableDestination:=Range("A3"), _
        TableName:="PivotTable2", DefaultVersion:=xlPivotTableVersion15
    Range("A3").Select
End Sub
```

The resulting pivot tables from these two subs have nothing in them. Each is just a "shell" of a pivot table. However, it is now possible to use the properties and methods of PivotTable objects to populate a blank pivot table. This is discussed next.

Manipulating Pivot Tables

To manipulate an existing pivot table, you rely heavily on the PivotFields collection. This is a list of all fields from the data set. There is also an AddFields method of a PivotTable object. This generally gives you two ways to add a field to an area of a pivot table. Specifically, suppose pivTab has been Set equal to an existing pivot table. Then either of the following two lines adds Gender to the Rows area:

```
pivTab.AddFields RowFields:="Gender"
```

or

```
pivTab.PivotFields("Gender").Orientation = xlRowField
```

The first statement uses the AddFields method, which takes arguments such as RowFields to specify where the added fields are placed. The second statement sets the Orientation property of a PivotField object to one of several possibilities: xlRowField, xlColumnField, xlPageField, xlDataField, and xlHidden.

The first statement can be generalized to add several fields at once, as in

```
pivTab.AddFields RowFields:="Gender", ColumnFields:="Age", PageFields:="Married"
```

In fact, you can even use it to add multiple fields to a given area by specifying an array, as in

```
pivTab.AddFields RowFields:=Array("Gender","Age"), ColumnFields:="Married"
```

However, the AddFields method cannot be used to place fields in the Values area. To do this, you must use the Orientation property, as in

```
pivTab.PivotFields("AmountSpent").Orientation = xlDataField
```

As long as you are at it, you might also want to set other properties of a Values field. These include the Function property, which specifies how the variable is summarized (Sum, Count, and so on), and the NumberFormat property, which uses the same format codes as regular number formatting. Here is one possibility:

```
With pivTab.PivotFields("AmountSpent")
    .Orientation = xlDataField
    .Function = xlSum
    .NumberFormat = "$#,##0.0"
End With
```

If you want to get rid of a field in some area on the pivot table, you can set its orientation to xlHidden, as in

```
pivTab.PivotFields("Gender").Orientation = xlHidden
```

If you have several fields in the Values area, you can get rid of all of them with the following line. (You might need to replace "Values" by "Data" in previous versions of Excel.) More generally, if you want to get rid of all pivot table fields, you can use the ClearTable method of a PivotTable object.

```
pivTab.PivotFields("Values").Orientation = xlHidden
```

15.4 An Example

Using the same sales data as in Section 15.2, I now illustrate a simple but useful application. (It is stored in the file **Sales Data with VBA.xlsm.**) It first uses the code illustrated in the previous section to create a pivot table named PivotTable1 on a sheet with name PT1. Alternatively, this step could be done manually. At this point there is a blank pivot table. The user then clicks a button on the Data sheet that runs a Report sub (listed later). This sub first shows two user forms, frmVariables and then frmItems. The first form, shown in Figure 15.18, allows the user to select a categorical variable for the Rows area, a numeric variable for the Values area, and a function to summarize by.

The second form, shown in Figure 15.19, lets the user select any of the items (categories) for the selected categorical variable. Note that the categories and the prompt are both based on the variable selected in the first form.

The program then fills a pivot table (behind the scenes), and for each item checked in the second form, it displays a message like the one shown in Figure 15.20. The pivot table itself is shown in Figure 15.21.

Figure 15.18 Variable Selection Dialog Box

Variables for pivot table   X

Choose a categorical variable to summarize by.

Choose a numeric variable to summarize and a summary function.

           OK

           Cancel

── Categorical variable ──
- ○ Age
- ○ Gender
- ○ OwnHome
- ○ Married
- ● Salary
- ○ Catalogs

── Numeric variable ──
- ○ NumberOrders
- ● AmountSpent

── Summary function ──
- ○ Sum
- ● Average
- ○ Minimum
- ○ Maximum

Figure 15.19 Item Selection Dialog Box

Selected items for Salary   X

Select the values of Salary you are interested in. (Check at least one.)

          OK

          Cancel

- ☑ Low
- ☐ Medium
- ☑ High

Figure 15.20 Typical Result

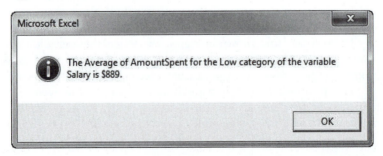

Microsoft Excel   X

ⓘ The Average of AmountSpent for the Low category of the variable Salary is $889.

          OK

Figure 15.21   Pivot Table That Results Are Based On

	A	B
1	Average of AmountSpent	
2	Salary ▼	Total
3	High	$916.19
4	Low	$889.15
5	Medium	$850.67
6	Grand Total	$877.79

The first form, frmVariables, is straightforward. Its event handlers are listed below. The ShowVariablesDialog function captures three variables, rowVariable, dataVariable, and summaryFunction, for later use.

```
Private cancel As Boolean

Public Function ShowVariablesDialog(rowVariable As String, _
        dataVariable As String, summaryFunction As String) As Boolean
    Call Initialize
    Me.Show
    If Not cancel Then
        Select Case True
            Case optAge.Value
                rowVariable = "Age"
            Case optGender.Value
                rowVariable = "Gender"
            Case optMarried.Value
                rowVariable = "Married"
            Case optOwnHome.Value
                rowVariable = "OwnHome"
            Case optSalary.Value
                rowVariable = "Salary"
            Case optCatalogs.Value
                rowVariable = "Catalogs"
        End Select
        Select Case True
            Case optNOrders.Value
                dataVariable = "NumberOrders"
            Case optAmtSpent.Value
                dataVariable = "AmountSpent"
        End Select
        Select Case True
            Case optSum.Value
                summaryFunction = "Sum"
            Case optAvg.Value
                summaryFunction = "Average"
            Case optMin.Value
                summaryFunction = "Min"
            Case optMax.Value
                summaryFunction = "Max"
        End Select
    End If
    ShowVariablesDialog = Not cancel
    Unload Me
End Function
```

```
Private Sub Initialize()
    optGender.Value = True
    optAmtSpent.Value = True
    optAvg.Value = True
End Sub

Private Sub cmdOK_Click()
    Me.Hide
    cancel = False
End Sub

Private Sub cmdCancel_Click()
    Me.Hide
    cancel = True
End Sub

Private Sub UserForm_QueryClose(cancel As Integer, CloseMode As Integer)
    If CloseMode = vbFormControlMenu Then cmdCancel_Click
End Sub
```

The second form, frmItems, is listed below. The Initialize sub sets up the checkboxes depending on the value of rowVariable. Note that the most categories in any categorical variable is 4, so the form has four checkboxes. However, some of these are hidden in case rowVariable has fewer than four categories. Then the ShowItemsDialog function captures the items checked and the number checked in the array rowItem and the variable nChecked. The Valid function ensures that the user selects at least one item.

```
Private cancel As Boolean

Public Function ShowItemsDialog(rowVariable As String, _
        rowItem() As String, nChecked As Integer) As Boolean
    Dim ctl As Control
    Call Initialize(rowVariable)
    Me.Show
    If Not cancel Then
        nChecked = 0
        For Each ctl In Me.Controls
            If TypeName(ctl) = "CheckBox" Then
                If ctl.Value Then
                    nChecked = nChecked + 1
                    ReDim Preserve rowItem(1 To nChecked)
                    rowItem(nChecked) = ctl.Caption
                End If
            End If
        Next
    End If
    ShowItemsDialog = Not cancel
    Unload Me
End Function

Private Sub Initialize(rowVariable As String)
    Me.Caption = "Selected items for " & rowVariable
    lblPrompt.Caption = "Select the values of " & rowVariable _
        & " you are interested in. (Check at least one.)"
```

```
            chk1.Value = True
            chk2.Value = False
            chk3.Value = False
            chk4.Value = False
            Select Case rowVariable
                Case "Age"
                    chk1.Caption = "Young"
                    chk2.Caption = "Middle-aged"
                    chk3.Caption = "Senior"
                    chk3.Visible = True
                    chk4.Visible = False
                Case "Gender"
                    chk1.Caption = "Male"
                    chk2.Caption = "Female"
                    chk3.Visible = False
                    chk4.Visible = False
                Case "Married"
                    chk1.Caption = "Yes"
                    chk2.Caption = "No"
                    chk3.Visible = False
                    chk4.Visible = False
                Case "OwnHome"
                    chk1.Caption = "Yes"
                    chk2.Caption = "No"
                    chk3.Visible = False
                    chk4.Visible = False
                Case "Salary"
                    chk1.Caption = "Low"
                    chk2.Caption = "Medium"
                    chk3.Caption = "High"
                    chk3.Visible = True
                    chk4.Visible = False
                Case "Catalogs"
                    chk1.Caption = "6"
                    chk2.Caption = "12"
                    chk3.Caption = "18"
                    chk4.Caption = "24"
                    chk3.Visible = True
                    chk4.Visible = True
            End Select
    End Sub

    Private Function Valid() As Boolean
        Dim ctl As Control
        Dim nChecked As Integer

        Valid = True
        For Each ctl In Me.Controls
            If TypeName(ctl) = "CheckBox" Then
                If ctl.Value Then
                        nChecked = nChecked + 1
                End If
            End If
        Next

        If nChecked = 0 Then
            Valid = False
            MsgBox "You must check at least one item.", vbInformation
```

```
    End If
End Function

Private Sub cmdOK_Click()
    If Valid Then Me.Hide
    cancel = False
End Sub

Private Sub cmdCancel_Click()
    Me.Hide
    cancel = True
End Sub

Private Sub UserForm_QueryClose(cancel As Integer, CloseMode As Integer)
    If CloseMode = vbFormControlMenu Then cmdCancel_Click
End Sub
```

The Report sub, listed below, shows the two forms and then fills the already existing pivot table. It first clears all fields in the data area by setting the Orientation property to xlHidden. It then adds the rowVariable field to the Rows area, and it adds the dataVariable field to the Values area, formatting it appropriately and setting its summarizing function to summaryFunction. For each item selected in the second form, it then uses the GetPivotData method of a PivotTable object. This method allows you to set a reference to a particular cell in the pivot table. You must supply enough information to specify the cell: the Values variable, the Rows variable, and the particular item for the Rows variable. (If there were also a Columns variable, you would have to specify information about it as well.) Finally, a message is displayed for each item the user specified in the second form.

```
Sub Report()
    Dim rowVariable As String, dataVariable As String, summaryFunction As String
    Dim rowItem() As String, nChecked As Integer

    Dim PT As PivotTable
    Dim tableItemCell() As Range
    Dim i As Integer

    ' Get user's choices.
    If frmVariables.ShowVariablesDialog(rowVariable, dataVariable, summaryFunction) Then
        If frmItems.ShowItemsDialog(rowVariable, rowItem, nChecked) Then

            ReDim tableItemCell(1 To nChecked)

            ' A pivot table with name PivotTable1 already exists in the PT1 sheet.
            Set PT = Worksheets("PT1").PivotTables("PivotTable1")
            With PT
                ' Clear all items from the pivot table.
                .ClearTable

                ' Add the selected row (categorical) field
                .AddFields RowFields:=rowVariable

                ' Add the selected numeric field, formatted and summarized appropriately.
                With .PivotFields(dataVariable)
```

```
                            .Orientation = xlDataField
                            If dataVariable = "NumberOrders" Then
                                  .NumberFormat = "0.0"
                            Else
                                  .NumberFormat = "$#,##0.00"
                            End If
                            Select Case summaryFunction
                                  Case "Sum"
                                        .Function = xlSum
                                  Case "Average"
                                        .Function = xlAverage
                                  Case "Min"
                                        .Function = xlMin
                                  Case "Max"
                                        .Function = xlMax
                            End Select
                      End With

                      ' Get the single summary data item from the pivot table.
                      For i = 1 To nChecked
                            Set tableItemCell(i) = _
                                  .GetPivotData(dataVariable, rowVariable, rowItem(i))
                      Next
                End With

                ' Display the results.
                For i = 1 To nChecked
                      MsgBox "The " & summaryFunction & " of " _
                            & dataVariable & " for the " & rowItem(i) _
                            & " category of the variable " & rowVariable & " is " _
                            & IIf(dataVariable = "NumberOrders", _
                            Format(tableItemCell(i), "0.0"), _
                            Format(tableItemCell(i).Value, "$#,##0")) & ".", vbInformation
                Next
          End If
      End If
End Sub
```

Note the IIf (Immediate If) function in the MsgBox statement. As mentioned briefly in Chapter 7, this is a very handy VBA function that works just like Excel's IF function. You supply a condition and then two arguments—one for when the condition is true and one for when it is false. This immediate If is used to format as decimal or currency depending on whether the dataVariable is NumberOrders or AmountSpent.

Clearly, if you know how to work with pivot tables manually, you could get these types of results much more easily than by writing a lot of VBA code. However, if your boss wants the results and doesn't know a thing about pivot tables, then he will really appreciate this type of application. In fact, you could hide the pivot table sheet, and your boss would never even know that it exists.

15.5 PowerPivot and the Data Model

Pivot tables are already powerful, but Microsoft added even more functionality in Excel 2013 with the introduction of PowerPivot. Actually, PowerPivot was available as a free add-in for Excel 2010, but two things changed in the Excel 2013 version. First, you no longer need to download a separate PowerPivot add-in. In Excel 2013, you can simply add it in by checking it in the add-ins list. Second, the details of PowerPivot have changed. Therefore, if you find a tutorial for the older PowerPivot add-in on the Web and try to follow it in Excel 2013, you will see that the new version doesn't work the same as before. So be aware that this section is relevant only for PowerPivot for Excel 2013 and *not* for the older version. (If you don't have Excel 2013 yet, and you want to try PowerPivot for Excel 2010, you can search the Web for "PowerPivot 2010 Excel." There is plenty of information out there.)

How is PowerPivot different from existing pivot table tools, and why is it necessary at all? The basic idea is that PowerPivot allows you to create a **data model** and then base pivot tables on it. The term *data model* is new in Excel 2013, but it is not at all a new concept. It is essentially a set of related tables, exactly like the relational databases discussed in Chapter 14 that have been around for decades. The new aspect is that PowerPivot provides you with the tools to create a data model entirely within Excel, with no need for Access or any other relational database system. Importantly, the tables for this model can come from a variety of sources. For example, one table could be a table from a worksheet within the workbook, another table could be an imported table from another workbook, another table could be imported data from a text file, and another table could be imported from an Access database. The only requirement is that these tables must have fields that can be used as primary and foreign keys, so that the usual relationships can be defined. Once this data model has been defined—the tables have been imported and the relationships have been created—pivot tables can be created in the usual way, with access to all of the fields in all of the tables.

There is not enough room here to explain the details of using PowerPivot, but if you perform a Web search for "PowerPivot 2013 tutorial," you should find plenty of useful information. (I learned it from the tutorial at http://office. microsoft.com/en-us/excel-help/tutorial-pivottable-data-analysis-using-a-data-model-in-excel-2013-HA102922619.aspx?CTT=3, which is hopefully still there. This site even includes a data set for practice.)

If you want to go a step farther with PowerPivot—that is, beyond learning how to implement it through the Excel interface—you can automate it with VBA. To see the possibilities, open the Object Browser, and in the Excel library, scroll down to the objects that begin with Model. These are all new to Excel 2013, and they can all be used to manipulate a data model. Unfortunately, these were evidently added fairly late to Excel 2013, as you can see if you request online help for any of them—help is virtually nonexistent. However, the object names, such as ModelTable, ModelTableColumn, and ModelRelationship, are fairly self-explanatory, so once you learn how to use PowerPivot through the Excel interface, you shouldn't have much trouble learning how to perform basic automations with VBA.

15.6 Working with Excel Tables Manually

As I stated in the introduction to this chapter, a table was a new feature of Excel 2007, and it exists in essentially the same form in later versions. Tables have always been around, and they were referred to as lists, data sets, or even tables in previous versions of Excel, but they now have "official" status with plenty of useful functionality. Tables are used primarily to sort, filter, and summarize data. They don't replicate the functionality of pivot tables—not by a long shot—but they enable you to perform relatively simple data analysis very easily. In this section, I illustrate some of the main features of Excel tables and how you can work with them manually. Then in the next section, I illustrate how you can automate these tasks with VBA. As with pivot tables, you might never need to use VBA to manipulate tables, given the ease of working with them through Excel's user interface, but it is good to know that everything you can do manually, you can also do with VBA.

The file I will use for illustration is **MBA Students.xlsx**. It contains information on a sample of 1,000 (fictional) MBA students, a small subset of which is shown in Figure 15.22. This is a typical table: a rectangular array of data, where each row has information about a student, each column is an attribute of the student, and the columns have names at the top. However, before you can use the new functionality of tables, you must *designate* the data set as a table. To do so, select any cell within the table and click the Table button on the Insert ribbon.[2] This does four things: (1) it colors the range nicely, (2) it inserts dropdown arrows next to each column name (see Figure 15.23), (3) it gives the resulting table a generic name such as Table1 (which you can change to something more descriptive), and (4) it gives you a new Table Tools Design ribbon that is visible when your cursor is inside the table (see Figure 15.24).

Although there are many things you can now do with the table, I will illustrate only the most common, and these are so easy that you can learn them with just a few minutes of practice. In the rest of this section, I will lead you through some operations. After you try these, you should be comfortable experimenting on your own.

Sorting

Suppose you want to sort first on Nationality, then (in case of ties) on Gender, with Males at the top, and finally (again in case of ties) on Age. To do this, you should proceed in *backwards* order. First, click the Age dropdown arrow and select the A-Z option. Next, click the Gender dropdown arrow and select the Z-A option (because you want Males at the top). Finally, click the Nationality dropdown arrow and select the A-Z option. If you would rather get back to the

---

[2] You can also click the Format as Table dropdown arrow on the Home ribbon and select a style to accomplish the same thing. An even quicker way is to press Ctrl+t.

Figure 15.22 MBA Student Data

	A	B	C	D	E	F	G	H	I	J	K	L
1	Student	Age	Gender	Nationality	Married	Children	Year in program	Undergrad major	GMAT score	Previous salary	Monthly expenses	School debt
2	1	28	Female	South America	No	0	2	Finance		55000	1210	32200
3	2	27	Male	US	No	0	2	Other business	663	44600	570	20000
4	3	28	Female	US	No	0	2	Engineering		43500	1850	53500
5	4	26	Male	China	Yes	1	2	Other business		37000	1300	91300
6	5	36	Male	US	No	0	1	Marketing	666	88600	1420	11100
7	6	29	Female	Europe	No	0	2	Marketing	658	41900	1310	49000
8	7	33	Female	US	Yes	1	1	Marketing		59000	1950	30400
9	8	37	Male	US	Yes	0	2	Other non-business	750	60400	870	19000
10	9	31	Male	Japan	No	0	2	Other business		49500	1090	32900
11	10	29	Female	US	Yes	1	1	Finance	669	65700	1570	18700

Figure 15.23 Table with Dropdown Arrows

	A	B	C	D	E	F	G	H	I	J	K	L
1	Studen	Age	Gende	Nationality	Marrie	Childre	Year in program	Undergrad majo	GMAT scor	Previous salar	Monthly expense	School det
2	1	28	Female	South America	No	0	2	Finance		55000	1210	32200
3	2	27	Male	US	No	0	2	Other business	663	44600	570	20000
4	3	28	Female	US	No	0	2	Engineering		43500	1850	53500
5	4	26	Male	China	Yes	1	2	Other business		37000	1300	91300
6	5	36	Male	US	No	0	1	Marketing	666	88600	1420	11100
7	6	29	Female	Europe	No	0	2	Marketing	658	41900	1310	49000
8	7	33	Female	US	Yes	1	1	Marketing		59000	1950	30400
9	8	37	Male	US	Yes	0	2	Other non-business	750	60400	870	19000
10	9	31	Male	Japan	No	0	2	Other business		49500	1090	32900
11	10	29	Female	US	Yes	1	1	Finance	669	65700	1570	18700

Figure 15.24 Table Tools Design Ribbon

original sort order, you can sort on the Student index in column A. (An index for the records, as this data set has in column A, is useful for exactly this purpose—to get data back to the original sort order.)

Note that you can even sort by color. I guess this could come in handy, and it certainly sounds cool, but I haven't yet found an example where I have really needed it.

Filtering

You might have used Excel's Autofilter in pre-2007 versions of Excel. This is basically what you get "for free" with Excel tables. Try the following.

- Filter out all but the US students. To do so, click the Nationality dropdown arrow and uncheck all nationalities but US. (A quicker way is to uncheck the Select All item and then check US.) You will see blue row numbers, meaning that some rows have been hidden—that is, filtered out. You will also see a filter icon in the Nationality dropdown arrow, indicating that a filter is in place. You could clear this filter by clicking the Nationality dropdown arrow and selecting the Clear Filter option, but don't do so yet.

- Filter out all students with "business" in the name of their undergraduate major. To do this, you could click the Undergrad Major dropdown arrow and uncheck the Other business and Other nonbusiness items, but a possibly better way is to select Text Filters. This provides a number of possibilities for filtering text. For now, select "Does not contain", and enter **business**.
- Filter out all students who are age 30 or older. To do this, click the Age dropdown arrow, and under the Number Filters, select "Less than" and enter **30**.

Note that you now see only US students with undergraduate majors in Finance, Marketing, or Engineering who are not yet 30 years old. As you see, the filters build upon themselves.

These few examples indicate just a few of the possibilities for filtering. Excel provides most of the options you will ever need, and they are very easy to implement. If you have a number of filters in place and you want to clear all of them, you can click the Clear button in the Sort & Filter group on the Data ribbon. (This is also available on the Home ribbon.)

Summarizing

Once you have filtered data, you might want to create summary measures for one or more columns *based on the filtered data only*. This was rather difficult in pre-2007 versions of Excel, but now it is really easy. First, it is useful to split the screen horizontally so that you can see the top and bottom of the table on the screen. Then in the Table Tools Design ribbon, check the Total Row option. You will see a new blue row at the bottom of the table. By default, it summarizes the *last* variable with the Sum function, but you can summarize *any* variable with any of several functions. As an example, select the total row cell for the Previous Salary variable and select the Average function from the resulting dropdown list. As another example, select the Count Numbers option for the GMAT column to see the number of nonmissing values. (If you look at the formulas entered in these cells, you will see that they use the SUBTOTAL function, along with a numeric code for the operation. For example, 101 corresponds to Average, 102 corresponds to Count Numbers, and so on.)

Again, these summary values are for the filtered data only, so if you change the filter, the summary measures will change. And if you don't want the total row, you can uncheck the Total Row option in the Table Tools Design ribbon.

Expandability

One final feature of tables is an extremely useful one. As you add data to a table, either to the right or to the bottom, the table automatically expands. In the MBA students data, try the following. Enter Marketing major in cell M1. It automatically gets its own dropdown arrow, meaning that it is automatically part of the table. Next, in the cell below, enter an IF formula to record a 1 if the student's undergraduate major is Marketing and a 0 otherwise. When you enter this formula, don't type the cell reference (H6, because rows 2–5 have been filtered out), but instead point to it. You will see the following formula: =**IF(Table1 [[#This Row], [Undergrad major]]** = **"Marketing", 1, 0)**. Although the usual =**IF(H6** = **"Marketing", 1,0)** would still work fine, this new syntax indicates exactly what the formula means.[3] Also, notice that as soon as you enter this formula, it automatically copies down. This is another advantage of a table. Finally, if you enter data for a new student at the bottom of the table, it will automatically be added to the table. (You might want to clear filters and remove the table row before doing this.)

This automatic expandability has a very important implication. Suppose you build a pivot table from a table. When you insert the pivot table, don't enter a range such as A1:L1001 for the pivot table range; enter the name of the table (Table1 in this case) instead. Now if you add more data, either to the right or to the bottom of the table, you can refresh the pivot table simply by clicking the pivot table Refresh button; you do *not need* to rebuild the pivot table. The same is true of a chart based on a table. It refreshes automatically as the table expands. People in the business world will *love* this new feature, at least once they learn that it exists!

15.7 Working with Excel Tables with VBA

When I say that tables were given "official" status in Excel 2007, this isn't entirely true. The Excel object model in previous versions of Excel had a ListObject object for working with lists—that is, tables. I didn't explore this object then, so I am not familiar with its original properties and methods, but there must have been a number of additions in Excel 2007 to deal with the new functionality available with tables. In any case, the ListObject object is the key to creating or manipulating tables with VBA.

To keep this section reasonably short, I will simply show the VBA code I obtained when I went through the exercises in the previous section with the VBA recorder on. Then I will show equivalent code I obtained by cleaning up the recorded code. Here is the recorded code. (You can find all of the code in the file **MBA Students.xlsm**.).

```
Sub RecordedCode()
    ActiveSheet.ListObjects.Add(xlSrcRange, Range("$A$1:$L$1001"), , xlYes).Name = _
        "Table1"
    Range("Table1[#All]").Select
    ActiveWorkbook.Worksheets("Data").ListObjects("Table1").Sort.SortFields.Clear
    ActiveWorkbook.Worksheets("Data").ListObjects("Table1").Sort.SortFields.Add _
        Key:=Range("Table1[[#All],[Age]]"), SortOn:=xlSortOnValues, Order:= _
        xlAscending, DataOption:=xlSortNormal
    With ActiveWorkbook.Worksheets("Data").ListObjects("Table1").Sort
        .Header = xlYes
```

---

[3] If you don't like this new syntax, go to Excel Options, select the Formulas group, and uncheck the "Use table names in formulas" option.

```
            .MatchCase = False
            .Orientation = xlTopToBottom
            .SortMethod = xlPinYin
            .Apply
    End With
    ActiveWorkbook.Worksheets("Data").ListObjects("Table1").Sort.SortFields.Clear
    ActiveWorkbook.Worksheets("Data").ListObjects("Table1").Sort.SortFields.Add _
        Key:=Range("Table1[[#All],[Gender]]"), SortOn:=xlSortOnValues, Order:= _
        xlDescending, DataOption:=xlSortNormal
    With ActiveWorkbook.Worksheets("Data").ListObjects("Table1").Sort
            .Header = xlYes
            .MatchCase = False
            .Orientation = xlTopToBottom
            .SortMethod = xlPinYin
            .Apply
    End With
    ActiveWorkbook.Worksheets("Data").ListObjects("Table1").Sort.SortFields.Clear
    ActiveWorkbook.Worksheets("Data").ListObjects("Table1").Sort.SortFields.Add _
        Key:=Range("Table1[[#All],[Nationality]]"), SortOn:=xlSortOnValues, Order _
        :=xlAscending, DataOption:=xlSortNormal
    With ActiveWorkbook.Worksheets("Data").ListObjects("Table1").Sort
            .Header = xlYes
            .MatchCase = False
            .Orientation = xlTopToBottom
            .SortMethod = xlPinYin
            .Apply
    End With
    ActiveWorkbook.Worksheets("Data").ListObjects("Table1").Sort.SortFields.Clear
    ActiveWorkbook.Worksheets("Data").ListObjects("Table1").Sort.SortFields.Add _
        Key:=Range("Table1[[#All],[Student]]"), SortOn:=xlSortOnValues, Order:= _
        xlAscending, DataOption:=xlSortNormal
    With ActiveWorkbook.Worksheets("Data").ListObjects("Table1").Sort
            .Header = xlYes
            .MatchCase = False
            .Orientation = xlTopToBottom
            .SortMethod = xlPinYin
            .Apply
    End With
    ActiveSheet.ListObjects("Table1").Range.AutoFilter Field:=4, Criteria1:= _
        "US"
    ActiveSheet.ListObjects("Table1").Range.AutoFilter Field:=8, Criteria1:= _
        "<>*business*", Operator:=xlAnd
    ActiveSheet.ListObjects("Table1").Range.AutoFilter Field:=2, Criteria1:= _
        "<30", Operator:=xlAnd
    ActiveSheet.ListObjects("Table1").ShowTotals = True
    ActiveWindow.Panes(3).Activate
    Range("Table1[[#Totals],[Previous salary]]").Select
    ActiveSheet.ListObjects("Table1").ListColumns("Previous salary"). _
        TotalsCalculation = xlTotalsCalculationAverage
    Range("Table1[[#Totals],[GMAT score]]").Select
    ActiveSheet.ListObjects("Table1").ListColumns("GMAT score").TotalsCalculation _
        = xlTotalsCalculationCountNums
    ActiveWindow.Panes(1).Activate
    Range("M1").Select
    ActiveCell.FormulaR1C1 = "Marketing major"
    Range("M4").Select
    ActiveCell.FormulaR1C1 = _
        "=IF(Table1[[#This Row],[Undergrad major]]=""Marketing"",1,0)"
    Range("A11").Select
    ActiveSheet.ListObjects("Table1").ShowTotals = False
```

```
ActiveWorkbook.Worksheets("Data").ListObjects("Table1").Sort.SortFields.Clear
ActiveSheet.ShowAllData
ActiveWindow.Panes(3).Activate
Range("A1002").Select
ActiveCell.FormulaR1C1 = "1001"
Range("B1002").Select
ActiveCell.FormulaR1C1 = "30"
Range("C1002").Select
ActiveCell.FormulaR1C1 = "Female"
Range("D1002").Select
ActiveCell.FormulaR1C1 = "US"
Range("E1002").Select
ActiveCell.FormulaR1C1 = "No"
Range("F1002").Select
ActiveCell.FormulaR1C1 = "0"
Range("G1002").Select
ActiveCell.FormulaR1C1 = "2"
Range("H1002").Select
ActiveCell.FormulaR1C1 = "Marketing"
Range("J1002").Select
ActiveCell.FormulaR1C1 = "51000"
Range("K1002").Select
ActiveCell.FormulaR1C1 = "850"
Range("L1002").Select
ActiveCell.FormulaR1C1 = "23000"
Range("M1002").Select
End Sub
```

As usual, this recorded code is ugly, and it is filled with unnecessary Select lines, but you can probably learn what you need from it for working with tables in your own code. Here is my cleaned up version.

```
Sub CleanedUpCode()
    Dim tbl As ListObject

    ' Create the table and give it a name.
    Set tbl = wsData.ListObjects.Add(Source:=wsData.Range("$A$1:$L$1001"), _
        XlListObjectHasHeaders:=xlYes)
    tbl.Name = "MBA_Table"

    With tbl
        With .Sort
            ' For each sort, first clear the SortFields list, then Add one,
            ' and then Apply it.
            .SortFields.Clear
            .SortFields.Add Key:=Range("MBA_Table[[#All],[Age]]"), _
                Order:=xlAscending
            .Apply
            .SortFields.Clear
            .SortFields.Add Key:=Range("MBA_Table[[#All],[Gender]]"), _
                Order:=xlDescending
            .Apply
            .SortFields.Clear
            .SortFields.Add Key:=Range("MBA_Table[[#All],[Nationality]]"), _
                Order:=xlAscending
            .Apply
            .SortFields.Clear
```

```
                ' Restore original sort order.
                .SortFields.Add Key:=wsData.Range("MBA_Table[[#All],[Student]]"), _
                    Order:=xlAscending
                .Apply
                .SortFields.Clear
        End With

        ' Apply filters.
        With .Range
            .AutoFilter Field:=4, Criteria1:="US"
            .AutoFilter Field:=8, Criteria1:="<>*business*"
            .AutoFilter Field:=2, Criteria1:="<30"
        End With

        ' Show Total Row and create a couple totals.
        .ShowTotals = True
        .ListColumns("Previous salary") _
            .TotalsCalculation = xlTotalsCalculationAverage
        .ListColumns("GMAT score") _
            .TotalsCalculation = xlTotalsCalculationCountNums

        ' Remove Total Row.
        .ShowTotals = False

    End With

    ' Clear filters.
    wsData.ShowAllData
    ' Create a new variable in column M.
    wsData.Range("M1").Value = "Marketing major"
    wsData.Range("M2").Formula = _
        "=IF(MBA_Table[[#This Row],[Undergrad major]]=""Marketing"",1,0)"

    ' Enter a new student at the bottom of the table.
    With wsData.Range("A1").End(xlDown).Offset(1, 0)
        .Value = .Offset(-1, 0).Value + 1
        .Offset(0, 1).Value = 30
        .Offset(0, 2).Value = "Female"
        .Offset(0, 3).Value = "US"
        .Offset(0, 4).Value = "No"
        .Offset(0, 5).Value = 0
        .Offset(0, 6).Value = 2
        .Offset(0, 7).Value = "Marketing"
        .Offset(0, 8).Value = ""
        .Offset(0, 9).Value = 51000
        .Offset(0, 10).Value = 850
        .Offset(0, 11).Value = 23000
    End With

    wsData.Range("A1").Select
End Sub
```

This is actually a great way to learn about a complex object such as the ListObject object. Turn on the recorder and record some typical operations. Then try to clean up the recorded code by eliminating everything but the essentials. (This will take some trial and error; at least it did for me.) You will not only realize how much unnecessary code the recorder adds, but you will learn a lot about the properties and methods of the object. For example, I learned that a ListObject object has a Sort property. From this, you move down the hierarchy to the Sort-Fields collection to add a field to sort on. But you must Clear the SortFields collection from one sort to the next, and you must use the Apply method to actually implement the sort. As another example, I tried to enter the typical IF formula in cell M2 *before* removing the filter. This produced an error because at that time, row 2 was filtered out. So evidently, you can't use VBA to enter a formula in a hidden cell. Live and learn.

15.8 Summary

If you have never explored pivot tables, you should take some time to do so. They provide one of the most powerful but yet simplest methods for analyzing data, and the PowerPivot tools introduced in Excel 2013 provide even more power. Although you might never feel the need to create or manipulate pivot tables with VBA—because Excel's tools for doing it manually are so simple—just remember that everything you can do manually, you can also do with VBA. It just takes some practice, experimentation, and a few trips to the Object Browser for help on the details. The same comments apply verbatim to tables in Excel 2007 and later versions.

EXERCISES

1. A human resources manager at Beta Technologies has collected current annual salary figures and related data for 52 of the company's full-time employees. The data are listed in the file **Beta.xlsx**. They include the employee's gender, age, number of years of relevant work experience prior to employment at Beta, number of years employed at Beta, number of years of postsecondary education, and annual salary. Use pivot tables and pivot charts to answer the following questions.
   a. What proportion of these employees are female?
   b. Is there evidence of salary discrimination against women at Beta?
   c. Is additional postsecondary education positively associated with higher average salaries at Beta?
   d. Is there evidence of salary discrimination against older employees at Beta?

2. The file **BusinessSchools.xlsx** contains enrollment data on the top-rated graduate business programs in the United States, as reported by *Business Week's Guide to the Best Business Schools*. Specifically, it reports the percentages of women, minority, and international students enrolled in each program, as well as the number of full-time students enrolled in each. Use pivot tables and pivot charts to answer the following questions.
   a. Do graduate business programs with higher proportions of female student enrollments tend to have higher proportions of minority student enrollments?
   b. Do graduate business programs with higher proportions of female student enrollments tend to have higher proportions of international student enrollments?

3. The file **HyTex.xlsx** contains data on the HyTex Company, a direct marketer of stereo equipment, personal computers, and other electronic products. HyTex advertises entirely by mailing catalogs to its customers, and all of its orders are taken over the telephone or through the Web. The company spends a great deal of money on its catalog mailings, and it wants to be sure that this is paying off in sales. Therefore, it has collected data on 1,000 customers at the end of the current year. Use pivot tables and pivot charts to find the following information about these customers.
   a. Find the percentage of homeowners, broken down by age, marital status, and gender.
   b. Find the percentage married, broken down by age, homeowner status, and gender.
   c. Find the average salary broken down by age, gender, marital status, and homeowner status.
   d. Find the percentages in the History categories, broken down by number of children and whether they live close to retail stores.
   e. Find the percentage receiving the various numbers of catalogs for each value of the History variable.
   f. Analyze the average amount spent in the current year, broken down by History, number of catalogs, and the various demographic variables.

4. Change the application in the file **Sales Data with VBA.xlsm** so that the user has no choice of summarizing function—it is always by Average—but the user gets to choose a Columns field as well as a Rows field, each from the same list. There should be another user form, just like frmItems, for the Columns variable, and there should be error checking to prevent the user from choosing the *same* variable for both the Rows and Columns areas.

5. Change the application in the file **Sales Data with VBA.xlsm** so that the user sees only a single form, frmVariables. It is an expanded version of the current frmVariables, where the user can also choose a Columns field and a Filters field. There should be error checking that prevents the user from choosing the *same* variable for the Rows, Columns, and Filters areas—they should all be different. Then, instead of reporting the results in one or more message boxes, the code should simply allow the user to see the resulting pivot table.

16
Working with Ribbons, Toolbars, and Menus

16.1 Introduction

Of all the chapters in this book, this is the one most affected by changes in post-2003 versions of Excel. Therefore, it is a good idea to start with a brief history of Excel's user interface. In version 2003 and earlier, the user interface included a variety of menus and toolbars, and virtually everything was customizable, either through the interface itself or with VBA. You could modify any of the menus or add your own custom menus. Similarly, you could modify any of the toolbars or create your own. There was even a built-in paint utility for designing your own toolbar icons. Many users loved this customizability, but it had its drawbacks. Specifically, users could change their userface so much that it barely looked like Excel. Worse yet, programmers who weren't careful could develop custom applications for others that changed the familiar Excel user interface beyond all recognition—and then forget to restore it after the application stopped running. You can imagine how upset users were when their familiar user interface disappeared and didn't return. In short, chaos was possible, and it often occurred.

In version 2007, Microsoft changed all of this. Many of the menus and toolbars were not only replaced by tabs and ribbons, but these tabs and ribbons were *fixed*. Users couldn't change them or develop their own. Actually, this isn't quite true. Custom developers *are* able to use a technology called **RibbonX** to modify, add, or hide ribbons. This requires them to write **XML** (extensible markup language) code, which is probably beyond the ability of typical Excel users. Even so, such changes are embedded in the custom files themselves. When these files run, the user interface changes according to the XML code, but when the file is closed, these changes disappear and the user interface reverts back to its original form. RibbonX and XML are discussed in this chapter. They can be used in either Excel 2007 or later versions.

Evidently, Microsoft got a lot of complaints about the lack of customizability in Excel 2007, so they restored *some* of it in Excel 2010. Now you can customize the ribbon structure without any RibbonX or XML. You can simply right-click a ribbon, select "Customize the Ribbon," and drag and drop to make changes. Any changes you make will remain intact—they are *not* a part of a particular file like RibbonX changes. I briefly discuss the changes you are allowed to make in this way.

On top of all this, much can still be done with VBA. Surprisingly, the **MSOffice** object model for modifying the user interface has *not* changed very much through the various versions of Office. The key objects continue to be the CommandBar object and the CommandBars collection. Roughly speaking, these contain menus and toolbars. In Excel 2003 and earlier, a programmer could manipulate these objects in VBA code to modify menus and toolbars. Such code still works in Excel 2007 and 2010. However, any customized menus and tool-bars it creates are added to the **Add-Ins** ribbon. This is primarily for backward compatibility. I discuss this topic only briefly. If you are a serious developer for post-2003 versions of Excel, you are much more likely to use RibbonX and XML than VBA to customize the user interface.

16.2 Customizing Ribbons

Customizing ribbons in Excel 2010 and later versions through the user interface—that is, without any XML or VBA—is easy. Just right-click any ribbon and select "Customize the Ribbon" to open the dialog box in Figure 16.1. On the left you see a list of all controls, including your own macros in the Macros group, that can be added to ribbons. On the right you see the existing tabs and their hierarchy of groups and controls. Depending on what you select, the Add and Remove buttons in the middle are either enabled or disabled. These allow you to change the ribbon structure as you like.

However, when Microsoft decided to let users customize the ribbons in Excel 2010, they didn't open the floodgates completely. There are certain things you can and can't do. Here are the rules, but you don't really need to memorize

Figure 16.1 Customizing the Ribbon

them. If some action is allowed, the corresponding Add and Remove buttons will be enabled; if it isn't allowed, they will be disabled.

- You are *not* allowed to delete or rename any built-in ribbons, and you are *not* allowed to delete or rename any groups or controls on these ribbons.
- You *are* allowed to add built-in Excel controls (the ones in the All Commands group) to existing ribbons. For example, there is a Zoom button on the View ribbon. You can drag this button to the Home ribbon, so that you can zoom from either the Home or View ribbon. However, you are *not* allowed to add buttons for your own macros (from the Macros group) to any of the built-in ribbons.
- You *are* allowed to create one or more "custom" tabs and then rename them. However, the term "(Custom)" will be tacked on to the names of all such tabs (and any groups on them). You have almost complete control of these custom tabs. You can create and name groups on them, and you can add built-in Excel buttons or buttons for your own macros to them.
- If you add one of your macros to a new custom tab, you can then click the Rename button to rename it (which becomes the tool tip you get when you hover the mouse over the button) and change the icon on the control. I will say more about the available icons in the next section. The default list contains only a limited number of icons.

Any changes you make to the ribbon structure in this way are completely independent of any files you have open. If you make any such changes, close Excel and reopen it, the ribbon changes will still be in effect.

16.3 Using RibbonX and XML to Customize Ribbons[1]

Recall that the extension for Excel files changed from .xls to .xlsx in Excel 2007. The extra "x" at the end stands for XML. Before Excel 2007, Excel files were in binary format, meaning that they could be read only by a special program—Excel. That changed dramatically in Excel 2007. Excel files (with either the .xlsx or .xlsm extensions) are now XML files, which means that they can be read in any text editor. The contents are pretty ugly, but they make sense. In fact, .xlsx and .xlsm are really *zipped* files. To prove this to yourself, try the following:

1. Locate an .xlsx or .xlsm file in Windows Explorer and rename it, adding .zip to the end. For example, if the file name is **Test.xlsx**, change it to **Test.xlsx.zip**. (You can ignore any warnings.)
2. Right-click the zip file and select Extract All. You will see something similar to Figure 16.2. This shows all of the files zipped into the **Test.xlsx** file, and you can open any of the files in any of these folders to see the corresponding

---

[1] This section applies to both Excel 2007 and later versions, but not to previous versions.

Figure 16.2 Contents of Zip File

XML contents. They will open in a text editor, not in Excel. Unless you know XML, the contents won't be very meaningful, but they won't be the gibberish you would see if you opened an .xls file in a text editor.

CustomUI Editor

This introduction sets the stage for customizing ribbons with XML. The technology for doing so is called **RibbonX** (again, "X" for XML), but it is all about writing XML code. This technology isn't for everyone, but after some practice, it really isn't very difficult. The best way to get started—by far—is to download a free utility called Custom UI Editor for Microsoft Office. (You can find it by searching the Web for the utility's name.) The RibbonX technology involves writing and modifying XML code in the files you see in Figure 16.2. The Custom UI Editor helps immeasurably to make sure it is all done correctly. When you open the Custom UI editor, all you see is what appears in Figure 16.3. However, once you open an Excel file in it, you can start typing XML code. Note the five buttons in the editor.

- The first two are the usual Open and Save buttons.
- The third button is for inserting an image (for icons) and will be discussed later.
- The fourth button is for checking the syntax of your XML. If you click this button and your XML has any errors, you will see what they are.
- The last button is for inserting "callbacks." I won't discuss this button because there is another way to do the same thing.

Figure 16.3   CustomUI Editor

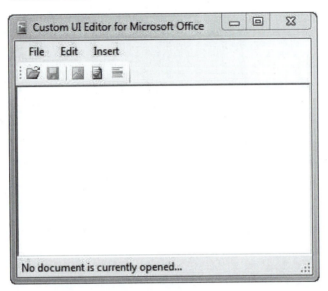

The following example leads you through the steps for creating a custom ribbon to run an application.

EXAMPLE 16.1   Creating an Application with Its Own Ribbon

The file **Car Loan with Ribbon.xlsm** is similar to the car loan application in Chapter 19. You might want to run that one first, just to see how it is structured. It contains a button on the Explanation worksheet. When you click it, you get a dialog box showing the various options. If you check the sensitivity option, you see another dialog box. In contrast, the version described here has no buttons on worksheets, and it has only a single user form, for getting inputs on the loan. You will run this application through its own ribbon. In fact, when you open the file, the *only* ribbon you will see is the one for this application (see Figure 16.4); you won't see any of the usual Excel tabs. Note that three of the sensitivity analysis "buttons" have been disabled. So as it stands, there are three enabled buttons:

Figure 16.4   Car Loan Ribbon

File	Car Loan		
Calc Payment	To Price	To Term	Create Table and Chart
	To Down Payment		
	To Interest Rate		
Monthly Payment	Sensitivity Analysis		Amortization Table

for calculating the monthly payment, for performing sensitivity on the price of the car, and for creating an amortization table and chart.

I created this application with the following steps.

1. I created an application very similar to the car loan application discussed in detail in Chapter 19. You can look at the VBA for the current version to see the logic, but the VBA code isn't the focus of the current example.
2. I closed the file in Excel and opened it in the Custom UI Editor. At that point, the editor appeared as in Figure 16.3—blank. Then I typed the XML code shown in Figure 16.5. I will say more about this code shortly.
3. I clicked the Save button and closed the Custom UI Editor.
4. I opened the file in Excel, got into the VBE, and added the argument control As IRibbonControl to all subs identified by the onAction attribute in the XML code. For example, the Sub line for the PaymentOnly sub is changed to

```
Sub PaymentOnly(control As IRibbonControl)
```

5. I saved the file, closed it, and reopened it in Excel. Now the custom ribbon is visible, and the various subs can be run by clicking the ribbon controls.

Here are a few comments about the XML code that will help you understand it and modify it for your own applications.

- As with any markup language (like HTML for Web pages), XML consists of **tags** for different elements, and tags come in pairs. If the beginning tag in a pair is <tabs>, the ending tag is the same except with the / character, as in </tab>. Also, there is a hierarchy of tags in RibbonX. You can see this hierarchy through the indentation: customUI, then ribbon, then tabs, then tab, then group, and finally button. Indenting isn't necessary, but as in VBA, it is

Figure 16.5 XML Code for Car Loan Application

```xml
<customUI xmlns="http://schemas.microsoft.com/office/2009/07/customui">
    <ribbon startFromScratch="true">
        <tabs>
            <tab id="CL" label="Car Loan">
                <group id="PO" label="Monthly Payment">
                    <button id="PY" label="Calc Payment" onAction="PaymentOnly" />
                </group>
                <group id="SE" label="Sensitivity Analysis">
                    <button id="PR" label="To Price" onAction="PriceSensitivity" />
                    <button id="DP" label="To Down Payment" onAction="DownPaymentSensitivity" enabled="false" />
                    <button id="IR" label="To Interest Rate" onAction="InterestRateSensitivity" enabled="false" />
                    <button id="TRM" label="To Term" onAction="TermSensitivity" enabled="false" />
                </group>
                <group id="AM" label="Amortization Table">
                    <button id="ART" label="Create Table and Chart" onAction="Amortization" />
                </group>
            </tab>
        </tabs>
    </ribbon>
</customUI>
```

C:\Users\Chris\Dropbox\My Books\VBA 4e\Example Files\Chpt16\Car Loan with Ribbon.xlsm   Ln 20 Col 12 *strongly* recommended for readability. Note that the button lines don't have any lines between them. In this case, you are allowed to include the beginning tag, <button, and the ending tag, />, in the same line.

- XML doesn't have a line continuation character for long lines. If your line is long, the Custom UI Editor will "word wrap" it to a second line, but this line is really a *single* line of XML. Don't press the Enter key unless you want a *new* line.

- XML is much fussier about case for its keywords (those in shades of red in the Custom UI Editor) than VBA. For example, startFromScratch in the second line must be spelled exactly this way. Either StartFromScratch or startfromscratch will produce an error.

- In XML terminology, each tag corresponds to an **element** (such as tab, group, and button), and each element has a number of **attributes**, such as id, label, and onAction. In the Custom UI Editor, the *names* of the attributes appear in red, and their *values* appear in blue. There are many possible attributes, but you need only a few for customizing ribbons. There is typically an id attribute, a unique identifier for each element; a label attribute that includes the text shown on the ribbon; an onAction attribute, the name of the macro attached to the button; and others. For example, you can see the enabled attribute set to "false" for three of the buttons. You can also see the startFromScratch set to "true" for the ribbon itself. If you wanted to see the standard Excel ribbons *in addition to* your ribbon, you would set the startFromScratch attribute to "false".

- After you type the XML in the code window, you should click the fourth button (Validate) in the Custom UI Editor. This will indicate whether you have valid (syntactically correct) XML code. If you don't, you can go back and fix your mistakes. For example, all id attributes must be unique, even if they are for *different* elements. This is a common error, and the editor will inform you of it.

Inserting Images for Icons

The ribbon in Figure 16.4 is not very fancy. Its buttons contain only text, and they don't look much like "buttons." If you want them to contain icons, you can set one of two attributes: imageMso or image (again, spelled exactly this way). The imageMso attribute identifies a built-in Office icon, whereas the image attribute identifies your own image from a picture file.

Where do you get the names of imageMso icons? I will show two possibilities. First, get into Excel, right-click a ribbon, select "Customize the Ribbon," and hover your mouse over one of the controls on the left. As shown in Figure 16.6, you see the name of the icon in parentheses, in this case ConditionalFormatting-Menu. Therefore, to use this control for your own custom button, you would specify the attribute imageMso="ConditonalFormattingMenu".

An even handier way is to borrow icons from the file **Office2007IconsGallery. xlsm.**[2] When you open this file in Excel, it installs nine dropdown lists on the

---

[2] I found this free file on the Web. I couldn't find a similar file for later versions of Office, but this one has *plenty* of icons.

Figure 16.6 Finding Icon Names in Excel

Figure 16.7 Galleries of Microsoft Office Icons

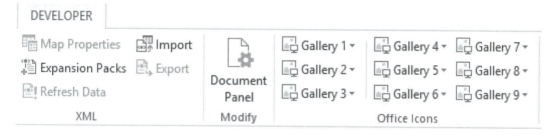

Developer ribbon, Gallery 1 to Gallery 9 (see Figure 16.7), and each has about 250 icons. If you hover your mouse over any of them, you will see its name. These too can be used as imageMso attributes.

You can also use your own images from picture files.[3] In this case, the Custom UI Editor really helps. (I read a description of how to do this *without* the editor, and it is quite complicated.) Here are the steps when using the Custom UI Editor (see Figure 16.8):

1. Open an Excel file in the Custom UI Editor.
2. Click the plus sign next to the file name to see an .xml file underneath.
3. Select this .xml file and click the **Insert Icons** button (the middle button).
4. Select a picture file from your hard drive. Its name will appear below the .xml file. In my example, the name is Bryn11.
5. Add an attribute to the button, in this case image="Bryn11".

---

[3] I am not sure which formats qualify and which don't, but standard formats such as .jpg certainly work.

Figure 16.8 Adding Your Own Image

```
Custom.xlam - Custom UI Editor for Microsoft Office                    ▢ ▣ ✕

File   Edit   Insert

☐ 🖫 🔳 🗎 ☰

☐ Custom.xlam          <customUI xmlns="http://schemas.microsoft.com/office/2009/07/customui">
  ☐ customUI14.xml        <ribbon startFromScratch="false">
      Bryn11                  <tabs>
                               <tab id="Tab1" label="Custom">
                                 <group id="Group1" label="Basic Actions">
                                   <button id="Button1" label="Calc Payment" image="Bryn11" />
                                 </group>
                               </tab>
                             </tabs>
                           </ribbon>
                         </customUI>

C:\Users\Chris\Dropbox\XLStart\Custom.xlam                              Ln 12  Col 1
```

16.4 Using RibbonX to Customize the QAT

I like to add buttons to my Quick Access Toolbar (QAT) that are attached to my
favorite macros in my Personal Macro Workbook. This process is exactly the same
as customizing ribbons, as explained in section 16.2. However, the default choice
of icons for the QAT buttons is rather limited (see Figure 16.9), and I had little
success with Web searches in finding ways to expand the list of icons. However,
I will now share a fairly simple method that does the job. Basically, I create an

Figure 16.9 Icon List for QAT Buttons

add-in (.xlam) file with my favorite macros, store it in my XLStart folder, create a new ribbon for them with XML code, add imageMso or image attributes for their buttons, and make this ribbon invisible. The effect is that the macros will always be available, and they and their icons will show up in the All Commands group when I customize my QAT. Here are the step-by-step directions.

1. Open a new Excel file, get into the VBE, insert a module in the new file, and copy your favorite macros (probably from your Personal Macro Workbook) into this module. For any macro you intend to associate with a ribbon button, add the argument control As IRibbonControl to the Sub line.

2. Save this file as an add-in (extension .xlam) in your XLStart folder. I call mine **Personal.xlam**. It is easy to do this wrong. As soon as you select "Excel Add-In (*.xlam)" as the type to save as, Excel tries to save the file in *its* Add-Ins folder. You have to override this by then selecting the XLStart folder.[4] You might wonder why I create this **Personal.xlam** file and don't just use the already existing **Personal.xlsb** file—the Personal Macro Workbook. The reason is that the .xlsb file is a *binary* file, not an XML file, so it can't hold the XML code necessary to make this procedure work. Also, I make it an .xlam file, not an .xlsm file, because .xlam files are essentially invisible when they are open in Excel. I want this Personal.xlam file to be as unobtrusive as possible.

3. Close Excel and open your new .xlam file in the Custom UI Editor. Proceed as described earlier in section 16.3 to add XML code. The beginnings of this code for my own .xlam file appear in Figure 16.10. Note the visible="false" attribute for the ribbon element itself. Not only will the .xlam file be invisible, but the ribbon for it will be invisible as well. Also, note the imageMso attributes for the buttons. I found the names of appropriate icons from the **Office2007IconsGallery.xlsm** I mentioned earlier. Alternatively, you could use the image attribute to use your own pictures for icons.

4. Open Excel. There will be no trace of the **Personal.xlam** add-in—no new worksheets and no new ribbons. However, assuming it really is in the XLStart folder, it is open and ready to use. (You should be able to see an entry for it in the VBE's Project Explorer.) To use it for the QAT, click the dropdown arrow to the right of the QAT and select More Commands. In the left side, select the All Commands group, *not* the Macros group, and scroll down for any of the label attributes in the XML code. For example, Figure 16.11 shows the "Move Text" command from the first button in Figure 16.10. Now click the Add button to move this command to your QAT. No other changes are necessary. You get the macro you want, together with a nice icon.

---

[4]To find the XLStart folder on your computer, get into the VBE, open the Immediate window, and type the command ?Application.StartupPath.

Figure 16.10 XML Code

Figure 16.11 Adding a Custom Command to the QAT

16.5 CommandBar and Related Office Objects[5]

All Office products have menus and toolbars, so the object model you need to learn here is the Office object model, not the Excel object model. A portion of this object model appears in Figure 16.12, taken from the Object Browser. As

---

[5] This material is basically a holdover from pre-2007 versions of Office, and you probably won't need it in Excel 2007 or later versions. It was kept for backward compatibility, so it still works. Just remember that if you use the type of code in this section to develop custom menus and/or toolbars in Excel 2007 or later versions, they will be placed in the Add-Ins ribbon.

Figure 16.12 Office Objects for Menus and Toolbars

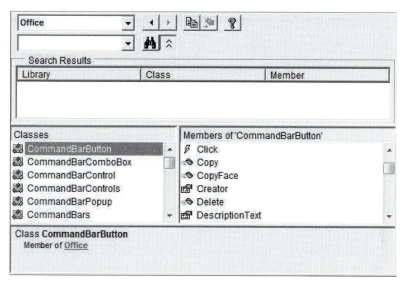

this figure indicates, the important objects for manipulating menus and toolbars with VBA are the CommandBar object and its related objects. Now that ribbons can be manipulated with XML, you are not likely to use CommandBar and related objects in VBA code, so I won't discuss them here. However, they are still available, and you can learn about them in the Object Browser if you ever need to.

16.6 A Grading Program Example

For my own use as an instructor, I developed a grading program. There are two versions of this with the book files. The first, written for Excel 2003, is called **Grading.xls**. The second, rewritten for Excel 2007 and later versions, is called **Grading.xlsm**. (When I wrote the latter, I added some extra functionality, but this is irrelevant for the current discussion.) I won't discuss the 2003 version, which uses CommandBar and related objects, but it is included with the files for this book if you would like to take a look.

The **Grading.xlsm** file, written especially for Excel 2007 and later versions, has the same basic functionality as the earlier version. However, it takes advantage of the RibbonX technology to provide a more modern look. When you open this file, you see the custom ribbon shown in Figure 16.13. As you can guess by now, this is accomplished with straightforward XML code that I entered in the Custom UI Editor. I won't show this code here, but you can open it yourself in the Custom UI Editor.

Fortunately, there is no worry of leaving this custom ribbon in the Excel user interface once the **Grading.xlsm** file closes. The XML code is *part* of the application, so when the application closes, the ribbon no longer exists in Excel.

Figure 16.13 Custom Grading Ribbon

Also, if you wanted this application to "take over" Excel by making all other ribbons invisible, only one change would be required—you would set the startFromScratch attribute of the ribbon to "true" in the XML code.

16.7 Summary

In this chapter, I have tried to walk the tightrope between the old and the new ways of modifying the user interface in Excel. In Excel 2003 and previous versions, working with menus and toolbars via VBA was a tricky undertaking. It is easy to get lost in the CommandBar labyrinth of objects. In Excel 2007 and later versions, VBA is not really necessary for modifying the ribbon interface. The RibbonX technology provides a better way to do it. Although this requires some knowledge of XML and some experimenting, it is fairly straightforward once you get used to it.

EXERCISES

Note: Exercises 1–7 are geared to pre-2007 versions of Excel. Skip these if you are using a later version.

1. Are there buttons on your Standard and Formatting toolbars that you absolutely never use? If so, get into Customize mode and drag them off, freeing up space for some you might find more useful. Then, still in Customize mode, explore the various categories of toolbar buttons in the Commands tab. You are bound to find a few that you could be useful to you. Drag them up to one of the visible toolbars. Now close Excel and reopen it. The work you just performed should be preserved.

2. Create (or record) one or more macros that do something you do often, such as formatting a cell as a number with 0 decimals or using the **File** → **Page Setup** to specify print settings. Store the macros in your Personal Macro Workbook file so that they are always available. Then get into Customize mode, create a new toolbar with name My Favorites, and populate it with buttons that run your new macros. Change the happy faces on your buttons to something more meaningful, and give your buttons tool tips (change their Name property).

3. In spreadsheet optimization models, it is helpful to designate input cells, changing cells, and the target cell in some way. I like to put blue borders around input cells, red borders around changing cells, and a black border around the target cell, but there is nothing special about my system. Devise your own color-coding scheme or borrow mine. Then proceed as in the previous exercise to create macros that color

code any selected range in the way you want (recording is a good option here), create a new toolbar named My Formatting, and add buttons to it with appropriate images and tool tips that run your macros. Finally, record one last button, and create an extra toolbar button for it that removes the formatting from any selected range. That way, you can remove any formatting you don't want. (*Hint:* Select a range *before* recording any macro. Then your formatting macros will work on *any* selected range.)

4. For either of the two preceding exercises, get into Customize mode and add a new menu called My Menu to the left of the Window menu. Then add menu items to this menu that correspond to the buttons on your toolbar. This will allow you to access the functionality of your macros from either a toolbar or a menu. (*Hint:* Examine the Macros and New Menu categories of the Commands tab in the Customize dialog box.)

5. Starting with a blank workbook, add code to the Workbook_Open and Workbook_BeforeClose event handlers in the ThisWorkbook object. The code in the Workbook_Open sub should hide the Standard and Formatting toolbars that are usually visible. The code in the Workbook_BeforeClose sub should make these toolbars visible. Save this workbook, close it, and then reopen it. The toolbars should be missing. Then close it and open another workbook. This time the two toolbars should be visible. (If your code messes everything up and you can't get the toolbars back, you can always do so manually through the **View → Toolbars** menu item.)

6. Starting with the macros from either Exercise 2 or 3, write a VBA sub that creates the toolbar in the earlier exercise and populates it with buttons that run the macros. (If you like, use the **Face IDs.xlsm** file to borrow appropriate icons for your buttons.)

7. Do the same as in the previous exercise, but this time use VBA code to create the menu requested in Exercise 4.

Note: The rest of the exercises are geared to Excel 2007 or later versions.

8. Example 16.1 illustrated a possible ribbon for the car loan application in Chapter 19. Choose any of the other applications in Part II of the book (Chapters 20–35) and create an appropriate ribbon for it. It can be all text or it can include images. Don't forget to include the control as IRibbonControl argument to any sub that is attached to a button on your ribbon.

9. Create a ribbon that looks like the one in Figure 16.14. All of its images are of the imageMso variety.

Figure 16.14 Custom Ribbon with Mso Images

17 Automating Solver and Other Applications

17.1 Introduction

There are many add-ins for Excel that have been developed by third-party software companies. Many of these companies have exposed object models or functions that programmers can use to manipulate the add-ins. Specifically, this is true of the Solver optimization add-in that is part of Microsoft Office. Solver can be manipulated not only through the familiar Excel user interface, but it can also be manipulated with VBA code. This chapter explains how to do it. In fact, the biggest part of this chapter deals with Solver. This is because I use Solver in many of the applications in Part II of the book.

Besides the Solver add-in, there are other Excel add-ins that can be manipulated with VBA. One example is the Analysis ToolPak that is part of Microsoft Office.[1] Another example is the @RISK simulation add-in from Palisade Corporation. In each case, programmers must search for built-in or online help that specifies the VBA functions available with the add-in. These functions are *not* part of Excel VBA, and they are not always well documented by the companies that have developed them. However, I will illustrate some of the possibilities for @RISK.

Finally, it is possible to *automate* other applications in Microsoft Office from Excel. This means that you can write VBA code in an Excel module to make the another application perform its functions. I will explain briefly how to do this for Word and Outlook. It is also possible to reverse the roles of the applications. For example, it is possible to write VBA code in a Word or Outlook module to automate Excel, and I will illustrate one possibility. To do any of this, you must have some familiarity with the object model for the application you are trying to automate. Unfortunately, knowledge of Excel's object model won't help you much in automating Word or Outlook; you need to understand *their* object models.

---

[1] If you have ever loaded the Analysis ToolPak and have then looked at the add-ins list, you have probably noticed that there is an Analysis ToolPak - VBA box you can check. This gives you access to the VBA functions that accompany the Analysis ToolPak.

17.2 Exercise

This exercise requires you to run Solver on an existing model with VBA code. Because the size of the problem can change based on the value of a user input, the VBA code must re-specify the Solver settings before running Solver.

Exercise 17.1 Scheduling Production

Consider a company that must plan its monthly production of footballs. It begins month 1 with a given number of footballs on hand, and at the beginning of each month it must decide how many footballs to produce. There are three constraints: (1) The quantity on hand after production must be at least as large as that month's (known) demand, (2) production in a month can never exceed production capacity, and (3) the ending inventory in any month can never exceed the storage capacity. You can assume that production and storage capacity remain constant through the planning period. There are two costs: (1) the unit production cost, which increases gradually through the planning period, and (2) the unit holding cost, which is a percentage of the unit production cost and is charged on each month's ending inventory.

The file **Production Scheduling.xlsx** contains a model for finding the company's minimum-cost production schedule for any planning period up to 12 months. (See Figure 17.1.) The inputs are in blue cells, the decision variables are in row 12, and cell B29 contains the total cost. The current model uses a planning period of 12 months, and the solution shown in Figure 17.1 is optimal for this planning period. The Solver settings appear in Figure 17.2. (This is from Solver for Excel 2010 or later.) Note that rows 12, 14, 16, 18, 20, 22, 26, and 27, columns B to M, have been range-named Produced, ProdCap, Onhand, Demand, EndInv, StorCap,

Figure 17.1 Production Planning Model

	A	B	C	D	E	F	G	H	I	J	K	L	M
1	Multiperiod production model												
2													
3	Input data												
4	Initial inventory	5000											
5	Holding cost as % of production cost	5%											
6													
7	Month	1	2	3	4	5	6	7	8	9	10	11	12
8	Unit production cost	$12.50	$12.55	$12.70	$12.80	$12.85	$12.95	$12.95	$13.00	$13.00	$13.10	$13.10	$13.20
9													
10	Production schedule												
11	Month	1	2	3	4	5	6						
12	Units produced	5000	20000	30000	30000	25000	10000	15000	30000	30000	30000	30000	25000
13		<=	<=	<=	<=	<=	<=	<=	<=	<=	<=	<=	<=
14	Production capacity	30000	30000	30000	30000	30000	30000	30000	30000	30000	30000	30000	30000
15													
16	On hand after production	10000	20000	35000	35000	25000	10000	15000	33000	32000	37000	31000	25000
17		>=	>=	>=	>=	>=	>=	>=	>=	>=	>=	>=	>=
18	Demand	10000	15000	30000	35000	25000	10000	12000	31000	25000	36000	31000	25000
19													
20	Ending inventory	0	5000	5000	0	0	0	3000	2000	7000	1000	0	0
21		<=	<=	<=	<=	<=	<=	<=	<=	<=	<=	<=	<=
22	Storage capacity	10000	10000	10000	10000	10000	10000	10000	10000	10000	10000	10000	10000
23													
24	Summary of costs												
25	Month	1	2	3	4	5	6	7	8	9	10	11	12
26	Production cost	$62,500	$251,000	$381,000	$384,000	$321,250	$129,500	$194,250	$390,000	$390,000	$393,000	$393,000	$330,000
27	Holding cost	$0	$3,138	$3,175	$0	$0	$0	$1,943	$1,300	$4,550	$655	$0	$0
28													
29	Total cost	$3,634,260											

Figure 17.2 Solver Settings for Model

ProdCosts, and HoldCosts, respectively. Also, cell B28 has the range name TotalCost. These range names are provided to make the Solver setup in Figure 17.2 and the formula for total cost easier to read.

The goal of the exercise is to develop a program that asks the user for a planning period from 4 to 12 months. (You could also have it ask for other inputs, such as the initial inventory and the holding cost percentage.) Based on the length of the planning period, the program should then rename the ranges in rows 14 to 27 appropriately, using only the months in the planning period, and reset Solver (the VBA equivalent of clicking the Reset All button in Figure 17.2). It should then re-specify the Solver settings in Figure 17.2, and finally it should run Solver. Note that if you rename the ranges appropriately, the Solver window will always end up looking like the one in Figure 17.2, but it *is* necessary to reset and then re-specify the settings when the physical ranges change. As an added touch, you might try hiding the columns that are not used—for example, columns L and M for a 10-month model.

The file **Production Scheduling Finished.xlsm** contains one possible solution. Feel free to open it and click its button to run it. However, do not look at the VBA code until you have tried writing it yourself.

17.3 Automating Solver with VBA

Many of the applications in Part II of the book are optimization models, where Excel's Solver is used to find an optimal solution. This section explains briefly how to do this. It makes two important assumptions. First, it assumes that you have some familiarity with Solver and know how to use it in the usual way through the Excel interface. Second, it assumes that an optimization model already exists. That is, the inputs and the formulas relating all quantities must already have been entered in a worksheet. This section deals only with specifying the Solver settings and running Solver; it does not deal with the optimization model itself.[2]

Solver is an add-in written by Frontline Systems, *not* by Microsoft.[2] It has a user-friendly Excel interface, shown by the dialog box in Figure 17.2, where you describe the model, set options, and eventually click the Solve button. If all goes well, you obtain the dialog box in Figure 17.3, indicating that an optimal solution has been found.

Fortunately, Frontline Systems has written several VBA functions that allow programmers to automate Solver with code. These functions enable you to specify the model (objective cell, decision variable cells, and constraints), set options, optimize, and even capture the message in Figure 17.3 (which might say that there is no feasible solution, for example).

Setting a Reference

To use these Solver functions in a VBA application, the first step is to set a **reference** to the Solver add-in in the VBE. Otherwise, VBA will not recognize the Solver functions and you will get a "Sub or function not defined" error message. You set the reference with the **Tools → References** menu item in the VBE. This brings up a long list of possible libraries of code to choose from. One of these should be Solver, as shown in Figure 17.4. (Your list might differ from the one shown here, depending on the software versions on your computer.) To add the reference, check its box and click the OK button. The reference will then appear in the Project Explorer window, as shown in Figure 17.5. Again, if you forget to set this reference and then try to use Solver functions in your code, you will get an error message.

---

[2] Starting with Excel 2010, Solver is significantly different from earlier versions, not only in the user interface you see in Figures 17.2 and 17.3, but also in the way its algorithms work. It is essentially the old "Premium" Solver. Also, starting in Excel 2010, Solver refers to *decision variable* cells rather than *changing* cells. However, these changes have virtually no effect on the VBA code required to run Solver. This part has hardly changed at all.

Figure 17.3 Solver Results Dialog Box

Figure 17.4 List of Potential References

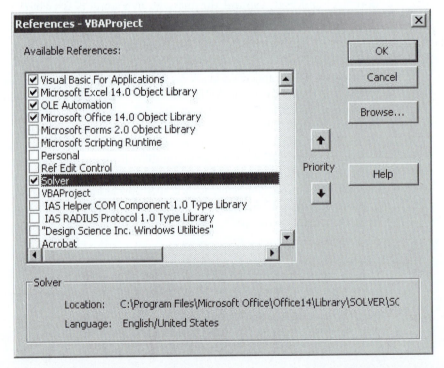

Figure 17.5 Reference to Solver in Project Explorer

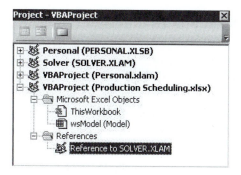

Solver Functions

All of the Solver functions begin with the word Solver. The ones used most often are SolverReset, SolverOk, SolverAdd, SolverOptions, and SolverSolve. This section explains each of these briefly. For more information, go to the Object Browser (after you set a reference to Solver), select the Solver library and then the VBA_Functions group. (See Figure 17.6.) This shows the names of the functions and the arguments each expects, but not much else. (If you click the question mark, nothing will happen.) If you need more help, you can go to the Frontline Systems Web site and search there.

Figure 17.6 Solver Help in Object Browser

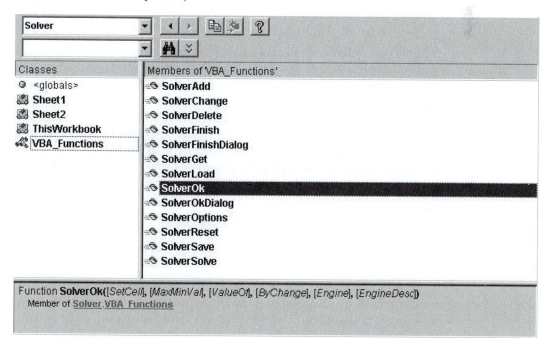

SolverReset Function

To reset Solver (which is equivalent to clicking the Reset All button in Figure 17.2), use the line

```
SolverReset
```

This clears all previous settings and lets you start with a clean slate.

SolverOk Function

This function does three things: (1) it identifies the objective cell; (2) it specifies whether the problem is a maximization or minimization problem; and (3) it identifies the decision variable cells. The following line is typical:

```
SolverOk SetCell:=Range("Profit"), MaxMinVal:=1, ByChange:=Range("Quantities")
```

Note that the MaxMinVal argument is 1 for a maximization problem and 2 for a minimization problem. Also, note that if there are several decision variable cell ranges (so that you would enter them, separated by commas, in the usual Solver dialog box), you can use Union in the ByChange argument. For example, you could write the following to indicate that there are two ranges of decision variable cells: the Quantities range and the Prices range.

```
SolverOk SetCell:=Range("Profit"), MaxMinVal:=1, _
    ByChange:=Union(Range("Quantities"), Range("Prices"))
```

The **SolverOk** function has two other optional arguments, **Engine** and **EngineDesc**. Either of these can be used to specify the solving method you want Solver to use. The **Engine** argument has possible values 1, 2, and 3. These correspond, respectively, to Simplex LP, GRG Nonlinear, and Evolutionary. The **EngineDesc** (Desc for descriptive) is similar, but instead of supplying integer values, you spell out the method: "Simplex LP", "GRG Nonlinear", or "Evolutionary" (including the quotes). If you use either of these arguments, you can omit the "AssumeLinear" argument of the SolverOptions function (see below) that was used in earlier versions of Excel Solver code. For example, the following code indicates that the LP Simplex method should be used.

```
SolverOk SetCell:=Range("Profit"), MaxMinVal:=1, ByChange:=Range("Quantities"), Engine:=1
```

SolverAdd Function

This function adds a new constraint each time it is called. It takes three arguments: a left side, a relation index, and a right side. The relation index is 1 for

"<=", 2 for "=", 3 for ">=", 4 for "integer", 5 for "binary", and 6 for "dif" (all different). (This is the same order in which they appear in the Solver Add Constraint dialog box. Also, note that there is no right-side argument for the latter three options.) The first and third arguments are specified differently. The left side must be specified as a range, whereas the right side must be specified as a string or a number. Here are several possibilities:

```
SolverAdd CellRef:=Range("Used"), Relation:=1, FormulaText:="Available"
SolverAdd CellRef:=Range("EndInventory"), Relation:=3, FormulaText:=0
SolverAdd CellRef:=Range("Investments"), Relation:=5
```

The first states that the Used range must be less than or equal to the Available range. The second states that the EndInventory range must be greater than or equal to 0. The third states that the Investments range must be binary.

SolverOptions Function

This function allows you to set various Solver options. The following line is typical:

```
SolverOptions AssumeNonNeg:=True
```

This indicates that the decision variable cells must be nonnegative. In general, *any* number of options can follow the SolverOptions function, all separated by commas. Most of these options correspond to those you see if you click the Options button in the main Solver dialog box. When you type SolverOptions and then a space, Intellisense indicates the names of the various arguments. Because they are all optional, you can list only the ones you want, and you can list them in any order. But to do so, you must specify the name and then :=, as in AssumeNonNeg:=True.

SolverSolve Function

This function is equivalent to clicking the Solve button in the Solver dialog box—it performs the optimization. There are two things you should know about SolverSolve. First, if it is used with the argument UserFinish:=True, the dialog box in Figure 17.3 will *not* appear. This dialog box could be a nuisance to a user, so it is often convenient to keep it from appearing with the line

```
SolverSolve UserFinish:=True
```

If you *want* the dialog box in Figure 17.3 to appear, just delete the UserFinish:=True part (or use UserFinish:=False, the default value).

Second, the SolverSolve function returns an integer value that indicates Solver's outcome. If this integer is 0, it means that Solver was successful, with the message in Figure 17.4. Actually, the integers 1 and 2 also indicate success, with slightly different messages. In contrast, the integer 4 means that Solver did not converge, and the integer 5 means that there are no feasible solutions. (More details can be found at Frontline Systems's Web site.) You can check for any of these and proceed accordingly. For example, the following lines are common. They run Solver, check for feasibility, and display an appropriate message if there are no feasible solutions.

```
Dim result As Integer
result = SolverSolve(UserFinish:=True)
If result = 5 Then
    MsgBox "There are no feasible solutions."
    Exit Sub
Else
    Worksheets("Report").Activate
End If
```

Note that when the result is captured in a variable, the UserFinish:=True argument must be inside parentheses. Actually, the result variable is not really necessary in this code; an alternative is the following:

```
If SolverSolve(UserFinish:=True) = 5 Then
    MsgBox "There are no feasible solutions."
    Exit Sub
Else
    Worksheets("Report").Activate
End If
```

Some applications require *only* the SolverSolve function. Their Solver settings can be set up manually with the Solver dialog box, not with VBA, at design time. Then all that is required at run time is to optimize with Solver-Solve. Other applications, such as Exercise 17.1, require a SolverReset line, and then SolverOk, SolverAdd, and SolverOptions lines, before SolverSolve can be called. That is, they must set up the model completely—at run time—before they can optimize. This is usually the case when the *size* of the model changes from run to run.

EXAMPLE 17.1   Optimal Product Mix

The file **Product Mix.xlsm** contains a typical product mix linear programming model. A company must decide how many frames of four different types to produce to maximize profit. There are two types of constraints: (1) resources used (labor hours, glass, and metal) must not exceed resources available, and (2) production must not exceed maximum quantities that can be sold. The model appears in Figure 17.7 with an optimal solution. (You can open the file and

Figure 17.7   Product Mix Model

	A	B	C	D	E	F	G	H	I	J	K	L
1	Product mix model											
2												
3	Input data						Sensitivity to multiples of maximum sales					
4	Hourly wage rate	$8.00		Run sensitivity analysis			Multiple	Frame1	Frame2	Frame3	Frame4	Profit
5	Cost per oz of metal	$0.50					0.50					
6	Cost per oz of glass	$0.75					0.75					
7							1.00					
8	Frame type	1	2	3	4		1.25					
9	Labor hours per frame	2	1	3	2		1.50					
10	Metal (oz.) per frame	4	2	1	2		1.75					
11	Glass (oz.) per frame	6	2	1	2		2.00					
12	Unit selling price	$28.50	$12.50	$29.25	$21.50		Unlimited					
13												
14	Production plan						Range names uses:					
15	Frame type	1	2	3	4		Available	=Model!$D$21:$D$23				
16	Frames produced	1000	800	400	0		MaxSales	=Model!$B$18:$E$18				
17		<=	<=	<=	<=		Multiples	=Model!$G$5:$G$12				
18	Maximum sales	1000	2000	500	1000		Produced	=Model!$B$16:$E$16				
19							Profit	=Model!$F$32				
20	Resource constraints	Used		Available			Used	=Model!$B$21:$B$23				
21	Labor hours	4000	<=	4000								
22	Metal (oz.)	6000	<=	6000								
23	Glass (oz.)	8000	<=	10000								
24												
25	Revenue, cost summary											
26	Frame type	1	2	3	4	Totals						
27	Revenue	$28,500	$10,000	$11,700	$0	$50,200						
28	Costs of inputs											
29	Labor	$16,000	$6,400	$9,600	$0	$32,000						
30	Metal	$2,000	$800	$200	$0	$3,000						
31	Glass	$4,500	$1,200	$300	$0	$6,000						
32	Profit	$6,000	$1,600	$1,600	$0	$9,200						

examine the various formulas. They are all quite straightforward.) The Solver dialog box, filled in manually, appears in Figure 17.8.

The goal of the example is to generate a sensitivity table in the range G4: L12, as indicated in Figure 17.7. Specifically, for each multiple in column G, the program should replace the original maximum sales values in row 18 by the multiple of these values, run Solver, and report the numbers of frames produced and the corresponding profit in the sensitivity table. Note that when the multiple is "unlimited," there is no maximum sales constraint at all. In this case, there should be only one constraint in the Solver dialog box. The results will appear as in Figure 17.9.

To develop this application, the first step is to open the VBE and add a reference to Solver. Then the following VBA code does the job. The MainProgram sub is attached to the button in Figure 17.8. Its basic function is to call a number of other subs to perform the various tasks. Note that three of these subs, ChangeModel, RunSolver, and StoreResults, are called within a For Each loop that loops over all cells in the Multiples range. Also, note how an argument is passed to each of these subs. More explanation on the various subs is provided below.

Figure 17.8 Solver Settings for Product Mix Model

Figure 17.9 Completed Sensitivity Table

	G	H	I	J	K	L
3	Sensitivity to multiples of maximum sales					
4	Multiple	Frame1	Frame2	Frame3	Frame4	Profit
5	0.50	500	1000	250	500	$7,500
6	0.75	750	1250	375	62	$8,688
7	1.00	1000	800	400	0	$9,200
8	1.25	1250	300	400	0	$9,700
9	1.50	1400	0	400	0	$10,000
10	1.75	1400	0	400	0	$10,000
11	2.00	1400	0	400	0	$10,000
12	Unlimited	1400	0	400	0	$10,000

```
Dim maxSales(1 To 4) As Single

Sub MainProgram()
    Dim cell As Range
    Dim multiple As Variant
    Dim iModel As Integer
    Dim includeConstraint As Boolean

    Application.ScreenUpdating = False
    Call SaveOriginalValues
    iModel = 0
    For Each cell In wsModel.Range("Multiples")
        iModel = iModel + 1
        multiple = cell.Value
        If IsNumeric(multiple) Then
            includeConstraint = True
        Else
            includeConstraint = False
        End If
        Call ChangeModel(multiple)
        Call RunSolver(includeConstraint)
        Call StoreResults(iModel)
    Next
    Call RestoreOriginalValues
End Sub
```

The first sub called, SaveOriginalValues, stores the original maximum sales values in the maxSales array for later use.

```
Sub SaveOriginalValues()
    Dim i As Integer
    For i = 1 To 4
        maxSales(i) = wsModel.Range("MaxSales").Cells(i)
    Next
End Sub
```

The ChangeModel sub takes the multiple argument and checks whether it is numeric with VBA's handy IsNumeric function. If it is, the sub multiplies the original maximum sales values by multiple and places these multiples in the MaxSales range.

```
Sub ChangeModel(multiple As Variant)
    Dim i As Integer
    If IsNumeric(multiple) Then
        For i = 1 To 4
            wsModel.Range("MaxSales").Cells(i) = multiple * maxSales(i)
        Next
    End If
End Sub
```

The RunSolver sub first resets Solver and then sets it up from scratch. It takes a Boolean argument, includeConstraint. If this value is True (because multiple is numeric), the maximum sales constraint is included; otherwise, it is not included. Note that if *all* values of multiple in column G were numeric, only the SolverSolve line of this sub would be required. This is because the Solver setup, developed manually as in Figure 17.9, would never change. You might argue that with only one possible change (the inclusion or exclusion of the maximum sales constraint), it should not be necessary to reset and then re-specify the *entire* Solver setup. This argument is correct. It is indeed possible to delete or add a single constraint to an existing Solver setup, but I have taken the "reset" route here, primarily to illustrate the various Solver functions.

```
Sub RunSolver(includeConstraint As Boolean)
    With wsModel
        SolverReset
        SolverOk SetCell:=.Range("Profit"), MaxMinVal:=1, _
            ByChange:=.Range("Produced"), Engine:=1
        SolverAdd CellRef:=.Range("Used"), Relation:=1, _
            FormulaText:="Available"
        If includeConstraint Then
            SolverAdd CellRef:=.Range("Produced"), Relation:=1, _
                FormulaText:="MaxSales"
        End If
        SolverOptions AssumeNonNeg:=True
        SolverSolve UserFinish:=True
    End With
End Sub
```

The StoreResults sub takes the Solver results in the Produced and Profit ranges and transfers them to the sensitivity table. It takes a single argument, iModel, that specifies how far down the table to place the results. Note that iModel is increased by 1 each time through the For Each loop in the MainProgram sub.

```
Sub StoreResults(iModel As Integer)
    Dim i As Integer
    With wsModel.Range("G4")
        For i = 1 To 4
            .Offset(iModel, i) = wsModel.Range("Produced").Cells(i)
        Next
        .Offset(iModel, 5) = wsModel.Range("Profit")
    End With
End Sub
```

Finally, the RestoreOriginalResults sub places the original maximum sales values back in the MaxSales range and runs Solver one last time. This is not absolutely necessary—by the time this sub is called, the sensitivity table is complete—but it is a nice touch. This way, the final thing the user sees is the solution to the original problem.

```
Sub RestoreOriginalValues()
    Dim i As Integer
    For i = 1 To 4
        wsModel.Range("MaxSales").Cells(i) = maxSales(i)
    Next
    Call RunSolver(True)
End Sub
```

17.4 Possible Solver Problems

There are a couple of peculiarities you should be aware of when you automate Solver with VBA.

Using a Main Sub

The problem described in this section was evidently fixed in Excel 2007's Solver. But I will retain this section for pre-Excel 2007 users.

It is common to name your "control center" sub Main. This can cause a strange problem in a program that has a reference to Solver. Try the following. In a pre-2007 version of Excel, open a new workbook, get into the VBE, add a module, and add a reference to Solver. Then add a sub in the module called Main. It doesn't have to do anything interesting, but it should be called Main. Now get back into Excel and open Solver. You will *not* see the Solver dialog box. To go one step farther, add a user form to your program (you can keep the generic name UserForm1), and add the following line to your Main sub:

```
UserForm1.Show
```

Again, get back into Excel and open Solver. Your new user form will appear! What is happening? The problem is that Solver has its own Main sub. So when you open Solver in Excel, it gets confused and invokes *your* Main sub instead of its Main sub. The fix is easy. If your program sets a reference to Solver, don't use the name Main for any of your subs. If you still like Main, use a name like MainProgram or something similar. This is my convention in all applications in the second part of the book that invoke Solver—just to be safe.

Missing Solver Reference

Let's say that someone (like me) writes a program that sets a reference to Solver. They give you that program, and you try running it—and you get an error. The chances are that you have a "missing Solver reference" problem. This is a common problem, one that I have gotten numerous e-mails about over the years. I finally went to the source—technical support at Frontline Systems—and got what I believe is a simple and reliable fix.[3]

---

[3] Thankfully, this problem seems to have disappeared, starting in Excel 2010.

According to my source at Frontline Systems, this problem happens because Solver is a "smart" add-in, which does not get loaded into memory until you use it. (This stems back to the days where start-up time and memory usage were bigger issues). When Solver has not been used in an Excel session, and the **Solver.xla** file has therefore not been opened yet, the following can happen.[4] You can open a workbook with a reference to Solver (because Solver functions are used in the workbook's code). Excel tries to restore the reference by opening the **Solver.xla** file, and it does this by following the path to this file stored in the workbook. If your **Solver.xla** file is located in a different place, Excel will fail and produce a "Missing: Solver.xla" in the references list, and the program won't run.

If you experience this problem, the simplest solution is to start Excel with a blank workbook and open the Solver dialog box once. This loads Solver into memory, and when your workbook now opens, the reference to Solver will be updated appropriately. If you then save the workbook, the reference is updated permanently, and you will not have any problems in the future.

The point is that the critical file **Solver.xla** is not stored in the same location on all computers. This is the source of the "missing Solver reference" problem. (Actually, this missing reference can occur for other reasons that I won't go into here.) However, to avoid this problem, all you have to do is open Solver and then close it. Then all of the VBA applications in this book should work fine. I call this "waking up Solver."

To help you remember this fix if you are using a pre-2010 version of Excel (where the problem tends to occur), all later applications in this book that require a reference to Solver show a message similar to that in Figure 17.10 when the application opens. This message is actually a user form, and I always call it frmSolver. If you are using Excel 2010 or a later version, you won't see this message.

Figure 17.10 Warning in Solver Applications

17.5 Programming with Risk Solver Platform

Writing programs to automate Solver should be straightforward, and it often is. But as I have found from experience with my SolverTable add-in (see http://www.kelley.iu.edu/albrightbooks/Free_downloads.htm), it can also be a never-ending source of headaches. The problem is that a programmer has to go by the rules Microsoft has set up for add-ins like Solver. But as Microsoft develops new versions of Excel, these rules change. Besides that, the rules have never been obvious, and it is difficult to find them written down anywhere. This is the reason for the fixes described on my Web site.

There is an alternative that I will briefly describe in this section. Frontline Systems has many products besides the "standard" Solver that ships with Excel. In particular, it has a Risk Solver Platform (RSP) that is *much* more powerful than Excel's built-in Solver.[5] Better yet, RSP has an improved API (application programming interface) for VBA programmers. This new API has an object model for controlling Solver models that is much more like other object models such as Excel's, complete with Intellisense. It takes some practice to get your code to work, but the structure is more logical than the Solver functions discussed in previous sections. And best of all, the code is much more stable than the original Solver code. For example, you don't have to "wake up" Solver or worry about where the user's Solver folder is located.

To take advantage of this new API, you must first purchase and install RSP. Next, you must set a reference to Risk Solver Platform x.x Type Library (where x.x is replaced by the version you are using) from the **Tools References** menu item in the VBE. (See Figure 17.11.)

Once you do this, you can get help from the Object Browser by selecting the RSP library. Some of this is shown in Figure 17.12. As usual, you can select an object or enumeration on the left and see more information on the right. Unfortunately, no extra help appears if you click the question mark, but I will try to supply the information you need here.[6]

The "top-level" object for RSP models is the Problem object. It essentially refers to an optimization model on a worksheet. Other key objects are the Solver, Function, and Variable objects. The Solver object contains all of the information about the optimizer used to optimize the model. A Function object refers to either the objective function or a group of constraint function cells. A Variable object refers to a range of decision variable cells. There is also a Variables collection object, the set of all decision variable cell ranges, and a Functions collection object, the set of all objective and constraint functions.

---

[5] We were allowed to include an academic version of RSP in the third edition of this book, but for contractual reasons, we are no longer allowed to do so. This decreases the importance of this section, but I have kept it mostly to illustrate another object model. The code in this section was written several years ago, so I won't guarantee that it still works exactly as is, but any necessary changes should be minor. For all applications in Part II of the book that use Solver, the original RSP versions (written at the time of the third edition) are included with the example files for this chapter.

[6] The online help was limited when I originally wrote this section a few years ago. The situation may have changed by now.

Figure 17.11 Setting a Reference to RSP

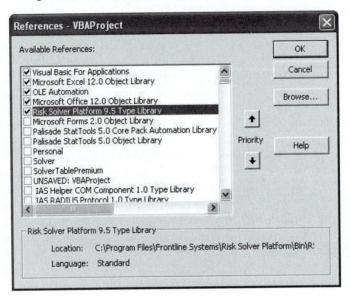

Figure 17.12 Object Browser for RSP Library

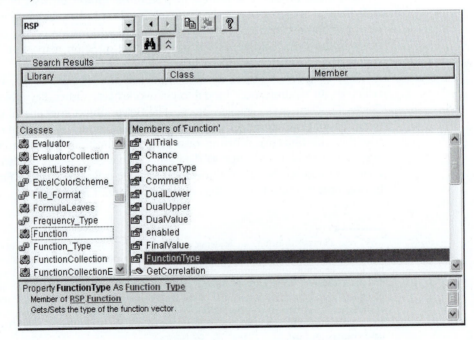

The following code illustrates how it works. This code can be used instead of the RunSolver code from Section 17.3 for the product mix application. (Again, this assumes that you have RSP on your computer.)

```vb
Sub RunSolver(includeConstraint As Boolean)
    Dim prob As New RSP.Problem
    Dim obj As New RSP.Function
    Dim dvCells As New RSP.Variable
    Dim constr1 As New RSP.Function
    Dim constr2 As New RSP.Function

    With prob
        .Variables.Clear
        .Functions.Clear

        ' Objective
        obj.Init Range("Profit")
        obj.FunctionType = Function_Type_Objective
        .Functions.Add obj

        ' MaxMin value
        .Solver.SolverType = Solver_Type_Maximize

        ' Decision variable cells
        dvCells.Init Range("Produced")
        dvCells.NonNegative
        .Variables.Add dvCells

        ' Constraints
        constr1.Init Range("Used")
        constr1.FunctionType = Function_Type_Constraint
        constr1.UpperBound.Array = "Available"
        .Functions.Add constrl

        If includeConstraint Then
            constr2.Init Range("Produced")
            constr2.FunctionType = Function_Type_Constraint
            constr2.UpperBound.Array = "MaxSales"
            .Functions.Add constr2
        End If

        ' Solve
        .Solver.Optimize
    End With
End Sub
```

Although this code is quite readable, here are a few comments.

- Each Problem, Function, and Variable object must be *instantiated*, which is done with the keyword New. The prefix RSP is used to indicate that these objects are part of the RSP library.
- The Functions and Variables collections should first be cleared.
- Note how the objective is set up. First, a new Function object is instantiated. Then the Init method is used to specify its range. Next, the FunctionType property is set. In this case, it is the Objective type, but later on in the code, it is the Constraint type. Finally, this function is added to the Functions collection of the Problem object.

- There is only one decision variable cell range in this model, so only one Variable object is required. If there were more decision variable cell ranges, extra Variable objects would be required. The Nonnegative property is used to ensure that the decision variable cells are nonnegative. After the properties of the Variable object are set, it is added to the Variables collection of the Problem object.
- The Problem object has a Solver property that returns the Solver that does the optimization. It has a SolverType property to specify whether the problem is a minimization or maximization, and it has an Optimize method to run the optimization.
- As in Section 17.3, the left and right sides of the constraints are treated differently. The Init method of a constraint function specifies the left side of the constraint as a range. The right side is specified by the UpperBound.Array (or LowerBound.Array) property, which is set to a string (either a range name or an address). Of course, UpperBound indicates a "$<=$" constraint, whereas LowerBound indicates a "$>=$" constraint. And if you want an equality constraint, you can set the LowerBound *and* UpperBound to the same value.

The above code is required if you need to reset the Solver settings several times through a loop, as in the product mix application. However, if the Solver settings never change during the execution of the program, you can set them up at design time interactively through the user interface. Then the only code you need is the following:

```
Dim prob As New RSP.Problem
prob.Solver.Optimize
```

17.6 Automating @RISK with VBA

The advantage of working with Solver is that it ships with Excel. When you purchase Microsoft Office, you get Solver as part of the package. However, there are many other Excel add-ins that can be purchased separately. Some of these add-ins (but certainly not all) expose VBA programming capabilities, just as I discussed with Solver. One set of add-ins I am particularly familiar with is the DecisionTools Suite from Palisade Corporation.[7] This suite includes, among others, @RISK for simulation modeling. In the same way that you can automate Solver with VBA, you can automate @RISK.

How can you learn how to automate add-ins in general? This depends entirely on the reference materials that accompany the add-in. For example, when you install the Palisade suite (version 6.0 or later) and open @RISK, you can find extensive help from its XDK (Excel Developer Kit) (see Figure 17.13). This includes not only reference materials but also a number of Excel example files with VBA code and videos explaining the code.[8]

---

[7] The academic version of this suite is available with my *Practical Management Science* and *Data Analysis and Decision Making* books.

[8] For the past several years, I have been working as a training consultant for Palisade, and in this role I have developed the example files and videos referenced in Figure 17.13.

Figure 17.13 @RISK XDK Help

To use @RISK functionality in a VBA program, you must first use the **Tools →
References** menu item to set the two references shown in Figure 17.14: one to
RiskXLA and the other to Palisade @RISK x.x for Excel Object Library. This allows
you to take advantage of everything that is explained in the help materials. It is then
"just" a matter of learning the functionality that @RISK provides. The rest of this
section illustrates some possibilities. (And remember that the examples indicated in
Figure 17.13 illustrate many other possibilities.)

If you have used any recent version of @RISK, you are aware that it has a
number of ways to produce results from a simulation. In fact, the variety of
possibilities can be bewildering. Therefore, I wrote a template to automate
one variation of the process. You can find this in the file **Simulation
Template.xlsm**. There is only one worksheet in this file, the Model worksheet
shown in Figure 17.15. (This sheet contains other text boxes to explain the
details.) It is quite generic and is set up so that you can enter any number of
inputs in the Inputs section, any number of outputs in the Outputs section,
and any simulation model in the Simulation section. I assume that you would
like to run a number of simulations, one for each combination of input values
to be tested, as listed in the Inputs section. In the case shown, there are $1 \times 2
\times 3 = 6$ input combinations, so 6 different simulations will be run. The pro-
gram does this in a clever way with @RISK's **RiskSimtable** function. In the
Outputs section, you can designate any statistical outputs desired, including
percentiles and targets. (@RISK uses the term *target* to mean a probability of
the "less than or equal to" type. So, for example, row 15 is requesting the
probability that the Output3 is less than or equal to 4.) The program runs the
required number of simulations, each for the requested number of iterations,
and creates separate worksheets for means, standard deviations, minimums,
maximums, percentiles, and targets.

Figure 17.14 @RISK References

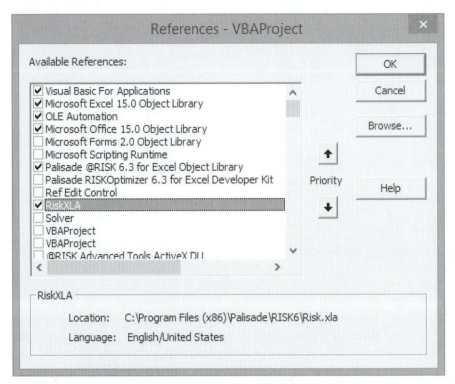

A lot of the code for this template contains nothing new, so I won't show it here. But the following is part of the code, where I have boldfaced the lines that rely on the @RISK object model. (There aren't many.) Note that I first had to set the @RISK references, as explained earlier. Otherwise, the boldfaced lines in the code wouldn't be recognized by VBA.

The first section of code illustrates how to change some @RISK simulation settings and how to designate cells as @RISK output cells. (There is no automatic way to perform this latter task. You have to manipulate the formula for the output to include **RISKOUT(*outputname*)+).**

```
' Change some @RISK settings.
With Risk.Simulation.Settings
    .AutomaticResultsDisplay = RiskNoAutomaticResults
    .NumIterations = Range("Number_of_iterations").Value
    .NumSimulations = nSimulations
End With

' Designate output cells as @RISK output cells if they're not already designated.
For i = 1 To nOutputs
    If InStr(1, outputCell(i).Formula, "RiskOutput") = 0 Then
        outputCell(i).Formula = "=RiskOutput(" & outputName(i) & ")+" _
            & Right(outputCell(i).Formula, Len(outputCell(i).Formula) - 1)
    End If
Next
```

Figure 17.15 Simulation Template

	A	B	C	D	E	F	G	H	I
1	Simulation Template								
2									
3	Number of iterations				Run Simulation				
4									
5	Inputs			Values to test					
6	Input1			5					
7	Input2			A	B				
8	Input3			0.50	0.75	1.00			
9	etc.								
10									
11				Tables requested					
12	Outputs			Mean	Stdev	Min	Max	Percentiles	Targets
13	Output1			Yes	Yes	Yes	Yes	.05,.50,.95	5,6
14	Output2			Yes	No	No	No	No	No
15	Output3			Yes	Yes	No	No	0.05	4
16	etc.								
17									
18									
19	Simulation								
20									
21									
22									
23									
24									
25									
26									

This file contains macros that run @RISK and generate requested tables of results for (1) any allowed number of iterations, (2) any number of (nonrandom) inputs in the blue cells, (3) any values of these inputs you want to test, and (4) any number of outputs in the gray cells. The Model sheet should be set up exactly as this. In particular, you shouldn't rename any of the bright yellow cells, and you should keep the headings in the light yellow cells right below the **Tables requested** label. To see a completed version of this template, open and run **NewsVendor Simulation.xlsm** or **World Series Simulation.xlsm**.

To run the simulation once it has been set up, only one line of code is necessary:

```
Risk.Simulation.Start
```

Finally, to get the requested statistical results in various worksheets, the following code is used. The key is Risk.Simulation.Results.GetSimulatedOuput(*output*). This returns a particular set of results, those for the designated *output*, from the Results collection of the Simulation object. From there, you can ask for the mean, the standard deviation, and other statistical summary measures.

```
Select Case statType
    Case "Mean", "Stdev", "Min", "Max"
        For i = 1 To nOutputs
            If Range("Tables_Requested") _
                .Offset(i + 1, index - 1).Value = "Yes" Then
            nRequested = nRequested + 1
            With Range("A1").Offset(0, j)
                .Value = outputName(i)
                For k = 1 To nSimulations
                    If statType = "Mean" Then
                        .Offset(k, 0).Value = Risk.Simulation.Results _
                            .GetSimulatedOutput(outputName(i), k).Mean
                    ElseIf statType = "Stdev" Then
```

```
                                .Offset(k, 0).Value = Risk.Simulation.Results. _
                                    GetSimulatedOutput(outputName(i), k).StdDeviation
                        ElseIf statType = "Min" Then
                                .Offset(k, 0).Value = Risk.Simulation.Results. _
                                    GetSimulatedOutput(outputName(i), k).Minimum
                        ElseIf statType = "Max" Then
                                .Offset(k, 0).Value = Risk.Simulation.Results. _
                                    GetSimulatedOutput(outputName(i), k).Maximum
                        End If
                    Next
                End With
                j = j + 1
            End If
        Next
    Case "Percentiles", "Targets"
        For i = 1 To nOutputs
            statString=Range("Tables_Requested") _
                .Offset(i + 1, index - 1).Value
            If statString < > "No" Then
                nRequested = nRequested + 1
                ' Parse the string of comma-delimited values.
                Call GetArrays(statString, arrayString, arrayNumber)
                For l = 1 To UBound(arrayString)
                    With Range("A1").Offset(0, j)
                        If statType = "Percentiles" Then
                            .Value = "Pctile " & arrayString(l) _
        •                       & " " & outputName(i)
                        ElseIf statType = "Targets" Then
                            .Value = "P(" & outputName(i) & " < = " _
                                & arrayString(l) & ")"
                        End If
                        For k = 1 To nSimulations
                            If statType = "Percentiles" Then
                                .Offset(k, 0).Value = Risk.Simulation.Results. _
                                    GetSimulatedOutput(outputName(i), k) _
                                        .PToX(arrayNumber(l))
                            ElseIf statType = "Targets" Then
                                .Offset(k, 0).Value = Risk.Simulation.Results. _
                                    GetSimulatedOutput(outputName(i), k) _
                                        .XToP(arrayNumber(l))
                            End If
                        Next
                    End With
                    j = j + 1
                Next
            End If
        Next
End Select
```

The code in this template can be used, exactly as is, on *any* simulation model that is set up as instructed in the template file. I have included two examples with the book files: **World Series Simulation.xlsm** and **Newsvendor Simulation.xlsm**. Open them and try them out. Just remember that @RISK must be loaded for them to work properly.

17.7 Automating Other Office Applications with VBA

It is also possible to automate one Office application from another. In this section I illustrate some possibilities, including the automation of Word and Outlook from Excel and the automation of Excel from Outlook. There are two basic steps required:

1. You first set a reference to the application you want to automate. As usual, you do this through the **Tools → References** menu item in the VBE. For example, if you are automating Word from Excel, you set a reference to the Microsoft Word x.x Object Library. As another example, if you are automating Excel from Outlook, you set a reference to the Microsoft Excel x.x Object Library. Note that Word and Outlook each have a VBE, and you get to them with **Alt+F11,** just as in Excel. Also, note that the references are "hard-coded" to the version of Office you are running. I wrote the examples for this chapter in Office 2013, so my references are to the version 15.0 object libraries. If you run them in Office 2007 or 2010, you will get an error about a missing reference. To fix it, select the **Tools → References** menu item, uncheck the Missing item, and check the similar item for your version of Office.

2. Create an instance of the application you want to automate. You can do this in one or two lines of code. To do it in a single line of code, the following is typical:

```
Dim olApp As New Outlook.Application
```

This does two things at once. It says that the variable olApp is of type Outlook.Application. It also creates an *instance* of Outlook with the keyword New. Alternatively, you can use two lines of code, one to indicate the type of variable and the other to create a new instance whenever you need it:

```
Dim olApp As Outlook.Application
' Other lines can go here.
Set olApp = New Outlook.Application
```

The method described here for automating another application is called **early binding**. By setting a reference to the other application's library, you get Intellisense on that application's objects, as well as access to its built-in constants such as **wdColumnWidthNarrow** in Word or **olFormatHTML** in Outlook.

A somewhat different method is to use **late binding**. In this case, you don't set a reference. Instead, you use lines such as the following to create an instance of the other application.

```
Dim WordApp As Object
Set WordApp = CreateObject("Word.Application")
```

One advantage of late binding is that the above code will work on a user's computer regardless of the *version* of Word the user has installed. However, late binding doesn't provide Intellisense or built-in constants. The examples in this section all use early binding.

EXAMPLE 17.2   Sending Grades in E-mails

As an instructor, I developed a handy application that automatically sends an email to each student in my class with their grade for an assignment or exam. I assume the students' usernames and grades are stored in an Excel file, set up as in Figure 17.16. (See the file **Sending Emails with Grades.xlsm**.) I first created a reference to the Microsoft Outlook 15.0 Object Library. Then the following code sends an email to each student with a message such as "You got grade B+ for the exam." It also sends an attachment that indicates what the student missed points for. You can adapt this code for your own needs.

```
Sub SendEMails()
    Dim topCell As Range
    Dim nStudents As Integer
    Dim i As Integer
    Dim userName As String
    Dim grade As String
    Dim pathStudents As String
    Dim fileName As String

    ' Create a new instance of Outlook.
    Dim olApp As New Outlook.Application
    Dim olMail As Outlook.MailItem

    ' Change this, depending on where your individual student
    ' folders are.
    pathStudents =ThisWorkbook.Path & "\Students\"

    Set topCell = wsGrades.Range("A1")
    With topCell
        nStudents = Range(.Offset(1, 0), .End(xlDown)).Rows.Count
    End With

    For i = 1 To nStudents
        userName = topCell.Offset(i, 0).Value
        grade = topCell.Offset(i, 1).Value
        ' Create a mail item for this student.
        Set olMail = olApp.CreateItem(olMailItem)
        With olMail
            .To = userName & "@stateuniversity.edu"
            .Subject = "Final exam"
            .Body = "Your grade for the exam is " & grade _
                & ". You can see what you missed in the attached file."
            ' The following assumes that each student has his own folder under
            ' the Students folder, with folder name equal to the student's
            ' username and including a file like Gradesheet_jbjones.xlsx.
            fileName = pathStudents & userName _
                & "\Gradesheet_" & userName & ".xlsx"
            .Attachments.Add fileName
            .Send
```

```
        End With
    Next

    ' Clean up.
    Set olMail = Nothing
    Set olApp = Nothing
End Sub
```

Figure 17.16　Student Exam Scores

	A	B
1	Username	Exam
2	jbjones	B+
3	crsmith	A–
4	tlwilson	C
5	fdblack	B
6	rsimmons	A

The key to the code is the olMail object. This is an Outlook MailItem object, declared with the line

```
Dim olMail As Outlook.MailItem
```

This object has all the properties and methods required to create and send an email from Outlook. However, you must first create an instance with the line

```
Set olMail = olApp.CreateItem(olMailItem)
```

Then you can use its To, Subject, and Body properties to create the email, and you can use its Send method to send the message.

Note the two lines at the bottom:

```
Set olMail = Nothing
Set olApp = Nothing
```

These are not necessary, but they illustrate good programming practice. The olMail and olApp take up some room in computer memory. These two lines, used after the objects have filled their purpose, free up the memory.

An alternative is to write essentially the same code in Outlook and use it to automate Excel. The following code shows how to do it. Just remember that this code lives in Outlook's VBE code window, and the reference is now to the Excel library.

```
Sub SendEMails()
    Dim topCell As Range
    Dim nStudents As Integer
    Dim i As Integer
    Dim username As String
    Dim grade As String
    Dim pathGradebook As String
    Dim pathStudents As String
    Dim fileName As String
    Dim olMail As MailItem
    ' Create an instance of Excel.
    Dim xlApp As New Excel.Application

    pathGradebook = "C:\My Course\"
    pathStudents = "C:\My Course\Students\"
    ' Note that Excel is used to qualify what a Workbook or Worksheet is.
    ' This isn't necessary (because a reference is set to Excel), but it
    ' is a good reminder that Excel is the automated application.
    Dim wb As Excel.Workbook
    Dim ws As Excel.Worksheet

    Set wb = xlApp.Workbooks.Open(pathGradebook & "Gradebook.xlsx")
    Set ws = wb.Worksheets("Grades")
    Set topCell = ws.Range("A1")
    nStudents = ws.Range("Usernames").Rows.Count

        For i = 1 To nStudents
            username = topCell.Offset(i, 0).Value
            grade = topCell.Offset(i, 1).Value
            ' Create a mail item for this student.
            Set olMail = CreateItem(olMailItem)
            With olMail
                .To = username & "@indiana.edu"
                .Subject = "Final exam"
                .body = "Your grade for the exam is " & grade _
                    & ". You can see what you missed in the attached file."
                On Error Resume Next
                fileName = pathStudents & username _
                    & "\Gradesheet_" & username & ".xlsx"
                .Attachments.Add fileName
                .Send
            End With
        Next

    ' Close and clean up.
    wb.Close
    Set olMail = Nothing
    Set xlApp = Nothing
End Sub
```

The following example shows that you can automate both Word and Outlook in the same Excel VBA program.

EXAMPLE 17.3   Sending Emails with Word Attachments

This example assumes there is an Excel file with a database of customers. (See Figure 17.17 and the file **Sending Overdue Notices.xlsm**.) The goal is to

Figure 17.17 Customer Database

	A	B	C	D	E	F	G	H	I	J	K	L
1	Customer info											
2				Generate and Send Notices					Purchase info			
3	First name	Last name	Greeting	Address	City	State	Zip	eMail	Amount	Date purchased	Due date	Date paid
4	Janice	Smith	Ms.	224 N. Edwards Lane	Bloomington	IN	47401	jsmith@fiction.com	$169.21	11/15/2014	1/14/2015	
5	Robert	Owens	Mr.	3352 First St	Los Angeles	CA	90012	rowens@fiction.com	$235.65	11/7/2014	1/6/2015	1/5/2015
6	Mary	Davis	Mrs.	413 E. Miller Ave	Chicago	IL	60602	mdavis@fiction.com	$106.07	11/1/2014	12/31/2014	12/22/2014
7	Wayne	Jacobs	Dr.	1616 Broad Ave	Fresno	CA	93727	wjacobs@fiction.com	$147.59	10/27/2014	12/26/2014	
8	Sam	Cummings	Mr.	543 S. Henderson St	Philadelphia	PA	19102	scumming@fiction.com	$387.48	10/27/2014	12/26/2014	
9	Linda	Fredericks	Ms.	6212 Blacksone Dr	Columbus	OH	43203	lfrederi@fiction.com	$572.56	10/18/2014	12/17/2014	12/10/2014
10	Don	Winkler	Dr.	751 Second Ave	St. Louis	MO	63112	dwinkler@fiction.com	$421.49	10/27/2014	12/26/2014	12/17/2014
11	James	Babich	Mr.	3325 Morningstar Dr	Houston	TX	77015	jbabich@fiction.com	$289.87	11/5/2014	1/4/2015	12/26/2014
12	Jennifer	Pohl	Mrs.	815 Churchill Lane	Seattle	WA	98118	jephohl@fiction.com	$492.12	11/7/2014	1/6/2015	
13	Tom	Shaw	Mr.	225 Walnut Ct	Atlanta	GA	30308	tomshaw@fiction.com	$192.14	11/8/2014	1/7/2015	12/31/2014

compose a Word document for each customer and then send it as an attachment in an email to the customer. If the customer has paid (column L is not blank), the Word document will contain a nice "appreciate your business" note. Otherwise, it will contain a past due warning. If you are interested in what the automatically generated Word documents contain, take a look at the files **Janice_Smith_01-31-15.docx** and **Robert_Owens_01-31-15.docx**, which I generated on January 31, 2015.

The code for this example is in Excel, so it is first necessary to set references to the Word and Outlook libraries. Then an instance of each must be created. The following code does it all. I admit to being a novice on this one because I don't know the Word object model very well. There may well be a more elegant way to compose the Word document instead of my repetitive wdSel lines. However, the bottom line is that this program works.

```
Sub GenerateAndSendNotices()
    Dim nCustomers As Integer
    Dim i As Integer
    Dim message As String
    Dim docName As String

    Dim wdDoc As Word.Document
    Dim wdSel As Word.Selection

    ' The next lines creates a new instance of Word and of Outlook.
    Dim wdApp As New Word.Application
    Dim olApp As New Outlook.Application

    Dim olMail As Outlook.MailItem

    With wsData.Range("A3")
        nCustomers = Range(.Offset(1, 0), .End(xlDown)).Rows.Count
    End With

    ' Uncomment the following line if you want to see Word doing its thing.
    'wdApp.Visible = True

    For i = 1 To nCustomers
        With wsData.Range("A3").Offset(i, 0)
            ' Compose the body of the letter depending on whether the
            ' customer has paid or not paid.
            If .Cells(1, 12).Value = "" Then ' hasn't paid yet
```

```
            message = "Your purchase on " & Format(.Cells(1, 10), "mmm-dd-yyyy") _
                & " for an amount " & FormatCurrency(.Cells(1, 9).Value, 2) _
                & " was due on " & Format(.Cells(1, 11), "mmm-dd-yyyy") _
                & " and is now " & Date - .Cells(1, 11) & " days late. " _
                & "We expect your payment within the next week."
        Else
            message = "Regarding your purchase on " & Format(.Cells(1, 10), _
                "mmm-dd-yyyy") & " for an amount " _
                & FormatCurrency(.Cells(1, 9).Value, 2) & "," _
                & " we received your payment on " _
                & Format(.Cells(1, 12), "mmm-dd-yyyy") & "." _
                & " Your account is now paid in full. We appreciate your business."
        End If

        ' Add a new document. The Selection is where you start typing.
        Set wdDoc = wdApp.Documents.Add
        wdDoc.Range.Select
        Set wdSel = wdDoc.ActiveWindow.Selection

        ' The following line sets spacing after paragraphs. I vary
        ' this through the sub.
        wdSel.ParagraphFormat.SpaceAfter = 0

        ' The next type of line adds text.
        wdSel.TypeText Text:=.Cells(1, 1).Value & " " & .Cells(1, 2).Value

        ' The next line is equivalent to pressing Enter.
        wdSel.TypeParagraph
        wdSel.TypeText Text:=.Cells(1, 4).Value
        wdSel.TypeParagraph
        wdSel.TypeText Text:=.Cells(1, 5).Value & ", " _
            & .Cells(i, 6).Value & " " & .Cells(i, 7).Value
        wdSel.ParagraphFormat.SpaceAfter = 10
        wdSel.TypeParagraph

        wdSel.TypeText Text:=Format(Date, "mmm-dd-yyyy")
        wdSel.TypeParagraph
        wdSel.TypeText Text:="Dear " & .Cells(1, 3).Value _
            & " " & .Cells(1, 2).Value & ":"
        wdSel.TypeParagraph

        wdSel.TypeText Text:=message
        wdSel.TypeParagraph
        wdSel.TypeText Text:="Sincerely,"
        wdSel.TypeParagraph
        wdSel.ParagraphFormat.SpaceAfter = 0
        wdSel.TypeText Text:="Chris Albright, Manager"
        wdSel.TypeParagraph
        wdSel.TypeText Text:="Albright Collection Agency"

        ' Save the document and close it.
        docName = ThisWorkbook.Path & "\" _
            & .Cells(1, 1).Value & "_" & .Cells(1, 2).Value _
            & "_" & Format(Date, "mm-dd-yy") & ".docx"
            wdDoc.SaveAs docName
            wdDoc.Close

            ' Email the document to this customer.
            Set olMail = olApp.CreateItem(olMailItem)
```

```
            olMail.To = .Cells(1, 8).Value
            olMail.Subject = "Purchase on " & Format(.Cells(1, 10).Value, "mmm-dd-yyyy")
            olMail.Body = .Cells(1, 3).Value & " " & .Cells(1, 2).Value _
                & ", please check the attached document. Thank you." _
                & vbCrLf & vbCrLf & "Albright Collection Agency"
            olMail.Attachments.Add docName
            olMail.Send
        End With
    Next

    ' Clean up.
    Set olMail = Nothing
    Set olApp = Nothing
    Set wdApp = Nothing
End Sub
```

17.8   Summary

This chapter has illustrated how you can take advantage of VBA functions written by third-party developers to run their add-ins. Specifically, I have discussed Solver functions that can be used to perform optimization for an existing optimization model. These functions allow you to set up and run Solver completely with VBA. I have also illustrated how to automate the Palisade @RISK add-in with VBA. I will take advantage of this ability in several of the applications in the second half of the book. Finally, I have illustrated how you can automate one or more Office applications from Excel or another Office application.

EXERCISES

1. The file **Product Mix.xlsx** contains a typical product mix model. A company needs to decide how many of each type of picture frame to produce, subject to constraints on resource availabilities and upper bounds on production quantities. The objective is to maximize profit. The model is set up appropriately, although the current solution is not optimal. The cells in blue are inputs, and the cells in red are decision variable cells. The range names being used are listed. Write a sub that sets up Solver and then runs it.

2. The file **Production Scheduling.xlsx** contains a multiperiod production scheduling model. A company has to schedule its production over the next several months to meet known demands on time. There are also production capacity and storage capacity constraints, and the objective is to minimize the total cost. The model is currently set up (correctly) for a 12-month planning horizon. The cells in blue are inputs, and the cells in red are decision variable cells. The range names currently being used are listed. This model can easily be changed, by deleting columns or copying across to the right, to make the planning horizon longer or shorter. You can assume that someone else does this. Your job is to write a sub that renames ranges appropriately, sets up Solver correctly, and then runs it. That

is, your sub should optimize the model in the worksheet, regardless of how many months are in its planning horizon.

3. The file **Facility Location.xlsx** contains a model for locating a central warehouse. There are four customers that send shipments to this warehouse. Their coordinates are given, as well as their numbers of annual shipments. The objective is to minimize the annual distance traveled, and there are no constraints. The cells in blue are inputs, and the cells in red are decision variable cells. The range names being used are listed. This is a nonlinear model, so it is conceivable that there is a local minimum in addition to the global minimum. If there is, then it is possible that the Solver solution could depend on the initial solution used (in the red cells). To test this, write two short subs and attach them to the two buttons. The first should generate "reasonable" random initial solutions. (Use VBA's Rnd function, which generates a uniformly distributed random number from 0 to 1, in an appropriate way. Make sure to put a Randomize statement at the top of the sub so that you get different random numbers each time you run the sub.) The second sub should then run Solver. (It doesn't need to set up Solver. You can do that manually, once and for all.) Then repeatedly click the first button and then the second button. Do you always get the same Solver solution?

4. The file **Transport.xlsx** contains a transportation model where a product must be shipped from three plants to four cities at minimal shipping cost. The constraints are that no plant can ship more than its capacity, and each city must receive at least what it demands. The model has been developed (correctly) on the Model worksheet. The company involved wants to run this model on five scenarios. Each of these scenarios, shown on the Scenarios worksheet, has a particular set of capacities and demands. Write a sub that uses a For loop over the scenarios to do the following: (1) it copies the data for a particular scenario to the relevant parts of the Model worksheet; (2) it runs Solver; and (3) it copies selected results to the Results worksheet. To get you started, the Results worksheet currently shows the results for scenario 1. This is the format you should use for all scenarios.

5. The file **Pricing.xlsx** contains a model for finding the optimal price of a product. The product is made in America and sold in Europe. The company wants to set the price, in Euros, so that its profit, in dollars, is maximized. The demand for the product is a function of price, and it is assumed that the elasticity of demand is constant. This leads to the formula for demand in cell B14, which depends on the parameters in row 10. (These parameters are assumed to be known.) The revenue, in dollars, equals price multiplied by demand. Of course, this depends on the exchange rate in cell B4. The company wants to perform a sensitivity analysis on the exchange rate. The results will be placed in the Sensitivity worksheet, which already lists the exchange rates the company wants to test. Do the following: (1) Enter *any data* in columns B, C, and D of the Sensitivity worksheet and use them to create three line charts (to the right of the data) that show price, demand, and profit versus the exchange rate; and (2) write a sub that substitutes each exchange rate into the model, runs Solver, and transfers the results to the Sensitivity worksheet. When you run your sub, the charts should update automatically with the new data. (That is why you manually set up the chart and link it to data columns—so that you don't have to do with it VBA code.)

6. The file **Stocks.xlsx** contains stock price returns for many large companies for a 5-year period. (Feel free to download more recent stock price data if you prefer.) Each company has its own worksheet, with the stock's ticker symbol as the name of the worksheet. There is also an S&P500 worksheet with the market returns. The Model worksheet uses the market returns and the returns from a given stock to estimate the equation Market = Alpha + Beta * Stock, where Market and Stock are the returns and Alpha and Beta are parameters to be estimated. The estimated Beta is especially useful to financial analysts. It is a measure of the volatility of the stock. The model is set up correctly (currently with data from American Express). The Alpha and Beta parameters are found by minimizing the sum of squared errors in cell E4. Write a sub that does the following: (1) It uses a **For Each** loop to go through all worksheets except the Results, Model, and S&P500 sheets, that is, all stock sheets; (2) it copies the stock's returns to column C of the Model worksheet, pasting them as values; (3) it runs Solver; and (4) it reports the results in a new line in the Results worksheet. At the end, the Results worksheet should have the ticker symbol and the Alpha and Beta for each stock. (*Note:* Your sub doesn't need to set up Solver. You can do that once and for all at design time, manually.)

7. The file **Planting.xlsx** contains a very simple model that a farmer could use to plant his crops optimally. The inputs are in blue, and the decision variable cells are in red. The purpose of this exercise is to develop a VBA application that allows the user to (1) choose any of the input cells as the cell to vary in a sensitivity analysis, (2) choose a range over which to vary this cell, (3) run Solver over this range, and (4) report the results in the Sensitivity worksheet. Here are some guidelines. For (1), you should develop a user form that has a list box with descriptive names of all input cells, such as Profit per acre of wheat, Workers used per acre of wheat, and so on. The user should be allowed to choose only one item from this list. For (2), you should develop a second user form where the user can enter a minimum value, a maximum value, and an increment. For example, the user might specify that she wants to vary the profit per acre of wheat from $150 to $350 in increments of $50. Perform error checks to ensure that numerical values are entered, the minimum value is less than the maximum value, and the increment is positive. For (3), store the current values of the selected input in a variable, run the sensitivity analysis, and then restore the current value. For (4), make sure you adjust the labels in cells A1 and A3 of the Sensitivity worksheet for the particular input chosen.

8. The Solver add-in contains some hidden secrets that can come in handy if you know them. (You might have to develop a friendship with someone in Frontline Systems' technical support group to learn them, as I did.) Here is one such secret. The decision variable cells in any Solver model are given the range name **solver_adj**. This name won't appear in the list of range names when you use Excel's Name Manager, but it is there. You can use it as follows. Open the file **Plant Location.xlsx**. This is a fairly large Solver model that can be used to find optimal locations of plants and warehouses. It is currently set up correctly, but it is not obvious where the decision variable cells are. (I didn't color the decision variable cells red as I usually do.) You could peek at the Solver dialog box to

find the decision variable cells, but instead, write a sub that displays, in a message box, the address of the range with name **solver_adj**.

9. Continuing the previous exercise, you might wonder whether there are any other hidden Solver range names. Open the **Plant Location.xlsx** file again. You will notice some headings out in columns AA and AB. Enter the following sub and run it. It finds all range names that start with Model!solver. You will see that Solver has stored quite a lot of information. What range name is given to the objective cell? (The part of the code that deals with errors is necessary because some of Solver's defined names do not refer to *ranges*. The On Error Resume Next statement says to ignore errors that would result because of these names.)

```
Sub ShowSolverRangeNamesO()
    Dim nm As Name
    Dim counter As Integer

    counter = 1
    With Range("AA1")
        For Each nm In ActiveWorkbook.Names
            On Error Resume Next
            If Left(nm.Name, 12) = "Model!solver" _
                    And Range(nm.Name).Address < > "" Then
                If Err.Number = 0 Then
                    .Offset(counter, 0) = nm.Name
                    .Offset(counter, 1) = Range(nm.Name).Address
                    counter = counter + 1
                End If
            End If
        Next
    End With
End Sub
```

10. Create an Excel file with a list of email addresses in column A of your best friends. Add any information you would like to send them in columns B, C, and so on (as many columns as you need, including only one). Then write a program in this file that automates Outlook and sends an appropriate message to each of your friends. You can use the information to the right of column A for the body and/or the subject line of the message.

18 User-Defined Types, Enumerations, Collections, and Classes

18.1 Introduction

By now, you have learned most of what you need to know to create powerful programs to automate Excel. This chapter, added in the fourth edition, discusses several more advanced topics that enable you to step up to the next level. You might never need to use the methods discussed in this chapter, but you might at least like to know what they are, and that they are available.

18.2 User-Defined Types

User-defined types are data types that you are allowed to create. They are typically used to store related information about a given entity. For example, you might want to store information about customers, such as first name, last name, address, and so on. Then you could create a user-defined type called Customer with the following code. Note that this definition of the type *must* be located outside of any subs. Typically, it will be at the top of a module, along with declarations of module-level variables. (The code for the examples in this section is in the file **User-Defined Types.xlsm**.)

```
Type Customer
    FirstName As String
    LastName As String
    City As String
    State As String
    CellPhone As String
    EMail As String
End Type
```

Once the user-defined type is defined, it can be used as in the following code. Note that you are allowed to have *arrays* of user-defined types, as is done here. Also, when you type favoriteCustomer and then a period, you get Intellisense, which lists the attributes of the type: FirstName, LastName, and so on.

```
Sub CreateCustomers()
    Dim favoriteCustomer As Customer
    Dim customers() As Customer
```

```
    Dim nCustomers As Integer
    Dim i As Integer

    With favoriteCustomer
        .FirstName = "Tiger"
        .LastName = "Woods"
        MsgBox "The name of your favorite customer is " _
            & .FirstName & " " & .LastName & "."
    End With

    ' The following assumes the data about customers is in a worksheet
    ' with code name wsData, starting in cell A2.
    With wsData.Range("A1")
        nCustomers = Range(.Offset(1, 0), .End(xlDown)).Rows.Count
        ReDim customers(1 To nCustomers)
        For i = 1 To nCustomers
            customers(i).FirstName = .Offset(i, 0).Value
            customers(i).LastName = .Offset(i, 1).Value
            customers(i).City = .Offset(i, 2).Value
            customers(i).State = .Offset(i, 3).Value
            customers(i).CellPhone = .Offset(i, 4).Value
            customers(i).EMail = .Offset(i, 5).Value
        Next
    End With

    With customers(4)
        MsgBox "The cell phone and email for the 4th customer are " _
            & .CellPhone & " and " & .EMail & "."
    End With
End Sub
```

Each of the attributes of a user-defined type has its own data type. In the example, they all happened to be String type, but this isn't necessary. One could be String, another Integer, another Boolean, and so on. It is even possible to have an attribute be another user-defined type, as in the following.

```
Type Address
    StreetAddress As String
    City As String
    State As String
    Zip As String
End Type

Type Customer
    FirstName As String
    LastName As String
    FullAddress As Address
    CellPhone As String
    EMail As String
End Type

Sub Favorite()
    Dim favoriteCustomer As Customer
    With favoriteCustomer
        .FirstName = "Peyton"
        .LastName = "Manning"
        With .FullAddress
```

```
            .StreetAddress = "Unknown"
            .City = "Indianapolis"
            .State = "IN"
            .Zip = "4620x"
      End With

      MsgBox "My favorite customer, " & .FirstName _
            & " " & .LastName & ", lives in " & .FullAddress.City _
            & ". His street address is " & .FullAddress.StreetAddress & "."
    End With
End Type
```

Note how the usual "dot" notation is used to go down the hierarchy, as in

```
favoriteCustomer.FullAddress.City
```

18.3 Enumerations

You have already seen enumerations many times. They are essentially named constants that are related. For example, go to the Object Browser and look up XlDirection in the Excel library. This is the *name* of the enumeration. On the right, you will see its four members: xlDown, xlToLeft, xlToRight, and xlUp. If you select any of these members, you will see its value at the bottom, such as −4162 for xlUp. Fortunately, you never need to know any of these weird values. Instead, you can refer to their more meaningful names, such as xlUp, in your code. You can even qualify a member's name by the enumeration name, as in XlDirection.xlUp, but this isn't necessary. Its only advantage is that it gives you Intellisense. As soon as you type XlDirection and then a period, you see a list of the member names.

As you can see from the Object Browser, there are *many* enumerations in the Excel library. All of them start with Xl and all of their members start with xl. Similarly, there are many VBA enumerations, with prefixes Vb and vb, and there are many Microsoft Office enumerations, with prefixes Mso and mso. These are all built-in constants that you can use in your code.

VBA also allows you to create your own enumerations. As with user-defined types, these must be declared outside of any sub, so you usually add them at the top of a module, along with declarations of module-level variables. The following is a possibility that might be used in a simulation of customer arrivals and departures at a bank.

```
Enum EventType
    Arrival
    Departure
    BankCloses
End Enum
```

You can supply *any* integer values to these event types, as in the following:

```
Enum  EventType
    Arrival  =  10
    Departure  =  20
    BankCloses  =  50
End  Enum
```

However, this is totally unnecessary because you are never going to refer to (or remember) the integer values anyway. If you omit values, VBA supplies them as consecutive integers, starting with 0.

The following code illustrates how you can use an enumeration in a program. I use the MsgBox statement only to prove that the three constants Arrival, Departure, and BankCloses are indeed equal to 0, 1, and 2. Note that nextEvent has been declared as type EventType. This ensures that the only possible values for nextEvent will be Arrival, Departure, and BankCloses. In fact, you even get Intellisense. As soon as you type nextEvent and then an equals sign, you get a list of the possible named values.

```
Enum  EventType
    Arrival
    Departure
    BankCloses
End  Enum

Sub  Simulation()
    Dim  nextEvent  As  EventType

    ' code to generate current value of nextEvent
    MsgBox EventType.Arrival & ", " & EventType.Departure _
        & ", " & EventType.BankCloses

    If nextEvent = Arrival Then
        ' code for an arrival
    ElseIf nextEvent = Departure Then
        ' code for a departure
    ElseIf nextEvent = BankCloses Then
        ' code for bank closure
    Else
        ' must be an error if you get here
    End If
End Sub
```

You might not create your own enumerations very often, but you should remember that their main purpose is to make your code more readable. It is much better to refer to a meaningful name such as xlUp or Arrival than to refer to a mysterious integer value.

18.4 Collections

A Collection object in VBA is essentially anything you can use a For Each construction to loop through. As with enumerations, collections are nothing new—you have been using them in virtually all of the preceding chapters. All of the plural objects, such as Workbooks, Worksheets, Charts, and even Range, are collections, and you have seen many For Each constructions to loop through them in code such as the following:

```
Dim ws As Worksheet

For Each ws In ThisWorkbook.Worksheets
    MsgBox ws.Name
Next
```

You can also create your own collections. There are two reasons for doing so. First, you can then loop through the items in the collection with a For Each loop. Second, all Collection objects have four built-in methods:

- Add (add a new item to the collection)
- Count (return the number of items in the collection)
- Item (refer to a particular item in the collection)
- Remove (remove an item from a collection).

Figure 18.1 illustrates these methods. After books is declared as a Collection, as soon as you type books and then a period, you see a list of the four methods. Note that the Item and Remove methods take one argument, the index of the item, as in Item(5) or Remove(2), where indexing starts at 1, not 0. I have no idea why, especially since arrays are 0-based by default.

The following self-explanatory code is typical. The main cause of error in such code is to omit the New keyword in the declaration of books as a Collection. In technical terms, you have to *instantiate* a new Collection object; otherwise, you get the ugly message "Object variable or With block variable not set". Another possible error is in the declaration of the generic book object. It must be declared as Variant. This actually makes sense, because *anything* can be added to the collection. Therefore, book must be declared as the most general type possible. Finally, because of 1-based indexing, the second MsgBox statement returns "Catcher in the Rye".

Figure 18.1 Methods of a Collection

```
Sub MyBooks()
    Dim books As Collection
    Dim aBook As Variant

    With books
        .|
    End ═◈ Add
End Sub ═◈ Count
        ═◈ Item
        ═◈ Remove
```

```
Sub MyBooks()
    Dim books As New Collection
    Dim book As Variant
    Dim counter As Integer

    With books
        .Add "War and Peace"
        .Add "Catcher in the Rye"
        .Add "David Copperfield"
        .Add "The World According to Garp"
        MsgBox "So far, the collection has " & .Count & " books."
        MsgBox "The second book is " & .Item(2) & "."
        .Remove 2
        MsgBox "Now the collection has " & .Count & " books, " _
            & "and the second book is " & .Item(2) & "."
    End With

    counter = 1
    For Each book In books
        MsgBox "Book " & counter & " is " & book & "."
        counter = counter + 1
    Next
End Sub
```

When you call the Add or Remove methods for a collection, you usually write lines as such as those above. However, you can also use the keyword Call as has been done in previous chapters. Then the arguments must be placed in parentheses, as in the following two lines. You are less likely to see this version, but it *is* possible.

```
Call .Add("War and Peace")
Call .Remove(2)
```

One drawback to referring to an item by its integer index is that it is hard to remember which item has which index. Fortunately, there is another way. The Add method of a Collection has the required Item argument, such as "Catcher in the Rye", but it also has an optional Key argument. If you supply a Key value, you can then refer to it in an Item or Remove line. The following lines illustrate one possibility. The second MsgBox statement returns the message in Figure 18.2.

Figure 18.2 Result of Using the Key Argument of Add

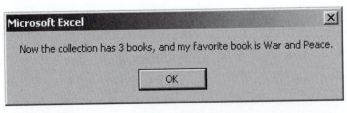

```
Sub MyBooks()
    Dim books As New Collection
    Dim book As Variant
    Dim counter As Integer

    With books
        .Add "War and Peace", "Tolstoy1"
        .Add "Catcher in the Rye", "Salinger1"
        .Add "David Copperfield", "Dickens1"
        .Add "Anna Karenina", "Tolstoy2"
        MsgBox "So far, the collection has " & .Count & " books."
        .Remove "Salinger1"
        MsgBox "Now the collection has " & .Count & " books, " _
            & "and my favorite book is " & .Item("Tolstoy1") & "."
    End With
End Sub
```

Another possibility is to use a loop to find the explicit item you want to remove. The following code indicates how you can do this. Instead of using a For Each loop, which is possible but would require an explicit counter variable, I have used a For loop, from 1 to the count of the collection. This works nicely because a For loop has its own built-in counter.

```
Sub MyBooks()
    Dim books As New Collection
    Dim book As Variant
    Dim i As Integer

    With books
        .Add "War and Peace"
        .Add "Catcher in the Rye"
        .Add "David Copperfield"
        .Add "The World According to Garp"

        ' Remove David Copperfield from the collection, assuming
        ' you don't know its index.
        For i = 1 To .Count
            If .Item(i) = "David Copperfield" Then
                .Remove i
                MsgBox "David Copperfield is item " & i _
                    & " and will now be removed."
                Exit For
            End If
        Next
    End With
End Sub
```

18.5 Classes

You may have heard the term **object-oriented programming**, abbreviated **OOP**. I think it is fair to say that this is the future direction of computer programming. In fact, for many programmers, this is the way they have been programming for years. This entire book talks about Excel's objects and how to manipulate them with VBA code, but this isn't really OOP. Excel's objects, such as Worksheet and Range objects, already exist, and they have properties and methods you can use in VBA code. However, OOP is all about creating your *own* objects. This section briefly describes how you can do this with VBA.

Many programmers complain that VBA is not a *true* OOP language, and they are correct. There are certain OOP operations that are possible—and useful—in true OOP languages such as VB.NET but are impossible with VBA. In fact, if you know one of these languages and then try to use OOP in VBA, it can be very frustrating. (I know, because I have tried to convert some of my VB.NET programs to VBA, and a lot of details have to be changed. The rules of the game are different and far from intuitive.) Nevertheless, warned with this disclaimer, there are some very interesting things you *can* do with OOP in VBA.

First, you have to understand the very important distinction between a **class** and an **object**. A class is basically a blueprint for the "thing" you want to create. For example, if you want to create a Customer class, you need to describe the properties and behaviors of customers you want them to have.[1] That is, you as the programmer need to define what you mean by a customer. In the example I will illustrate shortly, where customers enter a service system like a bank, a customer can arrive to the system, enter service, and leave the system. I call the corresponding methods ArriveToSystem, EnterService, and LeaveSystem. In my Customer class, these methods are subs (they could also be function subroutines) which contain the logical code. In my Customer class, there also two properties, SysClock and QueClock, which measure how long a customer stays in the system and stays in the queue, respectively. The point to understand here is that you get to decide which properties and methods you need to handle the logic you require. In short, you get to build your own world.

Once you create the class—the blueprint—you can then **instantiate objects** from this class. Here is an analogy that might help you with the idea. Think of the "human" class. This is a blueprint for what we humans are and how we behave. For example, we all have a EyeColor property and a Height property. Of course, we can all have different values for these properties. In addition, we all have methods such as Breathe and Eat. So each of us is cut from the same human blueprint, but each of us—each *instance* of the human class—is distinct. In the same way, you can define a class in OOP and then instantiate objects from this class. These instances then lead independent existences in computer memory.

At this point, you probably have two questions: (1) How do you do this in VBA?; and (2) Why would you want to do this at all? The former question is actually easier to answer, as I will do shortly. The latter question is harder to answer. As a non-OOP programmer myself for many years, I couldn't really see the advantage of creating my own classes of objects, and I resisted doing so. However, a "lightbulb" finally went on, and I began to see the huge opportunities that classes provide. In technical terms, they **encapsulate** the properties

---

[1] Classes can also raise events. However, I won't discuss this feature.

and behaviors of the objects—the "things"—you want your program to manipulate. This means that you can write the required logic you need in one place, and one place only, and you can then use it very compactly in your program. Every time you instantiate an object from a class, it "comes alive" knowing its properties and what it can do. I don't imagine that this brief explanation will sell you on classes, but read on—maybe the rest of this section will.

First, you create a class in VBA by selecting **Class Module** from the VBE's Insert menu. Then you can name the class in the Properties Window. Figure 18.3 shows an example where I have already created a class called Customer, and I am about to rename a second class as Server. They are called class *modules* because their code windows look just like those for modules—a big white space for your code. However, class modules are different from regular modules because you can instantiate from them.

The following code shows how to do so. This requires two distinct operations. First, you must declare a variable such as cust1 to be of type Customer (or whatever the class name is). Then you must instantiate a new object of this class with the keyword New. The following code shows how you can do both in a *single* line of code, and how you can do them in separate lines of code. You typically do the latter if you don't need the instance until later in the program, but either way works fine. Just remember that when you instantiate the object in a second line, you must use the keyword Set. Note that the code shown here is placed in a regular module, not a class module. The code in a class module defines the class, but the code used to manipulate instances of classes is placed in a regular module.

Figure 18.3 Naming Class Modules

```
Sub CreateNewCustomers()
    ' You can declare and instantiate an object in one line:
    Dim cust1 As New Customer

    ' You can also declare it and then instantiate it later on.
    ' Declare it.
    Dim cust2 As Customer

    ' Any number of intervening lines, and then...

    ' Instantiate it.
    Set cust2 = New Customer
End Sub
```

Figure 18.4 shows how Intellisense works with classes. Once you have a Customer class, Customer shows up in the list of variable types. This can be *very* helpful.

Class Properties

There are two ways to define a properties of a class. The first is simple. You do it with a line like the following at the top of a class module:

```
Public ArrivalTime As Single
```

If cust1 is an instance of the Customer class, you can then either write ("let") or read ("get") the property value with lines like the following in a regular module:

```
' Write (or "let") the property value.
cust1.ArrivalTime = 7.9

' Read (or "get") the property value.
MsgBox "The customer's arrival time is " & cust1.ArrivalTime
```

Figure 18.4 Intellisense with Classes

Although this way is easy, it has two potential drawbacks. First, *any* value can be given to the property, even values that make no sense like negative arrival times. Second, you might want the property to be read-only. That is, you might not want to allow the programmer to write his own value to the property.

To avoid these drawbacks, a more complex structure is possible. It involves private "member" variables, and Property Get, Property Let, and Property Set constructions. The private member variable, which by convention usually starts with m_, stores the value of the property privately, so that the outside world— code in any other module—can't get to it directly. Then a Property Get construction allows the outside world to *read* the value of the private variable, and a Property Let construction allows the outside world to *write* a given value to the private variable. (A Property Set construction is similar to a Property Let, except that the property is itself an object, so that it must be given a value with a Set statement. I won't use any Property Set constructions here.) If you want a property to be read-only, you simply omit the Property Let part. And in the more unusual case where you want a property to be write-only, you omit the Property Get part.

Assuming that you want the ArrivalTime property to be read-write, but you don't want it to have any negative values, the following code is appropriate. Note that Property Get has no arguments. Its purpose is to read the value of the private variable m_ArrivalTime. However, Property Let has the generic value argument. This is the value you want to give to m_ArrivalTime.

```
Private m_ArrivalTime As Single

Public Property Get ArrivalTime() As Single
    ArrivalTime = m_ArrivalTime
End Property

Public Property Let ArrivalTime(value As Single)
    If value < 0 Then
        MsgBox "You can't assign a negative arrival time value."
    Else
        m_ArrivalTime = value
    End If
End Property
```

This code, written inside a class module, allows a programmer in a regular module to write code like the following. To this programmer, ArrivalTime is the name of the property he sees; he knows nothing about the private m_ArrivalTime variable. However, when the line cust1.ArrivalTime=10 is executed, the value 10 is stored in m_ArrivalTime for the *first* customer. Similarly, when the line cust2.ArrivalTime=15 is executed, the value 15 is stored in m_ArrivalTime for the *second* customer. In this way, each new customer instance has his own m_ArrivalTime value. This is what I mean by instances having independent existences in memory. Finally, the third customer won't have a new value of m_ArrivalTime because the Property Let code doesn't allow a negative value.

```
Sub Test()
    Dim cust1 As Customer
    Dim cust2 As Customer
    Dim cust3 As Customer

    Set cust1 = New Customer
    cust1.ArrivalTime = 10
    MsgBox "The first customer arrived at time " & cust1.ArrivalTime

    Set cust2 = New Customer
    cust2.ArrivalTime = 15
    MsgBox "The second customer arrived at time " & cust2.ArrivalTime

    Set cust3 = New Customer
    ' The following line produces an error message.
    cust3.ArrivalTime = -10
End Sub
```

So, when you define properties in a class module, can you do it the easy one-line way or should you use the more complex multi-line way? My own rule of thumb is to do it the easy way whenever I can, maybe because I am lazy. But if I need more control, I use the more complex way.[2]

Class Methods

A method of a class is more straightforward. It is simply any sub or function subroutine. Here is a method for a Customer class. For now, the details inside the sub are not important. The point is that whenever a customer leaves the system, the LeaveSystem method can be called to take care of the required logic. Note the references to the keyword Me and the variable sim. You see many cases of Me in class modules. Me always refers to current instance of the class, in this case the customer who is about to leave. Each customer has a SysClock property, which is an instance of a Clock class, and the Clock class has a TurnOff method. So Me.SysClock.TurnOff turns off this customer's system clock.[3] Similarly, sim is an instance of a Simulation class, and each time I need to refer to one of *its* properties or methods, I have to use the sim prefix followed by a period.

```
Public Sub LeaveSystem()
    Call Me.SysClock.TurnOff
    Call sim.SysList.Remove(Me)

    ' Update customer stats.
    sim.TotalServed = sim.TotalServed + 1
```

---

[2] As I also found by trial and error, you cannot have a line like Public Prob(), where you want a public property to be an array. VBA simply disallows this, and you have to resort to a Property Let/Get workaround. By contrast, it *is* possible to have public array properties in VB.NET.

[3] Actually, the Me in Me.SysClock.TurnOff can be omitted; you can simply write SysClock.TurnOff. However, by typing Me and then a period, you get Intellisense, a very welcome addition.

```
        sim.TotalSysTime = sim.TotalSysTime + Me.SysClock.TimeSpent
        sim.TotalQueTime = sim.TotalQueTime + Me.QueClock.TimeSpent
End Sub
```

The LeaveSystem method has no arguments. However, just as with subs in general, subs in a class module can have arguments. Here is a possibility for a Server class. (You can think of a server as a teller at a bank.) There are several things to note about this method. First, CustomerServing is a public property of the Server class. Then a Customer object named cust is passed as an argument to the StartServing method, and the line Set Me.CustomerServing = cust sets this server's CustomerServing property to cust.

```
Public CustomerServing As Customer

Public Sub StartServing(cust As Customer)
    ' Remember customer starting service.
    Set Me.CustomerServing = cust

    ' Schedule service completion.
    Call sim.AddEvent(sim.CurrentTime + sim.ServiceTime, 2, Me)
End Sub
```

Constructors

A **constructor** is a sub inside a class module that runs automatically when a new member of the class is instantiated. (It is similar to the Workbook_Open sub that runs whenever the workbook is opened.) The name of this sub in VBA is always Class_Initialize. Here is an example for the Customer class, where I want each new customer to have her own system and queue clocks to keep track of their times. Note that a class is not required to have a constructor, but it is often useful for some type of initialization.

```
Public Sub Class_initialize()
    Set Me.SysClock = New Clock
    Set Me.QueClock = New Clock
End Sub
```

A Queueing Simulation Example

Now that you know class fundamentals, you can see how everything fits together in a nontrivial queueing simulation application. (See the file **Queueing Simulation with Classes.xlsm**.) This is actually the *same* application that is discussed in Chapter 29, but the code presented there makes no use of classes. In this sense, the Chapter 29 version is easier, but it is not as "cool" as the version here with classes. I will not list the code for this application here—it is fairly long—but you can learn a lot about OOP in VBA by studying it carefully.

Among other things, several of the classes in this application are collections. For example, the QueueList class is a collection of all customers currently waiting in the queue. By declaring this as a collection, I get to "borrow" the four methods (Add, Count, Item, Remove) built into all collections and then create my own versions of these methods. For example, when customers are added to a queue, I always want to add them to the *back* of the queue, and when a customer is removed from the queue (to enter service), I always want to remove the customer from the *front* of the queue.

18.6   Summary

If you are willing to take the plunge, user-defined types, enumerations, collections, and classes can take you to a whole new level in programming. However, as the queueing simulation application in the previous section indicates, it takes a lot of practice, perseverance, and visits to online help (or the Web) to master these new elements, especially classes. You have to think carefully about the "world" you want to create, and you have to deal with all the detailed rules that the language enforces. But the effort can result in some very compact and powerful applications—as well as a lot of reusable code.

EXERCISES

1. The file **Purchases 1.xlsx** contains a small data set on customer purchases. Write a program that creates a user-defined type called CustomerPurchase with an item (of the appropriate type) corresponding to each data column: Customer, Email, Cell, Date, Amount. Remember that this should be declared above any subs. Then write a Test sub to create an array purchase where each element of the array is of type CustomerPurchase, and fill this array with the data in the file. Finally, display the information about Sam Lafferty in a message box.

2. The file **Purchases 2.xlsx** is the same as the file from the previous problem except that it includes address data on the customers: street address, city, state, and zip. Repeat the previous exercise, but add another item in the CustomerPurchase type: Address. The Address item should be its own user-defined type, with items StreetAddress, City, State, and Zip. Again, fill an array of type CustomerPurchase with the data in the file, and display the information about Sam Lafferty in a message box.

3. Using the same **Purchases 1.xlsx** file as in Exercise 1, build an enum called SpendType that has three items: LowSpender, MediumSpender, and HighSpender. Then write a sub that creates an array customerType of type SpendType and then fills the array with the appropriate value from SpendType for each customer. You can assume that a purchase less than $75 is low, from $76 to $150 is medium, and above $150 is high.

4. Write a program that creates a collection called Cities and populates it with the *n* most recent cities you have visited, including the city where you live. (You can

choose *n*.) Then display the items in the collection in a message box. Finally, remove the city you live in, and display the count of the remaining cities in a message box.

5. Repeat Exercise 1, but this time create a CustomerPurchase class instead of a user-defined type. This class should have public properties Customer, Email, Cell, Date, and Amount. These can all be of the "easy" kind (no Property Get or Property Let required). In addition, it should have a write-only property Password, which means you need to create a Property Let. In this Property Let, write logic to require that each password must have at least eight characters and all characters must be alphanumeric. Then in a standard module, write a Test sub that creates an instance of the class for each customer in the **Purchases1.xlsx** file, provides a password (of your choice) to each customer, reads the other properties, and writes them to a message box. Then your code should read all the dates, and for all those that occurred on 1/25/2015, it should change them to 1/26/2015 in the spreadsheet. Here, the idea is that you can read and write (look at or even change) the data in the file, but once you set the passwords, you can't even look at them.

Part II

VBA Management Science Applications

This part of the book builds upon the VBA fundamentals in the first 18 chapters by presenting a series of management science applications. I have two objectives in this part of the book. First, I have attempted to present applications that are interesting and useful in the business world. Most of these are derived from similar models in my *Practical Management Science* book. Even if you ignore the VBA code in these applications completely, you can still benefit from the applications themselves. For example, you can use the transportation application in Chapter 24 to solve practically any transportation model, you can use the queueing simulation in Chapter 29 to simulate a wide variety of multiple-server queues, you can use the stock option model in Chapter 30 to price European and American options, you can use the portfolio application in Chapter 32 to find the efficient frontier for any group of stocks using live stock data from the Web, and you can use the AHP application in the online Chapter 34 to make a job decision.

The second objective in this part of the book is to illustrate a number of ways VBA can be used to convert a spreadsheet model into a decision support system (DSS). This is not always easy. Businesses want powerful applications, and power is not always easy to achieve. However, the VBA techniques illustrated in these applications are within the grasp of anyone who has mastered the VBA fundamentals from Part I of the book and is willing to make the effort. This effort should pay off handsomely in the job market.

The chapters in this part of the book can be read in practically any order, depending on your interests. The only exception is Chapter 19, which should be read first. It presents a number of guidelines for application development, and it illustrates these guidelines in a fairly straightforward car loan application.

Basic Ideas for Application Development with VBA

19

19.1 Introduction

It is now time to start using the elements of VBA from the first part of the book to develop modeling applications. This chapter establishes some guidelines for application development, and it also introduces a car loan application to illustrate some of these guidelines. The guidelines discussed here leave plenty of room for creativity. There are many ways to develop a successful application. From the user's standpoint, the main criteria for a successful application are that it be useful, clear, and, of course, correct. Beyond this, users appreciate an application that has the familiar look and feel of a Windows application. As later chapters illustrate, this leaves the door wide open for many possibilities, but it still provides some useful guidance.

I tend to use the term *application* for the programs in Part II of the book. As discussed briefly in Chapter 1, most of them could also be also called decision support systems (DSSs). They provide easy access to helpful information that could then be used by a decision maker to make well-informed decisions.

19.2 Guidelines for Application Development

The topic of software application development is a huge one, and whole courses are devoted to discussions of it. If you are a software developer in a large or even a small company, there are important issues you must be aware of, and there are important procedures you must follow. You are typically *not* the only person who is, or ever will be, working on any particular application. Other programmers are often working with you, and future programmers might need to update your programs to meet new requirements. Therefore, your programs must be readable and understandable by other programmers. Also, whenever possible, you should program with future extensions in mind. If new functionality is required of the program you write, another programmer should not have to start from scratch to incorporate this new functionality. In short, you need to write programs that are readable and reasonably easy to maintain.

This section is certainly not a complete manual on the application development process; this is well beyond the scope of the book. However, there are several simple guidelines provided here—and illustrated later on—that will help you write programs that are readable and maintainable. They are as follows.

1.   **Decide clearly what you want the application to accomplish.**

This is probably the single most important guideline. It is particularly important if you are developing the application for a client, but it is important even if you are working only for yourself. Application development can be a lengthy process, and you certainly do not want to spend your time going in the wrong direction. Decide ahead of time exactly what functionality your application should have and how you plan to implement it. For example, where will the input data come from—dialog boxes, worksheets, text files, or database files? What information will be reported? Will it be reported in tables or charts, or in both? Programming is always challenging, but if you don't even know which direction you are heading, it is impossible. And be on the watch for "feature creep." Most software developers, including myself, have a tendency to add more and more features to their programs as time evolves. At some point, you have to stop and get your software out the door to your customers.

2.   **Communicate clearly to users what the application does and how it works.**

You cannot assume that the eventual users will know what your application does and how it works. After all, the users have not been working on this application for several days (or weeks or months or years) as you have. They need a road map. In real applications, this is often done through printed materials and/or online help. Because the applications in this book are somewhat limited, their explanations are provided in an explanation worksheet that the user sees *first* upon opening the Excel file. If more explanations are required later on, they can be provided, for example, in dialog boxes. Users might have no idea what is going on behind the scenes—the technical part—but the explanations should leave no doubt about the *objectives of* the application and what the users need to do to make it work.

3.   **Provide plenty of comments.**

The best way to document your programs is to insert plenty of comments. It is a natural human tendency to plow through the coding process as quickly as possible and get the program to work, omitting the comments until the last minute—or altogether. Try to fight this impulse. Comments are useful not only to the next programmer who will have to read and maintain your code, but they are also useful to you as you are writing it. They remind you of the logical thought process you should be following. In this way, comments are analogous to an outline for an English composition—an organizational structure. Besides that, they are invaluable when you revisit your own program in a week or a month. It might be crystal clear to you, at the time you are writing, why you have done something in a certain way, but it is often a complete mystery a month later. And if it is a mystery to you, think how mysterious it will be to another programmer (or your instructor). So when there is any possibility for confusion, add comments. Of course, you can overdo it. As an example, the comment in the following lines is a waste of typing.

```
' Add 1 to the counter.
counter = counter + 1
```

4. Use meaningful names for variables, subs, and other programming elements.

There are unfortunately many existing programs that *consistently* use variable names such as i, j, k, n, and nn. They tend to be completely unreadable. (I confess that I still frequently use i, j, and k for loop counters, but otherwise I try to avoid meaningless variable names.) Fortunately, programmers are becoming increasingly careful about using meaningful names for variables and other programming elements. Names such as unitCost and totalProfit tend to make a program self-documenting. You can look at the names and figure out exactly what is going on.

As with comments, you can overdo naming. For example, if you want a variable name for the price paid by the first customer to enter your store, you could use priceForFirstCustomerToEnterStore. Unless you love to type, you will probably want to shorten this name to something like priceCust1 or price1.

5. Use a modular approach with multiple short subs instead of one long sub.

Beginning programmers tend to write one long sub to do everything. As discussed in Chapter 10, this is a bad habit for at least two reasons. First, it is hard to read one long sub that goes on and on, even if it is well documented with comments. It is much easier to read short subs, especially when each of them has a very specific objective. Second, programs are *much* easier to maintain, extend, and debug when they are written in a modular fashion. For example, suppose you have written a program that creates a sensitivity table of some type. Later on, you decide to accompany this with a chart. If your program has a Main sub that calls several other subs to do the work, all you need to do is create a CreateChart sub that has the specific objective of creating the chart and then call CreateChart from the Main sub. The rest of your program, if written properly, should not be affected at all.

6. Borrow from other programs that you or others have developed.

The concept of "shared" code is very important among programmers. The idea is that there is no need to reinvent the wheel each time you write a program. There are almost certainly elements of any program you write that are common to other programs you have written. Sometimes entire subs can be copied and pasted from one program to another. If this is not possible, it is still often possible to copy and paste specific lines of code. As for "borrowing" code written by others, this is a gray area from a legal/ethical standpoint. You should certainly not borrow a whole program or significant portions of a program written by someone else and claim it as your own. However, many programmers make much of their code available for others to use—with no strings attached.[1] If you know that this is the case, you can borrow and adapt this code for your own purposes, possibly with a comment or two to acknowledge the original programmer.

7. Decide how to obtain the required input data.

Almost every application you write (and almost all of the ones in this book) require input data. For example, the car loan application illustrated later in this chapter requires four inputs: the price of the car, the down payment, the annual interest rate, and the term of the loan. The question is how to obtain the data in the application. Perhaps the most natural way is to use one or more dialog boxes. This method is especially convenient when there are just a few data inputs, such as in the car loan application. However, there are times when it would be impractical to ask the user to type *numerous* inputs into a bulky dialog box. For example, the logistics model discussed in Chapter 24 can have literally hundreds of input values. The dialog box approach is totally impractical in this case.

When there is a lot of input data, the chances are that the data are stored in some type of database. Several possibilities are illustrated in later chapters. Each represents a different database format, and each must be handled in a particular way by the VBA code. The possible data locations include (1) a "data" worksheet in the same file as the application itself or in a different Excel file, (2) a text (.txt) file, (3) one or more tables in an Access (or other database) file, as discussed in Chapter 14, and (4) a Web page.

Getting the required data for an application is an extremely important issue, and several applications in later chapters have purposely been included to illustrate some of the possibilities. Of course, you should be aware that in many real applications, you have no control over where the data are located. For example, your company might have the data you require in a SQL Server database file. If this is the case, you must learn how to retrieve the required SQL Server data into Excel for your application.

8. Decide what can be done at design time rather than at run time.

This is a very important issue for you as a developer. Your skills with the Excel interface are probably greater than your programming skills. Therefore, you should develop as much of your application as possible with the Excel interface at *design* time. You can then write VBA to take care of other necessary details that are implemented at *run* time.

To illustrate, suppose you want to develop a linear programming model and then an accompanying report sheet and chart sheet based on the results of the model. It is certainly possible to do *all* of this with VBA code. Before the user runs the application, there would be *blank* Model, Report, and Chart sheets,

---

[1] If programmers really want to keep other users from borrowing their code, they will probably password protect it. This can be done easily through the Protection tab under the **Tools** → **VBA Project** menu item in the VBE.

and your VBA code would be responsible for filling them completely when the program runs. This is a demanding task. It is much easier for you to develop "templates" for these sheets at design time, using the Excel tools you are familiar with. Of course, you cannot fill in these templates completely because parts of them will depend on the inputs used in any particular run of the application. However, using VBA to fill in the missing pieces of a partially completed template is much easier than having to start from scratch with blank sheets.

This point is discussed for each of the applications in the following chapters. In each case, I indicate what can be created at design time—without any VBA.

9. Decide how to report the results.

The models in this book typically follow a three-step approach: (1) inputs are obtained; (2) a model is created to transform inputs into outputs; and (3) outputs are reported. There are many ways to implement the third step. The two basic possibilities are to report the results in tabular and in graphical form. You must decide which is more appropriate for your application. Often you will decide to do both. But even then, you must decide what information to report in the table(s) and what types of charts to create. A reasonable assumption is that many users are nontechnical, so they want the results reported in a user-friendly, nontechnical manner. A simple table and an accompanying chart frequently do the job, but you must use discretion in each application.

As for charts, there is a tendency among many beginning developers to create the fanciest charts possible—wild colors, three-dimensional design, and other "cool" features. My personal suggestion is to keep your charts as simple as possible. A three-dimensional chart might look great, but it sometimes portrays the underlying data less clearly than a "boring" two-dimensional chart. And please, use common sense with color combinations. Red lettering on a purple background might work in an art course, but most business users do not appreciate garish color combinations.

A final issue concerning charts is where they should be placed—on the same worksheet as the underlying data or on separate chart sheets. This is entirely a matter of taste. Many developers tend to favor separate chart sheets (along with navigational buttons, discussed in the next point) to reduce the clutter. You might disagree. However, if you decide to place charts on the same worksheets as the underlying data, you must decide whether to let them "cover up" the data. In other words, you will have to decide on proper placement (and sizing) of the charts on the worksheets. This can be tedious—and it might make you decide to place charts on separate chart sheets after all.

10. Add appropriate finishing touches.

There are a number of finishing touches you can add to make your applications more professional, although most of these are ultimately a matter of taste. Here are several possibilities.

- Add navigational buttons. For example, if there is a worksheet with tabular results and a chart sheet that contains a chart of the same results, it is useful to put a button on each sheet that, when clicked, takes the user to the other sheet. The code behind these buttons is simple, with lines such as:

```
Sub ViewReportSheet()
    With wsReport
        .Activate
        .Range("A1").Select
    End With
End Sub
```

- Hide sheets until the user really needs to see them. For example, there might be a Report sheet that contains results from a previous run of the application (if any). There is no point in letting users see this sheet until the application is run and *new* results are obtained. To implement this idea, the following code could be used to hide all sheets except for the Explanation sheet when the application workbook is opened. Then the Visible property of the Report sheet could be changed to True at run time, right after the new results are obtained.

```
Private Sub Workbook_Open()
    Dim sht As Object
    With wsExplanation
        .Activate
        .Range("F4").Select
    End With
    For Each sht In ActiveWorkbook.Sheets
        If sht.CodeName <> "wsExplanation" Then sht.Visible = False
    Next
End Sub
```

- Use the View tab to change some of the default settings on selected sheets. For example, it is possible to turn off gridlines, the formula bar, and/or row and column headers. Some programmers like to do this to make their applications look less like they actually reside in Excel. You might want to experiment with these options.

19.3   A Car Loan Application

This section presents a rather simple application for calculating the monthly payments on a car loan. This calculation is very easy to perform in Excel with the PMT function, but there are undoubtedly Excel users who are unaware of this function. Besides, users might just want a point-and-click application that gets them results with no Excel formulas required. The car loan application does this, and it illustrates many of the guidelines discussed in the preceding section. In addition, it has purposely been left incomplete. You will have a chance to fill in the missing pieces and thereby practice your VBA skills in the exercises.

Objectives of the Application

The car loan application has three primary functions:

1. It calculates the monthly payment and total interest paid for any car loan, given four inputs: the price of the car, the down payment, the annual interest rate, and the term (number of monthly payments) of the loan.
2. It performs a sensitivity analysis on any of the four inputs, showing how the monthly payment and total interest paid vary, both in tabular and graphical form.
3. It creates an amortization table and accompanying chart showing how the loan payment each month is broken down into principal and interest.

Basic Design of the Application

The application is stored in the file **Car Loan.xlsm**. (As you read the rest of this section, you should open the file and follow along.) The file consists of four worksheets and two chart sheets. The worksheets are named Explanation, Model, Sensitivity, and Amortization. The two chart sheets are named SensitivityChart and AmortizationChart. They all have code names, such as wsExplanation and chtSensitivity. All of these except the Explanation worksheet are hidden when the user opens the file. The others (except the Model worksheet) are revealed when necessary. The Explanation worksheet, shown in Figure 19.1, describes the application, and it has a button that the user clicks to run the application. (I like this design, so I use it in all of the applications in later chapters.)

There are three user forms that allow the user to select options or provide inputs. The first, named frmOptions and shown in Figure 19.2, provides users with the application's three basic options.

If the user selects the first option, the dialog box in Figure 19.3 appears, requesting the inputs for the car loan. (This user form is named frmInputs.) The initial values in this dialog box are those from the previous run, if any, and come from the hidden Model sheet. Of course, users can modify any of these inputs. Then the message box in Figure 19.4 displays the monthly payment and total interest paid for this loan.

If the user selects the second basic option, the sensitivity option, the dialog box in Figure 19.5 asks the user to indicate which of the four inputs to vary for the analysis. (This user form is named frmSensitivity.) It then displays frmInputs shown earlier in Figure 19.3. However, frmInputs is now slightly different, as indicated in Figure 19.6. Specifically, the explanation label at the top indicates that these inputs will now be used in a sensitivity analysis. The labels in dialog boxes should always be as clear as possible, to avoid any possible confusion.

Now that the user has asked to perform a sensitivity analysis on the price of the car, what price range should be used? This is an application design issue. The application could ask the user for this range, or it could choose a default range. This application uses the latter option, primarily to make the application easier to develop. The range chosen is displayed next in an informational message box (see Figure 19.7). The results are displayed graphically in the SensitivityChart sheet (see Figure 19.8) and in tabular form in the Sensitivity worksheet (see Figure 19.9). Note how the buttons in these figures allow for easy navigation through the application.

Figure 19.1 Explanation Worksheet

Car Loan Application

Run the application

This application can be used to find the monthly payment for a car loan. This payment depends on four inputs: the price of the car, the down payment, the annual interest rate on the loan, and the term (number of monthly payments) of the loan. It uses the PMT function (in the Model sheet) to calculate the monthly payment as a function of these inputs, and it also calculates the total interest paid on the loan.

The application provides the user with three options:

1. It calculates the monthly payment and total interest paid and reports these in a message box.

2. It performs a sensitivity analysis on any of the four inputs and reports the results in tabular form (in the Sensitivity sheet) and in graphical form (on the SensitivityChart sheet).

3. It creates an amortization table in the Amortization sheet and shows graphically (in the AmortizationChart sheet) how the amount of principal and the amount of interest in each payment vary through time.

Figure 19.2 Options Form

Figure 19.3 Inputs Form

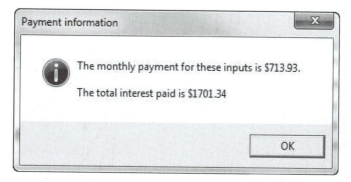

Figure 19.4 Payment Information

Finally, if the user selects the application's third option, an amortization table, frmInputs in Figure 19.3 is again displayed, using a slightly different explanation label appropriate for the amortization objective. (This version of the form is not shown here.) The amortization information is then shown graphically in the AmortizationChart sheet (see Figure 19.10) and in tabular form in the Amortization worksheet (see Figure 19.11). The results shown here are for a 24-month loan.

Figure 19.5 Sensitivity Form

Figure 19.6 Inputs Form with a Different Label

Design Templates

Most of this application can be set up at design time, using only the Excel interface—no VBA. The Model sheet, shown in Figure 19.12, is never displayed to the user, but it is the key to the application. It can be set up completely at design time, including range names and formulas, using any trial values in the input cells. The key formula in cell B11 is =**PMT(IntRate/12,Term,-Loan)**.

Figure 19.7   Information on Sensitivity Range

Figure 19.8   Sensitivity Chart

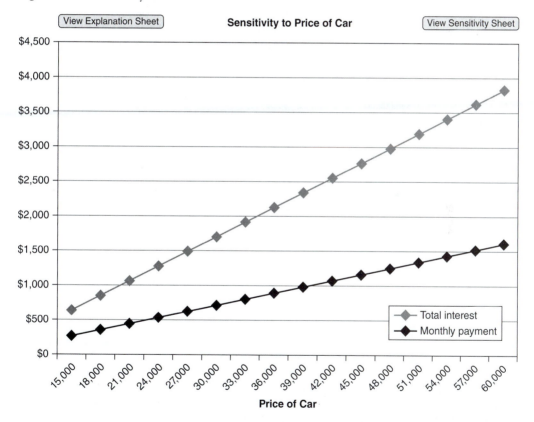

(If you want to examine this sheet more closely, you will need to unhide it. To do so, right-click any of the sheet tabs and select Unhide.)

In addition, templates can be created in the Sensitivity and Amortization sheets, as shown in Figures 19.13 and 19.14. The inputs in both of these sheets are linked to the input cells in the Model sheet. For example, the formula in cell C4 of Figure 19.13 is =**Price**. Therefore, when the user fills in the inputs form in

Figure 19.9 Sensitivity Table

Sensitivity analysis		

Basic inputs		
Price of car	$30,000	
Down payment	$6,000	
Annual interest rate	4.50%	
Term (months to pay)	36	

View Sensitivity Chart

View Explanation Sheet

Input to vary	Price

Price	Monthly payment	Total interest
$15,000.00	$267.72	$638.00
$18,000.00	$356.96	$850.67
$21,000.00	$446.20	$1,063.34
$24,000.00	$535.44	$1,276.01
$27,000.00	$624.69	$1,488.67
$30,000.00	$713.93	$1,701.34
$33,000.00	$803.17	$1,914.01
$36,000.00	$892.41	$2,126.68
$39,000.00	$981.65	$2,339.35
$42,000.00	$1,070.89	$2,552.01
$45,000.00	$1,160.13	$2,764.68
$48,000.00	$1,249.37	$2,977.35
$51,000.00	$1,338.61	$3,190.02
$54,000.00	$1,427.85	$3,402.69
$57,000.00	$1,517.09	$3,615.35
$60,000.00	$1,606.33	$3,828.02

Figure 19.10 Amortization Chart

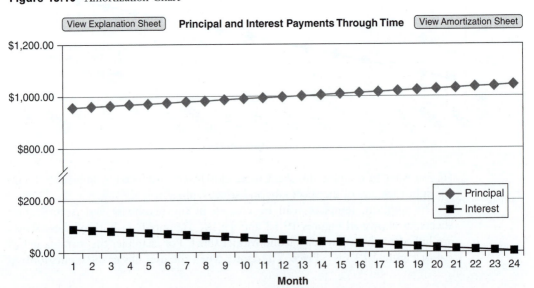

View Explanation Sheet   **Principal and Interest Payments Through Time**   View Amortization Sheet

Figure 19.11 Amortization Table

		Amortization schedule			

Basic inputs

Price of car	$30,000
Down payment	$6,000
Annual interest rate	4.50%
Term (months to pay)	24

View Amortization Chart

View Explanation Sheet

Month	Beginning balance	Payment	Principal	Interest	Ending balance
1	$24,000.00	$1,047.55	$957.55	$90.00	$23,042.45
2	$23,042.45	$1,047.55	$961.14	$86.41	$22,081.31
3	$22,081.31	$1,047.55	$964.74	$82.80	$21,116.57
4	$21,116.57	$1,047.55	$968.36	$79.19	$20,148.21
5	$20,148.21	$1,047.55	$971.99	$75.56	$19,176.22
6	$19,176.22	$1,047.55	$975.64	$71.91	$18,200.58
7	$18,200.58	$1,047.55	$979.30	$68.25	$17,221.29
8	$17,221.29	$1,047.55	$982.97	$64.58	$16,238.32
9	$16,238.32	$1,047.55	$986.65	$60.89	$15,251.67
10	$15,251.67	$1,047.55	$990.35	$57.19	$14,261.31
11	$14,261.31	$1,047.55	$994.07	$53.48	$13,267.25
12	$13,267.25	$1,047.55	$997.80	$49.75	$12,269.45
13	$12,269.45	$1,047.55	$1,001.54	$46.01	$11,267.91
14	$11,267.91	$1,047.55	$1,005.29	$42.25	$10,262.62
15	$10,262.62	$1,047.55	$1,009.06	$38.48	$9,253.56
16	$9,253.56	$1,047.55	$1,012.85	$34.70	$8,240.71
17	$8,240.71	$1,047.55	$1,016.64	$30.90	$7,224.07
18	$7,224.07	$1,047.55	$1,020.46	$27.09	$6,203.61
19	$6,203.61	$1,047.55	$1,024.28	$23.26	$5,179.32
20	$5,179.32	$1,047.55	$1,028.13	$19.42	$4,151.20
21	$4,151.20	$1,047.55	$1,031.98	$15.57	$3,119.22
22	$3,119.22	$1,047.55	$1,035.85	$11.70	$2,083.37
23	$2,083.37	$1,047.55	$1,039.73	$7.81	$1,043.63
24	$1,043.63	$1,047.55	$1,043.63	$3.91	$0.00

Figure 19.12 Model Worksheet

	A	B
1	**Car loan model**	
2		
3	**Inputs**	
4	Price of car	$30,000
5	Down payment	$6,000
6	Annual interest rate	4.50%
7	Term (months to pay)	24
8		
9	**Outputs**	
10	Amount financed	$24,000
11	Monthly payment	$1,047.55
12	Total interest paid	$1,141.14

Figure 19.13 Sensitivity Template

Sensitivity analysis	

Basic inputs	
Price of car	$30,000
Down payment	$6,000
Annual interest rate	4.50%
Term (months to pay)	24

View Sensitivity Chart

View Explanation Sheet

Input to vary	Price

Price	Monthly payment	Total interest

Figure 19.14 Amortization Template

Amortization schedule	

Basic inputs	
Price of car	$30,000
Down payment	$6,000
Annual interest rate	4.50%
Term (months to pay)	24

View Amortization Chart

View Explanation Sheet

Month	Beginning balance	Payment	Principal	Interest	Ending balance
1	$24,000.00	$1,047.55	$957.55	$90.00	$23,042.45
2	$23,042.45				

Figure 19.3, the values are transferred to the Model sheet, and they are then immediately available in the Sensitivity and Amortization sheets. Also, note the partially filled-in section of the Amortization table (rows 10 and 11). It is a good idea to enter the appropriate *formulas* at the top of this table at design time. VBA can then be used to copy them down at run time. As an example, the formula for interest in cell F10 is =**IntRate/12*C10**. (You can examine the **Car Loan.xlsm** file for more details on the formulas.)

I will now examine how the inner details of the application work, starting with the user forms and their event handlers.

frmOptions and Event Handlers

The design of frmOptions appears in Figure 19.15. It includes the usual OK and Cancel buttons, an explanation label, a frame for grouping, and three option buttons named optPayment, optSensitivity, and optAmortization. Of course, these controls have to be positioned and named appropriately (through the Properties window) at design time. The Initialize sub checks the first option by default. The ShowOptionsDialog function captures the user's choice in the variable analysisOption, which is 1, 2, or 3.

Figure 19.15 frmOptions Design

The code behind this form is straightforward and is listed below. (Recall that colons can be used to separate two short lines of code on the same physical line. This is often done in **Case** statements.)

```
Private cancel As Boolean

Public Function ShowOptionsDialog(analysisOption As Integer) As Boolean
    Call Initialize
    Me.Show
    If Not cancel Then
        Select Case True
            Case optPayment.Value: analysisOption = 1
            Case optSensitivity.Value: analysisOption = 2
            Case optAmortization.Value: analysisOption = 3
        End Select
    End If
    ShowOptionsDialog = Not cancel
    Unload Me
End Function

Private Sub Initialize()
    optPayment.Value = True
End Sub

Private Sub cmdOK_Click()
    Me.Hide
    cancel = False
End Sub

Private Sub cmdCancel_Click()
    Me.Hide
    cancel = True
End Sub
```

```
Private Sub UserForm_QueryClose(cancel As Integer, CloseMode As Integer)
    If CloseMode = vbFormControlMenu Then cmdCancel_Click
End Sub
```

frmInputs Design and Event Handlers

The design of frmInputs appears in Figure 19.16. It includes the usual OK and Cancel buttons, a label named lblExplanation at the top, three text boxes named txtPrice, txtDownPayment, and txtInterest (and corresponding labels), a frame for grouping, and five option buttons named opt12, opt24, opt36, opt48, and opt60. (Note that it was a *design* decision to limit the term of the loan to multiples of 12 months.) The lblExplanation at the top of the form has a blank caption at design time. The explanation that is inserted at run time depends on which option the user chooses. (Compare the labels in Figures 19.3 and 19.6, for example.)

The Initialize sub for this user form fills the three text boxes with the values currently in the Model sheet. (Alternatively, some programmers might elect to leave these boxes blank.) It also checks the appropriate option button, depending on what term is currently in the Model sheet, and it sets the Caption property of lblExplanation to explanation, a string variable that has, by this time, been defined in the module code (shown later on). After some straightforward error checking in a Valid function, the ShowInputsDialog function enters the user's inputs in the Model sheet. All of the code behind this form follows.

Figure 19.16 frmInputs Design

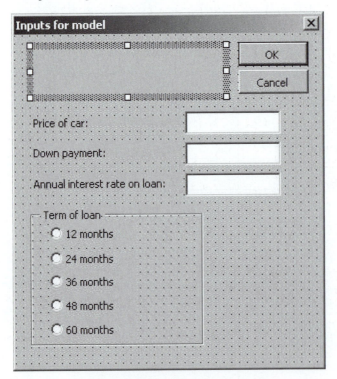

```
Private cancel As Boolean

Public Function ShowInputsDialog(explanation As String) As Boolean
    Call Initialize(explanation)
    Me.Show
    If Not cancel Then
        ' Enter the user's choices in the appropriate cells.
        With wsModel
            .Range("Price").Value = Val(txtPrice.Value)
            .Range("DownPayment").Value = Val(txtDownPayment.Value)
            .Range("InterestRate").Value = Val(txtInterestRate.Value)

            Select Case True
                Case opt12.Value: .Range("Term").Value = 12
                Case opt24.Value: .Range("Term").Value = 24
                Case opt36.Value: .Range("Term").Value = 36
                Case opt48.Value: .Range("Term").Value = 48
                Case opt60.Value: .Range("Term").Value = 60
            End Select
        End With
    End If
    ShowInputsDialog = Not cancel
    Unload Me
End Function

Private Sub Initialize(explanation As String)
    ' Enter the current values in the Model sheet in the text boxes.
    With wsModel
        lblExplanation.Caption = explanation
        txtPrice.Value = Format(.Range("Price").Value, "0")
        txtDownPayment.Value = Format(.Range("DownPayment").Value, "0")
        txtInterestRate.Value = Format(.Range("InterestRate").Value, "0.0000")

        ' Check the appropriate option button, based on the value in the Model sheet.
        Select Case .Range("Term").Value
            Case 12: opt12.Value = True
            Case 24: opt24.Value = True
            Case 36: opt36.Value = True
            Case 48: opt48.Value = True
            Case 60: opt60.Value = True
            Case Else: opt36.Value = True
        End Select
    End With
End Sub

Private Function Valid() As Boolean
    Dim ctl As Control, response As Variant

    Valid = True
    For Each ctl In Me.Controls
        If TypeName(ctl) = "TextBox" Then
            If ctl.Value = "" Or Not IsNumeric(ctl) Then
                Valid = False
                MsgBox "Enter a positive number in each box.", vbInformation
                ctl.SetFocus
                Exit Function
            End If
            If ctl.Value <= 0 Then
                Valid = False
                MsgBox "Enter a positive number in each box.", vbInformation
```

```
                ctl.SetFocus
                Exit Function
            End If
        End If
    Next

    If Val(txtDownPayment.Value) > Val(txtPrice.Value) Then
        Valid = False
        MsgBox "The down payment can't be greater than the price " _
            & "the car!", vbInformation, "Improper input"
        txtDownPayment.SetFocus
        Exit Function
    End If

    If Val(txtInterestRate.Value) > 0.25 Then
        response = MsgBox("You entered an annual interest rate greater than 25%. " _
            & "Do you really mean this?", vbYesNo, "Abnormal interest rate")
        If response = vbNo Then
            Valid = False
            txtInterestRate.SetFocus
            Exit Function
        End If
    End If
End Function

Private Sub cmdOK_Click()
    If Valid Then Me.Hide
    cancel = False
End Sub

Private Sub cmdCancel_Click()
    Me.Hide
    cancel = True
End Sub

Private Sub UserForm_QueryClose(cancel As Integer, CloseMode As Integer)
    If CloseMode = vbFormControlMenu Then cmdCancel_Click
End Sub
Private Sub btnCancel_Click()
    Unload Me
    End
End Sub
```

frmSensitivity Design and Event Handlers

There are no new concepts in frmSensitivity, so I will simply display its design in
Figure 19.17 and list its code below. Its purpose is to capture the variable sensiti-
vityOption, which has possible values 1, 2, 3, 4.

```
Private cancel As Boolean

Public Function ShowSensitivityDialog(sensitivityOption As Integer) As Boolean
    Call Initialize
    Me.Show
    If Not cancel Then
        Select Case True
```

```
                Case optPrice.Value: sensitivityOption = 1
                Case optDownPayment.Value: sensitivityOption = 2
                Case optInterestRate.Value: sensitivityOption = 3
                Case optTerm.Value: sensitivityOption = 4
            End Select
        End If
        ShowSensitivityDialog = Not cancel
        Unload Me
End Function

Private Sub Initialize()
    optPrice.Value = True
End Sub

Private Sub cmdOK_Click()
    Me.Hide
    cancel = False
End Sub

Private Sub cmdCancel_Click()
    Me.Hide
    cancel = True
End Sub

Private Sub UserForm_QueryClose(cancel As Integer, CloseMode As Integer)
    If CloseMode = vbFormControlMenu Then cmdCancel_Click
End Sub
```

Figure 19.17 frmSensitivity Design

Module Code

The module contains the VBA code that does most of the work. As usual, its Main sub acts as a control center, calling other subs to do most of the work, including showing the dialog boxes.

Main Code

The Main sub begins by showing frmOptions. Based on the user's response, it then uses a Case construct to perform one of three possible actions: (1) show frmInputs and calculate the monthly payment and total interest paid, (2) show frmSensitivity and perform a sensitivity analysis on the selected input, or (3) create an amortization table. Note that frmInputs is shown in each case, although the explanation string variable varies slightly. Also, note that for the sensitivity option, there is a nested Case construct that is based on the input variable chosen. (The comments in the code provide further details.)

```vb
Sub MainProgram()
    Dim analysisOption As Integer
    Dim explanation As String
    Dim sensitivityOption As Integer

    ' See which option of the application the user wants to run.
    If frmOptions.ShowOptionsDialog(analysisOption) Then
        Select Case analysisOption
            Case 1
                ' This explanation string will appear at the top of frmInputs.
                explanation = "Supply the following inputs and the application " _
                    & "will calculate the monthly car payment, along with total " _
                    & "interest paid."

                ' Get the user inputs and display the results in a message box.
                If frmInputs.ShowInputsDialog(explanation) Then
                    MsgBox "The monthly payment for these inputs is " _
                        & Format(Range("Payment").Value, "$0.00") & "." & vbCrLf _
                        & vbCrLf & "The total interest paid is " _
                        & Format(Range("TotalInterest").Value, "$0.00"), _
                        vbInformation, "Payment information"
                End If

            Case 2
                ' First, see which input to vary.
                If frmSensitivity.ShowSensitivityDialog(sensitivityOption) Then

                    ' This explanation string will appear at the top of frmInputs.
                    explanation = "Enter the following inputs. The sensitivity " _
                        & "analysis will use these as starting points."

                    ' Get the user's inputs.
                    If frmInputs.ShowInputsDialog(explanation) Then

                        ' Perform the sensitivity analysis for the selected input.
                        Select Case sensitivityOption
                            Case 1: Call PriceSensitivity
                            Case 2: Call DownPaymentSensitivity
                            Case 3: Call InterestRateSensitivity
                            Case 4: Call TermSensitivity
                        End Select
                    End If
                End If

            Case 3
                ' This explanation string will appear at the top of the InputsForm.
```

```
            explanation = "Enter the following inputs. The amortization " _
                & "table will be based on these."
            If frmInputs.ShowInputsDialog(explanation) Then
                Call Amortization
            End If
        End Select
    End If
End Sub
```

PriceSensitivity Code

The PriceSensitivity sub is called if the user wants a sensitivity analysis on the price of the car. It first unhides and activates the Sensitivity worksheet. Next, it clears the contents from the previous run, if any. Then it uses a For loop to cycle through prices as low as half the current price and as high as double the current price. For each of these, it substitutes the price into the Price cell of the Model sheet, captures the monthly payment and total interest paid from the corresponding cells of the Model sheet, and places these values in the Sensitivity worksheet. Note how the counter variable rowOffset keeps track of where to place these values in the Sensitivity worksheet. At the end of this loop, it puts the original price back in the Price cell of the Model sheet. Finally, it sets range variables for the ranges of the sensitivity data, and it calls the UpdateSensitivityChart sub (discussed below) with these ranges as arguments.

```
Sub PriceSensitivity()
    Dim currentPrice As Currency
    Dim price As Currency
    Dim rowOffset As Integer
    Dim i As Integer
    Dim dataRange As Range
    Dim xRange As Range

    With wsSensitivity
        .Visible = True
        .Activate

        ' Enter some labels and clear the sensitivity table from a previous run, if any.
        .Range("C9").Value = "Price"
        With .Range("B11")
            .Value = "Price"
            Range(.Offset(1, 0), .Offset(1, 2).End(xlDown)).ClearContents
        End With

        ' Capture the current price.
        currentPrice = .Range("C4").Value
        MsgBox "The price will be varied from half the current price " _
            & "to double the current price, in increments of 10% of the " _
            & "current price. (But it will never be less than the current " _
            & "down payment.)", vbInformation, "Price range"

        ' For each possible price, enter it in the Price cell (in the Model sheet)
        ' and then store the corresponding payment and total interest values in
        ' the sensitivity table.
        rowOffset = 0
        With .Range("B11")
```

```
        For i = -5 To 10
            price = currentPrice * (1 + i / 10)
            If price > = wsSensitivity.Range("C5").Value Then
                rowOffset = rowOffset + 1
                wsModel.Range("Price").Value = price
                .Offset(rowOffset, 0).Value = Format(price, "$0.00")
                .Offset(rowOffset, 1).Value = Format(wsModel.Range("Payment").Value, "$0.00")
                .Offset(rowOffset, 2).Value = Format(wsModel.Range("TotalInterest").Value, "$0.00")
            End If
        Next
    End With

    ' Restore the current price to the Price range (in the Model sheet).
    wsModel.Range("Price").Value = currentPrice

    ' Set the ranges for the sensitivity chart and then update the chart.
    With .Range("B11")
        Set dataRange = Range(.Offset(1, 1), .Offset(1, 2).End(xlDown))
        Set xRange = Range(.Offset(1, 0), .End(xlDown))
    End With
End With

Call UpdateSensitivityChart("Price of Car", dataRange, xRange)
End Sub
```

UpdateSensitivityChart Code

The UpdateSensitivityChart sub takes three arguments: a string for chart titles, a range for the source data, and another range for the horizontal axis variable. (Note how Range object variables can be passed as arguments, just like any other variables.) It then updates the already existing SensitivityChart sheet with these arguments. (If you are not sure exactly what part of the chart each of the lines changes, set a breakpoint at the Sub line. Then when you run the application, it will stop here, allowing you to step through the sub with the F8 key and examine the effect of each line.)

Keep in mind that the SensitivityChart sheet and the AmortizationChart sheet discussed below are created at design time, using Excel's chart tools in the usual way. Therefore, the only task required of VBA is to populate these charts with the current data, and this is relatively simple. It would be more tedious to create the chart sheets from scratch with VBA.

```
Sub UpdateSensitivityChart(inputParameter As String, dataRange As Range, _
        xRange As Range)
    With chtSensitivity
        .Visible = True
        .Activate
        .SetSourceData dataRange
        .SeriesCollection(1).Name = "Monthly payment"
        .SeriesCollection(2).Name = "Total interest"
        .SeriesCollection(1).XValues = xRange
        .Axes(xlCategory).AxisTitle.Caption = inputParameter
        .ChartTitle.Text = "Sensitivity to " & inputParameter
        .Deselect
    End With
End Sub
```

DownPaymentSensitivity, InterestRateSensitivity, and TermSensitivity Code

The next three subs are analogous to the PriceSensitivity sub. They are relevant for sensitivity analyses on the down payment, the interest rate, and the term, respectively. Their code has purposely *not* been supplied. They are left to you as an exercise. (Right now, they contain only messages that you can delete when you write your code.) Note that you should call the UpdateSensitivityChart sub from each of them, using appropriate arguments in each case.

```vba
Sub DownPaymentSensitivity()
    MsgBox "The code for this sensitivity analysis is not yet written. " _
        & "Try writing it on your own.", vbInformation, "Incomplete"
End Sub

Sub InterestRateSensitivity()
    MsgBox "The code for this sensitivity analysis is not yet written. " _
        & "Try writing it on your own.", vbInformation, "Incomplete"
End Sub

Sub TermSensitivity()
    MsgBox "The code for this sensitivity analysis is not yet written. " _
        & "Try writing it on your own.", vbInformation, "Incomplete"
End Sub
```

Amortization Code

The Amortization sub creates an amortization table. It first unhides and activates the Amortization worksheets and clears the contents of the previous run, if any. Because the amortization table will have as many rows as the term of the loan, the variable term is defined to help fill the table, and then the table is built. Its first column, the month number, is filled with the DataSeries method of a Range object. (This is equivalent to Excel's Fill tool. You can learn the syntax for the DataSeries line by using this tool with the macro recorder on.) The rest of the table is filled by copying the relevant formulas down their respective columns. (These formulas were entered in the template at design time. See rows 10 and 11 of Figure 19.14.) Finally, the sub sets Range variables for the ranges of the amortization table, and it calls the UpdateAmortizationChart sub with these ranges as arguments.

```vba
Sub Amortization()
    Dim term As Integer
    Dim dataRange As Range
    Dim xRange As Range

    With wsAmortization
        .Visible = True
        .Activate

        ' Clear out old table (but leave a few key formulas as is).
        With .Range("B10")
            Range(.Offset(2, 0), .Offset(2, 1).End(xlDown)).ClearContents
            Range(.Offset(1, 2), .Offset(1, 5).End(xlDown)).ClearContents
        End With
```

```
' Capture the term in a variable. It is the "length" of the amortization table.
term = Range("C7").Value

' Autofill the first column of the table (1,2,3,etc.). Then copy the
' formulas already supplied down the other columns.
With .Range("B10")
    .DataSeries Rowcol:=xlColumns, Step:=1, Stop:=term
    .Offset(1, 1).Copy Range(.Offset(2, 1), .Offset(term − 1, 1))
    Range(.Offset(0, 2), .Offset(0, 5)).Copy _
        Range(.Offset(1, 2), .Offset(term − 1, 5))
End With

' Set the ranges for the amortization chart and then update the chart.
With .Range("B9")
    Set dataRange = Range(.Offset(1, 3), .Offset(1, 4).End(xlDown))
    Set xRange = Range(.Offset(1, 0), .End(xlDown))
End With
End With

Call UpdateAmortizationChart(dataRange, xRange)
End Sub
```

UpdateAmortizationChart Code

The UpdateAmortizationChart sub takes two arguments: a range for the source data, and another range for the horizontal axis variable. It then updates the already existing AmortizationChart sheet with these arguments.

```
Sub UpdateAmortizationChart(dataRange As Range, xRange As Range)
    With chtAmortization
        .Visible = True
        .Activate
        .SetSourceData dataRange
        .SeriesCollection(1).Name = "Principal"
        .SeriesCollection(2).Name = "Interest"
        .SeriesCollection(1).XValues = xRange
        .Deselect
    End With
End Sub
```

Navigational Code

The remaining subs are attached to the buttons on the various sheets. They are for navigational purposes only.

```
Sub ViewExplanation()
    With wsExplanation
        .Activate
        .Range("F4").Select
    End With
End Sub
```

```
Sub ViewSensitivitySheet()
    With wsSensitivity
        .Activate
        .Range("B1").Select
    End With
End Sub

Sub ViewSensitivityChart()
    chtSensitivity.Activate
End Sub

Sub ViewAmortizationSheet()
    With wsAmortization
        .Activate
        .Range("B1").Select
    End With
End Sub

Sub ViewAmortizationChart()
    chtAmortization.Activate
End Sub
```

If you have used earlier editions of this book, you will observe that from the user's standpoint, this current car loan application acts *exactly* like previous versions, even though the code dealing with user forms is quite different. This is common in programming, and you have undoubtedly seen it many times without really being aware of it. Specifically, programs are often changed, usually to provide more efficient or up-to-date code, without changing what users see at all. After all, users really don't care how your code does what it does; they only care that it works in a consistent manner. But if you change the program so that users *see* something different, you risk incurring their wrath!

19.4   Summary

The car loan application is not the simplest one you will ever encounter, and there is no way you could develop it in, say, an hour. There are admittedly many details to take care of. As a tactical issue, you might want to try developing this application on your own in pieces. For example, you might omit the parts on sensitivity analysis and amortization, along with their charts, and develop only the part that displays the message box for the monthly payment in Figure 19.4. Once you get this working properly, you can develop the sensitivity analysis part of the application. You can then tackle the amortization table. The advantage of this approach is that you can work on several small and relatively easy subprojects, rather than one daunting large project, and gain confidence with your successes along the way. In addition, if you keep these small subprojects in separate subs, you can test them independently of one another, thereby eliminating bugs as you proceed.

If you keep this "divide and conquer" approach in mind, you will probably agree that there is no single piece of the application that you cannot master with some practice. Many applications in later chapters are like this one. They are fairly *long*, but they are not necessarily *difficult*. Just remember the claim in Chapter 1 that you can be a successful programmer if you persevere. In fact, to be a successful programmer, you *must* persevere.

EXERCISES

1. Complete the DownPaymentSensitivity, InterestRateSensitivity, and TermSensitivity subs that were left incomplete.

2. The charts in the application are currently line charts. Suppose the initial reaction from users is that they would rather see some other chart type such as stacked columns. Make the necessary changes. (Do you need to rewrite any of the code?)

3. Change the application so that the term of the loan can be *any* number of months from 12 to 60. Note that option buttons are no longer practical. Use a text box instead to capture the term of the loan.

4. Suppose all car loans are for 36 months. Then there is no need to obtain this input from the user, although it would be nice to inform the user of the term in a message box. Change the application appropriately to handle this situation.

5. Suppose a down payment of 20% is required for all car loans. Then there is no need to obtain this input from the user, although it would be nice to inform the user of the down payment in a message box. Change the application appropriately to handle this situation.

6. Change the application so that it is relevant for home loans (mortgages). Assume that the term of the loan can be any number *of years* from 5 to 30 (although the borrower makes *monthly* payments) and that a down payment of *at least* 10% of the price of the home is required. Make sure there are no leftover references to cars!

A Blending Application

20.1 Introduction

This application illustrates how a typical linear programming model, in this case an oil-blending model, can be transformed into an impressive decision support system with very little VBA coding. The key to the application is that it is a *fixed-size* model. Specifically, it works (in its present form) only if there are three types of crude oils blended into three gasoline products. This is certainly a limiting feature of the application. However, the fixed-size property allows the entire application to be set up at design time, without any VBA. The linear programming model can be developed, a report can be created, and several charts can be created. The only VBA tasks are to get the user's inputs for the model and to run Solver. There are many *Excel* details to take care of at design time, but the finished application is very straightforward, with a minimal amount of VBA code.

New Learning Objective: VBA

- To see how VBA can be used to develop a complete decision support system around a fixed-size optimization model by supplying input dialog boxes and charts and reports for the results.

New Learning Objective: Non-VBA

- To develop an understanding of linear programming blending models.

20.2 Functionality of the Application

The application provides the following functionality:

1. The application is based on a typical oil-blending model with three crude oils blended into three gasoline products. There are many inputs to the model, including crude oil availabilities, gasoline demands, minimum octane and maximum sulfur percentage requirements on the gasoline products, and others, all of which can change each time the model is run. The user has a chance to view all of these inputs and make any desired changes.

2. The model is developed in a Model worksheet and is optimized by Solver. The key outputs are reported in a Report worksheet. Various aspects of the solution are also displayed on several chart sheets. The user can view these chart sheets by clicking navigational buttons on the Report worksheet.

20.3 Running the Application

The application is stored in the file **Blending Oil.xlsm**. When this file is opened, the Explanation worksheet in Figure 20.1 is displayed.[1] When the user clicks the

Figure 20.1 Explanation Worksheet

Oil Blending Application

Run the application

This application finds the optimal blending plan for a problem of a fixed size. The "fixed size" means that the problem always has three crude oils being blended into three gasoline types. Because of this fixed size, the optimization model and all reports, including charts, can be set up with Excel -- no VBA required -- at design time. Then the application uses VBA to show the current inputs to the user and allows the user to change any of these. It then runs Solver with these inputs and displays the results in a report, with several optional charts that can be viewed.

The inputs come in three groups:

(1) Monetary inputs: the cost per gallon of purchasing each type of crude, the selling price per gallon for each type of gasoline, and the cost of transforming a gallon of any crude into any type of gasoline.

(2) Data related to octanes and sulfur percentages. Each crude has a certain octane rating and sulfur percentage. Each gasoline has a minimum required octane rating and a maximum allowable sulfur percentage.

(3) Data related to demands, availabilities, and production capacity. As for demand, this is the maximum amount of each type of gasoline that can be sold. (There is no incentive, therefore, to produce more than this.)

---

[1] Actually, assuming that a pre-2010 version of Excel is being used, the first thing the user sees upon opening the file is a Solver warning. This warning appears in all future applications that invoke Solver. It addresses the "missing Solver reference" problem discussed in Chapter 17. It indicates the necessary fix in case of a Solver problem. (It appears that this problem was fixed in Excel 2010, so the warning doesn't appear in Excel 2010 or later versions.)

button on this sheet, the dialog box in Figure 20.2 appears, which indicates that the inputs to the model are grouped into three categories. The user can view (and then change, if desired) the inputs in any of these categories by checking the appropriate options. If they are all checked, the dialog boxes in Figures 20.3, 20.4, and 20.5 appear sequentially. The inputs that appear initially in the boxes are those from the previous run of the model (if any). Of course, any of these inputs can be changed.

When the user has finished viewing/changing inputs, these inputs are substituted into the model in the (hidden) Model worksheet, and the model is optimized with Solver. The important inputs and outputs are displayed in a Report worksheet, as shown in Figure 20.6. This worksheet contains several buttons for navigating to the various chart sheets and back to the Explanation worksheet.

The available charts appear in Figures 20.7–20.13. Each of these charts contains a button that navigates back to the Report worksheet.

Figure 20.2 Initial Dialog Box

Figure 20.3 Dialog Box for Monetary Inputs

Figure 20.4 Dialog Box for Octane, Sulfur Inputs

Octane and sulfur inputs

The octane inputs include the octane rating of each crude and the minimum octane rating required in each gasoline. The sulfur inputs include the sulfur percentage in each crude and the maximum sulfur percentage allowed in each gasoline. For percentages, enter 0.10 for 10%, for example.

OK

Cancel

Octane ratings

Crude 1:	12
Crude 2:	10
Crude 3:	8

Sulfur percentages

Crude 1:	0.01
Crude 2:	0.005
Crude 3:	0.03

Minimum octane ratings

Gas 1:	11
Gas 2:	10
Gas 3:	9

Maximum sulfur percentages

Gas 1:	0.01
Gas 2:	0.03
Gas 3:	0.01

Figure 20.5 Dialog Box for Remaining Inputs

Demands, availabilities, and capacity inputs

These inputs, all expressed in gallons, include the demands for gasolines (the maximum amounts that can be sold), the availabilities of crudes, and production capacity.

OK

Cancel

Crude availabilities

Crude 1:	5000
Crude 2:	5000
Crude 3:	5000

Demands for gas

Gas 1:	3000
Gas 2:	2000
Gas 3:	1000

Production capacity: 15000

Figure 20.6 Report Worksheet

Report of optimal blending solution

Amounts of crudes purchased

	Purchased	Available	Purchase cost
Crude 1	1500	5000	$82,500
Crude 2	4300	5000	$150,500
Crude 3	200	5000	$5,000
Totals	6000	15000	$238,000

Amounts of gasolines produced (and sold)

	Produced	Demand	Production cost	Revenue
Gas 1	3000	3000	$15,000	$210,000
Gas 2	2000	2000	$10,000	$120,000
Gas 3	1000	1000	$5,000	$75,000
Totals	6000	6000	$30,000	$405,000

Blending plan (gallons of crudes used in different gasolines)

	Gas 1	Gas 2	Gas 3
Crude 1	1500.00	0.00	0.00
Crude 2	1500.00	2000.00	800.00
Crude 3	0.00	0.00	200.00

Octane requirements

	Obtained	Min required
Gas 1	11.00	11.00
Gas 2	10.00	10.00
Gas 3	9.60	9.00

Sulfur requirements

	Obtained	Max allowed
Gas 1	0.75%	1.00%
Gas 2	0.50%	3.00%
Gas 3	1.00%	1.00%

Monetary summary

Purchase cost	$238,000
Production cost	$30,000
Sales revenue	$405,000
Profit	$137,000

Figure 20.7 Chart of Crude Oils Purchased

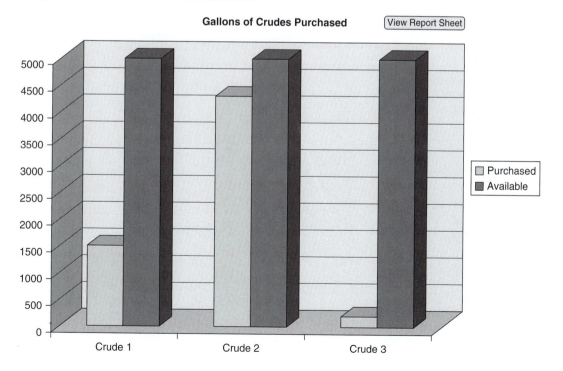

Figure 20.8 Chart of Crude Oil Purchase Costs

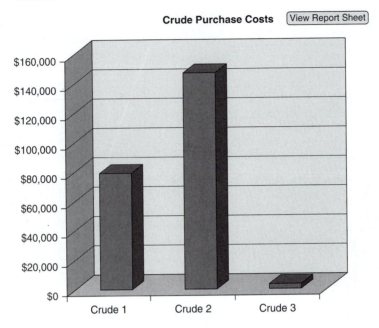

Figure 20.9 Chart of Gasolines Produced and Demands

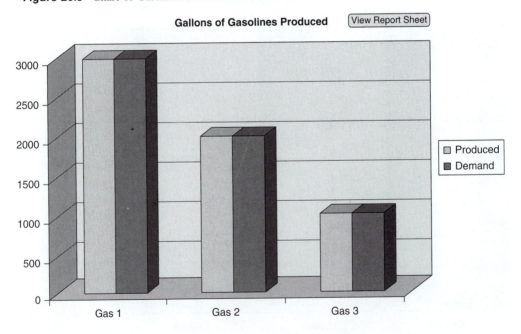

Figure 20.10 Chart of Production Costs and Gasoline Revenues

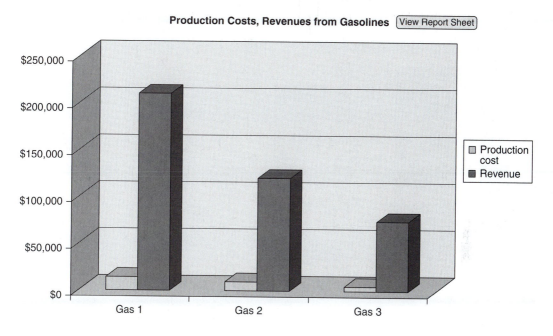

Figure 20.11 Chart of Blending Plan

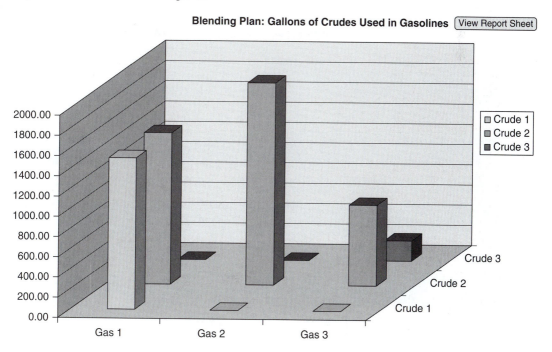

Figure 20.12 Chart of Octane Requirements

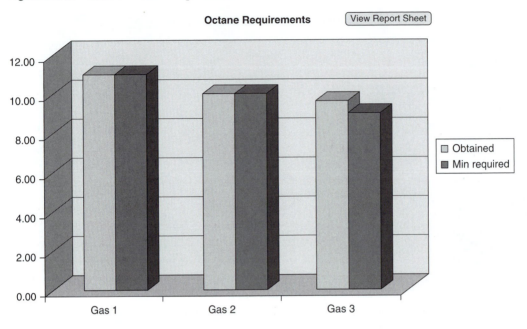

Figure 20.13 Chart of Sulfur Percentage Requirements

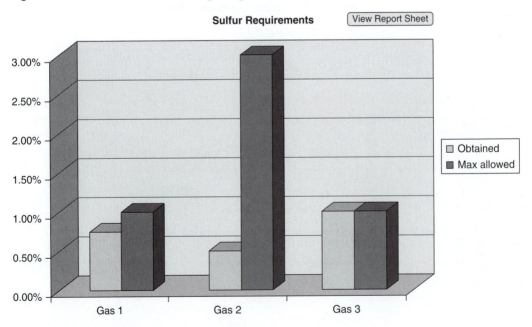

20.4 Setting Up the Excel Sheets

The **Blending Oil.xlsm** file contains three worksheets and seven chart sheets. *All* of these can be developed at design time, without any VBA. The three worksheets are the Explanation sheet in Figure 20.1, the Model sheet in Figure 20.14, and the Report sheet in Figure 20.6. Because of the fixed size of the problem (always three crude oils and three gasoline products), the structure of the model never changes; the only changes are new input values. Therefore, this model can be developed *completely*, including the Solver dialog box, at design time. Any inputs can be used for testing the model. (The model itself is a straightforward application of linear programming. You can open the **Blending Oil.xlsm** file, unhide the Model worksheet, and examine its formulas if you like.) Similarly, the Report worksheet can be developed, with links to appropriate cells in the Model worksheet, once and for all at design time. Finally, the charts in Figures 20.7 to 20.13 can be developed and linked to appropriate ranges in the Report worksheet at design time. After these worksheets and chart sheets are developed, they are ready and waiting for user inputs.

20.5 Getting Started with the VBA

The application includes four user forms, named frmInputTypes, frmInputs1, frmInputs2, and frmInputs3, a single module, and, because this application will be invoking Solver VBA functions, a reference to Solver.[2] (Remember that you set a reference with the **Tools→References** menu item in the VBE.) Once these items are added, the Project Explorer window will appear as in Figure 20.15. (As always, I have supplied meaningful code names for all of the sheets.)

Workbook_Open Code

To guarantee that the Explanation worksheet appears when the file is opened, the following event handler is placed in the ThisWorkbook code window. Note that it uses For Each loops to hide all sheets except the Explanation worksheet.

```
Private Sub Workbook_Open()
    Dim ws As Worksheet, cht As Chart
    With wsExplanation
        .Activate
        .Range("F4").Select
    End With
    For Each ws In ThisWorkbook.Worksheets
        If ws.CodeName <> "wsExplanation" Then ws.Visible = False
    Next
```

---

[2] It also contains the one other user form, frmSolver, that simply displays a message about possible Solver problems when the workbook is opened. This is included in all of the Solver applications in the remainder of the book, although users with Excel 2010 or later versions won't see it.

Figure 20.14 Model Worksheet

	A	B	C	D	E	F	G
1	**Oil blending model**						
2							
3	Purchase prices per gallon of crude			Sale price per barrel of gasoline			
4	Crude 1	$55		Gas 1	Gas 2	Gas 3	
5	Crude 2	$35		$70	$60	$75	
6	Crude 3	$25					
7							
8	Cost to transform one barrel of crude into one barrel of gasoline						
9		$5					
10							
11	Requirements for gasolines						
12		Gas 1	Gas 2	Gas 3			
13	Minimum octane	11	10	9			
14	Maximum sulfur	1%	3%	1%			
15							
16	Octane ratings			Sulfur content			
17	Crude 1	12		Crude 1	1.0%		
18	Crude 2	10		Crude 2	0.5%		
19	Crude 3	8		Crude 3	3.0%		
20							
21	Purchase/production plan						
22		Gas 1	Gas 2	Gas 3	Total purchased		Max Available
23	Crude 1	1500.00	0.00	0.00	1500	<=	5000
24	Crude 2	1500.00	2000.00	800.00	4300	<=	5000
25	Crude 3	0.00	0.00	200.00	200	<=	5000
26							
27	Demand for gasolines						
28		Gas 1	Gas 2	Gas 3			
29	Amount produced	3000	2000	1000			
30		<=	<=	<=			
31	Maximum Demand	3000	2000	1000			
32							
33	Constraint on total production						
34		Total produced		Max Capacity			
35		6000	<=	15000			
36							
37	Octane constraints	Gas 1	Gas 2	Gas 3			
38	Actual total octane	33000	20000	9600			
39		>=	>=	>=			
40	Required	33000	20000	9000			
41							
42	Sulfur constraints	Gas 1	Gas 2	Gas 3			
43	Actual total sulfur	22.5	10	10			
44		<=	<=	<=			
45	Required	30	60	10			
46							
47	Purchase costs	$238,000					
48	Production costs	$30,000					
49	Sales revenue	$405,000					
50							
51	Profit	$137,000					

```
        For Each cht In ThisWorkbook.Charts
            cht.Visible = False
        Next
        If Not (Application.Version = "15.0" Or Application.Version = "14.0") Then
        frmSolver.Show
    End Sub
```

Figure 20.15   Project Explorer Window

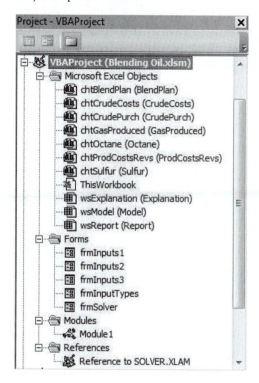

20.6 The User Forms

frmInputTypes

The design of frmInputTypes is shown in Figure 20.16. It contains the usual OK and Cancel buttons, an explanation label, and three check boxes named chkInputs1, chkInputs2, and chkInputs3. The design of the user forms for this application is completely straightforward. The text boxes must be positioned and named, the labels must be positioned and captioned, and so on—straightforward operations.

The event handlers for this user form are listed below. The Initialize sub checks each of the check boxes by default. The ShowInputTypesDialog function captures the user's entries in the check boxes in the Boolean variables blnInputs1, blnInputs2, and blnInputs3.

Figure 20.16 Design of frmInputTypes

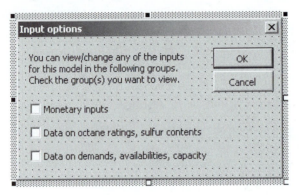

```
Private cancel As Boolean

Public Function ShowInputTypesDialog(inputType1 As Boolean, _
        inputType2 As Boolean, inputType3 As Boolean) As Boolean
    Call Initialize
    Me.Show
    If Not cancel Then
        inputType1 = chkInputs1.Value
        inputType2 = chkInputs2.Value
        inputType3 = chkInputs3.Value
    End If
    ShowInputTypesDialog = Not cancel
    Unload Me
End Function

Private Sub Initialize()
    ' Have all boxes checked initially.
    chkInputs1.Value = True
    chkInputs2.Value = True
    chkInputs3.Value = True
End Sub

Private Sub cmdOK_Click()
    Me.Hide
    cancel = False
End Sub

Private Sub cmdCancel_Click()
    Me.Hide
    cancel = True
End Sub

Private Sub UserForm_QueryClose(cancel As Integer, CloseMode As Integer)
    If CloseMode = vbFormControlMenu Then cmdCancel_Click
End Sub
```

frmInputs1

The design of frmInputs1 is shown in Figure 20.17. It contains OK and Cancel buttons, an explanation label, two frames for grouping inputs, and seven text boxes and corresponding labels. The three text boxes in the Unit crude costs group are named txtCrude1, txtCrude2, and txtCrude3. The three text boxes in the Unit gas prices group are named txtGas1, txtGas2, and txtGas3. Finally, the production cost text box is named txtProdCost.

The Initialize sub captures the values in the Model worksheet (from a previous run, if any) and enters them in the text boxes, and then the ShowInputs1Dialog function takes the user's choices and places them back in the Model worksheet. Note that it uses the Val function to convert a string (which is always the result from a text box) to a numeric value (which is required in the worksheet). Otherwise, arithmetic operations couldn't be performed on these cells in the worksheet. The Valid function performs some error checking to ensure that the user's inputs are numeric and positive.

Figure 20.17 Design of frmInputs1

```
Private cancel As Boolean

Public Function ShowInputs1Dialog() As Boolean
    Call Initialize
    Me.Show
    If Not cancel Then
        ' Enter the user inputs in the (hidden) Model sheet.
        With wsModel.Range("PurchCosts")
            .Cells(1).Value = Val(txtCrude1.Text)
            .Cells(2).Value = Val(txtCrude2.Text)
            .Cells(3).Value = Val(txtCrude3.Text)
        End With
        With wsModel.Range("SellPrices")
            .Cells(1).Value = Val(txtGas1.Text)
            .Cells(2).Value = Val(txtGas2.Text)
            .Cells(3).Value = Val(txtGas3.Text)
```

```
            End With
            wsModel.Range("ProdCost").Value = Val(txtProdCost.Text)
        End If
        ShowInputs1Dialog = Not cancel
        Unload Me
End Function


Private Sub Initialize()
    ' Initialize with the current values in the (hidden) Model sheet.
    With wsModel.Range("PurchCosts")
        txtCrude1.Text = .Cells(1).Value
        txtCrude2.Text = .Cells(2).Value
        txtCrude3.Text = .Cells(3).Value
    End With
    With wsModel.Range("SellPrices")
        txtGas1.Text = .Cells(1).Value
        txtGas2.Text = .Cells(2).Value
        txtGas3.Text = .Cells(3).Value
    End With
    txtProdCost.Text = wsModel.Range("ProdCost").Value
End Sub


Private Function Valid() As Boolean
    Dim ctl As Control
    Valid = True
    ' Check that the text boxes have positive numeric values.
    For Each ctl In Me.Controls
        If TypeName(ctl) = "TextBox" Then
            If ctl.Value = "" Or Not IsNumeric(ctl) Then
                Valid = False
                MsgBox "Enter positive numeric values in all boxes.", _
                    vbInformation, "Invalid entry"
                ctl.SetFocus
                Exit Function
            End If
            If ctl.Value < 0 Then
                Valid = False
                MsgBox "Enter positive numeric values in all boxes.", _
                    vbInformation, "Invalid entry"
                ctl.SetFocus
                Exit Function
            End If
        End If
    Next
End Function


Private Sub cmdOK_Click()
    If Valid Then Me.Hide
    cancel = False
End Sub


Private Sub cmdCancel_Click()
    Me.Hide
    cancel = True
End Sub


Private Sub UserForm_QueryClose(cancel As Integer, CloseMode As Integer)
    If CloseMode = vbFormControlMenu Then cmdCancel_Click
End Sub
```

frmInputs2 and frmInputs3

The other two input forms, frmInputs2 and frmInputs3, shown in Figures 20.4 and 20.5, are very similar. For example, frmInputs2 contains OK and Cancel buttons, an explanation label, four frames for grouping the inputs, and 12 text boxes and corresponding labels. The code behind these two forms is very similar to the frmInputs1 code, so it is not listed here.

20.7 The Module

In most applications, the VBA code in the module does the majority of the work. However, this is not the case here. There is a MainBlending module that "shows" the appropriate forms, which capture the user's inputs. Therefore, all the Main-Blending sub needs to do is show the forms and then run Solver. (Note that it must first unhide the Model worksheet. Solver cannot be run on a model in a hidden sheet.) Other than this, the module contains only navigational subs (not shown here). These are attached to the buttons on the Report worksheet and the various chart sheets.

MainBlending Code

```
Sub MainBlending()
    ' This sub runs when the user clicks on the button on the Explanation sheet.
    Dim inputType1 As Boolean, inputType2 As Boolean, inputType3 As Boolean
    Dim solverStatus As Integer

    ' Find which types of inputs the user wants to view/change.
    If frmInputTypes.ShowInputTypesDialog(inputType1, inputType2, inputType3) Then

        ' Show the input forms the user has requested.
        ' Exit if the user cancels from any of them.
        If inputType1 Then
            If Not frmInputs1.ShowInputs1Dialog Then Exit Sub
        End If
        If inputType2 Then
            If Not frmInputs2.ShowInputs2Dialog Then Exit Sub
        End If
        If inputType3 Then
            If Not frmInputs3.ShowInputs3Dialog Then Exit Sub
        End If

        Application.ScreenUpdating = False

        ' Unhide and activate the Model sheet, and run the Solver.
        With wsModel
            .Visible = True
            .Activate
        End With

        ' Call Solver and check for no feasible solutions.
        solverStatus = SolverSolve(UserFinish:=True)
        If solverStatus = 5 Then
```

```
                ' There are no feasible solutions, so report this and quit.
                MsgBox "There is no feasible solution to the problem with these " _
                    & "inputs. Try again with different inputs.", _
                    vbInformation, "Not feasible"
                wsModel.Visible = False
                Call ViewExplanation

        Else
                ' There is a solution, so report it in the Report sheet.
                wsModel.Visible = False
                With wsReport
                    .Visible = True
                    .Activate
                    .Range("A1").Select
                End With
        End If

            Application.ScreenUpdating = True
        End If
    End Sub
```

20.8   Summary

This application is a great example of the functionality you can achieve with very little VBA code. Although I don't necessarily encourage you to create all of the applications, starting from scratch, in the remaining chapters, I urge you to try developing this blending application on your own. There are at least two ways you can proceed. First, you can open a new, blank workbook and create the *entire* application—model, user forms, and code. Alternatively, you can make a copy of the **Blending Oil.xlsm** file. Then you can delete the user forms and the module from your copy and recreate them on your own, using the explanations in this chapter as a guide. In either case, you will find that there are no *difficult* steps in this application; there are just a lot of relatively simple steps. In fact, you will find that many of these steps are quite repetitive. Therefore, you should look for any possible shortcuts, such as copying and pasting, to reduce the development time.

EXERCISES

1. All of the charts in this application are types of three-dimensional column charts. Change the application so that they are different chart types. (You can decide which you prefer.) Do you need to rewrite any of the VBA code?

2. Continuing Exercise 1, suppose you want to give the *user* the choice of chart types. For example, suppose you want to give the user two choices: the current chart types or some other chart type. (You can choose the other type.) Change the application to allow this choice. Now you *will* have to add some new VBA code, along with another user form. However, you should never need to create any charts from scratch with VBA. You only need to modify existing charts.

3. Suppose there is another chemical additive—let's call it Excron—that is part of each crude oil. You know what percentage of each crude oil is Excron, and you know the *minimum* percentages of each gasoline product that must be Excron. That is, all of these percentages are inputs. Change the optimization model and the application to take Excron into account. (Expand the appropriate user form to capture the Excron inputs, and make all other necessary modifications.)

4. (More difficult) Changing the size of a model like this one can be quite tedious. Try the following to see what is involved. Assume that the model can have either two or three crude oils, and it can have either two or three gasoline products. First, create a new user form called frmSize to capture these size options. Then modify the rest of the application accordingly. (*Hints:* You can change the **Visible** property of controls on the user forms to hide them or unhide them, depending on whether they are needed. With VBA you can change the range names of the parts of the Model worksheet that will appear in the Solver dialog box. As discussed in Chapter 17, this will make all Solver setups *look* the same, but you will have to do a **SolverReset** and then respecify all settings because of changes in the physical locations of the ranges. Finally, you might want to remove the formatting from the Report worksheet—make it less fancy—to make modifications easier.)

21

A Product Mix Application

21.1 Introduction

This application is an example of the product mix model. It is a prototype model often used to introduce linear programming. The products illustrated here are custom-made pieces of wood furniture that require labor hours from senior and junior woodworkers, machine hours, and wood (measured in board feet). There are constraints on the availability of the resources. For some of the products, there are also constraints on the minimum and/or maximum production levels. The objective is to maximize profit: revenues minus costs.

The linear programming model in this application is, if anything, simpler than the blending model in the previous chapter. However, the VBA requirements are considerably more extensive. The model is no longer fixed in size because the user is allowed to include any number of products in the potential product mix. This means, for example, that the number of decision variable cells in the optimization model can change from one run to another. From a decision support point of view, this is much more realistic, but it also complicates the VBA. Only a limited part of the optimization model can be set up at design time. The rest must be developed at run time with VBA code.

New Learning Objectives: VBA

- To see how VBA can be used to get the data inputs from one worksheet and use them to build an optimization model in another worksheet.
- To illustrate how VBA can be used to develop an optimization model of varying size.
- To illustrate how a VBA program that must perform many tasks can be divided into several relatively small subroutines.
- To better understand how VBA can be used to enter formulas into cells.

New Learning Objectives: Non-VBA

- To develop an understanding of a prototype linear programming model: the product mix model.

21.2 Functionality of the Application

The application provides the following functionality:

1. It provides a database (on the Data worksheet) of all required inputs for the model. Before running the application, the user can change these inputs. In fact, it is possible to manually add or delete products and resources in the list. The VBA code will always capture the current data in the Data worksheet when it develops and solves the optimization model in the Model worksheet.
2. Given the set of all products listed in the Data worksheet, the user can select the products that will be included in the product mix model. If a product is not selected, it will not even be considered in the product mix.
3. Once the user selects the products to be included in the model, a product mix model is developed in the Model worksheet, and Solver is invoked to find the optimal product mix. The key results are then listed in a Report worksheet.

21.3 Running the Application

The application is in the file **Product Mix.xlsm**. When this file is opened, the explanation in Figure 21.1 appears.

Figure 21.1   Explanation Worksheet

Product Mix Application

Run the application

The Woodworks Company manufactures and sells custom-made furniture. The products, their unit prices, their unit resource usages, and their minimum and maximum production quantities for the next month appear on the data sheet. This sheet also lists the resources, their availabilities for the next month, and their unit costs. The problem is to find the mix of products that maximizes profit.

This application allows the user to choose which of the potential products to include in the product mix. (If a product is not chosen, it won't even be considered for the optimal product mix.) The product mix model is then formulated on a Model sheet, it is solved with Solver, and a report describing the optimal product mix is presented on a Report sheet.

The application searches the Data sheet for all product and resource data. Therefore, the user can add products and/or resources to this sheet, along with the corresponding data, and the application will include these new entries when it runs.

Figure 21.2 Data for the Products

	A	B	C	D	E	F	G	H	I	J	K
3	Data on products: unit price, resources required per unit, minimum and maximum units										
4	Product code	Description	UnitPrice	UnitCost	MinUnits	MaxUnits	SrLaborHrs	JrLaborHrs	MachineHrs	OakFt	CherryFt
5	1243	Oak end table	$190	$130	20	40	0.5	1.3	0.4	2.8	0
6	2243	Cherry end table	$203	$146		30	0.7	1.2	0.4	0	2.8
7	1456	Oak rocking chair	$371	$277	5	20	2.1	2.9	1.2	5.2	0
8	2456	Cherry rocking chair	$407	$308	5	15	2.5	2.7	1.2	0	5.2
9	1372	Oak coffee table	$238	$167	10	30	1.3	1.7	0.6	3.2	0
10	2372	Cherry coffee table	$259	$185		10	1.5	1.5	0.6	0	3.2
11	1531	Oak dining table	$837	$648			1.9	3.2	1.7	15.6	0
12	2531	Cherry dining table	$964	$724		10	2.1	2.8	1.6	0	15.6
13	1635	Oak desk	$1,084	$841	5		4.3	5.8	3.2	18.2	0
14	2635	Cherry desk	$1,214	$938	5		4.5	5.6	3.5	0	18.2
15	1367	Oak bookshelves	$401	$315	15	30	1.8	2.5	2.1	6.2	0
16	2367	Cherry bookshelves	$455	$349		40	1.9	2.5	2.2	0	6.2

Figure 21.3 Data for the Resources

	M	N	O
3	Data on resources		
4	Resource	UnitCost	Availability
5	SrLaborHrs	$20	263
6	JrLaborHrs	$12	450
7	MachineHrs	$15	225
8	OakFt	$35	488
9	CherryFt	$40	638

The data for the products and the data for the resources appear in Figures 21.2 and 21.3. The unit costs in column D of Figure 21.2 are actually calculated from formulas: Each is a sum of products of the unit usages in a product row of Figure 21.2 and the unit resource costs in column N of Figure 21.3. All other data are given values. The MinUnits and MaxUnits in columns E and F of Figure 21.2 prescribe lower and upper limits on the quantities of the products that can be produced. If a MinUnits value is blank, it is replaced by 0 in the model. If a MaxUnits value is blank, it is replaced by a suitably large value in the model (so that there is effectively no upper limit).

When the user clicks the button in Figure 21.1, the dialog box in Figure 21.4 appears. This allows the user to select the products that will be included in the model.

Once the products have been selected, VBA is used to develop the Model worksheet. Any results on this sheet from a previous run are cleared. Then a new model is developed, and Solver is set up and run. Finally, VBA unhides the Report worksheet, clears any results from a previous run, and reports the new solution. Typical Model and Report worksheets appear in Figures 21.5 and 21.6. I will not spell out the formulas in the Model sheet; it is a straightforward linear programming model. (To see these formulas, open the file, run the application once, unhide the Model sheet, and examine its formulas.)

Figure 21.4   Dialog Box for Selecting Products in the Model

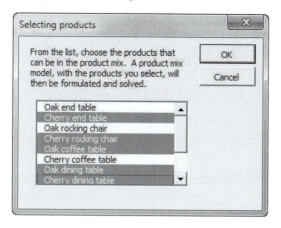

Figure 21.5   Model Worksheet

	A	B	C	D	E	F	G	H	I	J	K	L	M	N
3	**Product mix**													
4	Product code	2243	2456	1372	1531	2531								
5	Min	0	5	10	0	0								
6		<=	<=	<=	<=	<=								
7	Produced	30	15	30	25	10								
8		<=	<=	<=	<=	<=								
9	Max	30	15	30	31	10								
10														
11	UnitPrice	$203.00	$407.00	$238.00	$837.00	$964.00								
12	UnitCost	$146.40	$308.40	$167.40	$647.90	$723.60								
13	UnitProfit	$56.60	$98.60	$70.60	$189.10	$240.40								
14														
15	**Resource usage**					**Monetary summary**			**Resources used per unit of products**					
16	Resource	Used		Available		Total revenue	$49,900		Resource/Product code	2243	2456	1372	1531	2531
17	SrLaborHrs	166.0	<=	263.0		Total cost	$37,474		SrLaborHrs	0.7	2.5	1.3	1.9	2.1
18	JrLaborHrs	235.5	<=	450.0		Total profit	$12,427		JrLaborHrs	1.2	2.7	1.7	3.2	2.8
19	MachineHrs	106.5	<=	225.0					MachineHrs	0.4	1.2	0.6	1.7	1.6
20	OakFt	486.0	<=	488.0					OakFt	0	0	3.2	15.6	0
21	CherryFt	318.0	<=	638.0					CherryFt	2.8	5.2	0	0	15.6

Figure 21.6   Report Worksheet

	A	B	C	D	E	F	G	H	I	J	K
1	**Optimal product mix**										
2											
3	**Monetary summary**										
4	Total revenue	$49,900									
5	Total cost	$37,474									
6	Total profit	$12,427									
7											
8	**Product data**							**Resource data**			
9	Product code	Description	Units produced	Revenue	Cost	Profit		Resource	Used	Available	Left over
10	2243	Cherry end table	30	$6,090	$4,392	$1,698		SrLaborHrs	166.0	263.0	97.0
11	2456	Cherry rocking chair	15	$6,105	$4,626	$1,479		JrLaborHrs	235.5	450.0	214.5
12	1372	Oak coffee table	30	$7,140	$5,022	$2,118		MachineHrs	106.5	225.0	118.5
13	1531	Oak dining table	25	$20,925	$16,198	$4,728		OakFt	486.0	488.0	2.0
14	2531	Cherry dining table	10	$9,640	$7,236	$2,404		CherryFt	318.0	638.0	320.0

Figure 21.7   Model Worksheet Template

	A	B	C	D	E	F	G	H	I	J	K
1	Model formulation										
2											
3	Product mix										
4	Product code										
5	Min										
6											
7	Produced										
8											
9	Max										
10											
11	UnitPrice										
12	UnitCost										
13	UnitProfit										
14											
15	Resource usage					Monetary summary			Resources used per unit of products		
16	Resource		Used		Available	Total revenue			Resource/Product code		
17						Total cost					
18						Total profit					
19											

Figure 21.8   Report Worksheet Template

	A	B	C	D	E	F	G	H	I	J	K
1	Optimal product mix										
2											
3	Monetary summary										
4	Total revenue										
5	Total cost										
6	Total profit										
7											
8	Product data							Resource data			
9	Product code	Description		Units produced	Revenue	Cost	Profit	Resource	Used	Available	Left over
10											

21.4   Setting Up the Excel Sheets

The Model and Report worksheets cannot be set up entirely at design time because the number of products and the number of resources could change, depending on the data entered in the Data worksheet and the user's choice of potential products from the user form. However, they can be set up partially. The templates for the Model and Report worksheets appear in Figures 21.7 and 21.8.

21.5   Getting Started with the VBA

This application requires a user form named frmProducts, a single module, and a reference to Solver. Once these items are added, the Project Explorer window will appear as in Figure 21.9.[1]

---

[1] It also contains the usual frmSolver that displays a message about possible Solver problems when the workbook is opened, but only users of pre-2010 versions of Excel will see this message.

Figure 21.9 Project Explorer Window

Workbook_Open Code

To guarantee that the Explanation worksheet appears when the file is opened, the following code is placed in the ThisWorkbook code window. It also hides the Model and Report worksheets, and it shows the Solver warning for pre-2010 versions of Excel.

```
Private Sub Workbook_Open()
    With wsExplanation
        .Activate
        .Range("F4").Select
    End With
    wsModel.Visible = False
    wsReport.Visible = False
    If Not (Application.Version = "15.0" Or Application.Version = "14.0") Then frmSolver.Show
End Sub
```

21.6 The User Form

The design of frmProducts is shown in Figure 21.10. It has the usual OK and Cancel buttons, a label for explanation at the top, and a list box named lbProduct. The MultiSelect property for this list box should be changed to option 2 in the Properties window (see Figure 21.11). This enables the user to select *multiple* products from the list, not just a single product.

Figure 21.10   frmProducts Design

Figure 21.11   MultiSelect Property of the List Box

Once the user form has been designed, the appropriate code can be written. The Initialize sub indicates how the form should be presented initially to the user. It fills the list box with the product array (which will have been populated by this time with code in the module), and it selects the first product as the default. (Remember once again that the Selected array for a multi-type list box is 0-based. The first item in the list has index 0, the second has index 1, and so on.) The ShowProductsDialog function captures the user's selections in a Boolean isSelected array (1-based).

```
Private cancel As Boolean
Public Function ShowProductsDialog(product() As String, nProducts As Integer, _
        isSelected() As Boolean) As Boolean
    Dim i As Integer ' product index, 0-based
    Call Initialize(product, nProducts)
    Me.Show
    If Not cancel Then
        With lbProducts
            For i = 1 To nProducts
                isSelected(i) = .Selected(i - 1)
            Next
        End With
    End If
    ShowProductsDialog = Not cancel
    Unload Me
End Function

Private Sub Initialize(product() As String, nProducts As Integer)
    ' Add the product descriptions to the list.
    Dim i As Integer
    For i = 1 To nProducts
        lbProducts.AddItem product(i)
    Next
    ' Select the first item.
    lbProducts.Selected(0) = True
End Sub

Private Sub cmdOK_Click()
    Me.Hide
    cancel = False
End Sub

Private Sub cmdCancel_Click()
    Me.Hide
    cancel = True
End Sub

Private Sub UserForm_QueryClose(cancel As Integer, CloseMode As Integer)
    If CloseMode = vbFormControlMenu Then cmdCancel_Click
End Sub
```

21.7 The Module

Most of the work is performed by the VBA code in the module. This code is listed below. The application uses a modular design, as described in Chapter 10. After declaring the module-level variables at the top, the MainProductMix sub calls several other subs in a logical order. Some of these subs call other subs. Again, the purpose of dividing the overall program into so many small subs is to make it more readable—and easier to debug.

Note how a number of constants have been set to various cell addresses. These refer to "anchor" cells in the Data, Model, and Report worksheets that will be used in the code. If these worksheets were ever modified in some way, such as inserting blank rows, these anchor addresses could easily be changed in the Const lines.

Option Statements and Module-Level Variables

```
Option Explicit

' Definition of module-level variables:
'    nProducts - number of products listed in Data sheet
'    nResources - number of resources listed in Data sheet
'    product() - array of product names
'    resource() - array of resource names
'    isSelected() - Boolean array that indicates which products are selected
'        from the user form

' These variables are declared as module-level variables (but not
' Public variables) to avoid a lot of argument-passing in this module.
' Because they aren't Public, they still have to be passed to the form.
Dim nProducts As Integer, nResources As Integer
Dim product() As String, resource() As String
Dim isSelected() As Boolean

' Anchor cell addresses (created as constants so they could easily be changed).
' Note that these are used instead of range names.

' Data sheet
Const ProdAnchor = "A4"
Const ResAnchor = "M4"

' Model sheet
Const ProdMixAnchor = "A3"
Const ResUseAnchor = "A16"
Const MonSummAnchor = "F15"
Const UnitUseAnchor = "I16"

' Report sheet
Const ProdRepAnchor = "A9"
Const ResRepAnchor = "H9"
```

MainProductMix Code

The MainProductMix sub is the control center. It calls all of the other subs that do the real work. The button on the Explanation worksheet (see Figure 21.1) has the MainProductMix macro assigned to it. Note the feasible argument of the RunSolver call. The RunSolver sub determines whether there are any feasible solutions, and it passes this information back to the MainProductMix sub. There is no point in creating a report if there are no feasible solutions.

```
Sub MainProductMix()
    ' This sub runs when the user clicks on the button on the Explanation sheet.
    Dim feasible As Boolean

    Call GetProducts
    Call GetResources
```

```
    ReDim isSelected(1 To nProducts)
    If frmProducts.ShowProductsDialog(product, nProducts, isSelected) Then
        Application.ScreenUpdating = False
        Call SetupModel
        Call RunSolver(feasible)
        If feasible Then Call CreateReport
    End If
End Sub
```

GetProducts, GetResources Code

The GetProducts and GetResources subs find the numbers of products and resources from the Data worksheet, redimension the product, resource, and isSelected arrays appropriately, and fill them with the product and resource names from the Data worksheet. Note how the "anchor" cells are used. Everything is offset relative to them. This occurs many times throughout the application.

```
Sub GetProducts()
    ' This sub finds the number of products and their corresponding data.
    With wsData.Range(ProdAnchor)
        nProducts = Range(.Offset(1, 0), .End(xlDown)).Count
        ReDim product(nProducts)
        ReDim isSelected(nProducts)
        Dim i As Integer ' product index
        For i = 1 To nProducts
            product(i) = .Offset(i, 1).Value
        Next
    End With
End Sub

Sub GetResources()
    ' This sub finds the number of resources and their corresponding data.
    With wsData.Range(ResAnchor)
        nResources = Range(.Offset(1, 0), .End(xlDown)).Count
        ReDim resource(nResources)
        Dim j As Integer ' resource index
        For j = 1 To nResources
            resource(j) = .Offset(j, 0).Value
        Next
    End With
End Sub
```

SetupModel Code

The SetupModel sub first unhides and activates the Model worksheet (which at this point is only a template or contains data from a previous run), and then it calls seven other subs to develop the optimization model.

```
Sub SetupModel()
    ' This sub develops the optimization model through a series of subroutines.
    With wsModel
        .Visible = True
        .Activate
```

```
    End With
    Call ClearOldModel
    Call EnterProductData
    Call EnterResourceData
    Call EnterUsageData
    Call CalcMaxProduction
    Call CalcResourceUsages
    Call CalcMonetaryValues
End Sub
```

ClearOldModel Code

The ClearOldModel sub clears data, if any, from a previous run to return the Model worksheet to its "template" form. Note that it uses the ClearContents method. This deletes all values but leaves old formatting in place. Again, note how the "anchor" cells are used with offsetting.

```
Sub ClearOldModel()
    ' This sub clears all of the old data, but not formatting,
    ' from any previous model.
    With wsModel.Range(ProdMixAnchor)
        Range(.Offset(1, 1), .Offset(10, 1).End(xlToRight)).ClearContents
    End With
    With wsModel.Range(ResUseAnchor)
        Range(.Offset(1, 0), .Offset(1, 0).End(xlDown).Offset(0, 3)).ClearContents
    End With
    With wsModel.Range(MonSummAnchor)
        Range(.Offset(1, 1), .Offset(3, 1)).ClearContents
    End With
    With wsModel.Range(UnitUseAnchor)
        Range(.Offset(0, 0), .End(xlDown).End(xlToRight)).ClearContents
        .Value = "Resource/Product code"
    End With
End Sub
```

EnterProductData Code

The EnterProductData sub enters data about the selected products in the Model worksheet. It also names a few ranges for later reference.

```
Sub EnterProductData()
    ' This sub enters the product data for all products selected in the
    ' Product Mix part of the Model sheet.
    Dim i1 As Integer ' product index, selected products only
    Dim i2 As Integer ' product index, all products
    Dim minVal As Single

    ' Enter data only for the selected products
    i1 = 0
    With wsModel.Range(ProdMixAnchor)
        For i2 = 1 To nProducts
            If isSelected(i2) Then
                i1 = i1 + 1
```

```
                    ' Enter product code.
                    .Offset(1, i1).Value = wsData.Range(ProdAnchor) _
                        .Offset(i2, 0).Value

                    ' Enter minimum production level.
                    ' (Enter 0 if one isn't given in the Data sheet).
                    If wsData.Range(ProdAnchor).Offset(i2, 4).Value = "" Then
                        minVal = 0
                    Else
                        minVal = wsData.Range(ProdAnchor).Offset(i2, 4).Value
                    End If
                    .Offset(2, i1).Value = minVal
                    ' Set the initial values of the decision variable cells to 0.
                    .Offset(4, i1).Value = 0

                    ' Enter labels to identify constraints.
                    .Offset(3, i1).Value = "<="
                    .Offset(5, i1).Value = "<="

                    ' Enter unit price and unit cost.
                    .Offset(8, i1).Value = wsData.Range(ProdAnchor) _
                        .Offset(i2, 2).Value
                    .Offset(9, i1).Value = wsData.Range(ProdAnchor) _
                        .Offset(i2, 3).Value

                    ' Calculate unit profit.
                    .Offset(10, i1).FormulaR1C1 = "=R[-2]C-R[-1]C"
                End If
            Next

        ' Name various ranges.
        Range(.Offset(2, 1), .Offset(2, 1).End(xlToRight)).Name = "Model!MinProd"
        Range(.Offset(4, 1), .Offset(4, 1).End(xlToRight)).Name = "Model!Produced"
        Range(.Offset(8, 1), .Offset(8, 1).End(xlToRight)).Name = "Model!UnitRev"
        Range(.Offset(9, 1), .Offset(9, 1).End(xlToRight)).Name = "Model!UnitCost"
        Range(.Offset(10, 1), .Offset(10, 1).End(xlToRight)).Name = "Model!UnitProfit"
    End With
End Sub
```

EnterResourceData Code

The EnterResourceData sub enters the resource names and availabilities in the Model worksheet and names a couple of ranges for later use.

```
Sub EnterResourceData()
    ' This sub enters the resources availabilities in the Resource
    ' Usage part of the Model sheet.
    Dim j As Integer ' resource index

    With wsModel.Range(ResUseAnchor)
        For j = 1 To nResources
            ' Enter name of resource.
            .Offset(j, 0).Value = resource(j)

            ' Enter label to identify constraint.
            .Offset(j, 2).Value = "<="
```

```
            ' Enter resource availability.
            .Offset(j, 3).Value = wsData.Range(ResAnchor).Offset(j, 2).Value
        Next

            ' Name resource ranges.
            Range(.Offset(1, 1), .Offset(nResources, 1)).Name = "Model!Used"
            Range(.Offset(1, 3), .Offset(nResources, 3)).Name = "Model!Available"
        End With
End Sub
```

EnterUsageData Code

The EnterUsageData sub enters the table of unit resource usages (how much of each resource is used by a unit of each product) in the Model worksheet.

```
Sub EnterUsageData()
    ' This sub enters the unit usages of resources for selected products
    ' in the resource usage part of the Model sheet.
    Dim i1 As Integer ' product index, selected products only
    Dim i2 As Integer ' product index, all products
    Dim j As Integer ' resource index

    With wsModel.Range(UnitUseAnchor)
        ' Enter resource names.
        For j = 1 To nResources
            .Offset(j, 0).Value = resource(j)
        Next

        ' Enter data only for selected products.
        i1 = 0
        For i2 = 1 To nProducts
            If isSelected(i2) Then
                i1 = i1 + 1

                ' Enter product code.
                .Offset(0, i1).Value = wsData.Range(ProdAnchor) _
                    .Offset(i2, 0).Value

                ' Enter unit usages of all resources used by this product.
                For j = 1 To nResources
                    .Offset(j, i1).Value = wsData.Range(ProdAnchor) _
                        .Offset(i2, 5 + j).Value
                Next
            End If
        Next
    End With
End Sub
```

CalcMaxProduction Code

The CalcMaxProduction sub finds the maximum limit on production for each selected product and enters it in the Model worksheet. If no explicit maximum limit is given for a product in the Data worksheet, a suitable maximum limit is calculated in this sub by seeing which of the resources would be most constraining if *all* of the resource were committed to this particular product.

```
Sub CalcMaxProduction()
    ' This sub calculates the max production levels for all selected products.
    Dim i1 As Integer ' product index, selected products only
    Dim i2 As Integer ' product index, all products
    Dim j As Integer ' resource index
    Dim maxVal As Single
    Dim unitUse As Single
    Dim ratio As Single

    ' Enter data only for selected products, where i1 is a counter for these.
    i1 = 0
    With wsModel.Range(ProdMixAnchor)
        For i2 = 1 To nProducts
            If isSelected(i2) Then
                i1 = i1 + 1
                If wsData.Range(ProdAnchor).Offset(i2, 5).Value = "" Then
                    ' No maximum production level was given, so find how much of
                    ' this product could be produced if all of the resources were
                    ' devoted to it, and use this as a maximum production level.
                    maxVal = 1000000
                    For j = 1 To nResources
                        unitUse = wsModel.Range(UnitUseAnchor).Offset(j, i1).Value
                        If unitUse > 0 Then
                            ratio = wsModel.Range("Available").Cells(j).Value / unitUse
                            If ratio < maxVal Then maxVal = ratio
                        End If
                    Next

                    ' Enter calculated maximum production level
                    ' (rounded down to nearest integer).
                    .Offset(6, i1).Value = Int(maxVal)

                Else
                    ' The maximum production level was given, so enter it.
                    .Offset(6, i1).Value = wsData.Range(ProdAnchor) _
                        .Offset(i2, 5).Value
                End If
            End If
        Next

        ' Name the range of maximum production levels.
        Range(.Offset(6, 1), .Offset(6, 1).End(xlToRight)).Name = "Model!MaxProd"
    End With
End Sub
```

CalcResourceUsages Code

The CalcResourceUsages sub calculates the amount of each resource used by the current product mix and enters it in the Model worksheet. Pay particular attention to the following two lines, which are inside the For loop on j.

```
unitUseAddress = Range(.Offset(j, 1), .Offset(j, 1).End(xlToRight)).Address
wsModel.Range("Used").Cells(j).Formula = "=Sumproduct(Produced," & unitUseAddress & ")"
```

The goal is to enter a formula such as = **SUMPRODUCT(Produced,J17: N17)** in a cell. (For example, if j = 1, this would be the formula in cell B17 for the model in Figure 21.5.) To do this, I find the address for the second argument of the SUMPRODUCT function from the first line and store it in the string variable unitUseAddress. Then I use string concatenation to build the formula in the second line. Entering formulas in cells with VBA can be tricky, and it often involves similar string concatenation to piece together a combination of literals and string variables.

```
Sub CalcResourceUsages()
    ' This sub calculates the resource usages with a Sumproduct function.
    ' Note how the address of the row of unit usages for resource i is found first,
    ' then used as part of the formula string.
    Dim j As Integer ' resource index
    Dim unitUseAddress As String
    With wsModel.Range(UnitUseAnchor)
        For j = 1 To nResources
            unitUseAddress = Range(.Offset(j, 1), .Offset(j, 1).End(xlToRight)).Address
            wsModel.Range("Used").Cells(j).Formula = _
                "=Sumproduct(Produced," & unitUseAddress & ")"
        Next
    End With
End Sub
```

CalcMonetaryValues Code

The CalcMonetaryValues sub uses Excel's SUMPRODUCT function to calculate the total revenue, total cost, and total profit from the current product mix. It also names the corresponding cells for later reference.

```
Sub CalcMonetaryValues()
    ' This sub calculates the summary monetary values.
    With wsModel.Range(MonSummAnchor)
        .Offset(1, 1).Formula = "=Sumproduct(Produced,UnitRev)"
        .Offset(2, 1).Formula = "=Sumproduct(Produced,UnitCost)"
        .Offset(3, 1).Formula = "=Sumproduct(Produced,UnitProfit)"

        ' Name the monetary cells.
        .Offset(1, 1).Name = "Model!TotRev"
        .Offset(2, 1).Name = "Model!TotCost"
        .Offset(3, 1).Name = "Model!TotProfit"
    End With
End Sub
```

RunSolver Code

The RunSolver sub sets up Solver and then runs it.[2] It checks whether there are no feasible solutions. (Remember from Chapter 17 that the numerical code for no feasible solutions in the SolverSolve function is 5.) If the model has no feasible

---

[2] Even though the Solver setup will always *look* the same—for example, it will always have the constraint Used<=Available—it must be reset and then set up from scratch each time the application is run. If this is not done and the *size* of the model is different from the previous run, the Solver settings will be interpreted incorrectly.

solutions, then the Model and Report worksheets are hidden, the Explanation worksheet is activated, an appropriate message is displayed, and the application is terminated. Note that this code imposes integer constraints on the decision variable cells. Of course, if you do not want to impose integer constraints, you can delete (or comment out) the appropriate line in this sub.

```
Sub RunSolver(feasible As Boolean)
    ' This sub sets up and runs Solver.
    Dim solverStatus As Integer

    ' Reset Solver settings, then set up Solver.
    SolverReset
    SolverOk SetCell:=wsModel.Range("TotProfit"), MaxMinVal:=1, _
        ByChange:=wsModel.Range("Produced"), Engine:=1

    ' Add constraints.
    SolverAdd CellRef:=wsModel.Range("Produced"), Relation:=3, _
        FormulaText:=wsModel.Range("MinProd").Address
    SolverAdd CellRef:=wsModel.Range("Produced"), Relation:=1, _
        FormulaText:=wsModel.Range("MaxProd").Address
    SolverAdd CellRef:=wsModel.Range("Used"), Relation:=1, _
        FormulaText:=wsModel.Range("Available").Address

    ' Comment out the next line if you don't want integer constraints on production.
    SolverAdd CellRef:=wsModel.Range("Produced"), Relation:=4
    SolverOptions AssumeNonNeg:=True

    ' Run Solver and check for infeasibility.
    solverStatus = SolverSolve(UserFinish:=True)
    If solverStatus = 5 Then
        ' There is no feasible solution, so report this, tidy up, and quit.
        MsgBox "This model has no feasible solution. Change the data " _
            & "in the Data sheet and try running it again.", _
            vbInformation, "No feasible solution"
        With wsExplanation
            .Activate
            .Range("A1").Select
        End With
        wsModel.Visible = False
        wsReport.Visible = False
        feasible = False
    Else
        feasible = True
    End If
End Sub
```

CreateReport Code

The CreateReport sub first unhides and activates the Report worksheet (which at this point is only a template or contains results from a previous run). It then clears any previous results and transfers the important results from the Model worksheet to the appropriate places in the Report worksheet through a series of three short subs.

```
Sub CreateReport()
    ' This sub fills in the Report sheet, mostly by transferring the
    ' results from the Model sheet.
```

```
            ' Hide Model sheet.
            wsModel.Visible = False

            ' Unhide and activate Report sheet.
            With wsReport
                .Visible = True
                .Activate

                ' Enter results in three steps.
                Call EnterMonetaryResults
                Call EnterProductResults
                Call EnterResourceResults
                ' Make sure columns B and H are wide enough, then select cell A1.
                .Columns("B:B").Columns.AutoFit
                .Columns("H:H").Columns.AutoFit
                .Range("A1").Select
            End With
        End Sub
```

EnterMonetaryResults, EnterProductResults, and EnterResourceResults Code

These three short subs do exactly what their names imply: They transfer the key results from the Model worksheet to the Report worksheet.

```
Sub EnterMonetaryResults()
    ' This sub transfers the total revenue, total cost, and total profit.
    Dim i As Integer
    With wsReport.Range("B3")
        For i = 1 To 3
            .Offset(i, 0).Value = wsModel.Range(MonSummAnchor).Offset(i, 1).Value
        Next
    End With
End Sub
```

In addition to transferring the production quantities to the Report worksheet, the EnterProductResults sub also performs simple calculations to report the revenue, cost, and profit for each product individually.

```
Sub EnterProductResults()
    ' This sub transfers results for the products in the optimal product mix.
    Dim i1 As Integer ' product index, selected products only
    Dim i2 As Integer ' product index, all products

    With wsReport.Range(ProdRepAnchor)
        ' Clear old data (if any).
        Range(.Offset(1, 0), .Offset(1, 0).End(xlDown).End(xlToRight)) _
            .ClearContents

        ' Enter results for selected products only, where i1 is a counter for these.
        i1 = 0
        For i2 = 1 To nProducts
```

```
        If isSelected(i2) Then
            i1 = i1 + 1

            ' Enter product code, description, and number of units produced.
            .Offset(i1, 0).Value = wsData.Range(ProdAnchor).Offset(i2, 0).Value
            .Offset(i1, 1).Value = wsData.Range(ProdAnchor).Offset(i2, 1).Value
            .Offset(i1, 2).Value = wsModel.Range("Produced").Cells(i1).Value

            ' Calculate revenue, cost, and profit for the product.
            .Offset(i1, 3).Value = wsModel.Range("Produced").Cells(i1).Value * _
                wsModel.Range("UnitRev").Cells(i1).Value
            .Offset(i1, 4).Value = wsModel.Range("Produced").Cells(i1).Value * _
                wsModel.Range("UnitCost").Cells(i1).Value
            .Offset(i1, 5).Value = wsModel.Range("Produced").Cells(i1).Value * _
                wsModel.Range("UnitProfit").Cells(i1).Value
        End If
    Next
    End With
End Sub
```

In addition to transferring the resource usages and availabilities to the Report sheet, the EnterResourceResults sub also calculates the amount of each resource left over.

```
Sub EnterResourceResults()
    ' This sub transfers results about resource usage.
    Dim j As Integer ' resource index

    With wsReport.Range(ResRepAnchor)
        ' Clear old data (if any).
        Range(.Offset(1, 0), .Offset(1, 0).End(xlDown).End(xlToRight)).ClearContents
        For j = 1 To nResources

            ' Enter resource name, amount used, and amount available.
            .Offset(j, 0).Value = wsData.Range(ResAnchor).Offset(j, 0).Value
            .Offset(j, 1).Value = wsModel.Range("Used").Cells(j).Value
            .Offset(j, 2).Value = wsModel.Range("Available").Cells(j).Value

            ' Calculate amount left over.
            .Offset(j, 3).FormulaR1C1 = "=RC[-1]-RC[-2]"
        Next
    End With
End Sub
```

21.8 Summary

I promised in the introduction that this application is considerably more complex from a VBA point of view than the previous chapter's blending application. Although most of it involves Excel manipulations that are easy to do manually, a significant amount of programming is required to perform these same operations with VBA. An entire optimization model must be developed "on the fly" at run time. You can learn a lot of Excel VBA by carefully studying the code in this application. Better yet, open the file, split the screen so that you can see the Excel worksheets on one side and the VBA code on the other, step through the program with the F8 key, and keep watches on a few key variables. This can be *very* instructive. Finally, pay particular attention to how the overall program has been structured as a series of fairly small subs. This, taken together with a liberal dose of comments, makes the program much easier to read, understand, and debug.

EXERCISES

1. The application will work with *any* number of products in the Data worksheet, provided the data are entered appropriately. Convince yourself of this by adding a few more products to the section shown in Figure 21.2 and then rerunning the application.

2. Continuing the previous exercise, the application will also work for any number of resources, provided that you make space for them in the sections shown in Figures 21.2 and 21.3. Convince yourself of this by adding a new resource (glue, for example). What changes do you have to make to the overall file?

3. As the previous exercise illustrates, it might be inconvenient (and confusing) to require the user to insert new columns if more resources are added. I originally thought of putting the resource data in Figure 21.3 *below*, not to the right of, the product data in Figure 21.2, but this could also cause a problem if more products were added. (Then the user might need to insert extra rows.) Try the following alternative approach. Create *two* data worksheets, one for the product data in Figure 21.2, called Product Data, and one for the resource data in Figure 21.3, called Resource Data. Transfer the current data to these two worksheets, and make any necessary changes to the application. Now users will never have to insert any new rows or columns. Do you believe this new design has any drawbacks (from a user's, not a programmer's) point of view? Which design do you like best?

4. Change the application so that the user has no choice of the potential products in the product mix. That is, all products listed in the Data worksheet will be in the product mix model, and the user form in Figure 21.4 will no longer be necessary. However, the application should still be written to adapt to any number of products that might be listed in the Data worksheet.

5. Continuing the previous exercise, continue to assume that all products in the Data worksheet are potential products in the product mix. However, the company now wants, in addition to the current Report worksheet, a second report worksheet that shows how the optimal profit changes as the availability of all resources increases. Specifically, it should show a table and a corresponding chart, such as in Figure 21.12, on a Sensitivity Report worksheet. This table shows, for example, that when all of the resource availabilities increase by 30%, the new optimal profit is $23,392. Of course, your data might differ, depending on which products are on your Data worksheet. *(Hint:* Do as much as you can at design time. Then write VBA code to handle any tasks that must take place at run time.)

Figure 21.12   Sensitivity Analysis for Exercise 5

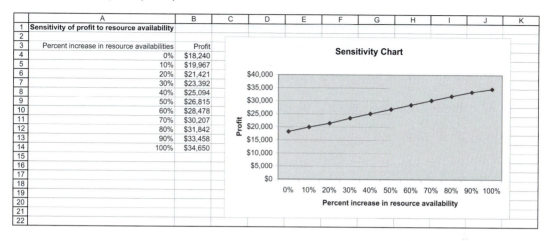

	A	B	C	D	E	F	G	H	I	J	K
1	Sensitivity of profit to resource availability										
2											
3	Percent increase in resource availabilities	Profit									
4	0%	$18,240									
5	10%	$19,967									
6	20%	$21,421									
7	30%	$23,392									
8	40%	$25,094									
9	50%	$26,815									
10	60%	$28,478									
11	70%	$30,207									
12	80%	$31,842									
13	90%	$33,458									
14	100%	$34,650									
15											
16											
17											
18											
19											
20											
21											
22											

Figure 21.13   Chart of Optimal Production Levels for Exercise 6

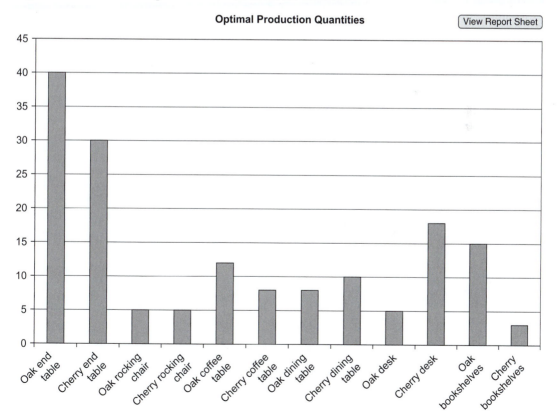

6. This application currently has no charts; it currently displays the outputs in tabular form only. Change the application so that it also displays a column chart (on a separate chart sheet) similar to the one in Figure 21.13, showing the amounts of the various products produced. As part of your changes, create buttons on the Report worksheet and the chart sheet, and write navigational subs to attach to them to allow the user to go back and forth easily. (*Hint:* Create the chart with Excel's chart tools only, not VBA, using representative data from the Report worksheet to populate it at design time. Then write VBA code to modify it appropriately at run time.)

22

A Worker Scheduling Application

22.1 Introduction

This application is based on a model for scheduling workers. A company needs to schedule its workers to meet daily requirements for a 7-day week, and each worker must work 5 days per week. Some of the workers can have nonconsecutive days off. For example, a worker could be assigned to work Monday, Wednesday, Thursday, Friday, and Sunday. This worker's 2 days off, Tuesday and Saturday, are nonconsecutive. However, there is a constraint that no more than a certain percentage of all workers can be assigned to nonconsecutive days-off shifts, where this maximum percentage is an input to the model. The objective is to minimize the weekly payroll, subject to meeting daily requirements, where the hourly wage rate on weekdays can differ from the wage rate on weekends.

New Learning Objectives: VBA

- To see how VBA can be used to conduct a sensitivity analysis for an optimization model.

New Learning Objectives: Non-VBA

- To learn how employee scheduling can be performed with an optimization model and how a sensitivity analysis can be performed on a key input parameter.

22.2 Functionality of the Application

This application provides the following functionality:

1. It allows a user to view and change the following inputs: daily requirements, weekday and weekend wage rates, and maximum percentage of nonconsecutive days off. For these given inputs, it finds the optimal solution to the model and reports it in a user-friendly form.
2. For given daily requirements and wage rates, it performs a sensitivity analysis on the maximum percentage of nonconsecutive days off and displays the results graphically.

22.3 Running the Application

The application is in the file **Worker Scheduling.xlsm**. When this file is opened, the explanation and button in Figure 22.1 appear. By clicking the button, the user can view and change the inputs in Figure 22.2. (The values shown are from the previous

Figure 22.1 Explanation Worksheet

Scheduling Workers

Run the application

The purpose of this application is to determine an optimal schedule for workers. All workers must work 5 days out of every 7-day week, and their 2 days off can be either consecutive or nonconsecutive. However, there is a constraint (an upper limit) on the percentage of workers who can have nonconsecutive days off. The model also allows the weekday wage rate to be different from the weekend rate. The objective is to meet given daily requirements at minimal weekly payroll cost.

The application allows you to view/change the inputs (daily requirements, hourly wage rates for weekdays and weekends, and maximum percentage of nonconsecutive days off) and then optimize the model with these inputs. Then you can perform a sensitivity analysis, with this maximum percentage nonconsecutive as the input varied, in which case the results are shown in graphical form.

Figure 22.2 Daily Requirements Dialog Box

Model inputs

Note that if there were values from a previous version of the model, these are shown. Feel free to change any of them.

OK

Cancel

Enter the required number of workers for each day of the week.

Monday	20	Friday	25
Tuesday	15	Saturday	15
Wednesday	25	Sunday	10
Thursday	20		

Enter the hourly wage rates for weekdays and weekend.

Weekday rate: 8

Weekend rate: 12

Enter the maximum percentage of workers that can be assigned nonconsecutive days off (e.g., enter .30 for 30%).

Max nonconsecutive pct: 1

Figure 22.3 Report of Optimal Solution

	A	B	C	D	E	F	G	H	I	J
1	Report of optimal solution									
2										
3	Weekly costs			Worker availabilities				Number of workers:		
4	Weekday	$6,720		Day	Available	Required		With consecutive days off		7
5	Weekend	$2,400		Mon	20	20		With nonconsecutive days off		19
6	Total	$9,120		Tue	15	15		Total		26
7				Wed	25	25				
8	Optimal assignments (positive assignments only)			Thu	20	20				
9	Days off	Number assigned		Fri	25	25				
10	Mon, Sun	6		Sat	15	15				
11	Tue, Sat	10		Sun	10	10				
12	Tue, Sun	1								
13	Wed, Sun	1								
14	Thu, Sun	6		Return to Explanation Sheet			Perform Sensitivity			
15	Fri, Sun	1								
16	Sat, Sun	1								

run, if any.) When the OK button is clicked, the user's inputs are placed in the appropriate range of the Model worksheet (see Figure 22.5 later in the chapter).

Once these inputs are entered and the user clicks OK, Solver is invoked and the optimal solution is reported in the Report worksheet, as shown in Figure 22.3.

If the user then clicks the Perform Sensitivity button, Solver is invoked several times, once for each maximum nonconsecutive percentage from 0% to 100% in increments of 10%, and important aspects of the optimal solutions appear graphically, as shown in Figure 22.4 Specifically, for each maximum percentage of

Figure 22.4 Results of Sensitivity Analysis

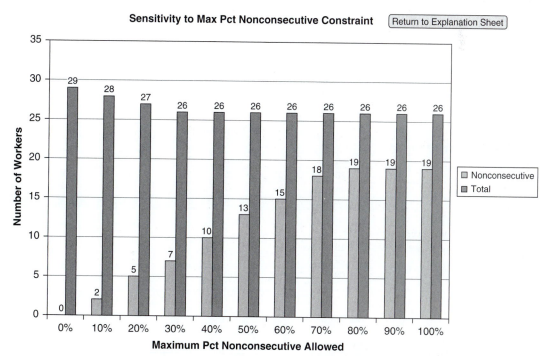

nonconsecutive days off, the report shows the total number of workers required and the number of these who are assigned nonconsecutive days off.

All of these results are based on the prebuilt model in the Model worksheet, shown in Figure 22.5. (Although the formulas for this model are reasonably

Figure 22.5   Scheduling Model

	A	B	C	D	E	F	G	H
1	Worker scheduling problem							
2								
3	Maximum percent with nonconsecutive days off					Hourly wage rates		
4		100%				Weekday	$8.00	
5						Weekend	$12.00	
6	Assignment of workers to days off pairs							
7	Days off	Consecutive	Assignments					
8	Mon, Tue	1	0					
9	Mon, Wed	0	0					
10	Mon, Thu	0	0					
11	Mon, Fri	0	0					
12	Mon, Sat	0	0					
13	Mon, Sun	1	6					
14	Tue, Wed	1	0					
15	Tue, Thu	0	0					
16	Tue, Fri	0	0					
17	Tue, Sat	0	10					
18	Tue, Sun	0	1					
19	Wed, Thu	1	0					
20	Wed, Fri	0	0					
21	Wed, Sat	0	0					
22	Wed, Sun	0	1					
23	Thu, Fri	1	0					
24	Thu, Sat	0	0					
25	Thu, Sun	0	6					
26	Fri, Sat	1	0					
27	Fri, Sun	0	1					
28	Sat, Sun	1	1					
29			26	<-- Total workers				
30	Daily constraints on workers							
31		Mon	Tue	Wed	Thu	Fri	Sat	Sun
32	Available	20	15	25	20	25	15	10
33		>=	>=	>=	>=	>=	>=	>=
34	Required	20	15	25	20	25	15	10
35								
36	Consecutive days off constraint							
37	Number nonconsecutive	19						
38		<=						
39	Maximum	26.00						
40								
41	Payroll							
42	Weekday	$6,720						
43	Weekend	$2,400						
44	Total	$9,120						

straightforward, you might want to examine them. To do so, you will need to unhide the Model worksheet.)

22.4 Setting Up the Excel Sheets

This optimization model always has the same size because there are always 7 days in a week. Therefore, most of the application can be developed with the Excel interface—without any VBA. It contains the following four sheets.

1. The Explanation worksheet in Figure 22.1 contains an explanation of the application in a text box, and it has a button for running the application.
2. The Model worksheet, shown in Figure 22.5, can be set up completely at design time, using any sample input values. Also, the Solver settings can be entered. Again, this is possible because the model itself will never change; only the inputs to it will change. You can look through the logic of this model in the **Worker Scheduling.xlsm** file. Most of it is straightforward. Pay particular attention to the formulas for worker availabilities in row 32. For example, the formula in cell E32 is =**SUM(AvailThu)**. Here, AvailThu is the range name used for a set of noncontiguous cells, namely, those decision variable cells where Thursday is *not* a day off. Giving range names to noncontiguous ranges is indeed possible and can sometimes be useful.
3. A template for the report shown in Figure 22.3 can be developed in the Report worksheet. This template appears in Figure 22.6. The costs section, worker availabilities section, and numbers of workers section have formulas linked to the Model worksheet, so they show the results from a previous run, if any. However, the optimal assignments section is left blank. It will contain the *positive* assignments only, and these will not be known until run time. The VBA code takes care of transferring the positive assignments from the Model worksheet to this section of the Report worksheet.
4. The chart in Figure 22.4 is located on a separate Chart sheet. This chart is linked to the data in a remote area of the Model worksheet (see Figure 22.7). This area contains the percentages in column AA and the counts from the optimization model in columns AB and AC. Columns AB and AC contain,

Figure 22.6 Report Template

	A	B	C	D	E	F	G	H	I	J
1	Report of optimal solution									
2										
3	Weekly costs			Worker availabilities				Number of workers:		
4	Weekday	$6,720		Day	Available	Required		With consecutive days off		11
5	Weekend	$2,400		Mon	20	20		With nonconsecutive days off		15
6	Total	$9,120		Tue	15	15		Total		26
7				Wed	25	25				
8	Optimal assignments (positive assignments only)			Thu	20	20				
9	Days off	Number assigned		Fri	25	25				
10				Sat	15	15				
11				Sun	10	10				
12										
13										
14					Return to Explanation Sheet			Perform Sensitivity Analysis		
15										

Figure 22.7 Data for Sensitivity Chart

	AA	AB	AC
1	Sensitivity of solutions to maxpct		
2	MaxPct	0	29
3	0%	2	28
4	10%	5	27
5	20%	7	26
6	30%	10	26
7	40%	13	26
8	50%	13	26
9	60%	15	26
10	70%	19	26
11	80%	19	26
12	90%	19	26
13	100%	19	26

respectively, the numbers of workers with nonconsecutive days off and the numbers of workers total in the optimal solutions. Any values can be used in columns AB and AC initially for the purpose of building the chart with Excel's chart tools. They will eventually be replaced with the optimal values by VBA when the sensitivity analysis is run.

22.5 Getting Started with the VBA

This application requires a user form named frmInputs, a module, and a reference to Solver. Once these items are added, the Project Explorer window will appear as in Figure 22.8.[1]

Workbook_Open Event Handler

To guarantee that the Explanation worksheet appears when the file is opened, the following code is placed in the ThisWorkbook code window. The GoToExplanation sub is actually in the module (see below), but it is perfectly acceptable to call a sub from a module in the Workbook_Open sub.

```
Private Sub Workbook_Open()
    Call GoToExplanation
    If Not (Application.Version = "15.0" Or Application.Version = "14.0") Then frmSolver.Show
End Sub
```

---

[1] It also contains the usual frmSolver that displays a message about possible Solver problems when the workbook is opened, but only users with pre-2010 versions of Excel will see this message.

Figure 22.8   Project Explorer Window

22.6 The User Form

The design of frmInputs uses 10 text boxes and accompanying labels, as shown in
Figure 22.9, along with the usual OK and Cancel buttons and a couple of explanation labels to their left. The "day" boxes are named txtDay1 to txtDay7 (for
Monday to Sunday), the wage rate boxes are named txtWeekday and txtWeekend,
and the percentage box is named txtMaxPct.

   The code behind frmInputs is listed below. The Initialize sub captures the existing inputs, if any, from the Model worksheet and uses them as starting values in
the text boxes. The ShowInputsDialog function then captures the user's inputs,
subject to passing the usual types of error checks in the Valid function. Note that
the Val function converts user responses (treated as *strings*) to numbers, which are
placed in the appropriate cells of the Model worksheet.

```
Private cancel As Boolean

Public Function ShowInputsDialog() As Boolean
    Dim ctl As Control
    Dim day As Integer ' day index, 1 to 7

    Call Initialize
    Me.Show
    If Not cancel Then
        ' Enter user's choices in Model sheet.
        For Each ctl In Me.Controls
            If TypeName(ctl) = "TextBox" Then
                If InStr(1, ctl.Name, "Day") > 0 Then
                    day = Right(ctl.Name, 1)
                    wsModel.Range("Required").Cells(day).Value = Val(ctl.Text)
                ElseIf ctl.Name = "txtWeekday" Then
                    wsModel.Range("WeekdayRate").Value = Val(ctl.Text)
```

```
                        ElseIf ctl.Name = "txtWeekend" Then
                                wsModel.Range("WeekendRate").Value = Val(ctl.Text)
                        Else
                                wsModel.Range("MaxPct").Value = Val(ctl.Text)
                        End If
                    End If
                Next
            End If
            ShowInputsDialog = Not cancel
            Unload Me
    End Function

    Private Sub Initialize()
        ' Enter values in the text boxes from the Model sheet.
        Dim ctl As Control
        Dim day As Integer

        For Each ctl In Me.Controls
            If TypeName(ctl) = "TextBox" Then
                ' Note that the boxes for Monday through Sunday have been named txtDay1
                ' through txtDay7. Therefore, these names all contain "Day" and the
                ' last character goes from 1 to 7.
                If InStr(1, ctl.Name, "Day") > 0 Then
                    day = Right(ctl.Name, 1)
                    ctl.Text = wsModel.Range("Required").Cells(day)
                ElseIf ctl.Name = "txtWeekday" Then
                    ctl.Text = wsModel.Range("WeekdayRate")
                ElseIf ctl.Name = "txtWeekend" Then
                    ctl.Text = wsModel.Range("WeekendRate")
                Else
                    ctl.Text = wsModel.Range("MaxPct")
                End If
            End If
        Next
    End Sub

    Private Function Valid() As Boolean
        Dim ctl As Control
        Dim day As Integer

        Valid = True
        For Each ctl In Me.Controls
            If TypeName(ctl) = "TextBox" Then
                If ctl.Text = "" Or Not IsNumeric(ctl.Text) Then
                    Valid = False
                    MsgBox "Enter a numeric value in each box.", _
                        vbInformation, "Improper entry"
                    ctl.SetFocus
                    Exit Function
                ElseIf InStr(1, ctl.Name, "Day") > 0 And ctl.Text < 0 Then
                    Valid = False
                    MsgBox "Enter a nonnegative integer in each day box.", _
                        vbInformation, "Improper entry"
                    ctl.SetFocus
                    Exit Function
                ElseIf InStr(1, ctl.Name, "Week") > 0 And ctl.Text <= 0 Then
                    Valid = False
                    MsgBox "Enter a positive wage rate in each wage box.", _
                        vbInformation, "Improper entry"
                    ctl.SetFocus
                    Exit Function
```

```
                    ElseIf ctl.Name = "txtMaxPct" And (ctl.Text < 0 Or ctl.Text > 1) Then
                        Valid = False
                        MsgBox "Enter a percentage between 0 and 1 in the percentage box.", _
                            vbInformation, "Improper entry"
                        ctl.SetFocus
                        Exit Function
                    End If
                End If
        Next
End Function

Private Sub cmdOK_Click()
    If Valid Then Me.Hide
    cancel = False
End Sub

Private Sub cmdCancel_Click()
    Me.Hide
    cancel = True
End Sub

Private Sub UserForm_QueryClose(cancel As Integer, CloseMode As Integer)
    If CloseMode = vbFormControlMenu Then cmdCancel_Click
End Sub
```

Figure 22.9   frmInputs Design

22.7 The Module

Most of the work in this application is performed by the VBA code in the module. This code is listed below. It proceeds in a modular manner, as described in Chapter 10.

MainScheduling Code

This MainScheduling sub is the control center and is assigned to the button on the Explanation worksheet. It calls other subs to do the real work.

```
Sub MainScheduling()
    ' This sub runs when the button on the Explanation sheet is clicked.
    If frmInputs.ShowInputsDialog Then
        Call RunSolver
        Call CreateReport
    End If
End Sub
```

RunSolver Code

The RunSolver sub unhides and activates the Model worksheet, and then it runs Solver. Note that Solver is already set up (this was done at design time), so SolverSolve is the only Solver function required. Also, note that there is no need to check for feasibility because it is always possible to hire enough workers to meet all daily requirements—it might just cost a lot.

```
Sub RunSolver()
    ' The Solver settings are already in place, so this sub just runs Solver.
    Application.ScreenUpdating = False
    With wsModel
        .Visible = True
        .Activate
    End With
    SolverSolve userfinish:=True

    wsModel.Visible = False
End Sub
```

CreateReport Code

This CreateReport sub unhides and activates the Report worksheet, clears old assignments, and then transfers *positive* assignments from the Model worksheet to the appropriate cells (below A9) in the Report worksheet.

```
Sub CreateReport()
    ' This sub transfers the optimal results from the Model sheet to the Report sheet.
    Dim iPair As Integer ' index of days off pair
    Dim nPositive As Integer
    Const nDaysOffPairs = 21

    Application.ScreenUpdating = False

    ' Unhide the Report sheet and activate it.
    With wsReport
        .Visible = True
```

```
            .Activate
      End With

      ' Clear out old assignments from a previous run (the part below A9).
      With wsReport.Range("A9")
          Range(.Offset(1, 0), .Offset(1, 1).End(xlDown)).ClearContents
      End With

      ' Transfer the positive assignments from the Model sheet to the Report sheet.
      ' nPositive counts the positive assignments.
      nPositive = 0
      With wsReport.Range("A9")
          For iPair = 1 To nDaysOffPairs
              If wsModel.Range("Assignments").Cells(iPair).Value > 0 Then
                  nPositive = nPositive + 1

                  ' Record the names of the days off and the number of workers assigned.
                  .Offset(nPositive, 0).Value = wsModel.Range("Assignments") _
                      .Cells(iPair).Offset(0, -2).Value
                  .Offset(nPositive, 1).Value = wsModel.Range("Assignments") _
                      .Cells(iPair).Value
              End If
          Next
      End With

      wsReport.Range("A1").Select
End Sub
```

Sensitivity Code

The Sensitivity sub unhides and activates the Model worksheet, and then it runs Solver 11 times for equally spaced values of the maximum percentage of nonconsecutive days off. The results are stored in cells under cell AA1 (in the Model worksheet). Because the prebuilt chart is linked to the data in these cells, the chart updates automatically.

```
Public Sub Sensitivity()
    ' This sub performs sensitivity analysis on the maximum percentage
    ' nonconsecutive by running Solver repeatedly and reporting the results.
    Dim iProblem As Integer ' index of problem
    Const nProblems = 11

    Application.ScreenUpdating = False

    ' Unhide and activate the Model sheet.
    With wsModel
        .Visible = True
        .Activate
    End With

    ' Solve problems for maximum percentage from 0 to 1 in increments of 0.1.
    For iProblem = 1 To nProblems
        wsModel.Range("MaxPct").Value = (iProblem - 1) * 0.1

        ' Enter the maximum percentage of days off, and reset all assignments
        ' (changing cells) to 0. Then run Solver.
        wsModel.Range("Assignments").Value = 0
        SolverSolve userfinish:=True
```

```
         ' Store the results in the range that the existing chart is linked to.
         With wsModel.Range("AA1")
              .Offset(iProblem + 1, 1).Value = wsModel.Range("Nonconsec").Value
              .Offset(iProblem + 1, 2).Value = wsModel.Range("TotalWorkers").Value
         End With
    Next

    ' Show the results.
    wsModel.Visible = False

    Application.ScreenUpdating = True
    With chtSensitivity
         .Visible = True
         .Activate
    End With
End Sub
```

GoToExplanation Code

The GoToExplanation sub (not shown here) is for easy navigation. It is attached to the corresponding buttons on the Model, Report, and Chart sheets.

22.8 Summary

This application is similar to the blending optimization model in Chapter 20 in that the size of the model never changes. Therefore, most of the application, including the entire optimization model, can be set up at design time. This decreases the amount of VBA code necessary. One objective here has been to show how to build sensitivity analysis into an application. This has been done for the maximum percentage of workers with nonconsecutive days off, but in general it can be done for any key input parameters. It is basically just a matter of running Solver inside a loop and reporting the results.

EXERCISES

1. Change the application so that there is another button on the Report worksheet. This is the option to perform a sensitivity analysis on the ratio of the weekend wage rate to the weekday wage rate. When you implement this, use the current value of the weekday wage rate from the Model worksheet, and let the ratio vary from 1 to 2 in increments of 0.1. In each case, capture the total cost. Then show the results of this sensitivity analysis (total weekly payroll cost versus the ratio) in graphical form, similar to that shown in Figure 22.4. (You can use the same general location of the Model worksheet, starting in column AF, say, to store your sensitivity results and a new chart sheet to show the results graphically. It should be transparent to the user.)

2. Repeat the previous exercise, but now add a third button on the Report worksheet that performs a sensitivity analysis on both parameters simultaneously. That is, it should use a nested pair of For loops to vary the maximum percentage of nonconsecutive days off from 0% to 100%, in increments of 10%, *and* to vary the ratio from the previous problem from 1 to 2, in increments of 0.1. (This will

Figure 22.10 Sensitivity Chart for Exercise 2

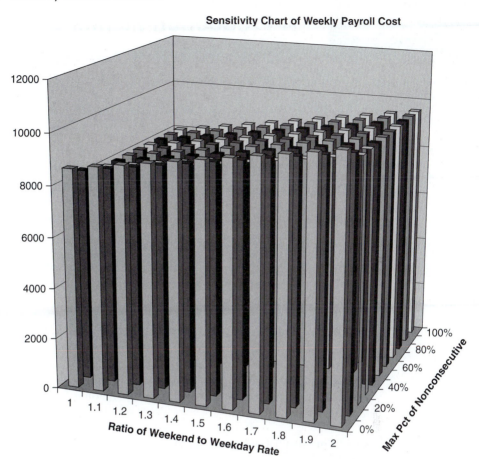

result in 11(11) = 121 Solver runs, and it will take awhile.) The total weekly pay-roll cost from each run should be captured and stored in some remote location of the Model worksheet, and a chart based on these results should be created and displayed. You can decide on the most appropriate chart type. One possibility might look like the chart in Figure 22.10.

3. Change the application so that there is no longer a sensitivity option. However, the user should now be allowed to select from approximately 10 different preset patterns of weekly requirements. For example, one pattern might be the weekend-heavy pattern 10, 10, 10, 10, 10, 30, 30 (where these are the requirements for Monday through Sunday), whereas another pattern might be the more stable pattern 15, 15, 15, 15, 20, 20, 15. You can make up any patterns you think are reasonable. Then allow the user to choose a pattern, along with weekday and weekend wage rates and the maximum percentage of nonconsecutive days off allowed, solve this particular problem, and present the results in a Report worksheet.

4. Change the model on the Model worksheet, and make any necessary modifications to the application as a whole when each worker works only 4 days of the week, not 5.

23 A Production-Planning Application

23.1 Introduction

This application finds an optimal multiperiod production plan for a single product. The objective is to minimize the sum of production and inventory costs, subject to meeting demand on time and not exceeding production and inventory capacities. This model is discussed in all management science textbooks, where the future demands and unit production costs are generally assumed to be known. In reality, these quantities, particularly the demands, must be forecasted from historical data. This application uses exponential smoothing to forecast future demands and unit production costs from historical data. Then it bases the optimal production plan on the forecasted values.

In addition, users can enter new data, update the forecasts, and then run the optimization model again. This allows the application to implement a rolling planning horizon. For example, it can optimize for January through June, then observe actual data for January and update forecasts, then optimize for February through July, then observe actual data for February and update forecasts, and so on. Because of these powerful features, this application is by far the most ambitious application discussed so far.

New Learning Objectives: VBA

- To learn how an application with several user forms, worksheets, charts, and various user options can be integrated within one relatively large VBA program.

New Learning Objectives: Non-VBA

- To learn how forecasts can be made with exponential smoothing methods and then used as inputs to a production-planning optimization model.
- To see how a rolling planning horizon can be implemented.

23.2 Functionality of the Application

The application has the following functionality:

1. It finds the optimal production plan for a 3- to 12-month planning horizon, using the data observed to date.

2. It allows users to view the historical data, along with the exponentially smoothed forecasts, in tabular and graphical form.
3. It allows users to append new demand and unit production cost data to the end of the historical period and update the forecasts.
4. It allows users to change any of the smoothing constants and update the forecasts.

The historical data included in the application are fictional monthly data for a period of several years. Demands are seasonal with an upward trend, so it is appropriate to use Winters' exponential smoothing method. Unit production costs are not seasonal, but they have an upward trend. Therefore, it is appropriate to use Holt's exponential smoothing method for the cost data. Users can replace these data with their own data (in the Data worksheet).

23.3 Running the Application

The application is stored in the file **Production Planning.xlsm**. When the file is opened, the Explanation sheet in Figure 23.1 appears. This explanation indicates two nonstandard features of the optimization model. First, the percentage of any month's production that is available to satisfy that month's demand can be *less* than 100%. For example, if this percentage is 70%, then 70% of this month's production can be used to satisfy this month's demand. The other 30% of this month's production is available only for *future* months' demands. Second, the inventory cost in any month can be based on the ending inventory for the month (the usual assumption), or it can be based on the average of the beginning and ending inventories for the month. Note also that the production and inventory capacities are assumed to be *constant* throughout the planning horizon. This assumption could be relaxed, but it would require additional user inputs.

When the button on the Explanation worksheet is clicked, the dialog box in Figure 23.2 appears. It indicates the four basic options for the application.

First Option

If the user selects the first option, the dialog box in Figure 23.3 appears. It requests the inputs for the production planning model. It then develops this model on the (hidden) Model worksheet, sets up and runs Solver, and reports the optimal solution in tabular and graphical form, as shown in Figure 23.4.

Second Option

Historical data are stored in the Data worksheet. The second option in Figure 23.2 allows users to view these data, as shown in Figure 23.5 (where several rows have been hidden). Note that the historical data appear in columns B and C, and their exponentially smoothed forecasts appear in columns G and J. (Some columns are hidden to shield the user from the exponential smoothing calculations.)

Figure 23.1 Explanation Worksheet

Production planning, using exponential smoothing for demand and cost forecasts

Run the application

This application uses exponential smoothing to forecast future demands and unit production costs from historical data. The future forecasts are inputs to a production planning optimization model, where the production quantities are the changing cells, total cost is the target, and the constraints are that demand must be met from available inventory, production cannot exceed production capacity, and ending inventory cannot exceed storage capacity.

There are four basic options:
1. Find an optimal production plan, with demand and unit cost forecasts based on all observed data so far.
2. View the demand and unit cost data, along with their forecasts.
3. Enter new observed demand and unit cost data, as would be done in a rolling planning horizon procedure.
4. Change the smoothing constants for forecasting.

Some other information about the model:
1. The Data sheet currently includes several years of monthly data on demands and unit production costs in columns B and C. Demand is assumed to be seasonal, with an upward trend. Unit production costs are not seasonal, but they are trending upward through time. To the right on the Data sheet (starting in column AA), parameters for the Winters' and Holt's exponential smoothing methods are listed (smoothing constants and initialization constants). If you like, you can enter new demand and unit cost data, as well as new smoothing constants and appropriate initilization constants, in place of the data here.

2. The unit holding cost is assumed to be a percentage of the unit production cost, where this percentage is a user input. The holding cost can be based on ending inventory or on the average of beginning and ending inventories.

3. Only a percentage of a month's production can be used to meet that month's demand. The rest goes into ending inventory. (This percentage can be 100%.)

4. Production capacity and storage capacity are assumed to be constant through time.

5. The planning horizon for the optimization model can be from 3 to 12 months.

Figure 23.2 Options Dialog Box

User options

Select one of the following options:

Options
- ● Find an optimal production plan
- ○ View demand and cost data
- ○ Enter new demand and cost data
- ○ Change smoothing constants

OK

Cancel

Figure 23.3 Inputs for Production Planning Model

Figure 23.4 Report of Optimal Production Plan

Summary of Optimal Production Plan

Month	Jan-16	Feb-16	Mar-16	Apr-16	May-16	Jun-16
Production	464.9	838.4	866.3	860.8	1354.7	947.7
Ending inventory	93.0	167.7	173.3	172.2	500.0	189.5

Total production cost	$637,859
Total holding cost	$15,520
Total cost	$653,380

View Explanation Sheet

Figure 23.5 Data Worksheet with Forecasts

	A	B	C	G	J	M	N	O	P	Q	R
1	Historical data on demands and unit production costs										
2											
3	Month	Demand	UnitCost	FCastDemand	FCastUnitCost		MAPE for historical data				
4	Jan-11	376	55.50	366.10	57.20		Demands	9.2%			
5	Feb-11	394	61.00	374.99	58.50		Unit costs	2.6%			
6	Mar-11	416	63.42	440.19	60.26						
7	Apr-11	437	57.17	446.75	62.16						
8	May-11	524	62.62	511.38	63.14						
9	Jun-11	672	65.66	697.03	64.56						
10	Jul-11	930	64.18	884.42	66.16						
11	Aug-11	945	69.37	906.15	67.41						
12	Sep-11	719	66.96	680.52	69.10						
13	Oct-11	444	65.87	444.37	70.33						
60	Sep-15	1208	115.17	1221.19	113.05						
61	Oct-15	667	114.29	721.16	114.10						
62	Nov-15	760	113.09	887.48	114.97						
63	Dec-15	1885	120.58	1448.84	115.59						

Buttons shown on the worksheet: View Demand Forecast Chart | View Unit Cost Forecast Chart | View Explanation Sheet | Find Optimal Production Plan

Note box: The exponential smoothing calculations and the absolute percentage errors are hidden in columns D-F, H-I, and K-M. Unhide them if you like. Smoothing constants and initialization constants are out in column AA.

When the left two buttons on the Data worksheet are clicked, the charts in Figures 23.6 and 23.7 appear. They show the actual data with the forecasts superimposed.

Third Option

If the user selects the third option in Figure 23.2, the dialog box in Figure 23.8 appears. It asks for the number of months of new data. Then the dialog box in Figure 23.9 is shown repeatedly, once for each new month.

The new data are automatically appended to the bottom of the historical period in the Data sheet (see Figure 23.10), and the exponential smoothing calculations are extended for this new period. If the user then asks for the new optimal production plan, the planning horizon starts *after* the period of the new data, as illustrated in Figure 23.11.

Fourth Option

Finally, if the user selects the fourth option in Figure 23.2, the dialog box in Figure 23.12 appears. It requests new smoothing constants. The updated MAPE (mean absolute percentage error) values are then reported in a message box, as shown in Figure 23.13. The smoothing constants, along with initialization values for Winters' method and Holt's method, are stored farther to the right in the Data worksheet, as shown in Figure 23.14.

Figure 23.6 Demand Data and Forecasts

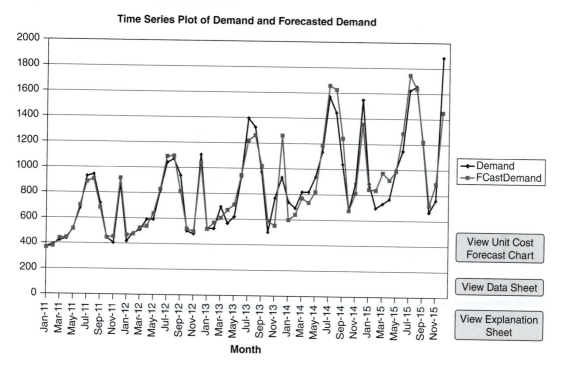

Figure 23.7 Unit Production Cost Data and Forecasts

Figure 23.8 First New Data Dialog Box

New data

Enter the number of months of new data.

Number of months: 1

OK

Cancel

Figure 23.9 Second New Data Dialog Box

New Data

Enter the newly observed demand and unit cost for Jan-2016

Demand: 940

Unit cost: 123

Add Data

Figure 23.10 Appended Data in Data Worksheet

	A	B	C	G	J
60	Sep-15	1208	115.17	1221.19	113.05
61	Oct-15	667	114.29	721.16	114.10
62	Nov-15	760	113.09	887.48	114.97
63	Dec-15	1885	120.58	1448.84	115.59
64	Jan-16	940	123	871.92	117.00

Figure 23.11 New Production Plan Report

Summary of Optimal Production Plan

Month	Feb-16	Mar-16	Apr-16	May-16	Jun-16	Jul-16
Production	338.6	1003.0	839.9	1091.3	1559.1	1608.9
Ending inventory	67.7	200.6	168.0	218.3	500.0	321.8

Total production cost	$784.889
Total holding cost	$18,008
Total cost	$802,897

View Explanation Sheet

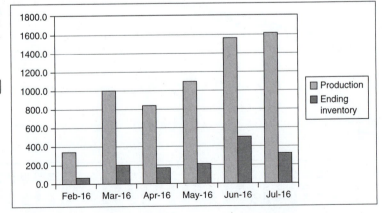

Figure 23.12 Smoothing Constant Dialog Box

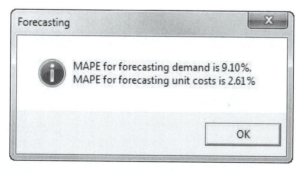

Figure 23.13 Updated MAPE Values

Possibility of No Feasible Solutions

There is always the possibility that the production planning model has no feasible solutions. This typically occurs when there is not enough production capacity to meet forecasted demands on time. In this case, the message box in Figure 23.15 is displayed.

Figure 23.14 Exponential Smoothing Information

	AA	AB	AC	AD	AE	AF	AG
3	Smoothing parameters for exponential smoothing						
4							
5	Winters' method (for demand)			Holt's method (for unit cost)			
6	Level	0.3		Level	0.2		
7	Trend	0.1		Trend	0.1		
8	Seasonality	0.4					
9							
10	Initialization values for Winters' method			Initialization values for Holt's method			
11	Level	512		Level	55.7		
12	Trend	11		Trend	1.5		
13							
14	Seasonal factors						
15	Jan	0.7					
16	Feb	0.7					
17	Mar	0.8					
18	Apr	0.8					
19	May	0.9					
20	Jun	1.2					
21	Jul	1.5					
22	Aug	1.5					
23	Sep	1.1					
24	Oct	0.7					
25	Nov	0.7					
26	Dec	1.4					

Figure 23.15 No Feasible Solutions Message

23.4 Setting Up the Excel Sheets

The **Production Planning.xlsm** file contains four worksheets, named Explanation, Data, Model, and Report, and two chart sheets, named Demand_Forecast and Cost_ Forecast. The Data worksheet can be set up completely at design time, as shown in Figures 23.5 and 23.14. Note that the hidden columns in Figure 23.5 must contain the exponential smoothing formulas for Winters' and Holt's methods. (See the **Production Planning.xlsm** file for details. If you need to review exponential smoothing, see the regression and forecasting chapter of *Practical Management Science*.)

The Model worksheet contains the linear programming production planning model. It must be developed almost entirely at run time. The completed version appears in Figure 23.16 for a 6-month planning horizon. Clearly, the number of

Figure 23.16 Completed Model Worksheet

⊿	A	B	C	D	E	F	G
1	**Production planning model**						
2							
3	**Inputs**						
4	Planning horizon	6					
5	Beginning inventory	500					
6	Production pct	80.0%					
7	Holding cost pct	10.0%					
8	Holding cost option	1					
9	Production capacity	2000					
10	Storage capacity	500					
11							
12	**Production plan**						
13	Month	Jan-16	Feb-16	Mar-16	Apr-16	May-16	Jun-16
14	Beginning inventory	500.0	93.0	167.7	173.3	172.2	500.0
15	Production	464.9	838.4	866.3	860.8	1354.7	947.7
16		<=	<=	<=	<=	<=	<=
17	Production capacity	2000	2000	2000	2000	2000	2000
18							
19	Available to meet demand	871.9	763.7	860.8	861.9	1255.9	1258.2
20		>=	>=	>=	>=	>=	>=
21	Demand	871.9	763.7	860.8	861.9	1026.8	1258.2
22							
23	Ending inventory	93.0	167.7	173.3	172.2	500.0	189.5
24							
25	Storage capacity	500	500	500	500	500	500
26	Average inventory	296.5	130.3	170.5	172.7	336.1	344.8
27							
28	**Cost summary**						
29	Month	Jan-16	Feb-16	Mar-16	Apr-16	May-16	Jun-16
30	Forecasted unit production costs	$117.00	$117.91	$118.82	$119.73	$120.64	$121.55
31							
32	Total production cost	$637,859					
33	Total holding cost	$15,520					
34	Total cost	$653,380					

Figure 23.17 Template for Report Worksheet

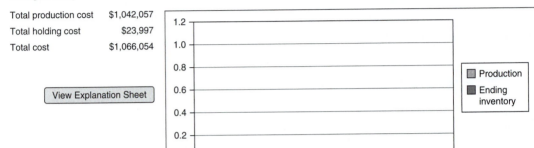

Summary of Optimal Production Plan

Month

Production

Ending inventory

Total production cost	$1,042,057
Total holding cost	$23,997
Total cost	$1,066,054

View Explanation Sheet

columns in this model depends on the length of the planning horizon, which is not known until run time. About the only parts that can be entered at design time are the labels in column A. (The formula in cell B34 is the one exception. It is always the sum of cells B32 and B33.)

A template for the Report worksheet shown earlier in Figure 23.4 *can* be developed at design time, as shown in Figure 23.17. In particular, the embedded chart can be created with Excel's chart tools. It can then be linked to the appropriate data in rows 3–5 at run time. Also, formulas in cells B7 to B9 can be entered at design time. These formulas are links to the appropriate Model worksheet cells.

Similarly, the chart sheets shown earlier in Figures 23.6 and 23.7 can be created at design time. Then they are linked to the appropriate data from the Data worksheet at run time.

23.5 Getting Started with the VBA

The application includes five user forms, named frmOptions, frmInputs, frmNewData1, frmNewData2, and frmSmConst, a single module, and a reference to Solver. Once these are inserted, the Project Explorer window will appear as in Figure 23.18.[1]

Workbook_Open Code

To guarantee that the Explanation sheet appears when the file is opened, the following code is placed in the ThisWorkbook code window. It also hides all sheets except for the Explanation worksheet, and it displays the usual Solver warning.

---

[1] It also contains the usual frmSolver that displays a message about possible Solver problems when the workbook is opened, but only users of pre-2010 versions of Excel will see this message.

Figure 23.18 Project Explorer Window

```
Private Sub Workbook_Open()
    Dim sht As Object
    With wsExplanation
        .Activate
        .Range("G4").Select
    End With
    For Each sht In ActiveWorkbook.Sheets
        If sht.CodeName <> "wsExplanation" Then sht.Visible = False
    Next
    If Not (Application.Version = "15.0" Or Application.Version = "14.0") Then frmSolver.Show
End Sub
```

23.6 The User Forms

frmOptions

The frmOptions form has the usual OK and Cancel buttons, an explanation label, a frame for grouping, and four option buttons named optOptimize, optViewData, optNewData, and optSmConst. Its design appears in Figure 23.19.

The code behind frmOptions is straightforward and is listed below. The whole purpose of the ShowOptionsDialog function is to capture the user's choice in the variable choice, with possible values 1 to 4.

Figure 23.19 frmOptions Design

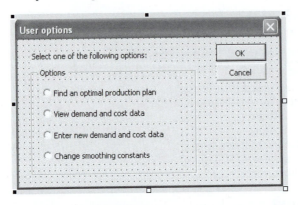

```
Private cancel As Boolean

Public Function ShowOptionsDialog(choice As Integer) As Boolean
    Call Initialize
    Me.Show
    If Not cancel Then
        ' Capture the user's choice.
        If optOptimize.Value Then
            choice = 1
        ElseIf optViewData.Value Then
            choice = 2
        ElseIf optNewData.Value Then
            choice = 3
        Else
            choice = 4
        End If
    End If
    ShowOptionsDialog = Not cancel
    Unload Me
End Function

Private Sub Initialize()
    optOptimize.Value = True
End Sub

Private Sub cmdOK_Click()
    Me.Hide
    cancel = False
End Sub

Private Sub cmdCancel_Click()
    Me.Hide
    cancel = True
End Sub

Private Sub UserForm_QueryClose(cancel As Integer, CloseMode As Integer)
    If CloseMode = vbFormControlMenu Then cmdCancel_Click
End Sub
```

frmInputs

The frmInputs form contains the usual OK and Cancel buttons; several explanation labels; a frame that contains two options buttons named optEndInv and

Figure 23.20   frmInputs Design

optAvgInv; and six text boxes, named txtNMonths, txtInitInv, txtProdPct, txtHoldPct, txtProdCap, and txtInvCap. Its design appears in Figure 23.20.

The code behind frmInputs is rather lengthy, but this is mostly because of error checking for the text boxes. The Initialize sub fills the dialog box with the previous settings from the Model worksheet. Then the ShowInputsDialog function captures the user's settings in several model input variables and their values are eventually entered in the appropriate cells of the Model worksheet. The Valid function performs the error checking.

```
Private cancel As Boolean

Public Function ShowInputsDialog(nMonths As Integer, initInv As Long, _
        prodPct As Single, holdPct As Single, prodCap As Long, _
        invCap As Long, holdOpt As Integer) As Boolean
    Call Initialize
    Me.Show
    If Not cancel Then
        nMonths = txtNMonths.Text
        initInv = txtInitInv.Text
        prodPct = txtProdPct.Text
        holdPct = txtHoldPct.Text
        prodCap = txtProdCap.Text
        invCap = txtInvCap.Text
        If optEndInv.Value Then
            holdOpt = 1
        Else
            holdOpt = 2
```

```
            End If
        End If
        ShowInputsDialog = Not cancel
        Unload Me
End Function

Private Sub Initialize()
    ' Enter values from the Model sheet.
    With wsModel
        txtNMonths.Text = .Range("NMonths").Value
        txtInitInv.Text = .Range("InitInv").Value
        txtProdPct.Text = Format(.Range("ProdPct").Value, "0.00")
        txtHoldPct.Text = Format(.Range("HoldPct").Value, "0.00")
        If .Range("HoldOpt").Value = 1 Then
            optEndInv.Value = True
        Else
            optAvgInv.Value = True
        End If
        txtProdCap.Text = .Range("ProdCap").Value
        txtInvCap.Text = .Range("InvCap").Value
    End With
End Sub

Private Function Valid() As Boolean
    Dim ctl As Control

    Valid = True
    ' Check for numeric values in text boxes.
    For Each ctl In Me.Controls
        If TypeName(ctl) = "TextBox" Then
            If ctl.Value = "" Or Not IsNumeric(ctl.Value) Then
                Valid = False
                MsgBox "Enter a numeric value in each box.", _
                    vbInformation, "Invalid entry"
                ctl.SetFocus
                Exit Function
            End If
        End If
    Next

    ' Check that txtNMonths is between 3 and 12.
    If txtNMonths.Text < 3 Or txtNMonths.Text > 12 Then
        Valid = False
        MsgBox "Make the planning horizon at least 3 months " _
            & "and no more than 12 months.", vbInformation, "Invalid entry"
        txtNMonths.SetFocus
        Exit Function
    End If

    ' Initial inventory cannot be negative.
    If txtInitInv.Text < 0 Then
        Valid = False
        MsgBox "Enter a nonnegative initial inventory.", _
            vbInformation, "Invalid entry"
        txtInitInv.SetFocus
        Exit Function
    End If

    ' The production percentage must be from 0 to 1.
    If txtProdPct.Text < 0 Or txtProdPct.Text > 1 Then
```

```
            Valid = False
            MsgBox "Enter a percentage (in decimal form) between 0 " _
                & "and 1.", vbInformation, "Invalid entry"
            txtProdPct.SetFocus
            Exit Function
        End If


        ' The holding cost percentage must be from 0 to 1.
        If txtHoldPct.Text < 0 Or txtHoldPct.Text > 1 Then
            Valid = False
            MsgBox "Enter a percentage (in decimal form) between 0 " _
                & "and 1.", vbInformation, "Invalid entry"
            txtHoldPct.SetFocus
            Exit Function
        End If


        ' Production capacity cannot be negative.
        If txtProdCap.Text < 0 Then
            Valid = False
            MsgBox "Enter a nonnegative production capacity.", _
                vbInformation, "Invalid entry"
            txtProdCap.SetFocus
            Exit Function
        End If


        ' Storage capacity cannot be negative.
        If txtInvCap.Text < 0 Then
            Valid = False
            MsgBox "Enter a nonnegative storage capacity.", _
                vbInformation, "Invalid entry"
            txtInvCap.SetFocus
            Exit Function
        End If
End Function

Private Sub cmdOK_Click()
    If Valid Then Me.Hide
    cancel = False
End Sub

Private Sub cmdCancel_Click()
    Me.Hide
    cancel = True
End Sub

Private Sub UserForm_QueryClose(cancel As Integer, CloseMode As Integer)
    If CloseMode = vbFormControlMenu Then cmdCancel_Click
End Sub
```

frmNewData1 and frmNewData2

The two user forms for new data, shown earlier in Figures 23.8 and 23.9, are straightforward, so their code is not listed here. The only new wrinkle is that an Add Data button replaces the usual OK and Cancel buttons on frmNewData2. Actually, this button has exactly the same functionality as the usual OK button; only its name and caption are different. The Cancel button is purposely omitted. By this time, new data rows have been added to the Data worksheet, so the user *must* enter demand and cost data for them.

frmSmConst

The frmSmConst form for the smoothing constants, shown earlier in Figure 23.12, also contains no new ideas, so its code is not listed here. It is initialized with the previous smoothing constants from the Model worksheet (see Figure 23.14). It then places the user's choice of smoothing constants in these same cells.

23.7 The Module

The module contains the code that does most of the work. As usual, the button on the Explanation worksheet is attached to a MainProductionPlanning sub that first shows frmOptions and then calls the appropriate sub, depending on the value of the variable choice. The module-level variables and the code for the MainProductionPlanning sub are listed below.

Option Statements and Module-level Variables

```
Option Explicit
Option Base 1

' Definitions of important variables:
'    choice: analysis to be run (1 to 4)
'    nMonths: number of months in planning horizon
'    initInv: initial inventory in first month of planning horizon
'    prodPct: percentage of a month's production that can be used to meet
'        that month's demand
'    holdPct: percentage of unit production cost used for unit holding cost
'    holdOpt: 1 or 2, depending on whether holding cost is based on ending
'        inventory or average of beginning and ending inventory
'    prodCap: production capacity, assumed constant each month
'    invCap: storage capacity, assumed constant each month
'    nMonthsNew: number of new data entries
'    newMonth: month for new data
'    newDemand: newly observed demand for newMonth
'    newUnitCost: newly observed unit cost for newMonth

' These variables are declared as module-level variables (but not
' Public variables) to avoid a lot of argument-passing in this module.
' Because they aren't Public, they still have to be passed to the forms.
Dim nMonths As Integer
Dim initInv As Long, prodPct As Single
Dim holdPct As Single, holdOpt As Integer
Dim prodCap As Long, invCap As Long
```

MainProductionPlanning Code

```
Sub MainProductionPlanning()
    ' This is the main program that runs when the user clicks the button
    ' on the Explanation sheet.
    Dim choice As Integer
    If frmOptions.ShowOptionsDialog(choice) Then
        Select Case choice
```

```
                    Case 1
                        Call  ProdModel
                    Case 2
                        Call  ViewData
                    Case 3
                        Call  NewData
                    Case 4
                        Call  SmConstants
                End Select
            End If
    End Sub
```

ProdModel Code

The ProdModel sub "shows" frmInputs, activates the Model worksheet, clears the contents of any previous model, and calls several subs (EnterForecasts, EnterFormulas, RunSolver, and CreateReport) to develop and optimize the production planning model and report the results.

```
Sub ProdModel()
    ' This sub is run when the user wants to find an optimal production plan,
    ' based on the historical data observed so far.
    Dim feasible As Boolean

    If frmInputs.ShowInputsDialog(nMonths, initInv, prodPct, holdPct, _
            prodCap, invCap, holdOpt) Then
        Application.ScreenUpdating = False

        ' Activate the Model sheet and get rid of any old model.
        With wsModel
            .Visible = True
            .Activate
            .Range("B13:M33").ClearContents
            ' Enter user inputs.
            .Range("NMonths").Value = nMonths
            .Range("InitInv").Value = initInv
            .Range("ProdPct").Value = prodPct
            .Range("HoldPct").Value = holdPct
            .Range("ProdCap").Value = prodCap
            .Range("InvCap").Value = invCap
            .Range("HoldOpt").Value = holdOpt
        End With

        ' Develop the model and optimize with Solver.
        Call EnterForecasts
        Call EnterFormulas
        Call RunSolver(feasible)

        ' If feasible, transfer selected results to the Report sheet.
        If feasible Then
            Call CreateReport
            wsModel.Visible = False
        End If
        Application.ScreenUpdating = True
    End If
End Sub
```

EnterForecasts Code

The purpose of the EnterForecasts sub is to calculate *future* forecasts of demands and unit costs, based on the data in the Data worksheet, and then enter these in the Model worksheet. Note that the Data worksheet contains forecasts for the *historical* period only. Therefore, forecasts for the planning horizon must be calculated in this sub.

Unless you thoroughly understand Holt's and Winters' forecasting models, you will probably not understand all of the details in this sub. In that case, it suffices to know that the relevant formulas have *already* been entered in the Data worksheet for the historical period. (This was done at design time.) This sub copies these formulas down for the planning period.

```
Sub EnterForecasts()
    ' This sub enters the forecasts of demand and unit cost in the Model sheet.
    ' They are calculated by Winters' and Holt's exponential smoothing models.
    Dim i As Integer
    Dim levelCell1 As Range, levelCell2 As Range, level1 As Single, level2 As Single
    Dim trend1 As Single, trend2 As Single
    Dim seasFactor As Single

    ' The levelCell1 and levelCell2 cells are the last values of "smoothed level"
    ' for demand and unit cost, respectively, in the Data sheet.
    Set levelCell1 = wsData.Range("A3").Offset(0, 3).End(xlDown)
    Set levelCell2 = wsData.Range("A3").Offset(0, 7).End(xlDown)

    ' The next four values are the basis for future forecasts.
    level1 = levelCell1.Value
    trend1 = levelCell1.Offset(0, 1).Value
    level2 = levelCell2.Value
    trend2 = levelCell2.Offset(0, 1).Value

    ' Fill up rows 13 and 29 of the Model sheet with the appropriate dates in the
    ' planning horizon. Dates are tricky to work with, but an easy way to do it here
    ' is to temporarily put the last historical date in cell A13, then use the
    ' AutoFill method to fill up the future dates in row 13, then replace the date
    ' in A13 with the label "Month", then copy row 13 to row 29.
    With wsModel.Range("A13")
        .Value = wsData.Range("A3").End(xlDown)
        .AutoFill Destination:=Range(.Offset(0, 0), .Offset(0, nMonths)), _
            Type:=xlFillDefault
        .Value = "Month"
        Range(.Offset(0, 1), .Offset(0, nMonths)).Copy Destination:=wsModel.Range("B29")
    End With

    ' For demand forecasts in row 21, project the most recent level upward by i
    ' times the most recent trend, then multiply by the appropriate seasonal factor.
    ' Do the same for unit costs in row 30, except that there is no seasonality.
    For i = 1 To nMonths
        seasFactor = levelCell1.Offset(i - 12, 2).Value
        wsModel.Range("A21").Offset(0, i).Value = (level1 + i * trend1) * seasFactor
        wsModel.Range("A30").Offset(0, i).Value = level2 + i * trend2
    Next

    ' Name some ranges for later use.
    With wsModel.Range("A13")
```

```
            Range(.Offset(0, 1), .Offset(0, nMonths)).Name = "Model!Months"
    End With
    With wsModel.Range("A21")
            Range(.Offset(0, 1), .Offset(0, nMonths)).Name = "Model!FDemands"
    End With
    With wsModel.Range("A30")
            Range(.Offset(0, 1), .Offset(0, nMonths)).Name = "Model!FCosts"
    End With
End Sub
```

EnterFormulas Code

The EnterFormulas sub is rather lengthy because it has to develop the optimization model on the fly at run time. It enters all of the formulas in the Model worksheet and names ranges appropriately. The comments spell out the details. (It is helpful to refer to Figure 23.16 when reading this code.)

```
Sub EnterFormulas()
    ' This sub enters all of the formulas for the production planning model.
    ' It uses the Formula or FormulaR1C1 property, depending on which is most natural.
    Dim i As Integer

    With wsModel
        For i = 1 To nMonths
            ' Calculate beginning inventories in row 14. Other than the first, these
            ' equal the previous ending inventory (9 rows below).
            If i = 1 Then
                .Range("A14").Offset(0, i).Formula = "=InitInv"
            Else
                .Range("A14").Offset(0, i).FormulaR1C1 = "=R[9]C[-1]"
            End If

            ' Row 15 contains the production quantities, the changing cells.
            ' Enter 0's initially.
            .Range("A15").Offset(0, i).Value = 0

            ' Enter <= labels in row 16 to denote constraints.
            .Range("A16").Offset(0, i).Value = "<="

            ' Enter a link to the ProdCap cell throughout row 17.
            .Range("A17").Offset(0, i).Formula = "=ProdCap"

            ' Calculate onhand inventory in row 19 as beginning
            ' inventory (5 rows up) plus production percentage times
            ' production (4 rows up).
            .Range("A19").Offset(0, i).FormulaR1C1 = "=R[-5]C+" & "ProdPct*R[-4]C"

            ' Enter >= labels in row 20 to denote constraints.
            .Range("A20").Offset(0, i).Value = ">="

            ' Calculate ending inventory in row 23 as the difference between onhand
            ' inventory (4 rows up) and demand (2 rows up), plus (1 minus the
            ' production percentage) times the production (8 rows up).
            .Range("A23").Offset(0, i).FormulaR1C1 = _
                "=R[-4]C-R[-2]C+" & "(1-ProdPct)*R[-8]C"

            ' Enter a link to the InvCap cel throughout row 25.
            .Range("A25").Offset(0, i).Formula = "=InvCap"
```

```
        ' Calculate the average of beginning inventory (12 rows up) and ending
        ' inventory (3 rows up) in row 26.
            .Range("A26").Offset(0, i).FormulaR1C1 = "=(R[-12]C+R[-3]C)/2"
    Next

    ' Name some ranges for later use.
    With .Range("A15")
        Range(.Offset(0, 1), .Offset(0, nMonths)).Name = "Model!Production"
    End With
    With .Range("A17")
        Range(.Offset(0, 1), .Offset(0, nMonths)).Name = "Model!ProdCaps"
    End With
    With .Range("A19")
        Range(.Offset(0, 1), .Offset(0, nMonths)).Name = "Model!Onhand"
    End With
    With .Range("A23")
        Range(.Offset(0, 1), .Offset(0, nMonths)).Name = "Model!EndInv"
    End With
    With .Range("A25")
        Range(.Offset(0, 1), .Offset(0, nMonths)).Name = "Model!InvCaps"
    End With
    With .Range("A26")
        Range(.Offset(0, 1), .Offset(0, nMonths)).Name = "Model!AvgInv"
    End With

    ' Calculate the total production cost.
    .Range("B32").Formula = "=Sumproduct(Production,FCosts)"
    ' Calculate the total holding cost.
    If holdOpt = 1 Then
        .Range("B33").Formula = "=Sumproduct(EndInv,HoldPct*FCosts)"
    Else
        .Range("B33").Formula = "=Sumproduct(AvgInv,HoldPct*FCosts)"
    End If

    ' The total cost in cell B34 already has a formula in it, which never changes.
    End With
End Sub
```

RunSolver Code

The RunSolver sub resets the Solver dialog box, sets it up appropriately, and runs Solver. A check is made for feasibility. If there are no feasible solutions, a message to this effect is displayed and the ProdModel sub is called. The effect is to let the user try again with new inputs.

```
Sub RunSolver()
    Dim solverStatus As Integer

    With wsModel
        SolverReset
        SolverOK SetCell:=.Range("TotalCost"), MaxMinVal:=2, _
            ByChange:=Range("Production"), Engine:=1
        SolverAdd CellRef:=.Range("Production"), Relation:=1, _
            FormulaText:="ProdCaps"
        SolverAdd CellRef:=.Range("OnHand"), Relation:=3, _
            FormulaText:="FDemands"
        SolverAdd CellRef:=.Range("EndInv"), Relation:=1, _
```

```
                    FormulaText:="InvCaps"
                 SolverOptions AssumeNonNeg:=True
                 ' Solve. If the result code is 5, this means there is no feasible solution, so
                 ' display a message to that effect and call ProdModel (to try again).
                 solverStatus = SolverSolve(UserFinish:=True)
                 If solverStatus = 5 Then
                     MsgBox "There is no feasible solution with these inputs. Try " _
                         & "larger capacities.", vbExclamation, "No feasible solution"
                     Call ProdModel
                     End
                 End If
             End With
        End Sub
```

CreateReport Code

The **CreateReport** sub copies the data on months, production quantities, and ending inventory levels from the Model worksheet to the Report worksheet. In the case of ending inventory levels, the Model worksheet contains formulas, so these are pasted as *values* in the Report worksheet. Finally, this sub updates the embedded chart on the Report worksheet with the new data.

```
Sub CreateReport()
    ' The Report sheet is already set up (at design time), so just copy (with
    ' PasteSpecial/Values when formulas are involved) selected quantities to
    ' the Report sheet.
    Dim i As Integer
    Dim cht As Chart

    ' Unhide and activate the Report sheet.
    With wsReport
        .Visible = True
        .Activate

        ' Clear old values.
        .Range("B3:M5").ClearContents

        ' Copy results to rows 3–5.
        wsModel.Range("Months").Copy Destination:=.Range("B3")
        wsModel.Range("Production").Copy Destination:=.Range("B4")
        wsModel.Range("EndInv").Copy
        .Range("B5").PasteSpecial xlPasteValues

        ' Name some ranges for later use.
        With .Range("A3")
            Range(.Offset(0, 1), .Offset(0, nMonths)).Name = "Report!RepMonths"
            Range(.Offset(1, 0), .Offset(1, nMonths)).Name = "Report!RepProd"
            Range(.Offset(2, 0), .Offset(2, nMonths)).Name = "Report!RepEndInv"
        End With

        ' Update the embedded chart on the Report sheet.
        Set cht = .ChartObjects(1).Chart
        cht.SetSourceData Source:=Union(.Range("RepProd"), .Range("RepEndInv"))
        cht.SeriesCollection(1).XValues = .Range("RepMonths")

        .Range("A1").Select
    End With
End Sub
```

NewData Code

The NewData sub "shows" frmNewDatal and frmNewData2 and appends the new data to the bottom of the historical data range in the Data worksheet. It then copies the exponential smoothing formulas down to these new rows, and it renames ranges to include the new rows. Finally, it calls the UpdateCharts sub to update the two chart sheets that show historical data with superimposed forecasts. Remember that the charts themselves were created with the Excel's chart tools at design time.

```vba
Sub NewData()
    ' This sub allows the user to enter newly observed demand and unit cost data.
    Dim nMonthsNew As Integer, newMonth As Date
    Dim newDemand As Long, newUnitCost As Single
    Dim i As Integer

    ' Unhide and activate the Data sheet.
    With wsData
        .Visible = True
        .Activate

        ' Get the number of new data values from the user.
        If frmNewData1.ShowNewData1Dialog(nMonthsNew) Then

            With .Range("A3").End(xlDown)
                ' Enter new dates in column A with the AutoFill method.
                .AutoFill Range(.Offset(0, 0), .Offset(nMonthsNew, 0))

                ' Get new demand and unit cost data and enter them below old data.
                For i = 1 To nMonthsNew
                    newMonth = .Offset(i, 0).Value
                    frmNewData2.ShowNewData2Dialog newMonth, newDemand, newUnitCost
                    .Offset(i, 1).Value = newDemand
                    .Offset(i, 2).Value = newUnitCost
                Next
            End With

            ' Copy formulas in columns D to L of the Data sheet down for new data.
            ' These implement the exponential smoothing methods.
            With .Range("A3").Offset(0, 3).End(xlDown)
                Range(.Offset(0, 0), .Offset(0, 8)).Copy _
                    Destination:=Range(.Offset(1, 0), .Offset(nMonthsNew, 8))
            End With

            ' Rename the ranges for various columns in the Data sheet.
            With .Range("A3")
                Range(.Offset(1, 0), .End(xlDown)).Name = "Data!Months"
                Range(.Offset(0, 1), .Offset(0, 1).End(xlDown)).Name = "Data!Demands"
                Range(.Offset(0, 2), .Offset(0, 2).End(xlDown)).Name = "Data!UnitCosts"
                Range(.Offset(0, 6), .Offset(0, 6).End(xlDown)).Name = "Data!DemFCasts"
                Range(.Offset(0, 9), .Offset(0, 9).End(xlDown)).Name = "Data!CostFCasts"
                Range(.Offset(1, 10), .Offset(1, 10).End(xlDown)).Name = "Data!_APE1"
                Range(.Offset(1, 11), .Offset(1, 11).End(xlDown)).Name = "Data!_APE2"
            End With
            ' Update the charts to include all data observed so far.
            Call UpdateCharts

            .Range("N9").Select
        End If
    End With
End Sub
```

UpdateCharts Code

The UpdateCharts sub resets the links to the data for the two chart sheets. This is done to accommodate the new data that were just appended to the historical data range.

```
Sub UpdateCharts()
    ' This sub updates the source data ranges for the two chart sheets.
    ' It is called only when the user enters new data.
    With chtDemandForecast
        .SetSourceData Source:=Union(wsData.Range("Demands"), wsData.Range("DemFCasts"))
        .SeriesCollection(1).XValues = wsData.Range("Months")
    End With
    With chtCostForecast
        .SetSourceData Source:=Union(wsData.Range("UnitCosts"), _
            wsData.Range("CostFCasts"))
        .SeriesCollection(1).XValues = wsData.Range("Months")
    End With
End Sub
```

SmConstants Code

The SmConstants sub "shows" the frmSmConst form and displays a message about the updated MAPE values. (Remember that the code behind frmSmConst enters the new smoothing constants in the Data worksheet.)

```
Sub SmConstants()
    ' This sub allows the user to change the smoothing constants. After choosing them,
    ' everything on the Data sheet recalculates automatically and a message box shows the
    ' updated MAPE values.
    If frmSmConst.ShowSmConstDialog Then
        With wsData
            MsgBox "MAPE for forecasting demand is " & _
                Format(.Range("MAPE1").Value, "0.00%") & "." _
                & vbCrLf & "MAPE for forecasting unit costs is " _
                & Format(.Range("MAPE2").Value, "0.00%"), vbInformation, "Forecasting"
        End With
    End If
End Sub
```

Navigational Code

The rest of the subs (not listed here) are for navigational purposes. They are attached to the buttons on the various sheets. You can see their code in the file.

23.8 Summary

This forecasting/optimization application is admittedly fairly long and complex, but this is the price paid for accomplishing so much. The application combines two traditional areas of management science. First, it implements exponential smoothing forecasting methods. Second, it uses the exponential smoothed forecasts as inputs to a production planning optimization model. In this way, the application can be used to implement the rolling planning horizon method used by many companies.

EXERCISES

1. The application currently creates a column chart of production quantities and ending inventories on the Report worksheet (see Figure 23.4). Change it so that two *separate* charts are created on the Report worksheet: one of production quantities and one of ending inventories. Also, make each of them *line* charts.

2. The planning horizon can currently be any number of months from 3 to 12. Suppose the company involved insists on a 6-month planning horizon—no more, no less. Would this make your job as a programmer easier or harder? Explain in words what basic changes you would make to the application.

3. Some programmers might object to my EnterFormulas sub, arguing that it is too long and should be broken up into smaller subs. Try doing this. You can decide how many smaller subs to use and what specific task each should have. Then test the application with your new code to check that it still works correctly.

4. I have used my own (fictional) historical data to illustrate the application. Try using your own. Specifically, enter your own data in columns A, B, and C of the Data worksheet (see Figure 23.5), and make sure the columns next to them (D-J) have the same number of rows as your new data. (Delete rows or copy down if necessary.) You will also have to enter "reasonable" initialization values for the smoothing methods. (See Figure 23.14 for the cells involved.) Now run the application to check that it still works correctly.

5. The third basic option in the application allows the user to enter *any* number of new observations. Change this so that only *one* new observation (of demand and unit cost) can be added on a given run. In this case, you won't need frmNewData1.

6. (More difficult, and only for those familiar with exponential smoothing) The fourth basic option in the application allows the user to enter *any* smoothing constants from 0 to 1. Delete this option. Instead, have the application choose the smoothing constants to minimize the root mean square error (RMSE), which is defined as the square root of the sum of squared differences between observations and forecasts. You will have to write code to set up and run Solver for this minimization. Write this as two subs, one for the demands and one for the unit costs (because each has its own set of smoothing constants). Then decide when these subs should be called and update other subs accordingly.

7. (More difficult, and only for those familiar with exponential smoothing) The application is written for a product with seasonal demand. This is the reason for using Winters' method. Change the application so that the user can choose (in an extra user form) which of three exponential smoothing methods to use for forecasting demand: simple, Holt's, or Winters'. Then the appropriate formulas should be used. (*Hint:* There are probably fewer required modifications than you might expect because the formulas for simple exponential smoothing and Holt's methods are special cases of the built-in Winters' method.)

A Transportation Application

24.1 Introduction

This application solves a well-known management science problem called the transportation problem. A company needs to ship a product from its plants to its retailers. Each route from a plant to a retailer has a unit shipping cost. The problem is to develop a shipping plan that gets the product from the plants to the retailers at minimum cost. There are plant capacity constraints and retailer demand constraints. There can be as many as 200 routes in the network.[1] In the usual management science terminology, the plants and retailers are called **nodes**, and the routes from plants to retailers are called **arcs**.

This problem requires extensive input data, including node data (names of plants and retailers, as well as capacities and demands) and arc data (unit costs for all plant/retailer combinations). The data for a real problem of this type might well reside on a database, not within Excel, so this possibility is illustrated here. The data are in three related tables (Capacity, Demand, and UnitCost) of an Access database called **Transportation.mdb**. This application illustrates how the Access data can be imported into an Excel worksheet to create a Solver model, which can then be optimized in the usual way. To do so, it uses Microsoft's ActiveX Data Objects (ADO) technology, discussed in Chapter 14, to import the data into Excel. You do not even need to *own* Access to make it work. Fortunately, ADO is quite easy to implement in VBA, as this chapter illustrates. This gives the developers of decision support systems a whole new level of power—the ability to access external databases from Excel.

New Learning Objective: VBA

- To learn how to import data from Access into an Excel application by using ADO, and to use the imported data to set up a model on the fly.

New Learning Objective: Non-VBA

- To learn about transportation models and how they can be optimized with Solver.

---

[1] This is due to a limitation of Solver, which allows at most 200 decision variable cells. This limitation is for the version of Solver that is built into Excel. Frontline Systems offers commercial versions of Solver with much larger limits.

24.2 Functionality of the Application

The application performs the following functions:

1. It presents a dialog box where the user can choose from two lists: a list of plants and a list of retailers. These lists are populated using ADO, which reads all of the plants from the Capacity table and all of the retailers from the Demand table. The resulting transportation model uses only the *selected* plants and retailers.
2. It again uses ADO, through VBA, to retrieve the data on capacities, demands, and unit costs from the Access tables to develop a transportation model for the selected plants and retailers. It then uses Solver to optimize this model.
3. It reports the minimum total cost and the positive amounts shipped on all arcs in a Report worksheet.

24.3 Running the Application

The application is in the file **Transportion.xlsm**. When this file is opened, the Explanation worksheet in Figure 24.1 appears. When the button is clicked, the user sees the dialog box in Figure 24.2. It has a list of all plants and retailers in the database, and the user can select any number of them from the lists. The data from the database for the selected plants and retailers are then imported into the (hidden) Model worksheet (see Figure 24.3), the transportation model is developed, Solver is set up and run, and the results are transferred to the Report worksheet. This Report

Figure 24.1 Explanation Worksheet

Transportation Model Application

Run the application

This application uses VBA code to get inputs for a user-selected set of plants and retailers. It imports the data an Access database and then solves a transportation model with these inputs.

The data are in three tables of the Access database. The Capacity table has capacities for each plant. The Demand table has demands for each retailer. The UnitCost table has unit shipping costs for each plant-retailer combination. The user specifies which plants and retailers to use in the model. Then the application imports the appropriate data from the database, enters this data into an optimization model, sets up the model formulas, and runs Solver to optimize.

The final report lists the total transportation cost, along with the quantities to ship between each selected plant and each selected retailer.

Figure 24.2 Dialog Box for Selecting Plants and Retailers

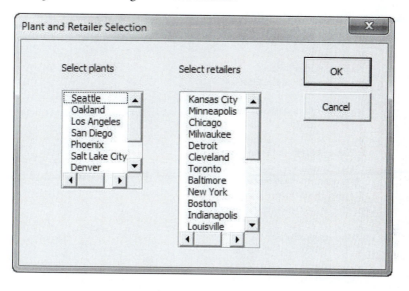

Figure 24.3 Transportation Model

	A	B	C	D	E	F	G	H	I	J	K	L
1	Transportation Model											
2												
3		Unit Costs		Retailers								
4				Chicago	Detroit	Cleveland	Toronto	New York	Boston	Indianapolis		Capacity
5		Plants	Seattle	$23.34	$27.14	$14.38	$19.76	$18.46	$24.64	$30.39		1300
6			Oakland	$16.67	$22.42	$24.09	$12.23	$10.48	$21.97	$25.16		1200
7			Los Angeles	$25.45	$31.54	$26.49	$27.70	$16.70	$25.81	$16.09		1000
8			San Diego	$26.41	$20.58	$21.70	$10.68	$17.67	$21.15	$15.25		1500
9			Phoenix	$23.36	$23.03	$22.62	$14.83	$14.31	$12.25	$20.55		1300
10			Salt Lake City	$13.11	$18.50	$18.44	$21.11	$21.98	$12.65	$20.07		1000
11												
12			Demand	500	450	200	500	500	300	450		
13												
14		Shipments									Sent out	
15				0	0	200	0	0	0	0	200	
16				0	0	0	0	500	0	0	500	
17				0	0	0	0	0	0	0	0	
18				0	0	0	500	0	0	450	950	
19				0	0	0	0	0	300	0	300	
20				500	450	0	0	0	0	0	950	
21			Sent in	500	450	200	500	500	300	450		
22												
23		Total Cost		$38,874								

worksheet, an example of which is shown in Figure 24.4, indicates all positive shipments, along with the total shipping cost. At this point, the user can run another problem (with a different selection of plants and/or retailers).

Figure 24.4 Report of Optimal Solution

	B	C	D	E	F	G	H	I
1	**Optimal Solution**							
2								
3	**Shipments from Seattle**					**Total shipping cost is $38,874**		
4		200 units to Cleveland						
5								
6	**Shipments from Oakland**							
7		500 units to New York				Run another problem		
8								
9	**No shipments from Los Angeles**							
10								
11	**Shipments from San Diego**							
12		500 units to Toronto						
13		450 units to Indianapolis						
14								
15	**Shipments from Phoenix**							
16		300 units to Boston						
17								
18	**Shipments from Salt Lake City**							
19		500 units to Chicago						
20		450 units to Detroit						

24.4 Setting Up the Access Database

The application depends entirely on the Access database. The application uses the database with the Capacity, Demand, and UnitCost tables shown in Figures 24.5, 24.6, and 24.7 (with some hidden rows in the latter). The tables are related through the PlantID and RetailerID fields, as indicated by the relationships diagram in Figure 24.8. The application will work for any database structured this way, provided the following are true:

- It should be named **Transportation.mdb**, and it should be located in the *same* folder as the **Transportation.xlsm** Excel file. Actually, the file name could be changed, but the appropriate line in the VBA module, where the name of the file is specified, would have to be changed accordingly.
- It should have three tables named Capacity, Demand, and UnitCost.
- The Capacity table should be structured as in Figure 24.5. It should have a record (row) for each plant, and it should have three fields (columns) named PlantID, Plant, and Capacity. The PlantID field is an AutoNumber primary key field, used to index the plants. (This means that it is automatically populated with consecutive integers.) The Plant field contains the name of the plant, and the Capacity field contains the capacity of the plant. The Demand table should be structured similarly for the retailers.
- The UnitCost table should be structured as in Figure 24.7. It should have a record for each plant-retailer pair, and it should have three fields named PlantID, RetailerID, and UnitCost. The PlantID and RetailerID fields are

Figure 24.5 Capacity Table in Access Database

Figure 24.6 Demand Table in Access Database

Figure 24.7 UnitCost Table in Access Database

PlantID	RetailerID	UnitCost
1	1	$13.24
1	2	$20.04
1	3	$23.34
1	4	$14.30
1	5	$27.14
1	6	$14.38
1	7	$19.76
1	8	$21.31
1	9	$18.46
1	10	$24.64
1	11	$30.39
1	12	$24.55
1	13	$15.26
1	14	$16.30
1	15	$25.30
1	16	$24.00
1	17	$20.88
1	18	$15.68
1	19	$18.43
1	20	$21.87
1	21	$23.01
1	22	$22.68
1	23	$20.76
1	24	$21.07
1	25	$23.59
2	1	$21.43
2	2	$22.37

Record: 1 of 250

Figure 24.8 Relationships Diagram for Access Database

foreign keys. They reference the corresponding rows in the Capacity and Demand tables. The UnitCost field contains the unit shipping cost for the associated plant-retailer route.

- The tables should be related as indicated in Figure 24.8.

Figure 24.9 Template for Model Worksheet

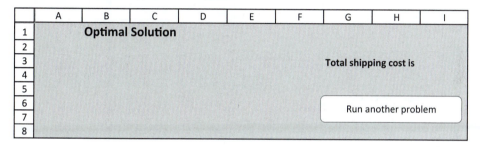

Figure 24.10 Template for Report Worksheet

24.5 Setting Up the Excel Sheets

The **Transportation.xlsm** file contains three worksheets: the Explanation worksheet in Figure 24.1, the Model worksheet in Figure 24.3, and the Report worksheet in Figure 24.4. The Model worksheet must be set up almost completely at run time because its size depends on the plants and retailers selected by the user. Therefore, the only template that can be formed in the Model worksheet at design time is shown in Figure 24.9. Similarly, the only template that can be set up in the Report worksheet at design time is shown in Figure 24.10.

24.6 Getting Started with the VBA

This application requires a module and a user form named frmInputs.[2] In addition, two references must be set. First, because Solver functions are used, a reference must be set to Solver. Also, because the ADO object model is being used, a reference must be set to it. To do so, select the **Tools→References** menu item in the VBE, scroll down the list for the Microsoft ActiveX Data Objects x.x Library

---

[2] It also contains the usual frmSolver that simply displays a message about possible Solver problems when the workbook is opened, but only users of pre-2010 versions of Excel will see this message.

items, and check one of their boxes.[3] (See Figure 24.11.) After this is done, the Project Explorer will look as shown in Figure 24.12. Note that there is no reference showing for ADO, only for Solver. Evidently, Microsoft lists only the *non-Microsoft* references in the Project Explorer.

Figure 24.11 References Dialog Box

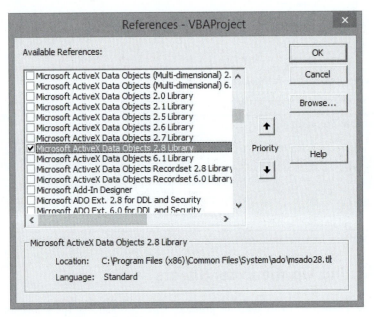

Figure 24.12 Project Explorer Window

---

[3] My PC lists versions 2.0, 2.1, 2.5, 2.6, 2.7, 2.8, and 6.1 of the ADO library. By the time you read this, there might be later versions. I have used version 2.8 in this application to be compatible with users who have earlier versions of Excel, but any of these versions, at least any from 2.5 on, should work fine.

Workbook_Open Code

To guarantee that the Explanation sheet appears when the file is opened, the following code is placed in the ThisWorkbook code window. It also hides the Model and Report worksheets, and it displays the usual Solver warning for pre-2010 versions of Excel.

```
Private Sub Workbook_Open()
    With wsExplanation
        .Activate
        .Range("G18").Select
    End With
    wsModel.Visible = False
    wsReport.Visible = False
    If Not (Application.Version = "15.0" Or Application.Version = "14.0") Then frmSolver.Show
End Sub
```

24.7 The User Form

The frmInputs form allows the user to select any subsets of plants and retailers from the sets of all plants and retailers in the database. It uses two list boxes, named lbPlants and lbRetailers, to do this. Each has its MultiSelect property set to 2-fmMultiSelectExtended so that the user can indeed select *several* items from each list. The design of this form is shown in Figure 24.13.

Recall from Chapter 11 that multi-select list boxes have a Selected property that is essentially a 0-based Boolean array. Each element indicates whether the corresponding item in the list has been selected. The ShowInputsDialog function uses this property to capture the selected plants and retailers in 1-based arrays, selectedPlant and selectedRetailer. (The Valid function also checks that the user selects at least one item from each list.) After it captures these arrays, it builds two strings, plantList and retailerList, that are used in a later SQL statement to get the required unit costs from the UnitCost table. For example, if the user selects the plants Seattle, Oakland, and Dallas, then plantList is "('Seattle','Oakland', 'Dallas')". The Initialize sub populates the list boxes with *all* of the plants and retailers from the database, which by this time have been stored in the arrays existingPlants and existingRetailers.

Figure 24.13 frmInputs Design

```
Private cancel As Boolean

Public Function ShowInputsDialog(existingPlant() As String, _
        existingRetailer() As String, _
        nSelectedPlants As Integer, selectedPlant() As String, _
        nSelectedRetailers As Integer, selectedRetailer() As String, _
        plantList As String, retailerList As String) As Boolean
    Dim i As Integer

    Call Initialize(existingPlant, existingRetailer)
    Me.Show
    If Not cancel Then
        ' Fill an array, selectedPlant, of the plants selected.
        nSelectedPlants = 0
        For i = 1 To lbPlants.ListCount
            If lbPlants.Selected(i - 1) Then
                nSelectedPlants = nSelectedPlants + 1
                ReDim Preserve selectedPlant(1 To nSelectedPlants)
                selectedPlant(nSelectedPlants) = lbPlants.List(i - 1)
            End If
        Next

        ' Build a string, plantList, that looks something like
        ' ('Seattle','Oakland','Dallas'), depending on plants selected.
        plantList = "("
        For i = 1 To nSelectedPlants
            If i < nSelectedPlants Then
                plantList = plantList & "'" & selectedPlant(i) & "',"
            Else
                plantList = plantList & "'" & selectedPlant(i) & "')"
            End If
        Next

        ' Fill an array, selectedRetailer, of the retailers selected.
        nSelectedRetailers = 0
        For i = 1 To lbRetailers.ListCount
            If lbRetailers.Selected(i - 1) Then
                nSelectedRetailers = nSelectedRetailers + 1
                ReDim Preserve selectedRetailer(1 To nSelectedRetailers)
                selectedRetailer(nSelectedRetailers) = lbRetailers.List(i - 1)
            End If
        Next

        ' Build a similar string, retailerList, depending on retailers selected.
        retailerList = "("
        For i = 1 To nSelectedRetailers
            If i < nSelectedRetailers Then
                retailerList = retailerList & "'" & selectedRetailer(i) & "',"
            Else
                retailerList = retailerList & "'" & selectedRetailer(i) & "')"
            End If
        Next
    End If
    ShowInputsDialog = Not cancel
    Unload Me
End Function

Private Sub Initialize(existingPlant() As String, existingRetailer() As String)
    ' Populate the listboxes with the arrays.
    lbPlants.List = existingPlant
    lbRetailers.List = existingRetailer
End Sub
```

```
Private Function Valid() As Boolean
    Dim nSelPlants As Integer, nSelRetailers As Integer
    Dim i As Integer

    Valid = True
    ' At least one plant and at least one retailer must be selected.
    nSelPlants = 0
    For i = 1 To lbPlants.ListCount
        If lbPlants.Selected(i - 1) Then
            nSelPlants = nSelPlants + 1
        End If
    Next
    If nSelPlants = 0 Then
        Valid = False
        MsgBox "You must select at least one plant.", vbInformation, _
            "Selection required"
        Exit Function
    End If

    nSelRetailers = 0
    For i = 1 To lbRetailers.ListCount
        If lbRetailers.Selected(i - 1) Then
            nSelRetailers = nSelRetailers + 1
        End If
    Next
    If nSelRetailers = 0 Then
        Valid = False
        MsgBox "You must select at least one retailer.", vbExclamation, _
            "Selection required"
        Exit Function
    End If
End Function

Private Sub cmdOK_Click()
    If Valid Then Me.Hide
    cancel = False
End Sub

Private Sub cmdCancel_Click()
    Me.Hide
    cancel = True
End Sub

Private Sub UserForm_QueryClose(cancel As Integer, CloseMode As Integer)
    If CloseMode = vbFormControlMenu Then cmdCancel_Click
End Sub
```

24.8 The Module

For a change, there are no module-level variables in the module. Instead, variables are passed from sub to sub, depending on where they are needed. This requires you to check exactly which variables are used in each sub, but it is a good programming practice.

The button on the Explanation worksheet is attached to the MainTransportation sub in the module. This sub calls other subs to retrieve the data from the

Access database, develop the transportation model, run Solver, and report the results. Note how it uses the keyword New to instantiate the Connection object cn. This is done exactly as explained in Chapter 14, so you can refer back to that chapter for details.

MainTransportation Code

```
Sub MainTransportation()
    ' This is the main macro that is run when the button on the
    ' Explanation sheet is clicked.

    ' The following variables could be declared as module-level, which
    ' would require much less passing of arguments below. However, the
    ' method used here shows how variables CAN be passed.
    Dim cn As New ADODB.Connection
    Dim existingPlant() As String, existingRetailer() As String
    Dim nSelectedPlants As Integer, nSelectedRetailers As Integer
    Dim selectedPlant() As String, selectedRetailer() As String
    Dim plantList As String, retailerList As String
    Dim feasible As Boolean

    Application.ScreenUpdating = False

    ' Open a connection to the database. This Excel workbook
    ' and the Access database should be in the same folder.
    With cn
        .ConnectionString = "Data Source=" & _
            ThisWorkbook.Path & "\Transportation.mdb"
        .Provider = "Microsoft.ACE.OLEDB.12.0"
        .Open
    End With

    ' Import the required data from the database.
    Call GetPlantAndRetailers(cn, existingPlant, existingRetailer)
    If frmInputs.ShowInputsDialog(existingPlant, existingRetailer, _
            nSelectedPlants, selectedPlant, nSelectedRetailers, _
            selectedRetailer, plantList, retailerList) Then
        If Not WithinSolverLimit(nSelectedPlants, _
            nSelectedRetailers) Then Exit Sub
        Call EnterModelData(cn, nSelectedPlants, selectedPlant, _
            nSelectedRetailers, selectedRetailer, _
            plantList, retailerList)

        ' Close the connection to the database.
        cn.Close
        Set cn = Nothing

        ' Set up and solver the model.
        Call EnterFormulas(nSelectedPlants, nSelectedRetailers)
        Call SetupAndRunSolver(feasible)
        If feasible Then
            Call CreateReport(nSelectedPlants, nSelectedRetailers, _
                selectedPlant, selectedRetailer)
        End If
    End If
End Sub
```

GetPlantsAndRetailers Code

The GetPlantsAndRetailers sub imports the data from the Capacity and Demand tables of the Access database. Because a connection to the **Transportation.mdb** database file is already open (from the MainTransportation code), it can immediately open a recordset based on a simple SQL statement: **Select Plant From Capacity**. Once this recordset is open, the code loops through the records and stores the plant names in the existingPlant array for later use in the Model worksheet. Then it performs similar steps for retailers.

You should refer to the general discussion of ADO in Chapter 14 as you examine this code. However, it is actually very straightforward once you see the big picture. Once a recordset based on an SQL statement is open, you move through each record of the recordset and extract data from its fields. For example, you reference .Fields("Plant").Value to get the value of the Plant field in the current record. Note that this reference is inside a With rs construction, where rs is the recordset. This means that the reference is really to rs.Fields("Plant").Value. Therefore, you see that the familiar "dot" notation used for Excel objects and properties carries over to ADO.

Several things are worth mentioning about this code. First, it uses a Do loop to step through the records (rows) of the recordset. The stopping condition is While Not .EOF, which is really short for While Not rs.EOF. This means to keep going until you reach the end of the file. Second, there *must* be a .MoveNext line inside the loop. Otherwise, the recordset will be stuck on its *first* record, creating an infinite loop. Finally, you should always close a recordset (rs.Close) when you're finished getting its data.

```
Sub GetPlantAndRetailers(cn As ADODB.Connection, _
        existingPlant() As String, existingRetailer() As String)
    ' This sub gets the potential plants and retailers from the database so that
    ' they can be entered in the listboxes.
    Dim nExisitingPlants As Integer, nExisitingRetailers As Integer
    Dim i As Integer, j As Integer
    Dim rs As New ADODB.Recordset
    Dim SQL As String

    ' Get the plants from the Capacity table to populate the array existingPlant.
    SQL = "Select Plant From Capacity"
    With rs
        .Open SQL, cn
        nExisitingPlants = 0
        Do While Not .EOF
            nExisitingPlants = nExisitingPlants + 1
            ReDim Preserve existingPlant(1 To nExisitingPlants)
            existingPlant(nExisitingPlants) = .Fields("Plant").Value
            .MoveNext
        Loop
        .Close
    End With

    ' Get the retailers from the Demand table to populate the array existingRetailer.
    SQL = "Select Retailer from Demand"
    With rs
        .Open SQL, cn
```

```
            nExisitingRetailers = 0
        Do While Not .EOF
            nExisitingRetailers = nExisitingRetailers + 1
            ReDim Preserve existingRetailer(1 To nExisitingRetailers)
            existingRetailer(nExisitingRetailers) = .Fields("Retailer").Value
            .MoveNext
        Loop
        .Close
    End With

    Set rs = Nothing
End Sub
```

WithinSolverLimit Code

After the user has selected plants and retailers from frmInputs, the WithinSolverLimits function checks whether the Solver limit of 200 changing cells has been exceeded. If so, the user is asked to make other selections.

```
Function WithinSolverLimit(nSelectedPlants As Integer, _
        nSelectedRetailers As Integer) As Boolean
    Dim nChangingCells As Integer

    nChangingCells = nSelectedPlants * nSelectedRetailers
    If nChangingCells > 200 Then
        MsgBox "With your selections, there are " & nChangingCells _
            & " changing cells in the model (" & nSelectedPlants & " x " _
            & nSelectedRetailers & "). The most Solver can handle is 200. " _
            & "Run the program again, and choose fewer plants or retailers.", _
            vbExclamation, "Model too large"
        WithinSolverLimit = False
    Else
        WithinSolverLimit = True
    End If
End Function
```

EnterModelData Code

The EnterModelData sub does the hard work. It uses three SQL statements to import the unit costs, the capacities, and the demands corresponding to the plants and retailers selected from frmInputs. It then places the imported data into the appropriate ranges of the Model worksheet (see Figure 24.3). The hardest part of this sub is the SQL statement for obtaining the unit costs. Although the unit costs obviously come from the UnitCost table, the SQL statement requires inner joins with the Capacity and Demand tables. This is because the UnitCost table stores only IDs (indexes) for the plants and retailers, whereas they need to be accessed by names such as Seattle. Also, the **Where** clause of this SQL statement uses the plantList and retailerList strings created earlier. It will look something like: **Where Plant In ('Seattle', 'Oakland', 'Dallas') And Retailer In ('Chicago', 'New York', 'Miami', 'Orlando', 'Little Rock', 'New Orleans')**. This clause filters out all unit costs except those for the cities listed. The rest of the code is fairly straightforward and is explained by the comments.

```
Sub EnterModelData(cn As ADODB.Connection, nSelectedPlants As Integer, _
        selectedPlant() As String, nSelectedRetailers As Integer, _
        selectedRetailer() As String, plantList As String, retailerList As String)
    ' The following macro uses ADO to place the appropriate data
    ' from the database in the appropriate cells of the Model sheet.
    Dim SQL As String
    Dim rs As New ADODB.Recordset
    Dim i As Integer, j As Integer
    Dim topCell As Range

    ' Clear everything from Model sheet (including formatting).
    With wsModel
        .Cells.Clear
        .Activate

        ' Enter labels.
        .Range("A1").Value = "Transportation Model"
        .Range("B3").Value = "Unit Costs"
        .Range("B5").Value = "Plants"
        .Range("D3").Value = "Retailers"

        Set topCell = .Range("C4")

    End With

' Add headings.
With topCell
    For i = 1 To nSelectedPlants
        .Offset(i, 0).Value = selectedPlant(i)
    Next
    For j = 1 To nSelectedRetailers
        .Offset(0, j).Value = selectedRetailer(j)
    Next
End With

' Get the data with the following SQL statement, and use the
' data to fill in the UnitCost range. The SQL statement requires a couple
' of inner joins. The reason is that the UnitCost table lists only the
' ID's of the plants and retailers. Their names, required in the Where clause,
' are stored in the Capacity and Demand tables.
SQL = "Select UC.UnitCost " _
    & "From (UnitCost UC Inner Join Capacity C On UC.PlantID = C.PlantID) " _
    & "Inner Join Demand D On UC.RetailerID = D.RetailerID " _
    & "Where C.Plant In " & plantList & " And D.Retailer In " & retailerList
With rs
    .Open SQL, cn
    For i = 1 To nSelectedPlants
        For j = 1 To nSelectedRetailers
            topCell.Offset(i, j).Value = .Fields("UnitCost").Value
            .MoveNext
        Next
    Next
    .Close
End With

' Name the range
With topCell
    Range(.Offset(1, 1), .Offset(nSelectedPlants, nSelectedRetailers)) _
        .Name = "UnitCosts"
End With
```

```
' Do the same type of operation to fill in the capacities.
Set topCell = wsModel.Range("C4").Offset(0, nSelectedRetailers + 2)
topCell.Value = "Capacity"

SQL = "Select Capacity From Capacity " & _
    "Where Plant In " & plantList
With rs
    .Open SQL, cn
    For i = 1 To nSelectedPlants
        topCell.Offset(i, 0).Value = .Fields("Capacity").Value
        .MoveNext
    Next
    .Close
End With

With topCell
    Range(.Offset(1, 0), .Offset(nSelectedPlants, 0)).Name = "Capacities"
End With

' Do the same type of operation to fill in the demands.
Set topCell = wsModel.Range("C4").Offset(nSelectedPlants + 2, 0)
topCell.Value = "Demand"

SQL = "Select Demand From Demand " & _
    "Where Retailer In " & retailerList
With rs
    .Open SQL, cn
    For j = 1 To nSelectedRetailers
        topCell.Offset(0, j).Value = .Fields("Demand").Value
        .MoveNext
    Next
    .Close
End With

Set rs = Nothing

With topCell
    Range(.Offset(0, 1), .Offset(0, nSelectedRetailers)).Name = "Demands"
End With
End Sub
```

EnterFormulas Code

By this time, ADO has done its job and is no longer needed. The required data from the database have now been placed in the Model worksheet. The EnterFormulas sub finishes the model by adding formulas to the Model worksheet. These are straightforward. (Again, see Figure 24.3.) Specifically, SUM formulas are required to calculate the total amounts shipped out of any plant and into any retailer. Also, a SUMPRODUCT formula is needed to find the total cost—the sum of unit costs times amounts shipped.

```
Sub EnterFormulas(nSelectedPlants As Integer, nSelectedRetailers As Integer)
    ' This sub puts the various formulas in the Model sheet, including
    ' the total shipped out of each plant and the total shipped into
    ' each retailer.
    Dim outOfRange As Range, intoRange As Range
```

```
        Dim topCell As Range

    With wsModel
        .Activate

        ' Set up changing cells (Shipments) range and enter 0's as initial values
        .Range("B4").Offset(nSelectedPlants + 4, 0).Value = "Shipments"

        Set topCell = .Range("C4").Offset(nSelectedPlants + 4, 0)
        With Range(topCell.Offset(1, 1), _
            topCell.Offset(nSelectedPlants, nSelectedRetailers))
            .Name = "Shipments"
            .Value = 0
            .BorderAround Weight:=xlMedium, ColorIndex:=3
        End With

        ' Enter formulas for row and column sums for "SentOut" and "SentIn" ranges.
        Set topCell = .Range("Shipments").Cells(1)
    End With

    With topCell
        .Offset(-1, nSelectedRetailers).Value = "Sent out"
        .Offset(nSelectedPlants, -1).Value = "Sent in"
        Set outOfRange = Range(.Offset(0, nSelectedRetailers), _
            .Offset(nSelectedPlants - 1, nSelectedRetailers))
        Set intoRange = Range(.Offset(nSelectedPlants, 0), _
            .Offset(nSelectedPlants, nSelectedRetailers - 1))
    End With

    With outOfRange
        .Name = "SentOut"
        .FormulaR1C1 = "=SUM(RC[-" & nSelectedRetailers & "]:RC[-1])"
    End With

    With intoRange
        .Name = "SentIn"
        .FormulaR1C1 = "=SUM(R[-" & nSelectedPlants &"]C:R[-1]C)"
    End With

    ' Calculate total cost in "TotalCost" range.
    Set topCell = wsModel.Range("SentIn").Item(1).Offset(2, 0)
    With topCell
        .Formula = "=SumProduct(UnitCosts,Shipments)"
        .Name = "TotalCost"
        .NumberFormat = "$#,##0_);($#,##0)"
        .Offset(0, -2).Value = "Total Cost"
    End With

    wsModel.Range("A1").Select
End Sub
```

SetupAndRunSolver Code

The SetupAndRunSolver sub sets up and then runs Solver. It checks for infeasibility (code 5 of the SolverSolve function). If there are no feasible solutions, a message to that effect is displayed and the user is asked to make different input selections.

```
Sub SetupAndRunSolver(feasible As Boolean)
    Dim solverStatus As Integer

    With wsModel
        .Visible = True
        .Activate

        SolverReset
        SolverAdd .Range("Shipments"), 3, 0
        SolverAdd .Range("SentOut"), 1, "Capacities"
        SolverAdd .Range("SentIn"), 3, "Demands"
        SolverOptions AssumeNonNeg:=True
        SolverOk SetCell:=.Range("TotalCost"), MaxMinVal:=2, _
            ByChange:=.Range("Shipments"), Engine:=1

        ' Run Solver. If there are no feasible solutions (code 5), call the
        ' MainTransport sub. The effect is to let the user try again.
        solverStatus = SolverSolve(UserFinish:=True)
        If solverStatus = 5 Then
            MsgBox "There is no feasible solution. Try a different combination of " _
                & "plants and retailers.", vbExclamation, "Infeasible"
            .Visible = False
            wsExplanation.Activate
            feasible = False
        Else
            feasible = True
            .Visible = False
        End If
    End With
End Sub
```

CreateReport Code

Finally, the CreateReport sub transfers the total shipping cost and the information about all routes with *positive* flows to the Report worksheet. If there are no shipments out of a particular plant, a note to this effect is included in the report. (See Figure 24.4 for an example.)

```
Sub CreateReport(nSelectedPlants As Integer, nSelectedRetailers As Integer, _
        selectedPlant() As String, selectedRetailer() As String)
    ' Finally, report the results in the Report sheet.
    Dim i As Integer, j As Integer
    Dim nShippedTo As Integer, amountShipped As Integer
    Dim topCell As Range

    ' Clear everything from Report sheet (including formatting), but not the button.
    With wsReport
        .Cells.Clear
        .Visible = True
        .Activate

        ' Enter heading and format.
        With .Range("B1")
            .Value = "Optimal Solution"
            With .Font
                .Size = 14
                .Bold = True
            End With
```

```
End With
With ActiveWindow
    .DisplayGridlines = False
    .DisplayHeadings = False
End With
.Cells.Interior.ColorIndex = 40
.Columns("B:B").Font.ColorIndex = 1
.Columns("C:C").Font.ColorIndex = 5
.Range("B1").Font.ColorIndex = 1

' For each route that ships a positive amount, print how much is shipped.
Set topCell = .Range("B3")
For i = 1 To nSelectedPlants
    If wsModel.Range("SentOut").Cells(i).Value > 0.1 Then
        With topCell
            .Value = "Shipments from " & selectedPlant(i)
            .Font.Bold = True
        End With
        nShippedTo = 0
        For j = 1 To nSelectedRetailers
            amountShipped = wsModel.Range("Shipments").Cells(i, j).Value
            If amountShipped > 0.01 Then
                nShippedTo = nShippedTo + 1
                topCell.Offset(nShippedTo, 1).Value = _
                    amountShipped & " units to " & selectedRetailer(j)
            End If
        Next
        Set topCell = topCell.Offset(nShippedTo + 2, 0)
    Else
        With topCell
            .Value = "No shipments from " & selectedPlant(i)
            .Font.Bold = True
        End With
        Set topCell = topCell.Offset(2, 0)
    End If
Next

' Record the total shipping cost.
With .Range("G3")
    .Value = "Total shipping cost is " & _
        Format(wsModel.Range("TotalCost").Value, "$#,##0;($#,##0)")
    .Font.Bold = True
End With

.Range("A1").Select
End With
End Sub
```

24.9   Summary

Virtually all of the VBA applications you will develop in Excel will require data, and it is very possible that the required data will reside in an external database format such as Access. (Actually, it is more likely that the data will reside in a server-based database such as SQL Server or Oracle, but the code would not change much from what I have presented here.) This chapter has demonstrated how to import the data from an Access database into Excel for use in a transportation model. This requires you to use the basic functionality of the ADO object model. It also requires you to know how to write SQL statements, the language of databases. However, the effort required to learn these is well spent. Knowing how to import data from an external database is an extremely valuable skill in today's business world, and it is likely to become even more valuable in the future.

EXERCISES

1. The application currently has no charts. Change it so that the user can view two charts (each on a separate chart sheet) after Solver has been run. The first should be a column chart showing the total amount shipped and the total capacity for each selected plant, something similar to that in Figure 24.14. Likewise, the second chart should show the total amount shipped to each selected retailer and the retailer's demand. (Actually, the latter two should be equal, given the way the transportation problem has been modeled. There is absolutely no incentive to send a retailer *more* than it demands.) As always, do as much at design time, and write as little VBA code, as possible.

2. I claimed that this application works with any data, provided that the database file is structured properly. Try the following. Open the **Transportation.mdb** file

Figure 24.14 Shipments from Plants for Exercise 1

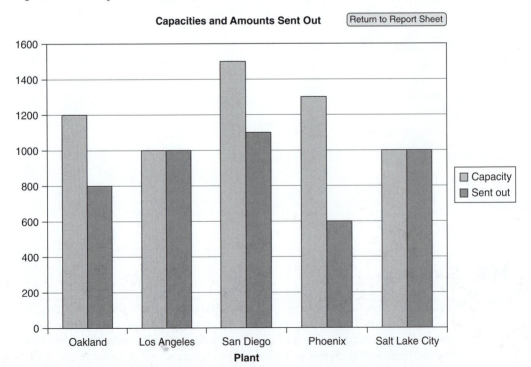

in Access and change its data in some way. (You can change names of plants, unit costs, and so on. You can even add some plants or retailers. Just be sure that there is a row in the UnitCost table for each plant-retailer pair.) Then rerun the application to check that it still works properly.

3. Repeat the previous exercise, but now create a *new* Access file called **MyData.mdb** (stored in the same folder as the Excel application), structured exactly as **Transportation.mdb**, and add some data to it. Then rerun the application to check that it still works properly. (Note that you will have to change one line of the VBA code so that it references the correct name of your new Access file.)

4. The previous problem indicates a "fix" that no business would ever tolerate—they would never be willing to get into the VBA code to change a file name reference. A much better alternative is to change the VBA code in the first place so that it asks the user for the location and name of the database file. You could do this with an input box (and risk having the user spell something wrong), but Excel provides an easier way with the FileDialog object, as illustrated in Chapter 13. Use this to change the application, so that it prompts the user for the name and location of the database file. Actually, you should probably precede the above line with a MsgBox statement so that the user knows she is being asked to select the file with the data. Then try the modified application with your own Access file, stored in a folder *different* from the folder containing the Excel application.

25 A Stock-Trading Simulation Application

25.1 Introduction

In *Practical Management Science*, we illustrate two ways to run spreadsheet simulations. Each method starts with a spreadsheet model that includes random quantities in selected cells. The first method creates a data table to replicate desired outputs. Summary measures and charts can then be obtained manually from this data table. The second method uses Palisade's @RISK simulation add-in. Once the user designates desired output cells, @RISK runs all of the replications and automatically creates summary measures, including charts, for these outputs. This application illustrates how VBA can be used to automate a simulation model, similar to the way @RISK does it. However, no data tables are created, and no add-ins are required.

The model itself simulates the trading activity of an investor in the stock market over the period of a year (250 trading days). This investor starts with a given amount of cash and owns several shares of a stock. The investor then uses a "buy low/sell high" trading strategy. The trading strategy implemented in the model is as follows: If the price of the stock increases 2 days in a row, the investor sells 10% of his shares. If it increases 3 days in a row, he sells 25% of his shares. In the other direction, if the price decreases 2 days in a row, the investor buys 10% more shares. For example, if he owns 500 shares, he buys 50 more shares. If the price decreases 3 days in a row, he buys 25% more shares. The only restriction on buying is that the investor cannot spend more than his current cash. The price of the stock is generated randomly through a lognormal model used by many financial analysts.

The simulation keeps track of five output measures: (1) the investor's cash at the end of the year, (2) the value of the investor's stock at the end of the year, (3) the gain (or loss) from the investor's cash/stock portfolio at the end of the year, relative to what he owned at the beginning of the year, (4) the lowest price of the stock during the year, and (5) the highest price of the stock during the year.

New Learning Objectives: VBA

- To illustrate how to automate a spreadsheet simulation model with VBA.
- To illustrate how the run time of a simulation can be affected by the recalculation mode.
- To show how to use VBA to enter an array function into an Excel range.

New Learning Objective: Non-VBA

- To show how simulation can be used to measure the effectiveness of a stock market trading strategy.

25.2 Functionality of the Application

The application has the following functionality:

1. It allows the user to specify a trading strategy. As written, the user can change the percentages to sell if the stock price increases 2 or 3 days in a row and the similar percentages to buy if the price decreases 2 or 3 days in a row. The model can be modified slightly to examine other types of trading strategies—buy high, sell low, for example—without any changes in the VBA code.
2. The simulation can be run for up to 1,000 replications. (This limit can easily be changed.) As it runs, it keeps track of the five outputs listed in the introduction. It then reports summary measures for these outputs (minimum, maximum, average, standard deviation, median, and 5th and 95th percentiles), and it creates histograms of the outputs. The application can be modified fairly easily to incorporate other outputs from the simulation.

25.3 Running the Application

The application is stored in the file **Stock Trading.xlsm**. When this file is opened, the user sees the Explanation worksheet in Figure 25.1.

Figure 25.1 Explanation Worksheet

Figure 25.2 Inputs Worksheet

	A	B	C	D	E	F	G	H	I	J	K	L
1	Inputs to simulation											
2												
3	Inputs			Recent stock prices				Trading strategy				
4	Initial cash	$75,000		3 days ago	$49.86			Buying: if change is negative				
5	Initial shares owned	500		2 days ago	$49.79			3 days in a row, buy		25%	of current shares	
6				1 day ago	$49.95			2 days in a row, buy		10%	of current shares	
7	Daily growth rate of stock price			Current	$50.00			Selling: if change is positive				
8	Mean	0.01%						3 days in a row, sell		25%	of current shares	
9	StDev	2.0%						2 days in a row, sell		10%	of current shares	
10												
11	Implication for the year (assuming 250 trading days per year)											
12	Mean	2.50%	(average annual growth rate of stock price)									
13	StDev	31.62%	(standard deviation of annual growth rate)									
14												
15												
16					Enter any new inputs in the blue cells. Then click on the button							
17					below to run the simulation with these inputs.							
18												
19					Run the simulation							
20												

If the user clicks the left button, the Inputs worksheet in Figure 25.2 appears. The various inputs appear in blue. The user can change any of these before running the simulation. In particular, a different trading strategy can be tried by changing the percentages in column J. Also, note that the current price (on day 1) and the prices on the 3 previous days are shown in column E. Because the investor's trading strategy depends on the three previous price changes, these past prices are required for the trading decisions on the first few days.

When the user clicks the button in Figure 25.2 (or the right button in Figure 25.1), the input box in Figure 25.3 is displayed. Here the user can choose any number of replications, up to 1000, for the simulation.

After the user clicks the OK button, the simulation runs. It recalculates the random numbers on the hidden Model worksheet (more about this later) for each replication, stores the outputs on the (hidden) Replications worksheet, and calculates summary measures, which are stored on the Summary worksheet, shown in Figure 25.4. This can take quite a while, so a replication counter placed on the Explanation worksheet shows the progress. This counter is certainly not necessary for the proper running of the simulation, but it is a nice touch for the user.

Each output has a corresponding histogram worksheet. These are created at design time, and they are then updated at the end of the simulation. As

Figure 25.3 Input Box for Number of Replications

Number of reps   ☒

How many replications of the year-long simulation do you want to run? (Enter an integer no greater than 1000.)

OK

Cancel

500

Figure 25.4 Summary Results from Simulation

	A	B	C	D	E	F
1	Summary results from the simulation					
2						
3		Ending cash	Ending stock value	Cum gain/loss	Min price	Max price
4	Min	$0	$38	($33,081)	$16.29	$50.00
5	Max	$121,307	$103,991	$31,821	$50.00	$137.98
6	Average	$90,039	$11,102	$255	$39.36	$63.60
7	Stdev	$22,940	$20,581	$8,418	$6.87	$13.49
8	Median	$100,002	$1,925	$1,923	$40.04	$59.69
9	5th percentile	$38,793	$53	($18,704)	$27.25	$50.18
10	95th percentile	$106,334	$62,013	$10,029	$49.50	$88.56
11						
12			For further results, take a look at any of the histogram sheets. They show			
13			histograms of the various output measures.			
14						

an example, the histogram for the cumulative gain/loss output appears in Figure 25.5.

If the user then returns to the Explanation worksheet and runs the simulation again, the results will differ, even if the same inputs are used, because *new* random numbers will be used in the simulation.

Figure 25.5 Histogram for Cumulative Gain/Loss

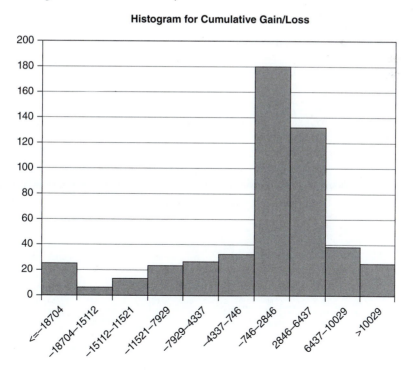

25.4 Setting Up the Excel Sheets

The **Stock Trading.xlsm** file contains 10 worksheets. These are named Explanation, Inputs, Model, Replications, Summary, and Histogram1 through Histogram5.

The Model Worksheet

The Model worksheet, shown in Figure 25.6 (with many hidden rows), can be set up *completely* at design time. From row 10 down, this worksheet models the trading activity for a 250-day period. I will discuss a few of the formulas in this sheet; you can open the file and examine the rest. First, the stock prices in column B are determined from the well-known lognormal stock price model. Specifically, the formula in cell B17, which is copied down column B, is

```
=ROUND(B16*EXP((GrMean−0.5*GrStdev^2)
  +GrStdev*NORMINV(RAND(),0,1)),2)
```

This formula uses the daily mean growth rate and standard deviation of growth rate (GrMean and GrStdev, from cells B8 and B9 of the Inputs worksheet), along with a standard normal random number—from NORMINV(RAND(),0,1)—to generate the day's price from the previous day's price in cell B16.

Second, the trading strategy is implemented in columns E and F with rather complex IF functions. For example, the number of shares bought in cell F16 uses the formula

Figure 25.6 Simulation Model and Outputs

	A	B	C	D	E	F	G	H	I	J	K	L
1	Stock Market Simulation											
2												
3	Outputs from one year-long simulation											
4	Ending cash	$101,386										
5	Ending value of stock owned	$62										
6	Cumulative gain/loss	$1,448										
7	Lowest stock price	$42.02										
8	Highest stock price	$71.85										
9												
10	Simulation											
11			Stock price		Trading activity				Value of stock/cash portfolio			
12		Day	Beginning price	Change from previous day	Beginning shares	Shares sold	Shares purchase	Ending shares	Beginning cash	Change in cash	Ending cash	Worth of shares	Cumulative gain/loss
13			$49.86										
14			$49.79	−$0.07									
15			$49.95	$0.16									
16		1	$50.00	$0.05	500	50	0	450	$75,000	$2,500	$77,500	$22,500	$0
17		2	$50.53	$0.53	450	113	0	337	$77,500	$5,710	$83,210	$17,029	$239
18		3	$51.63	$1.10	337	84	0	253	$83,210	$4,337	$87,547	$13,062	$609
19		4	$51.86	$0.23	253	63	0	190	$87,547	$3,267	$90,814	$9,853	$667
20		5	$52.90	$1.04	190	48	0	142	$90,814	$2,539	$93,353	$7,512	$865
261		246	$68.75	−$2.69	1	0	0	1	$101,386	$0	$101,386	$69	$1,455
262		247	$67.36	−$1.39	1	0	0	1	$101,386	$0	$101,386	$67	$1,454
263		248	$65.08	−$2.28	1	0	0	1	$101,386	$0	$101,386	$65	$1,451
264		249	$62.76	−$2.32	1	0	0	1	$101,386	$0	$101,386	$63	$1,449
265		250	$62.19	−$0.57	1	0	0	1	$101,386	$0	$101,386	$62	$1,448

```
=IF(AND(C14<0,C15<0,C16<0),MIN(ROUND(BuyPct3*D16,0),
   INT(H16/B16)),IF(AND(C15<0,C16<0),MIN(ROUND
   (BuyPct2*D16,0),INT(H16/B16)),0))
```

Here, BuyPct3 and BuyPct2 are 25% and 10%, respectively, from cells J5 and J6 of the Inputs worksheet. The formula first checks whether the price has decreased 3 days in a row. If it has, the investor buys the smaller of two quantities—the number of shares he would like to buy (25% of what he owns), and the number of shares he has cash for (his cash divided by the current stock price, rounded down to the nearest integer). If the price has not decreased 3 days in a row, the formula then checks whether it has decreased 2 days in a row. If it has, the investor again purchases the smaller of two quantities. If it hasn't, the investor buys nothing.

Finally, the cumulative gain/loss in column L is the current value of the cash/stock portfolio minus the initial value on day 1. For example, the formula for the last day in cell L265 is

```
=(J265+K265)−(InitCash+InitShares*InitPrice)
```

where InitCash, InitShares, and InitPrice refer to cells B4, B5, and E7 of the Inputs worksheet.

Once the 250-day model has been developed, the outputs in rows 4–8 can be calculated easily. For example, the formulas in cells B6 and B7 are **=L265** and **=MIN(B16:B265)**. Note that these outputs summarize a *single* 250-day replication.

The Replication Worksheet

When the simulation runs for, say, 500 replications, the VBA code forces the model to recalculate 500 times, each time producing new random numbers and therefore new outputs in the Model worksheet. It captures these outputs and stores them in the (hidden) Replications worksheet, as shown in Figure 25.7 (with many hidden rows). These outputs are then summarized in the Summary worksheet at the end of the simulation. Note that the Replications worksheet and the Summary worksheet (in Figure 25.4) have only labels, no numbers, at design time.

Figure 25.7   Replications Worksheet

	A	B	C	D	E	F
1	Results of individual replications					
2						
3	Replication	Ending cash	Ending stock value	Cum gain/loss	Min price	Max price
4	1	$104,408	$3,579	($912)	$46.01	$59.26
5	2	$103,063	$5,549	$6,586	$39.06	$61.87
6	3	$82,438	$3,617	($10,782)	$47.76	$70.13
7	4	$107,709	$247	$7,897	$46.62	$90.65
501	498	$103,899	$7,128	$1,173	$39.48	$62.43
502	499	$105,395	$54	$1,688	$42.17	$93.51
503	500	$41,788	$57	($2,553)	$44.44	$63.52

Data Sheets for Histograms

The histogram for each output is formed from a column of data in Figure 25.7 and from information on categories (usually called *bins*). The individual data, such as ending cash amounts, are placed into these bins and are then counted to obtain the histogram. The application uses 10 bins for each histogram. The first bin extends up to the 5th percentile for the output, the last extends beyond the 95th percentile, and the other eight bins are of equal width between the extremes. This information is summarized in a histogram sheet for each output at the end of the simulation.

For example, Figure 25.8 shows the data for the Cumulative Gain/Loss output. Column A contains the upper limit of each bin (other than the rightmost), column B contains horizontal axis labels (where –18704--15112, for example, means "from minus 18704 to minus 15112"), and column C contains the frequencies (obtained with Excel's FREQUENCY function, discussed below).

Note that sample data can be placed in these data worksheets, and histograms can be created from the sample data, at design time. The data in the histogram worksheets can then be updated at run time, and the histograms will change automatically.

25.5 Getting Started with the VBA

This application includes only a module—no user forms and no references. Once the module is inserted, the Project Explorer window will appear as in Figure 25.9.

Workbook_Open Code

The following code is placed in the ThisWorkbook code window. It activates the Explanation worksheet and hides all other worksheets.

Figure 25.8 Data for Cumulative Gain/Loss Histogram

	A	B	C
1	Frequency table for Cum gain/loss		
2			
3	Upper limit	Category	Frequency
4	-18704	<=-18704	25
5	-15112	-18704--15112	6
6	-11521	-15112--11521	13
7	-7929	-11521--7929	23
8	-4337	-7929--4337	26
9	-746	-4337--746	32
10	2846	-746-2846	180
11	6437	2846-6437	132
12	10029	6437-10029	38
13		>10029	25

Figure 25.9 Project Explorer Window

```
Private Sub Workbook_Open()
    Dim ws As Worksheet
    With wsExplanation
        .Activate
        .Range("G4").Select
    End With
    For Each ws In ThisWorkbook.Worksheets
        If ws.CodeName <> "wsExplanation" Then ws.Visible = False
    Next
End Sub
```

25.6 The Module

The module contains a Main sub, which calls several subs to do most of the work. The Main sub also does some work itself. It gets the number of desired replications from an input box, it clears the contents from the Replications worksheet from any previous run, and it places some (temporary) labels in row 21 of the Explanation worksheet. These are used to show the progress of the simulation as it runs.

Main Code

```
Option Explicit

Dim nReps As Integer

Sub Main ()
    ' This sub runs when the user clicks the "Run the simulation"
    ' button on the Explanation sheet (or the Inputs sheet).
```

```
    Dim i As Integer

    ' Get the number of replications (no greater than 1000).
    Do
        nReps = InputBox("How many replications of the year-long " _
            & "simulation do you want to run? (Enter an integer no " _
            & "greater than 1000.)", "Number of reps")
        If nReps > 1000 Then MsgBox "The number of reps should not " _
            & "exceed 1000.", vbExclamation, "Too many reps"
    Loop Until nReps <= 1000

    ' Clear previous results.
    With wsReplications.Range("A3")
        Range(.Offset(1, 0), .Offset(0, 5).End(xlDown)).ClearContents
    End With

    ' Enter labels for a replication counter on the Explanation sheet.
    With wsExplanation
        .Activate
        .Range("D21").Value = "Simulating replication"
        .Range("G21").Value = "of"
        .Range("H21").Value = nReps

        ' Run the simulation and collect the stats.
        Call RunSimulation

        ' Delete counters and turn off screen updating.
        .Range("D21:H21").ClearContents
        Application.ScreenUpdating = False

        Call CollectStats

        ' Delete the replication counter on the Explanation sheet.
        .Range("D18:H18").ClearContents

        ' Update the histogram data.
        Call UpdateHistograms
    End With

    ' Show the results.
    With wsSummary
        .Visible = True
        .Activate
        .Range("A2").Select
    End With

    ' Unhide the histogram sheets.
    For i = 1 To 5
        Worksheets("Histogram " & i).Visible = True
    Next

    Application.ScreenUpdating = True
End Sub
```

RunSimulation Code

The RunSimulation sub runs the simulation for the desired number of replications and stores the outputs in the Replications worksheet for later summarization.

The key to this sub is the Calculate method of the Application object (which is Excel itself). Each time this method is called, it forces a recalculation of the workbook, which generates new random numbers in the simulation model. It's that simple.

A note on Recalculation. Each recalculation takes a fraction of a second, but these fractions add up. The recalculations take place each time the Calculate method is called from VBA code, but also each time any change is made to the workbook. This means, for example, that each of the Offset lines below causes a recalculation—each time through the loop. The effect is that the simulation runs rather slowly. Fortunately, it is possible to change Excel's recalculation mode from **Automatic**, the default mode, to **Manual**. (To do this, use the Calculation Options dropdown list on the Formulas ribbon.) In Manual mode, recalculations take place only when the Calculate method is called from VBA (or the F9 key is pressed). I originally ran the simulation in Automatic mode. However, when I converted to Manual mode, the run time decreased dramatically (by a factor of about 7 for a 500-replication run). Try it yourself.

```
Sub RunSimulation()
    ' This sub runs the replications of the simulation. The simulation
    ' model is already set up, so all this sub has to do is force a
    ' recalculation of the sheet and record the results.

    ' Loop over the replications.
    Dim i As Integer
    For i = 1 To nReps

        ' Show the current replication number on the Explanation sheet.
        wsExplanation.Range("RepNumber").Value = i

        ' Force a recalculation.
        Application.Calculate

        ' Record outputs on the Replication sheet.
        With wsReplications.Range("A3")
            .Offset(i, 0).Value = i
            .Offset(i, 1).Value = wsModel.Range("EndCash").Value
            .Offset(i, 2).Value = wsModel.Range("EndStockVal").Value
            .Offset(i, 3).Value = wsModel.Range("CumGainLoss").Value
            .Offset(i, 4).Value = wsModel.Range("MinPrice").Value
            .Offset(i, 5).Value = wsModel.Range("MaxPrice").Value
        End With
    Next
End Sub
```

CollectStats Code

The CollectStats sub uses a For loop to go through the simulation outputs, one at a time. For each, it "sets" the repRange object variable to the range of data in the Replications worksheet to be summarized. It then uses Excel functions to calculate the summary measures and places them in the Summary worksheet. For example, WorksheetFunction.Average(repRange) uses Excel's AVERAGE function to calculate the average of the data in repRange.

```
Sub CollectStats()
    ' This sub summarizes the results of all replications of the simulation.
    Dim i As Integer
    Dim repRange As Range

    ' Loop over the output measures.
    For i = 1 To 5

        ' RepRange is the range on the Replications sheet to summarize.
        With wsReplications.Range("A3")
            Set repRange = Range(.Offset(1, i), .Offset(nReps, i))
        End With

        ' Use Excel's functions to calculate summary measures, and put
        ' them on the Summary sheet.
        With wsSummary.Range("A3")
            .Offset(1, i).Value = WorksheetFunction.Min(repRange)
            .Offset(2, i).Value = WorksheetFunction.Max(repRange)
            .Offset(3, i).Value = WorksheetFunction.Average(repRange)
            .Offset(4, i).Value = WorksheetFunction.StDev(repRange)
            .Offset(5, i).Value = WorksheetFunction.Median(repRange)
            .Offset(6, i).Value = WorksheetFunction.Percentile(repRange, 0.05)
            .Offset(7, i).Value = WorksheetFunction.Percentile(repRange, 0.95)
        End With
    Next
End Sub
```

UpdateHistograms Code

The UpdateHistograms sub also loops over the simulation outputs. For each, it updates the appropriate histogram worksheet (see Figure 25.8), using the results from the simulation.

A note on Array Functions. Pay particular attention to the line.

```
Range(.Offset(1, 2), .Offset(10, 2)).FormulaArray = _
    "=Frequency(Replications!" & repRange.Address & "," _
    & binRange.Address & ")"
```

Excel's FREQUENCY function is called an **array function**. To enter it manually in a worksheet, you need to highlight the range where the frequencies will be placed, type the formula, and press Ctrl+Shift+Enter. To do this in VBA, you specify the range where it will be entered and then use the FormulaArray property. Two other points about this formula are worth noting. First, it is not enough to specify RepRange.Address in the first argument. Because this range is on a *different* worksheet from where the formula is entered, it must be qualified by the worksheet name or code name. (I use the latter.) Second, the binRange required in the second argument is the range of upper limits for the bins. These are the values in column A of the relevant histogram worksheet.

```vba
Sub UpdateHistograms()
' This sub changes the settings for histograms of simulation
' data appropriately.

Dim i As Integer, j As Integer
Dim pct5 As Single, pct95 As Single, increment As Single
Dim repRange As Range, binRange As Range

' Loop over the output measures.
For i = 1 To 5

    ' The histograms each have 10 "bins". The lowest extends
    ' up to the 5th percentile, the last extends beyond the
    ' 95th percentile, and the remaining ones are equal length
    ' beyond these extremes.
    pct5 = wsSummary.Range("A9").Offset(0, i).Value
    pct95 = wsSummary.Range("A10").Offset(0, i).Value
    increment = (pct95 - pct5) / 8

    ' RepRange contains the data for the histogram.
    With wsReplications.Range("A3")
        Set repRange = Range(.Offset(1, i), .Offset(nReps, i))
    End With

    ' The histogram sheets contain the data for building the histograms.
    ' Column A has the bins, column B has labels for the horizontal axis,
    ' and column C has the frequencies (for the heights of the bars).
    With Worksheets("Histogram " & i).Range("A3")
        .Offset(1, 0).Value = Round(pct5, 0)
        .Offset(1, 1).Value = "<=" & .Offset(1, 0).Value
        For j = 2 To 9
            .Offset(j, 0).Value = Round(pct5 + (j - 1) * increment, 0)
            .Offset(j, 1).Value = Round(.Offset(j - 1, 0), 0) _
                & "-" & Round(.Offset(j, 0).Value, 0)
        Next
        .Offset(10, 1).Value = ">" & Round(.Offset(9, 0).Value, 0)
        Set binRange = Range(.Offset(1, 0), .Offset(9, 0))

        ' Excel's Frequency function is an array formula, so the
        ' appropriate property is the FormulaArray property.
        Range(.Offset(1, 2), .Offset(10, 2)).FormulaArray = _
            "=Frequency(Replications!" & repRange.Address & "," _
            & binRange.Address & ")"
    End With
Next
End Sub
```

ViewChangeInputs Code

The ViewChangeInputs sub unhides and activates the Inputs worksheet, allowing the user to view the inputs or enter different inputs before running the simulation.

```
Sub ViewChangeInputs()
    ' This sub runs when the user clicks the "View/change
    ' inputs" button on the Explanation sheet.

    ' Unhide and activate the Inputs sheet so that the user
    ' can view or change them.
    With wsInputs
        .Visible = True
        .Activate
    End With
End Sub
```

25.7 Summary

This application illustrates how to run a spreadsheet simulation model with VBA. You first develop a spreadsheet simulation model, including one or more cells with random functions, in a Model worksheet. To replicate this model, you use a For loop, inside which you call the Calculate method of the Application object to force a recalculation with new random numbers. The rest is a simple matter of recording selected outputs on a Replications worksheet and then summarizing them as desired at the end of the simulation. Because all of this can take a while, especially with many replications of a complex model, it is a good idea to set Excel's calculation mode to Manual, rather the Automatic, before running the simulation.

EXERCISES

1. Prove to yourself that the simulation runs much faster when Excel's calculation mode is set to Manual. Run the simulation in the current **Stock Trading.xlsm** file for about 250 replications, with calculation mode set to Manual. Then change the calculation mode to Automatic and run the simulation again. Keep track of the run time for each—you should see a noticeable difference.

2. Experiment with the same basic buy-low/sell-high trading strategy, but with different percentages in column J of the Inputs worksheet. Can you find any strategies that consistently outperform others?

3. Repeat the previous exercise, but now change the basic type of strategy to buy high/sell low. That is, if the price goes up, you buy more shares, whereas if it goes down, you sell. What changes do you need to make to the simulation model? Do you need to make any changes to the VBA code? Do these strategies tend to do better or worse than those in the previous exercise?

4. Change the application so that there is no limit on the shares the investor can buy. For example, if his strategy tells him to buy 25% more shares but he doesn't have enough cash to do so, he *borrows* the cash he needs. Now his cash positions in columns H and J of the Model worksheet can be negative, indicating that he owes money to the lender. Capture the maximum he ever owes during the year in an extra output cell, keep track of it, and summarize it, just like the other outputs, with your VBA code.

5. Change the application so that if the investor ever gets to a point where his cumulative gain for the year is above some threshold level, he sells his stock and does no more trading for the rest of the year. Your revised application should ask for the threshold with an input box. Also, it should add an extra output cell: the number of days it takes to reach the threshold (which is defined as 251 in case he never gets there). Keep track of this output and summarize it, just like the other outputs, with your VBA code.

26

A Capital Budgeting Application

26.1 Introduction

This application illustrates how VBA can be used to compare an optimal procedure with a good but nonoptimal heuristic procedure. This is done for a capital budgeting problem, where a company must decide which of several projects to undertake. Each project incurs an initial cost and provides a stream of future cash flows, summarized by a net present value (NPV). Each project is an all-or-nothing proposition—it cannot be undertaken partway. Other than that, the only constraint is that the sum of the initial costs of the projects undertaken cannot exceed a given budget. The objective is to find the subset of projects that maximizes the total NPV and stays within the budget.

One solution method is to solve the problem optimally with Excel's Solver, using binary decision variable cells to indicate which projects to undertake. Another possibility is to use an intuitive heuristic procedure that operates as follows. It first ranks the projects in decreasing order of the ratio of NPV to initial cost ("bang for buck"). Then it goes through the list of projects in this order, adding each as long as there is enough money left in the budget. The application compares the total NPVs obtained by these two methods.

New Learning Objectives: VBA

- To illustrate how a simple heuristic can be implemented in VBA with looping and arrays.
- To illustrate how random inputs for a model can be generated by VBA as formulas in a worksheet and how they can then be "frozen" with the Copy and PasteSpecial methods of Range objects.

New Learning Objectives: Non-VBA

- To compare a simple heuristic solution method with an optimal integer programming method.
- To show the effect of the Solver's Integer Optimality setting in an integer programming model.

26.2 Functionality of the Application

The application has the following functionality:

1. It first asks the user for the total number of projects, which can be any number up to 30. It then randomly generates the inputs for a model with this many projects—the initial costs, the NPVs, and the budget. It does this so that there is a large enough budget to undertake many, but not all, of the projects.
2. Given the inputs, a capital-budgeting model is developed in the (hidden) Model worksheet, and it is solved as a 0-1 integer programming model with Solver. The heuristic procedure is also used to solve the same problem. The outputs from both procedures are shown in the Report worksheet, including the heuristic's total NPV as a percentage of Solver's total NPV.
3. The program can be repeated as often as the user desires, using different random inputs on each run.
4. To show the effect of the Solver's Integer Optimality setting (which is set to 0 in all of the Solver runs), a worksheet named Interesting accompanies the file. It shows one problem where the optimal solution was *not* found by Solver when the Integer Optimality setting was set to 5%. (This worksheet is not really part of the VBA application, but it illustrates an interesting aspect of Solver.)[1]

26.3 Running the Application

The application is stored in the **Capital Budgeting.xlsm** file. Upon opening it, the user sees the Explanation sheet in Figure 26.1. When the button on this sheet is clicked, the dialog box in Figure 26.2 appears and asks the user for a number of projects (up to 30). It then randomly generates the inputs for a capital budgeting model with this many projects in the Model worksheet, solves it optimally with Solver, performs the heuristic on this same problem, and reports the results in the Report worksheet.

Typical Report worksheets from two separate runs of the application appear in Figures 26.3 and 26.4. Each of these problems has 30 potential projects. The first is a case where the heuristic obtains the optimal solution. The second is a case where the heuristic's NPV is only about 95% as large as the optimal NPV. By running the application on many problems of varying sizes, it becomes apparent that the heuristic is quite good, often finding the optimal solution and almost always coming within a few percentage points of the optimal solution.

The three buttons at the bottom of the Report worksheet give the user three options. The user can solve another problem by clicking the left button. Alternatively, the user can view the (hidden) Model worksheet, shown in Figure 26.5 (with several hidden columns), or the Interesting sheet (not shown here). Each of these worksheets has a button that leads back to the Report worksheet.

---

[1] Solver's Integer Optimality setting was previously called the *Tolerance*. Also, the previous default setting was 5%; now it is 1%.

Figure 26.1 Explanation Worksheet

Capital Budgeting Application

Run the application

This purpose of this application is to examine a capital budgeting model and see how close a simple heuristic solution is to the optimal solution using integer (0-1) programming. To do this, the application randomly generates the inputs to a model (NPVs, costs, and budget) with 30 possible capital budgeting projects. It then solves the problem using two methods. The first method uses Solver to find the optimal 0-1 solution. The second method is a simple heuristic. Here the investments are ranked in decreasing order of the NPV-to-unit-cost ratio. Starting at the top of this list and working down, a project is included as long as the remaining budget permits. The application shows that this heuristic is not always optimal, but that it is usually very close to optimal.

To find the optimal Solver solution, the Solver's Integer Optimality setting is set to 0. This guarantees an optimal solution (if one exists). See the Interesting sheet for an example where Solver solution is not optimal (because an Integer Optimality setting of 5% was used).

Figure 26.2 Number of Projects Input Box

Number of projects

Enter the number of potential capital budgeting projects.

Number of projects (up to 30): 30

OK

Cancel

Figure 26.3 Example Where Heuristic Is Optimal

Optimal Investment Policy

Investments	14,15,16,17,18,19,20,21,22,23,24,25,26,27,28,29,30
Leftover cash	$1,100
Total NPV	$416,700

Investment Policy from Heuristic Policy

Investments	14,15,16,17,18,19,20,21,22,23,24,25,26,27,28,29,30
Leftover cash	$1,100
Total NPV	$416,700

Suboptimal NPV as a % of optimal NPV

100.00%

Run another problem with new inputs   View Model sheet   View Interesting sheet

Figure 26.4 Example Where Heuristic Is Not Optimal

Optimal Investment Policy

Investments	3,4,5,6,7,8,9,10,11,12,14,15,16,17,18,19,20,21,22,23,25,26,27,28,29,30
Leftover cash	$600
Total NPV	$703,000

Investment Policy from Heuristic Policy

Investments	6,7,8,9,10,11,12,13,14,15,16,17,18,19,20,21,22,23,24,25,26,27,28,29,30
Leftover cash	$6,000
Total NPV	$667,600

Suboptimal NPV as a % of optimal NPV

	94.96%

Run another problem with new inputs	View Model sheet	View Interesting sheet

Figure 26.5 Optimization Model

	A	B	C	D	E	F	AD	AE
1	**Capital Budgeting Model**							
2								
3	Model							
4	Investment	1	2	3	4	5	29	30
5	Investment level	0	0	1	1	1	1	1
6	NPV	$24,100	25800	25300	$26,300	23200	$23,400	12500
7	Investment cost	$9,200	9800	9400	$8,800	7600	$2,500	1300
8	Bang-for-buck	$2.62	$2.63	$2.69	$2.99	$3.05	$9.36	$9.62
9								
10	Budget constraint	Spent		Available				
11		$137,800	<=	$137,900				
12								
13	Total NPV	$656,400						
14								
15	Note that the Solver Integer Optimality setting has been set to 0.							
16								
17			Return to the Report sheet					
18								

26.4 Setting Up the Excel Sheets

The **Capital Budgeting.xlsm** file has four worksheets: the Explanation sheet in Figure 26.1, the Report sheet in Figures 26.3 and 26.4, the Model sheet in Figure 26.5, and the Interesting sheet (not shown here, but just another version of the Model sheet). The Model and Report worksheets cannot be set up completely at design time because they depend on the number of projects. This number determines the number of columns that are necessary in the model. (See rows 4–8 in Figure 26.5.) However, it is possible to develop templates for these sheets. The Model template is shown in Figure 26.6, where the range names that can be created in the Model worksheet at design time are listed.

The Report worksheet template is shown in Figure 26.7, again with the range names used. Note that cell C15 contains the formula =TotNPVHeur/TotNPVOpt. Its current value is undefined (0 divided by 0) because both total NPVs are currently 0, but it reports correctly when the application runs.

Figure 26.6   Model Worksheet Template

	A	B	C	D	E	F	G
1	Capital Budgeting Model				Range names at design time:		
2					Budget	=Model!$D$11	
3	Model				TotCost	=Model!$B$11	
4	Investment				TotNPV	=Model!$B$13	
5	Investment level						
6	NPV						
7	Investment cost						
8	Bang-for-buck						
9							
10	Budget constraint	Spent		Available			
11			<=				
12							
13	Total NPV						
14							
15	Note that the Solver Integer Optimality setting has been set to 0.						
16							
17			Return to the Report sheet				
18							

Figure 26.7   Report Worksheet Template

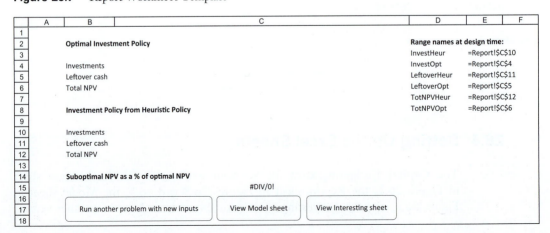

	A	B	C	D	E	F
1						
2		Optimal Investment Policy		Range names at design time:		
3				InvestHeur	=Report!$C$10	
4		Investments		InvestOpt	=Report!$C$4	
5		Leftover cash		LeftoverHeur	=Report!$C$11	
6		Total NPV		LeftoverOpt	=Report!$C$5	
7				TotNPVHeur	=Report!$C$12	
8		Investment Policy from Heuristic Policy		TotNPVOpt	=Report!$C$6	
9						
10		Investments				
11		Leftover cash				
12		Total NPV				
13						
14		Suboptimal NPV as a % of optimal NPV				
15			#DIV/0!			
16						
17		Run another problem with new inputs	View Model sheet	View Interesting sheet		
18						

VBA is then used to fill in these templates at run time. (Again, the Interesting worksheet is not really a part of the application; it is appended only to illustrate the effect of Solver's Integer Optimality setting. Therefore, it was created at design time and never changes.)

26.5 Getting Started with the VBA

This application requires a user form named frmProjects, a module, and a reference to Solver.[2] Once these items are added, the Project Explorer window appears as in Figure 26.8.

Workbook_Open Code

To guarantee that the Explanation worksheet appears when the file is opened, the following code is placed in the ThisWorkbook code window. It uses a For Each loop to hide all worksheets except the Explanation worksheet.

```vba
Private Sub Workbook_Open()
    Dim ws As Worksheet
    With wsExplanation
        .Activate
        .Range("F4").Select
    End With
    For Each ws In ThisWorkbook.Worksheets
        If ws.CodeName <> "wsExplanation" Then ws.Visible = False
    Next
    If Not (Application.Version = "15.0" Or Application.Version = "14.0") Then frmSolver.Show
End Sub
```

Figure 26.8   Project Explorer Window

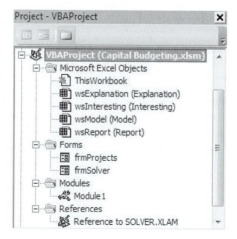

---

[2] It also contains the usual frmSolver that displays a message about possible Solver problems when the workbook is opened, but only users of pre-2010 versions of Excel will see this message.

Figure 26.9   frmProjects Design

26.6 The User Form

The frmProjects form, shown in Figure 26.9, contains the usual OK and Cancel buttons, an explanation label, and a text box named txtNProjects and an accompanying label. The code behind this form, listed below, is completely straightforward. The whole purpose is to capture the number of projects in the variable nProjects, a number that should be no larger than 30.

```
Private cancel As Boolean

Public Function ShowProjectsDialog(nProjects As Integer) As Boolean
    Call Initialize
    Me.Show
    If Not cancel Then
        nProjects = txtNProjects.Text
    End If
    ShowProjectsDialog = Not cancel
    Unload Me
End Function

Private Sub Initialize()
    txtNProjects.Text = ""
End Sub

Private Function Valid() As Boolean
    Dim nProj As Integer
    Valid = True
    ' Make sure the box is not empty and is numeric.
    If txtNProjects.Text = "" Or Not IsNumeric(txtNProjects.Text) Then
        Valid = False
        MsgBox "Enter a positive number of projects.", _
            vbInformation, "Invalid entry"
        txtNProjects.SetFocus
        Exit Function
    End If

    ' Check that the number of projects is from 1 to 30, the most
    ' allowed in this application.
    nProj = txtNProjects.Value
    If nProj < 1 Or nProj > 30 Then
        Valid = False
        MsgBox "Enter a number from 1 to 30.", _
            vbInformation, "Invalid entry"
        txtNProjects.SetFocus
    End If
End Function
```

```
Private Sub cmdOK_Click()
    If Valid Then Me.Hide
    cancel = False
End Sub

Private Sub cmdCancel_Click()
    Me.Hide
    cancel = True
End Sub

Private Sub UserForm_QueryClose(cancel As Integer, CloseMode As Integer)
    If CloseMode = vbFormControlMenu Then cmdCancel_Click
End Sub
```

26.7 The Module

The main work is performed by the code in the module. When the user clicks the button on the Explanation worksheet (or the left button on the Report worksheet), the MainCapitalBudgeting sub runs. It "shows" frmProjects and then calls other subs that perform the individual tasks.

Option Statements and Module-Level Variables

```
Option Explicit

' Definitions of module-level variables:
'    nProjects - number of potential projects (<=30)
'    zeroOne - binary array, indicates which projects are chosen by the heuristic
'    leftoverHeur - amount of budget left over using heuristic
'    totalNPVHeur - total NPV using heuristic
'    leftoverOpt - amount of budget left over from the optimal solution
'    totalNPVOpt - total NPV from the optimal solution

Dim nProjects As Integer
Dim zeroOne(1 To 30) As Integer
Dim leftoverHeur As Single, totalNPVHeur As Single
Dim leftoverOpt As Single, totalNPVOpt As Single
```

MainCapitalBudgeting Code

```
Sub MainCapitalBudgeting()
    ' The macro is run when the user clicks on the button on the Explanation sheet.

    Application.ScreenUpdating = False

    ' Get the number of potential projects.
    If frmProjects.ShowProjectsDialog(nProjects) Then
        ' Calculate random inputs for the model (NPVs, costs, and budget).
        Call GetInputs
        ' Sort projects on "bang for buck".
        Call SortProjects
        ' Calculate the optimal investments.
        Call RunSolver
        ' Calculate the investments based on the heuristic.
        Call Heuristic
```

```
              ' Report the results.
              Call CreateReport
      End If
End Sub
```

GetInputs Code

The GetInputs sub uses the combination of Excel's RAND and NORMINV functions to generate normally distributed values for the budget and for the initial costs and NPVs of the projects. The details are described in the comments below. Actually, this sub enters *formulas* for these random values, and it then "freezes" them with the Copy and PasteSpecial/Values method. (There is no particular reason for using the *normal* distribution here. I simply want to generate "representative" problems randomly, and the normal distribution works as well as any other distribution.) Finally, an initial solution of all 1's is used, so that all projects are initially undertaken. Actually, any other initial solution could be used, and the one used here almost certainly overspends the budget.

```
Sub GetInputs()
    ' This sub randomly generates inputs for a new version of the capital
    ' budgeting model.
    Dim i As Integer

    ' Unhide and activate the Model sheet.
    With wsModel
        .Visible = True
        .Activate

        With .Range("A4")
            ' Clear previous data and name some ranges.
            Range(.Offset(0, 1), .Offset(4, 1).End(xlToRight)).ClearContents
            For i = 1 To nProjects
                .Offset(0, i).Value = i
            Next
            Range(.Offset(1, 1), .Offset(1, nProjects)).Name = "InvLevel"
            Range(.Offset(2, 1), .Offset(2, nProjects)).Name = "NPV"
            Range(.Offset(3, 1), .Offset(3, nProjects)).Name = "InvCost"

            ' Calculate the ratio of NPV to investment cost (bang for buck).
            Range(.Offset(4, 1), .Offset(4, nProjects)).FormulaR1C1 = "=R[-2]C/R[-1]C"
        End With

        ' Randomly generate NPVs, costs, and budget. Use the Round function,
        ' with second argument -2, to round these to the nearest $100. The
        ' parameters used here have been chosen to generate "interesting" models.

        ' Each NPV is normal, mean $25000, standard deviation $6000.
        .Range("NPV").Formula = "=Round(NORMINV(RAND(),25000,6000),-2)"

        ' Each cost is between 10% and 40% of corresponding NPV.
        .Range("InvCost").Formula = "=Round(NPV*(.1+.3*RAND()),-2)"

        ' The budget is between 30% and 90% of the total cost of all investments.
        .Range("Budget").Formula = "=Round(SUM(InvCost)*(.3+.6*RAND()),-2)"

        ' "Freeze" the random numbers.
        With Union(.Range("NPV"), .Range("InvCost"))
```

```
            .Copy
            .PasteSpecial Paste:=xlValues
        End With
        With .Range("Budget")
            .Copy
            .PasteSpecial Paste:=xlValues
        End With

        ' Get rid of the dotted line around the copy range.
        Application.CutCopyMode = False

        ' Use all 1's as an initial solution.
        .Range("InvLevel").Value = 1

        ' Calculate the total investment cost and the total NPV.
        .Range("TotCost").Formula = "=Sumproduct(InvCost,InvLevel)"
        .Range("TotNPV").Formula = "=Sumproduct(NPV,InvLevel)"
    End With
End Sub
```

SortProjects Code

The SortProjects sub sorts the projects according to "bang for buck," putting those with the largest ratios of NPV to investment cost to the right. Note that the Orientation argument of the Sort method must be used because the values are in a row, not a column.

```
Sub SortProjects()
    ' This sub sorts the projects in increasing order of "bang for buck."
    With wsModel.Range("A4")
        Range(.Offset(1, 1), .Offset(4, nProjects)).Sort _
            Key1:=wsModel.Range("B8"), Order1:=xlAscending, _
            Orientation:=xlLeftToRight, Header:=xlNo
    End With
End Sub
```

RunSolver Code

The RunSolver sets up and then runs Solver. It must be reset and then set up each time through, just in case the size of the problem (the number of projects) has changed. Note how the Integer Optimality setting is set to 0 in the SolverOptions statement with the IntTolerance argument. This guarantees that Solver will continue to search until it has found the optimal solution. The nonoptimal solution on the Interesting sheet occurred because this setting was 5%. (The SolverWithout argument in this statement indicates that integer constraints should *not* be ignored.)

```
Sub RunSolver()
    ' Set up and run the Solver to find the optimal integer solution.
    With wsModel
        SolverReset
        SolverOK SetCell:=.Range("TotNPV"), MaxMinVal:=1, _
            ByChange:=.Range("InvLevel"), Engine:=1
```

```
        SolverOptions SolveWithout:=False, IntTolerance:=0
        SolverAdd CellRef:=.Range("TotCost"), Relation:=1, FormulaText:="Budget"
        SolverAdd CellRef:=.Range("InvLevel"), Relation:=5
        SolverSolve UserFinish:=True

        ' Capture the optimal total NPV and the amount of the budget left over.
        totalNPVOpt = .Range("TotNPV").Value
        leftoverOpt = .Range("Budget").Value - .Range("TotCost").Value
    End With
End Sub
```

Heuristic Code

The Heuristic sub implements the heuristic. It is a perfect example of looping and arrays. The first For loop sets all zeroOne array elements to 0. Then a single pass through the second For loop checks whether there is enough money left in the budget for each project, where the projects are examined in decreasing order of bang for buck. If enough money is left, the project's zeroOne value is set to 1, its investment cost is subtracted from the remaining budget, and its NPV is added to the total NPV for the heuristic.

```
Sub Heuristic()
    ' This sub finds the heuristic solution by choosing the investments in decreasing
    ' order of bang for buck.
    Dim i As Integer

    ' Initialize values so that no projects are undertaken and the whole budget is available.
    For i = 1 To nProjects
        zeroOne(i) = 0
    Next
    totalNPVHeur = 0
    leftoverHeur = Range("Budget").Value

    ' Loop through all projects in decreasing order of "bang for buck."
    ' Include the project only if its cost is no more than the remaining budget.
    With wsModel
        For i = nProjects To 1 Step -1
            If .Range("InvCost").Cells(i).Value <= leftoverHeur Then
                leftoverHeur = leftoverHeur - .Range("InvCost").Cells(i).Value
                totalNPVHeur = totalNPVHeur + .Range("NPV").Cells(i).Value
                zeroOne(i) = 1
            End If
        Next
    End With
End Sub
```

CreateReport Code

The CreateReport sub places the results from Solver and the heuristic in the Report worksheet. The main difficulty in doing this is creating *strings* that list the projects undertaken in each solution. (See the lists of investments in Figure 26.3, for example.) To see how this works, suppose the optimal solution undertakes projects 4, 6, 9, and 10. The string "4,6,9,10" is then created and placed in the InvestOpt cell of the Report worksheet. This string and the similar string for the heuristic solution are "built" one step at a time by using string concatenation and the For loop in the middle of the sub. Note that the number of projects undertaken must be known so that the For loop knows when to stop adding a comma to the string. (There is no comma after 10 in the above string.) Therefore, the first For loop in the sub counts the number of projects undertaken by each solution. Then this count variable can be used in an If construction in the second For loop to indicate when to stop adding the comma.

```vba
Sub CreateReport()
    ' This sub shows the results, so that a comparison of the optimal and
    ' heuristic solutions can be made.
    Dim i As Integer
    Dim investOpt As String, investHeur As String
    Dim nOpt As Integer, nHeur As Integer
    Dim counter1 As Integer, counter2 As Integer

    ' Hide the Model sheet, then unhide and activate the Report sheet.
    wsModel.Visible = False
    With wsReport
        .Visible = True
        .Activate
        Range("A1").Select

        ' Find the number of investments under the optimal plan (NOpt) and
        ' under the suboptimal plan (NHeur).
        nOpt = 0
        nHeur = 0
        For i = 1 To nProjects
            If wsModel.Range("InvLevel").Cells(i).Value = 1 Then
                nOpt = nOpt + 1
            End If
            If zeroOne(i) = 1 Then
                nHeur = nHeur + 1
            End If
        Next

        ' Create strings investOpt and investHeur that list the investments undertaken
        ' by the two plans. First, initialize strings and counters.
        investOpt = ""
        investHeur = ""
        counter1 = 0
        counter2 = 0

        ' Loop through all projects.
        For i = 1 To nProjects

            ' Check whether this project is in the optimal solution.
            If wsModel.Range("InvLevel").Cells(i).Value = 1 Then
                counter1 = counter1 + 1
                ' Add a comma to the string only if this investment is not the last one.
                If counter1 < nOpt Then
                    investOpt = investOpt & i & ","
                Else
                    investOpt = investOpt & i
                End If
            End If
```

```
        ' Check whether this project is selected by the heuristic.
        If zeroOne(i) = 1 Then
            counter2 = counter2 + 1
            ' Add a comma to the string only if this investment is not the last one.
            If counter2 < nHeur Then
                investHeur = investHeur & i & ","
            Else
                investHeur = investHeur & i
            End If
        End If
    Next

        ' Enter the results in the Report sheet, where the range names were created
        ' in this sheet at design time.
        .Range("InvestOpt").Value = investOpt
        .Range("InvestHeur").Value = investHeur
        .Range("LeftoverOpt").Value = leftoverOpt
        .Range("TotNPVOpt").Value = totalNPVOpt
        .Range("LeftoverHeur").Value = leftoverHeur
        .Range("TotNPVHeur").Value = totalNPVHeur
    End With
End Sub
```

Navigation Code

The remaining "View" subs (not shown here) allow for easy navigation through the application. They are attached to the corresponding buttons on the Model, Interesting, and Report worksheets.

26.8 Summary

This application has illustrated how VBA can be used to generate representative problems of a certain type and then compare the optimal Solver solutions for these problems to heuristic solutions. The context here is capital budgeting, but the same approach could be used to evaluate heuristics to other types of management science problems.

EXERCISES

1. The RunSolver sub sets the Integer Optimality setting to 0 to ensure that it gets the optimal solution. Change the application so that instead of running the heuristic, Solver is run once with this setting at 0, and it is run again with the intTolerance argument omitted in the SolverOptions statement (which will set the setting to its default value). Also, change labels appropriately on the Report worksheet. Now the report should compare a solution known to be optimal with one that might not be optimal. Then run the application a few times. Do the two solutions ever differ? (The solution on the Interesting sheet shows that they *can* differ, but it might not happen very often.)

2. The GetInputs sub generates random inputs with statements such as the following:

```
.Range("NPV").Formula = "=ROUND(NORMINV(RAND(),25000,6000),-2)"
```

This formula fills the NPV range in the Model worksheet with the specified formula. Later, it "freezes" these formulas by copying and then pasting special with the values option. Another possible approach is the following. Inside a For loop that goes over all investments, replace the above line by

```
randNPV = Round(Application.WorksheetFunction.NormInv(Rnd, 25000, 6000), -2)
```

This line also generates a random NPV and stores it in the variable randNPV. It does so with the VBA random number generator Rnd, not with Excel's RAND function, and it borrows Excel's NORMINV function to get a normally distributed random NPV. It should then place the randNPV value in the appropriate cell of the Model worksheet. However, no copying and pasting are necessary now. Change the GetInputs sub to implement this approach for all random inputs. If you want *different* random numbers each time you run the application, you should also insert a Randomize line near the top of the MainCapitalBudgeting sub. (This approach is not necessarily better or worse than the formula approach; it is simply an alternative.)

3. Change the heuristic so that it works as follows. First, it orders the investments in increasing order of their investment costs. Then it proceeds as before, scanning from left to right and choosing each investment as long as there is enough budget left to afford it. How does this heuristic compare with the optimal solution? What would you expect?

4. Repeat the previous problem, but now use the heuristic that orders the investments in decreasing order of their NPVs.

5. (More difficult) Change the model so that some investments incur an investment cost right away, some incur an investment cost a year from now, and some incur an investment cost right away *and* a year from now. There are now two budget amounts: the amount available right away and another amount that is allocated for a year from now. A decision on each investment must be made right away— to invest (and gain an NPV) or not to invest. The amount that can be spent a year from now includes the budget set aside for a year from now, plus any of the current budget not used. The following heuristic is proposed. It sorts the investments in decreasing order of the ratio of NPV to the *total* investment cost. It then goes through the investments from left to right and chooses each investment as long as there is enough money in each year's budget to afford it. (It never considers the possibility of having leftover money from the year 1 budget in year 2.) Develop an application similar to the one in the chapter that implements this new model and compares the heuristic to the optimal Solver solution for randomly generated problems. (If you like, you can use the method described in Exercise 2 to generate the random inputs.)

27

A Regression Application

27.1 Introduction

This application uses regression to estimate the relationship between any two variables, such as demand and price. It creates four scatterplots on separate chart sheets, each with a different type of trend line (linear, power, exponential, and logarithmic) superimposed, and calculates the parameters and the mean absolute percentage error (MAPE) for the best-fitting trend line of each type.

New Learning Objectives: VBA

- To illustrate how RefEdit controls can be used in user forms to specify ranges from a worksheet.
- To show how formulas can be entered in cells with the FormulaR1C1 property, using a combination of absolute and relative addresses.

New Learning Objectives: Non-VBA

- To illustrate how the relationship between two variables can be estimated by well-known and widely accepted trend lines, and how the fits from these trend lines can be compared with a measure such as MAPE.[1]

27.2 Functionality of the Application

This application provides the following functionality.

1. The user first selects data for two variables from the Data worksheet. (The sample price/demand data can be used, or the user can enter new data. In the latter case, the new data should be entered in the Data worksheet *before* running the application.) The data for the two variables should come in pairs (a price and a demand for each of several time periods, for example). One variable is designated as the independent variable; the other is designated as the dependent variable.

---

[1] Three of the four trend lines in this application are actually trend *curves*, but following Excel's terminology, I will refer to all of the as trend *lines*.

2. Four chart sheets named Linear, Power, Exponential, and Logarithmic are created. Each chart is a scatterplot of the two variables, with the appropriate trend line (linear, power, exponential, or logarithmic) superimposed.
3. All calculations are performed in the Report worksheet. This worksheet contains a copy of the data, logarithms of the data (required for all but the linear case), formulas for the parameters of the best-fitting trend line of each type, columns of absolute percentage errors in predicting one variable from the other for each trend line, and the MAPE for each trend line.

27.3 Running the Application

The application is in the file **Regression.xlsm**. When this file is opened, the explanation in Figure 27.1 appears. When the user clicks the button, the Data worksheet and the dialog box in Figure 27.2 appear. The user must supply the ranges for the two variables, which should contain variable names at the top. Note that the data set can contain more than two variables, but this application works with only two of them. The only requirement is that the two ranges identified in the dialog box must have equal numbers of cells, because the data (price and demand, for example) must come in pairs.

Once the ranges are specified, the application performs calculations on the Report worksheet and creates charts on four separate chart sheets named Linear, Power, Exponential, and Logarithmic. The completed Report worksheet appears in Figure 27.3. It shows the absolute percentage errors for the four fits in columns H, I, J, and K, and it shows summary measures of the fits in the range C5: F7. (The comments in cells C4 through F4 remind the user of the equation for each trend line.) Each chart sheet displays a scatterplot of the data, a superimposed trend line, and the equation of that trend line. For example, Figure 27.4 shows the scatterplot and the power trend line on the Power chart sheet.

Figure 27.1 Explanation Worksheet

Estimating a relationship between two variables

Run the application

This application takes a set of data on two variables, such as prices and corresponding demands, and then estimates the best-fitting linear, power, exponential, and logarithmic curves for these data. It shows each fit superimposed on a scatterplot of the data and calculates the corresponding mean absolute percentage error (MAPE).

Sample demand-price data appear on the Data sheet, but any data on any two variables can be substituted for these sample data before running the application. The only restriction is that, because logarithmic transformations are required, none of the data should be negative or 0.

Figure 27.2 Variable Ranges Dialog Box

Figure 27.3 Report Worksheet Results

	B	C	D	E	F	G	H	I	J	K
1	Calculations and report									
2							The values to the left and below show the parameters			
3	Parameters of best-fitting equations						of the best fits and the corresponding absolute			
4		*Linear*	*Power*	*Exponential*	*Logarithmic*		percentage errors and MAPEs. See the Linear, Power,			
5	a	6532.4110	1195683.7341	9925.9225	20645.2131		Exponential, and Logarithmic sheets for the			
6	b	-23.7515	-1.1990	-0.0081	-3530.0722		corresponding charts.			
7	MAPE	2.79%	2.97%	2.87%	2.86%					
8							Absolute percentage errors			
9	Price	Demand	Log(Price)	Log(Demand)			Linear	Power	Exponential	Logarithmic
10	127	3420	4.8442	8.1374			2.81%	4.97%	3.98%	3.65%
11	134	3400	4.8978	8.1315			1.48%	0.99%	1.16%	1.31%
12	136	3250	4.9127	8.0864			1.61%	1.75%	1.74%	1.64%
13	139	3410	4.9345	8.1345			5.25%	5.53%	5.36%	5.39%
14	140	3190	4.9416	8.0678			0.54%	0.12%	0.36%	0.34%
15	141	3250	4.9488	8.0864			2.05%	2.56%	2.29%	2.29%
16	148	2860	4.9972	7.9586			5.50%	4.48%	4.93%	5.06%
17	149	2830	5.0039	7.9480			5.78%	4.74%	5.18%	5.33%
18	151	3160	5.0173	8.0583			6.77%	7.69%	7.31%	7.16%
19	154	2820	5.0370	7.9445			1.94%	1.03%	1.38%	1.57%
20	155	2780	5.0434	7.9302			2.55%	1.69%	2.01%	2.21%
21	157	2900	5.0562	7.9725			3.33%	4.00%	3.78%	3.58%
22	159	2810	5.0689	7.9409			1.92%	2.42%	2.29%	2.08%
23	167	2580	5.1180	7.8555			0.55%	0.20%	0.25%	0.06%
24	168	2520	5.1240	7.8320			0.88%	1.86%	1.31%	1.48%
25	171	2430	5.1417	7.7956			1.68%	3.41%	2.54%	2.67%

Figure 27.4 Scatterplot and Power Trend Line

$y = 1E+06x^{-1.199}$

Power Fit

This equation implies that when X increases by 1%, Y changes by a constant percentage. (For this reason, it is called a "constant elasticity" equation.) This constant percentage is approximately the exponent of X.

27.4 Setting Up the Excel Sheets

This **Regression.xlsm** file contains three worksheets and four chart sheets. The worksheets are the Explanation sheet in Figure 27.1, the Data sheet in Figure 27.2, and the Report sheet in Figure 27.3. The Data sheet must contain data for at least two variables. A template in the Report sheet can be created at design time with *any* sample data, as indicated in Figure 27.5. The application always places the data in columns B and C of this sheet, starting in row 10 (with labels in row 9). Then four chart sheets, named Linear, Power, Exponential, and Logarithmic, can

Figure 27.5 Report Worksheet Template

	A	B	C	D	E	F	G	H	I	J	K
1		Calculations and report									
2											
3		Parameters of best-fitting equations						The values to the left and below show the parameters of the best fits and the corresponding absolute percentage errors and MAPEs. See the Linear, Power, Exponential, and Logarithmic sheets for the corresponding charts.			
4			*Linear*	*Power*	*Exponential*	*Logarithmic*					
5		a									
6		b									
7		MAPE									
8								Absolute percentage errors			
9		Price	Demand	Log(Price)	Log(Demand)			Linear	Power	Exponential	Logarithmic

be created at design time with Excel's chart tools, using the sample data in columns B and C of the Report sheet template as the source data for scatterplots. Also, the trend lines and the associated equations for them can be placed on the charts by using Excel's trendline option (found by right-clicking a chart series and selecting Add Trendline). The important point is that these charts can be created, along with any desired formatting, at design time. The only changes required at run time are to their source data, titles, and axis settings.

27.5 Getting Started with the VBA

This application requires a single user form named frmData and a module. Once they are inserted, the Project Explorer window will appear as in Figure 27.6.

Workbook_Open Code

To guarantee that the Explanation sheet appears when the file is opened, the following code is entered in the ThisWorkbook code window. This code also hides most of the other sheets.

```vba
Private Sub Workbook_Open()
    Dim cht As Chart
    With wsExplanation
        .Activate
        .Range("F4").Select
    End With
    wsReport.Visible = False
    For Each cht In ThisWorkbook.Charts
        cht.Visible = False
    Next
End Sub
```

Figure 27.6 Project Explorer Window

27.6 The User Form

The design of the frmData forms appears in Figure 27.7 It includes the usual OK and Cancel buttons, several labels, and two controls named rfeRange1 and rfeRange2 for the data ranges. These latter two boxes are called **RefEdit** controls. They are controls perfectly suited for allowing a user to select ranges. The RefEdit control is the lower left-hand control in the Control Toolbox in Figure 27.8.

 A Note about RefEdit Controls. Remember from Chapter 11 that RefEdit controls act somewhat differently from the other controls on the Control Toolbox in Figure 27.8. Specifically, if you use the Object Browser to look for online help on the RefEdit control under the MSForms library, you won't find it. The RefEdit control has its *own* library, which you can open by using the **Tools →** **References** menu item in the VBE and checking the RefEdit Control box. There you can find the desired online help under the RefEdit library. This brings up another curious point. You do *not* have to set a reference to the RefEdit Control to *use* one of these controls on a user form. As soon as you place a RefEdit control on a user form, the RefEdit Control box is automatically checked in the list of references.

Figure 27.7 frmData Design

Data Location

Specify the ranges that contain the data. They need not be in adjacent columns, but they should have the same number of values.

OK

Cancel

The first variable, the independent variable, will go on the horizontal axis, the second, the dependent variable, will go on the vertical axis.

Make sure to include cells containing variable names in the following ranges.

Independent variable data range:

Dependent variable data range:

Figure 27.8 Control Toolbox

Toolbox

Controls

The event handlers for frmData are listed below. The Initialize sub clears the two range boxes. The ShowDataDialog function captures the user's inputs after the Valid function checks for errors. (Other than checking for blank boxes, the only other error check is to ensure that the two specified ranges have the same number of cells.) Note that the specified ranges are captured in the Range variables range1 and range2. Then the variable names are captured in the variables var1Name and var2Name, and the data ranges are captured in the variables var1Range and var2Range. (The latter two must be captured with the keyword Set because they are *object* variables.)

Note that the Value (or Text) property of a RefEdit control returns the *address* of the designated range as a string. Then a line such as

```
Set range1 = Range(rfeRange1.Value)
```

can be used to define the Range object variable range1.

```
Private cancel As Boolean

Public Function ShowDataDialog(var1Name As String, var2Name As String, _
        var1Range As Range, var2Range As Range, nObs As Integer) As Boolean
    Dim ctl As Control
    Dim nCells As Integer
    Dim range1 As Range, range2 As Range

    Call Initialize
    Me.Show
    If Not cancel Then
        ' Capture names and ranges.
        Set range1 = Range(rfeRange1.Text)
        Set range2 = Range(rfeRange2.Text)
        ' By now, we know each range has the same number of cells.
        nCells = range1.Rows.Count

        var1Name = range1.Cells(1).Value
        var2Name = range2.Cells(1).Value
        Set var1Range = Range(range1.Cells(2), range1.Cells(nCells))
        Set var2Range = Range(range2.Cells(2), range2.Cells(nCells))
        nObs = nCells - 1
    End If
    ShowDataDialog = Not cancel
    Unload Me
End Function

Private Sub Initialize()
    rfeRange1.Value = ""
    rfeRange2.Value = ""
End Sub

Private Function Valid() As Boolean
    Dim ctl As Control
    Dim nCells1 As Integer, nCells2 As Integer
    Dim range1 As Range, range2 As Range

    Valid = True
    ' Check whether any box is empty.
    For Each ctl In Me.Controls
        If TypeName(ctl) = "RefEdit" Then
```

```
                    If ctl.Text = "" Then
                        Valid = False
                        MsgBox "Enter a range in each box.", vbInformation
                        ctl.SetFocus
                        Exit Function
                    End If
                End If
            Next

            ' Capture names and ranges.
            Set range1 = Range(rfeRange1.Text)
            Set range2 = Range(rfeRange2.Text)
            nCells1 = range1.Rows.Count
            nCells2 = range2.Rows.Count

            ' Check that both ranges are of the same length.
            If nCells1 <> nCells2 Then
                Valid = False
                MsgBox "Make sure the two ranges have equal numbers " _
                    & "of cells", vbExclamation, "Improper selections"
                rfeRange1.SetFocus
                Exit Function
            End If
End Function

Private Sub cmdOK_Click()
    If Valid Then Me.Hide
    cancel = False
End Sub

Private Sub cmdCancel_Click()
    Me.Hide
    wsExplanation.Activate
    Range("F4").Select
    cancel = True
End Sub

Private Sub UserForm_QueryClose(cancel As Integer, CloseMode As Integer)
    If CloseMode = vbFormControlMenu Then cmdCancel_Click
End Sub
```

27.7 The Module

Most of the work is performed by the VBA code in the module. This code is listed below. The Main sub is attached to the button on the Explanation worksheet. In turn, it first uses a DataSheetExists function to check whether there is a Data sheet, it shows the user form, and then it calls the subs Transfer-Data, ModifyCharts, and DoCalculations. The module-level variables are listed below. Just remember that index 1 is for the independent variable on the horizontal axis and index 2 is for the dependent variable on the vertical axis.

Option Statement and Module-Level Variables

```
Option Explicit

'  Definitions of module-level variables
'    nObs - number of observations for each variable
'    var1Range - range of the data on the horizontal axis
'    var1LogRange - range of logs of data in var1Range
'    var1Min - smallest observation in var1Range
'    var1Max - largest observation in var1Range
'    var1Name - descriptive name of horizontal axis variable
'    var2Range, var2LogRange, var2Min, var2Max,
'        var2Name - similar for vertical axis variable
'  chartDataRange - range containing both variables for use in scatterplot

Dim nObs As Integer
Dim var1Range As Range, var1LogRange As Range
Dim var1Min As Single, var1Max As Single, var1Name As String
Dim var2Range As Range, var2LogRange As Range
Dim var2Min As Single, var2Max As Single, var2Name As String
Dim chartDataRange As Range
```

Main Code

```
Sub Main()
    ' This sub runs when the user clicks on the button on the Explanation sheet.

    ' Specify the data on the Data sheet to be used.
    If DataSheetExists Then

        ' Note that the refEdit controls won't work correctly if
        ' ScreenUpdating is turned off.
        If frmData.ShowDataDialog(var1Name, var2Name, _
                var1Range, var2Range, nObs) Then
            ' Transfer the data to the Report sheet and perform the analysis.
            Application.ScreenUpdating = False
            Call TransferData
            Call ModifyCharts
            Call DoCalculations
            Application.ScreenUpdating = True
        End If
    End If
End Sub

Function DataSheetExists() As Boolean
    ' This sub gets the data on the two variables from the Data sheet.

    ' If there is a Data sheet, activate it.
    DataSheetExists = True
    On Error Resume Next
    wsData.Activate
    If Err.Number <> 0 Then
        DataSheetExists = False
        MsgBox "There should be a Data sheet that contains the " _
            & "data you want to analyze.", vbInformation
```

```
        With  wsExplanation
            .Activate
            .Range("F4").Select
        End  With
    End  If
End Function
```

TransferData Code

The TransferData sub copies the selected data in the Data worksheet to columns B
and C of the Report worksheet. When Excel creates a scatterplot (a scatter chart in
Excel's terminology), it automatically places the variable in the leftmost column on
the horizontal axis. Therefore, the variable designated as the independent variable is
copied to column B, and the variable designated as the dependent variable is copied
to column C. Note that the var1Range and var2Range object variables are set to the
data ranges in columns B and C. Then the chartDataRange variable is set to their
union—both columns B and C—for later use as the source range of the scatterplots.

```
Sub  TransferData()
    ' This sub transfers the data to the Report sheet, and sets up
    ' that sheet for further analysis.

    ' Unhide and activate the Report sheet.
    With  wsReport
        .Visible = True
        .Activate

        ' Clear any data from a previous run.
        .Range("B9").CurrentRegion.ClearContents
        With .Range("H9")
            Range(.Offset(1, 0), .End(xlDown).Offset(0, 3)).ClearContents
        End  With

        ' Add and format some labels.
        .Range("B9").Value = var1Name
        .Range("C9").Value = var2Name

        ' Copy the Data from the Data sheet to the Report sheet, with the first
        ' variable selected in column B and the second variable in column C.
        var1Range.Copy Destination:=.Range("B10")
        var2Range.Copy Destination:=.Range("C10")

        ' Set the pasted ranges and the chart range to Range object variables.
        With .Range("B9")
            Set var1Range = Range(.Offset(1, 0), .Offset(nObs, 0))
            Set var2Range = Range(.Offset(1, 1), .Offset(nObs, 1))
            Set chartDataRange = Union(var1Range, var2Range)
        End  With
    End  With

    ' Capture the min and max of the variables for charting purposes.
    var1Min = Application.Min(var1Range)
    var1Max = Application.Max(var1Range)
    var2Min = Application.Min(var2Range)
    var2Max = Application.Max(var2Range)
End Sub
```

ModifyCharts Code

The ModifyCharts sub modifies the properties of the charts that are affected by new data. (Recall that these charts are created at design time.) These properties include the source data, the titles, and the axes. For the latter, the application sets minimum and maximum values for the axes so that the data points fill up most of the chart. Specifically, it ensures that each axis extends from 10% below the smallest observation (on that axis) to 10% above the largest observation. (This was a design decision. It could be done differently.)

```
Sub ModifyCharts()
    ' This sub gets the chart sheets ready for the scatterplots of the
    ' data and the various trendlines.
    Dim cht As Chart

    ' Loop through all chart sheets.
    For Each cht In ActiveWorkbook.Charts

        ' Unhide and activate the chart.
        With cht
            .Visible = True
            .Activate

            ' Specify the source data for the chart.
            .SetSourceData Source:=chartDataRange, PlotBy:=xlColumns

            ' The xlCategory axis is the horizontal axis, and the xlValue axis is
            ' the vertical axis.
            With .Axes(xlCategory)
                .AxisTitle.Characters.Text = var1Name

                ' Set the min and max values on the horizontal axis. This is done
                ' so that the data will just about "fill" the chart.
                .MinimumScale = var1Min * 0.9
                .MaximumScale = var1Max * 1.1
            End With

            ' Set similar properties for the vertical axis.
            With .Axes(xlValue)
                .AxisTitle.Characters.Text = var2Name
                .MinimumScale = var2Min * 0.9
                .MaximumScale = var2Max * 1.1
            End With
        End With
    Next
End Sub
```

DoCalculations Code

The DoCalculations sub enters formulas in the appropriate ranges of the Report worksheet. It first creates logarithms of the data in columns D and E. Next, it uses formulas from regression to calculate the parameters of the best-fitting trend lines in the range C5:E6. It then calculates the absolute percentage errors in columns H, I, J, and K. Finally, it calculates the MAPE values in the range C7:F7.

A Note on the FormulaR1C1 Property. Pay particular attention to how the FormulaR1C1 property of ranges is used several times to enter formulas with relative and absolute addresses. For example, the *relative* reference RC[-2] refers to the same row and two columns to the left of the cell it is referenced by. If this is called from cell E5, say, it refers to cell C5; if it is called from cell G23, it refers to cell E23; and so on. In contrast, the reference R5C3, without brackets, is an *absolute* reference to the cell in row 5 and column C. It is equivalent to $C$5. The formulas for calculating absolute percentage errors toward the bottom of this sub use a combination of relative and absolute references. The relative parts are for the actual and estimated values of the variable; the absolute parts are for the parameters of the fitted equation. The FormulaR1C1 property is somewhat more difficult to learn than the Formula property, but it is often more convenient—it enables you to fill an entire range with formulas with a *single* line of code—no loops or copying are required.

```vba
Sub DoCalculations()
    ' This sub uses Excel's built-in regression functions to calculate
    ' the parameters of the various trendlines, and then it calculates some
    ' error measures to get tne MAPEs.
    Dim parameterRange As Range, APERange As Range
    Dim i As Integer

    With wsReport
        .Activate

        ' Enter labels for the log variables.
        .Range("D9").Value = "Log(" & var1Name & ")"
        .Range("E9").Value = "Log(" & var2Name & ")"

        ' Create logarithms of the two variables in columns D and E for later use.
        With .Range("D9")
            Range(.Offset(1, 0), .Offset(nObs, 1)).FormulaR1C1 = "=Ln(RC[-2])"
            Set var1LogRange = Range(.Offset(1, 0), .Offset(nObs, 0))
            Set var2LogRange = Range(.Offset(1, 1), .Offset(nObs, 1))
        End With
        ' Calculate the best-fitting parameters with formulas using Excel's
        ' Intercept and Slope functions, and place them in parameterRange.
        ' (The details won't be clear unless you know regression.)
        Set parameterRange = .Range("C5:E6")
    End With

    With parameterRange

        ' The linear fit uses original data.
        .Cells(1, 1).Formula = "=Intercept(" & var2Range.Address & "," _
            & var1Range.Address & ")"
        .Cells(2, 1).Formula = "=Slope(" & var2Range.Address &"," _
            & var1Range.Address & ")"

        ' The power fit uses logs of both variables.
        .Cells(1, 2).Formula = "=Exp(Intercept(" & var2LogRange.Address & "," _
            & var1LogRange.Address & "))"
        .Cells(2, 2).Formula = "=Slope(" & var2LogRange.Address & "," _
            & var1LogRange.Address & ")"
```

```
        ' The exponential fit uses original variable 1 and log of variable 2.
        .Cells(1, 3).Formula = "=Exp(Intercept(" & var2LogRange.Address & "," _
            & var1Range.Address & "))"
        .Cells(2, 3).Formula = "=Slope(" & var2LogRange.Address & "," _
            & var1Range.Address & ")"

        ' The logarithmic fit uses log of variable 1 and original variable 2.
        .Cells(1, 4).Formula = "=Intercept(" & var2Range.Address & "," _
            & var1LogRange.Address & ")"
        .Cells(2, 4).Formula = "=Slope(" & var2Range.Address &"," _
            & var1LogRange.Address & ")"
    End With

    ' Calculate the absolute percentage errors (with formulas) when predicting
    ' variable 2 from the four trend lines.
    With wsReport.Range("H9")
        Range(.Offset(1, 0), .Offset(nObs, 0)).FormulaR1C1 = _
            "=Abs(RC[-5]-(R5C3+R6C3*RC[-6]))/RC[-5]"
        Range(.Offset(1, 1), .Offset(nObs, 1)).FormulaR1C1 = _
            "=Abs(RC[-6]-R5C4*RC[-7]^R6C4)/RC[-6]"
        Range(.Offset(1, 2), .Offset(nObs, 2)).FormulaR1C1 = _
            "=Abs(RC[-7]-R5C5*Exp(R6C5*RC[-8]))/RC[-7]"
        Range(.Offset(1, 3), .Offset(nObs, 3)).FormulaR1C1 = _
            "=Abs(RC[-8]-(R5C6+R6C6*RC[-7]))/RC[-8]"
        Set APERange = Range(.Offset(1, 0), .Offset(nObs, 3))
    End With

    ' Calculate the MAPE values for the four trend lines.
    With wsReport.Range("B7")
        For i = 1 To 4
            .Offset(0, i).Formula = _
                "=Average(" & APERange.Columns(i).Address & ")"
        Next
    End With
End Sub
```

27.8 Summary

Finding a trend line that relates two variables, or finding the best of several such trend lines, is an extremely important task in the business world. Excel has several built-in tools for estimating such trend lines, including the ability to superimpose trend lines and their equations on a scatterplot. This application illustrates how the whole process can be automated with VBA. The charts indicate visually how well the trend lines fit the data, and the corresponding regression equations can be used for forecasting.

EXERCISES

1. The application currently calculates the MAPE for each trend line. Another frequently used measure of the goodness of fit is the mean absolute error (MAE). It is the average of the absolute differences between the actual and predicted

values. Change the application so that it reports the MAE for each trend line rather than the MAPE.

2. Repeat the previous exercise, but now report the root mean square error (RMSE) instead of the MAPE. This is defined as the square root of the average of squared differences between the actual and predicted values. It is another popular measure of the goodness of fit.

3. Change the application so that it reports all three goodness-of-fit measures for each trend line: the MAPE, the MAE from Exercise 1, and the RMSE from Exercise 2.

4. The application currently shows only the absolute percentage errors in columns H, I, J, and K of the Report worksheet. It doesn't explicitly show the predicted values from the regression equations, although it implicitly uses them in the equations for the absolute percentage errors. Change the application so that it enters the predicted values, with formulas, in columns H, I, J, and K, and then it enters the absolute percentage errors, again as formulas, in columns L, M, N, and O. Actually, you should be able to use a *single* FormulaR1C1 property to enter *all of* the errors in the latter four columns.

5. This application is typical in the sense that it requires input data. The question from the developer's point of view is where the data are likely to reside. Here I have assumed that the data reside in a Data worksheet in the same file as the application. This exercise and the next one explore other possibilities. For this exercise, assume that the data reside in some other worksheet but in the same file as the application. Change the application so that it can locate the data, wherever they might be. (*Hint*: The RefEdit control allows a user to select a range from *any* worksheet.)

6. For this exercise, assume that the data are in another Excel workbook. It will be up to the user to specify the workbook and then the data ranges in that workbook. Change the application so that (1) it informs the user with a message box that he is about to be prompted for the data file; (2) it uses the FileDialog object as illustrated in Chapter 13 to select the data file and then open this file; (3) it uses the same frmData as in Figure 27.2 to get the data ranges; (4) it enters the required data in the Report worksheet of the application file; (5) it closes the data file; and (6) it proceeds as before to analyze the data.

An Exponential Utility Application

28.1 Introduction

This application illustrates a rather surprising result that can occur when a decision maker is risk averse.[1] Suppose you can enter a risky venture where there will be either a gain of G or a loss of L. The probability of the gain is p and the probability of the loss is $1 - p$. You can have any share s of this venture, where s is a fraction from 0 to 1. Then if there is a gain, you win sG; if there is a loss, you lose sL. You must decide what share you want, given that you are risk averse and have an exponential utility function with risk tolerance parameter R. (The larger your R is, the more willing you are to take risks.)

The surprising result is that if the gain G increases and all other parameters remain constant, your optimal share s might *decrease*. In other words, you might want a *smaller* share of a better thing. The intuition is that if you are risk averse, you do not like risky ventures. However, as G increases, you can have less exposure to risk by decreasing your share s and still expect to do better in the venture.

In case this argument does not convince you, the application calculates the optimal share s for varying values of G and plots them graphically. The resulting chart shows clearly, at least for some values of the parameters, that the optimal value of s can decrease as G increases.

New Learning Objectives: VBA

- To learn how a VBA application, especially one that uses a chart, can illustrate a result that might be very difficult to understand—or believe—in any other way.

New Learning Objectives: Non-VBA

- To illustrate the role of risk in decision making under uncertainty.

---

[1] It is based on the article "Too Much of a Good Thing?" by D. Clyman, M. Walls, and J. Dyer, in *Operations Research*, Vol. 47, No. 6 (1999).

28.2 Functionality of the Application

The application is slightly more general than explained in the introduction. It does the following:

1. It first gets the inputs G, L, p, and R from the user in a dialog box. This dialog box also asks whether the user wants to vary G or L in a sensitivity analysis, and it asks for the range of values for the sensitivity analysis. Although the sensitivity analysis on the gain G is of primary interest, it might also be interesting to perform a sensitivity analysis on the loss L.
2. The user's expected utility from the risky venture, given a share s, is calculated in the Model worksheet, and then it is maximized with Solver (as a nonlinear model) several times, once for each value of G (or L) in the sensitivity analysis.
3. The Solver results are shown graphically in a chart sheet named SensitivityChart.
4. The model and chart show the optimal share s. They also show the corresponding certainty equivalent. This is the dollar equivalent of the risky venture, using the optimal share s. More specifically, it is the dollar amount such that the decision maker is indifferent between (1) receiving this dollar amount for sure and (2) participating in the risky venture. This certainty equivalent should increase as G increases, even though s might decrease. The chart indicates that this is indeed the case.

28.3 Running the Application

The application is stored in the file **Exponential Utility.xlsm**. When this file is opened, the Explanation worksheet in Figure 28.1 is displayed. Clicking the button on this sheet produces the dialog box in Figure 28.2 Its top four text boxes are filled with parameters from a previous run, if any. (To make things more interesting, you might want to think of the monetary amounts as expressed in *millions* of dollars.) The other options are set at chosen default values.

Once the OK button is clicked, the application runs Solver on the (hidden) Model worksheet several times, once for each value in the sensitivity analysis, and reports the results in the SensitivityChart sheet. For the parameters in Figure 28.2, the chart appears as in Figure 28.3. This chart shows clearly that the optimal share reaches its maximum of about 0.46 when the gain G has increased by about 60% above its original value of $68 million. As G increases further, the optimal share *decreases* slightly. However, the certainty equivalent continues to increase. This simply means that as G increases, the decision maker values the risky venture more.

The Model worksheet that is the basis for this chart appears in Figure 28.4. It is discussed in more detail below.

If the second option button in Figure 28.2 is selected, the sensitivity analysis is performed on the loss L, so that L varies and all other parameters remain

Figure 28.1   Explanation Worksheet

Risk Averseness: A Surprising Result

Run the application

Consider a risk averse decision maker about to become a partner in a risky venture. The venture will be a success, earning G, or a failure, losing L. The probability of success is p. The decision maker can have any share s of this venture, where s is a fraction from 0 to 1. Then the possible gain to him is sG, and the possible loss is sL. The decision maker wants to choose the share s that maximizes his expected utility, where the utility function is of the exponential form, with risk tolerance R. Then he wants to perform a sensitivity analysis to see how the optimal share s changes as G or L changes.

This application has the decision maker's model in the Model sheet. It is a straightforward Solver application. When you click the button above, you get to choose the input parameters: G, L, p, and R. You also get to choose the input parameter to change for sensitivity analysis, as well as the range of change (e.g., from 50% below to 100% above the current value). The application then runs Solver for each value inside this range (in 5% increments) and charts the results. The chart shows the optimal share s, as well as the associated "certainty equivalent." This is the equivalent dollar value, i.e., it is the value such that the decision maker would be indifferent between (1) taking the gamble (with the optimal s) and (2) getting the sure dollar value.

The surprising result is that for many input parameters, if you increase G (making the venture a more attractive one), the optimal share s decreases. In words, the decision maker wants a smaller percentage of a better deal! (However, the certainty equivalent always increases.) Here is the intuition behind this surprising result. Risk averse decision makers like to avoid risk, so they tend to prefer smaller shares of a risky venture. As the venture becomes more attractive (G increases), they can afford to have a smaller share and still make more money. Essentially, they can have their cake (smaller risk) and eat it too (higher certainty equivalent).

The idea for this application comes from the paper "Too Much of a Good Thing?" by Clyman, Walls, and Dyer, in Operations Research, Vol. 47, No. 6 (1999). They saw this phenomenon in the oil drilling industry, where they claim it is quite common.

constant. The chart from this analysis appears in Figure 28.5. This chart shows no surprises. As the loss increases, you want a smaller share of a bad thing, and your certainty equivalent also decreases steadily.

28.4   Setting Up the Excel Sheets

The **Exponential Utility.xlsm** file contains two worksheets: the Explanation worksheet in Figure 28.1 and the Model worksheet in Figure 28.4. It also contains the SensitivityChart chart sheet. Except for the sensitivity section (from row 17 down), a template for the Model worksheet can be formed at design time, as shown in Figure 28.6. (The input cells are shaded blue, and the decision variable cell is shaded red.) The formula in cell B12 calculates the expected utility for any share in cell B11, and the formula in cell B13 calculates the corresponding certainty equivalent. These formulas are listed after the charts below.

Figure 28.2 Inputs Dialog Box

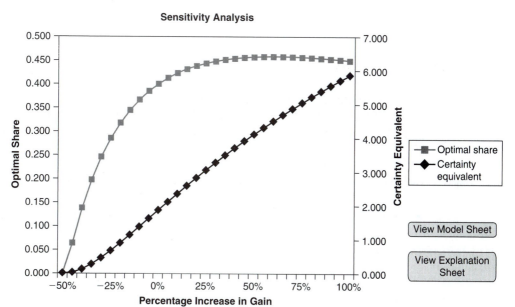

User inputs

Enter the following inputs (monetary values in $millions):

Expected gain from a successful project: 68.00

Expected loss from an unsuccesful project: 15.00

Probability that project is successful: 0.30

Risk tolerance: 50.00

Input to change for sensitivity analysis

● Expected gain from a successful project

○ Expected loss from an unsuccessful project

Enter the range of changes for the selected input. For example, if you want it to go as low as half its current value and as high as twice its current value, enter -0.5 in the first box and 1.0 in the second box. This indicates 50% below and 100% above. The percentage change will vary in increments of 5%.

Range of changes for sensitivity analysis

Percent below current value: -.5

Percent above current value: 1

OK

Cancel

Figure 28.3 Chart for Sensitivity Analysis on Gain

Figure 28.4 Optimization Model

	A	B	C	D	E
1	Decision model				
2					
3	Inputs			Original values	Pct change
4	Gain with success	68.00		68.00	0%
5	Loss with failure	15.00		15.00	0%
6	Probability of success	0.300			
7					
8	Risk tolerance	50.00			
9				View Chart	
10	Decision				
11	Share of project	0.400		View Explanation	
12	Expected utility	0.037		sheet	
13	Certainty equivalent	1.866			
14					
15	Optimal share and certainty equivalent as a function of percentage change in Gain				
16	Percentage change	Optimal share	Certainty equivalent		
17	-50%	0.000	0.000		
18	-45%	0.063	0.023		
19	-40%	0.137	0.118		
20	-35%	0.197	0.267		
21	-30%	0.246	0.453		
36	45%	0.456	3.915		
37	50%	0.457	4.117		
38	55%	0.458	4.314		
39	60%	0.458	4.505		
40	65%	0.458	4.691		
41	70%	0.457	4.872		
42	75%	0.457	5.048		
43	80%	0.456	5.220		
44	85%	0.454	5.387		
45	90%	0.453	5.549		
46	95%	0.451	5.707		
47	100%	0.449	5.861		

$$\text{=PrSuc*(1-EXP(-Share*Gain/RiskTol))+(1-PrSuc)*(1-EXP(-Share*(-Loss)/RiskTol))}$$

and

$$\text{=-RiskTol*LN(1-ExpUtil)}$$

(See the decision making under uncertainty chapter of *Practical Management Science* for a discussion of expected utility and exponential utility functions.) Then Solver is set up to maximize cell B12, with the single changing cell B11 constrained to be between 0 and 1. Because of the exponential utility function, this model must be solved as a *nonlinear* model.

Figure 28.5 Chart for Sensitivity Analysis on Loss

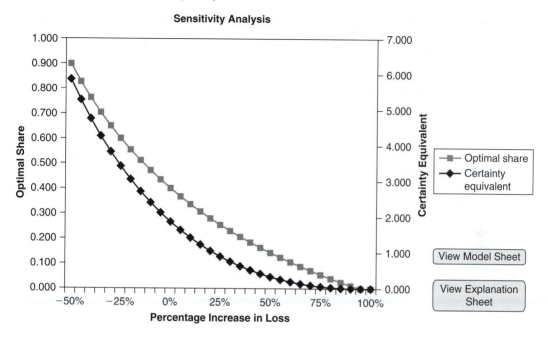

Figure 28.6 Model Worksheet Template

	A	B	C	D	E
1	**Decision model**				
2					
3	**Inputs**			Original values	Pct change
4	Gain with success	68.00		68.00	0%
5	Loss with failure	15.00		15.00	0%
6	Probability of success	0.300			
7					
8	Risk tolerance	50.00			
9				View Chart	
10	**Decision**				
11	Share of project	0.400			
12	Expected utility	0.037		View Explanation sheet	
13	Certainty equivalent	1.866			
14					
15	Optimal share and certainty equivalent as a function of percentage change in Loss				
16	Percentage change	Optimal share	Certainty equivalent		

The chart sheet can also be created at design time. To do this, you can enter *any* trial values in columns A, B, and C of the sensitivity section of the Model worksheet (see Figure 28.4) and then create the chart from these trial values. The VBA code will then update the chart with the appropriate values at run time.

28.5 Getting Started with the VBA

This application requires a user form named frmInputs, a module, and a reference to Solver.[2] Once these items are added, the Project Explorer window will appear as in Figure 28.7.

Workbook_Open Code

To guarantee that the Explanation worksheet appears when the file is opened, the following code is placed in the ThisWorkbook code window. It also hides all other sheets and displays the Solver warning.

```
Private Sub Workbook_Open()
    With wsExplanation
        .Activate
        .Range("F4").Select
    End With
    wsModel.Visible = False
    chtSensitivity.Visible = False
    If Not (Application.Version = "15.0" Or Application.Version = "14.0") Then frmSolver.Show
End Sub
```

28.6 The User Form

The design of frmInputs is shown in Figure 28.8. It includes the usual OK and Cancel buttons, two explanation labels, two frames for grouping controls, two option buttons named optGain and optLoss, and six text boxes with corresponding

Figure 28.7 Project Explorer Window

---

[2] It also includes the usual frmSolver form for displaying a warning about Solver, but only users of pre-2010 versions of Excel will see this message.

Figure 28.8 frmInputs Design

labels. These text boxes (from top to bottom) are named txtGain, txtLoss, txtPrSuccess, txtRiskTol, txtPctBelow, and txtPctAbove.

The code behind this user form is listed below. The Initialize sub captures the values from the Model worksheet from a previous run, if any, and places them in the top four text boxes. It then chooses the first option button by default, and it places the default values 0 and 1 in the bottom two text boxes. (Note how the Format function is used to ensure that the values in the top four text boxes are formatted as numbers with two decimals.) The ShowInputsDialog function captures the user's inputs for later use in the module. The Valid function does appropriate error checking for the various user inputs.

```
Private cancel As Boolean

Public Function ShowInputsDialog(gain As Single, loss As Single, _
        probSuccess As Single, riskTol As Single, inputToChange As String, _
        pctBelow As Single, pctAbove As Single) As Boolean
    Call Initialize
    Me.Show
    If Not cancel Then
        gain = txtGain.Text
        loss = txtLoss.Text
        probSuccess = txtPrSuccess.Text
        riskTol = txtRiskTol.Text
        If optGain.Value Then
            inputToChange = "Gain"
        Else
            inputToChange = "Loss"
        End If
        pctBelow = txtPctBelow.Text
        pctAbove = txtPctAbove.Text
    End If
    ShowInputsDialog = Not cancel
    Unload Me
End Function

Private Sub Initialize()
    ' Capture the values from the Model sheet in the first four boxes, and
    ' use appropriate default values for the others.
    With wsModel
        txtGain.Text = Format(.Range("OrigGain").Value, "0.00")
        txtLoss.Text = Format(.Range("OrigLoss").Value, "0.00")
        txtPrSuccess.Text = Format(.Range("PrSuccess").Value, "0.00")
        txtRiskTol.Text = Format(.Range("RiskTol").Value, "0.00")
    End With

    optGain.Value = True
    txtPctBelow.Text = 0
    txtPctAbove.Text = 1
End Sub

Private Function Valid() As Boolean
    Dim ctl As Control

    Valid = True
    ' Each text box must be numeric, the PctBelow box must not be positive,
    ' the PrSuccess must be between 0 and 1, and the other boxes must nonnegative.
    For Each ctl In Me.Controls
        If TypeName(ctl) = "TextBox" Then
            If ctl.Value = "" Or Not IsNumeric(ctl) Then
                Valid = False
                MsgBox "Enter numerical values in all of the boxes.", _
                    vbInformation, "Invalid entry"
                ctl.SetFocus
                Exit Function
            End If
            If ctl.Name = "txtPctBelow" Then
                If ctl.Value > 0 Then
                    Valid = False
                    MsgBox "Enter a nonpositive value in this box.", _
                        vbInformation, "Invalid entry"
                    ctl.SetFocus
                    Exit Function
                End If
```

```
            ElseIf ctl.Name = "txtPrSuccess" Then
                If ctl.Value < 0 Or ctl.Value > 1 Then
                    Valid = False
                    MsgBox "Enter a value between 0 and 1 in this box.", _
                        vbInformation, "Invalid entry"
                    ctl.SetFocus
                    Exit Function
                End If
            Else
                If ctl.Value < 0 Then
                    MsgBox "Enter a nonnegative value in this box.", _
                        vbInformation, "Invalid entry"
                    Valid = False
                    ctl.SetFocus
                    Exit Function
                End If
            End If
        End If
    Next
End Function

Private Sub cmdOK_Click()
    If Valid Then Me.Hide
    cancel = False
End Sub

Private Sub cmdCancel_Click()
    Me.Hide
    cancel = True
End Sub

Private Sub UserForm_QueryClose(cancel As Integer, CloseMode As Integer)
    If CloseMode = vbFormControlMenu Then cmdCancel_Click
End Sub
```

28.7 The Module

The module contains a MainExponentialUtility sub that first "shows" frmInputs and then calls several other subs to do the real work. The code is listed below.

Option Statement and Module-Level Variables

```
Option Explicit

' The following variables capture the user's inputs. Note that
' inputToChange will be "Gain" or "Loss". Also, pctBelow and pctAbove
' are the extremes in percentage changes for the sensitivity analysis.
Dim gain As Single, loss As Single, probSuccess As Single
Dim riskTol As Single
Dim inputToChange As String, pctBelow As Single, pctAbove As Single
```

MainExponentialUtility Code

The MainExponentialUtility sub gets the user inputs from frmInputs, enters these in the Model worksheet, performs the sensitivity analysis in the Model worksheet, and updates the chart.

```
Sub MainExponentialUtility()
    ' This is the sub that the user runs by clicking on the button on
    ' the Explanation sheet.

    ' Get the user inputs.
    If frmInputs.ShowInputsDialog(gain, loss, _
            probSuccess, riskTol, inputToChange, _
            pctBelow, pctAbove) Then

        Application.ScreenUpdating = False
        ' Enter the user inputs into the Model sheet.
        Call EnterInputs
        ' Run the sensitivity analysis in the Model sheet.
        Call Sensitivity
        ' Show and update the chart.
        Call UpdateChart
        Application.ScreenUpdating = True
    End If
End Sub
```

EnterInputs Code

The EnterInputs sub enters the user's inputs from frmInputs and enters them into named ranges of the Model worksheet. (Refer to Figure 28.4.) It enters an initial share of 0.5 in the decision variable cell, although any other initial share could be entered instead.

```
Sub EnterInputs()
    ' Enter the user inputs from the form into the Model sheet.

    ' Unhide and activate the Model sheet.
    With wsModel
        .Visible = True
        .Activate

        ' Enter the user's inputs into cells (already range-named) in the Model sheet.
        .Range("OrigGain").Value = gain
        .Range("OrigLoss").Value = loss
        .Range("PrSuccess").Value = probSuccess
        .Range("RiskTol").Value = riskTol

        ' Set the initial share to 0.5; Solver will find the optimal share.
        .Range("Share").Value = 0.5
    End With
End Sub
```

Sensitivity Code

The Sensitivity sub runs the sensitivity analysis on the chosen input parameter (gain or loss). To do this, it uses a Do loop to run through the various percentage changes for the selected input, and for each setting, it runs Solver to find the optimal share. As it does this, it records the optimal share and the corresponding expected utility and certainty equivalent in the sensitivity section of the Model worksheet. These values are the basis for the chart.

```
Sub Sensitivity()
    ' This sub runs a sensitivity analysis on the percentage change in the
    ' input (gain or loss) being changed.
    Dim rowOffset As Integer
    Dim currentPct As Single

    ' Enter an appropriate label.
    wsModel.Range("A15").Value = "Optimal share and certainty equivalent as a function " _
        & "of percentage change in " & inputToChange
    With wsModel.Range("A16")
        ' Clear out old values, if any, from the previous sensitivity table.
        Range(.Offset(1, 0), .Offset(1, 2).End(xlDown)).ClearContents

        ' rowOffset is the current number of rows below row 16, i.e., where the results
        ' from the current Solver run will be placed.
        ' currentPct is the current percentage change in the input being changed.
        rowOffset = 1
        currentPct = pctBelow

        ' Loop through the percentages to change, incrementing by 5% each time.

            ' Enter the current percentage in the sensitivity table and up above
            ' (in the PctGain or PctLoss cell), which ties it to the model.
            .Offset(rowOffset, 0).Value = currentPct
            wsModel.Range("Pct" & inputToChange).Value = currentPct

            ' Run Solver, which has already been set up.
            SolverSolve UserFinish:=True

            ' Enter the Solver results in the sensitivity table.
            .Offset(rowOffset, 1).Value = wsModel.Range("Share").Value
            .Offset(rowOffset, 2).Value = wsModel.Range("CertEquiv").Value

            ' Update rowOffset and currentPct for the next time through the loop (if any).

            rowOffset = rowOffset + 1
            currentPct = currentPct + 0.05

            ' The +0.001 in the next statement handles numerical roundoff. It ensures
            ' that the loop will be run when currentPct is equal to pctAbove.
        Loop While currentPct <= pctAbove + 0.001

        ' Run Solver one more time, using the original (user's input) values.
        ' (This isn't really necessary, but the user might want to see the model
        ' results with the original inputs.)
        wsModel.Range("Pct" & inputToChange).Value = 0
        SolverSolve UserFinish:=True
    End With

    ' Hide the Model sheet.
    wsModel.Visible = False
End Sub
```

UpdateChart Code

Recall that the chart has already been created and formatted as desired at design time. Therefore, the only purpose of the UpdateChart sub is to populate the chart with the data from the sensitivity analysis. It does this by using the SetSourceData method of the active chart. To label the horizontal axis appropriately, it sets the Text property of the Axes(xlCategory).AxisTitle.Characters object. To set the data range for the horizontal axis, that is, the range of percentage changes, it sets the XValues property of the SeriesCollection(1) object. (This object refers to the first of the two series plotted in the chart. Because they are both based on the same set of percentage changes, either could be used in this XValues statement.)

```
Sub UpdateChart()
    ' This sub updates the (already-created) chart to show the results of
    ' the sensitivity analysis.

    Dim chartData As Range, chartPcts As Range

    ' Define ranges for the parts of the sensitivity table used for the chart.
    With wsModel.Range("A16")
        Set chartData = Range(.Offset(0, 1), .Offset(0, 2).End(xlDown))
        Set chartPcts = Range(.Offset(1, 0), .End(xlDown))
    End With

    ' Unhide and activate the chart sheet.
    With chtSensitivity
        .Visible = True
        .Activate
    End With

    ' Update the chart, which was already set up at design time.
    With ActiveChart
        .Axes(xlCategory).AxisTitle.Characters.Text = _
            "Percentage increase in " & inputToChange
        .SetSourceData chartData
        .SeriesCollection(1).XValues = chartPcts
    End With
End Sub
```

Navigational Code

The remaining "View" subs (not shown here) allow for easy navigation through the application. They are attached to the corresponding buttons on the Model and SensitivityChart sheets.

```
Sub ViewModel()
    With wsModel
        .Visible = True
        .Activate
        .Range("A2").Select
    End With
End Sub

Sub ViewExplanation()
    With wsExplanation
        .Activate
        .Range("F4").Select
    End With
    wsModel.Visible = False
```

```
        chtSensitivity.Visible = False
    End Sub

    Sub ViewChart()
        wsModel.Visible = False
        chtSensitivity.Activate
    End Sub
```

28.8   Summary

This chapter has illustrated how a certain type of unexpected behavior can be demonstrated clearly to an unconvinced user. More generally, it has illustrated how a VBA application can perform a sensitivity analysis and present the results in a clear graphical format. This particular application allows users to run the sensitivity analysis with a variety of inputs to gain insight into the role risk aversion plays in risky ventures.

EXERCISES

1.   Change the application so that it is possible to perform a sensitivity analysis on the probability p of gain G. In this case, the user should be asked to select the range that p can vary over, in increments of 0.05, where the lower and upper limits of this range must be multiples of 0.05 from 0 to 1. The resulting chart should be like the ones illustrated in the chapter except that the horizontal axis should now show p.

2.   Change the application so that it is possible to perform a sensitivity analysis on the risk tolerance parameter R. In this case, the user should be asked to select the range that R can vary over. The resulting chart should be like the ones illustrated in the chapter except that the horizontal axis should now show R.

3.   Change the application so that it is possible to perform a sensitivity analysis on both L and G simultaneously. Specifically, the user should be asked for values of these parameters (as well as p and R). Then it should perform a sensitivity analysis where the possible loss and gain are of the form mL and mG, where m is a multiple that varies from 1 to 10 in increments of 1. The resulting chart should be like the ones illustrated in the chapter except the horizontal axis should now show the multiple m.

4.   Change the application so that the risky venture has three possible outcomes: a large gain G, a smaller gain g, and a loss L. The associated probabilities should be inputs that sum to 1. The user should now be allowed to perform a sensitivity analysis on G, g, or L. However, g should always be less than G.

29 | A Queueing Simulation Application

29.1 Introduction

As Chapter 25 illustrated, spreadsheet simulation usually means creating a spreadsheet model with random numbers in certain cells and then replicating the model with a data table, an add-in such as @RISK, or VBA. This chapter illustrates a simulation model that is very difficult to model with spreadsheet formulas because of the timing and bookkeeping involved. A more natural approach is to take care of all the model's logic in VBA and then simply report the results on a worksheet.

The model considered here is a multiserver queueing model. Customers arrive at random times to a service center, such as a bank. There are several identical servers (identical in the sense that they all have the same service time probability distribution). If a customer arrives and all servers are busy, the customer joins the end of a single queue. However, the model assumes that there is a maximum number of customers allowed in the queue. If the queue is already full when a customer arrives, this customer is turned away. At the beginning of the simulation, there are no customers in the system. The system is then simulated for a user-defined length of clock time. At this time, no further arrivals are allowed to enter the system, but customers already present are served. (This is analogous to a bank that locks its doors at 5:30 P.M. but allows customers already in the bank to finish.) The simulation terminates when the last customer departs. The model developed here assumes the times between arrivals and the service times are exponentially distributed, a very common assumption in queueing analysis, but other distributions could be used instead.

The purpose of the simulation is to simulate the system for the prescribed amount of time and, as it runs, collect statistics on the system behavior. At the end, the application reports measures such as the average amount of time in queue for a typical customer, the fraction of time a typical server is busy, the fraction of all arriving customers who are turned away, and others.

New Learning Objectives: VBA

- To learn how to use VBA to take care of the timing and bookkeeping details in a queueing simulation.

New Learning Objectives: Non-VBA

- To understand the effect of system inputs (arrival rate, mean service time, number of servers) on system outputs (average time in queue, average number in queue, and others) in a typical queueing model.

590

29.2 Functionality of the Application

The application allows the user to change six inputs to the queueing model: (1) the time unit (minute or hour, say), (2) the customer arrival rate to the system, (3) the mean service time per customer, (4) the number of servers, (5) the maximum number of customers allowed in the queue, and (6) the closing time (the time when no more customers are allowed to enter the system). The simulation then runs for the specified amount of time and keeps track of many interesting output measures, such as the average amount of time in queue for a typical customer, the fraction of time a typical server is busy, and the fraction of all arriving customers who are turned away. It also tabulates the probability distribution of the number of customers in the queue and shows this distribution graphically.

29.3 Running the Application

The application is stored in the file **Queueing Simulation.xlsm**. Upon opening this file, the user sees the Explanation worksheet in Figure 29.1. When the button on this form is clicked, the user sees the Report worksheet, the top part of which appears in Figure 29.2. This allows the user to change the inputs in the shaded cells.

The button allows the user to run the simulation. It runs for the simulated time shown in cell B9 of Figure 29.2, and then it continues until all customers currently in the system have finished service. When this occurs, statistical measures are calculated and reported in the bottom half of the Report worksheet, as in Figure 29.3. For example, during this 480-minute run, 524 customers arrived, 38 of them were turned away, the average time in the queue per customer was 4.10 minutes, and the longest time any customer spent in the queue was 14.71 minutes. Also, the typical server was busy 90.8% of the time, and there was no queue at all 25.83% of the

Figure 29.1 Explanation Worksheet

Multiserver Queueing System

View/Change Inputs

This application simulates a multiserver queueing system, such as at a bank, where arriving customers wait in a single line for the first available server. The system starts "empty and idle" and runs for a user-specified amount of time. The user specifies the arrival rate, the mean service time per customer, the number of (identical) servers, and the maximum number of customers allowed in the queue. (If a customer arrives when the system is full, this customer leaves.) The user also specifies the "closing" time. At this time, no further arrivals are permitted, but the customers already in the system are served.

Figure 29.2   Input Section of Report Worksheet

	A	B	C	D	E	F	G
1	Multiple Server Queueing Simulation						
2							
3	Inputs						
4	Time unit	minute		Change any of the inputs in the blue cells			
5	Customer arrival rate	1.000	customers/minute	and then click on the top button to run			
6	Mean service time	2.700	minutes	the simulation.			
7	Number of servers	3					
8	Maximum allowed in queue	10		**Measure of system congestion**			
9	Simulation run time	480	minutes	Traffic intensity	0.9		

Figure 29.3   Simulation Results

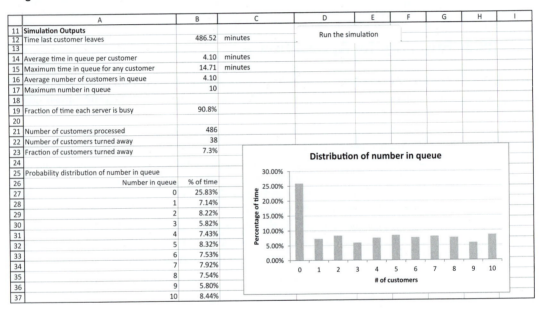

	A	B	C	D	E	F	G	H	I
11	Simulation Outputs								
12	Time last customer leaves	486.52	minutes		Run the simulation				
13									
14	Average time in queue per customer	4.10	minutes						
15	Maximum time in queue for any customer	14.71	minutes						
16	Average number of customers in queue	4.10							
17	Maximum number in queue	10							
18									
19	Fraction of time each server is busy	90.8%							
20									
21	Number of customers processed	486							
22	Number of customers turned away	38							
23	Fraction of customers turned away	7.3%							
24									
25	Probability distribution of number in queue								
26		Number in queue	% of time						
27		0	25.83%						
28		1	7.14%						
29		2	8.22%						
30		3	5.82%						
31		4	7.43%						
32		5	8.32%						
33		6	7.53%						
34		7	7.92%						
35		8	7.54%						
36		9	5.80%						
37		10	8.44%						

time. Finally, it took 6.52 minutes to service all customers who were in the system at time 480.

These results are for a *single* replication of the 480-minute simulation. Clicking repeatedly on the Run button causes different results to appear. As you can check, these results can differ dramatically, even with the same inputs. Some 480-minute days experience a lot of congestion, and some experience relatively little congestion—just as in real life. It would be possible to embed the current VBA code in a loop over a number of replications. For example, you could simulate 100 480-minute days, each starting empty and idle (no customers in the system). Then you could summarize output measures across days. (You will get a chance to do this in an exercise at the end of the chapter.)

29.4 Setting Up the Excel Sheets

The **Queueing Simulation.xlsm** file contains two worksheets, named Explanation and Report. The Report worksheet can be set up only as a template, with sample inputs in the inputs section and labels only in the outputs section. One measure, called the traffic intensity, can be calculated in cell E9 (see Figure 29.2) with the formula

=ArriveRate/(NServers/MeanServeTime)

This is actually the arrival rate divided by the *maximum* service rate of the system—when all servers are busy. If it is greater than 1 or only slightly below 1, the system is likely to experience long waiting times, and many arriving customers are likely to be turned away. However, if the traffic intensity is well less than 1, there is usually very little waiting in line, and the servers will tend to have a lot of idle time. The sample results in Figure 29.3 show that considerable congestion can occur even when the traffic intensity is "only" 0.9. Of course, the simulation outputs show exactly what happens on any given run.

The chart can be created at design time with Excel's chart tools, using any sample data in rows 27 down in the Report worksheet. Then it can be linked to the actual data at run time.

29.5 Getting Started with the VBA

The application includes only a module—no user forms and no references. Once the module is added, the Project Explorer window will appear as in Figure 29.4.

Workbook_Open Code

The Workbook_Open sub guarantees that the Explanation worksheet appears when the file is opened, and it hides the Report worksheet.

Figure 29.4 Project Explorer Window

```
Private Sub Workbook_Open()
    With wsExplanation
        .Activate
        .Range("E4").Select
    End With
    wsReport.Visible = False
End Sub
```

29.6 Structure of a Queueing Simulation

As stated in the introduction, there is no Model worksheet where the logic of the model is captured. Everything is done in memory with VBA. A worksheet is used only as a place to show the inputs and the eventual outputs. Therefore, the VBA code has to take care of all the timing and statistical bookkeeping as the simulation progresses. The general ideas are explained here.

The key idea is one of scheduled events. At any point in time, there is a list of scheduled events of two types. The first type is an arrival. Each time an arrival occurs, the *next* arrival is scheduled at some random time in the future. When it occurs, *another* arrival is scheduled, and so on. The second type of event is a service completion. Each time a customer goes into service (possibly after waiting in the queue), a service completion is scheduled at a random time in the future.

It is important to understand that *nothing happens,* in terms of computer code, between events. There is a simulation "clock" that is updated from one event time to the next. All of the action occurs at these event times.

The overall logic of the simulation is placed inside a **Do** loop, which continues until the arrivals have been cut off (because they would occur after closing time) and all customers have been cleared from the system. Each pass through the loop deals with a single event—the next (most imminent) event. It is implemented with the following four subroutines.

FindNextEvent Sub

This sub is the key to any queueing simulation. It scans through the list of all scheduled events and finds the most imminent one. For example, it might find that the next event is a departure from server 3 that will occur at clock time 100.47. It would then reset the clock to time 100.47 and return the information about the next event (a service completion from server 3). The next time through, the clock would be reset from 100.47 to the time of the *next* event.

UpdateStatistics Sub

This sub, always called right after the **FindNextEvent** sub, updates any statistical counters with information since the previous event time. As an example, suppose the clock has just been reset to time 100.47 and the previous clock time was 99.89. Also, suppose there were three customers in the queue from time 99.89 to time 100.47. (Remember that nothing happens between events, so the number in the queue has to remain constant during this time interval.) Then if there is a statistical variable that accumulates the total customer minutes spent in the queue, this sub adds three times the difference (100.47 – 99.89) to the previous value of this variable.

Arrival Sub

If the FindNextEvent sub determines that the next event is an arrival, the following logic is played out.

- Schedule the time of the *next* arrival. If this time is after closing time, disallow the next arrival and don't schedule any future arrivals.
- Check whether the queue is already full. If it is, turn this customer away, and add 1 to the number of customers turned away.
- Check whether all servers are busy. If they are, put this arrival at the end of the queue and keep track of his arrival time to the system (for later statistics). Otherwise, find an idle server, place this customer in service, and schedule a service completion.

Departure Sub

If the FindNextEvent sub determines that the next event is a departure from a particular server, then the following logic is played out:

- Increase the number of completed customers by 1.
- Check whether there is anyone in the queue. If there is no queue, decrease the number of busy servers by 1, and do *not* schedule a new departure event for the server who just finished. Otherwise, if there is at least one customer in the queue, keep this server busy with the customer at the front of the queue, move all other customers up one space in the queue, and schedule a departure event for this server.

Outputs

Once the clock time is past closing time and all customers have departed, the only thing left to do is report the outputs for the simulation. Some outputs must be calculated first. Other than counters such as the number of customers turned away, the outputs are of two types: **customer stats** and **time stats**.

A typical customer stat is the average time spent in queue per customer. To obtain this average, you keep track of a variable that sums the queueing times of all customers. Then at the end of the simulation, you divide it by the number of customers who have completed service to obtain the desired average.

A typical time stat is the average number of customers in the queue. To obtain this average, you keep track of a variable that sums the total number of customer-minutes spent in the queue. For example, if six customers wait in queue for half a minute each, this contributes three customer minutes to the total. Then at the end of the simulation, you divide this variable by the final clock time to obtain the desired average. (Can you convince yourself that this gives the desired average?)

Another typical time stat is the average server utilization, defined as the fraction of time a typical server is busy. To obtain this average, you keep track of a variable that sums the total number of server minutes spent serving customers. At the end of the simulation, you divide this variable by the final clock time to obtain the average number of servers busy, and you then divide this ratio by the number of servers to obtain the desired server utilization.

The Need for Careful Programming

The logic of most queueing simulations is really quite straightforward—you play out the events as they occur through time. However, the devil is in the details. Queueing simulations are difficult to get correct. Part of the reason is that there are so many interrelated details. Perhaps an even more important reason is that you don't know what the "answers" ought to be, so it is often not clear whether a queueing simulation is working correctly or not. (I can only imagine how many supposedly correct simulations in the business world are really wrong.) My intent is not to scare you away. Rather, it is to emphasize the need for careful programming. At the very least, variables and subroutines should be named meaningfully. A variable's name should leave little doubt about what it represents. Also, queueing simulations should probably be commented more extensively than any other programs in the book. This clearly helps people who read the program, but it also helps you, the programmer, to understand your own logic.

29.7 The Module

Now let's take a look at the code for this application. The following list separates the module-level variables into three categories for ease of interpretation. The system parameters are the user inputs. The system status indicators define the current status of the system at any point in time. The statistical variables are the "book-keeping" variables that are eventually used to calculate the simulation outputs. You should read these definitions carefully.

Option Statement and Module-Level Variables

```
Option Explicit

' Declare system parameters.
'    meanIATime - mean interarrival time (reciprocal of arrival rate)
'    meanServeTime - mean service time
'    nServers - number of servers
'    maxAllowedInQ - maximum number of customers allowed in the queue
'    closeTime - clock time when no future arrivals are accepted

Dim meanIATime As Single
Dim meanServeTime As Single
Dim nServers As Integer
Dim maxAllowedInQ As Integer
Dim closeTime As Single
```

```
' Declare system status indicators.
'   nInQueue - number of customers currently in the queue
'   nBusy - number of servers currently busy
'   clockTime - current clock time, where the initial clock time is 0
'   eventScheduled(i) - True or False, depending on whether an event of type i is
'       scheduled or not, for i>=0, where i=0 corresponds to arrivals and i from
'       1 to nServers corresponds to server i service completions
'   timeOfLastEvent - clock time of previous event
'   timeOfNextEvent(i) - the scheduled clock time of the next event of type i
'       (only defined when eventScheduled(i) is True)
'

Dim nInQueue As Integer
Dim nBusy As Integer
Dim clockTime As Single
Dim eventScheduled() As Boolean
Dim timeOfLastEvent As Single
Dim timeOfNextEvent() As Single


' Declare statistical variables.
'   nServed - number of customers who have completed service so far
'   nLost - number of customers who have been turned away so far
'   maxNInQueue - maximum number in the queue at any point in time so far
'   maxTimeInQueue - maximum time any customer has spent in the queue so far
'   timeOfArrival(i) - arrival time of the customer currently in the i-th
'       place in the queue, for i>=1
'   totalTimeInQueue - total customer-time units spent in the queue so far
'   totalTimeBusy - total server-time units spent serving customers so far
'   sumOfQueueTimes - sum of all times in the queue so far, where sum is over
'       customers who have completed their times in the queue
'   queueTimeArray(i) - amount of time there have been exactly i customers
'       in the queue, for i>=0
'

Dim nServed As Long
Dim nLost As Integer
Dim maxNInQueue As Integer
Dim maxTimeInQueue As Single
Dim timeOfArrival() As Single
Dim totalTimeInQueue As Single
Dim totalTimeBusy As Single
Dim sumOfQueueTimes As Single
Dim queueTimeArray() As Single
```

Main Code

The Main sub is attached to the button on the Report worksheet. It runs the simulation. It first calls VBA's Randomize function to ensure that *different* random numbers are used for each simulation run, it clears old results from the Report worksheet, it captures the inputs from the Report worksheet, and it calls the Initialize sub to initialize the simulation (see explanation below). Then it enters a Do loop, as explained in the previous section. This loop processes one event after another until the arrivals have been cut off and all customers have been cleared from the system. Finally, it calls the Report sub to calculate the outputs and place them on the Report worksheet.

```
Sub Main()
    ' This sub runs when the user clicks on the "Run the simulation" button on
    ' the Simulation sheet. It sets up and runs the simulation.
    Dim nextEventType As Integer
    Dim finishedServer As Integer

    ' Always start with new random numbers.
    Randomize

    ' Clear previous results, if any, from the Report sheet.
    Call ClearOldResults

    ' Get inputs from the Report Sheet.
    With wsReport
        meanIATime = 1 / .Range("ArriveRate").Value
        meanServeTime = .Range("MeanServeTime").Value
        nServers = .Range("nServers").Value
        maxAllowedInQ = .Range("MaxAllowedInQ").Value
        closeTime = .Range("CloseTime").Value
    End With

    ' The next two arrays have an element for arrivals (index 0)
    ' and one for each server.
    ReDim eventScheduled(nServers + 1)
    ReDim timeOfNextEvent(nServers + 1)

    ' Set counters, status indicators to 0 and schedule first arrival.
    Call Initialize

    ' Keep simulating until the last customer has left.

        ' Find the time and type of the next event, and reset the clock.
        ' Capture the index of the finished server in case the next event
        ' is a service completion.
        Call FindNextEvent(nextEventType, finishedServer)

        ' Update statistics since the last event.
        Call UpdateStatistics

        ' nextEventType is 1 for an arrival, 2 for a departure.
        If nextEventType = 1 Then
            Call Arrival
        Else
            Call Departure(finishedServer)
        End If
    Loop Until Not eventScheduled(0) And nBusy = 0

    ' Report the results.
    Call Report
End Sub
```

ClearOldResults Code

The ClearOldResults sub clears all outputs from a previous run from the output section of the Report worksheet.

```
Sub ClearOldResults()
    ' This sub clears the results from any previous simulation.
    With wsReport
        .Range("B12:B23").ClearContents
        With .Range("A26")
            Range(.Offset(1, 0), .Offset(0, 1).End(xlDown)).ClearContents
        End With
    End With
End Sub
```

Initialize Code

Most of the Initialize sub involves setting status indicators and statistical variables to 0. (Remember that the simulation starts at clock time 0 with no customers in the system—empty and idle.) Note in particular how the array queueTimeArray is initialized. By the time the simulation has finished, there should be an element in this array for each number of customers that have ever been in the queue. At time 0, however, there is no way to know how long the queue will eventually grow. Therefore, the queueTimeArray is initialized to have only one element, the 0 element. It will then be redimensioned appropriately as the queue grows later on.

The Initialize sub also schedules the first event—the time of the first arrival. It does this by setting eventScheduled(0) to True and generating a random time for this event in timeOfNextEvent(0). However, it sets eventScheduled(i) to False for i from 1 to nServers. This is because all of the servers are currently idle, so they should not have scheduled service completions. It is important to use careful indexing. Here, I have indexed an arrival with index 0 and service completions with indexes 1 to nServers. Other indexing could be used, but this one is fairly natural and easy to remember.

```
Sub Initialize()
    ' This sub initializes the simulation to the "empty and idle" state and
    ' sets all statistical counters to 0. It then schedules the first arrival.
    Dim i As Integer

    ' Initialize system status indicators.
    clockTime = 0
    nBusy = 0
    nInQueue = 0
    timeOfLastEvent = 0

    ' Initialize statistical variables.
    nServed = 0
    nLost = 0
    sumOfQueueTimes = 0
    maxTimeInQueue = 0
    totalTimeInQueue = 0
    maxNInQueue = 0
    totalTimeBusy = 0

    ' Redimension the queueTimeArray array to have one element (the 0 element,
    ' for the amount of time when there are 0 customers in the queue).
```

```
        ReDim queueTimeArray(1)
        queueTimeArray(0) = 0

        ' Schedule an arrival from the exponential distribution.
        eventScheduled(0) = True
        timeOfNextEvent(0) = Exponential(meanIATime)

        ' Don't schedule any departures because there are no customers in the system.
        For i = 1 To nServers
            eventScheduled(i) = False
        Next
End Sub
```

Generating Exponentially Distributed Random Numbers

The random interarrival times and service times in this simulation are all exponentially distributed.[1] (Again, this is an assumption frequently made in queueing models.) If an exponential distribution has mean m, you can generate a random number from it with the VBA expression

```
-m * Log(Rnd)
```

Here, Rnd is VBA's function for generating *uniformly* distributed random numbers from 0 to 1, and Log is VBA's natural logarithm function. (The minus sign is required because the logarithm of a number between 0 and 1 is *negative*.) Because exponentially distributed random numbers are generated several times in the program, I wrote the following function subroutine to take care of it.

```
Function Exponential(mean As Single) As Single
    ' This generates a random number from an exponential distribution
    ' with a given mean.
    Exponential = -mean * Log(Rnd)
End Function
```

FindNextEvent Code

The FindNextEvent sub is the key to the simulation. When it is called, there are typically several events scheduled to occur in the future (such as an arrival and several service completions). The nextEventTime variable captures the minimum of these—the time of the most imminent event. If the most imminent event is an arrival, nextEventType is set to 1. If it is a departure, nextEventType is set to 2, and finishedServer records the index of the server who just completed service.

---

[1] The term *interarrival time* means the time between two successive customer arrivals.

In either case, clockTime is reset to nextEventTime. This operation is crucial. If clock-Time were not updated, the simulation would never end.

```
Sub FindNextEvent(nextEventType As Integer, finishedServer As Integer)
    ' This sub finds the type (arrival, departure, or closing time) of the next
    ' event and advances the simulation clock to the time of the next event.
    Dim i As Integer
    Dim nextEventTime As Single

    ' nextEventTime will be the minimum of the scheduled event times.
    ' Start by setting it to a large value.
    nextEventTime = 10 * closeTime

    ' Find type and time of the next (most imminent) scheduled event. Note that
    ' there is a potential event scheduled for the next arrival (indexed as 0) and
    ' for each server completion (indexed as 1 to nServers).
    For i = 0 To nServers
        ' Check if there is an event schedule of type i.
        If eventScheduled(i) Then
            ' If the current event is the most imminent so far, record it.
            If timeOfNextEvent(i) < nextEventTime Then
                nextEventTime = timeOfNextEvent(i)
                If i = 0 Then
                    ' It's an arrival.
                    nextEventType = 1
                Else
                    ' It's a departure - record the index of the server who finished.
                    nextEventType = 2
                    finishedServer = i
                End If
            End If
        End If
    Next

    ' Advance the clock to the time of the next event.
    clockTime = nextEventTime
End Sub
```

UpdateStatistics Code

The UpdateStatistics sub first defines timeSinceLastEvent as the elapsed time since the previous event. At the end of the sub, it resets timeOfLastEvent to the current clock time (in anticipation of the *next* time this sub is called). In between, it updates any statistics with what has occurred during the elapsed time. For example, queueTimeArray(i) in general is the amount of time exactly i customers have been in the queue. During the time since the previous event, the number in the queue has been a constant value, nInQueue, so timeSinceLastEvent is added to the array element queueTimeArray(nInQueue). The next two lines add the number of customer-time units in the queue and the number of server-time units being busy, respectively, to the totalTimeInQueue and totalTimeBusy variables. If there were other outputs to keep track of, they would be updated similarly in this sub.

```
Sub UpdateStatistics()
    ' This sub updates statistics since the time of the previous event.
    Dim timeSinceLastEvent As Single

    ' timeSinceLastEvent is the time since the last update.
    timeSinceLastEvent = clockTime - timeOfLastEvent

    ' Update statistical variables.
    queueTimeArray(nInQueue) = queueTimeArray(nInQueue) + timeSinceLastEvent
    totalTimeInQueue = totalTimeInQueue + nInQueue * timeSinceLastEvent
    totalTimeBusy = totalTimeBusy + nBusy * timeSinceLastEvent

    ' Reset timeOfLastEvent to the current time.
    timeOfLastEvent = clockTime
End Sub
```

Arrival Code

The Arrival sub plays out the logic described in the previous section for an arrival event. The comments clarify the details. Note in particular the case where the arrival must enter the queue. A check is made to see whether this makes the queue length longer than it has ever been before. If it is, the maxNInQueue variable is updated, and the queueTimeArray and timeOfArrival arrays are redimensioned (to have an extra element). You can think of the timeOfArrival values as "tags" placed on the customers. Each tag shows when the customer arrived to the system. When a customer eventually goes into service, his tag is used to calculate how long he has spent in the queue: the current clock time minus his timeOfArrival value.

```
Sub Arrival()
    ' This sub takes care of all the logic when a customer arrives.
    Dim i As Integer

    ' Schedule the next arrival.
    timeOfNextEvent(0) = clockTime + Exponential(meanIATime)

    ' Cut off the arrival stream if it is past closing time.
    If timeOfNextEvent(0) > closeTime Then
        eventScheduled(0) = False
    End if

    ' If the queue is already full, this customer is turned away.
    If nInQueue = maxAllowedInQ Then
        nLost = nLost + 1
        Exit Sub
    End if

    ' Check if all servers are busy.
    If nBusy = nServers then

        ' All servers are busy, so put this customer at the end of the queue.
        nInQueue = nInQueue + 1
```

```
                    ' If the queue is now longer than it has been before, update maxNInQueue
                    ' and redimension arrays appropriately.
                    If nInQueue > maxNInQueue Then
                        maxNInQueue = nInQueue

                        ' queueTimeArray is 0-based, with elements 0 to maxNInQueue.
                        ReDim Preserve queueTimeArray(0 To maxNInQueue)

                        ' timeOfArrival is 1-based, with elements 1 to maxNInQueue.
                        ReDim Preserve timeOfArrival(1 To maxNInQueue)
                    End if

                    ' Keep track of this customer's arrival time (for later stats).
                    timeOfArrival(nInQueue) = clockTime

                Else
                    ' The customer can go directly into service, so update the number of servers busy.
                    nBusy = nBusy + 1

                    ' This loop searches for the first idle server and schedules a departure
                    ' event for this server.
                    For i = 1 To nServers
                        If Not eventScheduled(i) Then
                            eventScheduled(i) = True
                            timeOfNextEvent(i) = clockTime + Exponential(meanServeTime)
                            Exit For
                        End If
                    Next
                End If
            End Sub
```

Departure Code

The **Departure** sub plays out the logic described in the previous section for a service completion event. It takes one argument to identify the server who just completed service. Again, the comments clarify the details. The final **For** loop is important. The timeOfArrival "tags" should remain with the customers as they move up one space in the queue. Therefore, the timeOfArrival(1) value, the time of arrival of the first person in line becomes timeOfArrival(2) (because this person used to be second in line), timeOfArrival(2) becomes timeOfArrival(3), and so on.

```
Sub Departure(finishedServer As Integer)
    ' This sub takes care of the logic when a customer departs from service.
    Dim i As Integer
    Dim timeInQueue As Single

    ' Update number of customers who have finished.
    nServed = nServed + 1

    ' Check if any customers are waiting in queue.
    If nInQueue = 0 Then
```

```
            ' No one is in the queue, so make the server who just finished idle.
            nBusy = nBusy - 1
            eventScheduled(finishedServer) = False

        Else

            ' At least one person is in the queue, so take first customer
            ' in queue into service.
            nInQueue = nInQueue - 1

            ' timeInQueue is the time this customer has been waiting in line.
            timeInQueue = clockTime - timeOfArrival(1)

            ' Check if this is a new maximum time in queue.
            If timeInQueue > maxTimeInQueue Then
                maxTimeInQueue = timeInQueue
            End if

            ' Update the total of all customer queue times so far.
            sumOfQueueTimes = sumOfQueueTimes + timeInQueue

            ' Schedule departure for this customer with the same server who just finished.
            timeOfNextEvent(finishedServer) = clockTime + Exponential(meanServeTime)

            ' Move everyone else in line up one space.
            For i = 1 To nInQueue
                timeOfArrival(i) = timeOfArrival(i + 1)
            Next
        End If
End Sub
```

Report Code

The Report sub, called at the end of the simulation, calculates customer stats and time stats and then reports the results in named ranges in the Report worksheet. It also names two ranges where the probability distribution of queue length is stored, and it updates the chart.

```
Sub Report()
    ' This sub calculates and then reports summary measures for the simulation.
    Dim i As Integer
    Dim avgTimeInQueue As Single
    Dim avgNInQueue As Single
    Dim avgNBusy As Single
    Dim ser As Series

    ' Calculate averages.
    avgTimeInQueue = sumOfQueueTimes / nServed
    avgNInQueue = totalTimeInQueue / clockTime
    avgNBusy = totalTimeBusy / clockTime

    ' queueTimeArray records, for each value from 0 to maxNInQueue, the percentage
    ' of time that many customers were waiting in the queue.
    For i = 0 To maxNInQueue
```

```
            queueTimeArray(i) = queueTimeArray(i) / clockTime
        Next

        ' Enter simulate results in named ranges.
        With wsReport
            .Range("FinalTime").Value = clockTime
            .Range("NServed").Value = nServed
            .Range("AvgTimeInQ").Value = avgTimeInQueue
            .Range("MaxTimeInQ").Value = maxTimeInQueue
            .Range("AvgNInQ").Value = avgNInQueue
            .Range("MaxNInQ").Value = maxNInQueue
            .Range("AvgServerUtil").Value = avgNBusy / nServers
            .Range("NLost").Value = nLost
            .Range("PctLost").Formula = "=NLost/(NLost+NServed)"


            ' Enter the queue length distribution from row 27 down, and name the two columns.
            With .Range("A27")
                For i = 0 To maxNInQueue
                    .Offset(i, 0).Value = i
                    .Offset(i, 1).Value = queueTimeArray(i)
                Next
                Range(.Offset(0, 0), .Offset(maxNInQueue, 0)).Name = "Report!NInQueue"
                Range(.Offset(0, 1), .Offset(maxNInQueue, 1)).Name = "Report!PctOfTime"
            End With


            ' Update the chart.
            Set ser = .ChartObjects(1).Chart.SeriesCollection(1)
            ser.Values = .Range("PctOfTime")
            ser.XValues = .Range("nInQueue")

            .Range("A1").Select
        End With
End Sub
```

ViewChangeInputs Code

This last sub is for navigational purposes. It is attached to the button on the Explanation worksheet. It unhides and activates the Report worksheet so that the user can view and change any inputs before running the simulation. It also clears any old outputs from the Report worksheet. (These inputs could be obtained from a user form, but I have done it this way for variety.)

```
Sub ViewChangeInputs()
    ' This sub runs when the user clicks on the "View/Change Inputs" button on the
    ' Explanation sheet. It clears old results, if any, and lets the user see
    ' the Report sheet.
    With wsReport
        .Visible = True
        .Activate
    End With
    Call ClearOldResults
End Sub
```

29.8 Summary

A typical queueing simulation program, as illustrated in this chapter, is considerably different from most of the other applications in this book. The reason is that all of the logic must be done behind the scenes in VBA code—there is no spreadsheet model. Although the overall flow of the program is conceptually straightforward, there are many timing and bookkeeping details to keep straight, which means that a programmer must be extremely careful. However, this type of program provides an excellent way to sharpen your programming skills. Besides, a successfully completed queueing simulation program can provide many important insights into the system being modeled.

EXERCISES

1. Change the simulation so that there is no upper limit on the number allowed in the queue. This means that no customers will be turned away because the system is full. (Make sure you delete any variables that are no longer needed.)

2. Continuing the previous exercise, assume that each customer who arrives to the system looks at the queue (if there is one) and then decides whether to join. Assume the probability that a customer joins the queue is of the form r^n, where r is an input between 0 and 1 (probably close to 1), and n is the current number of customers in the queue. We say that a customer "balks" if she decides not to join. Keep track of the number of customers who balk.

3. Change the simulation so that the servers have different mean service times, so that some tend to be faster than others. Assume that an arrival always chooses the fastest idle server (if multiple servers are idle). Now report the fraction of time *each* server is busy.

4. Change the simulation so that all activity stops at closing time—the customers currently in the system are *not* serviced any further. Report the number of customers still in the system at closing time. (Make sure you update statistics from the time of the last event until closing time.)

5. (More difficult) This exercise is based on the "express" lines you see at some service centers. Assume that arriving customers are designated as "regular" or "express" customers when they arrive. The probability that an arrival is an express customer is an input between 0 and 1. Express customers have a relatively small mean service time. The mean service time for regular customers is larger. One of the servers is an "express" server. This server handles only the express customers. The other servers can serve *either* type of customer. The customers wait (at least conceptually, if not physically) in two separate lines. They are served in first-come, first-served order as servers become available, although the express server cannot serve a regular customer. If an express customer enters and a regular server and the express server are both idle, you can assume that the customer goes to the express server. Change the simulation appropriately to handle this situation, and keep track of separate statistics for express customers and regular customers, as well as for regular servers and the express server.

6. Change the program so that the current simulation is embedded in a For loop from 1 to 100. Each time through the loop, one simulation is run, and its outputs (you can select which ones) are reported on a Replications worksheet, one row per replication. After all 100 simulations have run, summarize the selected outputs on a Summary worksheet. For each output, report the following summary measures: minimum, maximum, average, standard deviation, median, and 5th and 95th percentiles. For example, if one of your outputs on any replication is the maximum number in queue, then you will get 100 such maximums, one for each replication. The Summary worksheet should summarize these 100 numbers: their average, their standard deviation, and so on. In this way, you can see how results vary from one replication to another.

30

An Option-Pricing Application

30.1 Introduction

This application prices European and American call and put options. A European *call option* on a certain stock allows the owner of the option to purchase 100 shares of the stock for a certain price, called the *exercise* (or *strike*) *price*, on a certain date in the future, called the *exercise date*. A *put option* is the same except that it allows the owner to *sell* 100 shares on the exercise date. An American option is similar, but it can be exercised on *any* date between the current date and the exercise date.

The owner of a call option hopes that the price of the stock will *increase* above the exercise price. The option can then be exercised, and the owner can make the difference by buying the stock at the exercise price and immediately selling it back at the actual price. The opposite is true for a put option. For a put option, the owner hopes that the price of the stock will *decrease* below the exercise price so that he can sell it for a relatively high price and immediately "cover his position" by buying it back at a cheaper price. The question answered by this application is how much these options are worth.

It is relatively easy to price European options. This is done with the famous Black-Scholes formula. American options are considerably more difficult to price. The usual method is to use a technique called binomial trees, as is done in this application. In addition, it can be shown that if no dividends are given, as is assumed here, it is never optimal to exercise an American call option early (before the exercise date). However, this is not true for American put options. For American puts, there is an early exercise boundary that specifies when the put should be exercised. Specifically, this boundary consists of a cutoff price for each date in the future before the exercise date. If the actual stock price falls below this cutoff price on any particular date, then the put should be exercised on that date. This application calculates the early exercise boundary for American put options (if the user requests it).

New Learning Objectives: VBA

- To gain practice working with dates, including the use of a user-defined function for calculating the number of days between two specified dates, excluding weekends, and to learn how to use the very handy calendar control in a user form.
- To learn how to manipulate Excel's status bar to indicate the progress of a program.
- To learn how to deal with literal double quotes inside a string.
- To learn how to use Excel's Goal Seek tool with VBA.

New Learning Objectives: Non-VBA

- To gain some knowledge of how options work and how they are priced, including the use of the Black-Scholes formula for European options and binomial trees for American options.

30.2 Functionality of the Application

The application has the following functionality:

1. It first asks the user for the inputs required to price any option. These include (1) the current price of the stock, (2) the exercise price, (3) the exercise date, (4) the annual risk-free rate of interest, (5) the volatility of the stock price (the standard deviation of its annual return), and (6) the type of option (European or American, call or put). It is assumed that the current date is the actual date the user runs the program, so that the exercise date must be *after* this. (Actually, the current date is taken to be the next Monday in case the user runs the program on a weekend.) Note that the current date can be found with Excel's TODAY function.[1]
2. It next calculates the price of the option and displays it in a message box.
3. If the option is an American put option, the user can also request the early exercise boundary.

There are two underlying assumptions. First, it is assumed that there are no dividends for the stock. If there were, the calculations would need to be modified. Second, it is assumed that trading days include weekdays but not weekends. This assumption is used to calculate the *duration* of the option, the number of trading days between the current date and the exercise date. It would be possible to exclude some weekdays as trading days (the Fourth of July, for example), but this would add complexity to the application, and it has not been done here.

This application uses a calendar control on the user form. See Section 11.3 of Chapter 11 for instructions on registering this control on your computer. The application won't work properly until you do so.

30.3 Running the Application

The application is stored in the file **Stock Options.xlsm**. Upon opening this file, the user sees the Explanation worksheet in Figure 30.1. When the button on this form is clicked, the dialog box in Figure 30.2 appears. The inputs on the left are the current values in the EuroModel worksheet (more about it later). Of course, any of these can be changed.

---

[1] All examples shown in this chapter were run on 8/19/2014, a Tuesday.

Figure 30.1 Explanation Worksheet

Option Pricing Application

Run the application

This application prices any European or American call or put option. The difference between these is that a European option can be exercised only at the exercise date, whereas an American option can be exercised at any time on *or before* the exercise date. The application uses the famous Black-Scholes formula to price European options. This is quite straightforward and is implemented on the EuroModel sheet. Pricing American options is considerably more complex. It requires a method called *binomial trees*, which is implemented on the AmerModel sheet.

For American *put* options, it is also possible to calculate the "early exercise boundary." For any day between now and the exercise date, the early exercise boundary indicates how low the current stock price must be to warrant exercising early on that date. The application provides the option of calculating this boundary. If this option is selected (which can require a few seconds of computing time), the results are shown on the Report sheet.

Other notes:
1. Why is there no early exercise boundary for American call options? It can be proved mathematically that unless there are dividends (which are not included in this application), an American call should never be exercised early.

2. Trading days are defined as all weekdays -- only Saturdays and Sundays are excluded. This application could be changed without too much difficulty to exclude holidays as well.

3. Options are usually for 100 shares, so the prices shown are for 100 shares.

If the user selects any type of option other than an American put, the price of the option is calculated in the EuroModel or the AmerModel worksheet, and the result is displayed in a message box, as shown in Figure 30.3.

For an American put option, the message box in Figure 30.4 appears. If the user clicks the No button, the same type of message as in Figure 30.3 appears. If the user clicks the Yes button, the early exercise boundary is calculated and is reported in the AmerPutReport worksheet, as shown in Figure 30.5. This particular example assumes that the exercise date is 9/4/2014 and the exercise price is $53. If this were a European put, the owner would wait until the exercise date and then exercise the option only if the actual stock price were less than $53. However, the report indicates that the American put should be exercised on, say, 8/22/2014 if it hasn't been exercised already and the actual price on 8/22/2014 is less than $46.88. By the way, the European put with these same inputs is priced at $347.10. The American option provides more flexibility, so it is priced slightly higher at $352.62.

Figure 30.2   Inputs Dialog Box

Figure 30.3   Message Box for Option Price

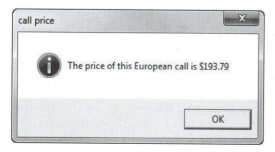

Figure 30.4   Request for Early Exercise Boundary

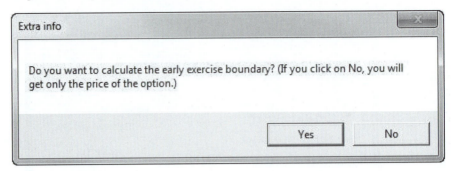

Figure 30.5   Early Exercise Boundary in AmerPutReport Worksheet

	A	B	C	D	E	F	G
1	Option price and early exercise boundary for the American put option						
2							
3	Price of option	$352.62	View Explanation Sheet				
4							
5	Early exercise boundary: exercise only if stock price on this day is below the value in column B.						
6	Trading date	Boundary price					
7	08/20/14	$46.11					
8	08/21/14	$46.37					
9	08/22/14	$46.88					
10	08/25/14	$46.87					
11	08/26/14	$47.32					
12	08/27/14	$47.85					
13	08/28/14	$47.92					
14	08/29/14	$48.54					
15	09/01/14	$49.46					
16	09/02/14	$50.55					
17	09/03/14	$51.74					
18	09/04/14	$53.00					

30.4 Setting Up the Excel Sheets

The **Stock Options.xlsm** file contains four worksheets: the Explanation sheet, the EuroModel sheet, the AmerModel sheet, and the AmerPutReport sheet. The EuroModel Worksheet, shown in Figure 30.6, can be set up completely at design time, using any trial values in the input cells. The current date is calculated in cell B7 with Excel's TODAY function. Actually, it uses an IF formula together with Excel's WEEKDAY function to return today's date or the following Monday in case today is a weekend day. The formula is

```
=IF(WEEKDAY(TODAY())=1,TODAY()+1,IF(WEEKDAY(TODAY())=7,
   TODAY()+2,TODAY()))
```

Figure 30.6 EuroModel Worksheet

	A	B	C	D	E
1	Black-Scholes model for pricing European puts, calls				
2					
3	Input data				
4	Type of option (1 for call, 2 for put)	1			
5	Stock price	$50.00			
6	Exercise price	$49.00			
7	Today's date	19-Aug-14			
8	Exercise date	28-Aug-14			
9	Riskfree interest rate	0.100			
10	StDev of annual return	0.400			
11					
12	Duration (trading days)	7			
13					
14	Quantities for Black-Scholes formula				
15	d1	0.38165033		N(d1)	0.64864
16	d2	0.31601732		N(d2)	0.624005
17					
18	Option price	$193.79			

Note that WEEKDAY of any date returns 1 for Sunday and 7 for Saturday. The duration of the option (number of trading days until the exercise date) is calculated in cell B12 with a function called TradeDays, written just for this application (see the code at the end of the chapter). The formulas in cells B15, B16, E15, E16, and B18 implement the Black-Scholes formula. (These formulas are rather technical. See the **Stock Options.xlsm** file for the details.)

A Note on Range Names.[2] The EuroModel and AmerModel worksheets each have input sections that use several of the same range names, such as RiskfreeRate for cell B9. If you want to use the *same* range names for different worksheets, you need to be careful. The best way is to precede them by their worksheet name when you define them. Specifically, to define the RiskfreeRate range name for the EuroModel sheet, first select cell B9 in this sheet and then select Excel's Name Manager on the Formulas ribbon. In the "Refers to" box, enter Euro-Model!RiskfreeRate. This creates a "worksheet-level" name. You can then proceed similarly to create the name AmerModel!RiskfreeRate for cell B9 of the AmerModel worksheet. Then VBA code such as wsAmerModel.Range("RiskfreeRate") can be used to refer to the appropriate range.

The AmerModel worksheet sets up a binomial tree for calculating the price of an American call or put. A finished version of this worksheet appears in Figure 30.7 for a call option with duration 4 days. The binomial tree calculations are performed in the two triangular ranges, which in general have as many rows and columns as the

---

[2] See Section 6.6 of Chapter 6 for a more complete discussion of this range name issue.

Figure 30.7 Finished AmerModel Worksheet

	A	B	C	D	E	F
1	Binomial tree model for pricing American calls, puts					
2						
3	Input data					
4	Type of option (1 for call, 2 for put)	2				
5	Stock price	$50.00				
6	Exercise price	$53.00				
7	Today's date	19-Aug-14				
8	Exercise date	25-Aug-14				
9	Riskfree interest rate	10%				
10	StDev of annual return	40%				
11						
12	Duration (trading days)	4				
13						
14	Parameters for binomial tree					
15	Up factor	1.025				
16	Down factor	0.975				
17	Probability of up	0.502				
18	Probability of down	0.498				
19						
20	Future prices		0	1	2	3	4
21		0	$50.00	51.25586	52.543264	53.863	55.21589
22		1		48.7749108	50	51.25586	52.54326
23		2			47.579839	48.77491	50
24		3				46.41405	47.57984
25		4					45.27682
26							
27	Option values		0	1	2	3	4
28		0	3.10171485	$1.99	0.983125	0.227572	0
29		1		4.22508918	3	1.74414	0.456736
30		2			5.4201615	4.225089	3
31		3				6.585952	5.420161
32		4					7.723179

duration plus one. Without going into the technical details, I will simply state that the option price is always in the upper-left corner of the bottom triangle—in this case, about $310.[3] (The value shown in the worksheet is the price per share. The $310 price is for 100 shares.) These triangular ranges must be calculated at run time. The only template that can be created at design time appears in Figure 30.8.

Finally, the AmerPutReport worksheet, shown earlier in Figure 30.5, must be filled in almost entirely at run time. The only template that can be set up at design time contains labels, as shown in Figure 30.9.

---

[3] A good explanation of binomial trees and how they can be implemented in Excel appears in Chapter 56 of Winston, W., *Financial Models Using Simulation and Optimization*, 3rd edition, Palisade Corporation, 2008.

Figure 30.8 AmerModel Worksheet Template

	A	B
1	Binomial tree model for pricing American calls, p	
2		
3	Input data	
4	Type of option (1 for call, 2 for put)	2
5	Stock price	$50.00
6	Exercise price	$53.00
7	Today's date	19-Aug-14
8	Exercise date	25-Aug-14
9	Riskfree interest rate	10%
10	StDev of annual return	40%
11		
12	Duration (trading days)	4
13		
14	Parameters for binomial tree	
15	Up factor	1.025
16	Down factor	0.975
17	Probability of up	0.502
18	Probability of down	0.498
19		
20	Future prices	

Figure 30.9 AmerPutReport Worksheet Template

	A	B	C	D	E	F	G
1	Option price and early exercise boundary for the American put option						
2							
3	Price of option	$80.41		View Explanation Sheet			
4							
5	Early exercise boundary: exercise only if stock price on this day is below the value in column B.						
6	Trading date	Boundary price					

30.5 Getting Started with the VBA

The application includes one user form named frmInputs and a module. The Solver add-in is never used, so no reference to it is necessary. (The Goal Seek tool *is* used, but no reference is necessary for it.) Once these items are added, the Project Explorer window will appear as in Figure 30.10.

Workbook_Open Code

To guarantee that the Explanation worksheet appears when the file is opened, the following code is placed in the ThisWorkbook code window. It also hides all other worksheets.

Figure 30.10 Project Explorer Window

```
Private Sub Workbook_Open()
    Dim ws As Worksheet
    With wsExplanation
        .Activate
        .Range("F12").Select
    End With
    For Each ws In ThisWorkbook.Worksheets
        If ws.CodeName <> "wsExplanation" Then ws.Visible = False
    Next
End Sub
```

30.6 The User Form

The design for frmInputs, shown in Figure 30.11, contains the usual OK and Cancel buttons, an explanation label, four text boxes and associated labels, a calendar and an associated label, and a frame that contains four option buttons. The text boxes are named txtCurrentPrice, txtExercisePrice, txtRiskfreeRate, and txtVolatility. The option buttons are named optEuroCall, optEuroPut, optAmerCall, and optAmerPut.

For the exercise price, I have used a calendar control. This is a very handy control for obtaining a date. It requires almost no work on the programmer's part, and it is very easy for the user. This control unfortunately disappeared in Office 2010, but as explained in Section 11.3 of Chapter 11, you can get it back. Once you register this control as explained there, you can right-click any blank gray area of the Control Toolbox (see Figure 30.12) and select Additional Controls. Then select the Calendar control, as shown in Figure 30.13, and the calendar control will be added to the Toolbox. Among other properties, the control has a Value property that returns the selected date (as a Date type). It also has Year, Month, and Day properties that return these values for the selected date. (Month returns 1 to 12.) The only annoying feature of this control is that if the

Figure 30.11 frmInputs Design

Figure 30.12 Additional Controls

Figure 30.13 Adding the Calendar Control

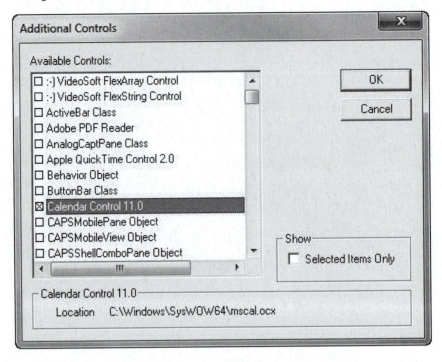

user changes the month or year, no day is selected, which leads to unexpected behavior. This is the reason for the prompt in the middle of Figure 30.11.

Most of the form code is straightforward. However, there is one twist. I want the four text boxes and the calendar to be filled with the inputs from the EuroModel worksheet if either of the first two option buttons is checked, and I want them to be filled with the inputs from the AmerModel worksheet if either of the bottom two option buttons is checked. Therefore, I added a utility sub called FillInputs that takes an argument country, which will be "Euro" or "Amer." The Initialize code checks the European Call option button by default and then calls FillInputs with argument "Euro." But this is not all. There are also event handlers for the Click event of each option button. Each of these calls FillInputs with the appropriate argument. This way, the text boxes and the calendar are filled with data from the appropriate worksheet regardless of which option button is checked.

```
Private cancel As Boolean

Public Function ShowInputsDialog(currentDate As Date, _
        exerciseDate As Date, currentPrice As Single, _
        exercisePrice As Single, riskfreeRate As Single, _
        volatility As Single, optionType As Integer) As Boolean
```

```
        Call Initialize
        Me.Show
        If Not cancel Then
            ' Capture the dates. Note that the current date is entered in the
            ' EuroModel and AmerModel sheets as today's date (or the next Monday
            ' if today is a weekend day.)
            currentDate = wsEuroModel.Range("B7").Value
            exerciseDate = calExerciseDate.Value

            ' Capture the other inputs.
            currentPrice = txtCurrentPrice.Text
            exercisePrice = txtExercisePrice.Text
            riskfreeRate = txtRiskfreeRate.Text
            volatility = txtVolatility.Text

            Select Case True
                Case optEuroCall.Value
                    optionType = 1
                Case optEuroPut.Value
                    optionType = 2
                Case optAmerCall.Value
                    optionType = 3
                Case optAmerPut.Value
                    optionType = 4
            End Select
        End If
        ShowInputsDialog = Not cancel
        Unload Me
End Function

Private Sub Initialize()
        ' Check the European call option and enter values
        ' for the other parameters from the EuroModel sheet.
        optEuroCall.Value = True
        With calExerciseDate
            .Year = Year(Date)
            .Month = Month(Date)
            .Day = Day(Date)
        End With
        Call FillInputs("Euro")
End Sub

Private Function Valid() As Boolean
        ' Perform error checking for user inputs.
        Dim ctl As Control
        Dim curDate As Date, exDate As Date

        Valid = True
        For Each ctl In Me.Controls
            ' Make sure the non-date boxes have positive numeric values.
            If ctl.Name = "txtCurrentPrice" Or ctl.Name = "txtExercisePrice" Or _
                ctl.Name = "txtRiskfreeRate" Or ctl.Name = "txtVolatility" Then
                If ctl.Value = "" Or Not IsNumeric(ctl) Then
                    Valid = False
                    MsgBox "Enter a positive value in this box.", _
                        vbInformation, "Invalid entry"
                    ctl.SetFocus
                    Exit Function
                End If
```

```
                If ctl.Value <= 0 Then
                    Valid = False
                    MsgBox "Enter a positive value in this box.", _
                        vbInformation, "Invalid entry"
                    ctl.SetFocus
                    Exit Function
                End If
            End If
    Next

    ' Capture the dates. Note that the current date is entered in the
    ' EuroModel and AmerModel sheets as today's date (or the next Monday
    ' if today is a weekend day.)
    curDate = wsEuroModel.Range("B7").Value
    exDate = calExerciseDate.Value

    ' Make sure the exercise date is after the current date.
    If curDate >= exDate Then
        MsgBox "The exercise date must be after the next trading day (" _
            & Format(curDate, "mm/dd/yyyy") & ").", _
            vbInformation, "Invalid dates"
            Valid = False
        calExerciseDate.SetFocus
        Exit Function
    End If
End Function

Private Sub FillInputs(country As String)
    Dim ws As Worksheet

    If country = "Euro" Then
        Set ws = wsEuroModel
    Else
        Set ws = wsAmerModel
    End If

    With ws
        txtCurrentPrice.Text = Format(.Range("CurrentPrice").Value, "0.00")
        txtExercisePrice.Text = Format(.Range("ExercisePrice").Value, "0.00")
        calExerciseDate.Value = .Range("ExerciseDate").Value
        txtRiskfreeRate.Text = Format(.Range("RiskfreeRate").Value, "0.000")
        txtVolatility.Text = Format(.Range("Volatility").Value, "0.000")
    End With
End Sub

Private Sub optAmerCall_Click()
    Call FillInputs("Amer")
End Sub

Private Sub optAmerPut_Click()
    Call FillInputs("Amer")
End Sub

Private Sub optEuroCall_Click()
    Call FillInputs("Euro")
End Sub

Private Sub optEuroPut_Click()
    Call FillInputs("Euro")
End Sub
```

```
Private Sub cmdOK_Click()
    If Valid Then Me.Hide
    cancel = False
End Sub

Private Sub cmdCancel_Click()
    Me.Hide
    cancel = True
End Sub

Private Sub UserForm_QueryClose(cancel As Integer, CloseMode As Integer)
    If CloseMode = vbFormControlMenu Then cmdCancel_Click
End Sub
```

30.7 The Module

The module consists of a Main sub that "shows" frmInputs and then calls the appropriate sub, EuroModel or AmerModel. The EuroModel sub is simple because the EuroModel sheet is already set up at design time. However, the AmerModel sub is considerably more complex. It has to create all of the formulas for the binomial tree method. In addition, it needs to calculate the early exercise boundary for an American put option. The details in the code are not spelled out here. They won't make much sense unless you thoroughly understand binomial trees and how they can be used to calculate the option price and the early exercise boundary.[4] I will simply present the code and let the comments speak for themselves.

Options Statement and Module-Level Variables

```
Option Explicit

' Definitions of module-level variables:
'    optionType: 1 (European call), 2 (European put),
'        3 (American call), or 4 (American put)
'    optionName: "call" or "put"
'    currentPrice: current stock price
'    exercisePrice: exercise price of option
'    currentDate: current date (when option is purchased)
'    exerciseDate: exercise date of option
'    riskfreeRate: riskfree rate (annual)
'    volatility: volatility of stock
'    duration: duration of option (in trading days)
'    cutoff(): an array showing the early exercise boundary for
'        an American put
'    optionPrice: price of the option
'    wantExtra: vbYes or vbNo, indicates whether the user wants to
'        calculate the early exercise boundary for an American put
'
```

---

[4] However, it is very instructive to read the Winston chapter referenced earlier and then see how the code in this application implements his method.

```
Dim optionType As Integer, optionName As String
Dim currentPrice As Single, exercisePrice As Single
Dim currentDate As Date, exerciseDate As Date
Dim riskfreeRate As Single, volatility As Single
Dim duration As Integer
Dim optionPrice As Single
Dim cutoff() As Variant, wantExtra As Integer
```

Main Code

```
Sub Main()
    ' This sub runs when the user clicks on the button on the Explanation sheet.

    ' Get the user inputs.
    If frmInputs.ShowInputsDialog(currentDate, exerciseDate, _
            currentPrice, exercisePrice, riskfreeRate, _
            volatility, optionType) Then

        ' Check if user wants the early exercise boundary (only for an American put).
        wantExtra = vbNo
        If optionType = 4 Then
            wantExtra = MsgBox("Do you want to calculate the early exercise boundary? " _
                & "(If you click on No, you will get only the price of the option.)", _
                vbYesNo, "Extra info")
        End If

        ' Define option name, depending on whether the user wants a call or a put.
        If optionType = 1 Or optionType = 3 Then
            optionName = "call"
        Else
            optionName = "put"
        End If

        ' Do the appropriate analysis, either for a European or an American option.
        If optionType <= 2 Then
            Call EuroModel
        Else
            Call AmerModel
        End If
    End If
End Sub
```

EuroModel Code

The EuroModel sub calls the EnterInputs sub to enter the user's inputs in the appropriate cells, gets the option price, and displays an appropriate message.

```
Sub EuroModel()
    ' This sub shows the EuroModel sheet, enters the user inputs in
    ' input cells, and displays the price of the option. The formulas
    ' for calculating the price are already in the sheet.
```

```
' Enter the inputs for the European model and get the result.
With wsEuroModel
    Call EnterInputs(wsEuroModel)
    optionPrice = .Range("B18").Value
End With

' Display the results.
MsgBox "The price of this European " & optionName & " is " _
    & Format(optionPrice, "$0.00"), vbInformation, optionName & " price"
End Sub
```

EnterInputs Code

The EnterInputs sub takes the user's inputs and enters them in the input cells of the specified worksheet. Because the input cells have the same range names in both the EuroModel and the AmerModel worksheets, this same code can be called from both the EuroModel and AmerModel subs. This means that it has to be written only *once*. Note that if the duration of the option is extremely long, the range for the binomial tree (for an American option) could extend beyond the right edge of the worksheet. (Of course, this is much less likely in Excel 2007 and later versions, which have *many* more columns.) A check is made for this by using ws.Columns.Count. This returns the number of columns in a worksheet.

```
Sub EnterInputs(ws As Worksheet)
    ' This sub enters the user's inputs into the appropriate sheet
    ' (EuroModel or AmerModel). This same sub is called for both the
    ' European and the American models.

    With ws
        If optionType <= 2 Then
            .Range("EuroOptType") = optionType
        Else
            .Range("AmerOptType") = optionType - 2
        End If
        .Range("CurrentPrice").Value = currentPrice
        .Range("ExercisePrice").Value = exercisePrice
        .Range("ExerciseDate").Value = exerciseDate
        .Range("RiskfreeRate").Value = riskfreeRate
        .Range("Volatility").Value = volatility
        duration = .Range("Duration").Value
    End With

    ' Check whether the duration would take the American model beyond the
    ' limits of a typical worksheet. If it does, quit.
    If optionType >= 3 And duration > ws.Columns.Count - 2 Then
        MsgBox "Excel cannot accommodate " & duration & " trading days. Its " _
            & "maximum is " & ActiveSheet.Columns.Count - 2 & ". " _
            & "Try again with less days till the exercise date.", _
            vbInformation, "Too many trading days"
        wsExplanation.Activate
        End
    End If
```

```
' Redim cutoff array in case the user wants the early exercise boundary
' for an American put.
If optionType = 4 And wantExtra = vbYes Then
    ReDim cutoff(1 To duration)
End If
End Sub
```

AmerModel Code

The AmerModel sub implements the American option pricing. It runs the same EnterInputs sub as above, and then calls the DevelopAmerModel sub to do most of the work. If the option is an American put and the user wants the early exercise boundary, this sub also calls the CreateAmerReport sub to report this information.

```
Sub AmerModel()
    ' This sub creates the binomial tree model for an American option.

    ' Enter the user inputs.
    Call EnterInputs(wsAmerModel)

    ' Develop the model
    Call DevelopAmerModel

    ' Display the option price unless it is a put option and the user
    ' wants the early exercise boundary. In this case, create a report.
    If optionType = 3 Or wantExtra = vbNo Then
        ' Hide the AmerModel sheet, activate the Explanation sheet,
        ' and display a message about the option's price.
        MsgBox "The price of this American " & optionName & " is " _
            & Format(optionPrice, "$0.00"), vbInformation, optionName & " price"

    Else
        ' This is an American put and the user wants the early exercise
        ' boundary, so it must be created.
        With wsAmerPutReport
            .Visible = True
            .Activate
        End With

        Call CreateAmerReport
    End If
End Sub
```

DevelopAmerModel Code

The DevelopAmerModel sub acts as its own control center, calling a number of subs (ErasePrevious, CalcFuturePrices, CalcValues, and, in the case of an early exercise boundary, EraseRowCol and RunGoalSeek) to set up the AmerModel worksheet and, if appropriate, calculate the early exercise boundary.

A Note on Status Bar Messages. The calculations for the early exercise boundary can take a while, so it is useful to indicate the progress to the user in the status bar at the bottom of the screen. Two properties of the Application object are useful here. The DisplayStatusBar property is Boolean; it is True if the status bar is visible, and it is False otherwise. The StatusBar property returns the message in the status bar. However, this property can also be set to False, which deletes the current message from the status bar.

To illustrate these properties, the next two lines capture whether the status bar was visible (in the Boolean variable oldStatusBar) and then ensure that it *is* visible.

```
oldStatusBar = Application.DisplayStatusBar
Application.DisplayStatusBar = True
```

The next line displays a progress indicator on the status bar that keeps changing as the program proceeds through a For loop.

```
Application.StatusBar = "Running Goal Seek on trading " _
    & "day " & Duration - i + 1 & " of " & Duration
```

Finally, the first of the next two lines removes the message, and the second restores the status bar to its original state (visible or not visible).

```
Application.StatusBar = False
Application.DisplayStatusBar = oldStatusBar
```

This technique can be very useful if your program takes a long time to run. Users will at least know that something is happening. Try running the program for an American put option with a duration of several months, and you will see what I mean.

Here is the DevelopAmerModel sub in its entirety.

```
Sub DevelopAmerModel()
    ' This sub develops the binomial tree model for an American option.
    Dim i As Integer
    Dim oldStatusBar As Boolean

    ' Clear any previous model.
    Call ErasePrevious
    ' Calculate the possible future stock prices in a triangular range.
    Call CalcFuturePrices
    ' Calculate the expected cash flows from the option by following an optimal strategy.
    Call CalcValues

    ' Calculate the early exercise boundary if the user requests it.
    If optionType = 4 And wantExtra = vbYes Then

        ' The StatusBar statements allow the user to track the progress of the calculations.
        oldStatusBar = Application.DisplayStatusBar
        Application.DisplayStatusBar = True
```

```
' The following loop solves a series of Goal Seek problems. Each finds the early
' exercise cutoff price (exercise only if current price is below this price) for a
' particular trading day. In this loop, i represents the row and column of the binomial
' tree "values" area that will be erased. This corresponds to trading day duration-i+1.
wsAmerModel.Range("A20").Offset(duration + 2, 0).Value = "Goal Seek set cell:"

For i = duration To 2 Step -1
    Application.StatusBar = "Running Goal Seek on trading " _
        & "day " & duration - i + 1 & " of " & duration
    Call EraseRowCol(i)
    Call RunGoalSeek
    cutoff(duration - i + 1) = wsAmerModel.Range("B21").Value
Next

' Delete the message from the status bar and restore it to its original state.
Application.StatusBar = False
Application.DisplayStatusBar = oldStatusBar

' The cutoff on the last day requires no calculation; it is the exercise price.
    cutoff(duration) = exercisePrice
    End If
End Sub
```

ErasePrevious Code

The ErasePrevious sub clears the contents of the triangular ranges in the Amer-Model worksheet from a previous run, if any.

```
Sub ErasePrevious()
    ' This sub clears the calculations from any previous model in the AmerModel sheet.
    With wsAmerModel.Range("A20")
        Range(.Offset(0, 0), _
            .End(xlToRight).End(xlDown).End(xlDown).End(xlDown)) _
            .ClearContents
    End With
End Sub
```

CalcFuturePrices Code

The binomial tree method is based on an approximation where the stock price can go up or down on any particular day. The CalcFuturePrices sub calculates all possible future prices in the first triangular array in the AmerModel worksheet. (Each column corresponds to a particular day in the future.)

```
Sub CalcFuturePrices()
    ' This sub sets up the possible future stock prices for the binomial tree
    ' method in a triangular region, starting in cell B21.
    Dim j As Integer

    With wsAmerModel.Range("A20")
        .Value = "Future prices"
```

```
' Enter headings in top row, left column.
For j = 0 To duration
    .Offset(j + 1, 0).Value = j
    .Offset(0, j + 1).Value = j
Next

' Get started by entering the current price in the top left cell
' of the triangular region.
.Offset(1, 1).Value = wsAmerModel.Range("CurrentPrice").Value

' Each entry in the top row is just UpFactor times the previous entry.
Range(.Offset(1, 2), .Offset(1, duration + 1)) _
    .FormulaR1C1 = "=UpFactor*RC[-1]"

' Each entry in other rows is (DownFactor/UpFactor) times the
' entry right above it.
Range(.Offset(2, 1), .Offset(duration + 1, duration + 1)) _
    .FormulaR1C1 = "=If(RC1<=R20C,(DownFactor/UpFactor)*R[-1]C,"""")"
    End With
End Sub
```

CalcValues Code

The key to the binomial tree method is that at the beginning of each day, the decision on whether to exercise or not is based on the maximum of two quantities: the value from exercising now and the *expected* value from waiting a day and then deciding whether to exercise. This permits a simple recursion that is implemented in the CalcValues sub. The FormulaR1C1 line in this sub enters the *same* formula (using relative addressing) in the entire second triangular range of the AmerModel worksheet.

A Note on Double Quotes Embedded in Strings. Suppose you want to use VBA to enter a formula such as **=IF(A5<=10,15, "NA")** in cell B5. This formula uses a pair of double quotes to enter a string in the cell B5 if the condition is false. It is tempting to write the following line of code:

```
Range("B5").Formula = "=If(A5<=10,15,"NA")"
```

This line enters the formula literally between the two outer double quotes. However, it will not work correctly. The problem is that VBA will read the formula up through "=If(A5<=10,15," and think it is finished because it has run into a second double quote. You need to indicate that the *inner* two double quotes should be treated as literals, not as double quotes enclosing the string that the formula consists of.

In general, if you want a double quote in a string to be treated as a literal and not as one of the double quotes enclosing the string, you need to precede it with *another* double quote. The following line does the job:

```
Range("B5").Formula = "=If(A5<=10,15,""NA"")"
```

The formula toward the bottom of the following sub illustrates how this technique is used. In fact, it can be used for any strings, not just formulas. For example, the following line illustrates how to handle double quotes around the word *strange* in a message box.

```
MsgBox "The results from this run were somewhat ""strange""."
```

Again, any two consecutive double quotes inside a string are interpreted as one *literal* double quote.

Here is the CalcValues sub in its entirety.

```
Sub CalcValues()
    ' This sub implements the binomial tree method in another triangular
    ' region, right below the previous one. Each formula says that the price
    ' of the option at any point of the time is the maximum of two quantities:
    ' the cash flow from exercising now and the expected value from waiting a
    ' day and then deciding.
    Dim j As Integer

    With wsAmerModel.Range("A20").Offset(duration + 3, 0)

    ' Enter headings.
        .Value = "Option values"
        For j = 0 To duration
            .Offset(j + 1, 0).Value = j
            .Offset(0, j + 1).Value = j
        Next

        ' Enter the ending value of the option in the last column.
        If optionType = 3 Then ' call option
            Range(.Offset(1, duration + 1), _
                .Offset(duration + 1, duration + 1)).FormulaR1C1 = _
                "=Max(R[-" & duration + 3 & "]C-ExercisePrice,0)"
        Else 'put option
            Range(.Offset(1, duration + 1), _
                .Offset(duration + 1, duration + 1)).FormulaR1C1 = _
                "=Max(ExercisePrice-R[-" & duration + 3 & "]C,0)"
        End If

        ' Enter the appropriate formula in the rest of the cells of the
        ' triangular region.
        If optionType = 3 Then ' call option
            Range(.Offset(1, 1), .Offset(duration, duration)).FormulaR1C1 = _
                "=If(RC1<=R20C,(PrUp*RC[1]+PrDown*R[1]C[1])/(1+RiskfreeRate/260),"""")"

        Else ' put option
            Range(.Offset(1, 1), .Offset(duration, duration)).FormulaR1C1 = _
                "=If(RC1<=R20C,Max(ExercisePrice-R[-" & duration + 3 & "]C," _
                & "(PrUp*RC[1]+PrDown*R[1]C[1])/(1+RiskfreeRate/260)),"""")"
        End If
```

```
             ' The option price is the top left entry of the region.
             optionPrice = .Offset(1, 1).Value * 100
        End With
    End Sub
```

EraseRowCol and RunGoalSeek Code

The calculation of the early exercise boundary, as explained in the Winston chapter referenced earlier, can be accomplished by a suitable modification of the second triangular range of the AmerModel worksheet and a call to Excel's Goal Seek tool. (Goal Seek is used in general to solve one equation in one unknown.) The following two subs implement this method.

```
Sub EraseRowCol(i As Integer)
    ' A quick way to get the early exercise boundary is to delete the bottom and
    ' leftmost row and column of the triangular "values" region and then run
    ' Goal Seek. This sub deletes row i and column i of the region.
    With wsAmerModel.Range("A20").Offset(duration + 3, 0)
        Range(.Offset(i + 1, 1), .Offset(i + 1, i + 1)).ClearContents
        Range(.Offset(1, i + 1), .Offset(i + 1, i + 1)).ClearContents
    End With
End Sub
```

A Note on Using Goal Seek in VBA. Goal Seek is an Excel tool (found in the What-If Analysis dropdown list on the Data ribbon) for solving one equation in one unknown. It requires you to specify three things: (1) a cell containing a formula that you want to force to some value, (2) the value you want to force it to, and (3) a "changing cell" that can be varied to force the formula to the required value. It is easy to invoke Goal Seek from VBA, using the GoalSeek method of a Range object. The following line illustrates how to do it.

```
Range("B20").GoalSeek Goal:=0, ChangingCell:=Range("B21")
```

This line forces the value in cell B20 to 0, using cell B21 as the changing cell. As this example shows, the GoalSeek method takes two arguments: the value to be forced to and the changing cell. It is used to calculate the early exercise boundary in the following RunGoalSeek sub.

```
Sub RunGoalSeek()
    ' This sub runs Goal Seek. (It would also be possible to run Solver, but
    ' Goal Seek is easier.) The changing cell is B21, which contains a trial
    ' value for the price of the stock. Initialize it to a value that is
    ' certainly too high: the exercise price.

    With wsAmerModel.Range("B21")
        .Value = exercisePrice
        .NumberFormat = "General"
    End With
```

```
' In between the two triangular regions (in column B), enter a formula:
' the difference between the cash flow from exercising now and the optimal
' cash flow. Then run Goal Seek, trying to drive the value from this
' formula to 0.
With wsAmerModel.Range("A20").Offset(duration + 2, 1)
    .Formula = "=ExercisePrice-B21-" & .Offset(2, 0).Address
    .NumberFormat = "General"
    .GoalSeek Goal:=0, ChangingCell:=wsAmerModel.Range("B21")
End With
End Sub
```

CreateAmerReport Code

Finally, the CreateAmerReport sub fills in the AmerPutReport worksheet with the information (calculated earlier and stored in the cutoff array) about the early exercise boundary. The most interesting part of this sub is the handling of dates. Note how the report in Figure 30.5 skips dates corresponding to weekend days (nontrading days). This is implemented in the sub with an If construct and Excel's WEEKDAY function, which returns 7 for a Saturday and 1 for a Sunday. Note that the thisDate variable needs to be declared as a Date variable to make this work properly.

```
Sub CreateAmerReport()
    ' This sub creates a report of the option price and the early exercise boundary, but
    ' only for an American put and only when the user requests the early exercise boundary.
    Dim i As Integer
    Dim thisDate As Date
    With wsAmerPutReport
        ' Record the option price.
        .Range("B3").Value = optionPrice

        ' Record the early exercise prices, starting in cell B7. Note that thisDate captures
        ' the actual date, but it excludes weekends.
        With .Range("A6")
            Range(.Offset(1, 0), .Offset(1, 1).End(xlDown)).ClearContents
            thisDate = currentDate
            For i = 1 To duration
                thisDate = thisDate + 1

                ' If thisDate is a Saturday, make it the next Monday.
                If Application.Weekday(thisDate) = 7 Then
                    thisDate = thisDate + 2

                ' If thisDate is a Sunday, make it the next Monday.
                ElseIf Application.Weekday(thisDate) = 1 Then
                    thisDate = thisDate + 1
                End If
                .Offset(i, 0).Value = thisDate
                .Offset(i, 1).Value = cutoff(i)
            Next
        End With

        .Range("A1").Select
    End With
End Sub
```

ViewExplanation Code

This sub is used for navigational purposes (from the button on the AmerPutReport worksheet).

```
Sub ViewExplanation()
    With wsExplanation
        .Activate
        .Range("F4").Select
    End With
    wsAmerPutReport.Visible = False
End Sub
```

TradeDays Function

Two inputs to the option pricing model are the current date and exercise date. The pricing models actually require the duration of the option, defined as the number of trading days until the exercise date. To calculate the duration, I created a TradeDays function specifically for this purpose, with the code listed below. It again uses Excel's WEEKDAY function to skip weekends. It can then be used in an Excel formula in the usual way. For example, the formula in cell B12 of the EuroModel worksheet (see Figure 30.6) is

```
=TradeDays(CurrentDate, ExerciseDate)
```

This is a perfect example of *creating* a function to perform a particular task when Excel doesn't have a built-in function to perform it. If you want to use this function in your own workbooks, you should insert a module in your workbook and copy the following code to it.

```
Function TradeDays(firstDate As Date, lastDate As Date) As Integer
    ' This function returns the number of trading days between two dates.
    ' It excludes weekends only, although with extra logic, it could be
    ' changed to exclude other days (such as Christmas). Note how it uses
    ' Excel's Weekday function, which returns 1 for Sundays, 7 for Saturdays.

    Dim nDays As Integer
    Dim i As Integer
    Dim currentDay As Integer

    ' Start with the number of days from FirstDate to LastDate
    nDays = lastDate - firstDate
    TradeDays = nDays

    ' Now subtract a day for every weekend day.
    For i = 1 To nDays
        currentDay = Application.WorksheetFunction.Weekday(firstDate + i)
        If currentDay = 1 Or currentDay = 7 Then
            TradeDays = TradeDays - 1
        End If
    Next
End Function
```

30.8   Summary

This application doesn't require a lot of inputs, and it doesn't produce a lot of outputs, but it does perform a number of rather complex calculations in the background to produce some very useful results. Considering that the options business in the financial community is a billion-dollar business annually, an application such as this one can be extremely valuable to financial analysts and investors.

EXERCISES

1. Develop a message box statement that displays the following message, exactly as it is written here:

When you want a literal double quote, ", in a string, you should use another double quote, as in "".

2. Consider the following formula that you want to enter, via VBA, in cell C3: **=If (A3="West","Los Angeles",If(A3="East","New York",""))**. Write a VBA statement to set the Formula property of cell C3 correctly.

3. The file **IRR.xlsx** contains data on an investment that requires an initial cost at the beginning of year 1 and then receives cash inflows at the ends of years 1 through 10. The net present value (NPV) of this investment is calculated in cell B11 for the discount rate in cell B3. The internal rate of return (IRR) of the investment is defined as the discount rate that makes the NPV equal to 0. Write a VBA sub, using the GoalSeek method, to calculate the IRR and display it in a message box, formatted as a percentage with two decimals. (*Note:* Excel has a built-in IRR function. It should obtain the same result as your VBA sub.)

4. The file **Certainty Equivalent.xlsx** contains the probability distribution of the monetary outcome for a given investment. Assume that a decision maker is risk averse and has an exponential utility function with the risk tolerance parameter R given in cell B3. Then the utility of any monetary outcome x is $e^{-x/R}$, the expected utility of an investment is the "sumproduct" of probabilities and utilities of monetary outcomes, and the certainty equivalent of the investment is the dollar amount such that its utility is equal to the expected utility of the investment. In words, the certainty equivalent is the monetary value such that the investor is indifferent between (1) getting this monetary value for sure and (2) getting into the risky investment. Write a sub that calculates the expected utility of the investment described from row 7 down and uses the GoalSeek method to calculate the certainty equivalent. Display both of these outputs in a message box. Write the sub so that it will work for *any* probability distribution listed from row 7 down and any risk tolerance given in cell B3.

5. Change the TradeDays function so that it also excludes the *fixed* dates January 1, December 25, and July 4. (In addition, you can exclude any other fixed dates you want to exclude. However, it would be much more difficult to exclude a "floating" holiday such as Thanksgiving, so don't worry about these.) Then change the CreateAmerReport sub so that it also excludes these fixed dates.

6. The preceding exercise claimed that it would be difficult to exclude "floating" holidays like Thanksgiving (the fourth Thursday in November). Is this true? Write a function subroutine called Thanksgiving that takes one argument called Year. (For example, this argument will have values like 2015.) It then returns the date that Thanksgiving falls on. Then redo the previous exercise, excluding Thanksgiving as well as the other fixed dates.

7. The file **City Sales.xlsx** contains sales of 100 products for five cities in California (each on a different sheet) for each day over a 2-year period. Write a sub that fills a two-dimensional array maxSale, where maxSale(i, j) is the maximum sale, over all days, for product j in city i. This will take a while to run, so display a message such as "Analyzing product 17 in San Diego" in the status bar that shows the current city and product being analyzed. Make sure the message disappears when all cities and products have been analyzed.

31

An Application for Finding Betas of Stocks

31.1 Introduction

The beta of a stock is a measure of how the stock's price changes as a market index changes. It is the coefficient of the market return when the returns of the stock are regressed on the market returns. If the beta of a stock is greater than 1, the stock is relatively volatile; if the market changes by a certain percentage, the stock's price tends to change by a *larger* percentage. The opposite is true when the beta of a stock is less than 1. This application calculates the beta for any company given historical price data on the company's monthly stock prices and a market index. It uses one of four possible criteria to find the best-fitting regression equation. More details on estimation of stock betas can be found in Chapter 7 of *Practical Management Science*.

The application also illustrates another way of getting data from an application—from another Excel file that is not currently open.

New Learning Objectives: VBA

- To illustrate how to capture data from one workbook for use in a VBA application in another workbook.
- To illustrate two features of list boxes: the use of two columns and the RowSource property for populating a list box.

New Learning Objectives: Non-VBA

- To learn how nonlinear optimization can be used to estimate the beta of a stock, using any of four possible optimization criteria.

31.2 Functionality of the Application

The application, stored in the file **Stock Beta.xlsm**, gets the required stock return data from another file, **Stock Data.xlsx**. The application is written so that these two files must be in the *same* folder. The **Stock Data.xlsx** file contains monthly stock price data for many large US companies from January 2009 through December 2013. It also contains monthly data on an S&P 500 market index during this same period. The user can choose any of these companies, a period of time containing at least 36 months (such as January 2011 to December 2013), and one of four criteria to minimize: sum of squared errors, weighted sum of squared errors, sum of absolute errors, or maximum absolute error. (I chose the 36-month limit somewhat arbitrarily.) The application then uses the company's returns and the market returns for this period, and it estimates the stock's beta using the specified criterion. It does this by estimating a regression equation of the form $Y = a + bX$, where Y is the stock return, X is the market return, and b estimates the stock's beta. It is also possible to view a time series plot of the stock's returns, with the predictions of its returns from the regression equation superimposed on the plot.

Each stock in the **Stock Data.xlsx** file has its own worksheet. You can add more worksheets for other stocks, and the application will automatically recognize them. If you want to run the application with more recent data on the included companies or any other companies, only a few changes in the VBA code are necessary. As it stands, it expects monthly returns from January 2009 through December 2013, but these can be changed easily in the code.

This application uses a calendar control on the user form. See Section 11.3 of Chapter 11 for instructions on registering this control on your computer. The application won't work properly until you do so.

31.3 Running the Application

When the **Stock Beta.xlsm** file is opened, the Explanation sheet in Figure 31.1 appears. After clicking on the button in this sheet, the user sees the dialog box

Figure 31.1 Explanation Worksheet

Application for Estimating Stock Betas

Run the application

This application uses monthly stock return data for several of the largest companies in the U.S. to find their "betas." The stock return data are in a separate file called Stock Data.xlsx, and this file should be in the same folder as the current workbook. The "beta" of the stock can be estimated for any of the companies in the Stock Data file, and it can be based on any period from January 2009 to December 2013 with at least 36 months. There are four possible optimization criteria: (1) sum of squared errors, (2) weighted sum of squared errors, (3) sum of absolute errors, and (4) minimax (minimize the maximum absolute error). Solver performs the appropriate optimization based on the criterion specified.

The Stock Data file is set up so that each company has its own data sheet, with monthly closing prices from December 2008 to December 2013, and corresponding returns from January 2009 to December 2014. Similar sheets for other companies can be added by the user. Any additional sheet should be named with the company's ticker symbol, and the name of the company should be entered in cell E1 of its sheet. There is also market data for the same time period in the S&P500 sheet of the Stock Data file.

Figure 31.2 Inputs Dialog Box

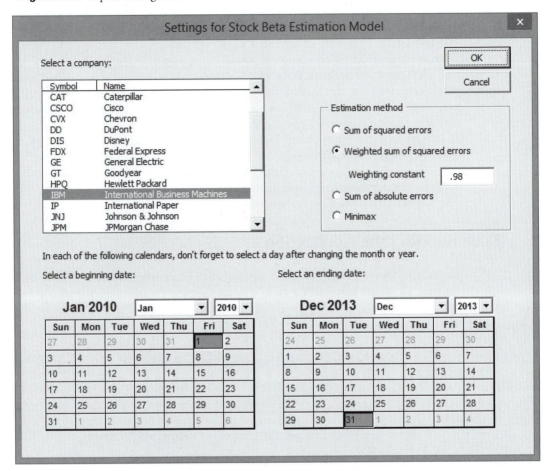

in Figure 31.2. As it is filled out here, it will find the beta for IBM, based on the returns from January 2010 to December 2013, using the weighted sum of squared errors criterion with a weighting constant of 0.98. Note that I have chosen to use calendar controls. Because the data are monthly, it doesn't matter which *day* of the month you choose in either of the calendars. However, a day *does* need to be chosen, or completely wrong dates will be returned.

At this point, the data from the IBM and S&P500 sheets in the **Stock Data.xlsx** file are copied to the Model worksheet in the **Stock Beta.xlsm** file. Then a Solver model is set up and optimized according to the specified criterion. The resulting beta is displayed in the message box in Figure 31.3, and the full details (with a number of hidden rows) appear in the Model worksheet in Figure 31.4.

When the left button on the Model worksheet is clicked, the chart in Figure 31.5 is displayed. It shows the stock's returns with the predictions from the best-fitting regression equation superimposed.

Figure 31.3 Beta for Selected Company

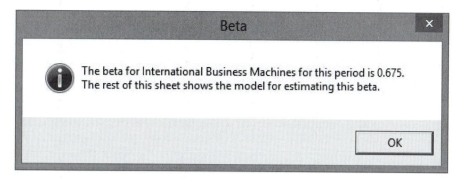

Figure 31.4 Completed Model Worksheet for Selected Company

	A	B	C	D	E	F	G	H	I	J	K	L
1	Estimation model for International Business Machines: period from 01/2010 to 12/2013, weighted sum of squared errors estimation method											
2												
3	Parameters											
4	Alpha	-0.0016		View Time Series Chart			View Explanation Sheet					
5	Beta	0.6754										
6												
7	Weighting constant	0.98										
8												
9	Optimization model											
10	Date	Mkt return	Stock return	Predicted	Error	SqError	AbsError	Weight		Objective for optimization		
11	Dec-2013	0.00693	0.00189	0.0031	-0.0012	0.00000	0.0012	1.0000		WSSE	0.0360801	
12	Nov-2013	0.02805	0.00802	0.0174	-0.0093	0.00009	0.0093	0.9800				
13	Oct-2013	0.04460	-0.03225	0.0285	-0.0608	0.00369	0.0608	0.9604				
14	Sep-2013	0.02975	0.01594	0.0185	-0.0026	0.00001	0.0026	0.9412				
15	Aug-2013	-0.03130	-0.06077	-0.0227	-0.0380	0.00145	0.0380	0.9224				
16	Jul-2013	0.04946	0.02057	0.0318	-0.0113	0.00013	0.0113	0.9039				
55	Apr-2010	0.01476	0.00584	0.0084	-0.0025	0.00001	0.0025	0.4111				
56	Mar-2010	0.05880	0.00858	0.0381	-0.0295	0.00087	0.0295	0.4029				
57	Feb-2010	0.02851	0.04362	0.0177	0.0260	0.00067	0.0260	0.3948				
58	Jan-2010	-0.03697	-0.06500	-0.0266	-0.0384	0.00148	0.0384	0.3869				

Figure 31.5 Time Series Plot of Returns and Predictions

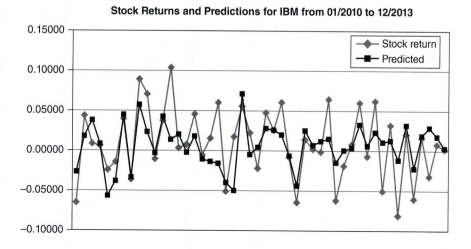

31.4 Setting Up the Excel Sheets

The **Stock Beta.xlsm** file contains an Explanation worksheet, a Model worksheet, and a chart sheet named TimeSeriesChart. The **Stock Data.xlsx** file contains an S&P500 worksheet and a separate worksheet for each company. These individual company worksheets are named by the company's ticker symbol (e.g., GE for General Electric, JNJ for Johnson & Johnson). A typical company worksheet is structured as in Figure 31.6. It contains dates (in reverse chronological order) in column A, monthly closing prices in column B, corresponding returns in column C, and the company's name in cell E1. (Note that many rows are not shown in the figure.) You can add sheets for additional companies in the **Stock Data.xlsx** file, but they should all be structured in this way. The S&P500 sheet is structured similarly, as shown in Figure 31.7. Note that the closing prices extend back to December 2008, whereas the returns extend back only to January 2009. This is because each return, being a percentage change, requires the *previous* closing price.

The Model worksheet in the **Stock Beta.xlsm** file can be set up at design time as a template, with the labels and range names shown in Figure 31.8. The body of

Figure 31.6 Typical Company Worksheet

	A	B	C	D	E
1	Monthly closing prices and returns for				Disney
2					
3	Date	Close	Return		
4	Dec-2013	72.40	0.03904		
5	Nov-2013	69.68	0.02849		
6	Oct-2013	67.75	0.06358		
7	Sep-2013	63.70	0.06008		
8	Aug-2013	60.09	-0.05904		
9	Jul-2013	63.86	0.02373		
10	Jun-2013	62.38	0.00112		
11	May-2013	62.31	0.00387		

Figure 31.7 S&P500 Worksheet

	A	B	C	D	E
1	Monthly closing prices and returns for				S&P 500
2					
3	Date	Close	Return		
4	Dec-2013	1818.32	0.00693		
5	Nov-2013	1805.81	0.02805		
6	Oct-2013	1756.54	0.04460		
7	Sep-2013	1681.55	0.02975		
8	Aug-2013	1632.97	-0.03130		
9	Jul-2013	1685.73	0.04946		
10	Jun-2013	1606.28	-0.01500		
11	May-2013	1630.74	0.02076		

Figure 31.8   Model Worksheet Template

	A	B	C	D	E	F	G	H	I	J	K	L
1	Estimation model for											
2												
3	Parameters											
4	Alpha			View Time Series Chart			View Explanation Sheet					
5	Beta											
6												
7	Weighting constant											
8												
9	Optimization model											
10	Date	Mkt return	Stock return	Predicted	Error	SqError	AbsError	Weight		Target for optimization		
11												
12												
13										Range names used:		
14										Alpha	=Model!$B$4	
15										AlphaBeta	=Model!$B$4:$B$5	
16										Beta	=Model!$B$5	
17										Objective	=Model!$K$11	
18										Weight	=Model!$B$7	

it must be filled in at run time. The TimeSeriesChart sheet can be created with Excel's chart tools at design time, using any trial data. It is then linked to the actual data on the Model worksheet at run time.

31.5 Getting Started with the VBA

The **Stock Beta.xlsm** file includes a single user form named frmInputs, a module, and a reference to Solver.[1] Once these items are added, the Project Explorer window will appear as in Figure 31.9.

Workbook_Open Code

To guarantee that the Explanation worksheet appears when the file is opened, the following code is placed in the ThisWorkbook code window. As usual, it hides all sheets except the Explanation worksheet, and it displays the Solver warning when used with pre-2010 versions of Excel.

```
Private Sub Workbook_Open()
    With wsExplanation
        .Activate
        .Range("E4").Select
    End With
    wsModel.Visible = False
    chtTimeSeries.Visible = False
    If Not (Application.Version = "15.0" Or Application.Version = "14.0") Then
    frmSolver.Show
End Sub
```

---

[1] It also contains the usual frmSolver that displays a message about possible Solver problems when the workbook is opened, but only users of pre-2010 versions of Excel will see this message.

Figure 31.9 Project Explorer Window

31.6 The User Form

The design of frmInputs appears in Figure 31.10. It contains the usual OK and Cancel buttons, several labels, a text box, a frame for grouping, four option buttons, a list box, and two calendar controls. (See Section 11.3 of Chapter 11 for a discussion of the calendar control.) The text is named txtWeight; the option buttons are named optSSE, optWSSE, optSAE, and optMinimax; the list box is named lbCompanies; and the calendars are named calBeginning and calEnding.

The text boxes and option buttons are standard. However, the list box presents two new features. Specifically, its ColumnCount property is set to 2 at design time. (See Figure 31.11.) This indicates that the list will contain two columns, one for the ticker symbols and one for the company names. The BoundColumn property of the list box then specifies which column the Value property refers to. For example, if you want to get an item from the list in the first column, you set the BoundColumn property to 1 before accessing the Value property. Finally, the RowSource property is set to the worksheet range named Companies at design time (using the Properties window). Then the list box is automatically populated with the list in this range.

The Initialize sub selects the first company in the list box, it sets the calendars to the earliest and latest dates in the data set, it checks the SSE option, and it clears the weight box and disables it. The Valid function performs a considerable amount of error checking before finally capturing the user's inputs in a number of variables. Note the use of VBA's DateDiff function in the Valid function. It takes three arguments: a time period (e.g., "m" for month) and two dates, and it returns the number of time periods between these two dates. For example, it returns 3 if the time period is a month and the dates are March 2013 and June 2013.

Figure 31.10 frmInputs Design

```
Private cancel As Boolean

Public Function ShowInputsDialog(ticker As String, _
        company As String, firstDate As Date, _
        lastDate As Date, method As String, weight As Single) As Boolean
    Call Initialize
    Me.Show
    If Not cancel Then
        ' Get the ticker symbol and company name from the user's selection.
        ' The BoundColumn of a list box indicates which column the Value
        ' property refers to.
        With lbCompanies
            .BoundColumn = 1
            ticker = .Value
            .BoundColumn = 2
            company = .Value
        End With
        firstDate = DateSerial(calBeginning.Year, calBeginning.Month, 1)
        lastDate = DateSerial(calEnding.Year, calEnding.Month, 1)
        ' Capture the method to use for optimization.
        Select Case True
            Case optSSE.Value: method = "SSE"
            Case optWSSE.Value
                method = "WSSE"
                weight = txtWeight.Value
```

```
                    Case optSAE.Value: method = "SAE"
                    Case optMinimax.Value: method = "Minimax"
            End Select
        End If
        ShowInputsDialog = Not cancel
        Unload Me
End Function

Private Sub Initialize()
    ' Note that the list box is populated by setting its ColumnCount property
    ' to 2 and its RowSource property to Companies. These are both set at
    ' design time in the Properties window. The Companies range (in the Model
    ' sheet) is populated, right before this user form is displayed, with the
    ' CreateCompanyList sub in Module1.
    lbCompanies.ListIndex = 0
    With calBeginning
        .Day = 1
        .Month = Month(EARLIEST_DATE)
        .Year = Year(EARLIEST_DATE)
    End With
    With calEnding
        .Day = 1
        .Month = Month(LATEST_DATE)
        .Year = Year(LATEST_DATE)
    End With
    optSSE.Value = True
    With txtWeight
        .Text = ""
        .Enabled = False
    End With
End Sub

Private Function Valid() As Boolean
    Dim ctl As Control
    Dim fDate As Date, lDate As Date
    Dim wt As Single

    Valid = True
    ' Make sure the dates are allowable.
    fDate = DateSerial(calBeginning.Year, calBeginning.Month, 1)
    lDate = DateSerial(calEnding.Year, calEnding.Month, 1)
    If fDate < EARLIEST_DATE Then
        Valid = False
        MsgBox "The beginning date cannot be before " & _
            Format(EARLIEST_DATE, "mm/dd/yyyy") & ". Choose again.", _
            vbExclamation, "Invalid date"
        calBeginning.SetFocus
        Exit Function
    ElseIf lDate > LATEST_DATE Then
        Valid = False
        MsgBox "The ending date cannot be after " & _
            Format(LATEST_DATE, "mm/dd/yyyy") & ". Choose again.", _
            vbExclamation, "Invalid date"
        calEnding.SetFocus
        Exit Function
    End If

    ' Use the VBA DateDiff function to get number of months between two dates.
    ' The first argument "m" means month, the second and third arguments are the
```

```
' first and last dates for the difference. Note that a literal month is again
' enclosed in pound signs.

' Check that the last date is at least 3 years after the first date.
If DateDiff("m", fDate, lDate) + 1 < 36 Then
    Valid = False
    MsgBox "Choose dates so that you have at least " _
        & "36 months of data", vbExclamation, "Invalid dates"
    calBeginning.SetFocus
    Exit Function
End If

' Check inputs in case WSSE is selected.
If optWSSE.Value Then
    ' Check that the weight box is not blank and is numeric.
    If Not IsNumeric(txtWeight) Or txtWeight.Text = "" Then
        Valid = False
        MsgBox "Enter a numerical weight between 0 and 1.", _
            vbInformation, "Invalid weight"
        txtWeight.SetFocus
        Exit Function
    Else
        wt = txtWeight.Text
        ' Check that the weight is between 0 and 1.
        If wt < 0 Or wt > 1 Then
            Valid = False
            MsgBox "Enter a weight between 0 and 1.", vbInformation, _
                "Invalid weight"
            txtWeight.SetFocus
            Exit Function
        End If
    End If
End If
End Function
Private Sub cmdOK_Click()
    If Valid Then Me.Hide
    cancel = False
End Sub

Private Sub cmdCancel_Click()
    Me.Hide
    cancel = True
End Sub

Private Sub UserForm_QueryClose(cancel As Integer, CloseMode As Integer)
    If CloseMode = vbFormControlMenu Then cmdCancel_Click
End Sub
```

There is also an event handler for each option button's Click event. This enables or disables the weight box, depending on which button has been checked. It makes no sense for the user to enter a value for the weight unless the weighted sum of squares criterion is selected. Remember that event handlers can be written for numerous events for *any* of the controls on a user form. The following subs illustrate how this works for the Click events of option buttons. Specifically, these subs enable or disable txtWeight, depending on which optimization method has been chosen. This text box should be enabled when the user clicks the WSSE option, and it should be disabled when the user clicks any of the other option buttons. To see the effect, run the application and click the various option buttons.

Figure 31.11 Properties of List Box

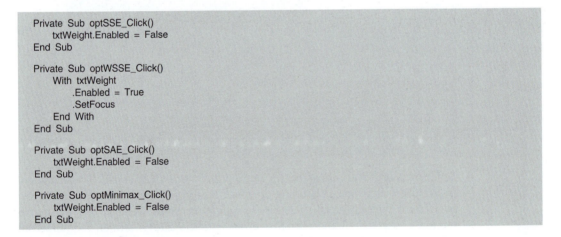

```
Private Sub optSSE_Click()
    txtWeight.Enabled = False
End Sub

Private Sub optWSSE_Click()
    With txtWeight
        .Enabled = True
        .SetFocus
    End With
End Sub

Private Sub optSAE_Click()
    txtWeight.Enabled = False
End Sub

Private Sub optMinimax_Click()
    txtWeight.Enabled = False
End Sub
```

31.7 The Module

The MainStockBeta sub is attached to the button on the Explanation worksheet. It first creates a list of companies by opening the **StockData.xlsx** file and looping through its worksheets. Then it "shows" frmInputs to get the user's inputs. Next, it sets up a model and optimizes it, and it updates the chart. It also takes care of closing the Stock Data.xlsx file when it is no longer needed.

Option Statement and Module-Level Variables

```
' Definition of module-level variables
'    ticker - ticker ticker of selected company
'    company - name of selected company
'    method - optimization method used
'    weight - weighting constant (for weighted least squares only)
'    firstDate - first date of selected time period
'    lastDate - last date of selected time period
'    nMonths - number of months in selected time period
'    firstDateRow - first row of data for estimation period (remember
'       that data are listed in reverse chronological order)
'    wbData - a workbook object variable for the Stock Data file

Dim ticker As String, company As String
Dim method As String, weight As Single
Dim firstDate As Date, lastDate As Date
Dim nMonths As Integer, firstDateRow As Integer
Dim wbData As Workbook

' Change the following if the dates in the data file change.
Public Const EARLIEST_DATE = #1/1/2009#
Public Const LATEST_DATE = #12/31/2013#
```

MainStockBeta Code

```
Sub MainStockBeta()
    ' This sub runs when the user clicks on the button in the Explanation sheet.

    ' Create a list of companies in the Companies range.
    Call CreateCompanyList

    ' Get user choices.
    If frmInputs.ShowInputsDialog(ticker, company, _
            firstDate, lastDate, method, weight) Then

        nMonths = DateDiff("m", firstDate, lastDate) + 1
        firstDateRow = DateDiff("m", lastDate, LATEST_DATE) + 1

        Application.ScreenUpdating = False

        ' Comment out the next line and run the program. You'll probably be
        ' asked about saving information on the clipboard – annoying, so
        ' I added the following line.
        Application.DisplayAlerts = False

        ' Set up the model in the Model sheet, use the Solver to optimize,
        ' and update the time series chart.
        Call SetupModel
        Call RunSolver
        Call UpdateChart
```

```
        Application.ScreenUpdating = True

        ' Display the beta in a message box.
        ' (Details are displayed to the user in the Model sheet.)
        MsgBox "The beta for " & company & " for this period is " _
            & Format(wsModel.Range("Beta"), "0.000") & ". The rest of this sheet " _
            & "shows the model for estimating this beta.", vbInformation, "Beta"
    Else
        Application.DisplayAlerts = False
        wbData.Close
        Application.DisplayAlerts = True
    End If
End Sub
```

CreateCompanyList Code

The CreateCompanyList sub opens the **Stock Data.xlsx** workbook and loops through all of its worksheets (other than the S&P500 worksheet) to see which companies are included. As it does this, it creates a list in columns AA and AB of the Model worksheet

Figure 31.12 Companies List in Model Worksheet

	AA	AB
1	Symbol	Name
2	AA	Aluminum Company of America
3	AAPL	Apple
4	AXP	American Express
5	BA	Boeing
6	CAT	Caterpillar
7	CSCO	Cisco
8	CVX	Chevron
9	DD	DuPont
10	DIS	Disney
11	FDX	Federal Express
12	GE	General Electric
13	GT	Goodyear
14	HPQ	Hewlett Packard
15	IBM	International Business Machines
16	IP	International Paper
17	JNJ	Johnson & Johnson
18	JPM	JPMorgan Chase
19	KO	Coca Cola
20	MCD	McDonalds
21	MMM	3M
22	MO	Altria Group
23	MRK	Merck
24	MSFT	Microsoft
25	PG	Procter & Gamble
26	T	AT&T
27	UTX	United Technologies
28	WMT	Walmart

in the **Stock Beta.xlsm** workbook and names the corresponding range Companies. (See Figure 31.12.) This range is the source for the list box in frmInputs because its RowSource property is set to Companies at design time. Note the error-handling code. If the **Stock Data.xlsx** file cannot be found, control passes to the MissingFile label. At that point, an error message is displayed, and the program ends. However, if there is no error—the file exists—an Exit Sub statement ensures that the lines following the label are *not* executed. This is the *one* time when it is accepted programming practice to use a GoTo statement.

```vba
Sub CreateCompanyList()
    ' This sub creates a list of companies in the Companies range
    ' (in columns AA, AB of the Model sheet) for populating the list box
    ' in the user form.
    Dim ws As Worksheet
    Dim i As Integer

    ' Clear old list.
    With wsModel
        .Range("Companies").ClearContents

        ' Open the Stock Data file. If it is not in the same folder as the
        ' Stock Beta file, an error occurs, and the program ends. Otherwise, make
        ' Stock Beta the active workbook. Remember that ThisWorkbook refers to
        ' the file that contains the code, i.e., this one.
        On Error GoTo MissingFile
        Set wbData = Workbooks.Open(ThisWorkbook.Path & "\Stock Data.xlsx")
        ThisWorkbook.Activate

        ' Go through all worksheets in the Stock Data file. If the name is not S&P500,
        ' add to the list. The sheet name is the ticker symbol, and its cell E1 should
        ' contain the company name. Note that the RowSource property of the list box in
        ' frmInputs is set to Companies. So as soon as the Companies range is populated,
        ' the list box is populated also.
        i = 0
        With .Range("AA1")
            For Each ws In wbData.Worksheets
                If ws.Name <> "S&P500" Then
                    i = i + 1
                    .Offset(i, 0).Value = ws.Name
                    .Offset(i, 1).Value = ws.Range("E1").Value
                End If
            Next
            Range(.Offset(1, 0), .Offset(i, 1)).Name = "Model!Companies"

            ' Sort the list on the ticker symbol.
            .Sort Key1:=.Cells(1, 1), Header:=xlYes
        End With
    End With
    Exit Sub

MissingFile:
    MsgBox "There is no Stock Data.xlsx file in the same folder as this " _
        & "workbook, so the application cannot continue.", _
        vbExclamation, "Missing file"
    End
End Sub
```

SetupModel Code

The SetupModel sub activates the Model worksheet and then calls two subs, Copy-Data and EnterFormulas, to set up the model for estimating the beta of the stock.

```
Sub SetupModel()
    ' This sub sets up the optimization model.

    ' Unhide and activate the Model sheet.
    With wsModel
        .Visible = True
        .Activate

        ' Set up the model.
        Call CopyData
        Call EnterFormulas

        .Range("A1").Select
    End With
End Sub
```

CopyData Code

At this point, the **Stock Data.xlsx** file is still open, so the CopyData sub copies the data on dates and monthly returns from the selected company sheet and the S&P500 sheet to the Model worksheet. It uses the PasteSpecial method to paste the monthly return *formulas* as values.

```
Sub CopyData()
    ' This sub copies the data from the S&P500 sheet and the sheet for the selected
    ' company to the Model sheet.

    ' First, clear any previous results from the Model sheet.
    With wsModel.Range("A10")
        Range(.Offset(1, 0), .End(xlDown).End(xlToRight)).ClearContents
    End With

    ' Copy the dates and returns from the S&P500 sheet of the StockData file to
    ' columns A and B of the Model sheet. Because the Returns columns of the
    ' stock sheets contain formulas, they are pasted special as values in the
    ' Model sheet.
    With wbData.Worksheets("S&P500").Range("A3")
        Range(.Offset(firstDateRow, 0), .Offset(firstDateRow + nMonths - 1, 0)).Copy _
            Destination:=wsModel.Range("A11")
        Range(.Offset(firstDateRow, 2), .Offset(firstDateRow + nMonths - 1, 2)).Copy
            wsModel.Range("B11").PasteSpecial xlPasteValues
    End With

    ' Similarly, copy the returns from the selected company to column C of the
    ' Model sheet.
    With wbData.Worksheets(ticker).Range("A3")
        Range(.Offset(firstDateRow, 2), .Offset(firstDateRow + nMonths - 1, 2)).Copy
            wsModel.Range("C11").PasteSpecial xlPasteValues
    End With
```

```
' Close the Stock Data file.
    wbData.Close
End Sub
```

EnterFormulas Code

The EnterFormulas sub is somewhat long, but it is straightforward. It enters the formulas for the optimization model, including the predicted returns, the errors, the squared errors, the absolute errors, the weights for the weighted sum of squares method (if applicable), and the appropriate objective for the criterion selected. The Case construct is used here to perform different tasks depending on the value of method.

```
Sub EnterFormulas()
    ' This sub enters all the required formulas in the Model sheet.
    Dim methodName As String

    ' First, enter an appropriate label in cell A1.
    Select Case method
        Case "SSE": methodName = "sum of squared errors"
        Case "WSSE": methodName = "weighted sum of squared errors"
        Case "SAE": methodName = "sum of absolute errors"
        Case "Minimax": methodName = "minimax"
    End Select

    With wsModel
        .Range("A1").Value = "Estimation model for " & company & ": period from " _
            & Format(firstDate, "mm/yyyy") & " to " & Format(lastDate, "mm/yyyy") _
            & ", " & methodName & " estimation method"

        ' Enter the weight in the Weight cell (if weighted least squares is selected).
        If method = "WSSE" Then
            .Range("Weight").Value = weight
        Else
            .Range("Weight").Value = "NA"
        End If

        ' Enter the predictions, errors, squared errors, and absolute errors with
        ' the appropriate formulas in columns D-G.
        With .Range("D10")
            Range(.Offset(1, 0), .Offset(nMonths, 0)).FormulaR1C1 = "=Alpha+Beta*RC[-2]"
            Range(.Offset(1, 1), .Offset(nMonths, 1)).FormulaR1C1 = "=RC[-2]-RC[-1]"
            Range(.Offset(1, 2), .Offset(nMonths, 2)).FormulaR1C1 = "=RC[-1]^2"
            Range(.Offset(1, 3), .Offset(nMonths, 3)).FormulaR1C1 = "=Abs(RC[-2])"
            If method = "WSSE" Then
                .Offset(0, 4).Value = "Weight"
                .Offset(1, 4).Value = 1
                Range(.Offset(2, 4), .Offset(nMonths, 4)).FormulaR1C1= "=Weight*R[-1]C"
            Else
                Range(.Offset(0, 4), .Offset(nMonths, 4)).Value = ""
            End If
        End With

        ' Name the appropriate range and then enter a formula for the appropriate
        ' objective in the Objective cell.
```

```
        Select Case method
            Case "SSE"
                With .Range("F10")
                    Range(.Offset(1, 0), .Offset(nMonths, 0)).Name = "Model!SqErrs"
                End With
                With .Range("Objective")
                    .Offset(0, -1).Value = method
                    .Formula = "=Sum(SqErrs)"
                End With
            Case "WSSE"
                With .Range("F10")
                    Range(.Offset(1, 0), .Offset(nMonths, 0)).Name = "Model!SqErrs"
                End With
                With .Range("H10")
                    Range(.Offset(1, 0), .Offset(nMonths, 0)).Name = "Model!Weights"
                End With
                With .Range("Objective")
                    .Offset(0, -1).Value = method
                    .Formula = "=Sumproduct(Weights,SqErrs)"
                End With
            Case "SAE"
                With .Range("G10")
                    Range(.Offset(1, 0), .Offset(nMonths, 0)).Name = "Model!AbsErrs"
                End With
                With .Range("Objective")
                    .Offset(0, -1).Value = method
                    .Formula = "=Sum(AbsErrs)"
                End With
            Case "Minimax"
                With .Range("G10")
                    Range(.Offset(1, 0), .Offset(nMonths, 0)).Name = "Model!AbsErrs"
                End With
                With .Range("Objective")
                    .Offset(0, -1).Value = method
                    .Formula = "=Max(AbsErrs)"
                End With
        End Select
    End With
End Sub
```

RunSolver Code

The RunSolver sub is particularly simple because Solver can be set up completely at design time and the *size* of the model never changes. Note that the Solver setup minimizes the Objective cell, has the AlphaBeta range as decision variable cells, and has *no* constraints. (With no constraints, there is no need to check for feasibility—there is bound to be a feasible solution.)

```
Sub RunSolver()
    ' Run Solver, which is developed once and for all at design time.
    SolverSolve UserFinish:=True
End Sub
```

UpdateChart Code

The time series chart is created at design time, so all the UpdateChart sub has to do is link the chart to the correct data and modify its title appropriately.

```
Sub UpdateChart()
    ' This sub updates the existing chart with the results of the optimization.
    Dim sourceData As Range, sourceDates As Range

    ' Set range variables for the dates and data ranges for the chart.
    With wsModel.Range("A10")
        Set sourceDates = Range(.Offset(1, 0), .Offset(nMonths, 0))
        Set sourceData = Range(.Offset(0, 2), .Offset(nMonths, 3))
    End With

    ' Update the chart, including its title.
    With chtTimeSeries
        .SetSourceData sourceData
        .SeriesCollection(1).XValues = sourceDates
        .ChartTitle.Text = "Stock returns and predictions for " & company _
            & " from " & Format(firstDate, "mm/yyyy") & " to " _
            & Format(lastDate, "mm/yyyy")
    End With
End Sub
```

Navigational Subs

The remaining subs are for navigational purposes and are not shown here.

31.8 Summary

This application illustrates another way to obtain data for a VBA application: from another Excel file. If the data are already stored in another Excel file, there is no point in appending all of the data to the file that contains the application. Instead, the data file can be opened (and later closed) programmatically, and the necessary data can be copied to the application file. This application also illustrates four common and useful estimation methods that can be used not only for estimating stock betas, but also for other estimation problems.

EXERCISES

1. The file **Sales Offices.xlsx** contains data on a company's sales offices. Each row lists the location of the office (country, state or province, if any, and city) and the sales for the current year. Open another file, and insert a user form and a module in this new file. The user form should contain the usual OK and Cancel buttons and a list box (with an appropriate label above the list box for explanation). The list box should contain three columns: one for country, one for state/province, and one for city. The user should be allowed to choose exactly one item from the list. There should then be a sub in the module that shows the user form

and then displays a message for the selected location, such as "The office in the city of Vancouver in the province of British Columbia in Canada has yearly sales of $987,000." Note that the part about the state/province will be absent for the offices not in the United States or Canada. This sub will also have to open the **Sales Office.xlsx** file (and close it at the end) with VBA code.

2. Repeat the previous exercise, but now allow the user to select any number of locations from the list. Then, inside a loop, the sub should display the same type of message for each location selected.

3. Change the application in this chapter and the data file as follows. For the data file, go to a suitable source (probably the Web), find monthly closing prices for the companies in the file for months after this application was written (from January 2014 on), and add them to the tops of the sheets in the **Stock Data.xlsx** file. You will also have to find the corresponding market index data. It has ticker symbol ^GSPC. Feel free to add worksheets for other companies as well if you like. Then make any necessary updates to the **Stock Beta.xlsm** file, including the code, to make it work with the expanded data set.

4. Suppose the **Stock Data.xlsx** file has stock price data for different months for different companies. For example, it might have data going back to 2007 for one company and data going back to only 2009 for another company. Rewrite the code in the **Stock Beta.xlsm** file to ensure that it uses only the data available. Should the dialog box in Figure 31.2 be redesigned? Should its event handlers be changed? These are design issues you can decide. In any case, you can assume that there are plenty of data for the S&P500 market index—it goes back at least as far as any of the companies—and that the most *recent* closing price date is the same for all companies.

5. The current **Stock Data.xlsx** worksheets all have stock *returns* calculated in column C. Suppose these are *not* yet calculated—each column C is blank. For example, this might be the case if you downloaded the closing prices from some source, and this source gave only the prices, not the returns. Change the VBA code as necessary so that it calculates the required returns on the fly.

6. Suppose the stock price data are in some file (in the same format as given here) in some folder, but the file name is not necessarily **Stock Data.xlsx** and the folder is not necessarily the same as the folder where the **Stock Beta.xlsm** file resides. Therefore, you need to give the user a way to locate the data file. You could do this with an input box (and risk having the user spell something wrong), but Excel provides an easier way with the FileDialog object discussed in Chapter 13. Use this latter method to change the application so that it prompts the user for the name and location of the data file. Actually, you should probably precede the above line with a MsgBox statement so that the user knows she is being asked to select the file with the data. Then try the modified application with your own Excel file, stored in a *different* folder from the folder containing the Excel application.

A Portfolio Optimization Application

32.1 Introduction

This application is probably the most ambitious application in the book, and it is possibly also the most exciting one. There is a Yahoo Web site that contains historical stock price data for many companies during any time period. The application retrieves the stock price data into an Excel file; calculates the means, standard deviations, and correlations for the corresponding stock returns; sets up a portfolio optimization model to minimize the portfolio variance (a measure of risk) for a given minimum required mean return; and solves this model for several minimum required mean returns to find the efficient frontier, which is shown in tabular and graphical form. The user can select any group of stocks and any time period. All of this is done in real time, so an active Web connection is required.

There is a price to pay for anything this powerful—the VBA code is lengthy and sometimes rather difficult. But if you have the perseverance to work through it, you are well on your way to becoming a real—and valuable—programmer.

Unfortunately, this application relies on a data source that we as programmers cannot control: the Web. The Yahoo site changes unpredictably from time to time, so there is no guarantee that the code presented here will always work. If I could fix this once and for all, I would; it has been a source of frustration for years. However, to avoid crashes, the current application performs an error check. If the Web query fails, then rather than present an obscure error message, the application continues with some fixed stock price data. (The fixed data are stored in a hidden worksheet called ClosingPricesFixed. You can substitute your own data for mine if you like.) Admittedly, the rest of the output will not be for the stocks or dates you requested, but it's better than a crash.

New Learning Objectives: VBA

- To learn how to run Web queries with VBA code.

New Learning Objectives: Non-VBA

- To gain some experience with portfolio optimization and efficient frontiers.
- To learn what Web queries are, and how to run them through the Excel interface.

32.2 Functionality of the Application

The application is stored in the **Stock Query.xlsm** file. At run time, this file contains no data except a list of companies and their stock symbols in the Stocks worksheet.[1] You can add to this list if you want. The application allows you to select any stocks from the current list and a time period, such as from January 2009 to December 2013. It then performs a Web query, which opens Yahoo Web pages for the selected stocks and time period, and imports the stock price data into the **Stock Query.xlsm** file. From that point, the Web part of the application is finished, and the necessary calculations leading to the efficient frontier are performed. (The Example Files folder also contains a scaled-down application called **Web Query Prices Only.xlsm**. This application allows you to download any historical stock prices, but it doesn't analyze them in any way.)

This application uses a calendar control on a user form. See Section 11.3 of Chapter 11 for instructions on registering this control on your computer. The application won't work properly until you do so.

32.3 Running the Application

The first step is to make sure a Web connection is available, but you do *not* have to open your browser or go to the Yahoo Web site. Next, when the **Stock Query.xlsm** file is opened, the Explanation worksheet in Figure 32.1 appears. When the user clicks the button on this sheet, the dialog box in Figure 32.2 is displayed, where the user can select any number of stocks from the list. (A portfolio will eventually be formed from the stocks selected.) Then the dialog box in Figure 32.3 appears, where the user can select a time period.

After these selections, there is no further user involvement. From here, the application does its work in steps. First, it retrieves the data from the Web. A new Query worksheet for each selected stock is created, and the Web data are imported into it. A sample appears in Figure 32.4. The only data on this page used in the application are the adjusted closing prices (adjusted for dividends and stock splits) in the last column. The next section discusses Web queries in some detail.

The data from this Query worksheet are transferred to the ClosingPrices worksheet, and then the Query worksheet is deleted. This is done for each selected stock. Next, the monthly *returns* (percentage changes in the adjusted closing prices) are calculated for all stocks on the Returns worksheet. Both the closing prices and returns are listed in *increasing* chronological order. (Note that the order is reversed in Figure 32.4. This is how it comes back from the Web.) Portions of the Closing-Prices and Returns worksheets appear in Figures 32.5 and 32.6.

The next step is to calculate summary measures (means, standard deviations, and correlations) for these historical returns. This is done in the SummaryMeasures

---

[1] The file might also contain some leftover data from a previous run, but these data are eventually deleted. Additionally, it includes the hidden StockPricesFixes worksheet discussed in the introduction.

Figure 32.1 Explanation Worksheet

Creating Optimal Portfolios Based on Data from the Web

Run the application

The purpose of this application is to get stock prices from the Web for any period of time and any chosen stocks. It brings the Web data into a temporary sheet, then it transfers all of the closing stock prices to the ClosingPrices sheet, and then it calculates the stock returns on the Returns sheet. Next, it creates summary data (means, standard deviations, and correlations) for the stock returns on the SummaryMeasures sheet. Finally, it sets up a portfolio selection optimization model on the Model sheet and runs Solver several times to obtain the efficient frontier. The results appear in tabular and graphical form in the EfficientFrontier sheet.

You must enter choices for the starting and ending time periods of interest, as well as a time interval (monthly, weekly, or daily). You must also select the stocks for which you want data. The Stocks sheet has a list of stocks you can choose from. Before running the application, you can add stocks to this list if you like. But see the note on the Stocks sheet about possible problems.

Due to the peculiarities of the Yahoo site that this application queries, the application fails to work sometimes. I am convinced that it has to do with browser settings or the Yahoo site, but I'm not sure which settings guarantee success (or failure). Rather than having the application fail with an obscure error message, I changed the application so that if the Web query fails, the *rest* of the application starts with *fixed* stock price data I downloaded when I created this application. (This fixed data is on the hidden StockPricesFixed sheet.) Of course, unless you replace this fixed data with new data, the application will give the same results every time you run it, but this is better than nothing!

worksheet, with the results shown in Figure 32.7. These summary measures are used as the input data for a portfolio optimization model, which is created in the Model worksheet, as shown in Figure 32.8. This optimization model finds the optimal weights (fractions of each dollar invested in the various stocks) that minimize the variance of the portfolio (in cell B19) subject to achieving a minimum required mean return (in cell D16).

Finally, the application solves this model for 11 equally spaced values of the minimum required mean return in cell D16. These values vary from the minimum return to the maximum return in row 5. This sweeps out the efficient frontier, which is reported in the EfficientFrontier worksheet in Figures 32.9 and 32.10. Note that this worksheet also shows the optimal weights for the various portfolios. For example, DuPont (DD) is in the optimal portfolio when a small mean return is required, but it is evidently too safe when a larger mean return is required. In contrast, American Express gets all of the weight when the largest mean return is required. It evidently has higher return—and higher risk. All of this occurs behind the scenes, and fairly quickly, when the user clicks

Figure 32.2 Stock Selection Dialog Box

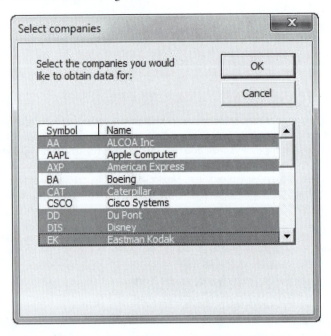

Figure 32.3 Dates Selection Dialog Box

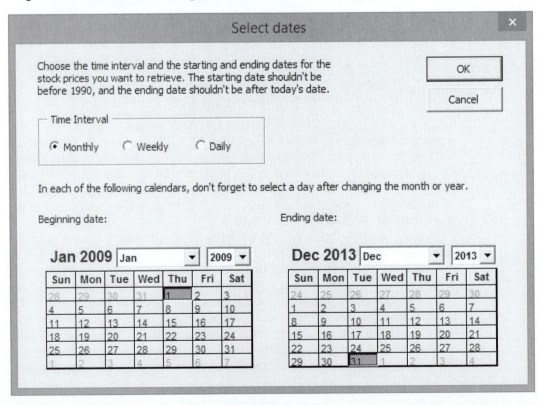

Figure 32.4 Data from Typical Web Query

Date	Open	High	Low	Close	Avg Vol	Adj Close*
Apr 1, 2013	212.80	213.50	211.25	212.38	4,289,000	205.65
Mar 1, 2013	200.65	215.90	199.36	213.30	3,988,600	206.54
Feb 6, 2013				0.85 Dividend		
Feb 1, 2013	204.65	205.35	197.51	200.83	3,622,800	194.47
Jan 2, 2013	194.09	208.58	190.39	203.07	4,320,300	195.81
Dec 3, 2012	190.76	196.45	186.94	191.55	4,200,200	184.71
Nov 7, 2012				0.85 Dividend		
Nov 1, 2012	194.68	198.00	184.78	190.07	4,134,700	183.28
Oct 1, 2012	208.01	211.79	190.56	194.53	4,867,000	186.76
Sep 4, 2012	196.61	208.32	193.25	207.45	4,329,000	199.17
Aug 8, 2012				0.85 Dividend		

Figure 32.5 ClosingPrices Worksheet

	A	B	C	D	E	F	G
1	Monthly closing prices from 01/01/2009 to 12/31/2013						
2							
3	Month	AA	AXP	CAT	DD	DIS	GT
4	1	7.19	15.22	26.76	18.45	19.35	6.12
5	2	5.87	10.97	21.35	15.34	15.69	4.4
6	3	6.92	12.4	24.26	18.26	16.99	6.21
7	4	8.55	23.26	31.27	22.81	20.49	10.9
8	5	8.72	22.92	31.16	23.62	22.66	11.35
9	6	9.76	21.59	29.03	21.26	21.83	11.16
10	7	11.12	26.32	39.2	25.66	23.5	16.87
11	8	11.42	31.42	40.32	26.83	24.36	16.35
12	9	12.43	31.66	45.67	27	25.69	16.88
13	10	11.77	32.54	49.35	26.73	25.61	12.77

Figure 32.6 Returns Worksheet

	A	B	C	D	E	F	G
1	Corresponding returns						
2							
3	Time period	AA	AXP	CAT	DD	DIS	GT
4	2	-0.184	-0.279	-0.202	-0.169	-0.189	-0.281
5	3	0.179	0.130	0.136	0.190	0.083	0.411
6	4	0.236	0.876	0.289	0.249	0.206	0.755
7	5	0.020	-0.015	-0.004	0.036	0.106	0.041
8	6	0.119	-0.058	-0.068	-0.100	-0.037	-0.017
9	7	0.139	0.219	0.350	0.207	0.077	0.512
10	8	0.027	0.194	0.029	0.046	0.037	-0.031
11	9	0.088	0.008	0.133	0.006	0.055	0.032
12	10	-0.053	0.028	0.081	-0.010	-0.003	-0.243
13	11	0.010	0.201	0.060	0.100	0.104	0.064

Figure 32.7 SummaryMeasures Worksheet

	A	B	C	D	E	F	G
1	Summary measures for stock returns						
2							
3	Stocks	AA	AXP	CAT	DD	DIS	GT
4	Means	0.0121	0.0378	0.0258	0.0245	0.0260	0.0362
5	Stdevs	0.1061	0.1374	0.1064	0.0831	0.0702	0.1758
6							
7	Correlations	AA	AXP	CAT	DD	DIS	GT
8	AA	1.000	0.507	0.704	0.672	0.658	0.596
9	AXP	0.507	1.000	0.634	0.696	0.608	0.706
10	CAT	0.704	0.634	1.000	0.837	0.620	0.699
11	DD	0.672	0.696	0.837	1.000	0.767	0.739
12	DIS	0.658	0.608	0.620	0.767	1.000	0.610
13	GT	0.596	0.706	0.699	0.739	0.610	1.000

Figure 32.8 Model Worksheet

	A	B	C	D	E	F	G	H	I	J	K	L
1	Portfolio selection model (solution shown is when required return is halfway between minimum and maximum of stock return											
2												
3	Stock	AA	AXP	CAT	DD	DIS	GT	Sum				
4	Weights	0	1	0	0	0	0	1				
5	Means	0.012064	0.037788	0.025848	0.024505	0.025975	0.036209					
6												
7	Covariances	AA	AXP	CAT	DD	DIS	GT					
8	AA	0.011074	0.007268	0.007816	0.00583	0.004815	0.010936					
9	AXP	0.007268	0.018554	0.009109	0.007816	0.005758	0.016771					
10	CAT	0.007816	0.009109	0.011128	0.007276	0.004549	0.01286					
11	DD	0.00583	0.007816	0.007276	0.006796	0.004397	0.01062					
12	DIS	0.004815	0.005758	0.004549	0.004397	0.004839	0.007401					
13	GT	0.010936	0.016771	0.0129	0.01062	0.007401	0.030386					
14												
15	Constraint on mean return											
16		0.037788	>=	0.037788								
17												
18	Portfolio variance											
19		0.018554										
20												
21	Portfolio standard deviation											
22		0.136215										

the OK button in Figure 32.3. The connection to the Yahoo site is made, the data are returned, the calculations are performed, and, like magic, the user sees the efficient frontier chart. (Again, remember that even if the Web query fails, the user will see all of these reports for the data in the StockPricesFixed worksheet.)

Figure 32.9 Efficient Frontier Data

	A	B	C	D	E	F	G	H	I	J
1	Efficient frontier									
2					Weights for these optimal portfolios					
3		PortStdev	ReqdReturn		AA	AXP	CAT	DD	DIS	GT
4		0.0691	0.0121		0.0000	0.0000	0.0000	0.1557	0.8443	0.0000
5		0.0691	0.0146		0.0000	0.0000	0.0000	0.1557	0.8443	0.0000
6		0.0691	0.0172		0.0000	0.0000	0.0000	0.1557	0.8443	0.0000
7		0.0691	0.0198		0.0000	0.0000	0.0000	0.1557	0.8443	0.0000
8		0.0691	0.0224		0.0000	0.0000	0.0000	0.1557	0.8443	0.0000
9		0.0691	0.0249		0.0000	0.0000	0.0000	0.1557	0.8443	0.0000
10		0.0726	0.0275		0.0000	0.1289	0.0000	0.0000	0.8711	0.0000
11		0.0831	0.0301		0.0000	0.3467	0.0000	0.0000	0.6533	0.0000
12		0.0983	0.0326		0.0000	0.5645	0.0000	0.0000	0.4355	0.0000
13		0.1164	0.0352		0.0000	0.7822	0.0000	0.0000	0.2178	0.0000
14		0.1362	0.0378		0.0000	1.0000	0.0000	0.0000	0.0000	0.0000

Figure 32.10 Efficient Frontier Chart

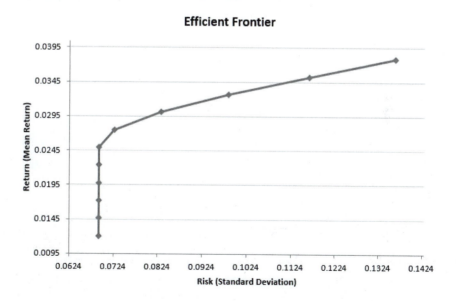

32.4 Web Queries in Excel

To understand this application, you must first understand a bit about Web queries. The application uses VBA to perform a Web query, but a Web query can be performed through the Excel interface, without any VBA. To do this, open a blank sheet in Excel and click the From Web button on the Data ribbon. This brings up

Figure 32.11 Web Query Dialog Box

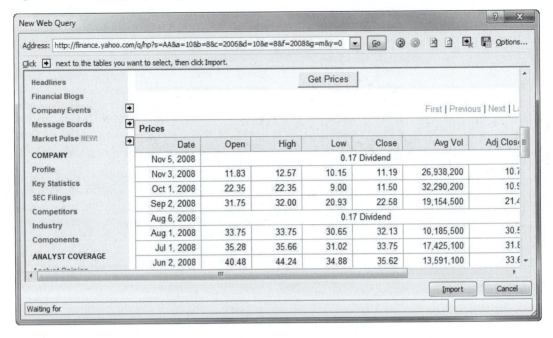

Figure 32.12 Web Site Request for Stock Prices

the dialog box in Figure 32.11, although the top box will depend on the home page for your browser. The essence of the procedure is that when you type a URL in the top box, the *tables* from the corresponding Web site are designated with yellow arrows. When you click any of them, it turns green. Then, when you click on Import, all the tables with green buttons are imported into Excel.

Sometimes the Web site, like the Yahoo site for this application, asks for parameters—the dates and the stock symbol, as in Figure 32.12. When you click the Go button in Figure 32.12, you get the requested data on a page with a URL like the following: http://finance.yahoo.com/q/hp?s=AA&a=10&b=8&c=2006 &d=10 &e=8&f=2008&g=m&y=0.

You have probably seen URLs like this, where there is a question mark followed by several "key-value" pairs, such as c=2006, separated by ampersands. The part following the question mark is called a **query string**. It indicates the information the user wants. This one has nine keys, named s, a, b, c, d, e, f, g, and y. The first indicates the stock symbol, the next three indicate the initial date requested (month, day, year), where for some reason the months are indexed 0 through 11. The next three indicate the ending date requested. The part g=m indicates that you want monthly data. Finally, y=0 has something to do with how many rows are returned per page.

This is simply the way the Yahoo site works, but you have to understand its query string to understand the code in the application. The code essentially fills in the pieces of the query string, depending on the user's choices from the user forms in Figures 32.2 and 32.3. Specifically, you will see the following code later on:

```
ConnectString = "URL;http://finance.yahoo.com/q/hp?" _
    & "s=" & tickerSymbol(iStock) _
    & "&a=" & Month(startDate) - 1 _
    & "&b=" & Day(startDate) & "&c=" & Year(startDate) _
    & "&d=" & Month(endDate) - 1 & "&e=" & Day(endDate) _
    & "&f=" & Year(endDate) & "&g=" & timeInterval
```

This line "builds" the URL required to access the stock data for a particular set of dates and a particular ticker symbol. (The part containing the "y" element isn't shown here, but it is in the application.) This connection string is the key to the whole process. It specifies where the data are located on the Web and which data you want from that site. Except for the fact that this string starts with URL and a semicolon, it is just like the URL in the dialog box in Figure 32.11.

This brief introduction gives you a taste of Web queries—how they can be performed through the Excel interface and what you need to perform them with VBA. This whole topic is still fairly new, and more user-friendly tools for extracting data from the Web into Excel are being developed. Right now, you typically must do some detective work on each Web site you want to query and then hope for the best. This stock application is not as "bulletproof" as the other applications discussed in this book. There is no guarantee that the Web sites will remain as they are, and there is no guarantee that they will return clean data or any data at all.

For these reasons, you might encounter problems when you run this application with new stocks or different time periods. In fact, you might experience problems I never even anticipated. Unfortunately, these are the perils of working with the Web.

32.5 Setting Up the Excel Sheets

The **Stock Query.xlsm** file contains the following worksheets at design time: Explanation, Stocks, ClosingPrices, Returns, SummaryMeasures, Model, Efficient-Frontier, and ClosingPricesFixed. There is very little that can be done at design time to set up these worksheets. The only steps possible are to list the stocks in

Figure 32.13 Stocks Worksheet

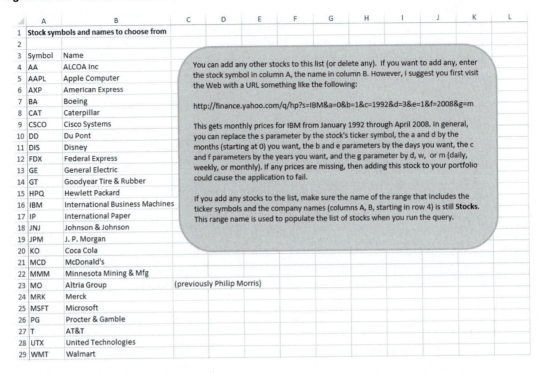

the Stocks worksheet, as shown in Figure 32.13, and to develop a scatter chart in the EfficientFrontier worksheet using any trial data. The chart will then be populated with the actual data at run time.

32.6 Getting Started with the VBA

The application requires two user forms, named frmStocks and frmDates, a module, and a reference to Solver.[2] Once these items are added, the Project Explorer window will appear as in Figure 32.14.

Workbook_Open Code

To guarantee that the Explanation worksheet appears when the file is opened, the following code is placed in the ThisWorkbook code window. For a change, it doesn't bother to hide any sheets.

```
Private Sub Workbook_Open()
    With wsExplanation
```

---

[2] It also contains the usual frmSolver that displays a message about possible Solver problems when the workbook is opened, but only users of pre-2010 versions of Excel will see this message.

```
        .Activate
        .Range("F4").Select
    End With
    If Not (Application.Version = "15.0" Or Application.Version = "14.0") Then frmSolver.Show
End Sub
```

Figure 32.14 Project Explorer Window

32.7 The User Forms

frmStocks

The design for frmStocks appears in Figure 32.15. It contains the usual OK and Cancel buttons, an explanation label, and a list box named lbCompanies. At design time, you should change three of the list box's properties: change the MultiSelect property to option 2 (so that multiple companies can be selected), change the ColumnCount property to 2, and change the RowSource property to Stocks. This is the range name in the Stocks worksheet where the list of companies and ticker symbols are located. (See Figure 32.13.)

The code behind this form is fairly straightforward. The Initialize sub selects the first company in the list by default. Then the ShowStocksDialog function uses the Selected array property of the list box to capture the names and ticker symbols of the selected stocks in the arrays stockName and ticker.

A Note on Multicolumn List Boxes. Like the user form from the previous chapter, this list box has two columns. You could use a combination of the

Figure 32.15 frmStocks Design

BoundColumn and Value properties to retrieve values from the two columns. (See the previous chapter for how this is done.) Alternatively, you can use the List property like a two-dimensional array, which is done here. The first index indicates how far down the list you are (starting with index 0 for the first item in the list), and the second index is 0 for the first column and 1 for the second column. With list boxes, there always seems to be more than one way to accomplish the same thing.

```
Private cancel As Boolean

Public Function ShowStocksDialog(nStocks As Integer, _
        tickerSymbol() As String, stockName() As String) As Boolean
    Dim i As Integer
    Call Initialize
    Me.Show
    If Not cancel Then
        ' Capture the number of stocks selected, their symbols, and their names.
        nStocks = 0
        For i = 0 To lbCompanies.ListCount - 1
            If lbCompanies.Selected(i) Then
                nStocks = nStocks + 1
                If nStocks = 1 Then
                    ReDim tickerSymbol(1 To 1)
                    ReDim stockName(1 To 1)
                Else
                    ReDim Preserve tickerSymbol(1 To nStocks)
                    ReDim Preserve stockName(1 To nStocks)
                End If
                tickerSymbol(nStocks) = lbCompanies.List(i, 0)
                stockName(nStocks) = lbCompanies.List(i, 1)
            End If
```

```
            Next
         End If
         ShowStocksDialog = Not cancel
         Unload Me
End Function

Private Sub Initialize()
      lbCompanies.Selected(0) = True
End Sub

Private Function Valid() As Boolean
      Dim i As Integer, nSel As Integer

         Valid = True
      nSel = 0
      For i = 0 To lbCompanies.ListCount - 1
         If lbCompanies.Selected(i) Then nSel = nSel + 1
      Next
      If nSel <= 1 Then
         Valid = False
         MsgBox "You should select at least two stocks for interesting results.", vbInformation
      End If
End Function

Private Sub cmdOK_Click()
      If Valid Then Me.Hide
      cancel = False
End Sub

Private Sub cmdCancel_Click()
      Me.Hide
      cancel = True
End Sub

Private Sub UserForm_QueryClose(cancel As Integer, CloseMode As Integer)
      If CloseMode = vbFormControlMenu Then cmdCancel_Click
End Sub
```

frmDates

The frmDates form, with design shown in Figure 32.16, contains OK and Cancel
buttons, some labels, three option buttons, and two calendar controls. The option
buttons are named optMonth, optWeek, and optDay, and the calendars are named
calStartDate and calEndDate. (See Section 11.3 of Chapter 11 for a discussion of
the calendar control.)

The code behind frmDates, listed below, contain no new ideas. Other than
some obvious checks on dates, it makes no other error checks. If the user requests
dates for which the Web site has no data, the program will not work correctly.

```
Private cancel As Boolean

Public Function ShowDatesDialog(startDate As Date, _
      endDate As Date, timeInterval As String) As Boolean
   Call Initialize
```

Figure 32.16 frmDates Design

```
        Me.Show
        If Not cancel Then
            startDate = calStartDate.Value
            endDate = calEndDate.Value
            Select Case True
                Case optMonth: timeInterval = "m"
                Case optWeek: timeInterval = "w"
                Case optDay: timeInterval = "d"
            End Select
        End If
        ShowDatesDialog = Not cancel
        Unload Me
End Function

Private Sub Initialize()
        ' Make the starting date two years before today's date.
        calStartDate.Value = DateSerial(Year(Date) - 2, Month(Date), Day(Date))
        calEndDate.Value = Date
        optMonth.Value = True
End Sub

Private Function Valid() As Boolean
        Dim sDate As Date, eDate As Date
```

```
        Valid = True
        ' Capture the dates for error checking.
        sDate = calStartDate.Value
        eDate = calEndDate.Value

        If sDate >= eDate Then
            Valid = False
            MsgBox "The starting date should be before the ending date.", _
                vbInformation, "Invalid dates"
            calStartDate.SetFocus
            Exit Function
        ElseIf sDate < EARLIEST_DATE Then
            Valid = False
            MsgBox "The starting date shouldn't be before 1990.", _
                vbInformation, "Start date too early"
            calStartDate.SetFocus
            Exit Function
        ElseIf eDate > Date Then
            Valid = False
            MsgBox "The ending date shouldn't be after today's date.", _
                vbInformation, "End date too late"
            calEndDate.SetFocus
            Exit Function
        End If
    End Function

Private Sub cmdOK_Click()
    If Valid Then Me.Hide
    cancel = False
End Sub

Private Sub cmdCancel_Click()
    Me.Hide
    cancel = True
End Sub

Private Sub UserForm_QueryClose(cancel As Integer, CloseMode As Integer)
    If CloseMode = vbFormControlMenu Then cmdCancel_Click
End Sub
```

32.8 The Module

The module must accomplish a long list of tasks. It starts with the MainStockQuery sub, which is attached to the button on the Explanation worksheet. This sub "shows" the two user forms and then calls a number of other subs to accomplish the various tasks. The module-level variables and the code for the MainStockQuery sub are listed below.

Option Statement and Module-Level Variables

```
Option Explicit

' Definitions of main variables:
'   nStocks: number of stocks chosen by user
'   tickerSymbol(): array of ticker symbols of stocks chosen by user
'   stockName(): array of company names for stocks chosen by user
```

```
'   startDate: starting date for data (user input)
'   endDate: ending date for data (user input)

' Variables from forms
Dim nStocks As Integer, tickerSymbol() As String, stockName() As String
Dim startDate As Date, endDate As Date, timeInterval As String

' Other module-level variables
Dim nWebQueries As Integer
Dim minReturn As Single
Dim maxReturn As Single

Public Const EARLIEST_DATE = #1/1/1990#
```

MainStockQuery Code

```
Sub MainStockQuery()
    Dim sIndex As Integer
    Dim oldStatusBar As Boolean
    Dim success As Boolean

    ' Name the range with the ticker symbols and company names.
    With wsStocks.Range("A3")
        Range(.Offset(1, 0), .Offset(1, 1).End(xlDown)).Name = "Stocks!Stocks"
    End With

    ' Get the user's choices of stocks and dates.
    If frmStocks.ShowStocksDialog(nStocks, tickerSymbol, stockName) Then
        If frmDates.ShowDatesDialog(startDate, endDate, timeInterval) Then

            ' Yahoo evidently returns 67 months or weeks per screen, but only 66 days.
            ' I figured this out with a lot of trial and error. Unfortunately, there is
            ' no guarantee that it won't change.
            Select Case timeInterval
                Case "m"
                    If DateDiff("m", startDate, endDate) + 1 Mod 67 = 0 Then
                        nWebQueries = (DateDiff("m", startDate, endDate) + 1) / 67
                    Else
                        nWebQueries = Int((DateDiff("m", startDate, endDate) + 1) / 67) + 1
                    End If
                Case "w"
                    If DateDiff("w", startDate, endDate) + 1 Mod 67 = 0 Then
                        nWebQueries = (DateDiff("w", startDate, endDate) + 1) / 67
                    Else
                        nWebQueries = Int((DateDiff("w", startDate, endDate) + 1) / 67) + 1
                    End If
                Case "d"
                    If (DateDiff("w", startDate, endDate) + 1) * 5 Mod 66 = 0 Then
                        nWebQueries = (DateDiff("w", startDate, endDate) + 1) * 5 / 66
                    Else
                        nWebQueries = Int((DateDiff("w", startDate, endDate) + 1) * 5 / 66) + 1
                    End If
            End Select

            Application.ScreenUpdating = False

            Call ClearOldData
```

```
        oldStatusBar = Application.DisplayStatusBar
        Application.DisplayStatusBar = True

        ' For each requested stock, add a new sheet and run a Web query. Show the
        ' progress in the status bar.
        For sIndex = 1 To nStocks
            Application.StatusBar = "Running web query for " & tickerSymbol(sIndex)
            Call RunQuery(sIndex, success)
            If Not success Then
                MsgBox "The Web query didn't succeed, so the rest of the application " _
                    & "will proceed with the fixed stock price data on the (hidden) " _
                    & "ClosingPricesFixed sheet.", vbInformation, "Web query failed"
                Exit For
            End If
        Next
        Application.StatusBar = False
        Application.DisplayStatusBar = oldStatusBar

        ' Add stock labels and sort appropriately.
        If success Then
            Call FinishClosingPrices
        Else
            ' Work with data on (hidden) ClosingPricesFixed sheet.
            With wsClosingPrices
                .Activate
                .UsedRange.ClearContents
                wsClosingPricesFixed.UsedRange.Copy _
                    Destination:=.Range("A1")
                With .Range("A3")
                    nStocks = Range(.Offset(0, 1), .End(xlToRight)).Columns.Count
                    ReDim tickerSymbol(1 To nStocks)
                    For sIndex = 1 To nStocks
                        tickerSymbol(sIndex) = .Offset(0, sIndex).Value
                    Next
                End With
            End With
        End If

        ' Calculate returns.
        Call Returns

        ' Calculate summary measures on the SummaryMeasures sheet.
        Call SummaryMeasures

        ' Create the portfolio optimization model and optimize.
        Call CreateModel
        Call RunSolver

        ' Create the chart of the efficient frontier and update its chart.
        Call EfficientFrontier
        Call UpdateChart
        Application.ScreenUpdating = True
    End If
  End If
End Sub
```

ClearOldData Code

The ClearOldData sub clears all previous data from ClosingPrices worksheet and adds some labels for the new data.

```
Sub ClearOldData()
    ' Clear contents from the ClosingPrices sheet.
    With wsClosingPrices.Range("A3")
        Range(.Offset(0, 0), .End(xlDown).End(xlToRight)).ClearContents
        Select Case timeInterval
            Case "m": .Value = "Month"
            Case "w": .Value = "Week"
            Case "d": .Value = "Day"
        End Select
    End With
End Sub
```

RunQuery Code

The RunQuery sub is the crucial sub. It creates a connection string (stored in the connectString variable), which is essentially the URL for the Web site, as discussed in Section 32.4. It then adds a QueryTable object to the active worksheet, with the output range starting in cell Al. (By this time, qryTable has been declared as a QueryTable object.)

This is followed by various properties of the QueryTable object. As the comment indicates, I discovered this code by creating the Web query through the Excel interface with the macro recorder on. The recorded code lists a lot of other properties of the QueryTable object, but after some experimenting, it appears that the ones shown below are the only ones required. Of course, you can look up more information on the properties of QueryTable objects in the Object Browser.

```
Sub RunQuery(iStock As Integer, successful As Boolean)
    ' This sets up a new Web query and runs it, placing the Web
    ' data into the active sheet.
    Dim connectString As String
    Dim qryTable As QueryTable
    Dim rowOffset As Integer
    Dim qIndex As Integer
    Dim foundNothing As Boolean

    rowOffset = 1
    foundNothing = False
    For qIndex = 1 To nWebQueries
        Worksheets.Add
        ActiveSheet.Name = "Query"
        ' The next line builds a long string that is essentially the URL
        ' (preceded by URL;). It is used to define the query. Note how it
        ' inserts the user's inputs into the string. The "keys", such as a, b,
        ' and so on) store the user's inputs (dates and ticker symbol). (For some
        ' unknown reason, Yahoo's month code is 0-based. E.g., 2 is for March.
        connectString = "URL;http://finance.yahoo.com/q/hp?" _
            & "s=" & tickerSymbol(iStock) _
            & "&a=" & Month(startDate) - 1 _
            & "&b=" & Day(startDate) & "&c=" & Year(startDate) _
            & "&d=" & Month(endDate) - 1 & "&e=" & Day(endDate) _
            & "&f=" & Year(endDate) & "&g=" & timeInterval
        If timeInterval = "m" Or timeInterval = "w" Then
            connectString = connectString & "&y=" & (qIndex - 1) * 67
        Else
            connectString = connectString & "&y=" & (qIndex - 1) * 66
        End If
```

```
    ' The next few lines create a QueryTable object with appropriate properties.
    ' I got this code by recording, then deleting parts that appeared unnecessary.
    Set qryTable = ActiveSheet.QueryTables.Add(Connection:=connectString, _
            Destination:=Range("A1"))
    On Error Resume Next
    With qryTable
        .WebSelectionType = xlAllTables
        .WebFormatting = xlWebFormattingAll
        .Refresh BackgroundQuery:=False
    End With

    If Err.Number = 0 Then
        successful = True
        Call TransferPrices(iStock, rowOffset, foundNothing)
    Else
        successful = False
    End If
    If foundNothing Then successful = False

    ' In any case, delete the Query sheet.
    Application.DisplayAlerts = False
    ActiveWorkbook.Connections(1).Delete
    Worksheets("Query").Delete
    Application.DisplayAlerts = True
    Next
End Sub
```

TransferPrices Code

The rest of the subs handle the details—and there are a lot of details. The comments provide most of the explanation you should need. In fact, in complex programs such as this one, extensive and well-written comments are crucial.

The TransferPrices sub must copy the data below the "Adj Close" label in the Query worksheet (see Figure 32.4) to the appropriate column in the ClosingPrices worksheet. Then it must transform the closing prices to returns (percentage changes) on the Returns worksheet. There are two problems that it encounters, both caused by the format of the imported Web data (over which I have no control). First, it is possible that some stocks will return no data. Second, there are several blank cells in the data below the "Adj Close" label because of dividends and stock splits. The VBA code must be written to skip over these blanks.

```
Sub TransferPrices(iStock As Integer, rowOffset As Integer, foundNothing As Boolean)
    ' This sub transfers the closing prices from the Query sheet to the
    ' ClosingPrices sheet. It puts the resulting prices in the correct format.
    Dim counter As Integer
    Dim adjCloseCell As Range
    Dim closeRange As Range

    ' Activate the ClosingPrices sheet.
    wsClosingPrices.Activate

    counter = 1

    ' Try to find the label "Adj Close" in this stock's sheet. This Find method
    ' returns a range object, which is set to adjCloseCell. If the Web query
```

```
' couldn't find any data for this stock (for whatever reason), this find
' will be unsuccessful and adjCloseCell will be set to Nothing.
Set adjCloseCell = Worksheets("Query").Cells.Find(What:="Adj Close")
If adjCloseCell Is Nothing Then
    foundNothing = True
    Exit Sub
End If
Set closeRange = Worksheets("Query").Range(adjCloseCell.Address)


' Loop through the rows until encountering a blank cell.
Do Until Left(closeRange.Offset(counter, -6).Value, 1) = ""
    ' rowOffset is how far down the Closing Prices sheet (below A3) we are.
    ' counter is how far down the Query sheet we are.
    If closeRange.Offset(counter, 0).Value <> "" Then
        ' Enter date indexes in column A of the Closing Prices sheet.
        If iStock = 1 Then _
            wsClosingPrices.Range("A3").Offset(rowOffset, 0).Value = rowOffset

        ' Transfer the closing price to the appropriate row and column of the
        ' Closing Prices sheet.
        wsClosingPrices.Range("A3").Offset(rowOffset, iStock).Value _
            = closeRange.Offset(counter, 0).Value

        ' Update rowOffset after every transfer.
        rowOffset = rowOffset + 1
    End If

    ' Update counter whether or not a blank was found in the
    ' Adj Close column.
    counter = counter + 1
Loop
End Sub
```

FinishClosingPrices Code

The FinishClosingPrices sub adds some labels and sorts the closing prices in increasing chronological order.

```
Sub FinishClosingPrices()
    'This sub finishes setting up the ClosingPrices sheet.
    Dim sIndex As Integer
    Dim sortRange As Range

    With wsClosingPrices
        ' Enter tickerSymbol symbols as headings.
        For sIndex = 1 To nStocks
            .Range("A3").Offset(0, sIndex).Value = tickerSymbol(sIndex)
        Next

        ' Sort the data from earliest to latest (the Web query brings them in
        ' in the opposite order).
        .Range("A3").Sort Key1:=Range("A:A"), Order1:=xlDescending, Header:=xlYes

        ' Put the date indexes back into increasing order.
        Set sortRange = Range(.Range("A3"), .Range("A3").End(xlDown))
        sortRange.Sort Key1:=.Range("A:A"), Order1:=xlAscending, Header:=xlYes
```

```
        Select Case timeInterval
            Case "m"
                .Range("A1").Value = "Monthly closing prices from " _
                    & Format(startDate, "mm/dd/yyyy") & " to " & Format(endDate, "mm/dd/yyyy")
            Case "w"
                .Range("A1").Value = "Weekly closing prices from " _
                    & Format(startDate, "mm/dd/yyyy") & " to " & Format(endDate, "mm/dd/yyyy")
            Case "d"
                .Range("A1").Value = "Daily closing prices from " _
                    & Format(startDate, "mm/dd/yyyy") & " to " & Format(endDate, "mm/dd/yyyy")
        End Select
    End With
End Sub
```

Returns Code

The Returns sub creates the stock returns (percentage changes) on the Returns worksheet.

```
Sub Returns()
    Dim rowOffset As Integer
    Dim sIndex As Integer

    With wsReturns
        .Cells.ClearContents
        .Range("A1").Value = "Corresponding returns"
        .Range("A3").Value = "Time period"
        For sIndex = 1 To nStocks
            .Range("A3").Offset(0, sIndex).Value = tickerSymbol(sIndex)
        Next
    End With

    With wsClosingPrices.Range("A3")
        rowOffset = 1
        Do
            If .Offset(rowOffset + 1, 0).Value <> "" Then
                wsReturns.Range("A3").Offset(rowOffset, 0).Value = rowOffset + 1
            End If
            For sIndex = 1 To nStocks
                If .Offset(rowOffset, sIndex).Value <> "" _
                        And .Offset(rowOffset + 1, sIndex).Value <> "" Then
                    wsReturns.Range("A3").Offset(rowOffset, sIndex).Value = _
                        .Offset(rowOffset + 1, sIndex).Value _
                            / .Offset(rowOffset, sIndex).Value - 1
                End If
            Next
            rowOffset = rowOffset + 1
        Loop Until .Offset(rowOffset, 0).Value = ""
    End With

    With wsReturns.Range("A3")
        For sIndex = 1 To nStocks
            With .Offset(0, sIndex)
                Range(.Offset(1, 0), .Offset(rowOffset – 2, 0)).Name = _
                    "Returns!" & tickerSymbol(sIndex)
            End With
        Next
    End With
End Sub
```

SummaryMeasures Code

The SummaryMeasures sub uses Excel's AVERAGE, STDEV, and CORREL functions to summarize the stock return data in the SummaryMeasures worksheet.

```
Sub SummaryMeasures()
    Dim sIndex1 As Integer, sIndex2 As Integer

    ' Enter formulas for averages and standard deviations (using Excel functions).
    With wsSummaryMeasures
        .Cells.ClearContents
        .Range("A1").Value = "Summary measures for stock returns"
        .Range("A3").Value = "Stocks"
        .Range("A4").Value = "Means"
        .Range("A5").Value = "Stdevs"
        .Range("A7").Value = "Correlations"
        For sIndex1 = 1 To nStocks
            .Range("A3").Offset(0, sIndex1).Value = tickerSymbol(sIndex1)
            .Range("A4").Offset(0, sIndex1).Formula = "=Average(Returns!" & tickerSymbol(sIndex1) & ")"
            .Range("A5").Offset(0, sIndex1).Formula = "=Stdev(Returns!" & tickerSymbol(sIndex1) & ")"
        Next

        ' Create a table of correlations (using Excel's Correl function).
        With .Range("A7")
            For sIndex1 = 1 To nStocks
                .Offset(sIndex1, 0).Value = tickerSymbol(sIndex1)
                .Offset(0, sIndex1).Value = tickerSymbol(sIndex1)
            Next
            For sIndex1 = 1 To nStocks
                For sIndex2 = 1 To nStocks
                    .Offset(sIndex1, sIndex2).Formula = _
                        "=Correl(Returns!" & tickerSymbol(sIndex1) & _
                        ",Returns!" & tickerSymbol(sIndex2) & ")"
                Next
            Next
        End With
    End With
End Sub
```

CreateModel Code

The CreateModel sub uses the summary measures from the previous sub as inputs to a portfolio optimization model (see Figure 32.8).

```
Sub CreateModel()
    ' This sub creates the portfolio optimization model in the Model sheet.
    Dim sIndex1 As Integer, sIndex2 As Integer

    With wsModel
        .Activate
        .Cells.ClearContents

        ' Enter title and headings.
        .Range("A1").Value = "Portfolio selection model (solution shown is when " _
            & "required return is halfway between minimum and maximum of stock returns)"
        With .Range("A3")
```

```
            .Value = "Stock"
            .Offset(1, 0).Value = "Weights"
            .Offset(2, 0).Value = "Means"
            For sIndex1 = 1 To nStocks
                .Offset(0, sIndex1).Value = tickerSymbol(sIndex1)

                ' Enter initial equal weights for the portfolio (Solver will find the optimal)
                ' weights and formulas for the average returns.
                .Offset(1, sIndex1).Value = 1 / nStocks
                .Offset(2, sIndex1).Formula = "=Average(Returns!" & tickerSymbol(sIndex1) & ")"
            Next
    End With

    ' Name some ranges.
    With .Range("A4")
        Range(.Offset(0, 1), .Offset(0, 1).End(xlToRight)).Name = "Model!Weights"
        Range(.Offset(1, 1), .Offset(1, 1).End(xlToRight)).Name = "Model!Means"
    End With

    ' Find the smallest and largest of the average returns, which will be used
    ' to create the efficient frontier.
    minReturn = WorksheetFunction.Min(.Range("Means"))
    maxReturn = WorksheetFunction.Max(.Range("Means"))

    ' Calculate the sum of weights (which will be constrained to be 1).
    With .Range("A3").Offset(0, nStocks + 1)
        .Value = "Sum"
        .Offset(1, 0).Name = "Model!SumWeights"
        .Offset(1, 0).Formula = "=Sum(Weights)"
    End With

    ' Calculate table of covariances (using Excel's Covar function).
    With .Range("A7")
        .Value = "Covariances"
        For sIndex1 = 1 To nStocks
            .Offset(sIndex1, 0).Value = tickerSymbol(sIndex1)
            .Offset(0, sIndex1).Value = tickerSymbol(sIndex1)
        Next
        For sIndex1 = 1 To nStocks
            For sIndex2 = 1 To nStocks
                .Offset(sIndex1, sIndex2).Formula = _
                    "=Covar(Returns!" & tickerSymbol(sIndex1) & _
                        ",Returns!" & tickerSymbol(sIndex2) & ")"
            Next
        Next
        Range(.Offset(1, 1), .Offset(nStocks, nStocks)).Name = "Model!Covar"
    End With

    ' Form lower bound constraint on mean portfolio return, using an intial lower
    ' bound halfway between the smallest and largest mean returns.  (This lower bound
    ' will be varied through the whole range when finding the efficient frontier.
    With .Range("A7").Offset(nStocks + 2, 0)
        .Value = "Constraint on mean return"
        .Offset(1, 1).Formula = "=Sumproduct(Weights,Means)"
        .Offset(1, 2).Value = ">="
        .Offset(1, 3).Value = (minReturn + maxReturn) / 2
        .Offset(1, 1).Name = "Model!MeanReturn"
        .Offset(1, 3).Name = "Model!RequiredReturn"

        ' Calculate the variance of the portfolio (using Excel's MMult and
        ' Transpose matrix functions.) Note that it uses the FormulaArray property.
        ' This is analogous to pressing Ctrl-Shift-Enter in Excel.
```

```
            .Offset(3, 0).Value = "Portfolio variance"
          With .Offset(4, 1)
                .FormulaArray = "=MMult(Weights,MMult(Covar,Transpose(Weights)))"
                .Name = "Model!PortfolioVariance"
          End With
          ' Calculate the standard deviation of the portfolio.
          .Offset(6, 0).Value = "Portfolio standard deviation"
          With .Offset(7, 1)
                .Formula = "=Sqrt(PortfolioVariance)"
                .Name = "Model!PortfolioStdev"
          End With
        End With
      End With

      ' Adjust width of column A.
      .Columns("A:A").ColumnWidth = 11
    End With
End Sub
```

RunSolver Code

The RunSolver sub is straightforward. It sets up Solver and then runs it. Note that it uses the GRG Nonlinear solving method (engine index 2) because the portfolio standard deviation is a nonlinear function of the stock weights.

```
Sub RunSolver()
    ' Set up and run Solver.
    With wsModel
        SolverReset
        SolverOk SetCell:=.Range("PortfolioVariance"), MaxMinVal:=2, _
            ByChange:=.Range("Weights"), Engine:=2
        SolverAdd CellRef:=.Range("SumWeights"), Relation:=2, FormulaText:=1
        SolverAdd CellRef:=.Range("MeanReturn"), Relation:=3, _
            FormulaText:="RequiredReturn"
        SolverOptions AssumeNonNeg:=True
        SolverSolve UserFinish:=True
    End With
End Sub
```

EfficientFrontier Code

The EfficientFrontier sub runs Solver several times and records the results in the EfficientFrontier worksheet. Each run uses a different minimum required mean portfolio return. Finally, it calls the UpdateChart sub to update the efficient frontier chart.

```
Sub EfficientFrontier()
    ' For each of 11 equally spaced values of the required mean portfolio return, run
    ' Solver and record the results on the EfficientFrontier sheet.
    ' Note the Model sheet is still the active sheet.
    ' The sheet with the Solver model must be active to run Solver.
    Dim sIndex As Integer
    Dim run As Integer

    With wsEfficientFrontier
        .Cells.ClearContents
```

```
        .Range("A1").Value = "Efficient frontier"
        .Range("B3").Value = "PortStdev"
        .Range("C3").Value = "ReqdReturn"
        .Range("E2").Value = "Weights for these optimal portfolios"
        With .Range("D3")
            For sIndex = 1 To nStocks
                .Offset(0, sIndex).Value = tickerSymbol(sIndex)
            Next
        End With

' Portfolio standard deviations and means are recorded in columns B and C.
' The corresponding portfolio weights are recorded from column E over.
' First, enter headings.
        For sIndex = 1 To nStocks
            .Range("D3").Offset(0, sIndex).Value = tickerSymbol(sIndex)
        Next
    End With

' Run the Solver 11 times and record the results.
    For run = 0 To 10
        wsModel.Range("RequiredReturn") = minReturn + run * (maxReturn – minReturn) / 10
        SolverSolve UserFinish:=True
        With wsEfficientFrontier.Range("B4")
            .Offset(run, 0).Value = wsModel.Range("PortfolioStdev").Value
            .Offset(run, 1).Value = wsModel.Range("RequiredReturn").Value
        End With
        With wsEfficientFrontier.Range("E4")
            For sIndex = 1 To nStocks
                .Offset(run, sIndex – 1).Value _
                    = wsModel.Range("Weights").Cells(sIndex).Value
            Next
        End With
    Next

    wsEfficientFrontier.Activate
    Call UpdateChart
End Sub
```

UpdateChart Code

The efficient frontier chart already exists as a scatter chart (of the type with the dots connected). The **UpdateChart** sub populates it with the newly calculated data in the EfficientFrontier worksheet.

```
Sub UpdateChart()
    ' This sub updates the efficient frontier chart.
    Dim sourceRange As Range
    Dim minX As Single, maxX As Single
    Dim minY As Single, maxY As Single
    Dim xLength As Single, yLength As Single

    ' Set minX, minY, etc. is for scaling the axes nicely.
    With wsEfficientFrontier
        Set sourceRange = .Range("B4:C14")
        minX = .Range("B4").Value
        maxX = .Range("B14").Value
        minY = .Range("C4").Value
        maxY = .Range("C14").Value
```

```
        xLength = maxX - minX
        yLength = maxY - minY
    End With

    ' Update the chart settings to update the chart.
    With wsEfficientFrontier.ChartObjects(1).Chart
        .SetSourceData sourceRange
        With .Axes(xlCategory)
            .MinimumScale = minX - 0.1 * xLength
            .MaximumScale = maxX + 0.1 * xLength
        End With
        With .Axes(xlValue)
            .MinimumScale = minY - 0.1 * yLength
            .MaximumScale = maxY + 0.1 * yLength
        End With
    End With

    wsEfficientFrontier.Range("A2").Select
End Sub
```

32.9 Summary

This application has been developed to impress—and to be useful to financial analysts and investors. To achieve anything this ambitious, a lot of code must be written, and it is not always straightforward. However, I hope you agree that it is well worth the effort. You should pay particular attention to the RunQuery sub, where the data from the Web site are retrieved. In fact, I suspect that many of you will be anxious to make appropriate modifications to this code to obtain data from other Web sites. The ability to access the mounds of data available on the Web and then analyze the data with Excel's many tools is indeed a powerful combination. But remember that you are at the mercy of the Web developers. If they change their site, they can easily break your code.

EXERCISES

1. Note that all summary measures are entered as *formulas* in the SummaryMeasures sub. There is no real need to do it this way. Change this sub so that all summary measures are entered as *values*.

2. The TransferPrices sub uses the Find method to find a cell with some specified value. There is also a FindNext method. (Each is a method of the Range object.) These can be used in VBA similar to the way they are used in the usual Excel interface to find a piece of information (or the next such piece of information). The file **Piano Orders.xlsx** contains a list of orders for Steinway pianos. It lists the date of the order and the state where the order was made. Write a sub that searches through the list of states to find each occurrence of California and colors the background of each such cell yellow. (*Hint*: Look up the Find and FindNext methods of the Range object in the Object Browser.)

3. Find a Web site that contains at least one table of data and allows the user to make a choice, such as I did in this application when I got to choose the period of

time and the ticker symbol. (If you can't find any of your own, try one like the following: http://www.cbssports.com/tennis/scoreboard/results/2010/0122, where the date is indicated at the end.) Then write a sub that retrieves the data specified by a user's choices. These choices can be obtained from an input box or a user form, whichever is more natural for the context. (For example, in this application I got the user's choices from the dialog boxes in Figure 32.2 and Figure 32.3.)

4. Sometimes you get lucky with Web sites. I was looking for current Major League Baseball rosters, and I found them at a Sports Network site with a typical URL such as follows: http://www.sportsnetwork.com/merge/tsnform.aspx?c=sports-network&page=mlb/teams/027/roster.aspx?team=027. This provides the roster for the team with index 27, which happens to be the Baltimore Orioles. Now try the following: (1) Run a Web query manually from one of these URLs. (2) Run it again with the recorder on. (3) Learning from the recorded code, write a VBA program that finds the current rosters for all teams and lists each on a separate team worksheet.

A Data Envelopment Analysis Application

33.1 Introduction

Data Envelopment Analysis (DEA) is a method for comparing the relative efficiency of organizational units such as banks, hospitals, and schools, where efficiency relates to the ability to transform inputs into outputs. For example, DEA could analyze several branch banks, where the inputs for each branch might be labor hours, square feet of space, and supplies used, and the outputs might be the numbers of loan applications, deposits processed, and checks processed during some time period. DEA could then use these data in several linear programming models, one for each branch, to see whether each branch can attach unit costs to its inputs and unit prices to its outputs to make itself appear efficient. By definition, a branch is "efficient" if the total value of its outputs is equal to the total value of its inputs. It is "inefficient" if the total value of its outputs is *less* than the total value of its inputs.

This application takes data from a text (.txt) file, sets up a Solver model, runs it for each of the organizational units, and reports the results. Among other things, this application illustrates how to import data from a text file into an Excel application.

New Learning Objectives: VBA

- To learn how the data from a comma-delimited text file can be imported into an Excel application (although this material was covered briefly in Chapter 13).
- To see how a comma-delimited string can be parsed by using appropriate loops and string functions.

New Learning Objectives: Non-VBA

- To learn how the DEA procedure can compare various organizational units for efficiency.

33.2 Functionality of the Application

The data for the application are in a file called **DEA.txt**. This is a simple text file that can be created with the Windows NotePad or any comparable text editor. It lists the names of the inputs and outputs, the names of the organizational units, and the inputs used and outputs produced by each unit. The application imports these data into the **DEA.xlsm** application file, where they are used as input data for a linear programming model. This model is solved for each organizational unit to see whether the unit is efficient. The results are then reported in a Report worksheet.

As the application is currently written, the **DEA.txt** and **DEA.xlsm** files should be stored in the same folder. The current **DEA.txt** file contains data on four organizational units (departments in a university), each with three inputs and two outputs. However, these data can be replaced with any data, with any numbers of organizational units, inputs, and outputs, and the application will respond appropriately. The format for the data in the **DEA.txt** file is discussed below.

33.3 Running the Application

When the **DEA.xlsm** file is opened, the Explanation worksheet in Figure 33.1 appears. When the button on this sheet is clicked, the application then opens the **DEA.txt** file, reads the data and stores it in arrays, sets up a linear programming

Figure 33.1 Explanation Worksheet

A Data Envelopment Analysis (DEA) Application

Run the application

This application automates DEA to see which of several organization units are efficient in their use of inputs to produce outputs. The user enters the number of organization units, the number of inputs, and the number of outputs, where it is assumed that all units have the same list of inputs and outputs. Then the application gets the actual data from a text (.txt) file named DEA.txt. This file contains the names for the units, inputs, and outputs, as well as the amounts of the inputs used by each unit and the amounts of the outputs produced by each unit. It then sets up a DEA linear programming model and runs Solver, once for each unit, to see which units are efficient. This is determined by maximizing the value for the unit's outputs, subject to constraining the value of its inputs to be 1. If this maximum output value is 1, the unit is efficient. Otherwise, it is inefficient. A list of the units and whether they are efficient or inefficient, as well as other pertinent infomation, is written to the Report sheet.

The DEA.txt file currently contains data for four units, each of which uses three inputs and produces two outputs. However, users can substitute their own data in this file (any number of units, inputs, and outputs), and the application will accept them.

Figure 33.2 Report Worksheet

Summary of analysis

View Explanation Sheet

Efficiency of units

Unit	LP maximum output	Efficient?
Business	1.000	Yes
Education	1.000	Yes
Arts & Sciences	1.000	Yes
HPER	0.848	No

Given data from text file

	Inputs used			Outputs produced	
Unit	Faculty	Support Staff	Supply Budget	Credit Hours	Research Pubs
Business	150.00	70.00	5.00	15.00	225.00
Education	60.00	20.00	3.00	5.40	70.00
Arts & Sciences	800.00	140.00	20.00	56.00	1300.00
HPER	30.00	15.00	1.00	2.10	40.00

Values from LP model

	Total costs of inputs used			Total values of outputs produced	
Unit	Faculty	Support Staff	Supply Budget	Credit Hours	Research Pubs
Business	0.597	0.403	0.000	0.875	0.125
Education	0.674	0.326	0.000	0.890	0.110
Arts & Sciences	0.798	0.202	0.000	0.819	0.181
HPER	1.000	0.000	0.000	0.152	0.696

model in a (hidden) Model worksheet, solves it once for each organizational unit, and reports the results in the Report worksheet shown in Figure 33.2.

There are three sections in this report. The one on the left indicates whether the units are efficient by reporting the maximum total output value from the linear programming model for each unit. Because the total input values are scaled to be 1, a unit is efficient only if its total output value is 1. For these data, all units are efficient except HPER. The section on the top right reports the original data. It shows the quantities of inputs used and outputs produced for each unit.

Finally, the section on the bottom right indicates input costs and output values from the linear programming model, where input costs are scaled so that they sum to 1 for each unit. For example, Education (internally) assigns *unit* costs to its inputs so that the total values of its faculty and support staff used are 0.674 and 0.326, respectively. It attaches zero value to its supply budget input. Similarly, it attaches *unit* prices to its outputs so that the total values of its credit hours and research pubs produced are 0.890 and 0.110, respectively. With these unit costs and unit prices, Education's total output value is equal to its total input value (both equal 1), which means that it is an efficient unit.

This report is based on the linear programming model shown in Figure 33.3. The version shown here is for checking the efficiency of unit 4 (HPER). It indicates the range names used. Of course, the actual ranges would change if there were different numbers of organizational units, inputs, or outputs.

The VBA code sets up this model at run time. It then substitutes the index for each organizational unit (1–4 in this example) in cell B3. The formulas in cells B21 and B24 are linked to this value through VLOOKUP functions so that they update automatically. Then Solver is run for each index in cell B3.

33.4 Setting Up the Excel Sheets and the Text File

The **DEA.xlsm** file contains three worksheets named Explanation, Model, and Report. However, there are no templates for the Model and Report worksheets. At design time, they are blank. The reason is that if the numbers of organiza-

Figure 33.3 Model Worksheet

	A	B	C	D	E	F	G	H
1	DEA model							
2								
3	Selected unit	4						
4								
5	Inputs used	Faculty	Support Staff	Supply Budget		Outputs used	Credit Hours	Research Pubs
6	Business	150	70	5		Business	15	225
7	Education	60	20	3		Education	5.4	70
8	Arts & Sciences	800	140	20		Arts & Sciences	56	1300
9	HPER	30	15	1		HPER	2.1	40
10								
11	Unit costs	0.033	0	0		Unit prices	0.0725	0.0174
12								
13	Constraints that input costs must cover output values					Range names used:		
14	Unit index		Input costs		Output values	InputCosts	=Model!$B$11:$D$11	
15		1	5	>=	5	InputsUsed	=Model!$B$6:$D$9	
16		2	2	>=	1.609	InputValues	=Model!$B$15:$B$18	
17		3	26.667	>=	26.667	LTable	=Model!$A$15:$D$18	
18		4	1	>=	0.848	OutputPrices	=Model!$G$11:$H$11	
19						OutputsProduced	=Model!$G$6:$H$9	
20	Constraint that selected unit's input cost must equal a nominal value of 1					OutputValues	=Model!$D$15:$D$18	
21	Selected unit's input cost	1	=		1	SelInputValue	=Model!$B$21	
22						SelOutputValue	=Model!$B$24	
23	Maximize selected unit's output value (to see if it is 1, hence efficient)							
24	Selected unit's output value	0.848						

tional units, inputs, or outputs change due to new data in the **DEA.txt** file, the Model and Report setups change dramatically. Therefore, it is easier to start with a clean slate and then fill these sheets completely—values, formulas, headings, and formatting—through VBA code at run time. The **DEA.txt** file should be structured as a comma-delimited file, as shown in Figure 33.4. The first row

Figure 33.4 Structure of Text File

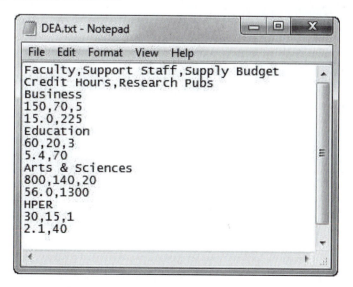

should contain the names of the inputs, separated by commas. The second row should contain the names of the outputs, separated by commas. There should then be three lines for each organizational unit. The first should contain the unit's name, and the second and third should contain its inputs used and outputs produced, respectively, with input values separated by commas and output values separated by commas. There should *not* be any spaces following the commas. If the data are not structured in this way, the application will either crash (with a "nice" error message) or yield misleading results.

33.5 Getting Started with the VBA

The application contains a single user form named frmInputs, a module, and a reference to Solver. Once these items are added, the Project Explorer window will appear as in Figure 33.5.[1]

Workbook_Open Code

To guarantee that the Explanation worksheet appears when the file is opened, the following code is placed in the ThisWorkbook code window. This sub also hides the Model and Report worksheets and displays the usual Solver warning when used with pre-2010 versions of Excel.

Figure 33.5 Project Explorer Window

---

[1] It also contains the usual frmSolver that displays a message about possible Solver problems when the workbook is opened, but only users of pre-2010 versions of Excel will see this message.

```
Private Sub Workbook_Open()
    With wsExplanation
        .Activate
        .Range("F5").Select
    End With
    wsReport.Visible = False
    wsModel.Visible = False
    If Not (Application.Version = "15.0" Or Application.Version = "14.0") Then frmSolver.Show
End Sub
```

33.6 Getting Data from a Text File

Perhaps the most interesting part of this application, at least from a VBA standpoint, is the way the data are obtained from the text file. To open the text file, the following line is required:[2]

```
Open ThisWorkbook.Path & "\DEA.txt" For Input As #1
```

The "#1" essentially means that this is the *first* text file opened. (If another were opened in the same session, it would be opened as #2, and so on.) Eventually, the file should be closed with the line

```
Close #1
```

To read a single line from the text file, the following code is required, where dataLine is a string variable:

```
Line Input #1, dataLine
```

Each time this line of code is executed, the next entire line of data is stored as a string in the dataLine variable. Typically, there are several pieces of data in a line of text, separated by commas. The individual pieces must then be parsed. Because this parsing operation is required several times, the program contains a ParseLine sub that is called whenever it is needed. The ParseLine sub takes three arguments: the dataLine string, the expected number of pieces of data, and an array (I've named it returnArray) to be filled with the individual pieces of data. It then passes the filled returnArray array *back* to a GetData sub, where its contents are put into array variables, such as inputName. The details appear in the next section.

---

[2] Although the steps for importing text data into Excel were discussed briefly in Chapter 13, they are repeated here for your convenience.

Summarizing, the steps required to import data from a text file are: (1) open the file; (2) read an entire line; (3) parse the line into its separate pieces of data; repeat steps (2) and (3) for each line in the text file; and (4) close the file.

33.7 The Module

Almost everything is done at run time with the code in the module. The button on the Explanation worksheet is attached to the MainDEA sub. This sub first captures the data from the text file in module-level arrays. Next, it sets up the linear programming model and solves it for each organizational unit. Finally, it creates the report. The module-level variables and the MainDEA sub are listed below.

Option Statements and Module-Level Variables

```
Option Explicit
Option Base 1

' Definitions of module-level variables:
'   nUnits: number of organization units
'   unitName(): array of names of units
'   nInputs: number of inputs for each unit
'   inputName(): array of names of inputs
'   inputUsed(): two-dimensional array of inputs used by units (first
'       dimension is the unit, second is the input)
'   nOutputs: number of outputs for each unit
'   outputName(): array of names of outputs
'   outputProduced(): two-dimensional array of outputs produced by units (first
'       dimension is the unit, second is the output)
'   totalInputCost(): two-dimensional array (first subscript is unit,
'       second is input) - e.g., TotalInputCost(1,3) is the unit cost
'       of input 3 multiplied by the amount of input 3 used by unit 1
'   totalOutputValue(): same as TotalInputCost array, except for outputs.
'   efficiencyIndex(): an array of maximum outputs from LP model, one for each unit

Dim nUnits As Integer, unitName() As String
Dim nInputs As Integer, inputName() As String, inputUsed() As Single
Dim nOutputs As Integer, outputName() As String, outputProduced() As Single
Dim totalInputCost() As Single, totalOutputValue() As Single
Dim efficiencyIndex() As Single
```

MainDEA Code

```
Sub MainDEA()
    ' This sub runs when the user clicks on the button in the Explanation sheet.
    Application.ScreenUpdating = False
    ' Get data from the DEA.txt file
    Call GetData
    ' Create the model in the Model sheet.
```

```
    Call CreateModel
    ' Set up and run the Solver several times, once for each unit.
    Call RunSolver
    ' Fill in the Report sheet.
    Call CreateReport
    Application.ScreenUpdating = True
End Sub
```

GetData Code

The GetData sub is responsible for importing the data from the text file into Excel. First, an attempt is made to open the text file. If there is an error (no such file exists, at least not in the same folder as the application file), an error message is displayed and the program ends. Otherwise, the file is read line by line. If there is ever an error of any type (probably because the text file isn't structured properly), control passes to the BadData label, a message is displayed, and the program ends. Note how the On Error statements discussed in Chapter 12 are used here to trap for these errors.

Pay particular attention to the ParseLine calls. (The code for the ParseLine sub is listed below.) For example, after the first line of the text file (the one with the names of the inputs) is stored in the dataLine string, the following line is called:

```
Call ParseLine(dataLine, nInputs, returnArray)
```

The second argument indicates the number of separate pieces of data that are expected in the dataLine string. This string is then parsed, and its pieces are placed in the returnArray array (this is done in the ParseLine sub) so that the array is available for the GetData sub.

```
Sub GetData()
    ' Read the data from the DEA.txt file and store it in arrays.

    Dim i As Integer, j As Integer
    Dim dataLine As String
    Dim returnArray() As String
    Dim nInputsRead As Integer, nOutputsRead As Integer

    ' Try to open the DEA.txt file, but check for an error in case it doesn't exist.
    On Error Resume Next
    Open ThisWorkbook.Path & "\DEA.txt" For Input As #1

    ' Quit if there is no DEA.txt file in the directory of this workbook.
    If Err.Number <> 0 Then
        MsgBox "There is no DEA.txt file in the same directory as " _
            & "this workbook, so the application cannot continue.", _
                vbInformation, "Missing file"
        End
    End If
```

```
' Quit if anything goes wrong reading the file.
On Error GoTo BadData

' The first line contains the names of the inputs.
Line Input #1, dataLine
Call ParseLine(dataLine, nInputs, returnArray)

' Transfer contents of returnArray array to inputName array.
ReDim inputName(nInputs)
For i = 1 To nInputs
    inputName(i) = returnArray(i)
Next

' Do it again, reading the second line for the output names.
Line Input #1, dataLine
Call ParseLine(dataLine, nOutputs, returnArray)
ReDim outputName(nOutputs)
For i = 1 To nOutputs
    outputName(i) = returnArray(i)
Next

' Now go through each organizational unit.
nUnits = 0
Do While Not EOF(1)

    ' Add another unit and redimension arrays appropriately. Note that
    ' only the second dimension of a two-dimensional array can be
    ' redimensioned dynamically with a Redim statement.
    nUnits = nUnits + 1
    ReDim Preserve unitName(nUnits)
    ReDim Preserve inputUsed(nInputs, nUnits)
    ReDim Preserve outputProduced(nOutputs, nUnits)

    ' The unit's name is in the first line - no parsing required.
    Line Input #1, dataLine
    unitName(nUnits) = dataLine

    ' The unit's inputs used are in the second line.
    Line Input #1, dataLine
    Call ParseLine(dataLine, nInputsRead, returnArray)

    ' Quit if the number of data items in this line is not the same
    ' as the number of inputs (which is known by now).
    If nInputsRead <> nInputs Then
        GoTo BadData
    End If

    ' Store the input data in this line for later use.
    For j = 1 To nInputs
        inputUsed(j, nUnits) = returnArray(j)
    Next

    ' Do the same for the unit's outputs produced, which are in the next line.
    Line Input #1, dataLine
    Call ParseLine(dataLine, nOutputsRead, returnArray)

    If nOutputsRead <> nOutputs Then
        GoTo BadData
    End If
```

```
      For j = 1 To nOutputs
           outputProduced(j, nUnits) = returnArray(j)
      Next
   Loop

   ' Close the data file.
   Close #1

   ' Now that we know the numbers of units, inputs and outputs,
   ' redimension other arrays.
   ReDim efficiencyIndex(nUnits)
   ReDim totalInputCost(nInputs, nUnits)
   ReDim totalOutputValue(nOutputs, nUnits)

   Exit Sub

BadData:
   MsgBox "The data file is not set up properly, so the application " _
      & "cannot continue.", vbInformation, "Invalid data"
   End
End Sub
```

ParseLine Code

To parse a string dataLine into its individual pieces of data, the ParseLine sub uses a For loop to go through the string one character at a time (from left to right), using the Mid function. Specifically, Mid(dataLine, i, 1) returns the character in position i of the string dataLine. As it reads these characters, it builds a currentText string. As it progresses, it checks whether each character is a comma or the last character in the dataLine string. In either case, it captures the characters stored in the currentText string as the next element of the returnArray array and resets currentText to an empty string. If it ever fills the array with the expected number of elements *before* parsing the entire dataLine string, it exits prematurely. (This could be the case if a text line contained more data than is required.)

It is very instructive to step through this sub one line at a time (with the F8 key) and keep a watch on the dataLine and currentText strings in the Watch window. This allows you to see exactly how the strings are parsed.[3]

```
Sub ParseLine(dataLine As String, nValues As Integer, returnArray() As String)
   ' This sub parses a line of data from the text file into individual pieces of data.
   ' It returns an array of the pieces of data and number of pieces (in nValues).

   Dim i As Integer
   Dim char As String
   Dim counter As Integer ' counts the pieces of data in the line
   Dim currentText As String ' text since last comma
```

---

[3] As mentioned in Chapter 13, I have included the parsing code because it is a great exercise in computing logic. However, there is a VBA function, Split, that makes most of this parsing code unnecessary. One of the exercises asks you to modify the application to take advantage of the Split function.

```
' Counter counts the number of pieces of data in the line.
counter = 1
ReDim returnArray(counter)

' currentText is any piece of data in the line, where the pieces
' are separated by commas.
currentText = ""

' Go through the string a character at a time.
For i = 1 To Len(dataLine)

    ' Get the character in position i.
    char = Mid(dataLine, i, 1)
    ' Check if the character is a comma or the last character in the string.
    If char = "," Then
        returnArray(counter) = currentText

        ' Get ready for the next piece of data.
        currentText = ""
        counter = counter + 1
        ReDim Preserve returnArray(counter)

    ElseIf i = Len(dataLine) Then
        ' Capture this last piece of data and return the number of pieces.
        currentText = currentText & Mid(dataLine, i, 1)
        returnArray(counter) = currentText
        nValues = counter
    Else
        ' Add this character to the currentText string.
        currentText = currentText & Mid(dataLine, i, 1)
    End If
    Next i
End Sub
```

CreateModel Code

The CreateModel sub clears the Model worksheet completely by using the Clear-
Contents method of the UsedRange. (Recall from Chapter 6 that the UsedRange
of a worksheet is basically the area of the worksheet that contains any data.) Then
it calls two subs, EnterInputsOutputs and CalcFormulas, to develop the linear programming model.

```
Sub CreateModel()
    ' This sub creates the LP model and reports the results.

    ' First, unhide and activate the Model sheet and clear all contents.
    With wsModel
        .Visible = True
        .Activate
        .UsedRange.ClearContents

        ' Enter labels. (Cell B3 will contain the index of the unit currently being
        ' analyzed for efficiency.)
        .Range("A1").Value = "DEA model"
        .Range("A3").Value = "Selected unit"
    End With
```

```
' Enter the user data.
Call EnterInputsOutputs

' Calculate all required formulas for the model.
Call CalcFormulas
End Sub
```

EnterInputsOutputs Code

The EnterInputsOutputs sub enters the data from the text file, which are by now stored in arrays (from the GetData sub), into the Model worksheet. It also enters descriptive headings. Keep in mind that the Model worksheet is practically blank when this sub and the next sub are called, so they have a considerable amount of work to do. Refer to Figure 33.3 and its list of range names as you read this code.

```
Sub EnterInputsOutputs()
    ' This sub enters the inputs for the DEA model.
    Dim i As Integer, j As Integer

    With wsModel
        ' Enter labels and data.
        With .Range("A5")
            .Value = "Inputs used"
            For j = 1 To nInputs
                .Offset(0, j).Value = inputName(j)
            Next
            For i = 1 To nUnits
                .Offset(i, 0).Value = unitName(i)
                For j = 1 To nInputs
                    .Offset(i, j).Value = inputUsed(j, i)
                Next
            Next

            ' Name the range of input amounts.
            ' It will be used for formulas in the Model sheet.
            Range(.Offset(1, 1), .Offset(nUnits, nInputs)).Name = _
                "Model!InputsUsed"

            ' Enter 0's as initial values for the input cost changing cells.
            With .Offset(nUnits + 2, 0)
                .Value = "Unit costs"
                For j = 1 To nInputs
                    .Offset(0, j).Value = 0
                Next

                ' Name the range of the changing cells for inputs.
                Range(.Offset(0, 1), .Offset(0, nInputs)).Name = _
                    "Model!InputCosts"
            End With
        End With

        ' Do the same for the outputs.
        With .Range("A5").Offset(0, nInputs + 2)
            .Value = "Outputs used"
            For j = 1 To nOutputs
                .Offset(0, j).Value = outputName(j)
```

```
            Next
            For i = 1 To nUnits
                .Offset(i, 0).Value = unitName(i)
                For j = 1 To nOutputs
                    .Offset(i, j).Value = outputProduced(j, i)
                Next
            Next
            Range(.Offset(1, 1), .Offset(nUnits, nOutputs)).Name = _
                "Model!OutputsProduced"
            With .Offset(nUnits + 2, 0)
                .Value = "Unit prices"
                For j = 1 To nOutputs
                    .Offset(0, j).Value = 0
                Next
                Range(.Offset(0, 1), .Offset(0, nOutputs)).Name = _
                    "Model!OutputPrices"
            End With
        End With
    End With
End Sub
```

CalcFormulas Code

The CalcFormulas sub continues the model development by entering all required formulas and naming various ranges. Again, refer to Figure 33.3 and its list of range names as you read this code.

```
Sub CalcFormulas()
    ' This sub calculates formulas for the Model, starting just below the changing
    ' cells from the previous sub.

    Dim i As Integer
    With wsModel.Range("A5").Offset(nUnits + 4, 0)

        ' Set up constraints that input costs incurred must be greater than
        ' or equal to output values achieved.
        .Value = "Constraints that input costs must cover output values"
        .Offset(1, 0).Value = "Unit index"
        .Offset(1, 1).Value = "Input costs"
        .Offset(1, 3).Value = "Output values"

        ' There is a constraint for each unit.
        For i = 1 To nUnits

            ' Labels in column A (1, 2, etc.) are needed for later on, to
            ' enable use of VLookup function.
            .Offset(1 + i, 0).Value = i

            ' The input cost incurred for any unit is the sumproduct of the changing
            ' cell range (UnitCosts) and the appropriate input data row. The same goes
            ' for output value. Note how the appropriate row is specified.
            .Offset(1 + i, 1).Formula = _
                "=Sumproduct(InputCosts," & Range("InputsUsed").Rows(i).Address & ")"
            .Offset(1 + i, 2).Value = ">="
            .Offset(1 + i, 3).Formula = _
                "=Sumproduct(OutputPrices," _
```

```
                & Range("OutputsProduced").Rows(i).Address & ")"
        Next

        ' Name appropriate ranges. LTable is for later on with the VLookup function.
        Range(.Offset(2, 1), .Offset(nUnits + 1, 1)).Name = "Model!InputValues"
        Range(.Offset(2, 3), .Offset(nUnits + 1, 3)).Name = "Model!OutputValues"
        Range(.Offset(2, 0), .Offset(nUnits + 1, 3)).Name = "Model!LTable"
    End With

    ' Set up constraint that the selected unit's total input cost is 1.
    With wsModel.Range("A5").Offset(2 * nUnits + 7, 0)
        .Value = "Constraint that selected unit's input cost must " _
            & "equal a nominal value of 1"
        .Offset(1, 0).Value = "Selected unit's input cost"

        ' Get the selected unit's total input cost with a VLookup.
        With .Offset(1, 1)
            .Formula = "=VLookup(B3,LTable,2)"
            .Name = "Model!SelInputValue"
        End With
        .Offset(1, 2).Value = "="
        .Offset(1, 3).Value = 1
        .Offset(3, 0).Value = "Maximize selected unit's output value " _
            & "(to see if it is 1, hence efficient)"
        .Offset(4, 0).Value = "Selected unit's output value"

        ' Get the selected unit's total output value with a VLookup.
        ' It is the target cell for maximization.
        With .Offset(4, 1)
            .Formula = "=VLookup(B3,LTable,4)"
            .Name = "Model!SelOutputValue"
        End With
    End With
End Sub
```

RunSolver Code

The RunSolver sub uses a For loop to go through each organizational unit and solve the appropriate model. (The particular unit being analyzed depends on the index placed in cell B3.) It then captures the Solver results in the arrays efficiencyIndex, totalInputCost, and totalOuputValue for later use in the report.

```
Sub RunSolver()
    ' This sub sets up and runs Solver once for each unit, first placing
    ' its index (1, 2, etc.) in cell B3.
    Dim i As Integer, j As Integer

    With wsModel
        For i = 1 To nUnits
            .Range("B3").Value = i
            SolverReset
            SolverOk SetCell:=.Range("SelOutputValue"), MaxMinVal:=1, _
                ByChange:=Union(.Range("InputCosts"), .Range("OutputPrices")), _
                Engine:=1
            SolverAdd CellRef:=.Range("InputValues"), Relation:=3, _
                FormulaText:="OutputValues"
```

```
            SolverAdd CellRef:=.Range("SelInputValue"), Relation:=2, FormulaText:=1
            SolverOptions AssumeNonNeg:=True
            SolverSolve UserFinish:=True

            ' Capture the quantities for the report in the totalInputCost,
            ' totalOutputValue, and efficiencyIndex arrays.
            For j = 1 To nInputs
                totalInputCost(j, i) = .Range("InputCosts").Cells(j).Value _
                    * inputUsed(j, i)
            Next
                For j = 1 To nOutputs
                totalOutputValue(j, i) = .Range("OutputPrices").Cells(j).Value _
                    * outputProduced(j, i)
            Next
            efficiencyIndex(i) = .Range("SelOutputValue").Value
        Next

            ' Hide the Model sheet.
        .Visible = False
    End With
End Sub
```

CreateReport Code

To create the report, the current Report worksheet is cleared completely. (Again, it is easier to start from scratch than to try to salvage anything from a previous report.) This provides a fresh start, but it means that all of the data transfers *and* all desired formatting must be done at run time through VBA code. There is nothing difficult about it, but there are a lot of steps. In the spirit of modularizing, the CreateReport sub does a few tasks and then calls three subs, FirstSection, SecondSection, and ThirdSection, to do the majority of the work.

```
Sub CreateReport()
    ' This sub creates a report of the Solver results.
    Dim i As Integer, j As Integer

    ' It's easier to start with a brand new Report sheet, so
    ' everything is cleared from the old one.
    With wsReport
        .Cells.Clear
        .Visible = True
        .Activate

        ' Shrink column width of column A and format the title in cell B2.
        .Columns("A:A").ColumnWidth = 3
        With .Range("B1")
            .Value = "Summary of analysis"
            .RowHeight = 40
            .VerticalAlignment = xlCenter
            .Font.Bold = True
            .Font.Size = 16
        End With

        ' Build the rest of the report in three sections with the following three subs.
        Call FirstSection
```

```
      Call SecondSection
      Call ThirdSection

      .Range("A1").Select
   End With
End Sub
```

FirstSection Code

Referring to the report in Figure 33.2, the first section is the section on the left, the second section is the top-right section, and the third section is the bottom-right section. Each of the following subs adds headings and data and then formats its section appropriately. (Interestingly, Excel 2007 and later versions no longer show an AutoFormat method for a Range in the Object Browser, but the old Auto-Format method still works.)

```
Sub FirstSection()
   ' This sub enters the efficiencies for the units.
   Dim i As Integer

   With wsReport
      ' Enter headings.
      With .Range("B3")
         .Value = "Efficiency of units"
         .Font.Bold = True
         .Font.Size = 12
      End With
      With .Range("B4")
         .Value = "Unit"
         .Offset(0, 1).Value = "LP maximum output"
         .Offset(0, 2).Value = "Efficient?"
         For i = 1 To nUnits
            .Offset(i, 0).Value = unitName(i)

            ' Enter target values from the optimization.
            .Offset(i, 1) = efficiencyIndex(i)

            ' Enter Yes or No depending on whether the target = 1 or < 1.
            If efficiencyIndex(i) < 1 Then
               .Offset(i, 2).Value = "No"
            Else
               .Offset(i, 2).Value = "Yes"
            End If
         Next

         ' Format appropriately.
         Range(.Offset(1, 1), .Offset(nUnits, 1)).NumberFormat = "0.000"
         Range(.Offset(0, 0), .Offset(nUnits, 2)).AutoFormat xlRangeAutoFormatClassic3
         .HorizontalAlignment = xlLeft
         Range(.Offset(1, 2), .Offset(nUnits, 2)).HorizontalAlignment = xlRight
      End With
   End With
End Sub
```

SecondSection Code

```
Sub SecondSection()
    ' This sub enters the given data from the DEA.txt file.
    Dim i As Integer, j As Integer

    With wsReport
        ' Enter headings.
        With .Range("F2")
            .Value = "Given data from text file"
            .Font.Bold = True
            .Font.Size = 12
        End With

        With .Range("F4")
            ' Enter more headings.
            .Value = "Unit"
            With .Offset(-1, 1)
                .Value = "Inputs used"
                .Font.Bold = True
            End With
            With .Offset(-1, nInputs + 1)
                .Value = "Outputs produced"
                .Font.Bold = True
            End With
            For i = 1 To nUnits
                .Offset(i, 0).Value = unitName(i)
            Next
            For j = 1 To nInputs
                .Offset(0, j).Value = inputName(j)
            Next

            For j = 1 To nOutputs
                .Offset(0, nInputs + j).Value = outputName(j)
            Next

            ' Enter the inputs used and outputs produced.
            For i = 1 To nUnits
                For j = 1 To nInputs
                    .Offset(i, j).Value = inputUsed(j, i)
                Next
                For j = 1 To nOutputs
                    .Offset(i, nInputs + j).Value = outputProduced(j, i)
                Next
            Next

            ' Format appropriately.
            Range(.Offset(1, 1), .Offset(nUnits, nInputs + nOutputs)) _
                .NumberFormat = "0.00"
            Range(.Offset(0, 0), .Offset(nUnits, nInputs + nOutputs)) _
                .AutoFormat xlRangeAutoFormatClassic3
            .HorizontalAlignment = xlLeft
        End With
    End With
End Sub
```

ThirdSection Code

```vb
Sub ThirdSection()
    ' This sub is almost the same as the previous sub, but now the data are
    ' total costs of inputs used and total values of outputs produced, as
    ' calculated from the LP model.
    Dim i As Integer, j As Integer

    With wsReport
        With .Range("F4").Offset(nUnits + 2, 0)
            .Value = "Values from LP model"
            .Font.Bold = True
            .Font.Size = 12
        End With

        With .Range("F4").Offset(nUnits + 4, 0)
            .Value = "Unit"
            With .Offset(-1, 1)
                .Value = "Total costs of inputs used"
                .Font.Bold = True
            End With
            With .Offset(-1, nInputs + 1)
                .Value = "Total values of outputs produced"
                .Font.Bold = True
            End With
            For i = 1 To nUnits
                .Offset(i, 0).Value = unitName(i)
            Next
            For j = 1 To nInputs
                .Offset(0, j).Value = inputName(j)
            Next
            For j = 1 To nOutputs
                .Offset(0, nInputs + j).Value = outputName(j)
            Next

            ' Enter the data from the LP runs. (These were calculated in the RunSolver sub.)
            For i = 1 To nUnits
                For j = 1 To nInputs
                    .Offset(i, j).Value = totalInputCost(j, i)
                Next
                For j = 1 To nOutputs
                    .Offset(i, nInputs + j).Value = totalOutputValue(j, i)
                Next
            Next
            Range(.Offset(1, 1), .Offset(nUnits, nInputs + nOutputs)) _
                .NumberFormat = "0.000"
            Range(.Offset(0, 0), .Offset(nUnits, nInputs + nOutputs)) _
                .AutoFormat xlRangeAutoFormatClassic3
            .HorizontalAlignment = xlLeft
        End With
    End With
End Sub
```

ViewExplanation Code

The ViewExplanation sub lets the user navigate back to the Explanation worksheet, and it hides the Report worksheet.

```
Sub ViewExplanation()
    With wsExplanation
        .Activate
        .Range("F5").Select
    End With
    wsReport.Visible = False
End Sub
```

33.8 Summary

This application has illustrated a very useful method, DEA, for comparing organizational units for relative efficiency. This method has been used in a number of real applications in various industries. (See the references in Chapter 4 of *Practical Management Science*.) In addition, this chapter has illustrated a method for importing data from a comma-delimited text file into Excel. This involves parsing data into its individual pieces, a technique that is very useful in its own right in a variety of contexts.

EXERCISES

1. If you ever try to open a text (.txt) file in Excel, you will see that it takes you through a wizard. One of the steps asks for the character delimiter. One choice is the comma (the one used here), and another is the tab character. Rewrite the ParseLine sub so that the separating character is the tab rather than the comma. Then get into Notepad, open the **DEA.txt** file, replace each comma with a tab (highlight the comma and press the Tab key), and rerun the application with your new ParseLine sub. You should get the same results as before. (*Hint:* Open the VBA library in the Object Browser and look under Constants to find the tab character.)

2. Rewrite the ParseLine sub so that it is slightly more general. It should receive an extra argument called separator, declared as String type. The separator is any single character that separates the pieces of the long string being parsed. In the application, the separator was the comma, but it might be another character in other applications.

3. Suppose a line from a text file uses a *single* comma to separate pieces of data, but it uses two *consecutive* commas to indicate that a comma is part of a piece a data. For example, the line 23,290,21,200 has three pieces of data: 23, 290, and 21,200. Rewrite the ParseLine sub to parse a typical line with this comma convention.

4. I claimed that this application works with any data, provided that the text file is structured properly. Try the following. Open the **DEA.txt** file in Notepad and change its data in some way. (For example, try adding another academic department and/or adding an input or an output.) Then rerun the application to check that it still works properly.

5. Repeat the previous exercise, but now create a *new* text file called **MyData.txt** (stored in the same folder as the Excel application), structured exactly as **DEA.txt**, and add some data to it. Then rerun the application to check that it still works properly. (Note that you will have to change the VBA code slightly, so that it references the correct name of your new text file.)

6. The previous exercise indicates a "fix" that no business would ever tolerate—they would never be willing to get into the VBA code to change a file name reference. A much better alternative is to change the VBA code in the first place so that it asks the user for the location and name of the database file. You could do this with an input box (and risk having the user spell something wrong), but Excel provides an easier way with the FileDialog object as illustrated in Chapter 13. Use this to change the application so that it prompts the user for the name and location of the data file. Actually, you should probably precede the above line with a MsgBox statement so that the user knows he's being asked to select the file with the data. Then try the modified application with your own text file, stored in a folder *different* from the folder containing the Excel application.

7. Put the ideas from Exercises 2 and 6 together to make the application fairly general. First, create a user form that allows the user to choose the separator character from a list of option buttons. (Make the choices reasonable, such as comma, tab, and semicolon.) Then pass the user's choice to the revised ParseLine sub discussed in Exercise 2 as the separator argument. Second, let the user select the text file with the data, as discussed in Exercise 6. Now the application should work with any text file with any separator in your list.

8. I mentioned in a footnote that VBA has a powerful String function called Split that does practically everything the complex ParseLine sub does. Look up Split in the Object Browser, and then modify the application to take advantage of this function. You should no longer need the ParseLine sub.

Index